Kansei Engineering and Soft Computing:

Theory and Practice

Ying Dai
Iwate Pref. University, Japan

Basabi Chakraborty
Iwate Prefectural University, Japan

Minghui Shi
Xiamen University, China

A volume in the Advances in Computer
and Electrical Engineering (ACEE) Book
Series

Director of Editorial Content:	Kristin Klinger
Director of Book Publications:	Julia Mosemann
Acquisitions Editor:	Lindsay Johnston
Development Editor:	Christine Bufton
Publishing Assistant:	Keith Glazewski
Typesetter:	Keith Glazewski
Production Editor:	Jamie Snavely
Cover Design:	Lisa Tosheff

Published in the United States of America by
Engineering Science Reference (an imprint of IGI Global)
701 E. Chocolate Avenue
Hershey PA 17033
Tel: 717-533-8845
Fax: 717-533-8661
E-mail: cust@igi-global.com
Web site: http://www.igi-global.com

Library of Congress Cataloging-in-Publication Data

Kansei engineering and soft computing : theory and practice / Ying Dai, Basabi
Chakraborty, and Minghui Shi, editors.
    p. cm.
  Includes bibliographical references and index.
  Summary: "This book focuses on the qualitative and quantitative evaluation of kansei, including the measurement and analysis of the impressions, emotions, and sense perceptions of groups and individuals, as well as the development of procedures for the representation, design and creation of products, machines and systems that embody the kansei of groups and individuals"--Provided by publisher.
  ISBN 978-1-61692-797-4 (hardcover) -- ISBN 978-1-61692-799-8 (ebook) 1. Human engineering. 2. Soft computing. 3. Senses and sensation. 4. System design--Psychological aspects. 5. Industrial design--Psychological aspects. I. Dai, Ying, 1963- II. Chakraborty, Basabi, 1956- III. Shi, Minghui, 1973-
  TA166.K363 2011
  006.3--dc22
                                        2009053466

This book is published in the IGI Global book series Advances in Computer and Electrical Engineering (ACEE) Book Series (ISSN: 2327-039X; eISSN: 2327-0403)

British Cataloguing in Publication Data
A Cataloguing in Publication record for this book is available from the British Library.

All work contributed to this book is new, previously-unpublished material. The views expressed in this book are those of the authors, but not necessarily of the publisher.

Advances in Computer and Electrical Engineering (ACEE) Book Series

Srikanta Patnaik
SOA University, India

ISSN: 2327-039X
EISSN: 2327-0403

MISSION

The fields of computer engineering and electrical engineering encompass a broad range of interdisciplinary topics allowing for expansive research developments across multiple fields. Research in these areas continues to develop and become increasingly important as computer and electrical systems have become an integral part of everyday life.

The **Advances in Computer and Electrical Engineering (ACEE) Book Series** aims to publish research on diverse topics pertaining to computer engineering and electrical engineering. **ACEE** encourages scholarly discourse on the latest applications, tools, and methodologies being implemented in the field for the design and development of computer and electrical systems.

COVERAGE

- Algorithms
- Applied Electromagnetics
- Chip Design
- Circuit Analysis
- Digital Electronics
- Electrical Power Conversion
- Optical Electronics
- Power Electronics
- Programming
- Qualitative Methods

IGI Global is currently accepting manuscripts for publication within this series. To submit a proposal for a volume in this series, please contact our Acquisition Editors at Acquisitions@igi-global.com or visit: http://www.igi-global.com/publish/.

Titles in this Series

For a list of additional titles in this series, please visit: www.igi-global.com

Agile and Lean Service-Oriented Development Foundations, Theory, and Practice
Xiaofeng Wang (Free University of Bozen/Bolzano, Italy) Nour Ali (Lero- The Irish Software Engineering Research Centre, University of Limerick, Ireland) Isidro Ramos (Valencia University of Technology) and Richard Vidgen (Hull University Business School, UK)
Information Science Reference • copyright 2013 • 312pp • H/C (ISBN: 9781466625037) • US $195.00 (our price)

Electromagnetic Transients in Transformer and Rotating Machine Windings
Editor, Charles Q. Su (Charling Technology, Australia)
Engineering Science Reference • copyright 2013 • 586pp • H/C (ISBN: 9781466619210) • US $195.00 (our price)

Design and Test Technology for Dependable Systems-on-Chip
Raimund Ubar (Tallinn University of Technology, Estonia) Jaan Raik (Tallinn University of Technology, Estonia) and Heinrich Theodor Vierhaus (Brandenburg University of Technology Cottbus, Germany)
Information Science Reference • copyright 2011 • 578pp • H/C (ISBN: 9781609602123) • US $180.00 (our price)

Kansei Engineering and Soft Computing Theory and Practice
Ying Dai (Iwate Pref. University, Japan) Basabi Chakraborty (Iwate Prefectural University, Japan) and Minghui Shi (Xiamen University, China)
Engineering Science Reference • copyright 2011 • 436pp • H/C (ISBN: 9781616927974) • US $180.00 (our price)

Model Driven Architecture for Reverse Engineering Technologies Strategic Directions and System Evolution
Liliana Favre (Universidad Nacional de Centro de la Proviencia de Buenos Aires, Argentina)
Engineering Science Reference • copyright 2010 • 460pp • H/C (ISBN: 9781615206490) • US $180.00 (our price)

www.igi-global.com

701 E. Chocolate Ave., Hershey, PA 17033
Order online at www.igi-global.com or call 717-533-8845 x100
To place a standing order for titles released in this series, contact: cust@igi-global.com
Mon-Fri 8:00 am - 5:00 pm (est) or fax 24 hours a day 717-533-8661

Table of Contents

Section 1
Basic Concepts, Frameworks and Techniques

Chapter 1

Siddhartha Bhattacharyya, The University of Burdwan, India
Ujjwal Maulik, Jadavpur University, India
Sanghamitra Bandyopadhyay, Indian Statistical Institute, India

Chapter 2

Yanping Lu, Xiamen University, China
Shaozi Li, Xiamen University, China

Chapter 3

Yasuhiro Yamada, Shimane University, Japan
Kanji Kato, GK Sekkei Incorporated, Japan
Sachio Hirokawa, Kyushu University, Japan

Chapter 4

Madhura Datta, University of Calcutta, India
C.A. Murthy, Indian Statistical Institute, India

Section 2
Measurement, Analysis, and Representation of Kansei

Detailed Table of Contents

Section 1
Basic Concepts, Frameworks and Techniques

Chapter 1

Siddhartha Bhattacharyya, The University of Burdwan, India
Ujjwal Maulik, Jadavpur University, India
Sanghamitra Bandyopadhyay, Indian Statistical Institute, India

The architecture of neural networks, the underlying concepts of fuzzy set theory and fuzzy logic, the heuristic search techniques [including genetic algorithm (GA), simulated annealing (SA), and ant colony optimization (ACO)], and an outline of the rough set theory are briefly discussed. The application of soft computing techniques in kansei-related issues is also discussed.

Chapter 2

Yanping Lu, Xiamen University, China
Shaozi Li, Xiamen University, China

New Particle Swarm Optimization (PSO) algorithms for clustering high-dimensional data and automatically determining the number of clusters for data mining applications are developed. As these algorithms are global search techniques, they can also be used to determine optimal feature subspace selection or to solve subspace clustering problems.

Chapter 3

Yasuhiro Yamada, Shimane University, Japan
Kanji Kato, GK Sekkei Incorporated, Japan
Sachio Hirokawa, Kyushu University, Japan

A brief survey of basic text mining techniques used to analyze interviews and questionnaires, including keyword extraction, word graphs, clustering of text and association rule mining, is introduced. Then, an example of text mining applied to interview and questionnaire analysis is provided. Finally, the advantages and disadvantages of text mining techniques are discussed.

Chapter 4

Madhura Datta, University of Calcutta, India
C.A. Murthy, Indian Statistical Institute, India

The development of a face recognition system for person authentication with a novel threshold selection technique for correct decision-making incorporating human cognitive behavior is presented. The effectiveness of the approach is demonstrated by simulation experiments with real data in a real-world environment.

Chapter 5

Tao Song, Huazhong University of Science and Technology, China
Xun Wang, University of Tsukuba, Japan
Shudong Wang, Shandong University of Science and Technology, China
Yun Jiang, Huazhong University of Science and Technology, China

The development of DNA computing, a form of biomolecular computing, is discussed, along with an introduction to the theoretical framework and formal models and a description of several models used to solve real-world problems. Practical problems regarding DNA encoding and the bottlenecks for this new tool are also discussed.

Chapter 6

Yaokai Feng, Kyushu University, Japan

After reviewing existing kansei retrieval systems, the general flow of kansei retrieval systems and the structure of a typical kansei database are presented. Furthermore, multidimensional index structures used in kansei retrieval systems, including the AR*-tree used to speed up the retrieval process, are described and discussed.

Shang-fei Wang, University of Science and Technology of China, China
Xu-fa Wang, University of Science and Technology of China, China

Advances in research on emotional semantic detection from multimedia are surveyed. A general overview of research is provided; research on emotional semantic detection from images, videos, and music, as well as their typical prototype systems, is introduced; and, finally, future research directions are identified.

Kamyar Mehran, Newcastle University, UK
Bashar Zahawi, Newcastle University, UK
Damian Giaouris, Newcastle University, UK

The fundamental concepts of non-smooth dynamical systems theory, together with case studies, are described, and a successful Takagi-Sugeno (TS) fuzzy modeling approach in modeling the dynamics of complex nonlinear systems is introduced. Then, a new type of TS-based fuzzy model is proposed to represent a non-smooth dynamical system, and the method of predicting the onset of instability leading to chaos for the non-smooth dynamical system is depicted.

Elisabeth Damour, Act & Be - Creative Management Consultancy, France

The relationship between human beings and humanoid robots, including some characteristic with their influence of future humanoids, such as immortality, cyber-body, human identity, and consciousness, are discussed. Further, strategies for making robots benevolent and grateful towards humans are presented.

Section 2
Measurement, Analysis, and Representation of Kansei

Shigekazu Ishihara, Hiroshima International University, Japan
Mitsuo Nagamachi, Hiroshima International University, Japan
Jun Masaki, Nagasaki Prefectural Government, Japan

Music-related research, classified into 6 categories, is described. Kansei evaluation experiments on modes, melodic ranges, and rhythms are introduced, and a real-time kansei music recognition system based on the results of analysis is developed. Further, internet-based music services incorporating kansei concepts are reviewed.

The usefulness of factor analysis, combined with the rough sets theory as an operational tool for linking participants' perceptions with the physical components of sidewalk environments, is illustrated. The methods of sidewalk photograph collection, field survey, and psychological survey are introduced. Furthermore, methods for extracting decision rules from data generated by factor analysis using the rough sets theory are presented in detail.

Chapter 12

The development of Ifbot, a kansei robot capable of communicating inner emotions through facial expressions, is discussed. The mapping of human emotions and facial expressions has been achieved using an auto-associative neural network, a soft computing tool. A method for creating personality using facial expressions is also proposed.

Chapter 13

The different effects of spatial (or temporal) ordered color sequences on the naturalness are examined. These effects were investigated by subjects who assessed the level of "naturalness" of linear, toroidal, or circular sequences of six colors. The relationship between sequence patterns and the impression of "naturalness" is explored, and some simple fuzzy rules are extracted by calculating the projected route area and the route complexity of a hexagonal diagram of six color sequences.

Chapter 14

Kitarou Nishida's theory of environment is adapted for the purpose of explaining the theory of scenery. In order to present the concept of a scenery narrative, this theory of scenery and Keiichi Noe's narrative theory are integrated. In the subsequent section, the theoretical relationship between scenery narratives and previous or current work experiences in the field are discussed. Finally, a hypothesis from the narrative theory of scenery is developed and tested in a case study.

Pierre Lévy, Eindhoven University of Technology, The Netherlands & Chiba University, Japan
Toshimasa Yamanaka, University of Tsukuba, Japan
Oscar Tomico, Eindhoven University of Technology, The Netherlands

An overview of the emerging approaches for kansei design based on its relation to psychophysiology has been presented. Tools and techniques are developed in order to incorporate human inspiration and mental images into the design process and are supported by real-world examples and applications.

Yusuke Manabe, Chiba Institute of Technology, Japan
Kenji Sugawara, Chiba Institute of Technology, Japan

A framework for analyzing handwriting as an example of a human skill with hidden elements of individuality is described. An approach for identity detection using handwriting captured by a computer pen tablet with the help of soft computing tools is presented and is supported by simulation experiments with benchmark data.

Shusaku Nomura, Nagaoka University of Technology, Japan

Biomarkers and biomarker studies, namely saliva sampling and quantitative determination of salivary biomarkers, are introduced. After describing the experimental procedure of biomarkers against short-term stressors, the results of subjects' salivary concentration changes and accumulative changes in task/break experiments are discussed. Then, a mathematical model reflecting biomarker response against intermittent short-term stressors is proposed.

Santoso Handri, Nagaoka University of Technology, Japan
Shusaku Nomura, Nagaoka University of Technology, Japan

Modes for acquiring several types of biosignals, including electrocardiogram (ECG) and ECG processing, are introduced. After an overview of the use of ECG as an indicator of fatigue, an experiment evaluating mental health problems is introduced. Approaches integrating PCA, HMM and NN are used to estimate human states of fatigue and vigor based on ECG, electroencephalogram (EEG), and thermograph data.

Chapter 19

Hugo de Garis, Xiamen University, China
Xiaoxi Chen, Xiamen University, China
Ben Goertzel, Novamente LLC, USA & Singularity Institute, USA & Xiamen University, China

The "Parcone" (Partially Connected Neural Evolutionary) model, which is used as the basis for all artificial brain projects, and the operating system software "IMSI" (Inter Module Signaling Interface) are described. The capabilities of the ABL's NAO robots and the interface between the IMSI operating system and NAO are introduced. A series of demos and discussions about the main aims and major challenges of this research project are presented. Finally, an improved model called CUDA-based partially connected neural evolutionary model, which is developed to speed up the evolution process, is presented in the appendix.

Foreword

The field of artificial intelligence evolves with the objective of developing intelligent machines that could think the way humans do. Perception-generated feelings and feeling-driven actions are two of the most important aspects of human intelligence. These require a knowledge system in which subjective impression and emotions of human's responses to the surroundings could be described and processed. Psychological impression or human emotions are unlikely to be fully captured, but these may be apparent at the subconscious level. Kansei Engineering has been developed to measure, analyze, and represent such information which is defined as Kansei. Research into Kansei involves determining which sensory attributes elicit particular subjective responses from people, and then designing a product, a machine or a system using the attributes which elicit the desired responses.

Among these technologies involved in Kansei Engineering, soft computing is undoubtedly the most popular and important approach of computational intelligence where artificial neural networks, fuzzy logic, rough set theory, evolutionary computation and other hybrid techniques are used to the knowledge representation and decision making of humans. Due to its tolerance to imprecision, uncertainty and partial truth, soft computing deals well with human related systems. Since the process of solving real world problems by inducing the concept of Kansei often interacts with human and involves human's affections with uncertainty, imprecision and dependence on the context, the recent advances in soft computing and Kansei engineering, and the fusion of these two fields are considered to be critical. The book, Kansei Engineering and Soft Computing: Theories and Practice, here KESC for short, is one of the first texts to focus on the topics related to these fields.

As soft computing steps into the field of Kansei engineering, one needs to go from the development and enhancement of modeling, algorithm development, computer simulation, and implementation in useful prototypes for rigorous testing and evaluation. Applications of soft computing to kansei related real world problems are sufficiently complex. This book, KESC, edited by Dr. Ying Dai, Dr. Basabi Chakraborty, and Dr. Minghui Shi, provides a comprehensive overview of the theories, methodologies, and recent developments in the field of Kansei engineering towards this end. The book covers such important topics as the framework of soft computing, up-to-date soft computing techniques and their applications in Kansei engineering, the practice in measuring, analyzing and representing Kansei, and the Kansei based product design.

KESC is a book well-organized, clearly presented and illustrated by many examples and many experiments. It is a must reading for ones interested in acquiring an understanding of what Kansei engineering is, developing an ability to employ it for human centric systems, and utilizing the soft computing techniques for real world problems with uncertainty and imprecision. The editors and contributors deserve our thanks and congratulations for producing a book, which adds so much and so importantly to the advancement of Kansei engineering and soft computing.

Nanning Zheng, Ph.D.
IEEE Fellow
Professor and Director
Institute of Artificial Intelligence and Robotics,
Xi'an Jiaotong University, China

Nanning Zheng *(IEEE SM'93-F'06) graduated from the Department of Electrical Engineering, Xi'an Jiaotong University, Xi'an, China, in 1975, and received the MS degree in information and control engineering from Xi'an Jiaotong University in 1981 and the PhD degree in electrical engineering from Keio University, Yokohama, Japan, in 1985. He jointed Xi'an Jiaotong University in 1975, and he is currently a Professor and the Director of the Institute of Artificial Intelligence and Robotics, Xi'an Jiaotong University. His research interests include computer vision, pattern recognition and image processing, and hardware implementation of intelligent systems. Dr. Zheng became a member of the Chinese Academy of Engineering in 1999, and he is the Chinese Representative on the Governing Board of the International Association for Pattern Recognition. He also serves as an executive deputy editor of the Chinese Science Bulletin.*

Preface

With the increasing concern regarding human factors in system development, the concepts of humanized technology and human-related systems have become the focus of more and more research. Kansei engineering and soft computing are the most representative research fields in this area.

The word *kansei* (derived from the Japanese 感性 [*kansei*]), refers to human feelings, such as impressions, affect, and emotions, derived by observing the surrounding environment. Such feelings can arouse people to act instinctively—for example, just as happiness results in laughter, enjoying something will motivate an individual to obtain it. In this way, the concept of kansei consists of two distinct aspects: perception-generated feelings and feeling-driven action. Both aspects include issues of uncertainty, diversity, and dependence on the environment. Kansei engineering aims to solve these problems while bringing together culture and technology through the establishment of an information society based on the concept of kansei—in other words, the harmonization of the social, cultural, and natural sciences and technology with human skills, and the creation and promotion of human happiness [1]. With this goal in mind, kansei engineering focuses on the qualitative and quantitative evaluation of kansei, including the measurement and analysis of the impressions, emotions, and sense perceptions of groups and individuals, as well as the development of procedures for the representation, design and creation of products, machines and systems that embody the kansei of groups and individuals. The theories and technologies of soft computing are therefore essential developmental tools in kansei engineering.

Soft computing, a consortium of tools and techniques suitable for dealing with the uncertainty and imprecision of human-centric computing, comprises artificial neural networks, fuzzy logic, the rough set theory, evolutionary computation and other hybrid techniques. Recently, soft computing tools have been developed to solve many real-world problems involving human behavior. Until now, kansei engineering and soft computing have developed as two independent fields.

This book offers the reader a comprehensive review of kansei engineering, soft computing techniques, and the fusion of these two fields from a variety of viewpoints. After introducing the traditional technologies, the book's focus shifts to the solution of real-world problems through the concept of kansei and the effective utilization of soft computing techniques, while such real world problems often involve uncertainty and imprecision, and are dependence on the context. Cutting-edge research on the measurement of kansei and its application in areas such as design, production, and healthcare is also introduced.

The book aims to reach professionals, researchers and students in the field of kansei information processing and soft computing, both in academia and industry. It will also serve as a reference book for professionals, researchers and students interested in studying existing kansei engineering and soft computing techniques from theoretical and practical viewpoints and obtaining insight into the application of kansei research in humanized technology or human-related systems.

The book is divided into two sections and comprises of 19 chapters. Section 1, "Basic Concepts, Framework and Techniques", consisting of 9 chapters, introduces the framework of soft computing, current soft computing techniques, the general process of constructing kansei retrieval systems, and the implementation of kansei factors in dynamic systems. Section 2, "Measurement, Analysis, and Representation of Kansei", consisting of 10 chapters, covers many critical kansei issues, such as the psychological and physiological measurement of kansei, representing kansei by analyzing the relationship between human's feelings and physical attributes of entities, and the incorporation of kansei into product design.

The first chapter provides an introduction to the three essential paradigms of soft computing: neural network, fuzzy logic and evolutional computation. These paradigms are integrated to provide a framework for flexible information processing, which is useful for processing kansei-related issues. In particular, the notions, methodologies, and some algorithms of neural networks, fuzzy set theory, and heuristic search techniques, which are utilized throughout the book, are mainly introduced and discussed. Furthermore, methods for applying soft computing techniques to real-world problems involving uncertainty, including kansei-related issues, are presented.

Chapter 2 presents the utility and efficiency of the Particle Swarm Optimization (PSO) technique, a recently developed soft computing tool, in solving real-world humanistic problems. This chapter proposes novel PSO algorithms for clustering high-dimensional data and automatically determining the number of clusters in data mining applications, supported by the results of simulation experiments with synthetic data sets. This chapter is useful in handling optimization and search problems while dealing with kansei databases and categorizing concepts related to kansei.

Chapter 3 introduces basic text mining techniques that help to analyze interviews and questionnaires, including keyword extraction, word graphs, clustering of text and association rule mining. In addition, a case study using text mining for the analysis of interviews and questionnaires revealing the opinions, concerns and needs of subjects is presented. This chapter is useful for learning the basics of text mining and how to use it to extract information such as the concerns and needs of subjects from questionnaire data.

Chapter 4 demonstrates an application of a human cognitive behavior model in developing an automatic biometric authentication system. Using set estimation, the authors developed a novel threshold selection technique for identifying individuals who are learned by the system, and differentiating humans from no-humans. This chapter deals with an important subset of cognitive system design involving human factors and demonstrates the possibility of successful design of such systems through simulation experiments in a real-world environment.

Chapter 5 introduces DNA computing, another emerging computational technique encompassing computer science, biological science and engineering. DNA computing, a variant of biomolecular computation, is now widely accepted as a new computing model for future computing devices. This chapter describes the theoretical framework and formal models of DNA computation and presents several DNA computing models used to solve real-world problems. DNA encoding may play a crucial role in designing successful human-centric computational paradigms that might be useful in kansei engineering.

Chapter 6 summarizes the general flow of kansei retrieval systems and presents the structure of a typical kansei database. Indexing technologies for kansei retrieval are then described and discussed. In particular, in order to speed up the retrieval process, the author proposes an original adaptive R*-tree method that is quite appropriated for the kansei database. This chapter not only helps readers to understand the mechanisms and methodology of kansei retrieval, but also to realize the importance of considering efficiency when constructing a kansei database and performing kansei retrieval.

Human moods are influenced by the multiple forms of media that surround us. Detection of emotions elicited by various media has emerged as an area of active research area in the past few decades. Chapter 7 surveys advances in this area, including a general overview of research on affective analysis of multimedia contents, recent research on detecting emotional semantics from images, videos and music, three typical archetypal systems related to the three fields of images, videos and music, several critical problems, and strategies for problem resolution. This chapter is helpful in understanding state-of-the-art research on kansei analysis regarding multimedia and the critical hurdles to overcome in constructing a kansei-based multimedia retrieval system.

Chapter 8 reviews the fundamental concepts of non-smooth dynamical systems, together with examples showing the diversity of their nonlinear behaviors, and introduces a Takagi-Sugeno fuzzy modeling concept, demonstrating how it could be extended to represent a non-smooth system and applied to a stability analysis to predict the onset of structural instability in the evolution of a dynamical system. This interesting topic implies the potentiality of inferring the bifurcation of kansei evaluation in processes such as product design, painting, or music video production, because they can be considered non-smooth dynamic systems following fuzzy decision rules.

Humanoid and android robots are expected to be one of the greatest new industries of the 21st century. We can therefore anticipate the presence of more and more robots not only in factories but also in our daily lives. Chapter 9 discusses the future relationship between humans and humanoid and android robots. How will robots change human society? Will the robots endanger us? How should we regulate the development of humanoid robots? This chapter is valuable for researchers and engineers who aim to explore the potential of robotic technology from the perspective of kansei.

Chapter 10 and Chapter 11 present the typical processing flow of kansei engineering by measuring and analyzing subjects' psychological states. After reviewing kansei engineering research on music, which is classified into six categories (kansei evaluation methodology, music psychological research, physiological measurement, music theoretical research, kansei music system and recommendation system), Chapter 10 presents approaches for kansei research on melody and rhythm from the perspective of music theory. Methods for analyzing relations between modes, melodic ranges, or rhythms and kansei evaluation based on principal component analysis are introduced, and how the arrangements of modes affects human impressions and feelings is revealed and applied in a real-time melody recognition system. This chapter helps readers to understand the basis of kansei engineering and how various approaches are applied.

To investigate the relationship between people's perceptions of sidewalk environments and their component elements, Chapter 11 adopts factor analysis and the rough sets approach to determine the most important attributes to people's perceptions, minimal attribute sets without redundancy, and a series of decision rules that represent the relationships between perceptions and the physical components of sidewalk environments. The analytical approach promotes better understanding of people's perceptions of sidewalk environments and then establishes a useful and constructive framework for discussion of walking environment design and management.

As an example of the application of kansei engineering, the development of a kansei communication robot, Ifbot, is presented in Chapter 12. Ifbot communicates with people by expressing emotions through facial expressions. Here, the authors present their development approach, including the association of facial expressions with human emotions using an auto-associative neural network, a soft computing tool. In addition, methods for generating expressive faces that convey human emotion in order to enhance the quality of human-robot communication are discussed. A method for creating personality through facial expressions has also been proposed. This study and its application represent an important development in the cooperation between kansei engineering and soft computing.

Chapter 13 describes how several color sequences (temporal or spatial) affect human impressions, and demonstrates how to develop a color sequence that reminds viewers of the natural world. A number of experiments have investigated the different effects of spatial (or temporal) ordered color sequences on the naturalness by calculating the projected route area and route complexity of a hexagonal diagram comprising six color sequences. Then, a simple fuzzy model of the colors used to give an impression of naturalness is achieved. The proposed techniques are also useful for investigating the effects of color order on other impressions, which play an important role in product design.

Chapter 14 examines how a particular narrative can become the narrative of an entire community, and thereby influence or control the behavior of all members of that community. This research extracts its hypothesis from the narrative theory of scenery, which holds that narratives are distinct with different work experiences and can be shared by people in the same community. These shared normative scenery narratives subsequently influence community members' behavior. Normative scenery narratives can be viewed as products of the general kansei of farmers in a community. This chapter helps readers to understand how general kansei is formed through sharing of group members' experiences and feelings, and how it controls the behaviors of the group.

An overview of the emerging approaches for incorporating kansei (human feelings) into system design is presented in Chapter 15. Three approaches involving the relationship between psychophysiology and the design process have been studied. Tools and methods are developed with a psychological basis with respect to human inspiration, behavior and mental images of the design process and requirements. Each of the proposed approaches is supported by real-world examples and applications. This chapter is highly educational in developing the field of kansei design.

Chapter 16 represents another application of a human cognitive action model in designing a person authentication system. This chapter focuses on handwriting as a primary coordinated activity of human movement and, with the help of soft computing tools, presents a framework for tacit handwriting skill analysis for the extraction of embedded knowledge. A technique for detecting human identity by analyzing handwriting captured by a computer writing pad is also presented and is supported by simulation experiments with benchmark data.

Chapter 17 and 18 introduce methods for measuring physiological signals and utilizing these signals to assess human mental states, such as stress, mood, or feelings. Chapter 17 explores salivary biomarkers and their potential to reveal the degree of stress accumulation, while Chapter 18 presents bioelectric signals and their application in estimating human mood states in combination with PCA, HMM and NN approaches . The contents of these two chapters demonstrate the possibility of measuring and analyzing kansei using physiological signals.

Chapter 19 presents a 4-year research project (2008-2011) currently underway at Xiamen University, China, to build China's first artificial brain. The project takes an "evolutionary engineering" approach, effectively evolving tens of thousands of neural net modules (or "agents" in the sense of Minsky's "Society of Mind") and connecting them to make artificial brains. These modules are evolved rapidly and are then connected according to the artificial brain designs of human "brain architects" (BAs). The artificial brain will eventually contain thousands of pattern recognizer modules and hundreds of decision modules that, when suitably combined, will be able to control the hundreds of behaviors of a robot. As a general research report, this chapter is worth reading to understand the construction of a system that is expected to develop functions rivaling the human brain in complexity.

We are confident that professionals, researchers and students in the fields of kansei information processing and soft computing will be able to use this book to learn more about the ways in which kansei research can be applied to different environments.

Ying Dai
Iwate Prefectural University, Japan

Basabi Chakraborty
Iwate Prefectural University, Japan

Minghui Shi
Xiamen University, China

ENDNOTE

[1]   Japan Society of Kansei Engineering, http://www.jske.org/

Acknowledgment

We wish to acknowledge all the people who have helped us directly or indirectly in completing the book. First, we would like to thank all chapter contributors for their innovative proposals, serious preparation and enthusiastic cooperation in the completion of all necessary chapters. We would also like to thank the reviewers, who took the time to review their assigned chapters in earnest and provided many constructive comments for improving the quality of the book. We are also grateful to Elizabeth Ardner and Christine Bufton from IGI Global for their technical support during all the phases of the book development process.

Ying Dai
Iwate Prefectural University, Japan

Basabi Chakraborty
Iwate Prefectural University, Japan

Minghui Shi
Xiamen University, China

Section 1
Basic Concepts, Frameworks and Techniques

Chapter 1
Soft Computing and its Applications

Siddhartha Bhattacharyya
The University of Burdwan, India

Ujjwal Maulik
Jadavpur University, India

Sanghamitra Bandyopadhyay
Indian Statistical Institute, India

ABSTRACT

Soft Computing is a relatively new computing paradigm bestowed with tools and techniques for handling real world problems. The main components of this computing paradigm are neural networks, fuzzy logic and evolutionary computation. Each and every component of the soft computing paradigm operates either independently or in coalition with the other components for addressing problems related to modeling, analysis and processing of data. An overview of the essentials and applications of the soft computing paradigm is presented in this chapter with reference to the functionalities and operations of its constituent components. Neural networks are made up of interconnected processing nodes/neurons, which operate on numeric data. These networks posses the capabilities of adaptation and approximation. The varied amount of uncertainty and ambiguity in real world data are handled in a linguistic framework by means of fuzzy sets and fuzzy logic. Hence, this component is efficient in understanding vagueness and imprecision in real world knowledge bases. Genetic algorithms, simulated annealing algorithm and ant colony optimization algorithm are representative evolutionary computation techniques, which are efficient in deducing an optimum solution to a problem, thanks to the inherent exhaustive search methodologies adopted. Of late, rough sets have evolved to improve upon the performances of either of these components by way of approximation techniques. These soft computing techniques have been put to use in wide variety of problems ranging from scientific to industrial applications. Notable among these applications include image processing, pattern recognition, Kansei information processing, data mining, web intelligence etc.

DOI: 10.4018/978-1-61692-797-4.ch001

1. INTRODUCTION

The field of *Soft Computing* is a synergistic integration of essentially three computing paradigms, viz. neural networks, fuzzy logic and evolutionary computation entailing probabilistic reasoning (belief networks, genetic algorithms and chaotic systems) to provide a framework for flexible information processing applications designed to operate in the real world. Bezdek [Bezdek92] referred to this synergism as *computational intelligence* [Kumar2004]. Soft computing technologies are robust by design, and operate by trading off precision for tractability. Since they can handle uncertainty with ease, they conform better to real world situations and provide lower cost solutions.

The three components of soft computing differ from one another in more than one way. Neural networks operate in a numeric framework, and are well known for their learning and generalization capabilities. Fuzzy systems [Zadeh65] operate in a linguistic framework, and their strength lies in their capability to handle linguistic information and perform approximate reasoning. The evolutionary computation techniques provide powerful search and optimization methodologies. All the three facets of soft computing differ from one another in their time scales of operation and in the extent to which they embed *a priori* knowledge.

Of late, rough set theory has come up as a new mathematical approach to model imperfect knowledge, crucial to addressing problems in areas of artificial intelligence. Apart from the fuzzy set theory pointed out in the previous paragraph, rough set theory proposed by Pawlak [Pawlak82] presents still another attempt to handle real world uncertainties. The theory has attracted attention of many researchers and practitioners all over the world, who have contributed essentially to its development and applications. The rough set approach seems to be of fundamental importance to artificial intelligence and cognitive sciences, especially in the areas of machine learning, knowledge acquisition, decision analysis, knowledge discovery from databases, expert systems, inductive reasoning and pattern recognition. The main advantage of rough set theory in data analysis is that it does not need any preliminary or additional information about data – like probability in statistics, or basic probability assignment in Dempster-Shafer theory, grade of membership or the value of possibility in fuzzy set theory.

2. NEURAL NETWORKS

A neural network is a powerful data-modeling tool that is able to capture and represent complex input/output relationships similar to a human brain. Artificial neural networks resemble the human brain in the following two ways:

* A neural network acquires knowledge through learning.
* A neural network's knowledge is stored within inter-neuron connection strengths known as *synaptic weights*.

The true power and advantage of neural networks lie in their ability to represent both linear and non-linear relationships and in their ability to learn these relationships directly from the data being modeled.

Artificial Neural Network

An artificial neural network [Haykin99], as the name suggests, is a parallel and layered interconnected structure of a large number of artificial *neurons*, each of which constitutes an elementary computational primitive. The distributed representation of the interconnections through massive parallelism achieved out of the inherent network structure, bestows upon such networks properties of graceful degradation and fault tolerance. These network structures differ from one to another in the topology of the underlying interconnections as well as on the target problem they are put to.

Since the essence of neural network operation is based on the behavior of human brain, these networks require a form of training or learning ability. Once these are trained with the different aspects of the problem at hand, they can be used to solve similar problems given the immense generalization capabilities embedded therein. Depending on the type of learning procedure adopted, different neural network architectures have evolved from time to time [Haykin99, Kumar2004].

In the most general form, an artificial neural network is a layered structure of neurons. It comprises seven essential components [Kumar2004], viz., (i) neurons, (ii) activation state vector, (iii) activation function, (iv) connection topology, (v) activity aggregation rule, (vi) learning rule and (vii) environment. These components are discussed in the following sections.

Neurons

Neurons are the processing units of a neural network. There are basically three types of neurons viz. input, hidden and output. The input neurons are designated to accept stimuli from the external world. The output neurons generate the network outputs. The hidden neurons, which are shielded from the external world, are entrusted with the computation of intermediate functions necessary for the operation of the network.

Activation State Vector

Neural network models operate in a real n-dimensional vector space R^n. The activation state vector, $X = (x_1, x_2, \ldots, x_n)^T \in R^n$, is a vector of the activation levels x_i of the individual neurons of the network. This state vector acts as the driving force for a neural network.

Activation Function

The characteristic activation functions are used to supplement the learning process of a neural network. These functions recognize specific range of input signals and selectively tune the neurons to respond to the input signals according some learning algorithm. Most of these activation functions take an input as an infinite range of activations $(-\infty, +\infty)$ and squashes/transforms them in the finite range $[0, 1]$ or $\{-1, 1\}$ [Leondes98]. Thus, these functions are able to map the input information into bipolar excitations. Though these functions may vary from neuron to neuron within the network, yet most network architectures are *field-homogeneous* i.e. all the neurons within a layer are characterized by the same signal function. Some of the common neural network signal functions [Kumar2004, Haykin99] include (i) binary threshold, (ii) bipolar threshold, (iii) linear, (iv) liner threshold, (v) sigmoid, (vi) hyperbolic tangent, (vii) Gaussian, (viii) stochastic [Kumar2004] etc.

Connection Topology

This refers to the interconnection topology of the neural network architectures. These connections may be either excitatory (+) or inhibitory (-) or absent (0). These connections, or synapses basically house the memory of the network. The behavior of neural network architecture is decided by its connection topology.

Activity Aggregation Rule

This rule aggregates the activities of the neurons at a given layer. It is usually computed as the inner product of the input vector and the neuron fan-in interconnection strength (weight) vector. An activation rule thereby, determines the new activation level of a neuron based on its current activation and external inputs.

Learning Rule

The neural network learning rules define an architecture-dependent procedure to encode *pattern information* into inter-neuron interconnections. This is a data driven process executed by modifying the connection weights. Two types of learning are in vogue; viz. *supervised learning* and *unsupervised learning*.

- *Supervised learning*: Supervised learning encodes a behavioristic pattern into a neural network by attempting to approximate the function that best describes the data set employed. For an input vector, $X_k \in R^n$ (a real n-dimensional vector space) related to an output vector $D_k \in R^p$ (in a real p-dimensional vector space), a supervised learning algorithm aims at deriving an unknown mapping function $f: R^n \rightarrow R^p$. The algorithm tries to reduce the error $(D_k\text{-}S_k)$ in the system response, where S_k is the actual response of the system by employing the desired output response of the system D_k (also referred to as the *teaching input*) and the associate of X_k. Thus, input-output sample pairs are used to train/teach the network through a simple form of error correction learning or gradient descent weight adaptation. Hence, the system generates an output D_k in response to an input X_k. The learning process achieves an association between D_k and X_k, when a stimulus X'_k close to X_k elicits a response S'_k sufficiently close to D_k.
- *Unsupervised learning*: This paradigm simply provides the system with an input X_k, and allows it to *self organize/self supervise* its parameters to generate internal prototypes of the sample vectors. Such a paradigm attempts to represent the entire data set by employing a smaller number of prototypical vectors. These prototypes are in a state of continual updating as newer system inputs enter into the system. This is often driven by a complex competitive-cooperative process where the individual neurons compete and cooperate with each other to

update their interconnection weights during the process of *self-organization*.

Environment

The operational environment of neural networks can be either deterministic (noiseless) or stochastic (noisy). A neural network N is a weighted directed graph, where the nodes are connected as either

- a *feedforward* architecture, in which the network has no loops. Examples include the perceptron, multilayer perceptron [Duda73], support vector machines [Cortes95] and radial basis function networks [Broomhead88], Kohonen's Self Organizing Feature Map (SOFM) [Kohonen95] etc., or
- a *feedback* (recurrent) architecture, in which loops occur in the network because of feedback connections. Examples include the Hopfield network [Hopfield84], BSB model [Hui92], Boltzmann machines [Ackley85], bidirectional associative memories [Kosko88], adaptive resonance theory [Carpenter95] etc.

The following sections discuss the basic philosophy of the supervised learning environment with reference to the simple artificial neuron and the multilayer perceptron.

Simple Artificial Neuron

The basic computational element of an artificial neural network model is often referred to as a node or unit. It receives inputs from some other units, or perhaps from an external source. The basic function of a single neuron is to add up its inputs, and to produce an output if this sum is greater than some value, known as the threshold value. The basic neuron model, also known as "perceptron" after Frank Rosenblatt [Haykin99, Rosenblatt58], is a binary classifier that maps real-valued vectored

Figure 1. A basic neuron

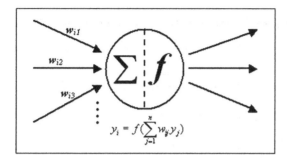

inputs to a single binary output value. It generally possesses the following features:

1. The output from a neuron is either on or off.
2. The output depends only on the inputs. A certain number of neurons must be on (or activated) at any one time in order to make a neuron fire. The efficiency of the synapses at coupling the incoming signal into a neuron can be modeled by having a multiplicative factor on each of the inputs to the neuron. This multiplicative factor, often referred to as the interconnection weight *w*, can be modified so as to model synaptic learning. A more efficient synapse, which transmits more of the signal, has a correspondingly larger weight, whilst a weak synapse has a smaller weight. Its output, in turn, can serve as input to other units. The basic neuron can be represented as shown in Figure 1.

Expressed mathematically, if there are n inputs with n associated weights on the input lines, then the ith unit computes some function f of the weighted sum of its inputs, given by

$$y_i = f(\sum_{j=1}^{n} w_{ij} y_j) \qquad (1)$$

where, w_{ij} refers to the weight from j^{th} to the ith unit. The function *f* is the unit's activation function. In

the simplest case, if *f* is the identity function the unit's output is just its net input. Thus, the node acts as a linear unit.

A variant of this architecture compares the computed sum to a certain value in the neuron called the threshold value. The thresholding process is accomplished by comparison of the computed sum to a predefined threshold value. If the sum is greater than the threshold value, then the network outputs a 1. On the other hand, if the sum is lesser than the threshold value, the network generates an output of 0. An example threshold function is shown graphically in Figure 2.

Equivalently, the threshold value can be subtracted from the weighted sum, and the resulting value then compared to zero. Depending on whether the difference yields a positive or negative result, the network outputs a 1 or 0. The output y_i of the ith neuron can then be written as:

$$y_i = f(\sum_{j=1}^{n} w_{ij} y_j - k) \qquad (2)$$

where, k the neuron's bias or offset, and *f* is a step function (actually known as the Heaviside function) and

$$f(x) = \begin{cases} 1 & \text{for } x > 0 \\ 0 & \text{for } x \le 0 \end{cases} \qquad (3)$$

Thus the threshold function produces only a 1 or a 0 as the output, so that the neuron is either activated or not.

Learning Algorithm

Since the single layer perceptron is a supervised neural network architecture, it requires learning of some a priori knowledge base for its operation. The following algorithm illustrates the learning paradigm for a single layer perceptron. It comprises the following steps.

Figure 2. A threshold function

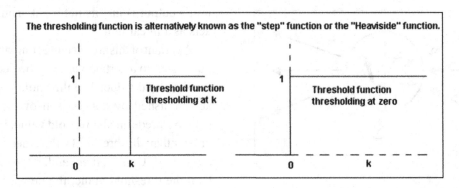

The thresholding function is alternatively known as the "step" function or the "Heaviside" function.

Threshold function thresholding at k

Threshold function thresholding at zero

- Initialization of the interconnection weights and thresholds randomly.
- Calculating the actual outputs by taking the thresholded value of the weighted sum of the inputs.
- Altering the weights to reinforce correct decisions and discourage incorrect decisions, i.e. reducing the error.

The weights are however, unchanged if the network makes the correct decision. Also the weights are not adjusted on input lines, which do not contribute to the incorrect response, since each weight is adjusted by the value of the input on that line x_i, which would be zero (see Table 1).

In order to predict the expected outputs, a loss (also called objective or error) function E can be defined over the model parameters to ascertain the error in the prediction process. A popular choice for E is the sum-squared error given by

$$E = \sum_i (y_i - d_i)^2 \qquad (4)$$

In words, it is the sum of the squared difference between the target value d_i and the perceptron's prediction y_i (calculated from the input value x_i) computed over all points i in the data set. For a linear model, the sum-squared error is a quadratic function of the model parameters. The loss function E provides an objective measure of predictive

error for a specific choice of perceptron model parameters. Minimizing the loss function would yield more accurate predicted outputs by the perceptron. This is solved by an iterative numerical technique called *gradient descent* [Haykin99, Snyman2005]. It comprises the following steps.

```
Choose some (random) initial values
for the network parameters
Repeat until G:=0
   Calculate the gradient G of the
error function with respect to each
parameter
   Change the parameters slowly in the
direction of the greatest rate of
decrease of the error, i.e., in the
negative direction of G i.e., -G
End
```

Computation of the Gradient

During the training process of neural networks by the gradient descent mechanism, the gradient G of the loss function (E) with respect to each weight w_{ij} of the network is computed [Haykin99, Snyman2005]. This gradient indicates as to how the small changes in the network weights affect the overall error E. Let, the loss function be represented for each p training sample, as

Table 1.

Begin
Initialize interconnection weights and threshold
Set $w_i(t=0)$, ($0 <= i <= n$), to small random values   *Interconnection weights from input i at time t*
Set $w_0 := k$ *k is the bias in the output node*
Set $x_0 := 1$ *x is the input to the network*
Present the inputs and the desired output to the network
Present $x_0, x_1, x_2, x_3, ..., x_n$ *$x_0, x_1, x_2, x_3, ..., x_n$ are the inputs to the network*
Present $d(t)$ *d(t) is the desired output*
Calculate the actual output
$y(t) := f(\sum_{i=1}^{n} w_i(t) x_i(t))$
Adapt interconnection weights
$w_i(t+1) := w_i(t) \pm x_i(t)$
End

$$E = \sum_p E^p \qquad (5)$$

where,

$$E^p = \frac{1}{2} \sum_o (d_o^p - y_o^p)^2 \qquad (6)$$

o refers to the range of the output units of the network. Then,

$$G = \frac{\delta E}{\delta w_{oi}} = \frac{\delta}{\delta w_{oi}} \sum_p E^p = \sum_p \frac{\partial E^p}{\partial w_{oi}} \qquad (7)$$

Generalizing for all training samples and decomposing the gradient into two factors using chain rule, one gets

$$\frac{\delta E}{\delta w_{oi}} = \frac{\delta E}{\delta y_o} \frac{\delta y_o}{\delta w_{oi}} \qquad (8)$$

The first factor of equation 8 can be obtained by differentiating equation 6.

$$\frac{\delta E}{\delta y_o} = -(d_o - y_o) \qquad (9)$$

Using $y_o = \sum_j w_{oj} y_j$, the second factor becomes

$$\frac{\delta y_o}{\delta w_{oi}} = \frac{\delta}{\delta w_{oi}} \sum_j w_{oj} y_j = y_i \qquad (11)$$

Hence,

$$\frac{\delta E}{\delta w_{oi}} = -(d_o - y_o) y_i \qquad (12)$$

The gradient G for the entire data set can be obtained by summing at each weight the contribution given by equation 12 over all the data points. Then, a small proportion μ (called the learning rate) of G is subtracted from the weights to achieve the required gradient descent.

The Gradient Descent Algorithm

The loss function minimization procedure during the training of a neural network involves the computation of the gradient of the loss function with time. The algorithm shown in Table 2 illustrates the steps in determining the gradient for attaining the minimum of the loss function [Haykin99, Snyman2005].

The algorithm terminates once the minimum of the error function, i.e., $G=0$ is reached. At this point the algorithm is said to have converged.

An important consideration is the learning rate (μ), which determines by how much the weights are changed at each step. If μ is too small, the algorithm will take a long time to converge. Conversely, if μ is too large, the algorithm diverges leading to imprecise learning.

However, the single layer perceptrons suffer from several limitations. They learn a solution if there is a possibility of finding it. They can separate linearly separable classes easily enough, but in situations where the division between the classes is much more complex, the single layer model fails abruptly.

Multilayer Perceptron

In order to overcome the shortcomings of the single layer perceptron model, the first and foremost way out is to resort to a multilayer model with the threshold function slightly smoothed out to provide some information about the nonlinearly separable inputs [Haykin99]. This means that the network will be able to adjust the weights as and when required. A possible multilayer neural network model comprising of three layers of nodes, viz., the input layer node, the hidden layer node and the output layer node along with their characteristic activation functions and inter-connection weights, is shown in Figure 3. In the figure, an extra node with a nonlinear activation function has been inserted between input and output. Since such a node is "hidden" inside the network, it is commonly referred to as a hidden unit. The hidden unit also has a weight from the bias unit. In general, all non-input neural network units have such bias weights. For simplicity however, the bias unit and weights are usually omitted from neural network diagrams. The sole output layer node shown in the figure is characterized by a linear activation function. Since the input layer node acts only as a

Table 2.

Begin	
Initialize w_{ij} **to small random values**	w_{ij} *are the interconnection weights*
Repeat until done	
For each weight w_{ij} **set** $\Delta w_{ij}:=0$	
For each data point $(x, t)^p$	
Set input units to x	
Compute value of output units	
For each weight w_{ij} **set** $\Delta w_{ij}:= \Delta w_{ij}+(d_i - y_i)y_j$	
For each weight w_{ij} **set** $w_{ij}:=w_{ij}+\mu\,\Delta w_{ij}$	μ *is the learning rate*
End	

Figure 3. Schematic diagram of a multilayer perceptron

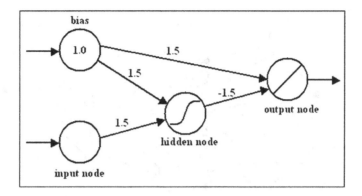

receptor of information from the external world, it is not driven by such activation mechanism.

As stated before, neural networks are often driven by nonlinear activation functions. The typical standard nonlinear hyperbolic tangent characteristic activation function is shown in Figure 4. Such a network model exhibits nonlinear behavior since theoretical results indicate that given enough hidden units.

A multilayer neural network architecture like the one shown in Figure 5 can approximate any nonlinear function to any required degree of accuracy. Hence, a multilayer neural network model is able to classify nonlinearly separable datasets. However, too many hidden layers can degrade the network's performance [Kumar2004].

Learning Algorithm

Since the target values for the hidden layers of multilayer networks are known, the gradient descent algorithm used for the training of linear networks (discussed earlier) cannot be applied to train multilayer neural networks. This inherent problem led to the sudden downfall of the neural networking paradigm after the 1950s until the *error backpropagation algorithm* [Haykin99, Rumelhart86, Chauvin95], or in short, *backprop* came to the rescue.

In principle, backprop provides a way to train networks with any number of hidden units arranged in any number of layers. The basic requirement of the backprop algorithm is to ensure that the network connection pattern must not contain any

Figure 4. Hyperbolic tangent function

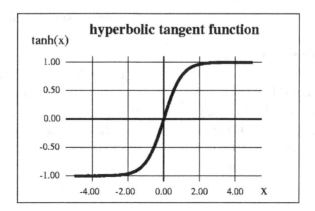

Figure 5. Schematic diagram of a multilayer perceptron with multiple hidden nodes

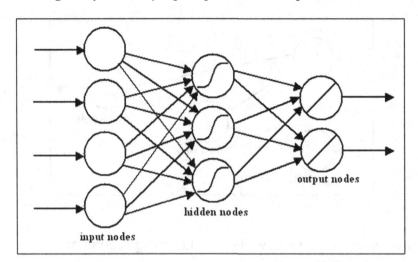

cycles. Networks that respect this constraint are called feedforward networks and their connection pattern forms a directed acyclic graph or dag.

For the purpose of training a multilayer feedforward neural network by gradient descent, a training dataset consisting of pairs (x, d) is considered. Here, vector x represents an input pattern to the network and vector d is the corresponding target output. The corresponding learning algorithm employing backprop is illustrated as shown in Table 3.

Neural networks are powerful and robust tools for the retrieval of incomplete data, finding patterns in datasets, and to mimic the human behavior when it comes to the analysis and interpretation of data. As such, they find wide use in processing, retrieval and recognition of data patterns.

3. FUZZY SETS AND FUZZY LOGIC

It may be pointed out that much of the information available in the real world exhibit vagueness, imprecision and uncertainty. In fact, the *fuzzy sets* approach fits in with the linguistic modes of reasoning that are natural to human beings. The fuzzy set theory, introduced by Zadeh [Za-deh65] explains the varied nature of ambiguity and uncertainty that exist in the real world. This is in sheer contradiction to the concept of crisp sets, where information is more often expressed in quantifying propositions.

The underlying concept behind the notion of *fuzzy sets* [Zadeh65] is that each and every observation, exists with a varied degree of containment in the universe of discourse. This degree of containment is referred to as the membership value of the observation. A fuzzy set is a mapping from an input universe of discourse into the interval [0, 1] that describes the membership of the input variable. This is referred to as *fuzzification*. The reverse mechanism to revert to the crisp world is termed as *defuzzification*. Thus, it can be inferred that

Whereas, crisp sets quantify quantities, fuzzy sets qualify qualities.

Fuzzy logic is a collection of conditional statements or fuzzy rules, which form the basis of the linguistic reasoning framework, which embodies representation of shallow knowledge. The fundamental atomic terms in this linguistic or natural language-reasoning framework are often modified with adjectives or "linguistic

Table 3.

Begin

Define $\delta_j := \dfrac{\delta E}{\delta net_j}$ *the error signal for unit j;* $\Delta w_{ij} := -\dfrac{\delta E}{\delta w_{ij}}$ *the (negative) gradient for weight w_{ij}.*

Let $A_i = \{j : \exists\, w_{ij}\}$ represents the set of preceding nodes to unit i and $P_j = \{i : \exists\, w_{ij}\}$ represents the set of succeeding nodes to unit j of the network.

Computation of the gradient

$$\Delta w_{ij} := -\frac{\delta E}{\delta net_{ij}} \frac{\delta net_{ij}}{\delta w_{ij}} \qquad \text{the first factor is the error of unit i.}$$

The second factor, $\dfrac{\delta net_{ij}}{\delta w_{ij}} := \dfrac{\delta}{\delta w_{ij}} \sum_{k \in A_i} w_{ik} y_k := y'_j$

So, $\Delta w_{ij} := \delta_i y'_j$

Forward activation

Remark: The activity of the input units is determined by the network's external input x. For all other units, the activity is propagated forward as

$$y_i := f_i \left(\sum_{j \in A_i} w_{ij} y_j \right)$$

Remark: The activity of all the preceding nodes A_i to unit i must be known before calculating the activity of i.

Calculation of output error

$$E := \frac{1}{2} \sum_o (d_o - y_o)^2 \qquad ; So,\ \delta_o := d_o - y_o \qquad \text{the error for output unit o.}$$

Error backpropagation

Remark: The output error is propagated back for deriving the errors of the hidden units in terms of the succeeding nodes.

$$\delta_j := -\sum_{i \in P_j} \frac{\delta E}{\delta net_i} \frac{\delta net_i}{\delta y_j} \frac{\delta y_j}{\delta net_j} \qquad \text{the first factor is the error of node i.}$$

The second factor, $\dfrac{\delta net_i}{\delta y_j} := \dfrac{\delta}{\delta y_j} \sum_{k \in A_k} w_{ik} y_k := w_{ij}$; *The third factor,* $\dfrac{\delta y_j}{\delta net_j} := \dfrac{\delta f_j(net_j)}{\delta net_j} := f'(net_j)$

If, the hidden units are characterized by the tanh activation function, then

$$f'(net_h) := 1 - y_h^2; So,\ \delta_j := f'(net_j) \sum_{i \in P_j} \delta_i w_{ij}$$

End

---

hedges". These linguistic hedges have the effect of modifying the membership function for a basic atom. The general form of a fuzzy rule [Zadeh65], which is similar to natural language expressions, can be written as

IF premise (antecedent) THEN conclusion (consequent)

It is generally referred to as the *IF-THEN* rule based form. It typically expresses an inference such that if a fact (premise, hypothesis or antecedent) is known, then another fact (conclusion or consequent) can be derived.

Fuzzy Set Theoretic Concepts

As already stated, all the elements in the universe of discourse X exhibit varying degrees of membership. This membership or containment of an element in a fuzzy set A is decided by a characteristic membership function, $\mu_A(x) \in [0,1]$. The closer is the membership value of an element to unity, the stronger is the containment of the element within the fuzzy set. Similarly, a lower membership value implies a weaker containment of the element within the set. A fuzzy set A, characterized by a membership function $\mu_A(x_i)$ and comprising elements $x_i, i = 1,2,3, ..., n$, is mathematically expressed as

$$A = \sum_i \frac{\mu_A(x_i)}{x_i}; i = 1, 2, 3, ..., n \qquad (13)$$

where, $\sum_i$ represents a collection of elements.

The resolution of a fuzzy set A is determined by the α-cut (or α-level set) of the fuzzy set. It is a crisp set A_α containing all the elements of the universal set U, that have a membership in A greater than or equal to α, i.e.

$$A_\alpha = \{x_i \in U \mid \mu_A(x_i) \geq \alpha\}, \alpha \in [0,1] \qquad (14)$$

If $A_\alpha = \{x \,\varepsilon\, U \mid \mu_A(x) > \alpha\}$, then A_α is referred to as strong α-cut. The set of all levels $\alpha \in [0, 1]$

that represents distinct α-cuts of a given fuzzy set A, is called a level set of A, i.e.,

$$\Lambda_A = \{\alpha \mid \mu_A(x) = \alpha, x \in U\} \qquad (15)$$

The support $S_A \in [0, 1]$, of such a fuzzy set A is defined as

$$S_A = \{\sum_{i=1}^{n} \frac{\mu_A(x_i)}{x_i} : x_i \in X \,\forall \mu_A(x_i) > 0\} \qquad (16)$$

The core (C_A) of a fuzzy set A represents all those constituent elements whose membership values are equal to unity, i.e.,

$$C_A = \{x_i \in U \mid \mu_A(x_i) = 1\} \qquad (17)$$

The bandwidth (BW_A) of a fuzzy set A is expressed as

$$BW_A = \{x_i \in U \mid \mu_A(x_i) \geq 0.5\} \qquad (18)$$

Figure 6 provides a graphical representation of the core, bandwidth, α-level and support of a fuzzy set.

The maximum of all the membership values in a fuzzy set A is referred to as the height (hgt_A) of the fuzzy set. If hgt_A is equal to 1, then the fuzzy set is referred to as a normal fuzzy set. If hgt_A is less than 1, then it is referred to as a subnormal fuzzy set. A normal fuzzy set is a superset of several nonempty subnormal fuzzy subsets.

A subnormal fuzzy subset (A_s) can be converted to its normalized equivalent by means of the normalization operator given by [Bhattacharyya2008]

$$\text{Norm}_{A_s(x)} = \frac{A_s(x)}{hgt_{A_s}} \qquad (19)$$

Figure 6. Representation of fuzzy set concepts

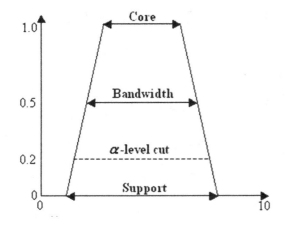

The corresponding denormalization operation is given by [Bhattacharyya2008]

$$\text{DeNorm}_{A_s(x)} = hgt_{A_s(x)} \times \text{Norm}_{A_s(x)} \qquad (20)$$

In general, for a subnormal fuzzy subset with support, $S_{As} \in [L, U]$, the normalization and the denormalization operators are expressed as [Bhattacharyya2008]

$$\text{Norm}_{A_s(x)} = \frac{A_s(x) - L}{U - L}; \quad \text{DeNorm}_{A_s(x)} = L + (U - L) \times \text{Norm}_{A_s(x)} \qquad (21)$$

Fuzzy Set Theoretic Operations

The fuzzy union, intersection and complement operations [Zadeh65] on two fuzzy sets A, B for an element x in the universe of discourse X, are defined as

$$\text{Union}: \quad \mu_{A \cup B}(x) = \max[\mu_A(x), \mu_B(x)] \qquad (22)$$

$$\text{Intersection}: \quad \mu_{A \cap B}(x) = \min[\mu_A(x), \mu_B(x)] \qquad (23)$$

$$\text{Complement}: \quad \mu_{\bar{A}}(x) = 1 - \mu_A(x) \qquad (24)$$

Fuzzy Cardinality

The scalar cardinality of a fuzzy set A is the summation of the membership grades of all elements of x in A. It is given by [Zadeh65, Ross95]

$$\mid A \mid = \sum_{x \in U} \mu_A(x) \qquad (25)$$

where, U is the universe of discourse. When a fuzzy set A has a finite support, its cardinality can be defined as a fuzzy set. This fuzzy cardinality is denoted by $|A_f|$ and is defined by Zadeh as [Zadeh65, Ross95]

$$\mid A_f \mid = \sum_{\alpha \in \Lambda_A} \frac{\alpha}{\mid A_\alpha \mid} \qquad (26)$$

where, α is the cut-off value, A_α is the α-level set of the fuzzy set and Λ_A is the corresponding level set.

Fuzzy Operators

Several operators are used to form the "linguistic hedges" in fuzzy logic. These are (i) Concentration (ii) Dilation and (iii) Intensification operators [Ross95, Bhattacharyya2006].

- Concentration: This operator tends to concentrate the elements of a fuzzy set by reducing the degree of membership of those elements that are "partly" in the set. It is expressed as

$$\mu_A(x) = \mu_A(x)^2 \quad \text{for} \quad 0 \leq \mu_A(x) \leq 1 \qquad (27)$$

- Dilation: This operator dilates or stretches a fuzzy set by increasing the membership of elements that are "partly" in the set. It is expressed as

Figure 7. Fuzzy operators

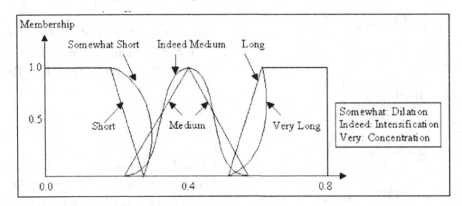

$$\mu_A(x) = d \times \mu_A(x) \quad \text{for} \quad 0 \le \mu_A(x) \le 1$$

(28)

where, d is the amount of dilation

- Intensification: This operator acts as a combination of the concentration and dilation operators. It is expressed as

$$INT(A) = \begin{cases} 2\mu_A(x)^2 & \text{for} \quad 0 \le \mu_A(x) \le 0.5 \\ 1 - 2[1 - \mu_A(x)]^2 & \text{for} \quad 0.5 < \mu_A(x) \le 1 \end{cases}$$

(29)

Thus, intensification increases the contrast between the elements, which have more than half-membership and those elements, which have less than half-membership. Figure 7 illustrates the operations of concentration, dilation and intensification for fuzzy linguistic hedges [*Short, Medium, Long*] on a typical fuzzy set A.

The resultant hedges are represented by [*Somewhat Short, Indeed Medium, Very Long*]. It is evident from the figure that the fuzzy operators tend to smooth out the hedges represented by the membership functions [*Short, Medium, Long*]. The steeper slopes of the hedges [*Short, Medium, Long*] are smoothed out to gradual variations. This change is attributed to the manipulation of the membership values of these hedges.

Due to the ability of handling uncertainties, fuzzy sets and fuzzy logic play a crucial role in decision-making processes. Fuzzy sets and fuzzy logic find application in modeling imprecise datasets, designing intelligently controlled systems, quantifying the varied amount of ambiguities in the domains of signal processing and computer vision, etc. They are also used to quantify the inherent vagueness/ambiguities often encountered in real life situations.

4. HEURISTIC SEARCH TECHNIQUES

This computing paradigm employs several search and optimization algorithms based on Darwinian laws of biological evolution. Several evolutionary algorithms are in vogue. These include (a) genetic programming (GP), which evolve programs, (b) evolutionary programming (EP), which focuses on optimizing continuous functions without recombination, (c) evolutionary strategies (ES), which focuses on optimizing continuous functions with recombination, and (d) genetic algorithms (GAs), which focuses on optimizing general combinatorial problems. Most of these evolutionary algorithms are characterized by a population of trial solutions and a collection of operators to act on the population. The basic philosophy behind these algorithms is to search the population space by the application of the embedded operators so as to arrive at an optimal solution space. Generally, two types of operators are used, viz. reproduction and evolution. The reproduction operator is guided by a selection mechanism. The evolution operator includes the crossover and mutation operators. The search technique is implemented through a series of iterations, whereby the different operators are applied in a loop on the initial population. Each iteration is referred to as a generation. Each generation produces a new solution space of parent individuals, which are selectively chosen for participating in the next generation of the optimization procedure. The selection of the participating parents for the next generation is decided by a figure of merit, often referred to as the objective function. This objective function is entrusted with the evaluation of the fitness of the candidate solutions in a particular generation to qualify for the next generation of operations. Other notable and related search techniques include:

- Quantum annealing [Apolloni89, Das2005], which uses "quantum fluctuations" instead of thermal fluctuations to get through high but thin barriers in the target function.
- Tabu search [Glover97], which normally moves to neighboring states of lower energy, but takes uphill moves when it finds itself stuck in a local minimum; and avoids cycles by keeping a "taboo list" of solutions already seen.
- Ant colony optimization (ACO) [Colorni91, Dorigo92], which uses many ants (or agents) to traverse the solution space and find locally productive areas.
- Harmony search, which mimics musicians in improvisation process where each musician plays a note for finding a best harmony all together.

- Stochastic optimization, which is an umbrella set of methods that includes simulated annealing and numerous other approaches.

The following sections discuss the operational procedures of three popular heuristic search techniques, viz., genetic algorithms, simulated annealing and ant colony optimization.

Genetic Algorithms

Genetic algorithms (GAs) [Goldberg89, Davis91, Michal92, Bandyopadhyay2007a] are efficient, adaptive and robust multi-point search and optimization techniques guided by the principles of evolution and natural genetics. They provide parallel near optimal and solutions of an objective or fitness function in complex, large and multimodal landscapes. GAs are modeled on the principles of natural genetic systems, where the genetic information of each individual or potential solution is encoded in structures called *chromosomes*. They use some domain or problem dependent knowledge for directing the search in more promising areas of the solution space; this is known as the fitness function. Each individual or chromosome has an associated fitness function, which indicates its degree of goodness with respect to the solution it represents. Various biologically inspired operators like selection, crossover and mutation are applied on the chromosomes to yield potentially better solutions.

Basic Principles and Features

A GA essentially comprises a set of individual solutions or chromosomes (called the *population*) and some biologically inspired operators that create a new (and potentially better) population from an old one. The different steps of a GA can be represented as follows.

```
Initialize the population
Do
  Encode the strings and compute
their fitness values
  Reproduce/select strings to create
new mating pool
  Generate new population by cross-
over and mutation
Loop while (not_termination)
```

The components of GAs are described in the following sections.

Encoding Strategy and Population

To solve an optimization problem, GAs start with the chromosomal representation of a parameter set which is to be encoded as a finite size string over an alphabet of finite length. For example, the string

```
1   0   0   1   1   0   1   0
```

is a binary chromosome (string of 0's and 1's) of length 8. Each chromosome actually refers to a coded possible solution. A set of such chromosomes in a generation is called a population, the size of which may be constant or may vary from one generation to another. The chromosomes in the initial population are either generated randomly or using domain specific information.

Evaluation Technique

The fitness function is chosen depending on the problem to be solved, in such a way that the strings (possible solutions) representing good points in the search space have high fitness values. This is the only information (also known as the payoff information) that GAs use while searching for possible solutions.

Genetic Operators

The frequently used genetic operators are the selection, crossover and mutation operators. These are applied to a population of chromosomes to yield potentially new offspring. The operators are described in the following sections.

Selection

The selection/reproduction process copies individual strings (called parent chromosomes) into a tentative new population (known as mating pool) for genetic operations. The number of copies that an individual receives for the next generation is usually taken to be directly proportional to its fitness value thereby mimicking the natural selection procedure to some extent. This scheme is commonly called the *proportional selection scheme. Roulette wheel parent selection, stochastic universal selection,* and *binary tournament selection* [Goldberg89, Michal92] are some of the most frequently used selection procedures. In the commonly used elitist model of GAs, the best chromosome seen up to the last generation is retained either in the population, or in a location outside it.

Crossover

The main purpose of crossover is to exchange information between randomly selected parent chromosomes by recombining parts of their genetic information. It combines parts of two parent chromosomes to produce offspring for the next generation. Single point crossover is one of the most commonly used schemes. Here, first of all, the members of the selected strings in the mating pool are paired at random. Then each pair of chromosomes is subjected to crossover with a probability μ_c where an integer position k (known as the crossover point) is selected uniformly at random between 1 and l-1 (l>1 is the string length). Two new strings are created by swapping all characters from position (k+1) to l.

For example, let the two parents and the crossover points be as shown below.

```
1   0   0   1   1 | 0   1   0
0   0   1   0   1 | 1   0   0
```

After crossover the offspring will be the following:

```
1   0   0   1   1   1   0   0
0   0   1   0   1   0   1   0
```

Some other common crossover techniques are two-point crossover, multiple point crossover, shuffle-exchange crossover and uniform crossover [Davis91].

Mutation

The main objective of mutation is to introduce genetic diversity into the population. It may so happen that the optimal solution resides in a portion of the search space, which is not represented in the population's genetic structure. Hence, the algorithm will therefore be unable to attain the global optima. In such a scenario, only mutation can possibly direct the population to the optimal section of the search space by randomly altering the information in a chromosome. Mutating a binary gene involves simple negation of the bit, while that for real coded genes are defined in a variety of ways [Eshelman93, Michal92].

For example in binary bit-by-bit mutation every bit in a chromosome is subject to mutation with a probability μ_m. The result of applying the bit-by-bit mutation on positions 3 and 7 of a chromosome is shown below.

```
1   0   0   1   1   0   1   0
1   0   1   1   1   0   0   0
```

Parameters of a Genetic Algorithm

There are several parameters in GAs that have to be tuned by the user. Some among these are the population size, probabilities of performing crossover (usually kept in the range 0.6 to 0.8) and mutation (usually kept below 0.1) and the termination criteria. Moreover, one must decide whether to use the generational replacement strategy where the entire population is replaced by the new population, or the steady state replacement policy where only the less fit individuals are replaced. Most of such parameters in GAs are problem dependent, and no guidelines for their choice exist in the literature. Therefore, several researchers have also kept some of the GA parameters variable and/or adaptive [Baker85, Srinivas94].

The cycle of selection, crossover and mutation is repeated a number of times till one of the following occurs:

1. average fitness of a population becomes more or less constant over a specified number of generations,
2. desired objective function value is attained by at least one string in the population,
3. number of generations is greater than some predefined threshold.

Simulated Annealing

Simulated annealing (SA) [Kirkpatrick83, Cerny85] is a probabilistic metaheuristic search technique useful for finding a good approximation to the global minimum of a given function in a large search space. It is generally efficient with a discrete search space. In situations, which demand an acceptably good solution in a fixed amount of time, SA has been found to be more effective than other exhaustive search techniques.

The term "simulated annealing" is derived from the common annealing process in metallurgy where subsequent heating and controlled cooling of a material are performed to increase the size of its crystals. Heating excites the material atoms and causes them to wander randomly in higher energy states. Subsequent slow cooling settles them to configurations with lower internal energy than the initial one.

Similarly, in the SA algorithm, each step replaces the current solution by a random neighboring solution. The probability of choosing such a neighboring solution depends on the difference between the corresponding energy function values and a global parameter T referred to as the temperature. This temperature is gradually decreased during the cooling process. Thus, the current solution changes almost randomly when T is large, but the rate of change of states goes down as T is reduced.

Overview of SA

The basic objective of SA is to minimize the system internal energy function $F(\rho)$, where ρ corresponds to each point of the search space. Thus, it aims to bring the system, from an arbitrary initial state, to a state with the minimum possible energy.

For this purpose, SA considers some user specified neighbors ρ' of the current state ρ, and probabilistically decides between migrating the system to either state ρ' or to retain in state ρ. The probabilities are chosen such that the system ultimately migrates to lower energy states. This step is repeated until the system reaches a state that is a good approximation to the required one, or until a prespecified limit to the approximation has been reached. The following sections highlight the important aspects of simulated annealing.

Acceptance Probabilities

This is the probability of migrating from the current state ρ to a candidate new state ρ'. This is decided by an acceptance probability function $P(g, g', T)$, where $g = F(\rho)$ and $g' = F(\rho')$ and T is the temperature (mentioned earlier). The acceptance probability is usually chosen such that the probability of allowing a transition decreases when the difference $(g'-g)$ increases. This means that smaller uphill migrations are more likely than the larger ones. P must be nonzero when $g' > g$,

which implies that the system may migrate to the new state even when it has a higher energy than the current one. This prevents the process from becoming stuck in a local minimum. When T goes to zero, the acceptance probability tends to zero if $g' > g$. P however, attains a positive value if $g' < g$.

Thus, the system favors transitions that go to lower energy values, and avoid those that go higher for sufficiently small values of T. When T becomes 0, the procedure will ensure making the migration only if it goes to lower energy. Thus, it is clear that the evolution of the state depends crucially on the temperature T. Roughly speaking, the evolution of a state ρ is sensitive to coarser changes of energy variations when T is large, and to finer changes of energy variations when T is small.

The Annealing Schedule

Another essential feature of the SA method is that the temperature (T) should be gradually reduced as the simulation proceeds [Kirkpatrick83, Cerny85]. Initially, T is set to a high value (i.e. ∞), and then it is decreased at each step according to some annealing schedule. The user generally specifies this schedule for the decrement of T. However, it must be ensured that the schedule should be such that it would end up with $T = 0$ towards the end of the annealing process.

Thus, the system is expected to migrate initially towards a broader region of the search space containing good solutions ignoring smaller features of the energy function in the process. Subsequently, it would drift towards the lower energy regions that become narrower and narrower. Finally, the system migrates downhill according to the steepest descent heuristic. However, the pure version of SA does not keep track of the best solution obtained in terms of the lower energy levels attained at any point of time.

SA Pseudocode

The pseudocode shown in Table 4 implements the simulated annealing heuristic, as described above, starting from state ρ_0 and continuing to a maximum of k_{max} steps or until a state with energy g_{max} or less is found.

Selection of Operating Parameters of SA

Several parameters need to be specified for the application of SA. These include the state space, the energy function F, the candidate generator procedure, the acceptance probability function P and the annealing schedule. The performance of SA depends on the suitability of the choice of these parameters. The following sections throw some light on the selection of these parameters.

Search Graph Diameter

Considering all the possible states of a simulated annealing process to be the vertices of a graph with the edges representing the candidate transitions, simulated annealing may be modeled as a search graph which aims to provide a sufficiently short path from the initial state to any intermediate state or the global optimum state. This implies that the search space must be small enough for an efficient implementation of the algorithm. In other words, the diameter of the search graph must be small to facilitate faster transitions between states. Hence, the choice of the search graph diameter is an essential criterion for successful operation of the simulated annealing algorithm.

Transition Probabilities

The migration from the current state ρ to the state ρ' is governed by another probability, viz., the transition probability. The transition probability depends on the current temperature (T_c), on the order of candidate transitions and on the acceptance probability function P.

Efficient Candidate Generation

It is evident that the current state is expected to have much lower energy than a random state after a few iterations of the SA algorithm. This observation is important in the selection of the candidate generator function. In practice, the generator function is sensitive towards those candidate migrates where the energy of the destination state ρ' is likely to be similar to that of the current state. This implies

Table 4.

Initialize state, energy and "best" solutions	
$\rho := \rho_0$; $g := F(\rho)$; $\rho_{best} := \rho$; $g_{best} := g$	*initial and best states, initial and best energy*
k:=0	*starting point*
Do	
Neighborhood selection and energy computation	
$\rho_{new} := \textbf{neighbor}(\rho)$	*new neighboring state*
$g_{new} := F(\rho_{new})$	*new energy*
if $g_{new} < g_{best}$ **then**	
$\rho_{best} := \rho_{new}$; $g_{best} := g_{new}$	*best state and energy*
if $P(g, g_{new}, T_c(k/k_{max})) > \varphi$ **then**	*T_c is current temperature and φ is a random number*
$\rho := \rho_{new}$; $g := g_{new}$	*updated states and energy*
$k := k + 1$	*next step*
Loop while $k < k_{max}$ *and* $g > g_{max}$	

that those candidate states ρ' for which $P[F(\rho), F(\rho'), T]$ is large should be opted for first.

Avoidance of Getting Stuck to Local Minima
Another aspect of the selection of the candidate generator function is to reduce the number of local minima, which may come up during the annealing process. Otherwise, the SA algorithm may be trapped in these minima with a high probability for a very long time. The probability of occurrence of such traps is proportional to the number of states achieved in the local minimal state of SA. The time of trapping is exponential on the energy difference between the local minimal state and its surrounding states. These requirements, however, can be met by resorting to slighter changes to the candidate generator function.

Cooling Schedule
The simulated annealing algorithm assumes that the cooling rate is always low enough such that the probability distribution of the current state remains near the thermodynamic equilibrium at all times. But the time required for attaining the equilibrium state (referred to as the relaxation time) after a change in temperature strongly depends on the nature of the energy function, the current temperature (T_c) as well as on the candidate generator.

Hence, there is no basis for selecting an ideal cooling rate for the algorithm. It should be estimated and adjusted empirically for a particular problem.

However, this problem has been taken care of by the thermodynamic simulated annealing algorithm, which adjusts the temperature at each step based on the energy difference between the two states according to the laws of thermodynamics instead of applying any cooling schedule.

Restarting of SA
Sometimes it is better to revert back to a solution that was significantly better rather than always migrate from the current state. This is called restarting. To do this ρ and g are set to ρ_{best} and g_{best}, respectively and the annealing schedule is restarted. The decision to restart could be based on a fixed number of steps, or based on the current energy being too high from the best energy so far.

Ant Colony Optimization

The ant colony optimization algorithm (ACO) is another probabilistic computational search technique useful for finding the best possible paths in search graphs. It is a member of the family of ant colony algorithms, which are referred to as swarm intelligence methods. Initially proposed by Marco Dorigo in 1992 in his PhD thesis [Colorni91, Dorigo92], the first algorithm was aimed at searching for an optimal path in a graph based on the behaviors exhibited by ants while searching for food out of their colony.

Overview of ACO

In their quest for food, ants generally start searching randomly through all possible paths that lead to food. Once food is found, they return to their colony leaving behind pheromone trails. If the following ants make the path, they do not hover randomly, instead follow the trail to find food.

This pheromone trail however, starts to evaporate with time, thereby reducing its attractive strength. The more time it takes for an ant to travel down the path and back again, the more time the pheromones have to evaporate. A short path, by comparison, gets marched over faster, and thus the pheromone density remains high as it is laid on the path as fast as it can evaporate.

The phenomenon of pheromone evaporation prevents the convergence of the algorithm to a local optimum. In absence of any pheromone evaporation the following ants would always be attracted to the paths traversed by the first/leading ant thereby leading to a constrained solution space.

This procedure adopted by real world ants is adapted in implementing the ant colony optimization algorithm, which always leads to the shortest one [Goss89, Deneubourg90] between two unequal length paths. This self-organized system adopted by ants, referred to as "Stigmergy", is characterized by both a positive feedback resulting out of the deposit of pheromone for attracting other ants and a negative one resulting out of the dissipation of the pheromone due to evaporation. A pseudocode for the ACO algorithm is listed below.

```
Do
    Generate_TrialSolutions()
    Update_Pheromone()
    Search_Paths()
Loop while (not_termination)
```

The generation of the trial solutions in the ACO algorithm by the **Generate_TrialSolutions()** procedure involves the selection of subsequent nodes in the search space. This process is referred to as edge selection. An ant will switch from node i to node j with probability

$$p_{ij} = \frac{\psi_{ij}^{\gamma}(t)\kappa_{ij}^{\delta}(t)}{\sum \psi_{ij}^{\gamma}(t)\kappa_{ij}^{\delta}(t)} \tag{30}$$

where, $\psi_{ij}(t)$ is the amount of pheromone on edge(i, j) at time t, κ_{ij}(ts the acceptability of edge(i, j) at time t, γ and δ control the influence of parameters κ_{ij} and ψ_{ij}, respectively.

The **Update_Pheromone()** procedure on a given edge(i, j) would yield the amount of pheromone at the next instant of time ($t+1$), It is determined as

$$\psi_{ij}(t+1) = (1-\varepsilon)\psi_{ij}(t) + \Delta\psi_{ij} \tag{31}$$

where, $\psi_{ij}(t+1)$ is the amount of pheromone on that edge at time ($t+1$), ε is the rate of pheromone evaporation and $\Delta\psi_{ij}$ is the amount of pheromone deposited. For the kth ant traveling on edge(i, j),

$\Delta\psi_{ij}^k = \frac{1}{C}$, where C is the cost/length of the kth ant's path. For all other ants, $\Delta\psi_{ij}^k = 0$.

Several variations of the ACO algorithm are in vogue. These include the Elitist Ant System, the Max-Min Ant System (MMAS) [Stutzle2000], the proportional pseudo-random rule [Dorigo97] and the Rank-Based Ant System (ASrank).

The evolutionary algorithms provide a platform for deriving at the global optimal solution to a problem by means of their searching capabilities. Notable application areas include the traveling salesman problem, determination of optimal clusters in a clustering algorithm etc.

5. ROUGH SET THEORY

Rough set theory [Pawlak82] is a comparatively new approach to explain vagueness/uncertainty inherent in real world datasets. The rough set theory, as an extension of the classical set theory, stems from Frege's idea of vagueness [Frege93]. Instead of the concepts of membership as used in fuzzy set theory, imprecision is expressed in rough sets by a boundary region of a set.

The underlying postulates of rough set theory are defined by means of two topological operations, viz., *interior* and *closure*, collectively referred to as *approximations*.

Let, for a given a set of objects U (the universe of discourse), an indiscernibility relation $R \subseteq U \times U$ exists, which can be used to represent the lack of knowledge about the elements of U. A subset P of U can then be characterized by approximations with respect to R as shown below.

- The *lower approximation* of P with respect to R is the set of all objects which can be certainly classified as belonging to P with respect to R,
- the *upper approximation* of P with respect to R is the set of all objects which can be

Figure 8. Rough set representation

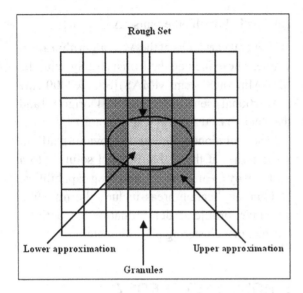

- *R-lower approximation* of *P* is given as

$$R_*(x) = \bigcup_{x \in U} \{R(x) : R(x) \subseteq P\} \tag{32}$$

- *R-upper approximation* of *P* is given as

$$R^*(x) = \bigcup_{x \in U} \{R(x) : R(x) \cap P \neq \varphi\} \tag{33}$$

- *R-boundary region* of *P* is given as

$$RN_R(x) = R^*(x) - R_*(x) \tag{34}$$

From the definition it is seen expressed in terms of granules of knowledge [Polkowski2002, Polkowski2001], the *lower approximation* of a set is union of all granules entirely included in the set. On the other hand, the *upper approximation* is the union of all granules having non-empty intersection with the set. The difference between the upper and lower approximations is the rough/boundary region of set. Figure 8 shows a generic representation of a rough set.

Rough sets can be also defined in terms of the rough membership function (μ_P^R) [Pawlak94] instead of the lower and upper approximations. The rough membership function indicates the degree with which x belongs to P given the knowledge of x expressed by R. It is defined as

$$\mu_P^R(x) = \frac{|P \cap R(x)|}{|R(x)|}; \quad \mu_P^R(x) \in <0, 1> \tag{35}$$

where, $|P|$ is the cardinality of P.

The lower and upper approximations and the boundary region of a set are then defined as

$$R_*(x) = \{x \in U : \mu_P^R(x) = 1\} \tag{36}$$

$$R^*(x) = \{x \in U : \mu_P^R(x) > 0\} \tag{37}$$

possibly classified as belonging to *P* with respect to *R* and

- the boundary region of a *P* with respect to *R* (i.e. the rough region) is the set of all objects which can be neither be classified as belonging to *P* nor as not belonging to *P* with respect to *R*.

Given the aforestated concepts, it can be inferred that *P* is a crisp set, i.e. it is exact with respect to *R* if the boundary region of *P* is empty. On the other hand, if the boundary region of *P* is nonempty, *P* is a rough set, i.e. it is inexact with respect to *R*. Thus, a set is defined as a rough set if it has nonempty boundary region, otherwise it is a crisp set.

The indiscernibility relation (*R*), as stated above, explains the lack of precise knowledge about the elements of the universe. Equivalence classes of *R* are referred to as the granules. The granules represent the elementary portion of knowledge perceivable due to *R*.

For *R(x)*, an equivalence class of *R* determined by element *x*, the following definitions of approximations and the boundary region hold.

$$RN_R(x) = \{x \in U : 0 < \mu_P^R(x) < 1\} \qquad (38)$$

Rough sets have flourished over the years, thanks to the approximating capabilities and the non-requirement of any a priori knowledge regarding the problem domain. This feature of rough sets has envisaged the use of these set theoretic concepts in several fields of engineering and scientific applications both with and without the conjunction of fuzzy set theory.

6. APPLICATIONS OF SOFT COMPUTING

The field of soft computing has been successfully applied in a variety of real life applications. Notable among these include image preprocessing and enhancement, pattern recognition, image segmentation, image analysis and understanding, image mining, Kansei information processing, networking, VLSI system design and testing, engineering design, information retrieval etc. The following sections illustrate the notable applications of the soft computing paradigm to image processing, pattern recognition and Kansei information processing.

Soft Computing Applications to Image Processing and Pattern Recognition

Neural networks have often been employed by researchers for dealing with the daunting tasks of extraction [Forrest88, Pham98, Hertz91, Lippmann87, Haykin99}, classification [Chua88a, Chua88b, Antonucci94, Egmont2002, Lippmann89, Pao89} of relevant object specific information from redundant image information bases, segmentation of image data [Tsao93, Bilbro88] and identification and recognition of objects from an image [Carpenter89, Parsi95, Tang96, Perlovsky97, Abdallah95, Egmont99,

Roth90, Scott97]. Several attempts [Amari88, Fukushima80] have also been reported where self-organizing neural network architectures are used for object extraction and pattern recognition.

Chiu et al. [Chiu90] applied artificial neural network architectures for the processing of photogrammetric targets. Carpenter et al. [Carpenter91} applied self-organizing neural networks for the recognition of patterns from images.

Neural networks of varying topology and assisted by fuzzy set theory, have also been widely used to deal with the problem of segmentation and clustering of image data, given the inherent features of susceptibility to dynamic environments [Baraldi2001, Leondes98, Tzeng98]. Tatem et al. [Tatem2001] applied a Hopfield neural network for the purpose of identification of super-resolution targets from remotely sensed images. Charalampidis et al. [Charalampidis2001] used a fuzzy ARTMAP to classify different noisy signals. Details of image and pattern classification approaches using neural networks are available in [Zhang2000].

Lin [Lin96] proposed an unsupervised parallel medical image segmentation technique using a fuzzy Hopfield neural network. In this approach, fuzzy clustering is embedded into a Hopfield neural network architecture for the purpose of segmentation of the images. In [Chen2003], a fuzzy neural network is used to classify synthetic aperture radar (SAR) images using the statistical properties of polarimetric data of the images. The images are clustered by the fuzzy c-means clustering algorithm based on Wishart data distribution. The clustered data is finally incorporated into the neural network for the purpose of classification. Boskovitz et al. [Boskovitz2002] developed an autoadaptive multilevel image segmentation and edge detection system using a neural network architecture similar to a multilayer perceptron. A fuzzy clustering technique is involved in selecting the labels required for the thresholding operation on the image.

Efforts have also been made by inducing multivalued logical reasoning to the existing neural networks for the purpose of classification of multidimensional data. Multilevel thresholding ability on input data has been induced in discrete-time neural networks by means of synthesis of multi-level threshold functions [Si91]. Other soft computing techniques like genetic algorithms have also been widely used in the domain of medical image segmentation. An extensive review is available in [Maulik2009].

Of late, the processing of multichannel information has assumed great importance mainly due to the evolving fields of remote sensing, GIS, biomedical imaging and multispectral data management. Color image segmentation is a classical example of multichannel information processing. The complexity of the problem of color image segmentation and object extraction is mainly due to the variety of the color intensity gamut. Due to the inherent parallelism and ability of approximation, adaptation and graceful degradation, neural networks are also suited for addressing the problem of color image processing. Lee et al. [Lee96] employed a CNN multilayer neural network structure for processing of color images following the RGB color model. In this approach, each primary color is assigned to a unique CNN layer allowing parallel processing of color component information. Zhu [Zhu94] however, transferred the RGB color space to Munsell color space and used an adaptive resonance theory (ART) neural network to classify objects into recognition categories. Roska et al. [Roska93] also applied a multilayer CNN structure for handling the enormous amount of data involved in the processing of color images. Self-organizing neural network architectures [Moreira96, Wu2000] have also been used for segmentation and classification of color images. The vagueness in image information arising out of the admixtures of the color components has often been dealt with the soft computing paradigm. In [Chen95], Chen et al. applied fuzzy set theory for proper analysis of uncertainty and vagueness in color image information. Color image segmentation techniques involving fuzzy set theory and fuzzy logic are also available in the literature [Gillet2002, Chung2003, Ito95, Choi95].

Soft Computing Applications to Kansei Information Processing

Another noteworthy application area where soft computing has made a mark is Kansei information processing [Schutte2004]. Kansei engineering invented in the 1970s by Professor Mitsuo Nagamachi of Hiroshima International University, is a method for translating feelings and impressions into product parameters. Kansei engineering essentially deals with the processing and manipulation of nonverbal information such as voice pitch, facial expressions, gestures as well as verbal information. Kansei encompass the total concept of senses, consciousness, and feelings that relate to human behavior in social living.

Since Kansei information has subjectivity, human linguistic understanding plays a central role in Kansei information processing. Fuzzy set theory [Zadeh65] has been effectively applied for explaining the ambiguity and vagueness in Kansei information [Yan2008]. In [Hayashida2002], Hayashida and Takagi proposed an evolutionary computation (EC) and interactive EC (IEC) system for visualizing individuals in a multi-dimensional searching space thereby enabling the envisioning of the landscape of an n-dimensional searching space. The proposed system has been found to be efficient than that obtained with the conventional genetic algorithm. Unehara and Yamada [Unehara2008] introduced an Interactive Genetic Algorithm (IGA) for the designing of products' shapes through evaluation by Kansei. Other notable applications of soft computing in Kansei information processing can be found in the literature [Onisawa2005, Nagata94].

Other Soft Computing Applications

Recently, soft computing tools are being widely used in the domain of data mining and bioinformatics. In data mining, genetic algorithms, neural networks and fuzzy logic are widely used in solving many problems of optimization, feature selection, classification and clustering [Bigus96, Cox2005, Bandyopadhyay2005]. In the domain of bioinformatics, soft computing tools have been used for sequence alignment, fragment assembly, gene and promoter identification, phylogenetic tree analysis, prediction of gene regulatory network, protein structure and function prediction, protein classification, molecule design and docking, to name just a few [Bandyopadhyay2007a, Bandyopadhyay2007b]. Web intelligence is another recent area that has seen a spurt of successful application of soft computing tools [Bandyopadhyay2007a].

7. CONCLUSION

A brief overview of the essence and applications of the soft computing paradigm is presented in this chapter. This computing framework is essentially built around several intelligent tools and techniques. Notable among them are the neural networks, fuzzy sets, fuzzy logic, genetic algorithms and rough sets. These tools form the backbone of this widely used computing paradigm meant for analysis and understanding of knowledge bases.

Neural networks are used for the analysis of numeric data. These networks comprise interconnected processing units or nodes in different topologies depending on the problem at hand. Fuzzy sets and fuzzy logic deal with the uncertainties inherent in data under consideration by representing the degree of vagueness in terms of linguistic information. Genetic algorithm, simulated annealing algorithm and ant colony optimization algorithm are random search techniques meant for arriving at an optimum probable solution to a problem. Rough sets also handle the underlying

uncertainties in data without even requiring any a priori information regarding the data content and distribution. These techniques are applied extensively in a wide variety of engineering and scientific problems with astounding results.

REFERENCES

Abdallah, M. A., Samu, T. I., & Grisson, W. A. (1995). Automatic target identification using neural networks. *SPIE Proceedings on Intelligent Robots and Computer Vision XIV, 2588*, 556–565.

Ackley, D. H., Hinton, G. E., & Sejnowski, T. J. (1985). A learning algorithm for Boltzmann Machines. *Cognitive Science, 9*, 147–169. doi:. doi:10.1207/s15516709cog0901_7

Amari, S. (1988). Mathematical theory of self-organization in neural nets. In Seelen, W. V., Shaw, G., & Leinhos, U. M. (Eds.), *Organization of Neural Networks: Structures and Models*. New York: Academic Press.

Antonucci, M., Tirozzi, B., & Yarunin, N. D. (1994). Numerical simulation of neural networks with translation and rotation invariant pattern recognition. *International Journal of Modern Physics B, 8*(11-12), 1529–1541. doi:.doi:10.1142/S0217979294000658

Apolloni, B., Caravalho, C., & De Falco, D. (1989). Quantum stochastic optimization. *Stochastic Processes and their Applications, 33*, 233–244. doi:. doi:10.1016/0304-4149(89)90040-9

Baker, J. E. (1985). Adaptive selection methods for genetic algorithms In J. J. Grefenstette (Ed.), *Proceedings of 1st International Conference on Genetic Algorithms* (pp. 101-111). Hillsdale, NJ: Lawrence Erlbaum Associates.

Bandyopadhyay, S., Maulik, U., Holder, L., & Cook, D. (Eds.). (2005). *Advanced Methods for Knowledge Discovery from Complex Data*. London: Springer.

Bandyopadhyay, S., Maulik, U., & Wang, J. T. L. (Eds.). (2007). *Analysis of Biological Data: A Soft Computing Approach*. Singapore: World Scientific.

Bandyopadhyay, S., & Pal, S. K. (2007). *Classification and Learning Using Genetic Algorithms: Application in Bioinformatics and Web Intelligence*. Germany: Springer.

Baraldi, A., Binaghi, E., Blonda, P., Brivio, P. A., & Rampini, A. (2001). Comparison of the multilayer perceptron with neuro-fuzzy techniques in the estimation of cover class mixture in remotely sensed data. *IEEE Transactions on Geoscience and Remote Sensing, 39*(5), 994–1005. doi:. doi:10.1109/36.921417

Bezdek, J. C. (1992). On the relationship between neural networks, pattern recognition and intelligence. *International Journal of Approximate Reasoning, 6*, 85–107. doi:10.1016/0888-613X(92)90013-P

Bhattacharyya, S., & Dutta, P. (2006). Designing pruned neighborhood neural networks for object extraction from noisy background. *Journal of Foundations of Computing and Decision Sciences, 31*(2), 105–134.

Bhattacharyya, S., Dutta, P., & Maulik, U. (2008). Self Organizing Neural Network (SONN) based gray scale object extractor with a Multilevel Sigmoidal (MUSIG) activation function. *Journal of Foundations of Computing and Decision Sciences, 33*(2), 131–165.

Bigus, J. P. (1996). *Data Mining With Neural Networks: Solving Business Problems from Application Development to Decision Support*. New York: Mcgraw-Hill.

Bilbro, G. L., White, M., & Synder, W.(n.d.). Image segmentation with neurocomputers. In Eckmiller, R., & Malsburg, C. V. D. (Eds.), *Neural computers*. New York: Springer-Verlag.

Boskovitz, V., & Guterman, H. (2002). An adaptive neuro-fuzzy system for automatic image segmentation and edge detection. *IEEE Transactions on Fuzzy Systems, 10*(2), 247–262. doi:. doi:10.1109/91.995125

Broomhead, D. S., & Lowe, D. (1988). Multivariate functional interpolation and adaptive networks. *Complex Systems., 2*, 321–355.

Carpenter, G. A. (1989). Neural network models for pattern recognition and associative memory. *Neural Networks, 2*(4), 243–258. doi:. doi:10.1016/0893-6080(89)90035-X

Carpenter, G. A., & Grossberg, S. (1991). *Pattern recognition by self-organizing neural networks*. Cambridge, MA: MIT Press.

Carpenter, G. A., & Ross, W. D. (1995). ART-EMAP: A neural network architecture for object recognition by evidence accumulation. *IEEE Transactions on Neural Networks, 6*(4), 805–818. doi:.doi:10.1109/72.392245

Cerny, V. (1985). A thermodynamical approach to the traveling salesman problem: an efficient simulation algorithm. *Journal of Optimization Theory and Applications, 45*, 41–51. doi:.doi:10.1007/BF00940812

Charalampidis, D., Kasparis, T., & Georgiopoulos, M. (2001). Classification of noisy signals using fuzzy ARTMAP neural networks. *IEEE Transactions on Neural Networks, 12*(5), 1023–1036. doi:. doi:10.1109/72.950132

Chauvin, Y., & Rumelhart, D. E. (1995). *Backpropagation: theory, architectures, and applications*. Hillsdale, NJ: L. Erlbaum Associates Inc.

Chen, C. T., Chen, K. S., & Lee, J. S. (2003). Fuzzy neural classification of SAR images. *IEEE Transactions on Geoscience and Remote Sensing, 41*(9), 2089–2100. doi:.doi:10.1109/TGRS.2003.813494

Chen, Y., Hwang, H., & Chen, B. (1995). *Color image analysis using fuzzy set theory*. Proceedings of International Conference on Image Processing. (pp. 242-245).

Chiu, W. C., Hines, E. L., Forno, C., Hunt, R., & Oldfield, S. (1990). Artificial neural networks for photogrammetric target processing. *SPIE Proceedings on Close-Range Photogrammetry Meets Machine Vision, 1395*(2), 794–801.

Choi, Y., & Krishnapuran, R. (1995). Image enhancement based on fuzzy logic. *Proceedings of International Conference on Image Processing.* (pp. 167-170).

Chua, L. O., & Yang, L. (1988). Cellular network: Applications. *IEEE Transactions on Circuits and Systems, 35*(10), 1273–1290. doi:. doi:10.1109/31.7601

Chua, L. O., & Yang, L. (1988). Cellular network: Theory. *IEEE Transactions on Circuits and Systems, 35*(10), 1257–1282. doi:. doi:10.1109/31.7600

Chung, F., & Fung, B. (2003). Fuzzy color quantization and its application to scene change detection. *Proceedings of MIR, 03*, 157–162.

Colorni, A., Dorigo, M., & Maniezzo, V. (1991). *Distributed Optimization by Ant Colonies, actes de la première conférence européenne sur la vie artificielle* (pp. 134–142). France: Elsevier Publishing.

Cortes, C., & Vapnik, V. N. (1995). Support vector networks. *Machine Learning, 20*, 273–297. doi:. doi:10.1007/BF00994018

Cox, E. (2005). *Fuzzy Modeling and Genetic Algorithms for Data Mining and Exploration*. San Francisco: Morgan Kaufmann.

Das, A., & Chakrabarti, B. K. (Eds.). (2005). Quantum Annealing and Related Optimization Methods. *Lecture Note in Physics (Vol. 679)*. Heidelberg: Springer. doi:10.1007/11526216

Davis, L. (Ed.). (1991). *Handbook of Genetic Algorithms*. New York: Van Nostrand Reinhold.

Deneubourg, J.-L., Aron, S., Goss, S., & Pasteels, J.-M. (1990). The self-organizing exploratory pattern of the Argentine ant. *Journal of Insect Behavior, 3*, 159. doi:.doi:10.1007/BF01417909

Dorigo, M. (1992). *Optimization, Learning and Natural Algorithms*. PhD thesis. Politecnico di Milano, Italie.

Dorigo, M., & Gambardella, L. M. (1997). Ant Colony System: A Cooperative Learning Approach to the Traveling Salesman Problem. *IEEE Transactions on Evolutionary Computation, 1*(1), 53–66. doi:.doi:10.1109/4235.585892

Duda, R. O., & Hart, P. E. (1973). *Pattern classification and scene analysis*. New York: Wiley.

Egmont-Petersen, M., & Arts, T. (1999). Recognition of radiopaque markers in X-ray images using a neural network as nonlinear filter. *Pattern Recognition Letters, 20*(5), 521–533. doi:. doi:10.1016/S0167-8655(99)00024-0

Egmont-Petersen, M., de Ridder, D., & Handels, H. (2002). Image processing using neural networks - a review. *Pattern Recognition, 35*(10), 2279–2301. doi:.doi:10.1016/S0031-3203(01)00178-9

Eshelman, L. J., & Schaffer, J. D. (1993). Real-coded genetic algorithms and interval schemata. In L. Whitley (Ed.), *Foundations of Genetic Algorithms* (pp 187-202). 2, San Mateo, CA: Morgan Kaufmann.

Forrest, B. M. (1988). Neural network models. *Parallel Computing, 8*, 71–83. doi:.doi:10.1016/0167-8191(88)90110-X

Frege, G. (1893). *Grundlagen der Arithmetik (Vol. 2)*. Jena: Verlag von Herman Pohle.

Fukushima, K. (1980). Neocognitron: A self-organizing multilayer neural network model for a mechanism of pattern recognition unaffected by shift in position. *Biological Cybernetics, 36,* 193–202. doi:.doi:10.1007/BF00344251

Gillet, A., Macaire, L., Lecocq, C. B., & Postaire, J. G. (2002). Color image segmentation by analysis of 3D histogram with fuzzy morphological filters. *Studies in Fuzziness and Soft Computing, 122,* 153–177.

Glover, F., & Laguna, M. (1997). *Tabu Search.* Norwell, MA: Kluwer.

Goldberg, D. E. (1989). *Genetic Algorithms: Search, Optimization and Machine Learning.* New York: Addison-Wesley.

Goss, S., Aron, S., Deneubourg, J.-L., & Pasteels, J.-M. (1989). The self-organized exploratory pattern of the Argentine ant. *Naturwissenschaften, 76,* 579–581. doi:.doi:10.1007/BF00462870

Hayashida, N., & Takagi, H. (2002). *Acceleration of EC convergence with landscape visualization and human intervention.* doi:10.1016/S1568-4946(01)00023-0.

Haykin, S. (1999). *Neural networks: A comprehensive foundation* (2nd ed.). Upper Saddle River, NJ: Prentice Hall.

Hertz, J., Krogh, A., & Palmer, R. G. (1991). *Introduction to the theory of neural computation.* Reading, MA: Addison-Wesley.

Hopfield, J. J. (1984). Neurons with graded response have collective computational properties like those of two state neurons. In *Proceedings of Nat* (pp. 3088–3092). U. S: Acad. Sci.

Hui, S., & Zak, S. H. (1992). Dynamical analysis of the Brain-State-in-a-Box (BSB) neural model. *IEEE Transactions on Neural Networks, 3,* 86–94. doi:.doi:10.1109/72.105420

Ito, N., Shimazu, Y., Yokoyama, T., & Matushita, Y. (1995). *Fuzzy logic based non-parametric color image segmentation with optional block processing* (pp. 119–126). ACM.

Kamgar-Parsi, B. (1995). *Automatic target extraction in infrared images* (pp. 143–146). NRL Rev.

Kirkpatrick, S., Gelatt, C. D., & Vecchi, M. P. (1983). *Optimization by Simulated Annealing.* Science. *New Series 220., 4598,* 671–680.

Kohonen, T. (1995). Self-organizing maps. *Springer Series in Information Sciences, 30.*

Kosko, B. (1988). Bidirectional associative memories. *IEEE Transactions on Systems, Man, and Cybernetics, 18*(1), 49–60. doi:.doi:10.1109/21.87054

Kumar, S. (2004). *Neural networks: A classroom approach.* New Delhi: Tata McGraw-Hill.

Lee, C.-C., & de Gyvez, J. P. (1996). Color image processing in a cellular neural-network environment. *IEEE Transactions on Neural Networks, 7*(5), 1086–1098. doi:.doi:10.1109/72.536306

Leondes, C. T. (1998). Neural network techniques and applications. In *Image processing and pattern recognition.* New York: Academic Press.

Lin, J.-S., Cheng, K.-S., & Mao, C.-W. (1996). A fuzzy Hopfield neural network for medical image segmentation. *IEEE Transactions on Nuclear Science, 43*(4), 2389–2398. doi:.doi:10.1109/23.531787

Lippmann, R. P. (1987). An introduction to computing with neural nets. *IEEE ASSP Magazine,* 3–22.

Lippmann, R. P. (1989). Pattern classification using neural networks. *IEEE Communications Magazine, 27,* 47–64. doi:.doi:10.1109/35.41401

Maulik, U. (2009). Medical Image Segmentation using Genetic Algorithms. *IEEE Transactions on Information Technology in Biomedicine, 13,* 166–173. doi:.doi:10.1109/TITB.2008.2007301

Michalewicz, Z. (1992). *Genetic Algorithms + Data Structures = Evolution Programs*. New York: Springer-Verlag.

Moreira, J., & Costa, L. D. F. (1996). *Neural-based color image segmentation and classification using self-organizing maps* (pp. 47–54). Anais do IX SIBGRAPI.

Nagata, T., Kakihara, K., Ohkawa, T., & Tobita, N. (1994). Concept Space Generation Oriented Design Using Kansei by Individual Subjectivity. *Journal of IEEJ, 116*(4).

Onisawa, T., & Unehara, M. (2005). Application of Interactive Genetic Algorithm toward Human Centered System. *Journal of SICE, 44*(1), 50–57.

Pao, Y. H. (1989). *Adaptive pattern recognition and neural networks*. New York: Addison-Wesley.

Pawlak, Z. (1982). Rough sets. *International Journal of Computer and Information Sciences, 11*, 341–356. doi:.doi:10.1007/BF01001956

Pawlak, Z., & Skowron, A. (1994). Rough membership function. In Yeager, R. E., Fedrizzi, M., & Kacprzyk, J. (Eds.), *Advances in the Dempster-Schafer Theory of Evidence* (pp. 251–271). New York: Wiley.

Perlovsky, L. I., Schoendor, W. H., & Burdick, B. J. (1997). Model-based neural network for target detection in SAR images. *IEEE Transactions on Image Processing, 6*(1), 203–216. doi:.doi:10.1109/83.552107

Pham, D. T., & Bayro-Corrochano, E. J. (1998). Neural computing for noise filtering, edge detection and signature extraction. *Journal of Systems Engineering, 2*(2), 666–670.

Polkowski, L. (2002). *Rough Sets, Mathematical Foundations*. Advances in Soft Computing, Physica – Verlag, A Springer-Verlag Company.

Polkowski, L., & Skowron, A. (2001). Rough mereological calculi granules: a rough set approach to computation. *International Journal of Computational Intelligence, 17*, 472–479.

Rosenblatt, F. (1958). The Perceptron: A Probabilistic Model for Information Storage and Organization in the Brain. *Cornell Aeronautical Laboratory. Psychological Review, 65*(6), 386–408. doi:. doi:10.1037/h0042519

Roska, T., Zarandy, A., & Chua, L. O. (1993). Color image processing using multilayer CNN structure. In Didiev, H. (Ed.), *Circuit theory and design*. New York: Elsevier.

Ross, T. J., & Ross, T. (1995). *Fuzzy logic with engineering applications*. New York: McGraw Hill College Div.

Roth, M. W. (1990). Survey of neural network technology for automatic target recognition. *IEEE Transactions on Neural Networks, 1*(1), 28–43. doi:.doi:10.1109/72.80203

Rumelhart, D. E., Hinton, G. E., & Williams, R. J. (1986). Learning representations by back-propagating errors. *Nature, 323*, 533–536. doi:. doi:10.1038/323533a0

Schutte, S., Eklund, J., Axelsson, J. R. C., & Nagamachi, M. (2004). Concepts, methods and tools in Kansei Engineering. *Theoretical Issues in Ergonomics Science, 5*(3), 214–232. doi:. doi:10.1080/1463922021000049980

Scott, P. D., Young, S. S., & Nasrabadi, N. M. (1997). Object recognition using multilayer Hopfield neural network. *IEEE Transactions on Image Processing, 6*(3), 357–372. doi:.doi:10.1109/83.557336

Si, J., & Michel, A. N. (1991). *Analysis and synthesis of discrete-time neural networks with multi-level threshold functions*. Proceedings of IEEE International Symposium on Circuits.

Snyman, J. A. (2005). *Practical Mathematical Optimization: An Introduction to Basic Optimization Theory and Classical and New Gradient-Based Algorithms*. New York: Springer Publishing.

Srinivas, M., & Patnaik, L. M. (1994). Adaptive probabilities of crossover and mutation in genetic algorithm. *IEEE Transactions on Systems, Man, and Cybernetics, 24*, 656–667. doi:. doi:10.1109/21.286385

Stutzle, T., & Hoos, H. H. (2000). MAX MIN Ant System. *Future Generation Computer Systems, 16*, 889–914. doi:10.1016/S0167-739X(00)00043-1

Tang, H. W., Srinivasan, V., & Ong, S. H. (1996). Invariant object recognition using a neural template classifier. *Image and Vision Computing, 14*(7), 473–483. doi:. doi:10.1016/0262-8856(95)01065-3

Tatem, A. J., Lewis, H. G., Atkinson, P. M., & Nixon, M. S. (2001). Super-resolution target identification from remotely sensed images using a Hopfield neural network. *IEEE Transactions on Geoscience and Remote Sensing, 39*(4), 781–796. doi:. doi:10.1109/36.917895

Tsao, E. C. K., Lin, W. C., & Chen, C.-T. (1993). Constraint satisfaction neural networks for image recognition. *Pattern Recognition, 26*(4), 553–567. doi:. doi:10.1016/0031-3203(93)90110-I

Tzeng, Y. C., & Chen, K. S. (1998). A fuzzy neural network to SAR image classification. *IEEE Transactions on Geoscience and Remote Sensing, 36*(1), 301–307. doi:. doi:10.1109/36.655339

Unehara, M., & Yamada, K. (2008). *Interactive Conceptual Design Support System Using Human Evaluation with Kansei*. Proceesings of 2nd International Conference on Kansei Engineering and Affective Systems, (pp. 175-180).

Wu, Y., Liu, Q., & Huang, T. S. (2000). *An adaptive self-organizing color segmentation algorithm with application to robust real-time human hand localization*. Proceedings of Asian Conference on Computer Vision.

Yan, H.-B., Huynh, V.-N., Murai, T., & Nakamori, Y. (2008). Kansei evaluation based on prioritized multi-attribute fuzzy target-oriented decision analysis. *International Journal of Information Sciences, 178*(21), 4080–4093.

Zadeh, L. A. (1965). Fuzzy sets. *Information and Control, 8*, 338–353. doi:. doi:10.1016/S0019-9958(65)90241-X

Zhang, G. P. (2000). Neural networks for classification: a survey. *IEEE Transactions on Systems, Man and Cybernetics. Part C, Applications and Reviews, 30*(4), 451–462. doi:. doi:10.1109/5326.897072

Zhu, Z. (1994). Color pattern recognition in an image system with chromatic distortion. *Optical Engineering (Redondo Beach, Calif.), 33*(9), 3047–3051. doi:. doi:10.1117/12.177509

Chapter 2
Particle Swarm Optimizer for High–Dimensional Data Clustering

Yanping Lu
Xiamen University, China

Shaozi Li
Xiamen University, China

ABSTRACT

This chapter aims at developing effective particle swarm optimization (PSO) for two problems commonly encountered in studies related to high-dimensional data clustering, namely the variable weighting problem in soft projected clustering with known the number of clusters k and the problem of automatically determining the number of clusters k. Each problem is formulated to minimize a nonlinear continuous objective function subjected to bound constraints. Special treatments of encoding schemes and search strategies are also proposed to tailor PSO for these two problems. Experimental results on both synthetic and real high-dimensional data show that these two proposed algorithms greatly improve cluster quality. In addition, the results of the new algorithms are much less dependent on the initial cluster centroids. Experimental results indicate that the promising potential pertaining to PSO applicability to clustering high-dimensional data.

1. INTRODUCTION

Clustering high-dimensional data is a common but important task in various data mining applications. A fundamental starting point for data mining is the assumption that a data object can be represented as a high-dimensional feature vector. Text clustering is a typical example. In text mining, a text data set is viewed as a matrix, in which a row represents a document and a column represents a unique term. The number of dimensions corresponds to the number of unique terms, which is usually in the hundreds or thousands. Another application where high-dimensional data occurs is insurance company customer prediction. It is important to separate potential customers into groups to help companies predict who would be interested in buying an insurance policy. Many other applications such as bankruptcy prediction, web mining,

DOI: 10.4018/978-1-61692-797-4.ch002

protein function prediction, etc. present similar data analysis problems.

Clustering high-dimensional data is a difficult task because clusters of high-dimensional data are usually embedded in lower-dimensional subspaces and feature subspaces for different clusters can overlap. In a text data set, documents related to a particular topic are characterized by one subset of terms. For example, a group of documents are categorized under the topic *electronics* because they contain a subset of terms such as *electronics*, *signal*, *circuit*, etc. The terms describing another topic, *athlete*, may not occur in the documents on *electronics* but will occur in the documents relating to *sports*.

Traditional clustering algorithms struggle with high-dimensional data because the quality of results deteriorates due to the curse of dimensionality. As the number of dimensions increases, data becomes very sparse and distance measures in the whole dimension space become meaningless. Irrelevant dimensions spread out the data points until they are almost equidistant from each other in very high dimensions. The phenomenon is exacerbated when objects are related in different ways in different feature subsets. In fact, some dimensions may be irrelevant or redundant for centain clusters and different sets of dimensions may be relevant for different clusters. Thus, clusters should often be searched for in subspaces of dimensions rather than the whole dimension space.

Clustering of such data sets uses an approach called subspace clustering or projected clustering, aimed at finding clusters from different subspaces. Subspace clustering in general seeks to identify all the subspaces of the dimension space where clusters are most well-separated {see for instance (Goill, 1999, Woo, 2004)}. The terms subspace clustering and projected clustering are not always used in a consistent way in the literature, but as a general rule, subspace clustering algorithms compute overlapping clusters, whereas projected clustering aims to partition the data set into disjoint clusters {See for instance (Procopiuc, 2002,

Achtert, 2008, Moise, 2008)}. Often, projected clustering algorithms search for clusters in subspaces, each of which is spanned by a number of base vectors (main axes). The performance of many subspace/projected clustering algorithms drops quickly with the size of the subspaces in which the clusters are found (Parsons, 2004). Also, many of them require domain knowledge provided by the user to help select and tune their settings, such as the maximum distance between dimensional values (Procopiuc, 2002), the thresholds of input parameters (Moise, 2008) and the minimum density (Agrawal, 2005), which are difficult to establish.

Recently, a number of soft projected clustering algorithms have been developed to identify clusters by assigning an optimal variable weight vector to each cluster (Domeniconi, 2007, Huang, 2005, Jing, 2007). Each of these algorithms iteratively minimizes an objective function. Although the cluster membership of an object is calculated in the whole variable space, the similarity between each pair of objects is based on weighted variable differences. The variable weights transform distance so that the associated cluster is reshaped into a dense hypersphere and can be separated from other clusters. Soft projected clustering algorithms are driven by evaluation criteria and search strategies. Consequently, defining the objective function and efficiently determining the optimal variable weights are the two most important issues in soft projected clustering.

Another fundamental difficulty in clustering high-dimensional data concerns how an algorithm automatically determines the number of clusters k in the data set. Most existing subspace algorithms require the number of clusters k as an input parameter, and this is usually very difficult to set where the structure of the data set is completely unknown. While a number of different clustering approaches to automatically determine the number of clusters have been proposed (Bandyopadhyay, 2001, Lai, 2005, Kumsawat, 2005, Handl, 2007), no reliable method exists for clustering high-dimensional data.

Developing effective algorithms for clustering high-dimensional data is the main focus of this chapter. The goal is to address two main problems, namely the variable weighting problem in soft projected clustering with a number of clusters k and the problem of automatic determination of k. Given a preset number of clusters k, the first of these is formulated as a nonlinear continuous optimization problem subjected to bound constraints. The aim is to find a set of variable weights for each cluster. The second problem is also formulated as a non-linear constrained continuous optimization problem. The aim is to find a set of cluster centers with the correct number of clusters. The objective criteria, the encoding of particles and search techniques are addressed. The inherent properties of high-dimensional data, such as sparsity and equidistance make cluster identification a rather tedious task. This emphasizes the need to develop modern tools to analyze and design algorithms for clustering high-dimensional data. In this chapter, the goal is to develop particle swarm optimization techniques as new heuristic methods with global search capabilities, to solve the problem of cluster identification. An attempt is made to modify the original PSO algorithm, in order to to explore its potential suitability for some of the optimization problems that exist in the area of clustering. Finally, the performance of the improved PSO algorithms is investigated and compared to that of other algorithms commonly used for clustering high-dimensional data.

2. BACKGROUND

Particle Swarm Optimization (PSO)

In PSO (Eberhart, 1995), each solution is regarded as a particle in the search space. Each particle has a position (usually a solution to the problem) and a velocity. The particles fly through the search space through their own effort and in cooperation with other particles.

The velocity and position updates of the ith particle are as follows:

$$V_i(t+1) = \alpha \cdot V_i(t) + c1 \cdot r1 \cdot (pBest_i - X_i(t)) \\ + c2 \cdot r2 \cdot (gBest - X_i(t))$$

$$\text{(1)}$$

$$X_i(t+1) = V_i(t+1) + X_i(t), \qquad \text{(2)}$$

where X_i is the position of the ith particle, V_i presents its velocity and $pBest_i$ is its personal best position yielding the best function value for it. $gBest$ is the global best position discovered by the whole swarm. α is the inertia weight used to balance the global and local search capabilities. $c1$ and $c2$ are the acceleration constants, which represent the weights pulling each particle toward the *pbest* and *gbest* positions, respectively. $r1$ and $r2$ are two random numbers uniformly distributed in the range [0, 1].

The original PSO algorithm was later modified by the researchers in order to improve its performance. Comprehensive Learning Particle Swarm Optimizer (CLPSO), one of the famous modifications of PSO, was proposed in (Liang, 2006) to efficiently optimize multimodal functions. The following velocity update was employed in CLPSO:

$$V_i(t+1) = \alpha \cdot V_i(t) + c1 \cdot r1 \cdot (CpBest_i - X_i), \qquad \text{(3)}$$

where $Cpbest_i$ is a comprehensive learning result from the personal best positions of some particles. $CpBest$ is obtained by a crossover operation between its own *pBest* and one of the personal best positions found by other particles in the swarm, represented here by *s_pBest*. The tournament mechanism is employed to select *s_pBest*, with the consideration that a particle learns from a good exemplar. First, two individuals, *pBest1* and *pBest2*, are randomly selected. Then their objective function values are compared: $s\_pBest = pBest1$ if $F(pBest1) < F(pBest2)$, $s\_pBest = pBest2$ otherwise. The crossover is done as follows. Each element at a position of *CpBest* is assigned the value either from *s_pBest* or from *pBest* at the corresponding position. This assignment is made randomly according to a user-defined probability value P_c (see the section Synthetic Data Simulations for further discussion). If, despite the random assignment process, all the elements of *CpBest* take values from its own *pBest*, one element of *CpBest* will be randomly selected and its value will be replaced by the value of the corresponding position from *s_pBest*. CLPSO achieves good diversity and effectively solves the premature convergence problem in PSO.

Soft Projected Clustering

Assuming that the number of clusters *k* is given and that all of the variables for the datasets are comparable, soft projected clustering algorithms (Domeniconi, 2007, Huang, 2005, Jing, 2007) have been designed to discover clusters in the full dimensional space, by assigning a weight to each dimension for each cluster. The variable weighting problem is an important issue in data mining. Usually, variables that correlate strongly with a cluster obtain large weights, which means that these variables contribute strongly to the identification of data objects in the cluster. Irrelevant variables in a cluster obtain small weights. Thus, the computation of the membership of a data object in a cluster depends on the variable weights and the cluster centroids. The most relevant variables for each cluster can often be identified by the weights after clustering.

The performance of soft projected clustering largely depends on the use of a suitable objective function and an efficient search strategy. The objective function determines the quality of the partitioning, and the search strategy has an impact on whether the optimum of the objective function

can be reached. Recently, several soft projected clustering algorithms have been proposed to perform the task of projected clustering and to select relevant variables for clustering.

C. Domeniconi *et al.* (Domeniconi, 2007) proposed the LAC algorithm, which determines the clusters by minimizing the following objective function:

$$F(w) = \sum_{l=1}^{k} \sum_{j=1}^{m} (w_{l,j} \cdot X_{l,j} + h \cdot w_{l,j} \cdot \log w_{l,j}),$$

$$X_{l,j} = \frac{\sum_{i=1}^{n} u_{i,l} \cdot (x_{i,j} - z_{l,j})^2}{\sum_{i=1}^{n} u_{i,l}}$$

$$(4)$$

$$s.t. \begin{cases} \sum_{j=1}^{m} w_{l,j} = 1, & 0 \le w_{l,j} \le 1, & 1 \le l \le k \\ \sum_{l=1}^{k} u_{i,l} = 1, & u_{i,l} \in \{0, 1\}, & 1 \le i \le n \end{cases}$$

$$(5)$$

where *k, n, m* are the number of clusters, the number of data objects and the number of dimensions, respectively. Throughout this paper, we will adopt the same notation. $u_{i,l}$ is the membership of data object *i* in cluster *l*. $x_{i,j}$ is the value of data object *i* on dimension *j* and $z_{l,j}$ is the centroid of cluster *l* on dimension *j*. *d* is the distance function measuring the similarity between two data objects. $X_{l,j}$ represents the squared variance of cluster *l* along dimension *j*. $w_{l,j}$ is a weight assigned to cluster *l* on dimension *j*. *U, Z,* and *W* represent the cluster membership matrix of data objects, the cluster centroids matrix, and the dimensional weights matrix, respectively. The LAC algorithm is summarized as follows:

```
Input:
    Select k well-scattered data
objects as initial centroids;
    Set w_{l,j} = 1 / m for each dimen-
```

sion in each cluster.
Repeat:
    Update the cluster memberships
of data objects U by (6);
    Update the cluster centroids Z
by (7);
    Update the dimension weights W
by (8);
Until: (the objective function obtains its local minimum value)

The LAC algorithm finds a solution that is a local minimum of the above objective function. In the LAC algorithm, U and Z are updated in the same way as in the k-means algorithm.

$$
\begin{cases} u_{l,i} = 1, \; if \; \sum_{j=1}^{m} w_{l,j} \cdot (x_{i,j} - z_{l,j})^2 \le \sum_{j=1}^{m} w_{t,j} \cdot (x_{i,j} - z_{t,j})^2 \; for \; 1 \le t \le k, \\ u_{t,i} = 0, \; for \; t \ne l. \end{cases}
$$

$$(6)$$

$$
z_{l,j} = \frac{\sum_{i=1}^{n} u_{l,i} \cdot x_{i,j}}{\sum_{i=1}^{n} u_{l,i}}, \quad for \quad 1 \le l \le k \quad and \quad 1 \le j \le m
$$

$$(7)$$

W is updated according to the following formula:

$$
w_{l,j} = \frac{\exp(-X_{l,j} / h)}{\sum_{t=1}^{m} \exp(-X_{l,t} / h)},
$$

$$(8)$$

where h is a parameter that is used to maximize or minimize the influence of X on $w_{l,j}$.

In LAC 2007, the authors employed a new objective function and a weight updating schema. Their work is similar to the work described in EWKM (2007). In LAC 2007, the authors also proposed a method based on well-scatter data to initialize the cluster centroids and an ensemble approach to overcome the difficulty of tuning the parameter h. However, their initialization needs to calculate the distance between high-dimensional data in the whole dimension space, whereas the very hypothesis of this work is that this distance is not reliable. It is not clear yet whether LAC is significantly improved by the new initialization schema.

Joshua Z. Huang *et al.* (Huang, 2005) proposed another objective function subjected to equation (5) and derived an algorithm called the *W-k*-means algorithm.

$$
F(w) = \sum_{l=1}^{k} \sum_{i=1}^{n} \sum_{j=1}^{m} u_{l,i} \cdot w_{j}^{\beta} \cdot d(x_{i,j}, z_{l,j}) \qquad (9)
$$

Here, β is a parameter greater than 1. The objective function is designed to measure the sum of the within-cluster distances along a subset of variables rather than over the entire variable (dimension) space. The variable weights in the W-k-means need to meet the constraints of the objective function in equation (5), too. The formula for updating the weights is also different and is written as follows:

$$
w_j = \begin{cases} 0, & if \quad D_j = 0, \\ \dfrac{1}{\sum_{t=1}^{m} \left[\dfrac{D_j}{D_t} \right]^{1/(\beta-1)}}, \end{cases}
$$

$$(10)$$

$$
D_j = \sum_{l=1}^{k} \sum_{i=1}^{n} u_{i,l} \cdot d(x_{i,j}, z_{l,j}).
$$

where the weight w_j for the j-th dimension is inversely proportional to the sum of all the within-cluster distances along dimension j. A large weight value corresponds to a small sum of within-cluster distances in a dimension, indicating that the dimension is more important in forming the clusters.

The W-k-means algorithm is a direct extension of the k-means algorithm. The W-k-means assigns a weight to each variable and seeks to minimize the sum of all the within-cluster distances in the same subset of variables. Furthermore, updating of variable weights is dependent on the value of the parameter β. In addition, the W-k-means algorithm does not utilize an efficient local search strategy. Consequently, it often has difficulty correctly discovering clusters which are embedded in different subsets of variables. Thus, the algorithm is inappropriate in the case of high-dimensional data where each cluster has its own relevant subset of variables.

Liping Jing *et al.* (Jing, 2007) proposed the entropy weighting k-means algorithm (EWKM), which employs a similar iterative process to that used by the W-k-means algorithm. The objective function in the EWKM algorithm takes both the within-cluster dispersion and the weight entropy into consideration. The function is described as follows:

$$F(w) = \sum_{l=1}^{k} \left[\sum_{i=1}^{n} \sum_{j=1}^{m} u_{i,l} \cdot w_{l,j} \cdot (x_{i,j} - z_{l,j})^2 + \gamma \cdot \sum_{j=1}^{m} w_{l,j} \cdot \log w_{l,j} \right]$$

(11)

The constraints of the above function are identical to those in the W-k-means algorithm. The formula for updating the weights is written as follows:

$$w_{l,j} = \frac{\exp(-D_{l,j} / \gamma)}{\sum_{t=1}^{m} \exp(-D_{l,t} / \gamma)},$$

(12)

$$D_{l,j} = \sum_{i=1}^{n} u_{i,l} \cdot (x_{i,j} - z_{l,j})^2$$

This objective function depends heavily on the value of parameter γ. If γ is too small, the entropy section has little effect on the function. On the other hand, if γ is too big, the entropy section could have too strong an effect on the function. Therefore, the value of γ is empirically determined and application-specific.

LAC, the W-k-means and EWKM all stem from the k-means algorithm and all three share some common problems. First, the constrained objective functions they provide have their drawbacks, which have been described above. Second, the cluster quality they yield is highly sensitive to the initial cluster centroids (see experiments). These algorithms employ local search strategies to optimize the objective functions with constraints. The local search strategies provide good convergence speed to the iterative process but greatly decrease the clustering quality.

Automatically Determining the Number of Clusters *k*

Another fundamental difficulty in cluster analysis is the determination of the number of clusters. Most popular clustering algorithms require the number of clusters to be provided as an input parameter, which is difficult to set when the structure of the data is not completely known *a priori*. In this situation, automatically estimating the number of clusters and simultaneously finding the clusters becomes a challenge.

Due to good performance of stochastic search procedures, one way to automatically determine the number of clusters is to make use of evolutionary techniques. In this regard, genetic algorithms (GA) have been the most frequently proposed for automatically clustering data sets. Basically, two types of GA representations for clustering solutions have been explored in the literatures: partition-based and centroid-based representations. Partition-based encodings directly represent the cluster membership of the ith data object by the ith gene. Although this is a straightforward encoding, it does not reduce the size of the search space and makes it difficult to design effective search operators. For this reason, many researchers have chosen to use centroid-based encodings, which borrow the idea of the popular k-means algorithm. The representation is encoded as the cluster centroids (Bandyopadhyay, 2001, Lai, 2005) and each data object is subsequently assigned to the closest cluster centroid.

In (Bandyopadhyay, 2001), Bandyopadhyay and Maulik proposed a genetic algorithm, in which a variable-length real-number string representation is used to encode the coordinates of the cluster centroids in the clustering problem. Chromosome i is encoded as $m*k_i$, where m denotes the number of data features and k_i denotes the number of clusters of the ith individual. New crossover and mutation operators are defined for tackling variable string lengths and real numbers. For one general clustering problem, Lai (Lai, 2005) employed another algorithm based on a hierarchical genetic algorithm, in which an individual is composed of two types of genes, the control and parameter genes. The control gene is encoded in binary digits, where the number of "1s" represents the number of clusters. The parameter gene is encoded in real numbers, which represent the coordinates of the cluster centroids. The parameter gene is governed by the control gene. Where the control gene is "1", the corresponding parameter gene is activated; otherwise, the associated parameter gene is disabled. In (Liu, 2008), Liu et al. employed a genetic algorithm with the same encoding $m*k_i$ as (Bandyopadhyay, 2001) to represent the coordinates of k_i cluster centroids. They designed two special operators, noising selection and division-absorption mutation, for the clustering problem. The proposed method can automatically provide the number of clusters and find the clustering partition.

In (Handl, 2007), Handl et al. employed a multiobjective genetic algorithm called MOCK to solve the clustering problem. For the encoding, they employed the locus-based adjacency representation, in which each individual consists of n genes, where n is the size of the data set, and each gene can take integer values j in the range of $[1, n]$. Thus, a value j assigned to gene i is meant as a link between two data objects i and j. In the result, they will be assigned to the same cluster. MOCK optimizes two complementary clustering objectives, within-cluster compactness and connectivity, and attempts to automatically estimate the number of clusters in the data set. MOCK has achieved high quality clustering results on the authors' data sets, which have complex cluster shapes, such as spherical, ellipsoidal or long datasets and overlapped clusters. However, it is not readily applicable on high-dimensional datasets where clusters are embedded in subspaces.

3. PSO FOR HIGH-DIMENSIONAL DATA CLUSTERING

PSO for Variable Weighting (PSOVW)

Our particle swarm optimizer for the variable weighting problem in soft projected clustering, termed PSOVW, performs on two main swarms of variable weights, the position swarm W and the personal best position swarm of variable weights *pBest*. The position swarm is the foundation of the search in the variable weights space, so the evolution of the position swarm pays more attention to global search, while the personal best position swarm tracks the fittest positions, in order to accelerate the convergence. In addition, it facilitates cooperation among the previous best positions in order to maintain the swarm diversity.

The Objective Function

We minimize the following objective function in PSOVW:

$$F(W) = \sum_{l=1}^{k}\sum_{i=1}^{n}\sum_{j=1}^{m} u_{l,i} \cdot \left(\frac{w_{l,j}}{\sum_{j=1}^{m} w_{l,j}}\right)^{\beta} \cdot d(x_{i,j}, z_{l,j})$$

(13)

$$s.t. \begin{cases} 0 \leq w_{l,j} \leq 1 \\ \sum_{l=1}^{k} u_{i,l} = 1, \quad u_{i,l} \in \{0,1\}, \quad 1 \leq i \leq n \end{cases}$$

(14)

Actually, the objective function in (13) is a generalization of some existing objective functions.

If β=0, function (13) is similar to the objective function used in the *k*-means. They differ solely in the representation of variable weights and the constraints.

If β=1, function (13) is also similar to the first section of the objective function in EWKM, differing only in the representation of variable weights and the constraints.

If $w_{l,j} = w_j,$ $\forall l$, function (13) is similar to the objective function in the W-*k*-means, which assigns a single variable weight vector, substituting different vectors for clusters. Again, the only difference is in the representation of variable weights and the constraints.

In PSOVW, β is a user-defined parameter. PSOVW works with all non-negative values of β. In practice, we suggest setting β to a large value (empirically around 10.0). A large value of β makes the objective function more sensitive to changes in weight values. It tends to magnify the influence of those variables with large weights on the within-cluster variance, allowing them to play a strong role in discriminating between relevant and irrelevant variables (dimensions).

In the existing algorithms, a *k**m variable weight matrix *W*, where a weight is a real number assigned to each dimension for each cluster, is usually a direct solution to the objective function and should simultaneously meet the equality constraints that the weights on each row should be normalized to 1. However, the greater the number of clusters, the greater the number of constraints and the harder it is to optimize the corresponding function. In PSOVW, a non-normalized matrix *W* is employed in the objective function, replacing the normalized matrix. Although the non-normalized representation in the constrained objective function (13) is redundant, the constraints can be loosened without affecting the final solution. As a result, the optimization procedure only needs to deal with bound constraints instead of many more

complicated equality constraints and it is greatly simplified. To sum up, the weighting schema is developed in a suitable way for the application of PSO.

Initialization

In the PSOVW algorithm, we initialize three swarms.

- The position swarm *W* of variable weights, which are set to random numbers uniformly distributed in a certain range *R*.
- The velocity swarm *V* of variable weights, which are set to random numbers uniformly distributed in the range [-*maxv*, *maxv*]. Here, *maxv* means the maximum flying velocity of particles and *maxv*=0.25*R.
- The swarm of cluster centroids *Z*, which are *k* different data objects randomly chosen out of all the data objects.

In all three swarms, an individual is a *k**m matrix. Actually, only the velocity swarm *V* is an extra swarm not included in *k*-means-type soft projected clustering algorithms.

Update of Cluster Centroids and Partitioning of Data Objects

Given the variable weight matrix and the cluster centroids, the cluster membership of each data object is calculated by the formula in Box 1.

Once the cluster membership is obtained, the cluster centroids are updated by

$$z_{l,j} = (\sum_{i=1}^{n} u_{l,i} \cdot x_{i,j}) / (\sum_{i=1}^{n} u_{l,i}),$$
$$for \quad 1 \leq l \leq k \quad and \quad 1 \leq j \leq m \qquad (16)$$

In our implementation, if an empty cluster results from the membership update by formula

Box 1.

$$\begin{cases} u_{l,i} = 1, & if \quad \sum_{j=1}^{m} (\frac{w_{l,j}}{\sum_{j=1}^{m} w_{l,j}})^{\beta} \cdot d(z_{l,j}, x_{i,j}) \leq \sum_{j=1}^{m} (\frac{w_{q,j}}{\sum_{j=1}^{m} w_{q,j}})^{\beta} \cdot d(z_{t,j}, x_{i,j}) \quad for \quad 1 \leq q \leq k, \\ u_{l,i} = 0, & for \quad q \neq l. \end{cases}$$

(15)

(15), we randomly select a data object out of the data set to reinitialize the centroid of the cluster.

Crossover Learning

Given a value for β, two extra swarms are kept to guide all the particles' movement in the search space. One is the personal best position swarm of variable weights *pBest*, which keeps the best position of the weight matrix W; i.e., *pBest* will be replaced by W if $F(W)<F(pBest)$. The other is the crossover best position swarm of variable weights *CpBest*, which guides particles to move towards better regions (Liang, 2006). *CpBest* is obtained by a crossover operation between its own *pBest* and one of the other best personal positions in the swarm, represented here by *s_pBest*, which is selected by the tournament mechanism.

The PSOVW algorithm can be summarized as follows:

```
Initialization:
    Randomly initialize the position
and velocity swarms, W and V.
    Partition the data objects.
    Evaluate the fitness of W by the
formula (13).
    Record the swarm pBest and the
best position gBest.
Repeat:
    Produce CpBest from pBest for
each particle.
    Update V and W by the equation
(3) and (2), respectively.
```

```
    If W is in the range of [0, 1],
evaluate its fitness by (13) and up-
date pBest and gBest.
Until: (the objective function reach-
es a global minimum value, or the
number of function evaluations reach-
es the maximum threshold.)
```

Synthetic Datasets

We generate high-dimensional datasets with clusters embedded in different subspaces using the synthetic data generator from Zait and Messatfa. The synthetic data generator has often been used to investigate the performance of subspace clustering algorithms. In these synthetic datasets, different clusters have their own relevant dimensions, which can overlap (Jing, 2007). The data values are normally distributed on the relevant dimensions of a cluster and the range of mean values is specified by the range [0, 100]. Random positive numbers are on the irrelevant dimensions and random values are uniformly distributed in the range [0, 10].

Two types of synthetic datasets are generated. They differ in the variance of clusters on their relevant dimensions. In type 1, we assign the same variance 0.9 to each relevant dimension in a cluster. In type 2, each relevant dimension is randomly assigned a variance and the cluster variances are randomly selected from the range [1, 10]. We generated a total of 16 synthetic datasets with varying numbers of dimensions and varying numbers of clusters. For each type of data, there are eight datasets, each of which has 4 or 10 clusters, combined with 20, 100, 1000 or 2000 dimensions. The datasets with 4 clusters have 50 data objects in a cluster, the clusters are well-separated and the percentage of overlapped relevant dimensions of clusters is low (near 0). The datasets with 10 clusters are more complicated: each cluster has 50 data objects and relevant dimensions of clusters are heavily overlapped (around 0.8).

Parameter Settings for Algorithms

We conducted experiments using *k*-means, LAC, W-*k*-means, and EWKM together with the PSOVW algorithm on synthetic datasets. In each algorithm, the Euclidean distance is used to measure the dissimilarity between two data objects for synthetic and real datasets. Here, we set β=10. The maximum number of function evaluations is set to 2,000 over all synthetic datasets in PSOVW and 500 in the other four algorithms. Given an objective function, PSOVW needs more iterations to get to its best optima than other algorithms. There are four additional parameters in PSOVW that need to be specified. They are the swarm size *s*, the inertia weight α, the acceleration constant *c*1 and the learning probability P_c. Actually, the four extra parameters have been fully studied in the particle swarm optimization field and we set the parameters in PSOVW to the values used in (Liang, 2006). *s* is set to 10. α is linearly decreased from 0.9 to 0.7 during the iterative procedure, and *c*1 is set to 1.49445. In order to obtain a better population diversity, particles in *PSOVW* are required to have different exploration and exploitation ability. So, P_c is empirically set to

$$P_c(i) = 0.5 * \frac{e^{f(i)} - e^{f(1)}}{e^{f(s)} - e^{f(1)}},$$

where $f(i) = 5 * \frac{i}{s-1}$ for each particle. The values of learning probability P_c in PSOVW range

from 0.05 to 0.5 as for CLPSO. The parameter γ in EWKM is set to 1.

Results for Synthetic Data

In order to compare the clustering performance of PSOVW with those of the *k*-means, LAC[1], the W-*k*-means and EWKM, we run these five algorithms on datasets of each type. Since PSOVW was randomly initialized and the other algorithms are sensitive to the initial cluster centroids to a certain degree, we run each algorithm ten trials on each dataset and record the average clustering accuracy that each algorithm achieved in Table 1. The clustering accuracy is the percentage of the data objects that are correctly recovered by an algorithm.

A number of observations can be made by analyzing the results in Table 1. First, PSOVW seems to perform much better than the other algorithms tested on both types of generated data sets. It correctly recovers clusters embedded in different variable subspaces of high-dimensional data and achieves 100 percent clustering accuracy on most of trials. The reason is that the synthetic datasets are not noisy. Noise-free datasets are appropriate for the purpose of this experiment. In particular, due to the PSO search strategy, PSOVW totally and correctly recovers clusters over the datasets with 4 well-separated clusters on each trial regardless of the shapes of these clusters and the variances of clusters along relevant dimensions. However, PSOVW occasionally misses an entire cluster on the more complicated, 10-cluster datasets. It sometimes fails to differentiate between two very close groups, whose relevant dimensions overlap considerably, and merges them into one cluster. For example, the relevant dimensions of one cluster in the Type 1 dataset with 10 clusters and 20 dimensions are {1 3 5 8 11} and those of another cluster in the same dataset are {1 3 5 11 17}.

W-*k*-means performs the next best on 12 out of 16 datasets. However, from the experimental results in Table 1, we cannot see much difference

Table 1. Average clustering accuracy of each algorithm over ten trials on each dataset

Datasets	k	n	m	k-means	LAC	W-k-means	EWKM	PSOVW
Type 1	4	200	20	68	70.3	86	77.4	**100**
			100	79.4	73	85.8	64.4	**100**
			1000	70.5	71.1	89.2	78.8	**100**
			2000	73.6	85.9	79.7	84.6	**100**
	10	500	20	61.3	74.5	75.1	74.5	**90.9**
			100	34.4	68.4	72.2	69.4	**94**
			1000	33.4	70.4	76.8	67	**91.2**
			2000	39.7	68.4	75.8	69.8	**86.8**
Type 2	4	200	20	63.1	83.4	78.2	89.3	**100**
			100	59.9	78.7	79	71.9	**100**
			1000	73.9	78.3	81.5	76.1	**100**
			2000	78.2	71.9	94.2	83.9	**100**
	10	500	20	34.4	66.1	77.7	63.9	**92.5**
			100	27.3	63	73.7	67	**94**
			1000	32.4	69.9	76.9	72.7	**88.2**
			2000	24	71.1	63.6	71	**90.3**

between the performance of the W-k-means and those of LAC and EWKM on Type 2 datasets. k-means performs the least well on complicated datasets, such as the datasets with 10 complicated clusters. We cannot see much difference between the results yielded by the k-means and those of LAC and EWKM on the Type 1 datasets with 4 clusters. However, the clustering accuracy of the k-means drops quickly as the variances of clusters along relevant dimensions increase. What is more, the k-means achieved very low clustering accuracy on complicated datasets, such as datasets with 10 clusters. The reason is that the k-means is not a subspace clustering algorithm, so that it fails to handle high-dimensional data due to the equidistance of such data in the whole dimensional space. The results of the k-means in Table 1 confirm that it was inferior to soft projected clustering algorithms in complex high-dimensional data clustering.

In order to further investigate the reasons why PSOVW achieves better performance than other algorithms on generated high-dimensional datasets, we also implemented the PSO method

with different objective functions presented in soft projected clustering algorithms, namely formula (4) in LAC, formula (9) in the W-k-means, formula (11) EWKM and formula (13) in PSOVW. PSO is a heuristic global search strategy, so it can be also employed to optimize other objective functions. Since PSO was randomly initialized, the PSO method with each function was run for 20 trials on each dataset. k and m represent the number of clusters and the number of dimensions, respectively. The average clustering accuracy yielded by the PSO method with each function is recorded in Table 2.

Table 2 gives the clustering results of the PSO method with different functions on the datasets with 10 clusters. In our experiments, we discovered that the PSO method with each of the four different objective functions performs pretty well on the datasets with 4 clusters and achieves 100 percent clustering accuracy on each trial. The reason is that clusters in these datasets are well-separated and the percentage of overlapped relevant dimensions is relatively low, although the

Table 2. Average clustering accuracy of the PSO method with different functions over 20 trials on datasets with 10 clusters

Datasets	n	k	m	Function (13) in PSOVW	Function (4) in LAC	Function (9) in W-k-means	Function (11) in EWKM
Type 1	500	10	20	**90.3**	87.2	89.4	86.5
			100	**93.6**	89.5	85.7	76.7
			1000	**91.9**	90.8	84.4	70.6
			2000	**87.0**	85.9	83.6	80.1
Type 2		10	20	93.2	**97.4**	92.4	85.9
			100	**92.3**	84.8	85.6	82.8
			1000	**87.6**	82.7	82.9	77
			2000	89.4	**90.8**	84.5	80.5

clusters are different shapes. Furthermore, we found out that the high clustering accuracy yielded by the PSO method with different functions benefits greatly from the non-normalized representation of variable weights presented in our objective functions, although we also tried several existing techniques to initialize feasible particles. For a fair comparison, we implemented the same representation as in Function (13) of PSOVW, where variable weights are only required to meet bound constraints, in the LAC, W-k-means and EWKM functions.

From Table 2, we can see that on average, except for the Type 2 datasets with 20 dimensions and 2000 dimensions, PSO with Function (13) always performs best on the synthetic datasets with 10 clusters, although PSO with LAC Function (4) is very close. The fact that Function (9) is less efficient than Functions (11) and (13) is understandable because it uses one weight per dimension; nevertheless, it performs better than Function (9). Obviously, the PSO method greatly improves the performances of LAC, the W-*k*-means and EWKM. The results reported in both Table 1 and Table 2 suggest that the good performance of PSOVW is due partly to the PSO method, and partly to the representation of our improved objective function.

Figure 1 illustrates the clustering results achieved by each algorithm on each type of dataset. The horizontal axis represents the datasets, while the vertical axes represents the variance of the clustering accuracies yielded by each algorithm in ten runs on each dataset.

From Figure 1, it can be readily seen that PSOVW yields the least variance in clustering accuracy on most of the datasets. The *k*-means achieved lower variance in clustering accuracy than PSOVW on some datasets with 10 clusters, because the clustering accuracy yielded by the *k*-means on these dataset is always very low. The other three soft projected clustering algorithms occasionally work well, achieving low variance in clustering accuracy on some datasets, but their variance is often high. What's more, it is difficult to tell for which type of datasets they are less sensitive to the initial centroids. From these above two graphs, we conclude that PSOVW was far less sensitive to the initial centroids than the other four algorithms.

Table 3 presents the average running time of each algorithm on the datasets, with varying k and m. All times are in seconds.

From Table 3, it is clear that the *k*-means runs faster than the other four soft projected clustering algorithms. Although LAC, EWKM and the W-*k*-means all extend the *k*-means clustering process

Figure 1. The variance of ten clustering results obtained by each algorithm on each dataset

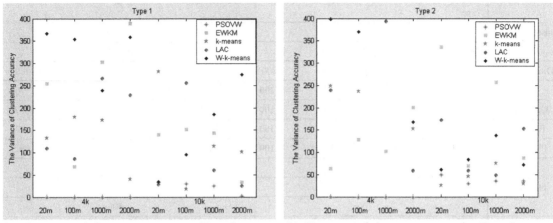

(a) *Variance of cluster accuracy on Type 1*   (b) *Variance of cluster accuracy on Type 2*

by adding an additional step in each iteration to compute variable weights for each cluster, LAC and EWKM are much faster algorithms than the W-*k*-means on datasets. The W-*k*-means required more time to identify clusters, because its objective function involves a much more complicated computation due to the high exponent. Based on the computational complexities of the various algorithms and the maximum number of function evaluations set in each algorithm, PSOVW was supposed to need 10~40 times the running time the W-*k*-means requires. In fact, it required only slightly more than ten times the running time that the W-*k*-means spent on the datasets with 20 and

100 dimensions, and around two times what the W-*k*-means spent on those with 1000 and 2000 dimensions. This is because the update of weights is simpler in PSOVW than in the other three soft projected clustering algorithms and particles are evaluated only if they are in the feasible closed space. We thus conclude that the much more complicated search strategy of PSOVW allows it to achieve the best clustering accuracy, at an acceptable cost in terms of running time.

Table 4 presents the comparison of PSO with the best result of LAC, EWKM and the W-*k*-means on multiple independent trials.

Table 3. The average running time of PSOVW vs. k-means, LAC, W-k-means, and EWKM

Datasets			Running Time (s)				
k	n	m	k-means	LAC	W-k-means	EWKM	PSOVW
4	200	20	**0.094**	1.531	2.031	1.234	7.828
		100	**0.453**	7.5	10.125	6.641	39.156
		1000	**4.422**	74.437	100.343	60.718	206.14
		2000	**8.843**	131.327	200.858	122.686	370.529
10	500	20	**0.172**	3	4.89	2.641	49.172
		100	**0.766**	14.875	24.125	13.203	92.358
		1000	**7.5**	149.249	257.467	132.749	408.451
		2000	**14.984**	298.826	514.684	264.186	700.902

Table 4 Comparison of PSOVW vs. LAC, W-k-means and EWKM

Datasets	Type 1							
	4 *k*				10 *k*			
	200*n*				500*n*			
Dimensions	20 *m*	100 *m*	1000 *m*	2000 *m*	20 *m*	100 *m*	1000 *m*	2000 *m*
LAC	89	93.5	89.5	**100**	83	92.5	81	76
W-*k*-means	**100**	**100**	**100**	**100**	85	85	86.5	**85.5**
EWKM	**100**	71.5	95.5	**100**	81	86	76	77
PSOVW	**100**	**100**	**100**	**100**	**100**	**100**	**100**	**85.5**
Datasets	Type 2							
	4 *k*				10 *k*			
	200*n*				500*n*			
	20 *m*	100 *m*	1000 *m*	2000 *m*	20 *m*	100 *m*	1000 *m*	2000 *m*
LAC	**100**	**100**	**100**	83.5	**88.5**	79	71.5	88.5
W-*k*-means	**100**	**100**	**100**	**100**	86.5	85	89.5	72.5
EWKM	**100**	**100**	91	96	76	80	**100**	83
PSOVW	**100**	**100**	**100**	**100**	87	**100**	86.5	**100**

Since PSOVW uses more resources than LAC, EWKM and the W-*k*-means, to ensure a very fair comparison of PSOVW with these three soft projected clustering algorithms, we independently ran LAC, EWKM and the W-*k*-means multiple times on each dataset and compared the best result out of the iterative trials with that of PSOVW. According to the average running time of each algorithm reported in Table 3, we ran PSOVW once on each dataset. On the datasets with 20 and 100 dimensions, LAC and EWKM were run 10 times and the W-*k*-means was run 4 times. On the datasets with 1000 and 2000 dimensions, LAC and EWKM were run 4 times and the W-*k*-means was run 2 times. The experimental results in Table 4 still show that PSOVW surpasses the other three algorithms on each data set except on the Type 2 datasets with 10 clusters and 20 and 2000 dimensions. This is because the particles in PSOVW do not work independently but cooperate with each other in order to move to better regions. The quality of the clustering is of prime importance and therefore the time taken to obtain it is at most secondary in many cluster-

ing applications. To sum up, the much more complicated search strategy allows PSOVW to achieve the best clustering accuracy, at a cost of longer running time, but the running time is acceptable

PSO Clustering with Auto-Determination of *k* (autoPSO)

In this section, we propose a particle swarm optimizer, called autoPSO, to automatically determine the number of clusters *k* and simultaneously identify clusters.

Encoding

To apply PSO to the clustering problem, one needs to choose an objective function and a suitable encoding of a partition. For the encoding, the position of each particle consists of two components, a real-number matrix M_{kmax*m} and a binary column vector Con_{kmax}. Here, *kmax* is the maximal number of clusters, which can be set by the users and *m* is the number of dimensions.

Each row in the matrix is coded as real numbers representing the coordinates of a cluster centroid. A "1" in the binary vector signifies that there is a cluster centroid row in the corresponding row of the matrix, while "0" signifies there is no center centroid in the corresponding row. Thus, the matrix is "supervised" by the vector. Where the binary vector value is "1", the associated row of the matrix is activated; otherwise the associated row is disabled.

In the autoPSO algorithm, we need to initialize three swarms.

In the position swarm, a position is a real-number matrix M. For a position i in the population, a random integer k in the range of $[2, kmax]$ is generated. Then, k different data objects are randomly chosen from the data set as k initial center centroids. These data objects are randomly distributed in rows of the matrix.

For example, assume that $m=4$, $kmax=6$, and random number $k_i=4$ for particle i. Then $k_i=4$ data objects are randomly chosen as 4 cluster centroids. Assume that these 4 cluster centroids are randomly distributed in rows 1, 5, 3, 6 in of the position matrix, respectively.

Let 4 data objects selected from the data set be

(2.4	4.3	5	0.1)
(10.7	8.2	3.1	2.9)
(2	1.9	8.2	4.4)
(12.9	13.1	5.3	2.8)

Then, the position matrix M_i for particle i will look like this:

(2.4	4.3	5	0.1)
(*	*	*	*)
(2	1.9	8.2	4.4)
(*	*	*	*)
(10.7	8.2	3.1	2.9)
(12.9	13.1	5.3	2.8)

In the velocity swarm, a velocity is also a $kmax*m$ matrix, which is set to random numbers uniformly distributed in the range $[-Vmax, Vmax]$. Here, $Vmax=0.25*(xu-xl)$, where xu and xl are the upper bound and the lower bound of the search space, respectively.

In the control parameter swarm, a control parameter is a binary vector Con. In the vector Con_i, if the jth element is 1, it indicates the presence of the associated cluster in the position matrix M_j. If the corresponding element is 0, it denotes the absence of the cluster.

For instance, the binary vector for the above example is:

1

0

1

0

1

1

This encoding scheme has several major advantages for our application. Most importantly, there is no need to set the number of clusters in advance. Hence, we can evolve and compare solutions with different numbers of clusters in one generation or adjacent generations of PSO. Furthermore, this real-number representation is well suited for the use of arithmetic operators in the original PSO and a complex crossover operator which will be introduced later into PSO.

The Objective Function

The Davies-Bouldin (DB) index is a popular internal validation index which captures both within-cluster scatter and between-cluster separation in a nonlinear combination and is employed as the objective function in autoPSO. It is defined as:

$$DB = \frac{1}{k} \cdot \sum_{i=1}^{k} R_i \quad (4\text{-}1)$$

where

$$R_i = \max_{i,j \neq i} \frac{S_i + S_j}{B_{ij}}$$

is the ratio of the sum of within-cluster scatter

$$S_i = \frac{1}{|C_i|} \cdot \sum_{x \in C_i} d(x, z_i)$$

to between-cluster separation

$$B_{i,j} = d(z_i, z_j).$$

Here, x is the data object and Z_i denotes the cluster centroid of cluster C_i, usually defined as $z_i = \frac{1}{|C_i|} \cdot \sum_{x \in C_i} x$, where $|C_i|$ is the number of data objects belonging to cluster C_i. d is the distance function which measures the dissimilarity between two data objects. DB takes values in the interval $[0, \infty]$ and needs to be minimized.

The use of the DB index has some major advantages. First, it is unbiased with respect to the number of clusters. It can measure the quality of partitions with similar or different numbers of clusters. Hence, we can compare solutions with different numbers of clusters. Second, values returned by the DB index are easier to interpret. The smaller the value of the DB index, the more compactness in individual clusters and the more separation between clusters.

Given a previous set of cluster centroids, the cluster membership of each data object is calculated by formula (6). Once the cluster membership is obtained, the cluster centroids are updated by fomula (7). In our implementation, if membership update by formula (6) results in an empty cluster, we randomly select a data object from the data set to reinitialize the centroid of the cluster. Then we can calculatse the fitness values, namely the values of the DB index, for the positions in the swarm.

Operators

In order to maintain population diversity and prevent premature convergence, autoPSO borrows the idea of using *CpBest* instead of *gBest* and *pBests* from (Liang, 2006). The arithmetic operators provided by the original PSO are very effective for the continuous function optimization. However, The arithmetic operators, such as the "-" operator between *CpBest* and X, needs special treatment in autoPSO because of the incorporation of the control parameter swarm. There are two values in control parameter vectors, namely "0" and "1". There are four combinations of the control parameter values between *CpBest* and X, as follows:

The control parameter of CpBest	- X	= result
0	0	= 0
0	1	= 0
1	0	= 1
1	1	= 1

Consequently, the result has the same control parameter vector as *CpBest*. However, the number of "1s" in the control parameter vector of the result sometimes happens to be less than 2 after the crossover operator: i.e. there are less than two cluster centroids in the corresponding result. In this situation, we keep the control parameter of X as the result, in order to guarantee that there are at least two clusters in the data set.

The autoPSO algorithm can be summarized as follows:

```
Initialization:
    Set the maximal number of clus-
ters, kmax=10.
```

```
        Set the parameters in PSO, namely
w, c1, Pc.
        For each particle i,
            Randomly choose k_i data ob-
jects from the data;
            Set as the initial cluster
centroids;
            Place these cluster cen-
troids in k_i random rows to construct
the position matrix;
            Construct the velocity ma-
trix vel, randomly uniformly distrib-
uted in the range [-mv, mv], where
v=0.25*(xu-xl), and xu, xl are the
upper and lower bounds of the dimen-
sion space.
        Evaluate the fitness value for
each position matrix by the DB index.
        Generate CpBest and its associ-
ated control parameter vector Con for
each position matrix.
Repeat:
        For each particle i,
            If the fitness value of a
position matrix isn't improved within
5 iterations,
                Update its associated
CpBest and Con.
            Update the velocity and po-
sition matrix, pos and vel.
            Confine vel in the range of
[-mv, mv].
            Confine pos in the range of
[xl, xu].
            Evaluate the fitness value
of each position.
            Update pBest, gBest, and
Con.
Until: Find the global fitness value
0, reach the maximal number of fit-
ness evaluations.
```

Contestant Algorithms

We study the performance of autoPSO by comparing the algorithm to:

- Three traditional clustering algorithms: k-means, Bisection k-means, and Graph-based clustering.
- PSOVW
- GA-based clustering (Bandyopadhyay, 2001)

The four clustering algorithms in the first two points require the number of clusters, k, to be provided by the user, while GA-based clustering allows us to automatically estimate the correct number of clusters as well as finding the clusters. The k-means is a conceptually simple and well-proven algorithm. The reason we have selected the Bisection k-means and Graph-based clustering algorithms for comparison is that both of them perform well on high-dimensional data sets, such as text data. PSOVW is an effective soft projected algorithm for clustering high-dimensional data based on variable weighting, already introduced in this chapter. Finally, the choice of GA-based clustering reflects our wish to demonstrate that autoPSO achieves a high level of performance not because it employs new objective functions, but rather because autoPSO introduces a more effective search strategy.

The *k-means* algorithm starts with a random partitioning and loops the following steps: 1) Compute the current cluster centroids, namely the average vector of each cluster in a data set in some cases; 2) Assign each data object to the cluster whose cluster centroid is closest to it. The algorithm terminates when there is no further change in the cluster centroids. By this means, k-means locally maximizes compactness by minimizing the within-cluster, namely the sum of squares of the differences between data objects and their corresponding cluster centroids. In our implementations, an empty cluster sometime occurs, so we reassign one data object randomly selected from the data set to it.

In order to generate *k* desired clustering solutions, *Bisection k-means* performs a series of *k*-means. Bisection *k*-means is initiated with the universal cluster containing all data objects. Then it loops: it selects the cluster with the largest variance and calls *k*-means, which optimizes a particular clustering criterion function in order to split this cluster into exactly two subclusters. The loop is repeated a certain number of times such that *k* non-overlapping clusters are generated. Note that this approach ensures that the criterion function is locally optimized within each bisection, but in general it is not globally optimized.

In the *Graph-based clustering* algorithm, the desired *k* clustering solutions are computed by first modeling the objects using a nearest-neighbor graph. Each data object becomes a vertex, and each data object is connected to the other objects most similar to it. Then, the graph is split into *k* clusters using a min-cut graph partitioning algorithm.

Finally, we compared against the *genetic algorithm* proposed by Bandyopadhyay. It starts with a randomly initialized population with fixed-length strings representing the centers of a number of clusters, where the value of this number may vary. The genetic clustering algorithm employs a conventional proportional selection, a modified single-point crossover and a special mutation. A cluster validity index such as the Davies-Bouldin (DB) index is utilized for computing the fitness of chromosomes. Experiments on four data sets, three artificial and one real-life, have demonstrated that GA-based clustering can automatically estimate the appropriate clustering of a data set.

High-Dimensional Synthetic Datasets

The clustering performance of the autoPSO algorithm was evaluated on the type 2 synthetic high-dimensional data sets selected from Section PSO for Variable Weighting.

Experimental Metric

The clustering performances of all of the above six algorithms, including autoPSO, were compared using the *Fscore* evaluation measure. Basically, this measure is based on the ideas of precision and recall from information retrieval. This function is an external function that compares the clustering solutions to the original class labels. Assume that a data set with *k* categories is grouped into *k* clusters and *n* is the total number of documents in the data set. Given a particular category L_r of size n_r and a particular cluster S_i of size m_i, n_{ri} denotes the number of documents belonging to category L_r that are assigned to cluster S_i. The *FScore* measure is defined as follows:

$$FScore = \sum_{r=1}^{k} \frac{n_r}{n} \cdot \max_{1 \le i \le k} \frac{2 \cdot R(L_r, S_i) \cdot P(L_r, S_i)}{R(L_r, S_i) + P(L_r, S_i)} \tag{17}$$

$$R(L_r, S_i) = \frac{n_{ri}}{n_r},$$

$$P(L_r, S_i) = \frac{n_{ri}}{m_i},$$

where *P* and *R* are the precision and recall for each class *i* and cluster *j*. *FScore* is limited to the interval [0,1] and should be maximized for the optimal clustering.

Experimental Results

Since *k*-means, Bisection *k*-means, PSOVW, GA-based and autoPSO are randomly initialized algorithms, we performed 20 runs of each algorithm on each data set and average the results obtained. We compare the different approaches in terms of the measure described in formula (17). For *k*-means, Bisection *k*-means, Graph-based and PSOVW, we set the proper number of clusters

Table 5. The FScore values of each algorithm on eight high-dimensional datasets.

High-dimensional data			autoPSO	GA-based	PSOVW	*k*-means	Bisection *k*-means	Graph-based
k	*n*	*m*						
4*k*	200	20*m*	100	100	100	64.9	100	88.7
		100*m*	100	100	100	62.1	100	85.6
		1000*m*	100	100	100	76.3	100	78.5
		2000*m*	100	100	100	72.4	100	87.3
10*k*	500	20*m*	100	90.5	93.2	35.1	92	86.4
		100*m*	100	87.8	92.4	33.4	92.5	85.5
		1000*m*	100	91.3	92.6	31.9	87	88.9
		2000*m*	100	88.9	94.8	36.2	86.2	81

for each dataset. GA-based and autoPSO do not require advance setting of this parameter. Table 5 reports the average value of the clustering solutions produced by each algorithm.

Figure 2 illustrates the distribution of the *FScore* values of Table 5.

From Table 5 and Figure 2, we note that autoPSO, GA-based, PSOVW and Bisection *k*-means attain comparable clustering results and all of them achieve 100 percent clustering accuracy on each trial over the data sets with 4 well-separated clusters. In our experiments on the data sets with 10 overlapped clusters, autoPSO performs most

robustly compared to its contestants. It reliably generates solutions that are comparable to or better than those of the other algorithms, showing that it explores high-quality clustering results on high-dimensional data sets. Evidently, it manages to cope with the complicated data sets where the relevant dimensions of individual clusters overlap considerably, while all of the other clustering methods fail on certain of these data sets. As can be expected, *k*-means performs very poorly in the absence of overlapped clusters, as it does in the data sets with 10 clusters. The clustering performance of the Graph-based algorithm

Figure 2. The FScore on high-dimensional datasets

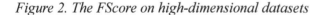
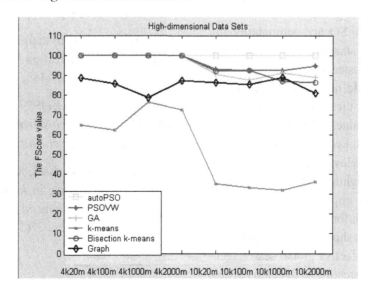

is little affected by the number of dimensions, because it employs the graph idea to find clusters. Bisection *k*-means produces a hierarchy by random binary splits, resulting in higher variance.

On all of the high-dimensional data sets, autoPSO reliably identifies the correct number of clusters. One should note the obvious difficulty of determining the number of clusters in high-dimensional data sets. In our experiments, the GA-based clustering algorithm is able to find the correct number of clusters as well as identifying clusters on the data sets with 4 clusters. However, its performance is inferior to that of autoPSO on the data sets with 10 clusters. The good performance of autoPSO in clustering high-dimensional data does not result from the objective function which is not new, but from its more effective search strategy.

4. CONCLUSION

PSO techniques for two specific tasks in clustering high-dimensional data have been developed and their performance has been analyzed in comparison to that of existing clustering approaches and several related projected clustering algorithms. The analysis has shown that particle swarm optimization can overcome some of the fundamental limitations of local search methods and may yield significant performance gains.

PSOVW and autoPSO are computationally more expensive than standard approaches such as *k*-means type of clustering algorithms.

Due to its heuristic nature, PSOVW is not guaranteed to obtain the most optimal weight vectors (where large values reflect the importance of the corresponding dimensions). Therefore, it is unable to recover the relevant dimensions totally, although the final weights it reaches do not have a significant negative impact on cluster quality. More effective methods for the selection of feature subsets for each cluster should thus be considered.

Since PSO is an effective global search technique, it would be interesting to develop particle swarm approaches to unsupervised feature selection and feature subspace selection for subspace clustering.

REFERENCES

Agrawal, R., Gehrke, J., & Gunopulos, D. (2005). Automatic Subspace Clustering of High Dimensional Data. *Data Mining and Knowledge Discovery, 11*(1), 5–33. doi:10.1007/s10618-005-1396-1

Bandyopadhyay, S., & Maulik, U. (2001). Nonparametric genetic clustering: comparison of validity indices. *IEEE Trans. on Systems, Man, and Cybernetics. Part C: Applications and Reviews, 31*(1), 120–125.

Davies, D. L., & Bouldin, D. W. (1979). A cluster separation measure. *IEEE Transactions on Pattern Analysis and Machine Intelligence, 1*(4), 224–227. doi:10.1109/TPAMI.1979.4766909

Domeniconi, C., & Gunopulos, D. (2007). Locally adaptive metrics for clustering high dimensional data. *Data Mining and Knowledge Discovery Journal, 14*, 63–97. doi:10.1007/s10618-006-0060-8

Eberhart, R. C., & Kennedy, J. (1995). A new optimizer using particle swarm theory. *Proc. 6th International Symposium on Micromachine and Human Science*, Japan, pp. 39-43.

Elke Achtert. & Christian B., et al. (2008). Detection and Visualization of Subspace Cluster Hierarchies. (*LNCS.* 4443, pp. 152-163).

Goil, S., & Nagesh, H. (1999). *Mafia: Efficient and scalable subspace clustering for very large data sets. Technical Report.* Northwestern University.

Huang, J. Z., & Michael, K. (2005). Automated dimension weighting in *k*-means type clustering. *IEEE Transactions on Pattern Analysis and Machine Intelligence, 27*(5), 1–12. doi:10.1109/TPAMI.2005.95

Jing, L., Ng, M. K., & Huang, J. Z. (2007). An entropy weighting *k*-means algorithm for subspace clustering of high-dimensional sparse data. *IEEE Transactions on Knowledge and Data Engineering*, *19*(8), 1026–1041. doi:10.1109/TKDE.2007.1048

Julia Handl & Joshua D. (2007). An Evolutionary Approach to Multiobjective Clustering. *IEEE Transactions on Evolutionary Computation*, *11*(1), 56–76. doi:10.1109/TEVC.2006.877146

Kumsawat, P., & Attakitmongcol, K. (2005). A new approach for optimization in image watermarking by using genetic algorithms. *IEEE Transactions on Signal Processing*, *53*(12), 4707–4719. doi:10.1109/TSP.2005.859323

Lai, C. (2005). A novel clustering approach using hierarchical genetic algorithms. *Intelligent Automation and Soft Computing*, *11*(3), 143–153.

Liang, J. J., Qin, A. K., Suganthan, P. N., & Baskar, S. (2006). Comprehensive learning particle swarm optimizer for global optimization of multimodal functions. *IEEE Transactions on Evolutionary Computation*, *10*(3), 281–295. doi:10.1109/TEVC.2005.857610

Liu Yongguo & Y. Mao. P. Jun. (2008). Finding the optimal number of clusters using genetic algorithms. *IEEE Conf. on Cybernetics and Intelligent Systems*(pp.1325-1330).

Moise, G., & Sander, J. (2008). Robust projected clustering. *Knowledge and Information Systems*, *14*(3), 273–298. doi:10.1007/s10115-007-0090-6

Parsons, L., & Haque, E. (2004). Subspace clustering for high dimensional data: A review. *SIGKDD Explorations Newsletter*, *6*, 90–105. doi:10.1145/1007730.1007731

Procopiuc, C. M., & Jones, M. PK. et al. (2002). A Monte Carlo algorithm for fast projective clustering. *Proc. of ACM SIGMOD Int. Conf. on Management of Data*. (pp.418 – 427).

Woo, Kyoung-Gu & Lee, Jeong-Hoon et al. (2004). FINDIT: A fast and intelligent subspace clustering algorithm using dimension voting. *Information and Software Technology*, *46*(4), 255–271. doi:10.1016/j.infsof.2003.07.003

Chapter 3
Text Mining for Analysis of Interviews and Questionnaires

Yasuhiro Yamada
Shimane University, Japan

Kanji Kato
GK Sekkei Incorporated, Japan

Sachio Hirokawa
Kyushu University, Japan

ABSTRACT

Interviews and questionnaires are the basis for collecting information about the opinions, concerns and needs of people. Analysis of those texts is crucial to understand the kansei of people. Text mining is an approach to discover useful and interesting patterns, knowledge and information from texts. This chapter contains two sections on text mining for beginners of it. The first section gives a brief survey of basic text mining techniques, such as keyword extraction, word graphs, clustering of texts and association rule mining. The second section demonstrates an example of text mining applied to interview analysis. Two text mining systems - the concept graph system and the matrix search system - are applied to analyze 2,409 remarks about products and services from 19 people. The analysis shows that text mining systems with a search function achieve interactive analysis of texts and an examination of various problems that we targeted.

1. INTRODUCTION

There are various approaches to understand the kansei of people. Brain waves, body temperatures and blood pressure are typical physiological data being used to measure kansei. Features of kansei appear in such data. Kansei are also reflected by the language that people use. This chapter deals with the study on patterns of language usage to understand kansei.

In order to understand opinions, concerns and needs of people, interviews and questionnaires are used as a standard approach. These opinions, concerns and needs are deeply related to the kansei of people. Sometimes, they are held in common by many people. At other times, they are unique to an individual. The kansei are implied by the form of the language, i.e. in sentences and in words.

DOI: 10.4018/978-1-61692-797-4.ch003

However, the kansei itself are behind these words and are not always expressed directly.

Interviews and questionnaires are stored in texts that can be analyzed by computers. Thanks to the progress of second storage capacity and the spread of the World Wide Web in the last decade, we can store and share a large amount of texts. Databases and search engines for texts help us to search easily and quickly. However, it is beyond the capability of one person to read, remember and manually analyze a large number of texts. At the very least, it requires a lot of time.

Even if an analyst was able to analyze a large amount of texts arising from interviews, the results may reflect the analyst's opinion and viewpoint. For example, they might depend on the analyst's personal knowledge, background and interest. Thus, if several researchers analyze a large amount of texts, the analyses are likely to be inconsistent from certain viewpoint. To eliminate bias, objective evidence is important. Traditionally, statistical methods have been used to support analysis. However, numeric analysis needs to be further interpreted. It should be explained as texts that can be readily understood.

Text mining is a technique to discover useful and interesting patterns, knowledge and information from texts. It is often able to discover information of which we are unaware. The results of mining are objective in the sense that they are obtained by the same method or algorithm even if input texts or analysts are different. Text mining techniques and systems are expected to help us analyze a large number of texts efficiently. Various such techniques and systems have been proposed.

This chapter contains two sections on text mining. The chapter assumes about readers which are going to use text mining for their research but do not know about it. The first section gives a brief survey of basic text mining techniques such as keyword extraction, word graphs, clustering of texts and association rule mining. Text mining techniques are classified into two types - statistical and semantic methods. Statistical methods are based on the frequencies of words in the texts. Semantic methods consider the meanings of words and how the words feature in the sentence structure. The first section describes also the statistical methods. This section is useful to start studying text mining.

The second section demonstrates an example of text mining applied to interview analysis. Two text mining systems - the concept graph system and the matrix search system - are applied to analyze interview. Search keywords are used, as with search engines, to specify the target and the circumstances of the analysis. The concept graph system visualizes a hierarchy of characteristic words in the texts. We can understand important words and relations among them in the texts before we actually read the texts. The matrix search system displays a matrix of the distribution of clustering of the texts from two different aspects. We can interpret the relation of the two aspects in the texts by combining various aspects. The two systems achieve multiple and dialogical analysis of interview. Therefore, the systems enable us to examine various problems that we choose as targets.

2. TEXT MINING TECHNIQUE

Preliminaries

This section reviews some notation used to describe text mining techniques. Let $D=\{d_1,d_2,...,d_n\}$ be a set of texts or documents. The number of texts in D is denoted by $|D|$. If w is a word that appears in some text d in D, we write $w \in D$. The term frequency of w in D, denoted by $tf(w, D)$, is the total number of occurrences of w in D. The document frequency of the word w in D, denoted by $df(w, D)$, is the number of texts in D that contain w. The number of texts containing both words u and v in D is denoted by $df(u*v,D)$.

This section describes the preprocessing of texts for text mining. Interviews and questionnaires are stored as texts in computers and are then transformed into "bags of words" by pre-processing. An English text is easy to divide into words, but it requires stemming to normalize the suffix of words. For example, "play," "plays" and "played" are transformed into the word "play." The Porter (Porter, 1980) and Paise/Hask (Paise, 1990) methods are well known. On the other hand, a Japanese or Chinese text needs special processes to divide it into words because the text does not have a space between two words.

Useless words in texts are removed in advance because they have a bad effect on text mining. Examples of useless words include function words such as a particles and auxiliary verbs. The SMART system (Salton, 1988) provides a list of useless words in English texts. The frequency of words determines their usefulness. Very frequent words are too general to characterize texts. On the other hand, very infrequent words are too special to be analyzed. Such words are often removed in advance. However, it is difficult to decide the boundary of frequency or infrequency.

Useless words in the situations above are called stop words.

Keyword Extraction

This section considers keyword extraction that characterizes the input texts. The extracted keywords play an important role in understanding and summarizing them. The frequency of a word is its most simple basic statistic. Assuming that keywords characterize texts exhaustively, the term frequency and the document frequency of words are appropriate measures of the characteristics of words in the texts. However, as noted above, very frequent words in the term frequency and the document frequency are often too general to characterize the texts.

Assume that a keyword characterizes the texts specifically. Then the inverse document frequency (idf) of the word is one of the appropriate measures of the characteristics of the word (Jones,

1972). The idf of the word w in a set D of texts is defined as follows.

$$idf(w, D) = \log \frac{|D|}{df(w, D)} + 1$$

Words with a high inverse document frequency appear in a small number of texts and are considered as special words.

Considering both the exhaustiveness and particularity of words in texts, tf-idf is commonly used as a standard measure in many information retrieval systems and clustering algorithms (Salton & McGill, 1983). The tf-idf of w in D, denoted by $tfidf(w, D)$, is defined as follows.

$$tfidf(w, D) = tf(w, D) \times idf(w, D)$$

The tf-idf is not the only measure for evaluating the characteristics of words in texts. Chujo and Utiyama (2006) introduced some measures which compare the frequency of words in two sets of texts. The measures evaluate words which are characteristic in one set but are not characteristic in another set. The measures are mutual information (Church & Hanks, 1990), the log-likelihood ratio (Dunning, 1993), the chi-square test and chi-square test with Yates' correction (Hisamitsu & Niwa, 2001), the Dice coefficient and Cosine (Manning & Schütze, 1999), a complete complementary similarity measure (Sawaki & Higata, 1996) and McNemar's test (Rayner & Best, 2001).

The co-occurrence of two words in the texts also helps us to understand the meaning of words and the texts. Church and Hanks (1990) proposed a method to measure word association by mutual information. Letting N be the total number of occurrences of words in a set D of texts and $tf_l(u*v,D)$ be the number of co-occurrences of words u and v within a window of size l which is the number of words between the two words, the mutual information $I(u, v)$ is defined as follows:

$$I(u, v) = \frac{P(u, v)}{P(u)P(v)}$$

where $P(u) = \dfrac{tf(u, D)}{N}$, $P(v) = \dfrac{tf(v, D)}{N}$ and

$$P(u, v) = \frac{tf_I(u * v, D)}{N}.$$

Further developments of this approach using word co-occurrence are mentioned in (Li et al., 2008; Matsuo & Ishizuka, 2004).

DIAMiningEX (Aikawa et al., 2003) is a system that analyzes texts such as questionnaires. It retrieves texts and analyzes them dialogically. The system shows a word co-occurrence table, which is a list of word frequencies.

Word Graph

The analysis of relations among words is more powerful than the analysis of a single word. Graphical visualization of such a relation is efficient for grasping the summary of a large number of texts without reading all the texts. The relation is often visualized as a directed or un-directed graph of words. This word graph consists of a set of nodes, which correspond to words, and a set of directed or un-directed edges each of which is a node pair. We can see that similar or related words form a group in the graph. We also can see upper and lower conceptual relations between words if the graph is directed.

KeyGraph is an un-directed graph of words generated from a given text (Ohsawa et al., 1998). The algorithm of KeyGraph has three extraction steps - foundations, columns and roofs. Firstly, the algorithm selects words with a high frequency and high association determined by the degree of co-occurrence of the words. Let d be a text consisting of some sentences. Then the association between two words u and v is defined as

$$assoc(u, v) = \sum_{s \in d} \min(|u|_s, |v|_s)$$

where $|w|_s$ denotes the number of occurrences of the word w in sentence s of d. High frequency words form the nodes of KeyGraph, and pairs of words with high association form the edges of KeyGraph. Maximal connected subgraphs in the graph determine the foundations. Secondly, the algorithm extracts roofs which are words connected with the foundations strongly. Finally, the algorithm adds the roofs to the graph as nodes. It also adds pairs of roofs and words in the foundations to the graph as edges.

A large volume of co-occurrence relations are constructed and maintained as a thesaurus. Some thesauruses capture not only co-occurrence but also upper and lower conceptual relations among words. The thesauruses are expressed as a hierarchy.

Niwa et al. (1997) proposed a method that automatically constructs a thesaurus from the retrieved texts. The user can analyze texts dialogically by constructing a thesaurus for each search result. The hypernym relation between words is defined by the document frequency and conditional probability of the frequency. The hypernym of a word is formulated as a more general word which maximizes the conditional probability. The method visualizes relations among words by linking edges from a word to all of its hypernyms.

Srinivasan (1992) considered a hierarchy of words according to the document frequencies of words. All words in the texts are divided into k groups $W_1, W_2, \ldots, W_k$ according to their document frequencies. The most frequent words form the highest level W_1. The range of the document frequency of each group is the same. The document frequency of the words in W_i is larger than that of words in $W_{i+1}, \ldots, W_k$. The similarity of words u and v is defined by

$$sim(u, v) = \frac{df(u * v, D)}{\sqrt{df(u, D) \times df(v, D)}}.$$

Figure 1. (a) hierarchical clustering and (b) non-hierarchical clustering

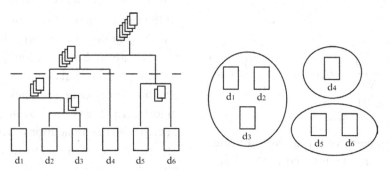

If $v \in W_{i+1}$ is most similar to $u \in W_i$, then v is a hyponym of u. After all words in W_{i+1} are linked with some word in W_i, when u has no hyponym in W_{i+1}, an identical dummy of u is copied to W_{i+1}. The method repeats the above steps from $i = 1$ to k-1.

Morita and Nakahara (2005) mined useful information from questionnaires about photographs of dishes using KeyGraph. They guessed that the size, color and shape of a dish are important factors from KeyGraph of the questionnaires. Ohsawa and Nara (2002) applied KeyGraph to analyze questionnaires about decision process in the real world and on the Internet. They compared it between US and Japanese people. An example result of the analysis was that Japanese people had negative attitude toward the Internet.

Clustering

Clustering is a technique to divide texts into several groups with the same or similar contents. Applying clustering to interviews and questionnaires, we can divide answers of questions into the same or similar ones. We can thus estimate the strength and importance of the answers by the number of similar answers. We also can cluster the interviewees. Therefore, clustering is useful to understand trends in the answers.

Rasmussen (1992) made a survey of clustering methods. A newer survey can be found in (Manning et al., 2008). There are two kinds of clustering methods which are hierarchical and non-

hierarchical. The result of hierarchical clustering is expressed as a binary tree structure (see Figure 1(a)). Leaves of the tree correspond to texts. The binary tree is called a dendrogram. A dendrogram indicates the status of coupling between clusters. Figure 1(a) is a dendrogram for six texts, where d_2 and d_3 are the most similar in all texts and the coupling starts from this pair. On the other hand, the result of non-hierarchical clustering is expressed by (generally disjoint) subsets in a plane (see Figure 1(b)). Figure 1(b) shows three clusters, each of which consists of three, two and one texts. In Figure 1, the hierarchical clustering at the dotted line gives the same result as non-hierarchical clustering.

Clustering algorithms utilize a vector space model. In the model, a text d is expressed by a word vector $d=(u_1,...,u_n)$ where u_i is a term weighting, for instance, the term frequency, the document frequency or the tf-idf weight which is defined by a word and a text.

The similarity of two texts is often calculated using the Euclidean distance, cosine distance, Dice coefficient or Jaccard coefficient (Salton, 1988; Rasmussen, 1992). Let $d_i=(u_1,...,u_n)$ and $d_j=(v_1,...,v_n)$ be two word vectors consisting of the weights of n words. The Euclidean distance between the two vectors is defined by

$$sim(d_i, d_j) = \sqrt{\sum_{k=1}^{n} (u_k - v_k)^2}.$$

The cosine distance is defined by

$$sim(d_i, d_j) = \frac{\sum_{k=1}^{n} u_k v_k}{\sqrt{\sum_{k=1}^{n} u_k^2 \sum_{k=1}^{n} v_k^2}}.$$

The dice coefficient is defined by

$$sim(d_i, d_j) = \frac{2\sum_{k=1}^{n} u_k v_k}{\sum_{k=1}^{n} u_k^2 + \sum_{k=1}^{n} v_k^2}.$$

The Jaccard coefficient is defined by

$$sim(d_i, d_j) = \frac{\sum_{k=1}^{n} u_k v_k}{\sum_{k=1}^{n} u_k^2 + \sum_{k=1}^{n} v_k^2 - \sum_{k=1}^{n} u_k v_k}.$$

In hierarchical clustering, given m texts, initially m clusters consisting of only one text are generated. Until the number of clusters becomes one, the most similar two clusters are combined into one cluster repeatedly by calculating the similarity of two clusters. There are several methods to measure the similarity of two clusters C_1 and C_2. The similarity in single linkage method (Sneath, 1957) is the similarity of the most similar texts, the first taken from C_1 and the second from C_2. The similarity in the complete linkage method (Sørensen, 1948) is the similarity of the furthest apart texts between C_1 and C_2. The similarity in the group average method (Sokal & Michener, 1958) is the average of similarities over all pairs from C_1 and C_2. Ward's method (Ward, 1963) considers the sum of squares of the similarities between the centroid of C_i which is the average of the word vectors in C_i and each text in C_i. The similarity in the Ward's method is the increase in the sum going from C_1 and C_2 to the new cluster obtained by merging C_1 and C_2.

The K-means algorithm is a non-hierarchical clustering algorithm (McQueen, 1967). Given a set D of texts and the desired number c of clusters, the procedure for the K-means algorithm is as follows: (1) select c texts randomly as initial clusters; (2) calculate the centroids of the clusters; (3) calculate the similarity between a text in D and the centroid for all texts and all centroids; (4) assign each text into its most similar cluster; (5) repeat from (2) to (4) until the generated clusters do not change. The result of the K-means algorithm depends on the selection of texts as initial clusters.

CLUTO is a free software package for clustering, made available by the University of Minnesota, (Karypis, 2003). CLUTO provides some functions for calculating the similarity of two texts and two clusters. CLUTO also produces a dendrogram when hierarchical clustering is performed. Willebrant et al. (2002) studied analysis of questionnaire for burn patients using hierarchical clustering and non- hierarchical clustering by the K-means algorithm. The questionnaire consists of 33 questions. They clustered 161 patients into three clusters.

Association Rule Mining

First, this section describes the problem of association rule mining, a procedure to find frequent associations between items in a database (Agrawal et al., 1993; Agrawal & Srikant, 1994). Let $I=\{i_1,...,i_m\}$ be a set of items. A set $X \subseteq I$ is called an itemset. A database D consists of a set of transactions, each element of which is a pair consisting of a transaction id and an itemset. An association rule is an expression of the form $X \rightarrow Y$, where $X \subset I$, $Y \subset I$ and $X \cap I = \phi$. The frequency of an itemset X is the number of transactions that involve X. The support of the rule $X \rightarrow Y$ is the frequency of $X \cup Y$ in D. The confidence of the rule $X \rightarrow Y$ is the ratio of the frequency of $X \cup Y$ to the frequency of X in D. In the association rule mining framework, the importance of an association rule is determined by comparing the thresholds of the support and the confidence. The problem of association rule mining is, given a database of transactions, a minimal support threshold and a minimal confidence threshold, to find all association rules which compare favorably with the thresholds in the database.

Applying the framework to texts, each item is replaced by a word, and a transaction is replaced by a text (Rajman & Besançon, 1998). An association rule represents frequent co-occurrence of words in the texts. An example of a discovered rule in (Rajman & Besançon, 1998) is (Iran, Nicaragua, Usa) →(Reagan) for a corpus of Reuter news articles. However, Rajman and Besançon (1998) stated that the obtained rules are often trivial or uninterpretable.

It is possible to take as basic unit items other than words. A term is a sequence of one or more words, to which a unit of meaning can be associated (Feldman et al., 1998). An episode, which also consists of a sequence of words, is the transformation of an association rule (Ahonen et al., 1997). In this framework, a text is considered as a sequence of words, not a set of words. The words in an episode appear nearby in the text. In Nahm and Mooney (2001), a text is considered to have multiple aspects. For example, a paper consists of title, author, affiliation, abstract, keywords and so on. An association rule in the framework distinguishes the same word from different aspects. An example of a rule is ("discovery" in title, "knowledge, discovery" in abstract)→ ("database, mining" in keywords). The studies reported that the rules obtained were more useful than those in the framework of simple words.

McNicholas et al. (2008) applied association rule mining to analysis of social questionnaire data collected from 1,490 Germans. The questionnaire consists of five questions each of which was answered yes or no. They extracted 38 association rules by setting a minimum support threshold to 20% and setting a minimum confidence threshold to 80%. An example of the found rules was that 95.1%, which is the confidence of the following rule, of those who did not agree that both "individuals are poor because of the lack of effort on

their part" and "poor people could improve their lot if they tried", did not also agree that "anyone can raise his standard of living if he is willing to work at it." The support of the rule was 26.2%

3. MULTIPLE ANALYSIS BY TEXT MINING OF THE REMARKS OF ELDERLY AND DISABLED PEOPLE

The purpose of the second section is to show a case study of an analysis of interviews using text mining. It describes an example of the flow of an analysis from texts of interviews to the result of text mining systems. It describes an analysis of needs determined from the remarks of elderly and disabled people (Yamada et al., 2007). The analysis utilizes two text mining systems, the concept graph system (Shimoji et al., 2008) and the matrix search system (Seki et al., 2007). The concept graph system is based on word graph in the first section of this chapter. The matrix search system is based on clustering.

In order to learn improved living conditions for elderly and disabled people, it is important to collect and analyze texts obtained from interviews and questionnaires. There are many needs revealed in remarks occurring in the texts. Some may be common to most of the participants. Others may occur rarely. The contents of the remarks depend on the individual interviewees. In order to discern the various needs, an analysis method is needed to interpret the collected texts from various viewpoints. Several aspects of interviewees should be considered. The needs of a person, the needs of people with the same disability, and their needs for a product should each be analyzed.

We can consider some important things in this analysis. It is difficult to understand a large amount of texts, therefore, it is important to figure out the texts roughly before we read the texts and analyze them. There are several aspects in the texts of interviews. The various combinations of two aspects achieve a multiple analysis. We consider the situation in which analysts examine various problems. For example, they are analysis of the needs of a person, the needs of people with the same disability, and their needs for a product. With a specialized system, which takes a keyword as input and outputs the result, like a search engine, analysts can analyze the texts dialogically.

The two text mining systems considered here analyze the remarks using an input keyword in a manner similar to search engines. The concept graph system constructs a thesaurus from the remarks as texts. Analysts can understand important words and relations among them in the remarks before they read them. The matrix search system displays a matrix of the distribution of clustering from two aspects of the remarks. Analysts can understand the relation between two aspects in the remarks by combining various aspects. The two systems allow multiple modes of analysis of the remarks, including a dialogical analysis. Therefore, these systems enable various targeted problems to be examined in several ways.

Elderly and Disabled Peoples' Remarks

This section describes the remarks of elderly and disabled people and the evaluation records which were transcribed from the remarks (Yamada et al., 2007). 2,409 remarks were collected from interviews of 19 subjects. The disabilities of subjects included completely blind, rheumatism, deaf and blind, the deaf-mute condition. The subjects also included healthy ones. The subjects were asked about 147 products and services, which are used in their daily life, such as mobile phones, remote controls and the train station. They were asked for reasons for liking or disliking these products and services. They were also asked about their day-to-day activities and opinions when they used these products and services.

In order to analyze the remarks multilaterally, remarks with meaningful content were transformed into texts with the following ten aspects.

1. Person: an interviewee, for example, a completely blind woman, a woman in her 20s, an elderly man,
2. Disability: a kind of disability, for example, complete blindness, rheumatism, deaf-muteness,
3. Operation / property: restriction by disability,
4. Evaluation factor 1: a factor which is common in the interviewee's life,
5. Evaluation factor 2: a factor which is common to other products and services,
6. Evaluation factor 3: a factor involving only the product or service,
7. Product / service: a target product and service for evaluation,
8. Part / function: a part and function of a product and service,
9. Positive keyword: a keyword based on a positive evaluation,
10. Negative keyword: a keyword based on a negative evaluation.

The transformed texts are called evaluation records. 680 evaluation records were constructed from all the remarks. The records were generated manually by reading the collected remarks and extracting keywords and sentences related to the ten aspects. This work was done by one interviewer.

Table 1 shows some of the evaluation records for a remote control (etc.). Some keywords and sentences related to the ten aspects could not be extracted from some remarks. The amount of extracted data in (1) is 680 out of 680 records, (2) is 312, (3) is 219, (4) is 220, (5) is 177, (6) is 167, (7) is 498, (8) is 218, (9) is 434, and (10) is 269. Table 2 shows the frequent words for each aspect.

The collected remarks and evaluation records were written in Japanese. Note that all figures and tables in the second section of this chapter were originally written in Japanese. The sentences and words in the figure and tables are translated into English. However, some words which are difficult to translate are deleted in the figures and tables.

Table 1. The five evaluation records for a remote control

ID	(1)	(2)	(3)	(4)	(5)
1	completely blind woman	completely blind	I check by touch and hearing.		
2	completely blind woman	completely blind	I check by touch and hearing.		
3	completely blind man	completely blind	I check by touch.	I want to do by myself.	I don't want to make a mistake.
4	completely blind man	completely blind	I cannot check by my eyes.	I want to do by myself.	
5	man using a wheel-chair	limb movement disorder	I use my favorite products.	I want to use products that healthy subjects use.	using my initiative
ID	(6)	(7)	(8)	(9)	(10)
1		remote control etc.	switch	I prefer a remote control with an announce function.	I don't prefer a remote control with only a beep because I don't know how to use it.
2		remote control etc.	switch	I prefer a remote control with the sign of sound.	I don't prefer a remote control which stays in the same state when I turn the power on or off.
3	I want to use my favorite products.	remote control	button	I prefer a remote control whose buttons are not flat and are different between different operations.	I don't prefer a small and flat remote control.
4		remote control			I don't prefer a remote control whose number of buttons is too many.
5		remote control			

Table 2. Frequent words for each aspect

(1)	(2)	(3)	(4)	(5)
woman	completely blind	wheelchair	thing	thing
man	rheumatism	confirmation	use	design
wheelchair	insult	movement	self	use
completely blind	neck	application	brand	self
couple	extremity	TV	product	brand
(6)	(7)	(8)	(9)	(10)
thing	bag	switch	can	button
design	remote control	button	thing	digital
use	fax machine	body	function	display
remote control	mobile phone	color	button	design
helper	phone	design	design	blue

The Concept Graph System

This section describes the concept graph system which is an automatic thesaurus construction system for texts (Shimoji et al., 2008). Given a search keyword, the system first retrieves the set of texts that satisfy the search keyword. Then, it generates a directed acyclic graph whose nodes are characteristic words of the texts and whose edges represent upper and lower relations of the words. The construction of a concept graph consists of three processes – (1) the extraction of characteristic words, (2) the construction of upper and lower relations between the words, (3) the construction of direct upper relations. The characteristic words are determined by their document frequencies and the upper and lower relations are determined by the co-occurrence of characteristic words.

Firstly, the system extracts characteristic words from texts. A word has different meanings and levels of importance according to the context where the word is used. Let U be the set of whole texts. Given a search keyword q, $D(q)$ denotes the set of texts which satisfy the search keyword q. Let w be a word appearing in $D(q)$. A word w is characteristic in $D(q)$ if

$$\frac{df(w, D(q))}{df(w, U)} > \alpha,$$

where a is a supplied threshold. Thus, if $a = 0.5$, a word w is characteristic in the search result $D(q)$ when the number of texts containing the word w in $D(q)$ is more than half of texts containing w in U. The system extracts all characteristic words of $D(q)$.

Secondly, the system extracts upper and lower relations between the extracted characteristic words. The semantic relation between two words also depends on the context where they are used. Hypernym and hyponym relations between words are formulated in terms of the document frequencies of the word. A word u is a hypernym of v with

respect to $D(q)$ if the following two conditions are satisfied:

$$df(u, D(q)) > df(v, D(q)) \text{ and } \frac{df(u * v, D(q))}{df(v, D(q))} > \beta,$$

where β is a supplied threshold. A word u is a hypernym of v, if u occurs more often than v in $D(q)$ and most texts with v contain u. The system extracts all hypernym and hyponym pairs of the extracted characteristic words.

Finally, the system constructs direct upper relations. Some words have many hypernyms and the graph may contain overlapping edges. Given a word v, the set $UP(v)$ of upper words of v and the set $DUP(v)$ of direct upper words of v are defined as follows.

$$UP(v) = \left\{ u \in D(q) \mid u \text{ is a hypernym of } v \right\}$$

$$DUP(v) = \left\{ u \in UP(v) \mid \forall w \in UP(v), u \notin UP(w) \right\}$$

A hypernym u of v is a direct upper hypernym if there are no other hypernyms of v between u and v. Visualization of a concept graph can be obtained by placing words of high frequency on the left side and ones of lower frequency on the right side.

Figure 2 shows part of the concept graph for evaluation records in which the word "wristwatch" appears. The denominator in a node stands for the document frequency of the word in the node in all records. The numerator stands for the document frequency of the word in the retrieval records. The number of records retrieved was 21. Words on the left are hypernyms of words connected to their right. For example, we see that the word "wristwatch" is a hypernym of "sense," "money," "balance" and so on. We also see that "sense" is a hypernym of "winding button," "actual feeling," "wind" and "no feeling." We can infer that some subjects talking about a wristwatch talked

Figure 2. The concept graph for "wristwatch"

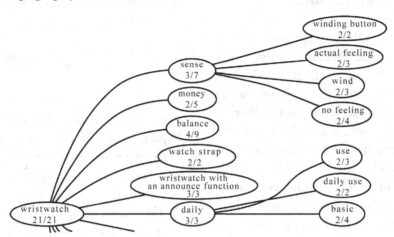

about the sense of winding the winding button of a wristwatch.

We can see words associated with a search keyword in retrieval records. The system is useful to understand the abstract of the records without reading the records. If the two thresholds are set to be large, we can see only words associated with each other strongly. If they are set to be small, a lot of words are displayed in a concept graph. The graph informs us noteworthy words in the retrieval. The words will be useful for next analysis.

The Matrix Search System

This section describes the matrix search system (Seki et al., 2007). It is an interactive system for analyzing texts from several points of view. Many of the current search engines merely display a list of texts containing search keywords. However, it is difficult to determine the significance of material appearing in the search result and to interpret it. Clustering is a useful method to understand any tendencies in the results.

In a text with multiple aspects, the content of each aspect is separated from the contents of other aspects. For example, a paper consists of title, author, affiliation, abstract, keywords and so on. The answer of interviews and questionnaires is often structured as a list of answers to each question. Analyzing the relation between two aspects in retrieved texts helps us to understand any tendencies in the texts.

The matrix search system retrieves texts of an indicated search aspect and displays a matrix of the distribution of the clustering from two aspects of the retrieved texts. A user selects a search aspect, two aspects as rows and columns for the matrix, the required number of clusters and enters search keywords through the interface of the system. The retrieved results are displayed as a matrix. If a retrieved text belongs to cluster i of the row and cluster j of the column, it becomes an element of the (i, j)-th cell in the matrix. The number of texts contained in each cell is displayed in the matrix.

This system allows users to freely change the search keywords, the search aspect, the row and column aspects, and the number of clusters for a multiple-view search. The characteristic words of each cluster are displayed in the matrix. They support the understanding of the meaning of the cluster and extension of the search. The system implements a zooming function, which refers to a recursive matrix generation that clusters texts in a cell. Thus, various retrieval conditions for a search keyword can be attempted interactively and continuously.

The system implements three types of grouping of texts. Firstly, the system divides numeric data

Figure 3. The result for "button" using the matrix search system

		small, high, position, eye, fan	digital display, button, time, minute, combination	power-on, power-off, state, difficult, understand	button, small, menu, item, many		
product / service	elevator	0	0	0	1		
	timer	0	1	0	0		
	fax machine	0	0	0	1		
	remote control	0	0	0	5		
	clothing	0	0	0	1		
	home electronics	0	0	1	0		
	air fan	1	0	1	0		
	vending machine	0	0	0	1		
	rice cooker	0	0	0	1		
	microwave	0	1	0	0		
				negative keyword			

into groups with the same range. For example, if the numeric data (10, 20, 22, 28, 40) is divided into two groups, the range is (40-10)/2=15. Therefore, the generated clusters are (10, 20, 22) and (28, 40). Secondly, for an aspect consisting of a small number of fixed values such as country or month, the content of a generated group is a constant value. Finally, for other types of data such as sentences, the system clusters the data by hierarchical clustering. The relation of clusters is displayed by a dendrogram.

Figure 3 shows an output of the system. The search keyword was "button." The target search aspect was all aspects. The row was "product / service." The column was "negative keyword." The number of evaluation records assigned to a cell is displayed in the table. The characteristic words of each cluster on the column are also displayed. They support the understanding of the features of a cluster without reading the records. Figure 3 omits part of the result matrix, some of characteristic words and the dendrogram of the clustering due to limitations of text space.

From Figure 3, we can infer that there is the same need that we observed earlier between "air

fan" "home electronics." The need concerns "power-on," "power-off" and "state." The fourth cluster in the negative keyword aspect is the largest cluster in the result. It contains various record contents, so it does not seem to be a cluster with the same meaning. The reason for this result is that the number of clusters in the column is small. In order to analyze the cluster, it is useful to re-cluster using the zooming function to focus on the cluster.

We can get more information by clustering of two aspects rather than it of one aspect. A matrix result shows records which belong to one cluster in one aspect but which belong to some different clusters in another aspect. We can also see records which do not belong to multiple clusters in both aspects. Interviews and questionnaires often consist of a variety of questions. Therefore, the discovery of the commonality and the independent is useful for analysis.

Analysis

This section shows an example of analysis of the elderly and disabled peoples' evaluation records using the concept graph system and the matrix search system. The example analysis is to find positive and negative keywords which are common to multiple disabilities when the target search aspect is "disability." The selected 4 disabilities, which appear frequently in the evaluation records, are "completely blind," "rheumatism," "limb movement disorder" and "deaf."

Figure 4 shows the concept graph of the records of completely blind. The denominator in the node stands for the number of records of the word in the node in all records. The numerator

stands for the number of records of the word in the node in the 138 records of completely blind. We see that person and disability associated with completely blind are extracted as characteristic words in the graph. We also see that words associated with completely blind are extracted as characteristic words, for example, "display,"

Figure 4. The concept graph for completely blind

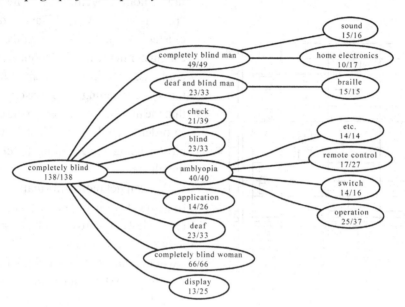

"check," "sound," "braille" and "operation." We can infer that the complete blind man talked about home electronics with sounds. We also can infer that subjects with amblyopia talked about the operation of a remote control and a switch.

Analysis using the matrix search system was performed by changing search keywords, re-clustering using the zooming function and changing the number of clusters. Figure 5 shows the output of the matrix search system when the search keyword was "completely blind OR rheumatism OR limb movement disorder OR deaf," the row aspect was "disability," and the column aspect was "negative keyword." The OR searching means that the retrieval records involve one or some of the four words. Figure 5 is generated by re-clustering a certain cluster using the zooming function repeatedly. The matrix shows that the third cluster of the negative keyword aspect determines a need that is common to "completely blind" and "completely blind and amblyopia." In the three records of the cluster, the document frequency of the word "operation result" is three. Therefore, we can infer that the need is about operation result. Actually, the three records state that it is

not desirable if a subject cannot understand the operation result.

Figure 6 is constructed by selecting important information from the results of the matrix search system using the four words and integrating it manually. The five positive and negative keywords which are common to multiple disabilities are displayed. The number in Figure 6 shows the number of evaluation records which are related to two aspects. A line without a number stands for one record. For instance, there exist three records which describe that it is not desirable if a subject cannot understand the operation result. A subject with complete blind talked it once, and

Figure 5. The result for disability using the matrix search system

disability	completely blind	0	1	1
	completely blind and amblyopia	0	0	2
	limb movement disorder	1	0	0
		paper quality, soft, tissue, constant, skin	understand, amount, hot water, fast, hot-water supply	operation result, button, understand, selection, eyesight
			negative keyword	

Figure 6. The result of analysis of disability

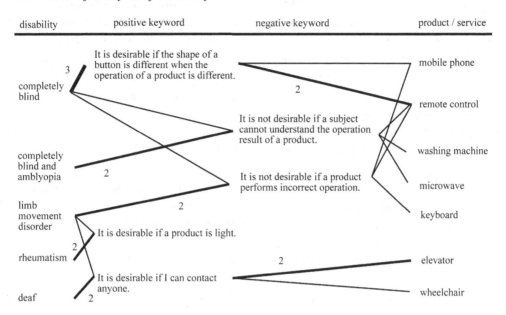

a subject with complete blind and amblyopia talked it twice. A result matrix of the system enables us to understand the degree of need because a cell in the matrix displays the number of records. The third cluster in the negative keyword aspect of Figure 5 shows that the number of records of a subject with completely blind is one and that of a subject with completely blind and amblyopia is two in the above 3 records. Figure 6 also describes the products associated with the keywords. We can analyze and determine the relations among "disability," "positive keyword," "negative keyword" and "product."

The concept graph system is useful to understand the abstract of records without reading all the records. Analysts can understand important words and the relations of the words. Words in a concept graph imagine a next target of analysis. A problem of the concept graph system is that a result graph is too simple and trivial if a text is short or the number of retrieved texts is small. The matrix search system is useful to analyze the relations between multiple aspects. We can combine the results of both systems to achieve an interactive analysis of the records. A problem of

the matrix search system is that the numbers of texts in clusters vary greatly. For example, the numbers of texts in some clusters are quite large but those of other clusters are quite small.

The case study in the second section of the chapter shows that a text mining system can be useful in the analysis of interviews and questionnaires. In particular, using text mining systems with a search function can achieve interactive analysis of texts and examination of various problems that analysts target by inputting keywords. We have to search target texts manually if we cannot use the search function. It takes a long time to search target texts that we want to analyze. The search function reduces the time for searching. We can also analyze texts from a variety of angles by combining some different text mining techniques and systems.

4. CONCLUSION

This chapter contained an introduction to basic text mining techniques which help to analyze interviews and questionnaires. The techniques introduced were keyword extraction, word graph, clustering and association rule mining. The chapter demonstrated an example of a case study in interview analysis. It described an analysis of the remarks of elderly and disabled people by using two text mining systems.

Text mining technique can treat with a large amount of texts. It reduces the burden of analysts. The results of text mining are not reflected by the analyst's opinion and viewpoints, for example, the analyst's personal knowledge, background and interests. The results have objectivity and reproducibility. The results are often displayed with numbers such as frequency. It helps us to compare to other results. Especially, text mining systems with a search function achieve interactive analysis of texts and an examination of various problems that we targeted.

The disadvantage of text mining is that it depends on analysts or tasks of analysis to judge whether found fact is useful or not. The found fact may be sometimes mediocrity and trivial. Other disadvantage is that words talked in interviews and questionnaires depend on subjects. Sometimes, different subjects use different words in a sentence with the same meaning. Word count based approaches recognize the sentence as different. In order to treat with such sentence, it is needed to be formalized as preprocessing. It is often performed manually.

The remarks of people are reflected by the kansei of the people. The kansei appears in interviews and questionnaires as their opinions, concerns and needs. In order to understand the diversity of them, we should consider the multi-faceted understanding of users. Text mining finds useful information from interviews and questionnaires and helps us to discover facts of which we are unaware. The found facts lead to understand users. This chapter introduced some text mining techniques and their basic knowledge. There are a variety of text mining techniques and systems except for them in this chapter. Each of them has its own characteristic that other techniques do not have. Therefore, analysts should select one or some of the techniques which are suitable for the task of their analysis. The authors believe that this chapter is useful to select text mining techniques and to learn the basic.

REFERENCES

Agrawal, R., Imielinski, T., & Swami, A. (1993). Mining Association Rules between Sets of Items in Large Databases. *Proceedings of the 1993 ACM SIGMOD International Conference on Management of Data* (pp. 207-216). ACM.

Agrawal, R., & Srikant, R. (1994). Fast Algorithms for Mining Association Rules in Large Databases. *Proceedings of the 20th International Conference on Very Large Data Bases* (pp. 487-499). ACM.

Ahonen, H., Heinonen, O., Klemettinen, M., & Verkamo, A. I. (1997). *Applying Data Mining Techniques in Text Analysis* (Technical Report C-1997-23). University of Helsinki.

Aikawa, T., Itoh, T., Takayama, Y., Suzuki, K., & Imamura, M. (2003). A Proposal of a Method of Analysis of Questionnaires Using Text Mining Based on Concept Extraction. *IPSJ SIG Notes*, 2003-FI-70-1, (pp. 1-6). (in Japanese)

Chujo, K., & Utiyama, M. (2006). Selecting level-specific specialized vocabulary using statistical measures. [Elsevier.]. *System*, *34*, 255–269. doi:10.1016/j.system.2005.12.003

Church, K. W., & Hanks, P. (1990). Word Association Norms, Mutual Information, and Lexicography. [Cambridge, MA: MIT Press.]. *Computational Linguistics*, *16*(1), 76–83.

Dunning, T. (1993). Accurate Methods for the Statistics of Surprise and Coincidence. [Cambridge, MA: MIT Press.]. *Computational Linguistics*, *19*(1), 61–74.

Feldman, R., Fresko, M., Kinar, Y., Lindell, Y., Liphstat, O., Rajman, M., et al. (1998). Text Mining at the Term Level. *Proceedings of the Second European Symposium on Principles of Data Mining and Knowledge Discovery* (pp. 65-73). Springer-Verlag.

Hisamitsu, T., & Niwa, Y. (2001). Topic-Word Selection Based on Combinatorial Probability. *Proceedings of the Sixth Natural Language Processing Pacific Rim Symposium* (pp. 289-296).

Jones, K. S. (1972). A statistical interpretation of term specificity and its application in retrieval. *The Journal of Documentation, 28*(1), 11–21. doi:10.1108/eb026526

Karypis, G. (2003). *CLUTO: A Clustering Toolkit Release 2.1.1.* (Technical Report: #02-017). University of Minnesota.

Li, X., Wu, X., Hu, X., Xie, F., & Jiang, Z. (2008). Keyword Extraction Based on Lexical Chains and Word Co-occurrence for Chinese News Web Pages. *Proceedings of the 2008 IEEE International Conference on Data Mining Workshops* (pp. 744-751). IEEE Computer Society.

Manning, C. D., Raghavan, P., & Schütze, H. (2008). *Introduction to Information Retrieval.* Cambridge, UK: Cambridge University Press.

Manning, C. D., & Schütze, H. (1999). *Foundations of Statistical Natural Language Processing.* Cambridge, MA: MIT Press.

Matsuo, Y., & Ishizuka, M. (2004). Keyword Extraction from a Single Document using Word Co-occurrence Statistical Information. *International Journal of Artificial Intelligence Tools, 13*(1), 157–169. doi:10.1142/S0218213004001466

McNicholas, P. D., Murphy, T. B., & O'Regan, M. (2008). Standardising the lift of an association rule. [Elsevier.]. *Computational Statistics & Data Analysis, 52,* 4712–4721. doi:10.1016/j.csda.2008.03.013

McQueen, J. (1967). Some Methods for Classification and Analysis of Multivariate Observations, *Proceedings of the Fifth Berkeley Symposium on Mathematical Statistics and Probability* (pp.281-297).

Morita, H., & Nakahara, T. (2005). Data mining from photographs using the KeyGraph and genetic algorithms, *Journal of Economics. Business and Law, 7,* 73–85.

Nahm, U. Y., & Mooney, R. J. (2001). Mining Soft-Matching Rules from Textual Data. *Proceedings of the Seventeenth International Joint Conference on Artificial Intelligence* (pp. 979-984).

Niwa, Y., Nishioka, S., Iwayama, M., Takano, A., & Nitta, Y. (1997). Topic Graph Generation for Query Navigation: Use of Frequency Classes for Topic Extraction. *Proceedings of Natural Language Processing Pacific Rim Symposium, 97,* 95–100.

Ohsawa, Y., Benson, N. E., & Yachida, M. (1998). KeyGraph: Automatic Indexing by Co-occurrence Graph based on Building Construction Metaphor. *Proceedings of the IEEE International Forum on Research and Technology Advances in Digital Libraries* (pp. 12-18). IEEE Computer Society.

Ohsawa, Y., & Nara, Y. (2002). *Modeling the Process of Chance Discovery by Chance Discovery on Double Helix.* AAAI Fall Symposium Technical Report FS-02-01, American Association for Artificial Intelligence, pp.33-40.

Paise, C. D. (1990). Another Stemmer. [ACM.]. *ACM SIGIR Forum, 24*(3), 56–61. doi:10.1145/101306.101310

Porter, M. F. (1980). An algorithm for suffix stripping. *Program, 14*(3), 130–137.

Rajman, M., & Besançon, R. (1998). Text Mining - Knowledge extraction from unstructured textual data. *Proceedings of 6th Conference of International Federation of Classification Societies* (pp. 473-480).

Rasmussen, E. M. (1992). Clustering Algorithms. In Frakes, W. B., & Baeza-Yates, R. (Eds.), *Information Retrieval: Data Structures & Algorithms* (pp. 419–442). Upper Saddle River, NJ: Prentice-Hall.

Rayner, J. C. W., & Best, D. J. (2001). *A Contingency Table Approach to Nonparametric Testing*. Boca Raton, FL: Chapman & Hall/CRC.

Salton, G. (1988). *Automatic Text Processing*. Reading, MA: Addison-Wesley Longman Publishing.

Salton, G., & McGill, J. M. (1983). *Introduction to Modern Information Retrieval*. New York: McGraw Hill New York.

Sawaki, M., & Hagita, N. (1996). Recognition of Degraded Machine-Printed Characters Using a Complementary Similarity Measure and Error-Correction Learning. *IEICE Transactions on Information and Systems*, *79*(5), 491–497.

Seki, T., Wada, T., Yamada, Y., Ytow, N., & Hirokawa, S. (2007). Multiple Viewed Search Engine for e-Journal - a Case Study on Zoological Science. *Proceedings of the 12th International Conference on Human-Computer Interaction*, Vol. 4553/2007 (pp. 989-998). Springer-Verlag.

Shimoji, Y., Wada, T., & Hirokawa, S. (2008). Dynamic Thesaurus Construction from English-Japanese Dictionary. *Proceedings of the 2008 International Conference on Complex, Intelligent and Software Intensive Systems* (pp. 918-923). IEEE Computer Society.

Sneath, P. H. A. (1957). The Application of Computers to Taxonomy. *Journal of General Microbiology*, *17*, 201–226.

Sokal, R. R., & Michener, C. D. (1958). A Statistical Method for Evaluating Systematic Relationships. *University of Kansas Scientific Bulletin*, *28*, 1409–1438.

Sørensen, T. (1948). A method of establishing groups of equal amplitude in plant sociology based on similarity of species content and its application to analyses of the vegetation on Danish commons. *Biologiske Skrifter*, *5*, 1–34.

Srinivasan, P. (1992). Thesaurus Construction. In Frakes, W. B., & Baeza-Yates, R. (Eds.), *Information Retrieval Data Structures & Algorithms* (pp. 161–218). Upper Saddle River, NJ: Prentice-Hall.

Ward, J. H. (1963). Hierarchical Grouping to Optimize an Objective Function. *Journal of the American Statistical Association*, *58*(301), 236–244. doi:10.2307/2282967

Willebrand, M., Andersson, G., Kildal, M., & Ekselius, L. (2002). Exploration of coping patterns in burned adults: cluster analysis of the coping with burns questionnaire (CBQ). [Elsevier.]. *Burns*, *28*, 549–554. doi:10.1016/S0305-4179(02)00064-5

Yamada, Y., Katoh, K., & Hirokawa, S. (2007). Multiple Analysis of Remarks of Elderly and Disabled People by Text Mining. *Proceedings of the International Conference on Kansei Engineering and Emotion Research 2007*.

Chapter 4

Intra–Class Threshold Selection in Face Space Using Set Estimation Technique

Madhura Datta
University of Calcutta, India

C. A. Murthy
Indian Statistical Institute, India

ABSTRACT

Most of the conventional face recognition algorithms are dissimilarity based, and for the sake of open and closed set classification one needs to put a proper threshold on the dissimilarity value. On the basis of the decision threshold, a biometric recognition system should be in a position to accept the query image as client or reject him as imposter. However, the selection of proper threshold of a given class in a dataset is an open question, as it is related to the difficulty levels dictated in face recognition problems. In this chapter, the authors have introduced a novel thresholding technique for a real life scenario where the query face image may not be present in the training database, i.e. often referred by the biometric researchers as the open test identification. The theoretical basis of the thresholding technique and its corresponding verification on several datasets has been successfully demonstrated in the article. The proposed threshold selection is based on statistical method of set estimation and is guided by minimal spanning tree. It has been found that the proposed technique performs better than the ROC curve based threshold selection mechanism.

1. INTRODUCTION

A hypothetical face recognition task can be viewed in general as combinations of two phases i.e. face authentication or verification and face identification. Several evaluation protocols (Philips, 2003; Jain, 2004; Blackburn, 2004) have been designed

DOI: 10.4018/978-1-61692-797-4.ch004

earlier for measuring the performance of different existing algorithms. Among those popular methods, appearance based methods (Zhao, 2003; Moghaddam, 2004; Solar, 2005; Maltoni 2005) are generally based on dissimilarity, where the query image is either put in the class for which the dissimilarity is minimal or from which the maximum number of matches are found. This is a classical approach of identification and known as *closed test identification* where the test face always exists in the client database. However, in a real life scenario the identification system may face a situation where the query face image may not be present in the database, i.e. often referred by the biometric researchers as the open test identification. In case of *open test identification* the system should identify the face as imposter to the system. A way of achieving such a task is to put a threshold on the dissimilarity value at the identification stage. On the basis of the *decision threshold*, a *biometric recognition* system should be in a position to accept the query image as client or reject him as imposter. The problem of threshold selection in face recognition has not been properly understood. The understanding has been ambiguous, vague, and imprecise. That problem is modeled as a set estimation problem here. Modeling of ambiguous and imprecise phenomena is one of the subject matters of soft computing, though the usual soft computing techniques are not used here. Additionally, since the feelings of the authors are modeled mathematically, and the subject pertains to human beings, this method of selecting threshold in this article gives the flavor of *Kansei Engineering*.

Selection of proper threshold of a given class in a dataset is an open question, as it is related to the difficulty levels dictated in face recognition problems. A difficulty level is likely to change from situation to situation. In a face recognition problem for an ideal security system, three difficulty levels may be ascertained. These are (i) zero effort attack, (ii) minimal effort attack and (iii) organized effort attack. Depending on the demand imposed on security system, the difficulty levels are decided.

Mansfield (2002) used a method of selecting threshold based on false acceptance rate (FAR) and false rejection rate (FRR). FAR is defined as the percentage of images which are incorrectly matched by the system and FRR is the percentage of images which are rejected as unknown face images although they exist in the training set.

The threshold value is determined using receiver operating characteristic (*ROC*) curve which in turn, is based on the different values of FAR and FRR. The point on the ROC curve that satisfies the condition of the equal error rate (EER), when FAR = FRR, is selected as the operating threshold for subsequent tests. *Martin* (1997) proposed the use of detection error trade-off (*DET*) curve which is nothing but a non-linear transformation of ROC curve. In principle, both the curves for threshold determination work well, if the threshold value is computed over a large number of test images. In practice, however, obtaining recognition results on a large number of test images is computationally expensive.

In any face recognition problem, the given query image may be attributed into one of the following categories with respect to the given training set. These categories are (a) the query image is a non face image, (b) the query image is a face image of a doll or statuette or some such object (c) the query image is that of a human being but no image of that person is in the training set and (d) at least an image of the person in the query image is in the training set. All that is needed for the purpose of face recognition is a procedure to obtain good estimates of FAR and FRR values. Finding a good estimate of FAR is not always possible, as we are supposed to cover ALL or at least a representative set of the images of objects or of living beings falling into categories (a), (b) and (c). In reality, a system can have extremely few examples of genuine access and relatively few imposter accesses as found in the literature. As a result user specific threshold selection is very unreliable to involve FAR and FRR. Again the common practice is to use the global threshold for a system rather than using user dependent versions of ROC.

In the current problem we are interested in finding the threshold values for the facial classes when the attacks are with zero effort. Face class consists of all possible face images of a person. "All possible face images of a person" would mean, theoretically, face images taken under all possible conditions. That is, these conditions include (i) different artifacts on face, (ii) different illuminations of face, (iii) different head positions with respect to the camera, (iv) different expressions on face, and (v) all different combinations of the above said four possibilities. After projection of "ALL" face images from image space to the face space, the face class of a particular person will form a "universal set" in the face space. And theoretically the set will contain infinite number of face points. But in reality we have the sets formed by the training face points which are not able to provide full information for a person because in real life it is not possible to have ALL variations of a single human being. We will only have finitely many points from each of the face classes in face space. Having all these limitations one may try to estimate the set with the help of few training face points in the face space R^m where m is the number of extracted features. The method of *set estimation* mainly used to find the pattern class and its multivalued shape/boundary from its sample points in two dimensional Euclidean space R^2 (*Murthy*,1995). Some investigation on estimation of α−shapes for point sets in R3 had been proposed by E*delsbrunner* (1983), and later M*andal* et al. (1997) extended the method to Rm and found it very useful in developing a multivalued recognition system. As one can get the shape or boundary of a given set, this procedure of s*et estimation* also generates the intuition for determination of the class thresholds of the set. As a tool of set estimation, m*inimal spanning tree* (MST) is proposed to calculate threshold value (Murthy, 1988).

In this paper we proposed two types of threshold values namely (i) global, (ii) local or user specific.

Here two types of decisions can be made by the system. *Global threshold* will provide whether the query image belongs to the given collection of face classes. The local or *intra-cluster local threshold* will identify the user as it should belong to one of the training classes in the database. These two thresholds will satisfy a biometric system in both the closed and open test identification cases.

For the purpose of reducing the *dimensionality*, we need to extract features by using any one of the *subspace methods*. Three types of feature extraction methods of the images in the face database are explored. They are (i) *principal component analysis* (PCA) (ii) *wavelet based PCA,* and (iii) *linear discriminant analysis* (LDA) in combination with PCA.

2. MATHEMATICAL PRELIMINARIES FOR THE THRESHOLD SELECTION

The intuition for the proposed threshold selection mechanism is provided in the next subsection. We assume that the feature extraction step has already been carried out either in spatial or in the wavelet domain using any subspace method.

Intuition for the Method

In each class of the database we may have a few face images, such as images of same person having different expressions. The images of the same person, giving the same expression at different times, may differ even if the lighting and other peripheral conditions remain invariant. Let us assume that we have n images corresponding to a particular expression of a particular person P. We also assume that there are infinitely many images corresponding to the same expression P. This is due to the fact that, for the same expression, there may be different small changes in muscle movements in face. For example, movement of eye brows, different locations of iris, twitching of nose, different muscle movements in cheeks and mouth portions when a person is in joyous mood. Note that, for the same expression of P, the corresponding set, intuitively, is to be connected too since for two different images of the same expression, P must be able to provide the intermediary images of that expression (a path connecting the two points is completely contained in the set.). If we represent an image of an expression of P by a vector x_0 then the set corresponding to the small variations in the same expression may be assumed to be a *disc* of radius $\varepsilon > 0$ The set corresponding to an expression of the same person

P may be taken as $\bigcup_{i=1}^{n} \{x \in \Re^m : d(x_i, x) \leq \varepsilon\}$

where $x_1, x_2,...x_n$ are the n vectors corresponding to the given n images. The set corresponding to the union of all possible expressions of a person may also be taken as a connected set. The face class of a person is nothing but the set of all possible expressions of that person.

A general formulation of the face class, probably, would have the radius value depending on the center of the disc. Here, that possibility is not considered because of the complicated nature of the formulation. The radius value is taken to be independent of the the center of the disc here.

In the above formulation, as the number of face images of the same person increases, we shall be obtaining more information regarding the face class, and hence the radius value needs to be decreased. Thus the radius value needs to be a function of the number of images. Several issues may arise out of the previous intuitive formulation. (i) How does one know whether the method works? (ii) Is there any mathematical basis for the above formulation? (iii) What is the value of ε? Usually one may want to *"estimate"* a set on the basis of the given finitely many points. The set to be estimated may have some "nice" properties. *Grenander* (1981) has formulated the set estimation problem as the problem of finding consistent estimate of a set.

Definition: Let $X_1, X_2, ...X_n, ...$ be a sequence of independent and identically distributed random vectors which follow some continuous distribution over the set $\alpha \subseteq \Re^m$ where α is an unknown quantity. Let α_n be an estimated set based upon the random vectors $X_1, X_2, ... X_n$. Then α_n is said to

be a consistent estimate of α_n, if $E_\alpha[\mu(\alpha_n \Delta \alpha)] \to 0$ as $n \to \infty$, where Δ denotes symmetric difference, μ is the *lebesgue measure* and E_α denotes the "expectation" taken under α.

Result: *Let* $X_1, X_2,...,X_n,...$ be independent and identically random vectors, which follow uniform distribution over $\alpha \subseteq \Re^2$ where α is unknown. Let α be such that $cl(Int(\alpha)) = \alpha$ and $\mu(\delta\alpha) = 0$ where $\delta\alpha$ denotes the boundary of α, cl denotes closure, and Int denotes the interior. Let $\{\varepsilon_n\}$ be a sequence of positive numbers such that $\varepsilon_n \to 0$ and $n\varepsilon_n^2 \to \infty$ as $n \to \infty$.

Let $\alpha_n = \bigcup_{i=1}^{n} \{x \in \Re^2 : d(x, X_i) \leq \varepsilon_n\}$;

$$(1)$$

where 'd' denotes the Euclidean distance. Then α_n is a consistent estimate of α.

Remarks:

i. *The above theorem did not mention a way of finding εn.*

ii. Let the sequence $\{\varepsilon_n\}$ satisfy $\varepsilon_n \to 0$ and $n\varepsilon_n^2 \to \infty$ as $n \to \infty$. Let $\varepsilon_{1n} = \beta\varepsilon_n$ where $\beta > 0$ is a constant. Then $\varepsilon_{1n} \to 0$ and $n\varepsilon_{1n}^2 \to \infty$ as $n \to \infty$ Thus there are several sequences with these two properties. α_n will be a consistent estimate for every one of these sequences. Thus, one needs to choose the radius judiciously.

iii. The intuition, *which wa*s discussed earlier, is expressed in equation (1).

Murthy (1988) developed a way of finding ε_n for points in two dimensional spaces. He also generalized the method to any continuous density function on α, where α is a path connected set. His method is given as Method 1. The method has been used extensively in different applications and for different problems and in different fields

Murthy 1995, Edelsbrunner (1983), Mandal et al. (1997), S. K. Pal (1997).

Method 1:

i. Find minimal spanning tree (MST) of $S = \{X_1, X_2, \ldots\ldots X_n\}$ where the edge weight is taken to be the Euclidean distance between two points and S is a finite set of points. Note that the MST of S would be an uncountable set of points. Let us denote MST of S by G_n.

ii. Let l_n denote the sum of edge weights of MST, and

iii. Let $\varepsilon_n = \sqrt{\dfrac{l_n}{n}}$

iv. $A_n = \bigcup\limits_{x \in G_n} \{y \in \Re^2 : d(x, y) \leq \varepsilon_n\}$. (2)

Then A_n is a consistent estimate of α.

Remarks:

i. α is taken to be a path connected set here. If one needs to estimate a set $E = E_1 \cup E_2$ then we would prefer to estimate E_1 and E_2 separately and take their union. This would make the assumption of path connectedness effective.

ii. The method 1 can be easily generalized to m dimensions and for any continuous distribution on α. Then the parameter ε_n is given by

$\varepsilon_n = (l_n/n)^{1/m}; \; m \geq 2$ (3)

Note that as $n \to \infty$, $\varepsilon_n \to 0$ and $n\varepsilon_n^m \to \infty$.

iii. The value of m may change from one data set to another.

3. PROPOSED SET ESTIMATION METHOD

In the present problem, a dimensionality reduction method is implemented initially. It is followed by the set estimation method. Determination of the

set A_n given by the equation 3 is a difficult task since the union of all the disks with centers on MST has to be taken into account. The estimated set is to be path connected and connectivity is preserved by MST. There are several ways in which we can make the estimated set connected. We shall describe a generic way (Method 2) of making the estimated set connected, where only finite union of disks is considered.

Method 2:

a. Take δ_n as (Maximum of the $(n\text{-}1)$ edge weights of MST)/2.

b. Let $\beta \geq 1$ be a constant. Let $\varepsilon_n(\beta) = \beta \delta_n$.

c. Take the estimate $A_n(\beta)$ as

$$A_n(\beta) = \bigcup\limits_{x \in S}^{n} \{y : d(x, y) \leq \varepsilon_n(\beta)\} .$$ (4)

Remarks: (i) Every $\beta \geq 1$ will make $A_n(\beta)$ a connected set. $\beta < 1$ will make the set disconnected. (ii) Value of β needs to be chosen judiciously. (iii) $\varepsilon_n(\beta)$ is not dependent on the dimension m. (iv) In method 1, MST has been considered as a set. It is considered as a finite union of line segments. Note that, in every line segment there are infinitely many points. A disc is considered for each point on MST. Thus, infinitely many discs (in fact uncountable number of discs) are considered and their union is taken as an estimate. It is extremely difficult to write a program for taking union of infinitely many discs. In the proposed method, unlike the method 1, union of infinitely many closed discs need not be taken into account. Note that $A_n(\beta)$ is a union of n number of discs since S is a finite set (equation 4).

Application of Proposed Set Estimation Method on Artificial Data Set

In order to demonstrate the utility of the method 2, an artificial data set is created. Points are ran-

Figure 1. Set a = the letter P

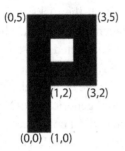

domly selected from the set and the set is estimated using those randomly generated points. Let the set α under consideration is union of ten squares and figuratively represents the alphabet P shown in Figure 1. α is union of 4 sets. Each set is a subset of the two dimensional Euclidean space $\Re^2$. In the 1st set the value of x is ranging from 0 to 1 and y is ranging from 0 to 5. In the 2nd set x ranges from 1 to 2 and y takes values from 2 to 3. In totality it provides the letter P shown in Figure 1 and is given by

$\alpha = ([0,1] \times [0,5]) \cup ([1,2] \times [2,3]) \cup ([1,2] \times [4,5]) \cup ([2,3] \times [2,5])$

The alphabet P is selected as it contains a "hole". n number of points are selected randomly from α where n = 50, 100, 200, and 400. For each n, MST was computed and its maximal edge weight is obtained. The set has been estimated in two different ways (Method 2) by considering two different values for β. They are $\beta=1$ and $\beta=2$. The results are given in Figure 2 and Figure 3 for $\beta=1$ and Figure 4 and Figure 5 for $\beta=2$, for different values of n. It may be noted that, as n increases, estimated set is tending towards the original set shown in Figure 1. To elaborate it further, the difference sets, $A_n \Delta \alpha$ for different values of n are constructed as shown in Figure 3 and Figure 5, which reflects that the area of the difference (denoted by white colour) is decreasing as n increases.

4. THRESHOLD INCORPORATED FACE CLASSIFICATION

To establish the usefulness of the method 2 in face classification problem, several face images

Figure 2. Estimated set for different values of n for β=1

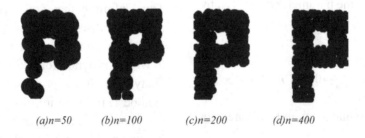

(a)n=50   (b)n=100   (c)n=200   (d)n=400

Figure 3. Difference between Original Set and Estimated sets for β=1. White parts denote the difference

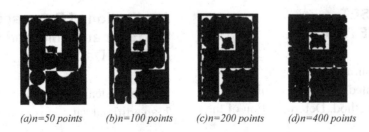

(a)n=50 points   (b)n=100 points   (c)n=200 points   (d)n=400 points

Figure 4. Estimated set for different values of n for β=2

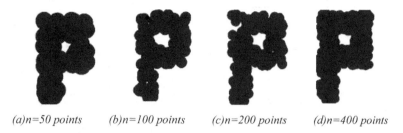

(a)n=50 points   (b)n=100 points   (c)n=200 points   (d)n=400 points

for the same human being are considered. The number of classes is same as the number of human beings. Let us consider M human beings and for each human being we have N face images of same size and same background. If we represent an image by a vector $\underline{x}$, then we are considering all possible such vectors corresponding to a human being. Let us represent such a set by α. This set denotes the face class of that human being. It can be noted that we don't know α completely. Only a few points of α like the different expressions of a face are known to us. Initially we apply one of the feature extraction methods described earlier to reduce the number of dimensions for m. Thus every face now is an m dimensional vector. For every one of M human beings, we have N number of such m dimensional vectors.

The proposed set estimation method can be utilized in two ways in face recognition problem as described in the next subsection.

Local Threshold Based Recognition

Here we assume that we have M classes, each class denoting a human being. Each class consists of N vectors of m dimensions. Here for each class we calculate MST of the respective N vectors and find its maximal edge weight. Let us denote the maximal edge weight of the MST of the ith class by ξ_i for any m dimensional vector $\underline{x}$ in the following way. For this scheme, we have considered β to be 2 since the number images for each class is a small number. Note that, $\beta=2$ will make, according to method 2, the value of threshold for the ith class as ξ_i. The recognition method is described below.

a.   The total number of given vectors is MN. For each class i, find the minimum distance of $\underline{x}$ with all the N points in the class. Let the minimal distance be ρ_i

b.   If there does not exist any i such that $\rho_i \leq \xi_i$ then the given image does not fall in any one of the given face classes.

Figure 5. Difference between Original Set and Estimated sets for β=2. White parts denote the difference

(a)n=50 points   (b)n=100 points   (c)n=200 points   (d)n=400 points

Figure 6. Block diagram of the proposed method for training and testing phases

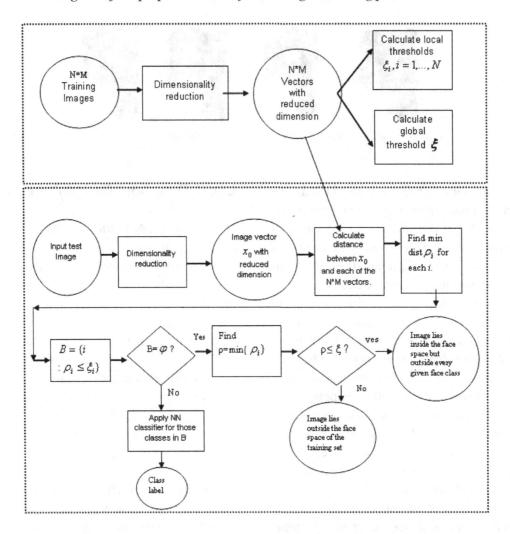

c. If there exists exactly one i such that $\rho_i \leq \xi_i$ then put x in the ith class. If the number of such i's is more than one, then the query image belongs to at least two classes, resulting in an overlap between the classes. In such a case, one can provide all those class labels as result of classification, or one can further proceed to get a unique classification among those labels using any existing classifier. Here, we considered the later option and used nearest neighbor classifier. Block diagram of this process is shown is Figure 6.

If the given image does not fall into any of the given face classes, it may still lie within the given face space. In order to analyze this possibility, the global thresholding scheme is formulated.

Global Threshold Based Recognition

This method is useful when we have a large number of images in the database, and we need to know whether the query image can be taken to be a member of the database. A threshold value, larger than the individual thresholds is necessary for such classification problem. Thus we have taken β as

1 here. For determining the global threshold, we have the following algorithm.

a. Find MST of MN points and find half of its maximal edge weight. Let it be ξ

b. Find $\rho = \underset{i=1,2,...n}{Min} \rho_i$

c. If $\rho < \xi$ then the image is a face image and will form a new face class in the face space. If $\rho > \xi$ then the given vector $\underline{x}$ does not belong to the given face space. Here the image is either a non face image or a face image not belonging to the given face space. Note that $\xi_i \leq \xi, \forall i$ is true generally but not for any set of MN *points*.

Remarks:

1. Depending on the problem at hand, we may use (i) only the global thresholding scheme, or (ii) only the local thresholding scheme, or (iii) both the schemes. Local thresholding scheme discriminates between the given face classes, whereas the global scheme provides an ``upper approximation'' of given database of face images. We used both the schemes in the recognition procedure for different purposes. Block diagram of the proposed thresholding scheme is given in Figure 6.

2. For a better understanding on local and global thresholds, a figure (Figure 7) has been constructed. The process of applying global and local thresholds is depicted in Figure 7. In Figure 7, two classes are considered in $\mathfrak{R}^2$, where five points are considered from each class. In the same figure we have two local MSTs for the two classes and the global MST of the 10 points, where the edge weight is the Euclidean distance. For each class, the edge having the maximal edge weight (ξ_1, ξ_2) is denoted by a bold line. The line with dashes indicates the edge with maximal edge weight (ξ) of the global MST.

5. EXPERIMENTAL DESIGN AND RESULT ANALYSIS

The proposed method has been used for face recognition and tested over three well known face databases namely (ORL, Yale, AR). We also used one object (i.e., non face) database namely, the COIL-100 Database (Nene, 1996) for verifying the utility of the threshold based classification. For AR database (Martinez, 1998) we have taken the first 10 images from each of 68 classes and the only the face portions are manually cropped to dimension 128X128. the images are then transformed to gray level. To form the face space from the image space we have used three well known feature selection methods (i) principal component analysis (PCA), (ii) wavelet based PCA, and (iii) linear discriminant analysis (LDA) in combination with PCA. There are several parameters to be chosen for the experiments on face databases. They are (i) number of training images, (ii) procedure for choosing those images, and (iii) number of principal components to be taken. The construction of the face space with several face datasets are described in the talbe1.

After the dimensionality reduction, we have divided each face dataset into two parts, namely (i) training set, and (ii) test set. Each training dataset contains data corresponding to 5 images of each face class in the database. Remaining data points are considered to be in the test set.

Figure 7. MST based global and local thresholds for two classes

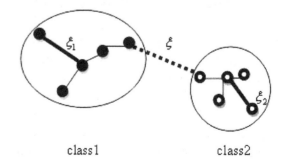

class1   class2

Figure 8.

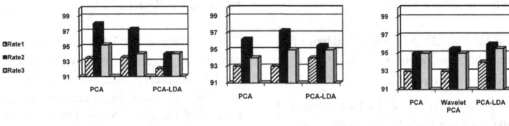

Chart 1: Results on ORL   Chart 2: Results on YALE   Chart 3: Results on AR

Now the proposed MST based method of threshold selection is applied on the each training set of face points. Local thresholds and global threshold are computed for each face data set. Note that the numbers of nodes of MSTs are 200, 75, 340 for ORL dataset, YALE, and AR respectively because of the number of training faces are converted to the face points which have been considered to be the nodes of MST. It may be noted that the value of global threshold is generally more than every one of the class thresholds. For each value of dimension, the experiment is repeated 10 times by varying the images in the training set randomly and the average result is given in the Charts 1-3 (Figure 8).

Since the proposed method derives local or user specific thresholds there are several recognition rates denoting different aspects of the proposed scheme. Additionally, an image may be put in more than class according to the proposed formulation. In such a case, to get unique classification, we used the nearest neighbor (NN) rule for all those classes to which the image is classified. Thus there are several recognition rates denoting different aspects of the proposed scheme.

Recognition rates in percentages are provided in three different ways. The recognition rate I denotes the recognition rate using the nearest neighbor (NN) classifier. No thresholding mechanism is used to obtain this rate. The recognition rate II denotes the recognition rate using the class thresholds where one of the classes to which an image is classified is the correct one. The recogni-

tion rate III is the recognition rate obtained using NN classifier among all those classes to which the image is classified after using the class thresholds. Thus theoretically recognition rate II is necessarily greater than or equal to recognition rate III.

It is observed from Figure 8 (charts 1-3) the recognition rate with threshold (i.e., recognition rate (3)) is more than the recognition rate without threshold (i.e., recognition rate (1)) in each case. The system is based upon the local user specific threshold. For each case it is observed that the recognition rates are better than the non threshold based systems.

Description and Result Analysis Using Two Different Databases

To perform stress testing upon the proposed method, we import the COIL-100 database (and perform the above classification. Columbia Object Image Library (COIL-100) contains 7200 color images of 100 objects with uniform background. The objects are rotated through 360 degrees to vary object pose with respect to a fixed camera. The images are taken at a pose interval of five degrees, and this corresponds to the 72 poses. We however transformed the color images to gray level images and used them for our purpose. The first five images in each class of each training face dataset are considered for the training set.

Table 2 provides the results of taking COIL-100 database as the test set where the training dataset is a face dataset. It is apparent from this table that

Table 1. Construction of the face space

Database	Number of subjects	Number of face images per subject and the number of images in the training set per class	Total number of images in the training set	Size of images	Reduced Dimension of face space (Method applied)
ORL	40	10 and 5	200	112x92	120 (PCA), 39 (PCA-LDA), 120 (Wavelet PCA)
YALE	15	11 and 5	75	100X100	30 (PCA), 14 (PCA-LDA), 30 (Wavelet PCA)
AR	68	10 and 5	340	128X128	275 (PCA), 67 (PCA-LDA), 275 (Wavelet PCA)

no image in the COIL-100 dataset is classified to one of the face classes of the training set.

It may also be noted that the proposed procedure may not classify an image to one of the existing classes. We denote it by classification to NULL class. Here there are two possible ways in which an image may be placed in null class. In the first case, the distance is more than the threshold value of each class, but it is less than the global threshold. That is, the image is within the face space of the training set, but outside each face class. In the second case, the distance is more than the global threshold. That is, the image is outside the face space of the training set. In the tables, the rates corresponding to these possibilities are denoted respectively by "Null class rate (within face space)", and "Null class rate (outside face space)".

We have also performed experiments where the images in one face dataset are considered for training and the images in other face dataset are considered for testing. The first five images in each class of each training face dataset are considered for the training set. The results using PCA (with the number of dimensions 120) are provided in table 3. The other values of dimensions and the other methods of dimensionality reduction are observed to provide similar results.

From table 3, it is clear that no image of a test face data set is falling under the class of a training dataset. At least 96% of the test images are classified as faces but outside the face classes of the

Table 2. Results on COIL dataset

Methods Applied	Training Database	Total no. of classes	No. of training images per class	Null class rate (inside face space)	Null class rate (outside face space)
PCA	ORL	40	5	0	100
PCA	AR	68	5	0	100
PCA	YALE	15	5	0	100
Wavelet PCA	ORL	40	5	0	100
Wavelet PCA	AR	68	5	0	100
Wavelet PCA	YALE	15	5	0	100
PCA-LDA	ORL	40	5	0	100
PCA-LDA	AR	68	5	0	100
PCA-LDA	YALE	15	5	0	100

Table 3. Comparison using separate test and training face databases

Training Database	Test Database	Null class rate (within the face space of the training set)	Null class rate (outside the face space of the training set)	% of points falling within the threshold of at least a training class
YALE	ORL	4	96	0
YALE	AR	2	98	0
ORL	YALE	1	99	0
ORL	AR	1	99	0
AR	ORL	0	100	0
AR	YALE	0	100	0

training dataset. This validates the main point of threshold selection of this paper.

Comparison with ROC Based Method of Threshold Selection

The proposed method of threshold selection using set estimation is compared with the ROC based age old biometric authentication system. Both the authentication methods are applied on the face space formed using the dimensionality reduction techniques discussed earlier. To observe the performance of the two methods, several dataset configurations are designed. The configurations follow the division ratio of the Lausanne protocol. The face datasets have been divided into three parts namely *(i) training set, (ii) evaluation set, and (iii) test set.* The training set is used to build the client model; evaluation set is used to compute client and imposter scores defining two well known parameters FAR and FRR, and the test set is used to compare the performance. The definitions of FAR and FRR are given below.

- FAR = Number of successful fraud attempts / Number of all fraud attempts.
- FRR = Number of false rejections / Number of all client accesses.

When setting a certain similarity rating as a threshold for determination of authorized versus non authorized users, the False Acceptance Rate (FAR) is the number of non authorized users for whom the Euclidian distances fall below the threshold compared to all such attempts. On the other hand, False Rejection Rate (FRR) is the number of authorized users for whom the Euclidian distances fall above this threshold compared to all such attempts. We see that FAR and FRR are dependant on the adjustable adopted threshold. If we increase the value of threshold, the proportion FAR will increase, while FRR will decrease. When we decrease the value of threshold, the proportion FAR will decrease, while FRR increases. The intersection point [Equal error rate (EER)] of these two curves is chosen as the threshold for the whole system. With the help of the threshold, the system makes either of the two decisions: (i) accept the person as client, or (ii) reject him as imposter. Then the test set is used to simulate a real authentication scenario.

It may be noted that one needs to get a good estimate of FAR and FRR to calculate EER. In order to obtain a good estimate of FAR, one needs to consider all those elements which don't belong to the given classes (i.e., the complementary set). Usually, this set is a very large set. The classifier which uses FAR and FRR would vary with the size and choice of complementary set. Ideally, one would like to develop a classifier without considering the complementary set. In this article, such a method has been developed.

We proposed two types of thresholds namely class specific thresholds, and global threshold for

Table 4. TVT configuration

TVT Configuration	Training Set No. of classes * No. of faces from each class	Evaluation set		Test set	
		No. of imposters	Number of Clients	Number of imposters	Number of Clients
TVT-1	ORL 40*5	YALE 15*6	ORL 40*3	YALE 15*5	ORL 40*2
TVT-2	ORL 40*5	AR 68*5	ORL 40*3	AR 68*5	ORL 40*2
TVT-3	YALE 15*5	ORL 40*5	YALE 15*3	ORL 40*5	YALE 15*3
TVT-4	YALE 15*5	AR 68*5	YALE 15*3	AR 68*5	YALE 15*3
TVT-5	AR 68*5	ORL 40*5	AR 68*3	ORL 40*5	AR 68*2
TVT-6	AR 68*5	YALE 15*6	AR 68*3	YALE 15*5	AR 68*2
TVT-7	ORL1 20*5	ORL2 20*5	ORL1 20*3	ORL2 20*5	ORL1 20*2
TVT-8	ORL2 20*5	ORL1 20*5	ORL2 20*3	ORL1 20*5	ORL2 20*2
TVT-9	AR1 34*5	AR2 34*5	AR1 34*3	AR2 34*5	AR1 34*2
TVT-10	AR2 34*5	AR1 34*5	AR2 34*3	AR1 34*5	AR2 34*2

the system. For a fair comparison between ROC based scheme and the proposed method, we considered below the global threshold of the proposed scheme since the ROC based method has only one threshold for the system. In order to compare the performance of the proposed method with ROC based threshold selection method, we considered several combinations of training, validation, and test (TVT) sets as shown in table 4 and results on table 5. Additionally, here, we considered the first five images of every class (as mentioned in the TVT table) as training set. AR1, AR2, and ORL1, ORL2 are the odd and even class divisions of AR and ORL datasets respectively. Here ORL1 and AR1 are the odd numbered classes (i.e., 1,3,5,7,…) of faces whereas ORL2 and AR2 are the even numbered classes (2,4,6,…) of faces of the corresponding datasets respectively.

The recognition rate for each such TVT combination is calculated as follows:

Recognition rate: Let m_1 be the number of client accesses correctly classified out of a total of m client accesses. Let n_1 be the number of successful fraud attempts out of a total of n attempts. Then the recognition rate is defined as $(m_1+n-n_1)\times 100/(m+n)$. The obtained recognition rates for the two schemes are shown in table 4 for each TVT combination. It can be clearly seen that the performance of the proposed method is better than the ROC based scheme for all the 10 TVT combinations.

From Table 5, it may be seen that the proposed method outperforms ROC based threshold selection methods for each TVT configuration. Another significant observation is that the global threshold remains same for each training dataset but in ROC based method the threshold varies as the number of imposters in the validation set changes. Note that the training sets in TVT1 and TVT2 are same and the corresponding thresholds in ROC based

Table 5. Comparison table

TVT Configuration	Proposed Method (set estimation)		EER as threshold	
	Recognition rate	Global threshold	Recognition rate	Global threshold
1	97.25	1.5437e+003	95	2.1987e+003
2	98	1.5437e+003	94	2.3567e+003
3	96	1.3012e+003	95	1.9997e+003
4	98	1.3012e+003	93	2.546e+003
5	98.25	1.4824e+003	96.25	1.8234e+003
6	97.25	1.4824e+003	94.5	2.5897e+003
7	96	1.1808e+003	95	1.6787e+003
8	97	1.1732e+003	94	2.1523e+003
9	98	1.1564e+003	96.5	2.1437e+003
10	98	1.1895e+003	95	1.1527e+003

method are different. Similarly for TVT3, TVT4 and TVT5, TVT6.

For a proper choice of threshold selection in ROC curve based method, one needs to get training images for all those objects which are not faces and for all those persons who are not present in the training set. It is very difficult to obtain such ALL large validation set. Additionally, the more the number of non face images considered for obtaining ROC curve, the more is its complexity. By the proposed method, this drawback has been successfully removed. The validity of the proposed method has been additionally shown in the tables 2 and 3, where the test images are objects or persons whose images are not present in the training database. Here, unlike for ROC based recognition, the set estimation method does not require any representative non-face dataset.

6. CONCLUSION

A method is proposed for threshold selection for MST based face recognition scheme. The method has been applied on ORL, Yale, AR databases and it is found to give better results than those methods without threshold. We have also tested

the utility of the method, where the training and the test datasets are different (Tables 1 and 2). It has been found conclusively that the thresholds are helpful in finding whether a query image belongs to the given face class, or belongs to the given collection of face classes. The global threshold is found to be useful (Tables 4 and 5) when the training and test datasets are different. It has also been observed from the previous section that the proposed method of threshold selection outperforms the ROC based scheme of threshold selection.

One has to take care of several inherent issues regarding the subspace based methods like the number of dimensions chosen, number of training images per class etc. The experimental demonstration of the utility of the proposed scheme has been provided in section 5 by considering different dimensions and varying the training set. The proposed method is seen to outperform the methods without threshold.

For future work, one can try the proposed method on other PCA based subspace methods like 2DPCA, KPCA, 2DLDA, KLDA, modular PCA, etc. The proposed threshold selection mechanism can be developed for those schemes with suitable modifications.

The proposed method can be applied to classification problems in other domains. As the number of points in the training set increases, the accuracy of set estimation procedure increases, and thus the classification performance increases. If the number of sample points is very small, the uncertainty is large, and thus the performance may not be appropriate. To some extent, this difficulty has been overcome by considering path connectivity and hence MST. The authors suggest that the number of images in the training set for each class should never be less than 5. The more the number of images in the training set for each class, the more is the accuracy, and the less is the uncertainty.

There are several classification methods in literature. There are also many problems in which these classification methods are applied. The article proposes a classification scheme based on set estimation. The proposed method can easily be applied on other data sets too, including other biometric data sets, where there is no difference between the units of two different features. i.e., If one feature is measured in meters, and the other one is measured in kilograms, the proposed method can't be directly used. There are several theoretical results regarding this classification scheme. Under certain regularity conditions, it can be shown theoretically that the proposed scheme provides `good' classification results.

REFERENCES

A. J. Mansfield &J. L. Wayman (2002), Best Practices in Testing and Reporting Performance of Biometric Devices, Version 2.01. *Centre for Mathematics and Scientific Computing, National Physical Laboratory, Queens Road, Teddington, Middlesex, TW11 OLW*.

Blackburn, D. M. (2004). *Biometrics 101, version 3.1*. Federal Bureau of Investigation.

Edelsbrunner, H., Kirkpatrickand, D. G., & Seidel, R. (1983). On the Shape of a Set of Points in a Plane. *IEEE Transactions on Information Theory, IT-29*, 551–559. doi:10.1109/TIT.1983.1056714

Grenander, U. (1981). *Abstract Inference*. New York: John Wiley.

Jain, A. K., Ross, A., & Prabhakar, S. (2004). An introduction to biometric recognition. *IEEE Transactions on Circuits and Systems for Video Technology, 14*(1). doi:10.1109/TCSVT.2003.818349

Maio, D., & Maltoni, D. (2005). Real-time face location on gray-scale static images. *Pattern Recognition, 33*(9), 1525–1539. doi:10.1016/S0031-3203(99)00130-2

Mandal, D. P., & Murthy, C. A. (1995). Selection of alpha for alpha-hull and formulation of fuzzy alpha-hull in R^2, *Int. J. of Uncertainty. Fuzziness and Knowledge Based Systems, 3*(4), 401–417. doi:10.1142/S0218488595000207

Mandal, D. P., & Murthy, C. A. (1997). Selection of alpha for alpha-hull in R^2. *Pattern Recognition, 30*(10), 1759–1767. doi:10.1016/S0031-3203(96)00176-8

Mandal, D. P., Murthy, C. A., & Pal, S. K. (1997). Determining the Shape of A Pattern Class From Sampled Points: Extension To R^N. *International Journal of General Systems, 26*(4), 293–320. doi:10.1080/03081079708945187

A. Martin, G. Doddington, T. Kamm, M. Ordowski, M.Przybocki (1997). The DET curve in Assessment of Detection Task Performance. *Proc. Of Eurospeech'97, 4*, 1895-1898.

A.M. Martinez & R. Benavente (1998). *The AR Face Database*. CVC Technical Report #24.

Murthy, C.A. (1988). *On Consistent Estimation of Classes in R^2 in The Context of Cluster Analysis*, Ph.D Thesis, Indian Statistical Institute, Calcutta India.

Nene, S. A., Nayar, S. K., & Murase, H. (1996) *Technical Report CUCS-006-96.*

*Olivetti face database,*Retrieved from <http://www.cam-orl.co.uk/facedatabase.html>.

Phillips, P. J., Grother, P., Micheals, R. J., Blackburn, D. M., Tabassi, E., & Bone, J. M. (2003). *FRVT 2002: Evaluation Report,* from http://www.frvt.org/DLs/FRVT_2002_Evaluation_Report.pdf

Ruiz-del-Solar, J., & Navarrete, P. (2005). Eigenspace-based face recognition: a comparative study of different approaches. *IEEE Transactions on Systems, Man and Cybernetics. Part C, 35*(3), 315–325.

Shakhnarovich, G., & Moghaddam, B. (2004). Face Recognition in Subspaces. In Li, S. Z., & Jain, A. K. (Eds.), *Handbook of Face Recognition.* New York: Springer-Verlag.

*Yale face database,*Retrieved from <http://cvc.yale.edu/projects/yalefaces/yalefaces.html>.

Zhao, W., Chellappa, R., Rosenfeld, A., & Phillips, J. (2003). *Face Recognition: A Literature Survey. Technical Report, CS-TR4167.* Univ. of Maryland.

Chapter 5
DNA Computing

Tao Song
Huazhong University of Science and Technology, China

Xun Wang
University of Tsukuba, Japan

Shudong Wang
Shandong University of Science and Technology, China

Yun Jiang
Huazhong University of Science and Technology, China

ABSTRACT

DNA computing is widely accepted as a new computing framework all over the world. In this chapter, the background of DNA computing is firstly introduced by solving a Hamilton Path problem. Then three research directions are proposed according to the current development of it, including the theoretical framework, practical DNA computing models and DNA encoding. In each part of the three research directions, many recent results are involved. In the theoretical framework, DNA computing is proved to be computationally universal by four formal DNA computing models. In practical DNA computing models, DNA computing is shown to solve NP-complete problems and work well in other fields, such as medical science. In DNA encoding, some DNA codes and encoding methods are introduced to avoid the false positive phenomenon. And they have a final purpose in common: constructing a universal Biomolecular computing model, which is also called as biomolecular computer, to solve intractable problems for electrical computers. Finally, some further research directions are shown in each part for the design of biomolecular computer.

1. INTRODUCTION

Biomolecular computing, especially DNA computing, is a biologically inspired computing method. Biomolecular and bio-chemistry operations are introduced in solving hard problems in

DNA computing. So it is quite a great advancement of soft computing in the 20th century and it also plays an important role in constructing low energy costing and huge information storing computing models. Nowadays it has been widely accepted as a new computing model for future computing devices in computer science. As we know, NP-

DOI: 10.4018/978-1-61692-797-4.ch005

hard and NP-complete problems are intractable to be solved in polynomial time by electrical computers when the size of problems becomes large. DNA computing was firstly proposed to solve these computationally hard problems by biological models. It is novel to solve problems by taking DNA molecules as computing paradigms and bio-chemistry operations as tools in realistic world. More and more computationally hard problems are considered to be solved by this novel computing device. The hugely storing information ability, parallel computing ability and lower computing energy cost make DNA computing to be a perfect computing paradigm. DNA computer based on DNA computing earn much attention all over the world.

In this chapter, DNA computing is mainly discussed as a new computing method. In section 2, the birth and development of DNA computing are introduced. Three research aspects of DNA computing and their relationship are introduced in detail in this section too. The theoretical framework of DNA computing, including formal DNA computing models and theoretical DNA computing models, are discussed in section 3. Three main formal DNA computing models are proved to be computational universal and their computing complexities are considered. In section 4, some DNA computing models which are used to solve realistic problems, such as Benenson Automata, are introduced. DNA encoding, including DNA encoding metrics and methods, are involved in section 5. Finally, some further researching directions are discussed in section 6.

2. THE BIRTH AND DEVELOPMENT OF DNA COMPUTING

DNA computing, firstly proposed to solve HPP with seven vertexes, is quite a new method in solving NP-complete problems. DNA computing is proved to be much more effective in solving NP-complete problems. Since then it has attracted important attention from scientific community with contributions to mathematics, biology, chemistry and computer science, enriching each other with results, opening problems and promising new research lines. The eventual purpose of DNA computing is to design DNA computers, also called biological computers, which are universal computing devices and much more powerful than electrical computers. There are three main research aspects in DNA computing: theoretical framework of DNA computing, DNA computing models in practice and DNA encoding. The above three researching aspects together contribute to the invention of DNA computer.

Adleman's DNA Computing Algorithm

In 1994, Adleman [Adleman94] firstly proposed DNA computing algorithm, by which a Hamilton Path Problem (HPP) with 7 vertexes is solved only using DNA molecular and biochemistry operations. Three steps were mainly introduced in Adelman's algorithm: encoding all paths, deleting unsatisfactory paths and reading out satisfactory paths. The involved bio-chemistry operations include hybridization, melting, filtrating, PCR amplification, probe detecting, DNA sequencing technology, etc. The HPP solved by Adleman is shown in Figure 1 and the flowchart of Adleman's algorithm in Figure 2.

In Adleman's algorithm, each vertex is encoded into 20-bases DNA strand randomly. Then all the seven DNA strands are put into an initial tube labeled tube1. Since there are thirteen edges in Figure 1, thirteen 20-bases long edge single DNA molecules are designed according to the molecules encoding the seven vertexes and added into the tube1. Now tube1 is known as the initial solutions space of the HPP. According to the Watson-Crick principle(A&T bonded and G&C bonded), single DNA molecules can hybridize to double DNA molecules in a very short time

Figure 1. The HPP solved by Adleman

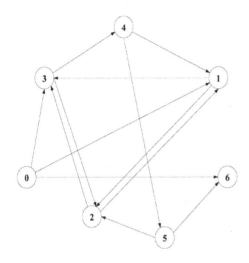

Figure 2. The flowchart of Adleman's algorithm

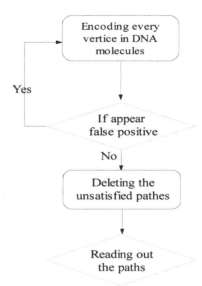

under reasonable circumstance, then all the possible paths could be created in just a few seconds.

For instance, three of the seven vertexes in Adleman's algorithm are encoded randomly as follows:

v_2=TATCGGATCGGTATATCCGA,
v_3=GCTATTCGAGCTTAAAGCTA and
v_4=GGCTAGGTAGGTACCAGCATCGTT.

The edge $e_{2\to3}$ between v_2 and v_3 is designed as $e_{2\to3}$=CATATAGGCTCGATAAGCTC, and the edge between v_3 and v_4 as $e_{3\to4}$=GAATTTCGATCCGATCCATG is. After $e_{2\to3}$ and $e_{3\to4}$ are added into tube1, the path $p_{2\to3\to4}$ is formed by hybridization in a very short time as in Figure 3.

Obviously, when all the edge represented by single DNA strands are added into the tube1, all the candidate paths are formed in a very short time in the form of double DNA strands with sticker ends (two ends of the double DNA strings are single strings), also called double sticking DNA strands.

Subsequently, we delete the unsatisfactory paths. Double sticking DNA strands that are longer than 140 in length are filtered and cleaned from tube1 by the gel electrophoresis. Furthermore, by DNA probe technology paths containing at least more than two same vertexes are deleted. A small number of DNA molecules maybe left in tube1, so PCR amplification is used to duplicate the remaining DNA molecules. Finally, we detect if there are molecules remained and read out the paths by DNA sequencing technology.

In six hours, Adleman successfully solved the HPP shown in Figure 1 and finally found a long DNA string with sticker ends, which is corresponded to the Hamilton Path shown as follows $v_0 \to v_1 \to v_2 \to v_3 \to v_4 \to v_5 \to v_6$. It is the

Figure 3.

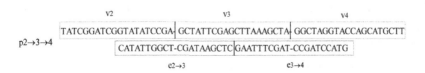

Figure 4. The relationships among the three main research fields

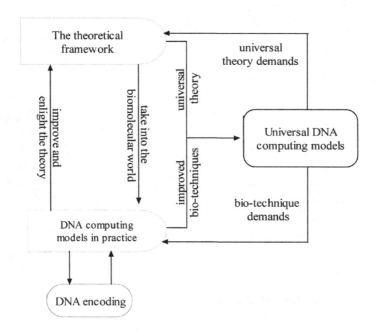

first time that DNA molecules were used to solve mathematic problems, which attracts interesting of many experts all over the world.

Three Main Research Fields and their Relationships

Since DNA computing was proposed in 1994, it has been considered as a framework for solving mathematical and combinatorial problems. For example, Lipton [Lipton96] proposed the DNA-based algorithm for 3-SAT problems and Ouyang [Ouyang97] proposed the algorithm by DNA computing to solve the maximal clique problem.

Although variant DNA computing algorithms were proposed to solve different problems, there are no essential differences among them. They have a drawback in common: when the size of the problem increases, the algorithms become unavailable. So experts interested in DNA computing divided into 2 main groups, one paid their attentions to finding more feasible computing models by new bio-chemistry technology to solve intractable problems, such as NP-complete problems with big

size, while the other hammered at constructing theoretical universal DNA computing models. Also, by repeating the Adleman's experiment, it was found that if the vertexes were encoded by 20-bases molecules randomly, the false-positive and secondary structure of DNA molecules would make the computation failed. So they committed themselves to designing reasonably encoding methods to avoid false-positive and secondary structure phenomenon. Reasonable DNA codes could ensure the computing progress proceeding as it was presupposed. The main purpose of research in DNA computing is always to find a universal DNA computer, by which hard problems can be easily solved.

Now there are three main research fields in DNA computing: the theoretical framework of DNA computing, DNA computing models in practice and the DNA encoding. They work together for designing the universal DNA computer. If the three aspects are greatly improved, then DNA computer will be on the corner. Their relationships are shown in Figure 4.

3. THE THEORETICAL FRAMEWORK OF DNA COMPUTING

Although several DNA computing models have been designed and practiced in real-world to solve intractable problems, there hasn't been a universal DNA computer model that can solve all the problems. Just like Turing Machine gave a strong theoretical support for the invention of electrical computers, it is necessary to prove the computability is universal. That is to say we should know if the DNA molecular could solve universal problems. The answer is attractive. Formal DNA computing models based on the recombinant behavior of DNA molecules are used to prove the computational universality and completeness of DNA computing.

Although the biomolecular can store huge information and parallel compute in nano scale, there are still some limitations of it. So the optimum theories are also needed in DNA computing such as the time and space complexity and how to lower them, including concepts and algorithms.

Simple gates and circuits based on DNA molecular and bio-chemistry operations have been designed. They can be used to solve some simple problems, but more complex circuits are needed to solve real-world problems. More theories should be involved in conceiving biomolecular gates and circuits. We should firstly prove it to be feasible, such as the reversible gates and circuits [Song2008b]. More computing models must be designed for hard problems.

The Computational Completeness of DNA Computing

Formal models of DNA computing are based on the recombinant behaviors of DNA molecules under various enzymes. Sticker system, Sticker model, Splicing system and Insert-Delete system are four famous formal models, whose computability have been proved no less than Turing Machine. They

are the vital evidences for "DNA computer is conclusive being there waiting for us".

As we know, Turing Machine is the theoretical model of the electrical computer with the highest computability among the known computing models. According to the theory of formal language and automata, as a result the recursively enumerable language is and only is accepted by Turing Machine. When a grammar (language producer) on some alphabet can produce the recursively enumerable language, its computability is equal to Turing Machine's. It is said to be computation universal and complete. Sticker system [Roweis96], Insert-Delete system and Splicing system [Paun96] are all language producers, with elements being strings on the alphabet {A,T,C,G}. They can produce the recursively enumerable language, so the computability of DNA computer in one of the above three forms is no less than Turing Machine. We will subsequently introduce them.

The Sticker System

There are eight kinds of structure of DNA molecular with or without sticking ends as shown in Figure 5. Mathematical form proposed by Păun are shown in Figure 6. In Figure 5, x, y and z are single strings on the alphabet {A,T,C,G}, while $\bar{x}$, $\bar{y}$ and $\bar{z}$ are the complementary DNA molecules of x, y and z. By hybridization x, y, z and $\bar{x}$, $\bar{y}$, $\bar{z}$ can form double strands and sticking double strands as shown in Figure 5. In Figure 6, λ is denoted as the "empty molecular". Take the eight kinds of DNA structure as the initial words to produce recursively enumerable language. The bio-chemistry operations are corresponding to rewriting rules. As a language producer, the Sticker system can generate the recursively enumerable language. So the the Sticker system is equal to the Turing Machine.

If the DNA computer is constructed in the form of the Sticker system, then its computability is no less than the Turing Machine's. However, it's very

Figure 5. Eight kinds of structure of DNA molecular

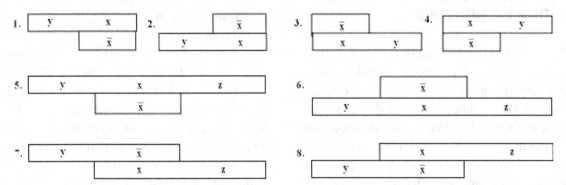

hard to construct it in real world, since the bio-chemistry hasn't reached the level to perform the complex operations needed in Sticker system. Recently, lots of improved Sticker system has been designed, but no one could be work in real word.

Two examples are shown in Figure 7 with the hybridization being rewriting rule.

The Sticker Model

In the theory of formal language and automata, if a language on the alphabet $\{0,1\}$ is a recursively enumerable one, then it is accepted by a one-tape Turing Machine with tape alphabet $\{0,1,B\}$. That is the theoretical basis of electrical computer and the reason why binary strings are the input and output of it. To simulate one-tape Turing Machine, the Sticker model designs a one-to-one mapping between DNA molecules and binary strings, called DNA binary strings. By the initial DNA binary strings, others can also be generated by rewriting rules. Then the recursively enumerable language

Figure 6. Eight kinds of structure of DNA molecular in mathematic forms

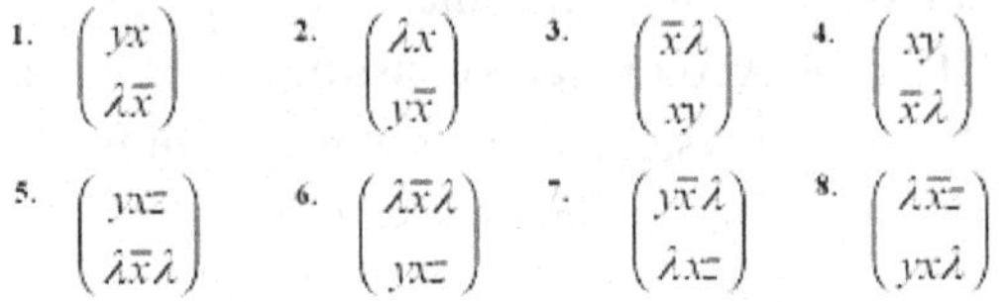

1. $\begin{pmatrix} yx \\ \lambda \bar{x} \end{pmatrix}$ 2. $\begin{pmatrix} \lambda x \\ y\bar{x} \end{pmatrix}$ 3. $\begin{pmatrix} \bar{x}\lambda \\ xy \end{pmatrix}$ 4. $\begin{pmatrix} xy \\ \bar{x}\lambda \end{pmatrix}$

5. $\begin{pmatrix} yxz \\ \lambda\bar{x}\lambda \end{pmatrix}$ 6. $\begin{pmatrix} \lambda\bar{x}\lambda \\ yxz \end{pmatrix}$ 7. $\begin{pmatrix} y\bar{x}\lambda \\ \lambda xz \end{pmatrix}$ 8. $\begin{pmatrix} \lambda x z \\ yx\lambda \end{pmatrix}$

on alphabet $\{0,1\}$ can be produced by the Sticker model. Also, the rewriting rules are corresponding to the bio-chemistry operations, such as melting and hybridization.

The one-to-one mapping between DNA molecules and binary strings is constructed as follows. Each bit of a binary string is denoted by a fixed length DNA molecular composed by $\{A,T,C,G\}$: 1 is corresponding to double DNA molecular, while 0 is to single one. Generally, the fixed length of DNA molecular is four. It has been proved that all the words in the recursively enumerable language on the alphabet $\{0,1\}$ can be produced by the Sticker model with reasonable initial words and rewriting rules. So the Sticker model's comput-ability is no less the one-tape Turing Machine with tape alphabet $\{0,1,B\}$. That is to say the Sticker model is computation universal. An example of Sticker system is shown in Figure 8. There are 2^3 binary strings with three bits in all.

The Splicing System

The operation mostly used in Sticker system and Sticker model is hybridization, by which "long strings" are formed from "short strings". So the "short strings" should be designed formally as the initial words. In brief, it is a progress from "short" to "long". While the computing progress of the Splicing system is quite a backward progress. A long DNA molecular can be cut into two or more

Figure 7. Two examples of rewriting rules

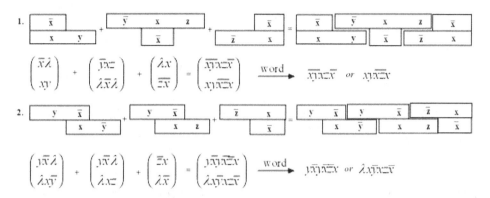

short DNA molecules with sticker ends or blunt ends by restricted enzymes. And then they can reform to other DNA molecules. So it's another method to produce the recursively enumerable language by DNA molecules. Also DNA molecules are seen as strings on the alphabet {A,T,C,G}.

Taking random DNA molecules as initial words and some special enzymes as tools, recursively enumerable language can be easily produced. Since a restricted enzyme recognize only one cutting site, so cutting different molecules at different cutting site needs different restricted enzymes. There are about 3000 kinds of restricted enzymes, but it is not enough when they are used in producing recursively enumerable language.

In Figure 9, computing progresses of Splicing system are presented in three examples. It is not difficult to get the conclusion that the recursively enumerable language on the alphabet {A,T,C,G} can be produced by the Splicing system. Then the splicing rules are corresponding to restricted enzyme cutting and reforming.

The splicing operations were firstly proposed by Head [Head1987, Head2000], which was a

Figure 8. The mapping between binary strings and DNA binary strings with length

binary string 0 1 0 ◄──► DNA binary string $\begin{array}{c} \text{GCTA-ATCG-TTCA} \\ \text{TAGC} \end{array}$

binary string 0 1 1 ◄──► DNA binary string $\begin{array}{c} \text{GCTA-ATCG-TTCA} \\ \text{TAGC-AAGT} \end{array}$

1. $\begin{array}{c} \text{GCTA-ATCG-TTCA} \\ \text{TAGC} \end{array}$ + CGAT + AAGC $\xrightarrow{\text{hybridization}}$ $\begin{array}{c} \text{GCTA-ATCG-TTCA} \\ \text{CGAT-TAGC-AAGT} \end{array}$ ◄──► binary string 1 1 1

2. $\begin{array}{c} \text{GCTA-ATCG-TTCA} \\ \text{TAGC-AAGT} \end{array}$ $\xrightarrow{\text{melting}}$ $\begin{array}{c} \text{TAGC-AAGT} \\ + \\ \text{GCTA-ATCG-TTCA} \end{array}$ $\xrightarrow{\text{filter}}$ GCTA-ATCG-TTCA ◄──► binary string 0 0 0

$\begin{array}{c} \text{GCTA-ATCG-TTCA} \\ \text{TAGC} \end{array}$ $\xrightarrow{\text{melting}}$ $\begin{array}{c} \text{TAGC} \\ + \\ \text{GCTA-ATCG-TTCA} \end{array}$ $\xrightarrow{\text{filter}}$ GCTA-ATCG-TTCA

3. GCTA-ATCG-TTCA + GCAT + TAGC $\xrightarrow{\text{hybridization}}$ $\begin{array}{c} \text{GCTA-ATCG-TTCA} \\ \text{CGAT TAGC} \end{array}$ ◄──► binary string 1 0 0

4. GCTA-ATCG-TTCA + AAGT $\xrightarrow{\text{hybridization}}$ $\begin{array}{c} \text{GCTA-ATCG-TTCA} \\ \text{AAGT} \end{array}$ ◄──► binary string 0 0 1

5. GCTA-ATCG-TTCA + AAGT + CGAT $\xrightarrow{\text{hybridization}}$ $\begin{array}{c} \text{GCTA-ATCG-TTCA} \\ \text{CGAT AAGT} \end{array}$ ◄──► binary string 1 0 1

6. GCTA-ATCG-TTCA + TAGC + CGAT $\xrightarrow{\text{hybridization}}$ $\begin{array}{c} \text{GCTA-ATCG-TTCA} \\ \text{CGAT TAGC} \end{array}$ ◄──► binary string 1 1 0

Figure 9. Three examples of the Splicing system computing progresses

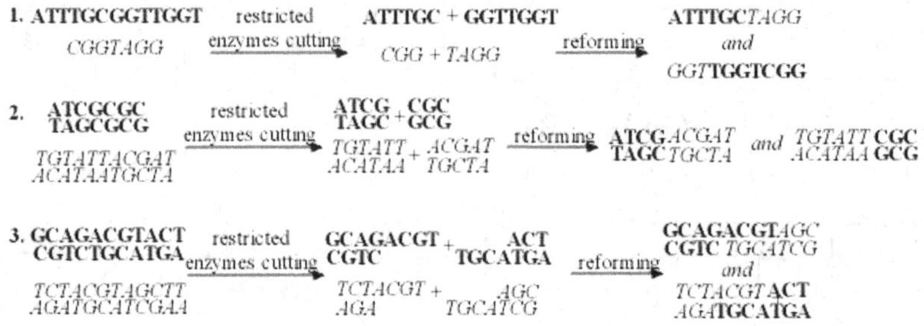

formal computing model based on the recombinant behaviors of DNA molecules. The theories of Formal Language and Automata were used in analyzing the languages generated by Splicing systems.

Let $x = w_1 w_2$ and $y = w_3 w_4$ be two strings on the alphabet $\{A, T, C, G\}$. When using the splicing rule $r = w_1 \# w_2 \$ w_3 \# w_4$, we get $z_1 = w_1 w_4$ and $z_2 = w_3 w_2$, where $\#$ denotes the enzyme cutting positions. Obviously, r can be regarded as a string on the alphabet $\{A, T, C, G\} \cup \{\#, \$\}$. The above progress is called running splicing operation once and written as $(x, y) \to_r^1 z$, where $z \in \{z_1, z_2\}$ and the superscript 1 means running splicing rule r only once.

For instance, in Figure 9, number 1 denotes the following splicing progress:

$x = w_1 w_2 =$ ATTTGCGGTTGGT, then
$w_1 =$ ATTTGC and $w_2 =$ GGTTGGT;

$y = w_3 w_4 =$ CGGTAGG, then $w_3 =$ CGG and $w_4 =$ TAGG;

$r =$ ATTTGC#GGTTGGT$CGG#TAGG.

So the splicing progress is $(\text{ATTTGCGGTTGGT}, \text{CGGTAGG}) \to_r^1 z$, in which z belong to

$\{\text{ATTTGCTAGG}, \text{CGGTGGTCGG}\}$.

So when given the initial words set and splicing rules set, the recursively enumerable language on the alphabet $\{A, T, C, G\}$ can also be produced by using splicing rules several times. Then we get the conclusion that the Splicing system can compute as the Turing Machine does.

The Insert-Delete System

The Insert-Delete system generate languages over $\{A, T, C, G\}$ based on the insert and delete operations on the single DNA molecules. These insert and delete operations are present in mathematical form as follows:

$5' - x_1 v x_2 z - 3' \to 5' - x_1 u v x_2 z - 3'$, u is inserted into $5' - x_1 v x_2 z - 3'$ to form $5' - x_1 v x_2 z - 3'$, where u, v, x_1, x_2, z are short DNA molecules;

$5' - x_1 u v x_2 z - 3' \to 5' - x_1 v x_2 z - 3'$, u is deleted from the left molecule to form the right side one, where u, v, x_1, x_2, z are short DNA molecules.

The insert operation on single DNA strands is shown in Figure 10 and the delete operation is shown in Figure 11. In Figure 10, short DNA molecule $\bar{y}$ is inserted into $5' - x_1 u v x_2 z - 3'$ to form $5' - x_1 u \bar{y} v x_2 z - 3'$. In Figure 11, short DNA molecule y is deleted from $5' - x_1 u y v x_2 z - 3'$ to form $5' - x_1 u v x_2 z - 3'$. By insert and delete operations, the Insert-Delete system can also generate recursively enumerable language over $\{A, T, C, G\}$. So the Insert-Delete system is computation universal.

Figure 10. The insert operation in the Insert-Delete system

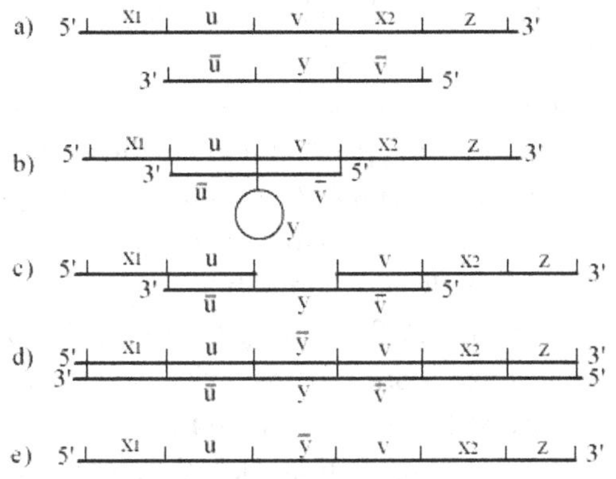

Figure 11. The delete operation in the Insert-Delete system

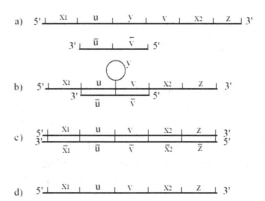

Outlooks

Though the above formal DNA computing models are computationally universal, their computing progresses are too difficult to come true in biology. So the computing models need improvement. Recent years, variants of formal DNA computing models are designed such as the distributing Splicing system, extended Splicing system and circular Splicing system and so on. There weren't a universal computing model in the real world till now.

Nowadays, various of DNA computing models have been proposed in order to find a feasible model for DNA computer, such as the sticker computer, Watson-Crick automata insertion-deletion system. By associated with nowadays biological level, some special DNA computers are proposed such as Benenson automata [Benenson2004] for medicine and surface DNA computing models for disease detecting. However, which one is the most feasible for DNA computer and how it comes true are still open questions. The biological technique is an obstacle in the development of DNA computer. In the future, feasible research and models' design should be considered in the purpose of making the DNA computing models more simple and reliable.

All the above formal models have proved that the computability of DNA computer is no less than that of Turing Machine. That is to say DNA computing is computation universal. With the development of biological, chemical and computer science, some computing models may come true, which are seemed to be impossible today. Theoretical supports are still the vital power of the development of DNA computer. The more feasible models are designed the more easily it can come to our lives.

The Computing Complexity of DNA Computing

In computer science, the running time of a program is called its time complexity and its storing space in RAM is named as its space complexity. If its running time is non-polynomial or storing space is immense, then the program is unavailable. That is to say it can't work in real. So the program is invaluable at all. These concepts also work in DNA computing. People would ask what the time and space computing complexity are in DNA computing. Till now there aren't uniform definitions for time and space complexity in DNA computing. Many kinds of them have been proposed for different computing models, but none is accepted as a universal one. It is still an open question for biomolecular researchers.

The Time Complexity of DNA Computing

There are 2 main definitions of time complexity that are widely accepted. One is computed by adding all the time cost in bio-chemical reactions. It's an ideal method, for only the time cost in pure biological progress is considered. It's always such a small number, that the computing time of DNA computing frequently was ignored by those who hold the first definition.

The other definition considered the question more practically. They took the first one as a fixed part of the time complexity. The time spent in bio-chemistry operations were also involved including the time spent in preparing and operating these experiments. For that is quite the time cost in solving some problem by DNA computing. The time is much bigger than that of the first one, so it could not be ignored. When solving a problem by DNA computing, the bio-chemistry operations can be done sequentially, but they also can be done parallel. There is no doubt that parallel operating is more time saving than orderly operate. Many effective operating algorithms have been designed, but there is not a universal one which is available for all the models.

For the Sticker system, Sticker model and Splicing system, their time complexity are considered as the using times of rewriting rules or splicing rules without losing any computability. So how to construct the above formal models with the smallest time complexity is still an open question.

The Space Complexity of DNA Computing

When it comes to space complexity, there are 2 main widely accepted conceptions. The first one is noted as the mol number of molecules used in the computing progress. If more than $o(6.02 \times 10^{23})$ molecules are needed when solving some problem, then it can not be solved by DNA computing. For the concentration of molecular is 6.02×10^{23} mol/L, i.e., no more molecules than 6.02×10^{23} mol can work as computing paradigm in one liter. That is also a bottle-neck of DNA computing. Two open questions are given: 1. How to cut down the mol number to the least when solving a problem by DNA computing? 2. If more than $o(6.02 \times 10^{23})$ molecules can work together with development of biology and chemistry in the future?

The second conception takes the mol number of molecules as one part of the space complexity. The remaining part is the number of tubes used in DNA computing progress. If too many tubes are involved in a computing progress, then it's hard for biologist to perform these experiments and get the result. That is to say the computing progress only works in theory and there is no value for solving realistic problems. So after an algorithm has been constructed, its space complexity should be completely considered. What is the feasible universal method in decreasing the every computing model's space complexity is still an open question.

The space complexity of the above four formal DNA computing models are composed of the size of initial word set, rewriting rules set and the medium strings set. Their outputs are the recursively enumerable language, so their output sizes are equal to each other. The attentions of how simple their space complexity are paid on simplifying and deceasing the medium strings.

4. DNA COMPUTING MODELS IN PRACTICE

After the computability of DNA computing has been proved to be no less than that of the Turing Machine, many attentions are paid to designing feasible DNA computing models with the biological and chemical technology. The speed of DNA computing models in practice is much slower theoretical models. For instance, the 3-SAT problem with n variables has been solved in 1995, seven years later the 3-SAT problem with 20 variables could be solved in practice. With the development of biology science and technology, more and more DNA computing models could work in real world. There are three main research fields in DNA computing models in practice: The molecular based gates and circuits, surface based DNA computing models and DNA self-assemble computing models.

DNA Computing Models

During the fifteen years' development of DNA computing, plenty of mathematical and combinational problems have been solved by it and in practice, and some of them have been proved feasible in real world with small sizes. In 1995, Lipton [Lipton95] proposed a DNA algorithm for the 3-SAT problem. The order of the solution space is 2^n, with n being the length of DNA molecular. Bach [Bach98] presents a more effective algorithm which reduces the order to 1.51^n when computing the independent set problem. The simulation of Boolean circuits by DNA computer is achieved. Breaking DES by DNA computing was proposed by Boneh [Boneh96]. Some combinational problems are solved, such as the China postman problem, graph coloring problem, maximal clique problem and so on.

Briefly speaking, many DNA computing models have been designed and lots of combinational problems have been solved. But very little can work in realistic word and there is not a universal one. More theoretical DNA computing models with more feasibility should be conceived. And how to construct a universal DNA computing model in both theory and realistic world is still an open question.

The Molecular Based Gates and Circuits

As we all know, the electrical computer is based on the logic gates and circuits, the inputs and outputs of which are both binary strings. The computing progress of the Boolean function is simulated by DNA molecules and bio-chemistry operations. In biological labs, simple DNA Boolean functions are used in solving some easy problems. The gates of $\wedge$ *(and)*, $\vee$ *(or)* and $\neg$ *(not)* are involved in molecular based gates. The complexities of those circuits are given by fan-in, fan-out, the size and the depth. The computing progress has been proved feasible and the molecular based circuits are successfully designed. With the development of biology science, a little more complex DNA molecular based gates and circuits are invented in China, Japan and American etc. It is regarded as a successful example from theory to practice in DNA computing. And it's also seemed as the initial computing models of DNA computer.

Though some models have been designed and practiced in real-world applications, there hasn't been a universal one that can solve every kind of problems in reality. And the circuits are too simple to solve hard problems. The problems that can be solved by them are quite easy for electrical computers. More theories about circuits should be involved in the construction of bimolecular circuits. For instance, the reversible gates and circuits have been proved feasible by Song [Song2008b] in 2008. More improved theories are also needed in the evolution of the DNA computer. There are two open questions: 1. How to construct a DNA computing circuit with more computably power? 2. How to design molecular based gates and circuits which more suitable for DNA computing and DNA computer?

Figure 12. The construction of the Fredkin gate

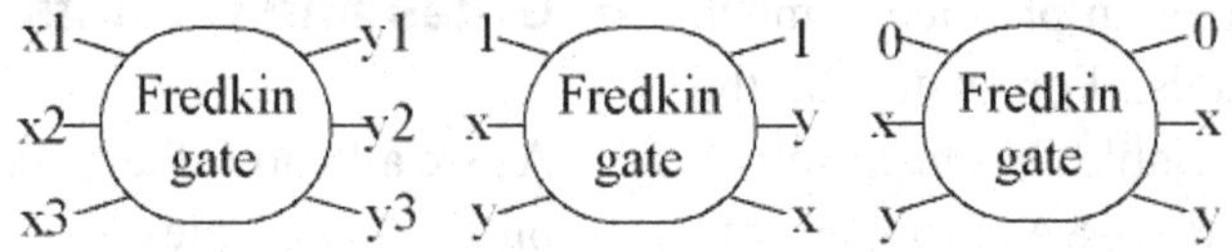

The Reversible Gates and Circuits in DNA Computing [Song2008b]

For irreversible logic computations, Landauer has proposed that each bit of information lost generates $KT\ln2$ joules of heat energy in electronic computing, where K is the Boltzmann's constant and T is the absolute temperature. And that is also known as the main bottleneck in the development of electronic computers. While reversible circuits formed by reversible gates do not lose information, i.e. they generate less heat, and then their computing efficient is almost the highest in all the known computing models, which plays an important role in quantum computing. Both Fredkin and Toffoli gate are famous reversible gates. Himanshu has proposed that we can also use the DNA molecules to construct the reversible gates and reversible sequential circuits.

The reversible gates and reversible sequential circuits generate unique output vector from each input vector, and verse visa, i.e. that is a one-to-one mapping between input and output vectors. A Fredkin gate is shown in Figure 12.

The DNA Fredkin gates are constructed by simulating the binary input and output of the Fredkin gate in DNA strands in two forms as shown in Figure 13 and Figure 14 respectively.

By Sticker model and Splicing system in DNA computing, the Fredkin gate is simulated. That must be a new computing model in both DNA computing and quantum computing.

Surface Based DNA Computing Models

The surfaced based technology was firstly proposed by Liu [Liu2000] in 2000, which takes DNA

Figure 13. Simulating Fredkin gate by Sticker model

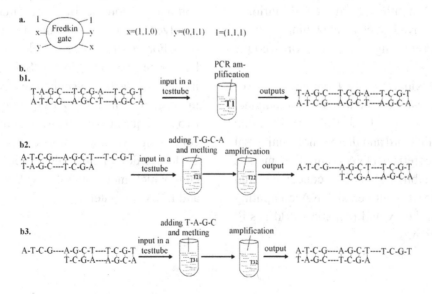

Figure 14. Simulating Fredkin gate by Splicing system

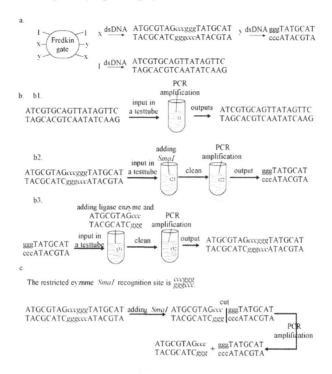

molecules from tubes to a surface. That also the first time that the circumstance of DNA computing is changed to dry from wet. It also makes genetic clip becoming true. In Figure 15, the progress from tubes to surface is given, which is easily operated in biology. Glasses, silicon, even the plastic can be used as the material of the surface.

Another advantage of surface based technology is that DNA molecules are still alive on the surface, i.e., they can be operated by bio-chemistry operations as well. For instance the fixed

DNA molecules can hybridize to its complementary molecules and more operations are shown in Figure 16. There are 4 main operations for the surface based DNA molecular technology. Extracting: extracting DNA molecules from the tube; magnetization: adding magnetic balls on one end of every DNA molecular; fixing: fixing the molecules with magnetic balls on the magnetic surface; cleaning or destroying: removing the molecules from the surface and cleaning the surface. And the surface could be circular used in different

Figure 15. Surface based DNA technology

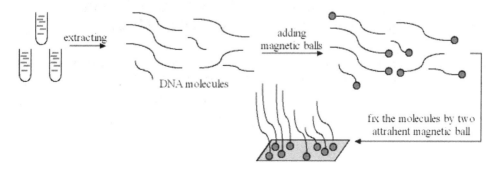

Figure 16. Surface based molecular operations

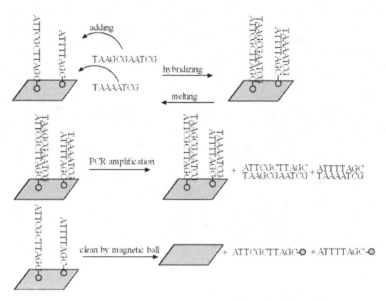

surfaced based DNA computing models. After the surface based technology come to use in practice, many DNA computing models designed in tubes are extended to surface and some of them can really work in solving realistic problems, such as 3-SAT with 20 variables. The surfaced DNA molecules can also work as a logic gate, so it's called the gene clips. It might make DNA computer out of the tubes in the future.

Now the surfaced based molecular technology is chiefly used in genetic disease detecting. Firstly, the genes (long DNA molecular is called gene) whose expression is some diseases are known. Then the genes are extracted, after the magnetic balls are added on each of them, they can be fixed on a surface. Subsequently, we extract the DNA molecules from someone's body and put them into a tube. Then we pour the DNA molecular solutions through the surface. By detecting the molecular on the surface we can get the conclusion that whether the man has got some disease. The detailed progress is shown in Figure 17.

Outlooks

The surface based DNA molecular technology is regarded as a great development in DNA computing. It takes the DNA molecular to dry circumstance from wet tubes. It also makes DNA computer to work out of tubes possible. Now researchers apply themselves to surface based DNA computing models and the application in other fields such as medicine science and disease detecting. There are 2 open questions for surface based DNA computing: 1. How to design a universal surface based DNA computing model, which can solve every problem? 2. Finding more fields which surface based DNA molecular can work quite well.

The DNA Self-Assemble Computing Model

Based on biological properties of DNA molecules, the DNA self-assemble computing model was proposed and now it is becoming a hot researching field in DNA computing.

Figure 17. The surface based disease detecting model

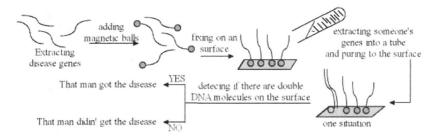

The principle of DNA self-assemble computing model is "to tell DNA molecules what to do". In IBM biological lab, the DNA molecules can form a "sweet smiling face" and other figures in nanoscale. Obviously, it's an easy job to draw a DNA picture. But people would like to do more complex things by DNA molecules. DNA self-assemble computing models could also be used in solving various problems: molecular components such as simulating AND, OR, and NOT gates, it also could be chemically attached to DNA tiles and subsequent self-assembly would proceed to display the tiles in some rules. The processes could be regarded as functional devices.

Summary and Prospects

DNA-based self-assembly appears to be a robust, readily programmable phenomenon. Periodic two-dimensional crystals have been demonstrated for tens of distinct types of DNA tiles, illustrating that in these systems the sticky ends drive the interactions between tiles. However several factors limit immediate applications. Unlike high-quality crystals current DNA tile lattices are often slightly distorted, with the relative position of adjacent tiles jittered by a nanometer and lattice defect rates of 1 percent or more. Some DNA tiles are designed to form two-dimensional sheets. Furthermore, procedures have yet to be worked out for reliably growing large (greater than 10 micron) crystals and depositing them nondestructively on the substrate of choice.

Although one and two dimensional algorithmic self-assembly has been demonstrated, per-step error rates between 1 and 10 percent preclude the execution of complex algorithms. Recent theoretical work has suggested the possibility of error-correcting tile sets for self-assembly, which, if demonstrated experimentally, would significantly increase the feasibility of interesting applications. A second prevalent source of algorithmic errors is undesired nucleation (analogous to programs starting by themselves with random input). Thus controlling nucleation, through careful exploitation of super saturation and tile design, is another active topic of research. Learning how to obtain robustness to other natural sources of variation lattice defects, ill formed tiles, poorly matched sticky-end strengths, changes of tile concentrations, temperature and Buffers will also be necessary.

Thus, DNA self-assembly can be seen as one step in the quest to harness biochemistry in the same way we have harnessed the electron. Electronic computers are good at (and pervasive at) embedded control of macroscopic and microscopic electromechanical systems. We do not yet have embedded control for chemical and nanoscale systems. Programmable, algorithmic biochemical systems may be our best bet.

Benenoson Automata [Benenson2004]

The Benenson's autonomous molecular computer is proposed for logical control of gene expression in 2004. By using biological molecules as input and active molecules as output, it could produce a system for logic control of biological progresses.

Figure 18. The progress of the benenson autonomous molecular treating diseases

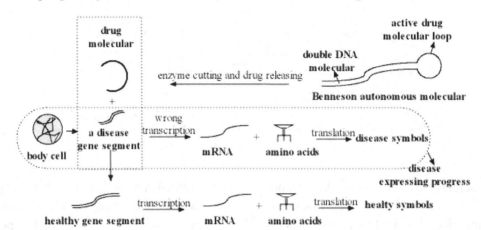

Especially for the gene expression, which is mainly controlled by gene and mRNA. The autonomous molecular computer logically analysis the levels of mRNA and in response produce molecules affecting levels of gene expression. The Benenson automata have been working in the lab for treating diseases which is aroused by some genes' wrongly express. It plays an important role in disease diagnosing and treating. Also it has lots of enlighten principle in the researching of the genetic engineering and biomolecular computer. The progress of autonomous molecular computer is shown in Figure 18, by which the wrongly expressed gene is corrected and the disease is controlled.

The Benenson autonomous model demonstrates a robust and flexible molecular computer, which is capable of logical analyzing of mRNA disease indicator in vitro and controlling administration of biologically active single string DNA molecular, including drugs. The design of modularity improves each computer component independently. It is also an important DNA computer model except for formal models. And it's more useful in medicine science and disease diagnosing and treating. One of the main aims of gene engineering is to diagnose and control the cancer by gene drug, so the Benenson autonomous molecular computer plays a vital role in gene engineering. Also, the Benenson automata have been used in

computing Boolean function and shallowing Boolean circuits. It is considered as a more feasible model in DNA computing. There are 2 open questions for Benenson automata: 1. How to control the cancer by what means? 2. How to use it as a universal computing model which can solve realistic problems autonomous?

Problems Solved by DNA Computing Models

In 1997, Frutos [Frutos97] proposed surface based DNA computing theories. In 1998, Kari [Kari98] solved a boundary China postman problem on the surface. In the same year, Sakomata solved a 3-SAT problem by the hairpin structure of DNA molecules. Wu [Wu2001] improved the surface based DNA molecular technology, which made it more feasible by computing with surface DNA molecules. Cukras [Cukras98] proposed a RNA computing model, by which the chess game was solved in the lab. A computing algorithm with DNA by operating on plasmids was practiced by Head, which is used to solve the maximal clique problem. In 2002, a 3-SAT problem with 20 variables was solved in biological lab, which was known as the hardest problem solved by DNA computing.

Chinese researchers have also made contributions to the developments of DNA computing.

In 2005, the vertex coloring problem was solved by Wang [Wang2005] in DNA computing. Some more combinational problems have also been solved, such as 0-1 linear programming; inter linear programming etc. The most famous DNA computing model invented by Chinese researcher was the DNA surface based logic circuit in 2002. That was considered as the initial DNA computer, which could solve some simple problems. Now it was used in various fields such as code breaking and Boolean function computing.

Nowadays, researchers all over the world apply themselves in constructing a universal DNA computing model which can compute lots of problems just like the electrical computer.

5. DNA ENCODING

DNA encoding is to design the DNA molecules which are used to represent realistic problems. It was proposed by researchers when they repeated Adleman's DNA computing algorithm. They found that if the DNA molecules used to represent the vertexes and edges are randomly selected, the computing progress would drastically fail without any solutions. The reason was that inappropriate single DNA molecules would hybridize to form double DNA molecules which is called false-positive phenomenon. It is one of the most difficult problems in DNA computing. Reasonable DNA codes could improve the reliability and stability of experiment as well as the rate of successful computation. There are many metrics for DNA encoding, including distance like value, GC content, melting temperature and Gibb's free energy. Many DNA encoding metrics have been designed, which are more suitable in DNA encoding, such as H-metric [Garzon97], H-measure, Watson-Crick Hamming distance [Song2008a], DNA encoding matrix and so on. Based on those metrics, many DNA encoding methods have been proposed, and some DNA codes were designed.

But the known codes weren't good enough to avoid the false-positive phenomenon in practice.

DNA Encoding Metrics

Some distance-like metrics are introduced firstly, and then others are presented.

Distance-Like Metrics

Hamming Distance: The Hamming Distance of two DNA stands is the number of corresponding places where two characters differ. Let x,y be 2 strings then the Hamming Distance between them is $H(x,y)$, which is given by lining up x to the reverse complement of y and subtracting from their common length the number of identical matches.

H-measure: The H-measure between two n-length DNA strings x and y is given by

$$\left|x, y\right| = \min_{-n<k<n} H\left(x, \sigma^k\left(\bar{y}\right)\right),$$

where $\sigma(\sigma^{-1})$ is the left(right)-shift and $H(*,*)$ is the ordinary Hamming Distance.

H-Distance: The H-Distance between two sets of DNA stands X,Y is given by:

$$\left|X, Y\right| = \min_{x\in X, y\in Y}\left|x, y\right|,$$

where $\left|*,*\right|$ is the ordinary H-measure defined above.

Watson-Crick Hamming Distance: Let x,y be two n-length DNA stands. Then its Watson-Crick Hamming Distance is $H'\left(x, y\right) = \sum_{i=1}^{n} f\left(x_i, y_i\right)$, in which

$$f\left(x_i, y_i\right) = \begin{cases} 1, & x_i \neq y_i, x_i \neq \bar{y}_i \\ 0, else \end{cases}, i=1,2,\ldots,n,$$

101

with $\bar{y}_i$ being the Watson-Crick complementary base of y_i.

The distance like metrics are used to choose good DNA codes for DNA computing, and distance like metrics can all be noted as τ, then the DNA encoding problem is expressed by mathematical language as follows:

A DNA code is a set with finite n-length DNA stands on the alphabet $S=\{A,T,C,G\}$. K is positive integer and τ is the encoding metric, which is seemed as a mapping from S^* to Z^+. Then a good DNA code C is a subset of S such that $\forall x,y \in C, \tau(x,y) \geq K$. So the purpose of DNA encoding is to find such a good DNA code. It has been proved that the bigger K is, the less possible to occur false-positive phenomenon.

Many methods have been designed and some "good" codes are achieved. But they can not work as a perfect paradigm in practice, so many metrics have been proposed, which is not only distance like metrics, such as GC content and Gibb's free energy of the DNA stands.

GC Content

GC content: The GC content of an n-length DNA stand is the rate between the number of G&C and n.

In molecular biology science, the higher the GC content of a DNA string is, the more energy is needed when melting. The relationship of melting temperature and GC content are given as follows:

$$\begin{cases} T_m = 4(G+C) + 2(A+T), n \leq 18\text{bp}; \\ T_m = 81.5 - 16.6 \log_{10}\left[Na^+\right] + 0.41\%(G+C) - \dfrac{600}{n}, 14\text{bp} \leq n \leq 70\text{bp} \end{cases}$$

If a DNA code with some n-length strings, the GC content of each string is quite different. In DNA computing progress, they can not be well controlled. That may make some inaccuracy for the computing, especially for hybridization and PCR amplification. Generally, a good DNA code is defined as that the GC content of each strings in it is almost 50%. So the GC content are considered when designing good DNA codes.

Stacking Energy

In DNA encoding, it is believed that the strings in the same DNA code should have the same biological structure. The DNA code is quite a good one, for the complexity of biological operation could be lower by using them. Based on different kinds of experimental data, several models for estimating DNA structure have been devised. Every pair of bases has a Stacking energy value. If two n-length DNA molecules are with almost the same stacking energy value, then the two DNA molecules have biological properties almost in common. That is also the aim of constructing DNA codes, so when designing DNA codes the stacking energy should be considered detailed. The stacking energy values of every neighboring base are given in table1.

Consider a sequence of $n+1$ nucleotides $A_1 \ldots A_{n+1}$ and corresponding to sequences of propeller twist values $(a_1 \ldots a_n)$. The inverse complementary sequence on the opposite string is $A_{n+1} \ldots A_1$ with the scale sequence $(a_n \ldots a_1)$. We would like to find an encoding $E\left(A_1 \ldots A_{n+1}\right) = E\left(a_1 \ldots a_n\right)$ with two properties. First, it must be string invariant: $E\left(A_1 \ldots A_{n+1}\right) = E\left(\bar{A}_{n+1} \ldots \bar{A}_1\right) = E\left(a_n \ldots a_1\right)$. Second, we must be able to recover the sequence itself from the encoding mapping E. It is known as the other mathematical definition for DNA encoding. A good DNA code should be designed by considering the two properties, GC content and some distance like metrics.

Gibb's Free Energy

In bio-chemistry, each chemical progress is two-directional reaction. That is when A met B we got C is noted as the positive direction, also C was broken into A and B at the same time. So if A and B are two single DNA molecular and the reaction is defined as the hybridization, then C is the double DNA molecular. The Gibb's free energy of A and B is bigger than C, the reaction among them is rely to the positive direction. If

Table 1. The stacking energy values of every neighboring base

Base pair	Stacking energy (kcal/mole)	Propeller twist (degree)	Base pair	Stacking energy (kcal/mole)	Propeller twist (degree)
AA	-5.37	-18.66	GA	-9.81	-13.48
AC	-10.51	-13.10	GC	-14.59	-11.08
AG	-6.78	-14.00	GG	-8.26	-8.11
AT	-6.57	-15.01	GT	-10.51	-13.10
CA	-6.57	-9.45	TA	-3.82	-11.85
CC	-8.26	-8.11	TC	-9.81	-13.48
CG	-9.69	-10.03	TG	-6.57	-9.45
CT	-6.78	-14.00	TT	-5.37	-16.66

the Gibb's free energy of C is much bigger than A and B, then there are very little C appearing in that reaction. Because DNA encoding can not completely ensure the reaction's direction, more bio-chemical conditions should also be taken into account. For example, suppose that more C are needed to be hybridized, we can add A and B during the reaction and also can higher the temperature. If A and B can successfully hybridize C without any secondary structure and wrong hybridizations, then the false-positive will be solved. But till now there are no perfect DNA codes can avoid it.

DNA Encoding Methods

It is known that there are 4^n DNA strands with n-length, for there are 4 kinds of bases. The DNA encoding metrics can be worked as a "filter", by which good DNA codes are chosen from all the 4^n DNA stands. The progress of finding good DNA codes is DNA encoding. For 4^n is quite a huge solution space, so DNA encoding problem may be also a NP-hard problem. Because finding good codes in such a huge space is quite difficult for the recent computing ability. Just as solving other NP-hard and NP-complete problems, some new optimizing algorithms are involved.

By genetic algorithm, a small size DNA code was achieved. But when coming to the larger one,

the genetic algorithm is unavailable for DNA encoding. By PSO algorithm [Cui2007], a "good" DNA code was achieved, but no bio-chemical proof was operated for its advantage. Now when solving a problem by DNA computing, the DNA code should be checked and fixed many times for avoiding the false-positive phenomenon as most as possible. The most popularly used DNA codes was got by software designed in Germany. There are not quite useful algorithms or tools for DNA encoding and each of them is only efficient in some field. So DNA encoding method itself is quite an open question urgently needed to be solved in DNA computing.

Triple Elements DNA Encoding Method [Song2008a]

As we know that DNA strands are usually seemed as strings over {A,T,C,G}. Triple elements DNA encoding method focus on designing DNA strands on {A,T,G} or {T,C,A}. For DNA strands on {A,T,G} or {T,C,A} are more effective in avoiding false-positive phenomenon. All most every proposed distance-like metric works on the alphabet {A,T,C,G}, among which Watson-Crick Hamming Distance [Song2008a] is the more powerful in describing the differences between two DNA strands. So it is mainly considered in triple elements DNA encoding method. We also use a matrix to define a set of DNA codes, and each row or column in the matrix is noted as a DNA strand.

Algorithm 1: Triple elements DNA encoding method.

Step0. Let $k=k_0, y_0 = y_{01}y_{02}\ldots y_{0n} \in \{A,G,T\}^*$, $h=h(y_0) > k$, $Y = \{1,2,\ldots,n\}$, $\alpha = 0,1, s=1$, $Y_s = \varnothing$ and $Y_\alpha = \{i \mid g(y_{0i}) = \alpha, i=1,2,\ldots,n\}$. Obviously, $Y_1 \cap Y_0 = \varnothing$, $Y_1 \cup Y_0 = Y$.

Step1. If $|Y_1| \geq k$, turn to Step2; else stop. Then $\{y_1, y_2, \ldots, y_s\}$ is the set of DNA codes.

Step2. Randomly select $i_1, i_2, \ldots, i_k$, where $i_1 < i_2 < \ldots < i_k$, from Y_1. For $\forall j \in \{1,2,\ldots,k\}$, at least one $i_{j+m} - i_{j+m-1} \geq 3$ is true when $m=1,2,3$. Then change the $i_j th$ bit of y_0 into G, for $j=1,2,\ldots k$, with other bits being randomly selected from $\{A,T\}$. Then we get y_s. Let $Y_1 = Y_1 \backslash \{i_1, i_2, \ldots, i_k\}, s=s+1$, then turn to Step1.

It is not hard to get that Algorithm 1 will stop in $l = \left\lfloor \dfrac{h}{k} \right\rfloor$ steps, and there are at most k selections and k substitutions in each step. So there are $l \times 2k$ computations in all, then Algorithm 1 is an effective algorithm.

Example: Let $k=3$, $y_0 = $ATGAATGAATGAATGTATGTTA, then $n=22$, $h=17$, $l=5$ and $t=h(\mathrm{mod}\,k)=2$. According to Algorithm 1, then $Y_1 = \{1,2,4,5,6,8,9,10,12,13,14, 16,17,18,20,21,22\}$. The firstly selected three bits in Y_1 is $\{1,8,12\}$, then changing the three bits into G with other bits being randomly selected from $\{A,T\}$. Then we get y_1. Next, selecting $\{2,4,9\}$ from $Y_1 = Y_1 \backslash \{1,8,12\}$ and changing the three bits into G with other bits being randomly selected from $\{A,T\}$, we get y_2. Selecting $\{5,6,16\}$ from $Y_1 = Y_1 \backslash \{1,2,4,8,9,12\}$ and changing the three bits into G with other bits being randomly selected from $\{A,T\}$, we get y_3. After $l=5$ steps, the algorithm stops. Finally, we get y_1, y_2, y_3, y_4, y_5 as follows:

$y_1 = $GTATTTAGTTAGTATTAATATA,

$y_2 = $AGTGTTAAGTATTTATATTAAT

$y_3 = $TATAGGTTAATTAATGTATATT,

$y_4 = $TATAAATTAGATGTGATTTAAT

$y_5 = $ATATTAGTATGTTATATATGAA.

And the matrix is as follows:

$$D = \begin{pmatrix} G\,T\,A\,T\,T\,T\,A\,G\,T\,T\,A\,G\,T\,A\,T\,T\,A\,A\,T\,A\,T\,A \\ A\,G\,T\,G\,T\,T\,A\,A\,G\,T\,A\,T\,T\,T\,A\,T\,A\,T\,T\,A\,A\,T \\ T\,A\,T\,A\,G\,G\,T\,T\,A\,A\,T\,T\,A\,A\,T\,G\,T\,A\,T\,A\,T\,T \\ T\,A\,T\,A\,A\,A\,T\,T\,A\,G\,A\,T\,G\,T\,G\,A\,T\,T\,T\,A\,A\,T \\ A\,T\,A\,T\,T\,A\,G\,T\,A\,T\,G\,T\,T\,A\,T\,A\,T\,A\,T\,G\,A\,A \end{pmatrix}$$

Adding Elements DNA Encoding Method [Song2008a]

In triple elements encoding method, DNA strands are designed over $\{A,T,G\}$, so the GC content of the DNA strands generated by Algorithm 1 is $\dfrac{k}{n}$. If $\dfrac{k}{n} < \dfrac{n}{2}$, then it can not satisfy the condition that the GC content of DNA strands should be more than 50%. So adding elements DNA encoding method is constructed to increase the GC content of them.

Algorithm 2: Adding elements DNA encoding method.

Step0. Let D be the matrix generated by Algorithm 1 and $H_{j_1}, H_{j_2}, \cdots, H_{j_t}$ be the columns of D with all bits being A or T. Changing all the bits of $H_{j_1}, H_{j_2}, \cdots, H_{j_t}$ into G or C, then we get a new D. Let $i=0$ and turn to Step1.

Step1. Compute the GC content in each row of D. If GC%$<c\%$, then let $i=i+1$ turn to Step2; else stop. All the rows of D make up a set of DNA codes.

Step2. Delete the ith row of D, then there are k more columns $H_{j_1}, H_{j_2}, \cdots, H_{j_k}$, whose bits are all A or T. Change all the bits of $H_{j_1}, H_{j_2}, \cdots, H_{j_k}$ into G or C and turn to Step1.

Obviously, Algorithm 2 will stop in $\frac{n \cdot c\% - t}{k} - 1$ steps and there are k selections and k substitutions in each step. So there are $\left(\frac{n \cdot c\% - t}{k} - 1\right) \times 2k$ computations in all. Then Algorithm 2 is an effective algorithm. Finally, the set of DNA strands generated by Algorithm 1 and 3 satisfy that the GC content is GC%$\geq c$% and the Watson-Crick Hamming distance of every two DNA stands is $2k$. Many results are proposed by Song [Song2008a].

DNA Golay Code [Wang2009]

A lot of designed DNA codes are enlightened from the Code theory in information science. DNA Golay code is designed from the Golay code.

In 1949, Marcel Golay firstly proposed a kind of linear code note as G_{24} with length 24 based on the generating matrix P, where $P = (I_{12}, U)$ with

$$U = \begin{pmatrix} 0 & 1 & 1 & 1 & 1 & 1 & 1 & 1 & 1 & 1 & 1 & 1 \\ 1 & 1 & 1 & 0 & 1 & 1 & 1 & 0 & 0 & 0 & 1 & 0 \\ 1 & 1 & 0 & 1 & 1 & 1 & 0 & 0 & 0 & 1 & 0 & 1 \\ 1 & 0 & 1 & 1 & 1 & 0 & 0 & 0 & 1 & 0 & 1 & 1 \\ 1 & 1 & 1 & 1 & 0 & 0 & 0 & 1 & 0 & 1 & 1 & 0 \\ 1 & 1 & 1 & 0 & 0 & 0 & 1 & 0 & 1 & 1 & 0 & 1 \\ 1 & 1 & 0 & 0 & 0 & 1 & 0 & 1 & 1 & 0 & 1 & 1 \\ 1 & 0 & 0 & 0 & 1 & 0 & 1 & 1 & 0 & 1 & 1 & 1 \\ 1 & 0 & 0 & 1 & 0 & 1 & 1 & 0 & 1 & 1 & 1 & 0 \\ 1 & 0 & 1 & 0 & 1 & 1 & 0 & 1 & 1 & 1 & 0 & 0 \\ 1 & 1 & 0 & 1 & 1 & 0 & 1 & 1 & 1 & 0 & 0 & 0 \\ 1 & 0 & 1 & 1 & 0 & 1 & 1 & 1 & 0 & 0 & 0 & 1 \end{pmatrix}.$$

By deleting the last bit of G_{24}, we get G_{23}. G_{24} and G_{23} play an vital role in information science. From the Golay code, DNA Golay codes are denoted as D_{24} and D_{23}. For G_{24} and G_{23} are binary codes, D_{24} and D_{23} are designed based on a mapping f in the form of $f: \{0,1\} \rightarrow \{A,T,C,G\}$.

Firstly, let $\sum = \{A,T,C,G\}$, $\sum_1 = \{A,T\}$ and $\sum_2 = \{C,G\}$. The mapping $f: \{0,1\} \rightarrow \{A,T,C,G\}$ is constructed as follows: for any binary code $x = x_1 x_2 \ldots x_{24} \in G_{24}$, if $x_i = j$, then $f(x_i) \in \sum_j$, where $i = 1, 2, \ldots, n$ and $j = 0, 1$. The $f(x)$ is a DNA Golay corresponding to the binary code x. By the mapping f, binary Golay code G_{24} maps to DNA Golay code D_{24}. We can also get DNA Golay code D_{23}. Obviously, the length of D_{24} and D_{23} are 24 and 23 respectively. After constructing D_{24} and D_{23}, we also get some results.

Theorem 1. DNA Golay D_{24} and D_{23} are linear codes.

Theorem 2. H'(D_{24})=8 and H'(D_{23})=7, which means that the least Watson-Crick Hamming distance of every two codes in D_{24} and D_{23} is 8 and 7, respectively.

Theorem 3. DNA Golay D_{23} is a perfect code.

The proofs of the above three theorems are given by Wang [Wang2008]. There are 2576 DNA codes in DNA Golay code D_{24} with code weight at least 12 and 1288 DNA codes in D_{23} with code weight at least 11. The DNA codes in DNA Golay code D_{24} with GC content 50% and in DNA Golay code D_{23} with GC content 47.82%. These are both perfect for DNA computing to avoid false-positive phenomenon.

In Tulpan [Tulpan2001], by randomly searching method, after about 6×10^5 steps 2193 codes with length 24, Hamming distance 12 and GC content 50% are obtained. And after about 5×10^5 steps, 2000 codes with length 23, Hamming distance 11 and GC content 50% are obtained. Obviously, the method used to generate DNA Golay codes is more powerful.

Novel IWO DNA Encoding Method [Zhang2009]

Recently, a new methodology based on the IWO algorithm is developed to optimize encoding sequences. Firstly, the mathematics models of constrained objective optimization design for encoding problems based on the thermodynamic criteria are set up. Then a modified IWO method is developed by defining the colonizing behavior of weeds to overcome the obstacles of the original IWO algorithm, which cannot be applied to discrete problems directly. The experimental results show that the proposed method is effective and convenient for the user to design and select effective DNA sequences in silicon for controllable DNA computing.

The original IWO algorithm can only optimize problems in which the elements of the solution are continuous real numbers, while it can not be applied to discrete problems directly. Focusing on this encoding problem, a modified IWO method by defining the colonizing behavior of weeds is developed.

Let n DNA sequences of m-mers form a DNA sequences set. It is denoted as a plant. The detailed steps are given below.

1. Initializing a population: A population of seeds is being randomly dispersed over the feasible search area. We could calculate each seed's fitness by putting its position into a designated objective function.

2. Reproduction: Some members of the population of plants are allowed to produce seeds depending on their own and the colony's lowest and highest fitness. The number of seeds each plant produced increases linearly from the minimum possible seed production to its maximum. The numbers of seeds ith produces can be calculated by

$$Num\_Seeds[i]=(F_i-F_w)(F_g-F_w)\times(S_{max}-S_{min})+S_{min},$$

where F_g is the best fitness of the colony, F_w is the worst fitness of the colony and F_i is fitness of the ith weed.

3. Spatial dispersal: The generated seeds are being randomly distributed over the d dimensional search space by normally distributed random numbers with mean equal to zero, but varying variance. This means that seeds will be randomly distributed such that they lie close to the parent plant. Accordingly, the position of new seed is given as follows

$$\begin{cases} \sigma_{it} = \left[\left(it_{max} - it\right)/it_{max}\right]^n \times \left(\sigma_i - \sigma_f\right) + \sigma_f \\ NewS_i = \text{Mod}\left(\text{Parent's position } w_i + \sigma_{it} \times Random\left(0,1\right), 4\right) \end{cases}$$

where the Mod (number, divisor) function returns the remainder after a number is divided by a divisor, Random(0, 1) is a normally distributed random number with mean equal to 0 and variance to 1.

4. Competitive exclusion: If a plant leaves no offspring then it would go extinct. When the maximum number of weeds in a colony is reached, each weed is allowed to produce seeds according to the mechanism mentioned in step (2). The produced seeds are then allowed to spread over the search area according to step 3. When all seeds have found their position in the search area, they are ranked together with their parents (as a colony of weeds). Next, weeds with lower fitness are eliminated to reach the maximum allowable population in a colony.

By this method, parameters used in IWO are given in Figure 19 and some results are shown in Figure 20 and Figure 21.

The mathematics models of constrained objective optimization design for encoding problems based on the thermodynamic criteria are set up. A novel IWO algorithm provides a new solution for the encoding problem. However, it is an attempt to investigate how to solving the encoding problem using IWO. To be useful in practical applications, this effect should be further explored in different scenarios. In future work, the algorithm should be investigated for adapted so that much larger sets, such as used in microarray applications, can be designed efficiently. In addition, the time complexity of the algorithm which calculates

Figure 19. IWO parameter values for DNA encoding

Symbol	Quantity	Value
N_0	Number of initial population	10
it_{max}	Maximum number of iterations	10000
p_{max}	Maximum number of plant population	30
s_{max}	Maximum number of seeds	3
s_{min}	Minimum number of seeds	0
n	Nonlinear modulation index	3
$\sigma_{initial}$	Initial value of standard deviation	5
σ_{final}	Final value of standard deviation	1
x_{ini}	Initial search area	0–3

Figure 20. The sequences designed by IWO and compared with Deator

IWO	Deator et al.
AGACGCTACTCTGTGATGCC	ATAGAGTGGATAGTTCTGGG
TAGTACGATATGGCGATGTC	CATTGGCGGCGCGTAGGCTT
AGCATCGTTGAGGATTAGTG	CTTGTGACCGCTTCTGGGGA
TAAGACTGAGACTCCCGTTT	GAAAAAGGACCAAAAGAGAG
ATGTTCGCTCGAATACGGAG	GATGGTGCTTAGAGAAGTGG
CCGGTCGCGCTAACGAATTA	TGTATCTCGTTTTAACATCC
CATGTTTGCCAGCAAAGTCT	TTGTAAGCCTACTGCGTAGC

minimum free energy is high. It will further improve the accuracy of algorithms and reduce the complexity of calculation if combined with other methods.

6. CONCLUSION

In this chapter, DNA computing is mainly introduced from three aspects: the theoretical framework of DNA computing, computing models in practice and the DNA encoding.

In the section of the theoretical framework of DNA computing, the computability of DNA computing is mainly discussed. Four theoretical DNA computing models are introduced and they are all proved to be computationally universal. How to make the DNA computer come true is the eventual purpose of DNA computing. Nowadays it is still very hard to construct a universal DNA computer in the form of Sticker models, Insert-Delete system and other theoretical DNA computing models. According to new bio-chemical technologies, more theoretical models in DNA

Figure 21. The sequences designed by IWO and compared with Shin

IWO	Shin et al.
GCAGATTCCCGGATACTCAG	GTGACTTGAGGTAGGTAGGA
GATGGATTTACCTTGCACCT	ATCATACTCCGGAGACTACC
CTGGAAGCGTTTGCTAACTT	CACGTCCTACTACCTTCAAC
CCTTCTCTCGTCTTCATACA	ACACGCGTGCATATAGGCAA
ACGATCGATTAATGGGAGTC	AAGTCTGCACGGATTCCTGA
ATAAGTAGGGACTGCTCTAC	AGGCCGAAGTTGACGTAAGA
CCTAAGAACACAGGGCATAG	CGACACTTGAAGCACACCTT
GTCCACTGTCAACGGTGAAA	TGGCGCTCTACCGTTGAATT
ACGTCGGAGACCTCTGTTTA	CTAGAAGGATAGGCGATACG
ACTCGCTATCGGTCATCTAT	CTTGGTGCGTTCTGTGTACA
CATTGATATTGGCGGCGGTA	TGCCAACGGTCTCAACATGA
CCTATAATTCGCCCACCCTC	TTATCTCCATAGCTCCAGGC
GAGTGTGAGGAGGAAACCAG	TGAACGAGCATCACCAACTC
GTACGACCAAGCTAGGCTAG	CTAGATTAGCGGCCATAACC

computing should be designed. Those theoretical DNA computing models will play an important role in designing of DNA computer.

In the section of DNA computing models in practice, many DNA computing models used in practice are introduced in different fields. By DNA computing, a lot of NP-hard and NP-complete problems in small size are solved. But when the size of them becomes large, almost all the algorithm by DNA computing is unavailable. Much more powerful DNA computing models in practice are necessary by new bio-chemical technologies. Including solving mathematical problems, DNA computing also works in medical science, such as Benenson Automata and Gene chip. We should found more fields, in which DNA computing is much powerful than traditional methods. In order to construct the DNA computer, DNA based logic gates and circuits and designed, such as reversible logic gates and circuits. In the future, we need more DNA computing models with much more power that can work in realistic world and solve hard problems for people.

DNA codes are vital for DNA computing, so many encoding metrics and method are involved in DNA encoding. By different ways, lots of "good" DNA codes have been designed. By triple elements and adding elements DNA encoding method, we got a set with small size of stable DNA codes in avoiding false-positive phenomenon. Recently, some optimization algorithms are used to design DNA codes, such as IWO and genetic algorithm. Although many DNA codes have been designed, DNA encoding problem is a NP problem, which is intractable to be solved. So much more useful algorithms are still needed in DNA encoding.

REFERENCES

Adleman, L. (1994). Molecular Computation of Solution to Combinatorial Problems. *Science*, *266*(11), 1021–1024. doi:10.1126/science.7973651

Bach, E., Condon, A., & Glaser, E. (1998). DNA Models and Algorithms for NP-Complete Problems. *Journal of Computer and System Sciences*, *57*(2), 172–186. doi:10.1006/jcss.1998.1586

Benenson, Y., & Gil, B. (2004). An Autonomous Molecular Computer for Logical Control of Gene Expression. *Nature*, *429*, 423–429. doi:10.1038/nature02551

Boneh, C. (1996). Breaking DES Using a Molecular Computing. *DNA based. Computer*, 37–66.

Braich, S., Johnson, C., Rothemund, W. K., & Adleman, L. (2001). Solution of a Satisfy Problem on a Gel-based DNA Computer. *The 6th International Workshop on DNA Based Computing, London: Springer-verlag*, 27-42.

Cui, G., Li, C., & Zhang, X. (2009). Application of DNA Computing by Self-assembly on 0-1 Knapsack Problem. *Advances in neural networks*, (5583), 684-693.

Cui, G., Niu, Y., Wang, Y., & Pan, L. (2007). A New Approach Based on PSO Algorithm to Find Good Computational Encoding Sequences. *Progress in Natural Science*, (17): 712–716.

Cukras, A., Faulhammer, D., & Lipton, R. (1998). Chess Games: A Model for RNA-based Computation. *The 4th International Meeting on DNA based Computer. Baltimore, Penns*, 159-162.

Elsenda, F., Anna, S., & Ramon, E. (2001). Synthesis and Hybridization Properties of DNA and PNA Chimeras Carrying. *Bioorganic & Medicinal Chemistry*, *8*, 291–297.

Freud, R., & Păun, G. (1997). Watson-Crick finite Automata. *Proc of the Third Annual DIMACS symp, on DNA Based Computers, Philadephia*, 305-317.

Frutos, A. G. (1997). Demonstration of a Word Design Strategy for DNA Computing on Surface. *Nucleic Acids Research*, *25*(23), 4748–4757. doi:10.1093/nar/25.23.4748

Garzon, M., & Neathery, P. (1997). A New Metric for DNA Computing. *Proceedings of the 2nd Annual Genetic Programming Conference GP-97*, 472-487.

Gatterdam, R. (1989). Splicing System and Regularity. *Computer Math, 31*, 63–67.

Head, T. (1987). Formal Language Theory and DNA: An Analysis of the Generative Capacity of Specific Recombinant Behaviors. *Bulletin of Mathematical Biology, 49*, 737–759.

Head, T., Kaolan, P. D., & Bladergroen, R. (2000). Computing with DNA by Operating on Plasmids [J]. *Bio Systems, 57*, 87–93. doi:10.1016/S0303-2647(00)00091-5

Kari, L., & Resenberg. (1998). DNA Computing, Sticker System and Universality. *Acta Informatica, 35*(5), 401–420. doi:10.1007/s002360050125

Kari, L., & Păun, G., & Resenberg. (1998). DNA computing, Sticker System and Universality. *Acta Informatica, 35*(5), 401–420. doi:10.1007/s002360050125

Karl-Heize, Z. (2002). Efficient DNA Sticker Algorithm for NP Complete Graph Problems. *Computer Physics Communications, 81*, 1–9.

Kim, B., Song, J., & Wang, K. (2009). Prostate Cancer Classification Processor Using DNA Computing Technique. *IEICE Elutriations express*, (6), 581-586.

Lipton, R. (1995). DNA based computers. *Proc of a DIMCS workshop, Princeton.* Kari, L. (1991). On insertion and deletion in formal languages. *University of Turku.*

Lipton. (1996). DNA Solutions of Hard Combinational Problems. *Science, 268*, 542-548.

Liu, Q., & Frutos, A. G. (2000). DNA Computing on Surface. *Nature, 403*, 175–179. doi:10.1038/35001232

Martin, C., & Păun, G. (1998). Cooperating Distribute Splicing Systems. *Workshop on molecular computing, Mangalia Romania.*

Melkikh, A. (2008). DNA Computing, Computation Complexity and Problem of Biological Evolution Rate. *Acta Biotheoretica, 56*(4), 285–295. doi:10.1007/s10441-008-9055-8

Ouyang, Q., Kaplan, P. D., & Liu, S. (1997). DNA Solution of the Maximal Clique Problem. *Science, 278*, 446–449. doi:10.1126/science.278.5337.446

Păun, G. (1996). Regular Extended H systems are Computationally Universal. *Journal of Automata, Languages. Combinatorics, 1*, 27–36.

Păun, G., Rozenberg, & Salomaa, A. (1996). Computing by Splicing. *Theoretical Computer Science, 2*, 332–336.

Roweis, S., Winfree, E., & Burgoyne, R. (1996). A Sticker Based Architecture for DNA Computation. *In Proceeding of Second Annual Meeting on DNA Based Computers, DIMACS: Series in Discrete Mathematics and theoretical Science*, 1123-1126.

Saaid, M., & Ibrahim, Z. (2008). Fuzzy C-Meaus Clustering for DNA Computing Readout Method Implemented on Light Cycler System. *Proceedings of SICE annual conference*, 641-646.

Sakomata, Y., & Kobayashi, S. (2001). Sticker System with Complex Structure. *Soft Computing, 5*, 114–120. doi:10.1007/s005000000074

Song, T., Wang, S., & Ma, F. (2008a). *Triple Elements and Adding Elements DNA Encoding Methods.* System Engineering and Electrical Technology. (in Chinese)

Song, T., Wang, S., & Wang, X. (2008b). The Design of Reversible Gate and Reversible Sequential Circuit based on DNA Computing. *Proceedings of 2008 third International Conference on Intelligent System and Knowledge Engineering, IEEE*, 114-118.

Tulpan, D., Hoos, H., & Condon, A. (2002). Stochastic Local Search Algorithm for DNA Word Design. *DNA Computing: 8th International Workshop on DNA-Based Computers*, 229—241.

Wang, S. (2005). Solved Graph Coloring by DNA Sticker Model. *System Engineering and Electrical Technology*, 27(3), 568–573.

Wang, S., Song, T., & Li, E. (2009). The Design and Analysis of DNA Golay Codes [in Chinese]. *Acta Electronica Sinica*, 7, 1542–1545.

Wang, X., Bao, Z., & Hu, J. (2008). DNA Computing Solves the 3-SAT Problem with a Small Solution Space. *Current nanoscience, 4* (6), 354-360.

Wu, H. (2001). An Improved Surface-Based Method for DNA Computing. *Bio Systems*, *59*, 1–5. doi:10.1016/S0303-2647(00)00133-7

Xu, J. (2004). Stickerter Model(II): Applications. *Chinese Science Bulletin*, 2, 223–225.

Yang, Y. X., Wang, A. M., & Ma, J. L. (2009). A DNA Computing Algorithm of Addition Arithmetic. *Proceedings of the first international workshop on education technology and computer science*, 1056-1059.

Yokomori, T., & Kobayashi, S. (1997). On the Power of Circular System and DNA Computing. *IEEE*. 219-224.

Zhang, X., Wang, Y., & Cui, G. (2009). Application of a novel IWO to the design of encoding sequences for DNA computing. *Computers & Mathematics with Applications (Oxford, England)*, *57*(11), 2001–2008. doi:10.1016/j.camwa.2008.10.038

Zhang, Z., Shi, X., & Liu, J. (2008). A Method to Encrypt Information with DNA Computing. *The third international conference on bio-inspired computing: theory and application*, 155-159.

Chapter 6
Kansei Database and AR*–Tree for Speeding up the Retrieval

Yaokai Feng
Kyushu University, Japan

ABSTRACT

Along with Kansei information being successfully introduced to information retrieval systems, particularly multimedia retrieval systems, many Kansei retrieval systems have been implemented in the past two decades. And, it has become clear that the traditional multimedia retrieval systems using key-words or/and other text information are not enough in many applications, because that they can not deal with sensitive words reflecting user's subjectivity. In this chapter, Kansei retrieval systems efficiently taking user's subjectivity into account will be discussed in detail. Like many traditional retrieval systems, Kansei retrieval systems are also based on databases system, which are called Kansei databases. After roughly introducing some existing Kansei retrieval systems is a general flow for designing Kansei retrieval systems. Also, we will discuss how to speed up the Kansei retrieval systems by using multidimensional indexing technologies and you will learn that our proposed multidimensional index structure, Adaptive R*-tree (AR*-tree for short), is more suitable to Kansei retrieval systems than the traditional multidimensional indexing technologies.

1. INTRODUCTION

Information retrieval systems are certainly user-oriented, where how to reflect *user's subjectivity* becomes an important and hard problem. When a user wants to search for something, for instance a passenger car or a costume, he/she normally have a kind of feeling such as "graceful and looks intelligent, but not so expensive." This feeling is called as *"Kansei"* in Japanese, which means the user's psychological feeling as well as the physiological issues. Unfortunately, traditional information retrieval systems cannot efficiently deal with the search requests given with Kansei words.

In recent decades, Kansei retrieval systems that can process Kansei words and Kansei in-

DOI: 10.4018/978-1-61692-797-4.ch006

formation have attracted many attentions. Like many *traditional retrieval systems*, the Kansei retrieval systems are also based on databases (called *Kansei databases*) and Kansei is usually expressed with emotional words such as beautiful, romantic fantastic, comfortable, calm, and so on. For instance, image retrieval systems having an ability to handle subjective expressions are useful especially when the users, who have not enough knowledge about contents of the image database and have no specific query image, try to retrieve unknown images using some *Kansei words* (e.g., " beautiful", "calm", etc.). However, because the key-words processes in traditional retrieval systems are registered by operators and they are influenced by the operators' subjectivities, it is difficult to obtain the data based on user's feeling or Kansei by using the traditional key-word retrieving methods. This means that the traditional retrieval systems using key-words or/and other text information cannot deal with sensitive words reflecting user's subjectivity. Thus, they are not enough in many applications.

In this chapter, after briefly introducing some existing Kansei retrieval systems, a general flow for designing Kansei retrieval systems is presented. Then, we will discuss how to speed up Kansei retrieval processes using multidimensional indexing technologies. Some existing *multidimensional index structures* that are possibly used to Kansei retrieval systems are introduced. From the discussions and experimental result, you will learn that our proposed index structure, *Adaptive R*-tree* (*AR*-tree* for short), is more suitable to Kansei retrieval systems than others. Finally, we will briefly summarize this chapter.

2. SOME EXISTING KANSEI RETRIEVAL SYSTEMS

Many *Kansei retrieval systems* aiming at specific applications have been proposed in the last two decades. Some selected examples are briefly introduced here.

Kurita (1992) proposed a retrieval method on image databases using sensitive words reflecting *user's subjectivity*. Because the user's subjectivity such as visual impressions (e.g., fantastic, nice…) may be very different from each other even to the same picture, it is difficult to register each picture along with the visual impressions of all the possible users. The authors adopted a learning stage, in which some typical pictures are selected for the users learning. And a relationship (user's model) can be obtained between the *sensitive words* of each user and the features of the pictures. This relationship can be used for future Kansei retrievals.

Fukuda (1995, 1996) proposed a method for a textile-design *image database system*. In this method, a relationship was built between Kansei words and the features of the images (e.g., the color or the pattern shape). This is similar to the idea in the work of Kurita (1992). In addition, a new human interface based on "Kansei" retrieval method using user models was developed for a distributed image database systems of textile designing. This method provided an easy and flexible access to the image database by specifying certain Kansei words that make users more satisfied with the retrieval result. Furthermore, the user model would be updated after evaluating the difference between his/her Kansei and objective model based on knowledge-base.

Harada (1999) proposed a method for retrieving the relevance between Kansei words and the shape features of images. Their purpose is to study a methodology for building an image data retrieval system. The system can accept natural language sentences that contain subjective expressions. In this method, images are retrieved interactively using comparative sentences. In order to interpret sentences including subjective expressions and match the images, a space that binds subjective expressions and image features is introduced. The conditions that the space should satisfy and a method to construct such a space are discussed. As an example, a process for constructing and evaluating the shape feature space of "chairs" is proposed, and an experimental image retrieval system for office chairs was developed, which can deal with natural language including *subjective expressions*.

Endo (2001) implemented a Kansei database for Ise Katagami (one kind of Japanese paper) design using lattices and unit structures. In this system, the concept of "layers" is introduced to create the perceived characteristics of Ise Katagami. A five-layer structure is used to characterize each kind of Ise Katagami. For example, Layer 3 indicates surface grating and layer 4 is unit structure. After processing the auto-correlation function, luminescent spots in each image represent a plane grate, and each area enclosed in the luminescent spots represents a unit structure. By use of this method, even plane grates also can be extracted easily. Consequently, this system provides an easy way to retrieve Ise Katagami, which is usually difficult by traditional pattern matching.

Miura (2002) proposed a music retrieval system which could estimate individual characteristics of music data based on users' sensibility. It estimates each user's interest (*user model*) from the history about which data he/she had accessed and it also estimates characteristics of music data (music title model) from the history about which users have accessed.

Tsutsumi (2004) proposed a method to retrieve a building name from the users' impression to the buildings.

Baek (2006) proposed an image retrieval system based on Kansei of colors, in which natural language was used for *Kansei representations* even including the image structures. A method for background image retrieval using Kansei words to represent the sensibility of colors was proposed. In order to process Kansei information, an adaptive Lesk algorithm (Banerjee, 2002) in WordNet (George, 1995) was used and, according to the experiment result, the average user's satisfaction rate was reportedly up to 63%.

Ogino (2006) proposed a method (called Kansei System Modeling) for designing Kansei retrieval systems, which retrieves multimedia contents that can meet individual's subjective criteria about similarity or impressions to multimedia contents. In this method, Kansei Framework Diagram and Kansei System Process are proposed for system engineers designing and developing Kansei retrieval systems. The Kansei Framework Diagram can simulate an individual's evaluation process of similarities or impressions on multimedia contents.

3. GENERAL FLOW OF KANSEI RETRIEVAL SYSTEMS

Most of the existing Kansei retrieval systems aim at specific applications and they are very different from each other. Anyway, according to my investigations and analysis, it has been found that the designing efficiency and system performance can be improved much if a general flow is followed in the designing phase. For example, a relationship should be built between Kansei (subjective) expressions and features of the objects such as images, videos, music, and so on. In order to build this relationship, a large number of objects along with their features and their Kansei (subjective) expressions (words) from different people should be obtained in advance. In addition, since the *Kansei expressions* may vary much from different people, the selected users should be grouped and an above-mentioned relationship should be built for each of user groups. The relationships for user groups are called user models. A general structure of Kansei retrieval systems is shown in Figure 1.

This system can be divided into two parts: *registration part* and *query part*. In the registration part, the quantitative features are extracted from every original object (images, videos, music and so on), which is called "*pattern extracting*". After

Figure 1. A typical structure of databases –based Kansei retrieval systems

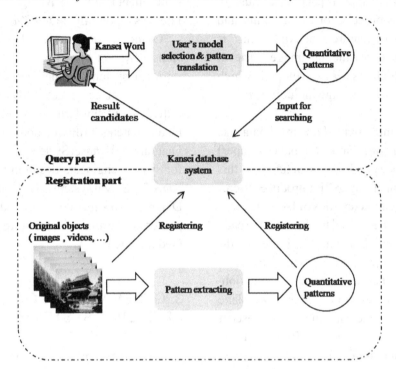

that, every original image and its corresponding *quantitative features* are registered in the database system. There are many kinds of features can be used in this process of pattern extracting. For example, histogram, texture, local autocorrelation features, local contrast, and so on (Ogino, 2006).

In the query part, because Kansei words vary much from different users even to the same object. Thus, the user model selection is necessary. That is, after the user gives some Kansei (subjective) words (e.g., calm, romantic, and etc.) to the system for query, a specific user model is selected for this user. Then, the translation function will create a specific *quantitative pattern* according to the given Kansei words, which is used to implement a specific search in the database system. For the users that have already been known by the system, the corresponding user model can be found easily. For such users that the system does not know, by asking the user some prepared questions, the system can determine which user group the cur-

rent user should belong to and which user model should be used for this user.

Obviously, the *user models* play an important role for the query result. Here, let's see how to build the user models. Although there are actually many specific methods to build the user models, the following four phases are generally needed: 1) selecting sample objects and users, 2) collecting primitive *Kansei words*, 3) clustering users, and 4) learning. The four phases are shown in Figure 2.

In Phase 1 of selecting sample objects and users, some typical objects distributed in a broad range are selected as samples. Clustering all the objects in advance may be helpful. At the same time, some potential users (or say, user representatives) having different backgrounds are also selected. In Phase 2 of collecting primitive Kansei words, every selected object is labeled with *Kansei words* by the selected potential users. There are some different methods to conduct Phase 2. The examples include (1) *SD (Semantic Differential) method*: a rating scale designed to measure

Figure 2. General flow for building users' models

the connotative meaning of objects, events, and concepts. The connotations are used to derive the attitude towards the given objects, events or concepts. The selected potential users are asked to choose where their positions lie, on a scale between two bipolar adjectives. SD method is today one of the most widely used scales in the measurement of attitudes, (2) *keyword method*. The selected people only need to select one or some of keywords from a decided keyword set for each of such selected objects, and (3) *weighted keyword method*. This method is extended from the above keyword method. The selected people need to decide a weight for each of their decided keywords to indicate the degree to which the current object meets this keyword.

In Phase 3, all the selected people are clustered according to the Kansei words collected from them about the selected objects. And, all the people having similar Kansei are clustered into the same group. After that, Phase 4 will build a user model for each of the user groups obtained in Phase 3. In this phase, learning is needed to find the relationship for each of user groups between Kansei words and the contents of the objects. The technologies that can be used in this learning phase include regression analysis, particularly multiple regression analysis, canonical correlation analysis, *discriminant analysis*, principal components analysis, statistical factor analysis, and so on.

Briefly, when the user uses this system for *Kansei retrieval*, he/she only needs to submit to this system some Kansei words or natural language reflecting his/her subjectivity. After that, the part of *users' models and Translation* in this system plays the role of transforming the user-given request into corresponding pattern (quantitative

features) that the database system can recognize. The *quantitative pattern* will be sent to the database system for retrieving. Finally, the retrieval results (actually result candidates) are presented to the user.

Now, let's see the last part in Figure 1: the Kansei database system, which should be able to efficiently manage the original objects along with their corresponding *quantitative features* (or say feature vectors), and can answer the query requests using quantitative patterns translated from the Kansei words that reflect the users' real purposes. Most of relational database management systems (*RDBMSs*) can be used here. However, the key technology is indexing. Since the quantitative feature vectors of original objects are all with many feature values, multidimensional index technology can be used to speed up the query processing. Thus,, we need to choose one from the existing *multidimensional index structures* or design a new indexing structure for every specific Kansei database system. This topic will be discussed in the next section.

4. INDEXING TECHNOLOGIES FOR SPEEDING UP KANSEI RETRIEVAL

Besides the user's *satisfaction rate*, the *response time* is also an important factor for any retrieval systems. It is explained in this section how to improve the *response time* of Kansei retrieval systems using multidimensional indexing technologies. At first, it will be pointed out that the retrievals in Kansei database systems can be regarded as range queries in *multidimensional spaces*. Then, some multidimensional index structures that

Figure 3. Every query in Kansei database systems is a range query

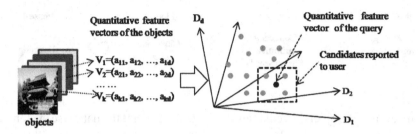

can be applied for *Kansei database systems* are introduced. After detailed discussion and experiments on performance comparison, we will learn that our proposed index structure (AR*-tree) has efficiently considered the features of Kansei retrievals and is more suitable to *Kansei retrieval systems* than others.

Regarding Queries in Kansei Database Systems as Range Queries

In the *Kansei database systems*, the registered quantitative feature values for each of the objects form a vector, called quantitative feature vector. Each of *quantitative feature vectors* can be regarded as one point in a *multidimensional space* (called *feature vector space*) and the dimensionality of the *feature vector space* is the number of values in each of quantitative feature vectors. In this way, the quantitative feature vectors of all the objects registered in the database form a set of points in the multidimensional vector space (see Figure 3). When querying, the user-given Kansei words are translated into a *quantitative feature vector* which can also be mapped into one point in the vector space. In Kansei retrieval systems, exact queries trying to find the objects that exactly match quantitative feature vectors of the input queries are generally unrealistic and unnecessary for most cases. Obviously, all the similar objects to the quantitative feature vector translated from the user-given *Kansei words* should be reported to the user as candidates (see Figure 3). Here, it should be noted that the similar

objects will be mapped into neighboring points in the vector space.

In this way, the queries in the *Kansei database systems* become *range queries* in the multidimensional vector space. That is, all the objects in the feature vector space that are distributed near to the point mapped from the query feature vector (translated from the user-given Kansei words) should be reported to the user.

Since the queries in Kansei database systems can be implemented by multidimensional range queries, the *multidimensional indexing technologies* can be used to speed up the query process. However, to the best of my knowledge, no study has been done on introducing multidimensional indexes to *Kansei database systems*.

Many index structures have been proposed in the database community in the recent decades. Examples include *R*-tree* (Beckmann, 1990), X-tree (Berchtold, 1996), SR-tree (Katayama, 1997) and A-tree (Sakurai, 2000). Gaede and Gunther (1998) conducted a survey on multidimensional indices and a more recent survey has been presented by Cui (2003). Some of these index structures (esp. R-tree family) have been popularly used in researches and several commercial database products (Informix, 2004; Adler, 2001).

Using R*-Tree for Kansei Database Systems

R*-tree is a famous and popular variant of above-mentioned *R-tree* family and it can be efficiently used for many kinds of applications for indexing

Figure 4. (a) Multidimensional data space; (b) structure of R*-tree; (c) Structure of R*-tree node; (d) Expression of MBR in R*-tree node

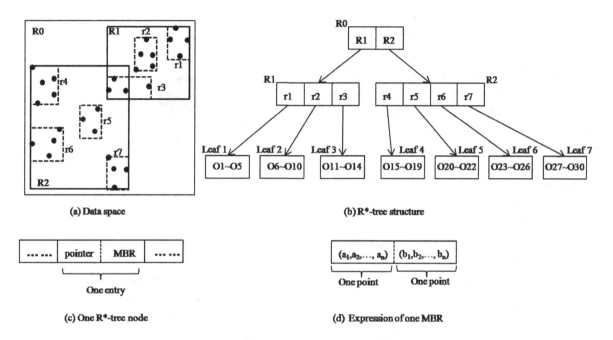

multidimensional data. It is also can be used in *Kansei database systems*.

R*-tree is a hierarchy of nested multidimensional *MBRs (Minimum Bounding Rectangles)*. Each non-leaf node of the R*-tree contains an array of entries, each of which consists of a pointer and an *MBR*. The pointer refers to one child node of this node and the *MBR* is the minimum bounding rectangle of the child node referred to by the pointer. When the R*-tree is used for a range query, only the nodes intersecting the *query range* are accessed and their entries are checked. The other nodes can be skipped. Figure 4 shows an example of R*-tree.

In the example shown in Figure 4, the entire data space is divided into subspace recursively (Figure 4 (a)) and each of the subspaces corresponds to one R*-tree node (Figure 4 (b)). The entire data space corresponds to the root node of the R*-tree and each subspace corresponds to one of the entries of its parent node and each of the entries in R*-tree nodes is expressed into the MBR

of its corresponding subspace of the data space (Figure 4 (c)). In each R*-tree node, every MBR is expressed by two points: one is the point that has the minimum coordinate in each axis among all the points in this subspace and the other point is the one that has the maximum coordinate in each axis among all the points in this subspace (Figure 4 (d)).

Disadvantages of Using R*-Tree or Other Naïve Methods for Kansei Database Systems

According to my investigations, the required range queries in Kansei database systems are special. Concretely, the importance degree (or say "weight") of the features (dimensions in the data space) are probably different from each other, which means that the users usually emphasize only part of the features of the objects in each of specific queries. Thus, partial dimensions (not all) of the entire *multidimensional index space* are usually enough for actual Kansei retrievals. That is, the quantitative feature vectors in the database system tend to have many feature values, only part of which, however, are necessary in each of actual retrievals. Such queries are called partially-dimensional (PD) range queries in this chapter. In these queries, the query ranges are given only in some dimensions (not all) of the *index space*. On the contrary, those having query ranges given in all the dimensions of the feature vector space are called all-dimensional (AD) range queries.

Because every node of the R*-tree contains the information of its entries at all of the index dimensions, when R*-tree in the entire n-dimensional index space is used for a PD range query with d ($d < n$) query dimensions, the *PD range query* can be evaluated by simply extending the query range in each of the other (n-d) irrelevant index dimensions to the entire data range.

The advantage of this approach is that only one index is necessary. However, each of the *R*-tree* nodes contains n-dimensional information of all its entries and only d-dimensional information of them is necessary for a PD range query using d ($d < n$) query dimensions. This means that a great deal of unnecessary information, i.e., the information in the irrelevant (n-d) dimensions, also has to be read from disk, which obviously degrades the query performance. A rough mathematical analysis will be given later.

There are still the following two naïve methods for the PD range queries in the Kansei database systems: multi-Btree and multiple multidimensional indices.

1. Multi-Btree

In this naïve approach, using the projections of the quantitative feature vectors on each of the index dimensions, one *B-tree* (or a variant thereof) is constructed for each index dimension. For a PD range query, the corresponding B-trees are used individually and their results are intersected to obtain the final query result. In total, n B-trees should

Figure 5. A PD range query using multi-Btree

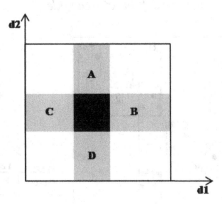

be constructed in advance for an n-dimensional index space.

Figure 5 is an example of a PD range query evaluated using the multi-Btree, where the two dimensions (d_1 and d_2) are used as query dimensions and the thick shadow region is the given query range. In this example, two B-trees constructed on the dimensions of d_1 and d_2 are used. At first, two range queries are evaluated on the two B-trees, respectively. All of the objects located in the vertical shadow region and the horizontal shadow region are reported as intermediate results, R_1 and R_2. The final result of this range query is given by intersecting them.

The disadvantage of multi-Btree is that queries on different B-trees are evaluated independently without any mutual reference. That is, during searching on every B-tree, the algorithm cannot realize the query ranges in the other index dimensions. Thus, unnecessary checks such as those in regions A, B, C, and D in Figure 5 cannot be pruned. Many unnecessary investigations are thus performed, a great deal of irrelevant information is read from disk and many unnecessary intermediate results are reported by every B-tree. In addition to the unnecessary I/O operations, the intersection phase is also very time-consuming. Considering a dataset having 1,000,000 data points uniformly distributed in a six-dimensional space. Assume that the given PD range query has four

Figure 6. General structure of AR*-tree

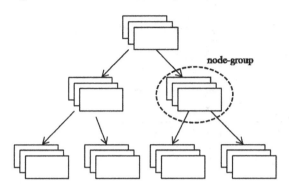

Figure 7. General structure of node-groups in an n-dimensional AR*-tree

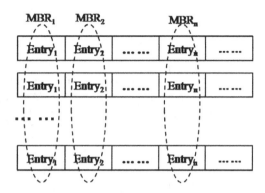

query dimensions and the query range in each of the four query dimensions is 1/6 of the entire data range. In this case, the final result of this query has only $1,000,000/6^4 = 771$ objects (quantitative feature vectors). However, the query result on each of the four B-trees has $1,000,100/6=166,666$ objects! The total number of intermediate results is 666,666! Even if the query range in each of the query dimensions is decreased to 1/10 of the data range, the above three numbers are 100, 100,000 and 400,000, respectively. That is, although only 100 objects are in the final result, up to 400,000 objects are reported as intermediate results. Another disadvantage of the multi-Btree approach is that managing/updating many disk-resident B-trees requires additional costs.

2. Multiple Multidimensional Indices

It is a nature question that *"Why do not we prepare one index for each possible combination of query attributes?"* Since there are many possible actual combinations of index dimensions (quantitative features) used in the actual retrievals on Kansei database systems, it is not always feasible in applications with large datasets that one index is built for each of such possible combinations. This is because (1) numerous indices have to be constructed and managed, (2) many feature values are repeatedly included in different indices, which is too space-consuming for large datasets

and results in a large update cost, and (3) the combinations of index dimensions that are possibly used in the range queries of Kansei database systems are often unpredictable. Note that, there are a total of (2^n-1) different combinations for n index dimensions. Thus, this naïve method is not considered in this chapter.

Using Adaptive R*-Tree for Kansei Database Systems

Our proposal for *PD range queries* which is called Adaptive *R*-tree* or *AR*-tree* for short can be efficiently used for *Kansei database systems*.

1. General Structure

The key concept of the *AR*-tree* is that, instead of *n*-dimensional *R*-tree* nodes, the AR*-tree consists of *node-groups*, each of which have *n* one-dimensional nodes. Every node of node-groups holds information of its entries in only one dimension and each node-group holds the information in all the *n* dimensions. Note that each of the R*-tree nodes holds information of its entries at all of the dimensions. The general structure of the AR*-tree is depicted in Figure 6 and the structure of every node-group is shown in Figure 7. The structure of every node is generally the same as that of the R*-tree and the only difference is that

Figure 8. Example of entries of node-groups in a two-dimensional space

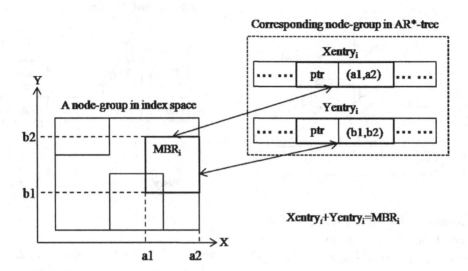

only one-dimensional information is contained in each of the AR*-tree node (not node-groups).

Here we note that the AR*-tree is not obtained by simply dividing each of R*-tree nodes into a node-group. This is because 1) the size of each node in node-groups of the AR*-tree is also one disk page, which is the same as the R*-tree nodes. And, different nodes in (even the same) node-groups are stored in a separate disk pages, and 2) *n*-dimensional information of each entry is contained in every *R*-tree node*. However, only one-dimensional information of each entry is contained in every AR*-tree node. Thus, the number of entries in each of the *AR*-tree* nodes (not node-groups) is much larger than that in each of R*-tree nodes. Actually, several *R*-tree nodes* correspond to one node-group in the *AR*-tree*.

Figure 7 shows one *node-group* of the *AR*-tree*. All of the entries in the same place of the *n* different nodes of this *node-group* form a complete *n*-dimensional *MBR* in the index space. Whereas every entry in R*-tree nodes includes MBR information in all of the dimensions, every entry in the nodes of the AR*-tree includes only one-dimensional information. This means that each entry only corresponds to an MBR edge.

The term *entry of node-group* is used hereinafter, which refers to the set of entries having the same index distributed in all the different nodes of one node-group (see Figure 7). Every entry of each node-group corresponds to a complete MBR in the index space, such as $Xentry_i + Yentry_i$ in Figure 8. In Figure 7, all of the entries in an ellipse form an entry of this node-group. Figure 8 shows an example of entries in the node-group of the AR*-tree in a two-dimensional index space. In this example, each complete MBR is divided into two parts, which are separately contained in two nodes of one node-group. In this way, each entry in the nodes of the AR*-tree includes only one-dimensional information.

The question may arises that whether or not the number of nodes in the *AR*-tree* increase greatly. The answer is No. This is because the maximum number of entries in each node of the AR*-tree increases greatly since only one-dimensional information is contained in each node. According to the experiments, the number of nodes increases less than 10%.

The structure of the *AR*-tree* guarantees that it can be applied to *PD range queries* (retrievals in the Kansei database systems) with any combina-

Table 1. Algorithm for range query on the AR*-tree

```
Procedure RangeQuery (rect, node-group)
Input:    rect: query range
      node-group: initial node-group of the query

Output: result: all the tuples in rect

Begin
  For each entry e*) in node-group Do
    If e INTERSECT rect in all the query dimensions**) Then
      If (node-group is not at leaf) Then
        RangeQuery (rect, e.child);
        //e.child: the child node-group corresponding to e
      Else result     result+e
  EndFor
End
```

* An entry of a node-group includes all of the entries with the same index in the different nodes of this node-group and it corresponds to a complete *MBR*.

** When an entry of a node-group (corresponding to a *MBR*) is checked to determine whether it intersects the query range or not, only the nodes in the query dimensions are accessed and the other nodes even in the same node-group are skipped. Moreover, in many cases that an entry of a node-group is checked, even not all of the nodes in the query dimensions need to be checked. This is because that the investigation is done dimension by dimension, so it can stop if the current entry (*MBR*) is found not to intersect the query range in the current query dimension.

tions of the index dimensions and that only the information in the relevant dimensions is visited. Here we note that the AR*-tree is also able to deal with the retrievals in which all the dimensions of the index space (all the features in the feature vectors) are necessary. Thus, the *AR*-tree* is suitable for *Kansei database systems*.

2. Algorithms of AR*-Tree

The insert algorithm of the AR*-tree is a simply extensions of the counterparts of the R*-tree. After the new quantitative pattern reaches the leaf node-group, it is divided according to dimensions and stored in different nodes of the leaf node-group. If some node-group must be split, then all of its nodes have to be split at the same time and the split may be up propagated. After a delete operation, if the node-group under-flowed, then all of its nodes should be deleted at the same time and all of its entries are inserted to the AR*-tree again. That is,

Table 2. Symbols and their descriptions

n	Dimensionality of the entire index space
d	Number of the query dimensions
S	Volume of the entire index space
S_q	Volume of the extended query range of PD range query
M_r	Maximum number (capacity) of entries in each leaf node of R*-tree
M_g	Maximum number (capacity) of entries in each leaf node-group of AR*-tree
N_l	Number of leaf nodes in the case of R*-tree
N_g	Number of leaf node-groups in AR*-tree

all of the nodes in every node-group must be born and die simultaneously. A range query algorithm for the AR*-tree is shown in Table 1.

Starting with the root node-group, each entry of the current node-group needs to be checked to decide whether its *MBR* intersects the query range. If its MBR intersects the query range, and the current node-group is not at the leaf level, then this algorithm is invoked recursively with its child node-groups.

Mathematical Analysis on Performance of R*-Tree and AR*-Tree

In this section, under the assumption of uniform distribution, the performance of the *AR*-tree* for *PD range queries* is examined mathematically by comparing with the R*-tree. The number of accessed leaf nodes is estimated and compared since it is the most important factor with regard to query performance in many applications, especially for those having large datasets. The symbols used in this section are described in Table 2. Note that the extended query range of one PD range query refers to the *n*-dimensional range obtained by extending the unused (*n-d*) dimensions to their entire data ranges.

In the case of the R*-tree, the average number of leaf-node accesses (i.e., the number of leaf nodes intersecting the query range), R_l, can be given by

$$R_l = \frac{S_q}{S} \times N_l .$$

If the AR*-tree is used, then the average number of leaf node groups intersecting the query range, AR_g, can be given by

$$AR_g = \frac{S_q}{S} \times N_g .$$

Since the node sizes of the R*-tree and the AR*-tree are the same (on the basis of one node one disk page), the maximum number of entries in each leaf node of the AR*-tree is roughly n times that in each leaf node of the R*-tree. This is easy to understand considering that only one-dimensional information of each entry is contained in each of the AR*-tree nodes. In addition, considering that the clustering algorithms (insert algorithms) of the R*-tree and the AR*-tree are the same, we have

$$\frac{N_g}{N_l} \approx \frac{M_r}{M_g} \approx \frac{1}{n} .$$

In each accessed node-group, at most d nodes are visited for each d-dimensional PD range query. This is because that, although this query is relevant to d dimensions, investigation of each entry of node-group may stop midway. Thus, the number of leaf nodes (not the node-groups) that must be visited, AR_p can be given by

$$AR_l \leq AR_g \times d \approx \frac{S_q}{S} \times N_g \times d$$
$$\approx \frac{S_q}{S} \times \frac{1}{n} \times N_l \times d = \frac{d}{n} \times R_l < R_l \qquad (when \ d < n).$$

The last equation indicates that, for *PD range queries* with $d < n$, the number of accessed leaf nodes in the case of the AR*-tree is less than that in the case of the R*-tree. Even if $d = n$ (AD queries), then the number of accessed leaf nodes is approximately the same or the AR*-tree needs less accesses of leaf nodes than the R*-tree. Moreover, for a fixed n, the lower the number of query dimensions, d, the bigger the advantage of the AR*-tree compared to the R*-tree.

The last equation can be explained as follows. Because the capacity of each leaf node-group in the AR*-tree is roughly n times that of each leaf node in the R*-tree, the number of accessed leaf node-groups in the AR*-tree is approximately $1/n$ times that of the accessed leaf nodes in the R*-tree. However, in each of the accessed leaf node-groups of the AR*-tree, at most d nodes must be visited.

Experimental Comparison on Performance between R*-Tree and AR*-Tree

A dataset having 200,000 points in a six-dimensional space having Zipf distribution (the constant is 1.5) is used to examine the behavior of the AR*-tree for PD range queries (retrievals in Kansei database systems).

The page size of my system is 4096 bytes. Query performance is measured in term of the number of leaf node accesses. Although the price of main memory chips continues to drop and the size of main memory in many systems has increased greatly in recent years, indices (especially their leaf nodes) for large relational datasets still tend to be stored in secondary storage. That is, the I/O cost is still the performance bottleneck for many indexing systems having large datasets. Thus, many works on the disk-resident indexing systems use the number of node accesses, especially the number of leaf node accesses, as an important factor of search performance.

PD range queries are tested with different numbers of query dimensions (query dimensionalities) ranging from 1 to 5. Without loss of generality, the query ranges in all the query dimensions are

Table 3. The comparison experimental results (the numbers of leaf node accesses)

Query dimensionality	R*-tree vs AR*-tree	Size of query ranges					
		10%	20%	30%	40%	50%	60%
d=1	R*-tree	1389	2190	2561	3002	3484	4126
	AR*-tree	205	487	498	592	674	793
d=3	R*-tree	509	1480	1590	1924	2506	3498
	AR*-tree	124	412	487	690	996	1479
d=5	R*-tree	118	980	1096	1379	2108	3065
	AR*-tree	204	254	295	496	981	1680

set equally from 10% to 60% in increments of 10%. The range query for the range of the same size is repeated 100 times with random locations, and the averages are presented. The experimental result is shown in Table 3, in which *query dimensionality* means the number of dimensions (features) used in the specific retrievals and *size of query ranges* is the size (or say length) of one specific query range in each of the dimensions. Note that, we assume that all of the query ranges in the experiments are hyper-cubes. That means that the query range of every specific query has the same side length in all the query dimensions.

The result shows that the *AR*-tree* has better *query performance* than the *R*-tree* in any cases. And we can know that the performance of *PD range queries* on the *R*-tree* becomes better as the number of query dimensions increases. This is because the *search region* can be limited in more dimensions as the number of *query dimensions* increases.

5. SUMMARY AND FUTURE WORK

In this chapter, it was pointed out that the traditional multimedia retrieval systems using key-words or/ and other text information are not enough in many applications because that they can not deal with *sensitive words* reflecting user's subjectivity. After briefly introducing some existing *Kansei retrieval systems*, we proposed a general flow for building Kansei retrieval systems. Also, we discussed

how to speed up the retrieval process of Kansei retrieval systems using *multidimensional indexing technologies* and we learned that our proposed multidimensional index structure (called AR*-tree) seems to be more suitable to *Kansei retrieval systems* than the famous *multidimensional index structure* R*-tree. In the future, we are going to apply and evaluate the AR*-tree in real Kansei retrieval systems.

ACKNOWLEDGMENT

The author would like to thank Mr. Zhibin Wang, who conducted some of the experiments.

REFERENCES

Adler, D. W. (2001). DB2 Spatial Extender-Spatial Data with the RDBMS. In *Proceedings International Conference on Very Large Data Bases (VLDB)*, pp. 687-690.

Baek, S., Cho, M., Hwang, M., & Kim, P. (2006). *Kansei-based Image Retrieval Associated with Color. Lecture Notes in Artificial Intelligence (LNAI) 3849* (pp. 326–333). New York: Springer-Verlag.

Banerjee, T. P. (2002). An Adapted Lesk Algorithm for Word Sense Disambiguation Using WordNet. *In Proceedings the Third International Conference on Intelligent text Processing and Computational Linguistics*, pp. 136-145.

Beckmann, N., & Kriegel, H. (1990). The R*-tree: An Efficient and Robust Access Method for Points and Rectangles. In *Proceedings ACM SIGMOD International Conference*, pp. 322-331.

Berchtold, S., Keim, D., & Kriegel, H. (1996). The X-tree: An Index Structure for High- dimensional data. In *Proceedings the 22nd International Conference on Very large Data Bases (VLDB)*, pp. 28-39.

Chen, D., & Bovik, A. C. (1990). Visual Pattern Image Coding. *IEEE Transactions on Communications, 38*(12), 2137–2146. doi:10.1109/26.64656

Cui, Y. (2003). High-dimensional Indexing. [LNCS]. *Lecture Notes in Computer Science,* 2341.

Endou, Y., Ojika, T., Sato, H., & Harada, A. (2001). Construction of Kansei Database with Ise Katagami Lattice and Unit Structure: Extraction and Use of Cognitive Characteristics on Pattern Design. *Bulletin of Japanese Society for Science of Design, 48*(3), 119–124.

Feng, Y., & Makinouchi, A. (2006). Dfficient Evaluation of Partially-Dimensional Range Queries Using Adaptive R*-tree. In *Proceedings International Conference on Database and Expert Systems Applications (DEXA),* pp. 687-696.

Fukuda, M., Katsumoto, A., & Shibata, Y. (1995). Kansei Retrieve Method based on User Model. *Transactions of Information Processing Society of Japan, DPS, 95*(13), 43–48.

Fukuda, M., & Shibata, Y. (1996). Kansei Retrieval Method Reflecting Shape Pattern of Design Images. *Transactions of Information Processing Society of Japan. DPSWS, 96*(1), 267–274.

Gaede, V., & Gunther, O. (1998). Multidimensional Access Methods. *ACM Computing Surveys, 30*(2), 170–231. doi:10.1145/280277.280279

George, A. M. WordNet (1995): a Lexical database for English. *Communications on the ACM.* http://wordnet.cs.princeton.edu/

Harada, S., Itoh, Y., & Nakatani, H. (1999). On Constructing Shape Feature Space for Interpreting Subjective Expressions. *Transactions of Information Processing Society of Japan, 40*(5), 2356–2366.

Informix (2004). *Informix Spatial DataBlade Module.* ww306.ibm.com/software/data/ Informix /blades/spatial/rtree.html).

Katayama, N., & Satoh, S. (1997). The SR-tree: An Index Structure for High-Dimensional Nearest Neighbor Queries. In *Proceedings ACM SIGMOD International Conference*, pp.369-380.

Kurita, T., Kato, T., Fukuda, I., & Sakakura, A. (1992). Sense Retrieve on an Image Database of Full Color Paintings. *Transactions of Information Processing Society of Japan, 33*(10), 1373–1383.

Miura, M., Mitsuishi, T., Sasaki J., & Funyu, Y. (2002). A Music Retrieval System which Estimates Characteristics of Data based on Users' Sensibility. *Information Processing Society of Japan, SIG Notes, 2002*(3), 129-136.

Motomura, Y., Yoshida, K., & Fujimoto, K. (2000). Generative user models for adaptive Information Retrieval. In *Proceedings IEEE International Conference on System, Man and Cybernetics*, pp. 665-670.

Ogino, A., & Kato, T. (2006), Kansei System Modeling: Design Method for Kansei Retrieval Systems. *Transactions of Information Processing Society of Japan, 47.(SIG4) (TOD29)*, pp. 28-39.

Sakurai, Y. (2000), The A-tree: An Index Structure for High-Dimensional Space Using Relative Approximation. In *Proceedings the 26th International Conference on Very Large Data Bases (VLDB)*, pp. 516-526.

Tsutsumi, K. (2004). A Development of the Building Kansei Information Retrieval System. In Proceedings *the International Conference on Computing in Civil and Building Engineering, pp.* 174-181.

Zhang, C. (2001). On Supporting Containment Queries in Relational Database Management Systems. In *Proceedings ACM SIGMOD International Conference*, pp. 425-436.

KEY TERMS AND DEFINITIONS

Multimedia Database: A database that hosts one or more primary media file types such as documents, images, videos, audio, etc.

Kansei Words: Such words that reflect the subjective feelings of people. For example, calm, romantic, simple, gorgeous, etc.

Kansei Retrieval: In Kansei retrieval, the user uses Kansei words as query input. That is, the systems can response to the queries given using some Kansei words.

Kansei Database: A database that hosts objects along with the Kansei information about them from people. And, it can deal with Kansei retrieval.

Multidimensional Index: A data structure built in multidimensional space in order to speed up the retrieval process for multidimensional data.

Multidimensional Range Query: The user gives a range in the multidimensional index space and the query tries to retrieve all the objects in this range.

Multidimensional MBR: Abbreviation of Minimum Bounding Rectangles. It is the minimum multidimensional rectangles that can hold all the multidimensional objects in an object group (e.g., node).

R*-Tree: A famous multidimensional index structure. It is a hierarchical structure of nested multidimensional MBRs.

Chapter 7
Emotional Semantic Detection from Multimedia:
A Brief Overview

Shang-fei Wang
University of Science and Technology of China, China

Xu-fa Wang
University of Science and Technology of China, China

ABSTRACT

Recent years have seen a rapid increase in the size of digital media collections. Because emotion is an important component in the human classification and retrieval of digital media, emotional semantic detection from multimedia has been an active research area in recent decades. This chapter introduces and surveys advances in this area. First, the authors propose a general frame of research on affective multimedia content analysis, which includes physical, psychological and physiological space, alongside the relationships between the three. Second, the authors summarize research conducted on emotional semantic detection from images, videos, and music. Third, three typical archetypal systems are introduced. Last, explanations of several critical problems that are faced in database, the three spaces, and the relationships are provided, and some strategies for problem resolution are proposed.

1. INTRODUCTION

In recent times, with the development of many kinds of multimedia, our moods are continually being influenced by them. A change in mood is particularly anticipated when watching TV, seeing a movie, or playing an electronic game. Interestingly, multimedia may bring pleasure, tension, and even fear that audience members want to enjoy. However, inappropriate audiovisual stimuli may also cause unnecessary harm. For instance, on December 16, 1997, at around 6:50 p.m., 685 Japanese children and some adults fainted suddenly while watching a popular animated TV program called *Pocket Monsters*. The reason for the fainting was photosensitive epilepsy (Tobimatsu, Zhang, Tomoda, Mitsudome, & Kato, 1999). Therefore, it is important to investigate the relationships between multimedia and users' emotional response, which calls for the interdisciplinary study of people and multimedia that would embrace psychology, psychophysiology,

DOI: 10.4018/978-1-61692-797-4.ch007

aesthetics, and information science. This chapter focuses mainly on recent advances from the viewpoint of information science.

With the rapid growth in types of multimedia, an efficient method for organizing, browsing, searching, and retrieving elements such as images, videos, and music becomes crucial. Emotion is an important natural component in human classification of information, beyond feature and cognitive level (Hanjalic, 2001). Therefore, emotional semantic detection from multimedia, known as affective multimedia content analysis, has become a new and promising area of research in the past decades. It will be beneficial to various applications, including the following:

- Personal recommendation. If we can identify tense, relaxed, sad, or joyful parts of a movie, or the highlight of a soccer game, we may recommend it to users who are interested in these things.
- Digital entertainment. We can enhance users' feelings when they play electronic games through music, images, or video with a fixed emotion.
- Psychotherapy. A tool that would be capable of detecting emotion from multimedia could be helpful for a psychotherapist who seeks music or videos that would motivate a patient who is doing recovery exercises.
- Green information environment. By removing unpleasant segments from videos, we can provide a healthy environment, for example, avoiding the *Pocket Monsters* event.
- Multimedia retrieval. Users typically rely on concepts and semantics to retrieve information. Emotion is one of these ways. For example, a beautiful image, romantic music, or an exciting video segment. We are able to provide emotion-based multimedia retrieval if we can efficiently identify emotion in media.

2. A GENERAL FRAME OF RESEARCH ON AFFECTIVE MULTIMEDIA CONTENT ANALYSIS

Because research deals with multimedia and the human emotion induced by them, the framework should consist of physical, psychological, and physiological space, in addition to the relationships between the three (see Figure 1). Physical space is used to represent multimedia, while psychological and physiological space represent subjective and physiological emotional responses, respectively. For each space, we should consider the content of the space. For their relationships, we should focus on users' modeling and individualizing models.

Physical Space

Physical space should include several sensitive visual and audio features to represent multimedia. Although many kinds of visual- and audio-feature extraction methods have been proposed, little is known about the relationship between the features and human emotion. Therefore, selecting sensitive features is a key issue when building physical space.

Domain knowledge in the fields of art, advertising, cinematography, and psychophysiology is useful for feature selection. The influence of several features on human affective states have been investigated, such as color and lines in art images, motion and shot length in film, etc. Most researchers propose their features after considering the domain knowledge. However, there is no authoritative comparison to evaluate the effectiveness of these features. Furthermore, there is no evidence about whether these features can be used for general occasions. Therefore, the machine learning method is another choice for feature selection, such as Multivariate Analysis of Variance (MANOVA), and Stepwise Backward Selection Method (SBSM), among others.

Figure 1. A framework of research on affective multimedia content analysis

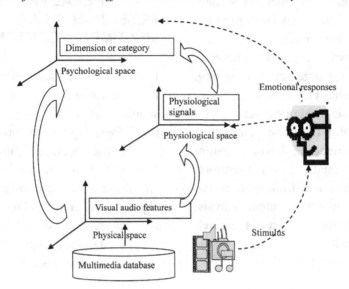

Psychological Space

Psychological space is adopted to represent a user's subjective response. In studies of emotion, there are two primary theoretical frameworks. One conceptualizes emotion discretely, while the other regards emotion as a dimensional construction. Therefore, the psychological space may be either discrete or continuous.

Many emotion theorists have claimed that there is a set of basic emotions. Different theorists have proposed different types of basic emotions. Although psychologists have yet to yield commonly agreed-on definitions for the prototypes of emotion, Ekman's six basic emotions are the most salient and frequently used categories in the field of information science, which include happiness, sadness, anger, disgust, fear, and surprise. Adjectives, from beautiful to ugly, are also often used to describe users' subjective response to images or music. In this case, factor analysis is adopted to obtain an orthogonal space.

Dimensional views of emotion have been advocated and applied by a large number of researchers through the years. Most researchers agree that three dimensions are enough to describe subjec-

tive response. However, a consensus has not been reached on the labels of the dimensions. Terms such as valence and arousal are frequently used in the field of information science (Hanjalic & Xu, 2005). Pleasure, arousal, and dominance are also used in some research (Arifin & Cheung, 2007).

Physiological Space

Physiological space is adopted to represent physiological emotion response. It may include the physiological signals that have been shown to be useful in assessing emotions, such as galvanic skin resistance (GSR), electrocardiogram (ECG), electromyograms (EMG), and electroencephalogram (EEG).

Most present researchers of affective multimedia content analysis only focus on humans' subjective response using emotional categories or dimensions, which have been labeled artificially. Subjective assessment is an easy and direct method. But it has some problems, such as an inaccurate definition, indeterminacy of the opinion scale and the response bias to true feeling. Physiological signals, as a kind of objective data, may avoid these problems, and can be useful supplements to emotional subjective assessment. Only a few studies introduce physiological signals to analyze the relationships between emotion and multimedia (J. Kim & Andre, 2008; Money & Agius, 2009; Mohammad Soleymani, Guillaume Chanel, Joep J.M. Kierkels, & Thierry Pun, 2008; Toyosawa & Kawai, 2009). With the advancement of wearable systems that record physiological signals, it is becoming feasible to employ these signals to analyze multimedia and the emotion they induce.

Relationships

There exist three relationships among the three spaces: physical vs. psychological space, physical vs. physiological space, and physiological vs. psychological space. The last belongs to the research of emotion recognition from physiological signals, which is beyond the scope of this chapter (R.W. Picard, E. Vyzas, & Healey, 2001; Wagner, Kim, & Andre, 2005). Because only a few studies introduce physiological signals into emotional semantic detection from multimedia, most research only focuses on the relationship between physical and psychological space, which is called "user modeling" in this paper. Variants

of well-known learning methods have been employed, such as Neural Networks (NN), Support Vector Machine (SVM), fuzzy theory and Hidden Markov Models (HMM). Emotion is subjective and user-dependent, so the pre-modeled relationship may be not suitable for everyone and the individualizing process is necessary. Similar to people understanding each other through communication, this individualizing process should also be interactive, dynamic, and adaptive.

3. EMOTIONAL SEMANTIC DETECTION FROM IMAGES

Emotional semantic detection from images was first studied in Japan in the 1990s. They uses the Japanese word "Kansei" instead of emotional or affective at that time. Table 1 provides an overview of the research from 1998 to present, with respect to the utilized features, feature selection, emotion presentation, classifier, performance, database, and individuation. A missing entry means that the matter at hand was either not reported or remained unclear from the available literature.

Table 1. Emotional semantic detection from images

References	Features	Feature Selection	Emotion Presentation	Classifier	Performance	Database	Individualized
(Hayashi & Hagiwara, 1998)	RGB color, projection distributions, spectrum		27 adj: sunny, cloudy, soft, hard, rich, solemn, hot, warm, cool, cold, dry, fresh, pretty, pleasant, strong, rustic, romantic, lonely, mysterious, urban, clear, peaceful, calm, young, elegant, severe, active. 8words: spring, summer, fall, winter, sunset, night, country, marchen	NN	RR:75.5%	120 images	
(Yoshida, Kato, & Yanaru, 1998)	intensity of luminance, color balance between red and green, color balance between yellow and blue		10adj: warm, soft, natural, clear, elegant, chic, authentic, classic, gorgeous, dynamic.	canonical correlation analysis		200 color paintings	Adjust weights by users feedback

continued on following page

Table 1. continued

References	Features	Feature Selection	Emotion Presentation	Classifier	Performance	Database	Individualized
(Bianchi-Berthouze & Catarci, 2003)	color, tone, intensity, morphology, position, area, length, direction, texture		increasable	NN	P:38.9%	From web	Adapt ion through relevance feedback
(Shibata & Kato, 1999)	color: RGB and lab spaces direction: a horizontal, a vertical and two diagonal ones	factor analysis	23 pairs of adj: likable/unlikable, beautiful/ugly, comfortable/uncomfortable, calm/restless, reliable/anxious, relaxing/dense, deep/shallow, spacious/confined, dispersed/crowed, soft/hard, warm/cold, orderly/disorderly, unified/not unified, light/heavy, varied/monotonous, feminine/masculine, new/old, modern/historical, novel/old-fashioned, clear/unclear, large-scale/small-scale, cheerful/gloomy, impressive/not impressive.	regression analysis		68 street landscape images	
(S. Wang, 2002; S. F. Wang, Chen, Li, & Wang, 2001)	color, shape, texture	PCA	18 pairs of adj: likable/unlikable, beautiful/ugly, coordinated/uncoordinated, romantic/not romantic, hot/cold, warm/cool, light/dark, soft/hard, orderly/disorderly, clear/unclear, quiet/noisy, impressive/unimpressive, relaxing/repressive, varied/monotonous, vivid/bleak, spacious/confined.	SVM	P:84%	1004 images	Interactive Genetic algorithm
(Mao, Chen, & Muta, 2003)	fractal dimensions(FD)		7 pairs of adj: monotonous/mussy, noisy/quiet, oppressive/active, worldly/elegant, decadent/inspiring, artificial/natural, ugly/beautiful.			500 images	
(Wang Weining, 2005)	color weighted line direction-length Vector		16 pairs of adj: modern/historical, strong/weak, light/dark, dreamlike/practical, simple/complex, active/oppressive, ornate/simple, dynamic/static, relaxing/dense, vivid/bleak, warm/cool, showy/elegant, clear/unclear, happy/sad, comfortable/uncomfortable	SVM	SR:78.0% RR:87.3%	85 images 110 images	
(W. Lu & Ni, 2005)	color, entropy features of region of interest		18 adj: beautiful,wet,modern,likable ,romantic,pleasant,bright,lively,complex,cold,quiet,grand ,broad,impressive,orderly,clear.vivid,dense.	NN	P:77.63%	300 scenic images	

continued on following page

Table 1. continued

References	Features	Feature Selection	Emotion Presentation	Classifier	Performance	Database	Individualized
(S.-J. Kim, Kim, Jeong, & Kim, 2006)	color, texture		6 pairs of adj: warm/cold, light/dark, cheerful/dismal, fun/sober, strong/weak, hard/soft.	fuzzy rule based	RR:84.8%	160 textile images	
(Datta, Joshi, Li, & Wang, 2006)	light and colorfulness, saturation and hue, familiarity measure, the rule of thirds, wavelet-based texture, size and aspect ratio, region composition, low depth of field indicators, shape convexity	one-dimensional SVM	aesthetics scores in the range of (1.0-7.0)	tree-based approaches	RR: 70.12%	3581 images	
(YOO, 2006)	30 color patters color code gray code		13 pairs of adj: like/dislike,beautiful/ ugly,natural/unnatural,dynamic/ static,warm/cold,gay/ sober,cheerful/dismal,unstable/ stable,light/dark,strong/ weak,gaudy/plain,hard/ soft,heavy/light.	similarity measurement	RR:64%	450 images	relevance feedback algorithm
(H. Li, Li, Song, & Chen, 2007)	texture: directionality, contrast coarseness		12 pairs of adj: homogeneous/ nonhomogenous, geometrical/ non-geometrical, soft/rough, fine/coarse, with lines/without lines, flat/non flat, regular/irregular, symmetrical/asymmetrical, clear/dark, simple/complex, defined/diffuse, natural/artificial.	fuzzy recognize degree-clustering		200 MIT texture images	
(Eun-Jong & Joon-Whoan, 2008)	edge histogram, descriptor homogeneous texture descriptor color structure descriptor color layout descriptor scalable color descriptor	different feature for different adj.	3 pairs of adj.: static/dynamic, light/heavy, cool/warm.		retrieval satisfaction > 90% in the 3.15-th retrieval	5625 natural images	consistency feedback and construction of multiple queries
(Fu & Cao, 2008; Jianning & Restrepo, 2008)	texture direction, the coarseness of texture, the texture color hue and brightness, the contrast and the intensity of the texture		2 adj. ornate/simple	BPNN	RR:84.51%	165 wood images	

continued on following page

Table 1. continued

References	Features	Feature Selection	Emotion Presentation	Classifier	Performance	Database	Individualized
(Jianning & Restrepo, 2008)	shape features by FFT		36 pairs: simple/complex, ordinary/extraordinary, traditional/modern, balance/imbalance, static/dynamic, lying/erect, symmetrical/asymmetrical, personal/impersonal, harmonious/inharmonious, organic/geometric, heavy/light, natural/artificial, fragile/strong, elegant/inelegant, gradual/sudden, orderly/disorderly, lovely/unlovely, loose/tight, high-tech/low-tech, variational/formalistic, friendly/unfriendly, moving/still, male/female, hard/soft, rounded/angular, rational/sensible, boring/lively, rough/smooth, acute/obtuse, stable/unstable, warm/cool, familiar/strange, regular/irregular, liberal/conservative,active/inactive, likable,/unikable.	a linear multiple regression analysis		6 shapes	
(Na Yeon, Yunhee, Youngrae, & Eun Yi, 2008)	color pattern		10adj: romantic, clear, natural, casual, elegant, chic, dynamic, classic, dandy, modern.	NN	P: 100% R: 99%	389 textile images	
(Yanulevskaya, et al., 2008)	Gabor features Wiccest features		valence arousal	SVM	RR:>50%	IAPS	
(Yongjie Hu, Shangfei Wang, Rui Ding, 2008)	color shape and texture		arousal	CBA	RR:>70%	IAPS	

For psychological space, most researchers adopt adjectives or adjective pairs to express emotion. The number of adjectives or pairs varies from two to 36. For physical space, many kinds of features have been extracted from images including color, shape, and texture. Some research uses factor analysis, Principal Component Analysis (PCA), or one-dimensional SVM to select features. Others introduce the sensitive features by consulting domain knowledge. Eun-Jong proposed different features for different adjectives (Eun-Jong & Joon-Whoan, 2008). For user modeling, two kinds of classifiers are adopted: machine learning and rule-based methods. Several researchers consider the individualizing process using Interactive Genetic Algorithm(IGA) (Cho & Lee, 2002; S. Wang, 2002) and Relevance Feedback(RF) (Bianchi-Berthouze & Catarci, 2003; Eun-Jong & Joon-Whoan, 2008; Yoo, 2006).

Researchers have used their own databases to evaluate the effectiveness of their approach. The size of the databases ranges from 6 to 5,625. Some researchers (S.F. Wang & Hu, 2009; Yanulevskaya et al., 2008) used the International Affective Picture System (IAPS), which was developed by Lang (Lang, Bradley, & Cuthbert, 2008) and is often used in psychological research. The performance measurements are different, such as Recognition Rate (RR)/ Accuracy Rate (AR), Precision Rate (PR), Satisfaction Rate (SR), and Recall Rate (R). Therefore, we cannot rank the performances of the surveyed approaches.

4. EMOTIONAL SEMANTIC DETECTION FROM VIDEOS

Emotional semantic detection from videos was first studied in the beginning of this century. In 2001, Chitra Dorai proposed *Computational Media Aesthetics* (CMA), defined as

the algorithmic study of a number of image and aural elements in media and the computational analysis of the principles that have emerged underlying their use and manipulation, individually or jointly, in the creative art of clarifying, intensifying, and interpreting some event for the audience. (Nack, Dorai, & Venkatesh, 2001)

The core trait of CMA is to interpret the data with its maker's eye. It laid the foundation for the later study on affective content analysis from video. Almost all researchers adopt domain knowledge to introduce and select features, except Kang (Kang, 2003), who used the AdaBoost method. Table 2 provides an overview of the research from 2001 to the present, with respect to the utilized features, emotion presentation, classifier, performance, and database.

For psychological space, researchers adopt either classes or dimension. For physical space,

Table 2. Emotional semantic detection from videos

Reference	Features	Emotion presentation	Classifier	Performance	Database
(Moncrieff, Dorai, & Venkatesh, 2001)	7 component energy dynamic label	4 type sound energy events	rules	RR: 82%	sections of 4 films: the mummy, pitch black, aliens, and scream.
(Kang, 2002)	intra-scene context, inter-scene context	fear, sadness, joy	using formula	RR:62%	3 video sequences: i know what you did last summer, when harry met sally and dying young
(Kang, 2003)	color, motion, shot cut rate ada-boost method for selection features	fear, sadness, joy	adaboost classifier	RR:63.13%	6 30-minute video data: i know what you did last summer, home alone, dying young, ring, titanic and when harry met sally
(M. C. Xu, L.-T.; Jin, J.;, 2005)	mel-frequency cepstral coefficient, energy, delta, acceleration	comedy: 5, canned laughter, dialogue, silence, music and others, horror: 4, horror sounds, dialogue, silence and others	HMM	R: above 90% P: above 90%	40 minutes comedy soap opera (friends). 40 minutes of horror films (korea, face).
(Wei, Dimitrova, & Chang, 2004)	movie palette histogram, mood dynamics histogram, dominant color, ratio, pace, family histogram	eight mood types	c-svc SVM	RR:81.2%	15 full length feature films

continued on following page

Table 2. continued

Reference	Features	Emotion presentation	Classifier	Performance	Database
(Arifin & Cheung, 2007)	proposed visual feature computed from the color emotional response, attention and tempo information of the video. audio: tempo histogram, daubechies wavelet cumulative histogram, mel frequency cepstral coefficients, root mean square energy, spectral flux, spectral rolloff and zero crossing rate	pleasure, arousal, dominance	2 models using DBN	R:74% for model 1 R: 80% for model 2	34 videos, 7381 shots, 7 hours, 4 minutes and 7 seconds.
(Sun & Yu, 2007)	motion, shot length, sound energy, speech rate, pitch average, pitch range, sound energy, silence ratio and color features	joy, anger, sadness and fear	video affective tree+hmms	P: 68.1% R: 78.78%	10 feature films, titanic, a walk in the clouds, love letter, raiders of the lost ark, con air, pirates of the caribbean, scary movie, spider-man, lord of the rings and the lion king
(C. W. Wang, Cheng, Chen, Yang, & Wu, 2007)	light, color, movement, rhythm, sound	action, drama, and romance	aesthetic intensity curves using domain knowledge	R:74% P:57%	5 movies, hitch, ghost, hero, the promise, and charlie's angels ii
(Yoo & Cho, 2007)	average color histogram, average brightness, average edge histogram, average shot duration, gradual change rate	action, excitement, suspense, quietness, relaxation, and happiness	IGA	R: 70% in the tenth generation	300 TV commercials
(Watanapa, Thipakorn, & Charoen-kitkarn, 2008)	visual-spatial features, visual-temporal features, audio feature	excitement, joy and sadness	a unique sieving-structured nn	RR: 87.67%	120 scenes from 24 movies.
(M. Xu, Jin, Luo, & Duan, 2008)	arousal features: duration, duration relationship, short-time energy, mel frequency cepstral coefficients. valence features: brightness, lighting, color energy and pitch	fear, anger, happy, sad and neutral	fuzzy c-mean clustering to arousal + HMM	RR:80.7%	8 movies, 6201 video shots, 720 minutes
(Zhang et al., 2008)	arousal features: motion intensity, shot switch rate, sound energy, zero crossing rate, tempo, and beat strength. valence features: rhythm regularity, pitch, lighting, saturation and color energy.	arousal, valence	clustering: affinity pre	P:64.2% R:66%	156 English pop music videos
(Zhang, Huang, et al., 2008)	arousal features: motion intensity, short switch rate, zero crossing rate, music tempo and beat strength. valence features: lighting, saturation, color energy, rhythm regularity and pitch.	arousal, valence	svr using user's profile for individual process.		552 music videos in mpeg format

many kinds of visual and audio features are introduced, including motion intensity, the rate of switching from shot to shot, sound energy, tempo, lighting, saturation, and color. For user modeling, some researchers introduce their own formula after consulting domain knowledge. Others use machine learning methods, such as HMM, Dynamic Bayesian Networks (DBN), etc. Only a few researchers consider the individualizing process by using users' profile data (Mohammad Soleymani, Jeremy Davis, & Thierry Pun, 2009; Zhang, Huang, Tian, Jiang, & Gao, 2008) or by building a model for each user (Sun & Yu, 2009).

For physiological space, a few researchers began to consider the possibility of employing physiological signals for video affective content analysis. Pun demonstrated a first step toward benefiting from physiological responses to determine personalized emotional profiles and subsequently to permit affective based video indexing (Mohammad Soleymani, Guillaume Chanel, Joep J. M. Kierkels, & Thierry Pun, 2008). Five peripheral physiological signals, including GSR, EMG, blood pressure, respiration pattern and skin temperature, were acquired. Money and Agius (2009) investigated whether user physiological response may serve as a suitable basis for a video summarization technique by analyzing electro-dermal response, respiration amplitude, respiration rate, blood volume pulse and heart rate, in response

to a range of video content in a variety of genres including horror, comedy, drama, sci-fi, and action. Toyosawa and Kawai (2009) measure impression by the degree of arousal based on two measures of heart activity: deceleration of heart rate and activation of the higher frequency component of the heart rate variability.

Researchers have used their own databases to evaluate the effectiveness of their approach. Because the performance measurements differ as well, it is difficult to compare their performances.

5. EMOTIONAL SEMANTIC DETECTION FROM MUSIC

Emotion and music have been studied for many years; it would be hard work to provide an exhaustive overview. Table 3 reviews advances made in the past five years.

For psychological space, many researchers consult several well-known emotion music models. For example, Hevner discovered eight clusters of adjective sets describing music emotion and

Table 3. Emotional semantic detection from music

References	Features	Feature Selection	Emotion Presentation	Classifier	Performance	Database
(Dan Liu, 2003; L. Lu, Liu, & Zhang, 2006)	timbre, intensity, rhythm		contentment, depression, exuberance, and anxiety	GMM	AR: 86.3% R: 84.1%	acoustic music 20s long clips 200 for each classes
(Tien-Lin Wu, 2006)	rhythmic, timbre texture, pitch, sound level, frequency spectrum and spatial features, dissonance and pitch, loudness.	MANOVA	valence -arousal	SVM	AR:98.67%	75 musical segments
(Yang, et al., 2007)	114, PsySound(44), Marsyas(30), Spectral contrast(12), DWCH(28) Or 15PsySound(15)		arousal valence	ML SVR AdaBoost.RT	arousal: AR:76.84%-86.84% valence: AR:61.58%-67.89%	195 popular songs from western, Chinese, and Japanese.25s segment

continued on following page

Table 3. continued

References	Features	Feature Selection	Emotion Presentation	Classifier	Performance	Database
(Yang, Liu, & Chen, 2006)	15, PsySound	SBSM	Thayer's model, 4 quadrants	FKNN FNM	AR: FKNN: 70.88% FNM:78.33%	195 as above
(C.-C. Liu, Yang, Wu, & Chen, 2006)	15, PsySound	remove one after another	Thayer's model of mood	The Nearest-Mean Classifier	AR:78.97%	195 as above
(M. Wang, Hang, & Zhu, 2004a; M. Wang, et al., 2006)	18, statistical and perceptual features		joyous, robust, restless, lyrical, sober, gloomy	SVM	AR average: 74.11%	western tonal music, MIDI files, 20s clips
(T. Li & Ogihara, 2004)	35 Mel-Frequency Cesptral Coefficients (MFCC), other timbre features, daubechies wavelet coefficient histograms		cheerful-depressing, relaxing- exciting, and comforting-disturbing	SVM	AR: >70%	235 sound files, 30s segments
(Dan Yang, 2004)	24 acoustic attributes, timbre features, and another 12 attributes		music emotion intensity	SVM	emotional intensity was highly correlated with rhythm and timbre features	500 rock song, 20s segments
(Xuan Zhu, Shi, Kim, & Eom, 2006)	timbre feature set, and a novel tempo feature set		sad, calm, pleasant and excited	AdaBoost	AR: 90.5%	200 songs MP3 files, >=30s
(Korhonen, Clausi, & Jernigan, 2006)	18 dynamics, mean pitch, pitch variation, timbre, harmony, tempo, texture		valence and arousal	linear model	average R^2 statistic: 21.9% for valence 78.4% for arousal	6 musical selection, Western art musical style
(Shi, Zhu, Kim, & Eom, 2006)	segmental features: intensity and timbre; supraseg-ment feature: Log-scale Modulation Frequency Coefficients(LMFC)		sad, excited, pleasant, calm	Adaboost	AR: Segmental:86.1% LMFC:90.2% Segmental & LMFC: 92.8%	194, MP3 frame
(B. Zhu, Liu, & Tang, 2008)	10 midi features average of pitch, average of intensity, velocity, variance of pitch, variance of interval, variance of intensity, direction of intensity, direction of pitch, span of interval, density of note.		dignified, sad, dreaming, soothing, graceful, joyous, exciting, vigorous	IGEP PLS BP	AR: IGEP:95.7% BPNN:91.2% PLS:86.2%	270, MIDI Chinese music
(Cheng, Yang, Lin, Liao, & Chen, 2008)	chord features low-level features spectral flatness measure, and spectral crest factor		valence (positive valence and negative valence)	k-NN	AR:63.08%	195 popular songs from western, Chinese, and Japanese, 25s segment
(He et al., 2008)	language features; unigrams, bigrams, trigrams.	a simple feature elimination method, feature weighting	love lovelorn	NBC, MEC, SVM.	AR: the best:89.65%	1903 Chinese pop music

continued on following page

Table 3. continued

References	Features	Feature Selection	Emotion Presentation	Classifier	Performance	Database
(Laurier, Grivolla, & Herrera, 2008b)	audio features & lyrics features		happy, sad, angry, relaxed	SVM	AR: 81.5% - 98.1% for audio 77.9% - 84.4% for lyrics 91.7% - 98.3% for mixed	1000 songs having English lyrics and an entry in LyricWiki
(D. Liu, Zhang, & Zhu, 2003)	5 pitch, length, timbre, tempo, velocity		sober, gloomy, laughing, lyrical, sprightly, joyous, exciting, robust	fuzzy classifier, 40 rules	AR average:85.55%	6 famous waltz centos
(Pao et al., 2008)	45 15 PsySound features, 19 timbre texture features, 6 rhythmic content features, 5 pitch content features.		thayer's arousal-valence emotion plane	W-D-KNN	AR:96.7%	60 25s segments, convert to WAV file
(K. C. Wang & Chen, 2007)	56 26 timbre features, 30 tempo features.		calm, sad, exciting, pleasant	AdaBoost	AR:97.5%	163
(Wen & Lingyun, 2008)	30 pitch content feature set, rhythm content feature set and timbre content feature set		anxious depression contentment exuberance	Bayesian network classifier	AR: 40.0% - 88.9% with Chinese traditional music 63.6% - 100% with Western classical music	20 Chinese traditional instrumental music 20 Western classical music, single channel
(Alicja Wieczorkowska, 2006; Synak & Wieczorkowska, 2005; A. Wieczorkowska & Synak, 2006; A. Wieczorkowska, Synak, Lewis, & Ras, 2005; A. A. Wieczorkowska, 2005)	29 frequency, level, tristimulus1, 2, 3, evenharm and oddharm, brightness, irregularity, frequency1, ratio1, ..., 9, amplitude1, ratio1, ..., 9.		happy and fanciful graceful and dreamy pathetic and passionate dramatic, agitated, and frustrated scared and spooky dark and bluesy	k-NN	AR: for 303 samples: 62.67% - 92.33% for all 870 samples: 64.02% - 95.97%	870 audio simples, 30s segments, songs and classic music pieces.

created an emotion cycle for these categories. Thayer's model consists of two axes. The horizontal axis describes the amount of stress and the vertical axis is the amount of energy. Others use other adjective and pairs or valence-arousal. For physical space, many kinds of timbre, rhythm, and pitch features have been introduced. Laurier proposed lyrics features besides audio features (Laurier, Grivolla, & Herrera, 2008a). Several kinds of software for musical feature extraction and analysis from audio have been developed, such as PsySound (Cabrera, 1999), Marsyas (Tzanetakis, 2009) and MIRToolBox (Olivier, Petri, & Tuomas, 2009). Some researchers use a one-way MANOVA or the SBSM to select features. For user modeling, most researchers adopt a machine leaning method as the classifiers, such as Gaussian mixture model (GMM), Multiple Linear Regression (MLR), Fuzzy k-NN classifier, Fuzzy Nearest-Mean classifier (FNM), Linear Discriminant Function (LDF), Gene Expression Programming (IGEP), Partial Least Squares (PLS), Naïve Bayes Classifier (NBC), and Maximum Entropy Classification (MEC). Several researchers consider the individualizing process by grouping users based on their profiles (Yang, Lin, Su, & Chen, 2007, 2008), or building a model for each user (M. Wang, Hang, & Zhu, 2004b; M. Wang, Zhang, & Zhu, 2006).

For physiological space, Loviscach and Oswald (2008) measured five physiological signals to help select the upcoming song: galvanic skin response, skin temperature, heart rate, breath rate and volume.

Each researcher used different mood categories and different datasets, making comparison on previous work a virtually impossible mission. As a solution, Music Information Retrieval Evaluation eXchange (MIREX) builds the first ever community available test set and proposes a contest on music mood classification (MIREX, 2009).

6. CURRENT ANTETYPE SYSTEMS

Several prototype systems of emotional semantic detection from multimedia have been developed (Bertini, Cucchiara, Del Bimbo, & Prati, 2004; Inder, Bianchi-Berthouze, & Kato, 1999; Mohammad Soleymani, et al., 2009; Yoshida, et al., 1998;

Xuan Zhu, et al., 2006). Especially for music, there exist several commercial systems (Google, 2009; musicovery, 2009). We only introduce three prototype systems of emotion detection from image, video, and music as study examples.

The emotional information acquiring system designed by the University of Science and Technology of China(USTC) is a double-level emotion scenery and fashion image retrieval system, which is composed of both common emotion retrieval and individual emotion retrieval(S. Wang, 2002). Domain color, shape, and gray–level distribution of scenery images, and also the color, style, length, and materials of costumes have been extracted from images to construct the feature space. A common emotional space is constructed based on the idea of "dimension" in psychology. After that, emotional annotations have been provided, SVMs map images from the low-level feature space to the high-level emotional space, and automatically annotate unevaluated images based on the users' common emotion. When a user requests images with subjective parameters, the common emotion image retrieval grasps the user's emotion quickly by indexing images in the common emotion space. This process can greatly reduce the workload of online learning. Then, the visualized interactive genetic algorithm realizes the individual emotional image retrieval to make the model more adaptive to individual variation. The dataset consists of 1,007 scene images and 1,486 costume images.

Thierry Pun et al. in the University of Geneva have developed a collaborative affective video retrieval system (Mohammad Soleymani, Jeremy Davis, & Thierry Pun, 2009). A dataset of 155 video clips extracted from Hollywood movies are annotated by the emotion felt by participants in both a valence-arousal and label based approach. Collaborative filtering of a weighted k-Nearest Neighbor (KNN) is adopted to find the closest clips to an affective query. The ability of the user profiling and using the tags from the users with similar taste is considered to improve the retrieval results.

Zhu et al. (2006) at the Samsung Advanced Institute of Technology have proposed an integrated music recommendation system, which contains the functions of automatic music genre classification, automatic music emotion classification, and music similarity query. They chose five genre classes (classical, pop & rock, jazz & blues, Hip-hop, and mental & punk), and four music emotion classes (sad, calm, pleasant, and excited) for their system. A timbre feature vector consisting of 26 components with 13-ms time resolution and a tempo feature vector containing 60 components with 1-second time resolution are extracted. A classifier with AdaBoost algorithm including two layers, which are responsible for timbre features and tempo features respectively, is designed. The dataset is composed of 1,000 songs.

7. FUTURE RESEARCH DIRECTIONS

Database for Emotion Multimedia Classification

Having enough labeled data of emotion multimedia is a prerequisite in media emotion classification. However, it is difficult to obtain large amounts of samples because the data are usually acquired from subjects' self-report experiments. Collecting data from Web sites such as Flickr.com may be a potential way to solve this problem (Hajime, Takano, & Hagiwara, 2008; Stefanie Schmidt & Wolfgang G. Stock, 2009). Semi-supervised learning may be another solution, since it make use of both labeled and unlabeled data for training - typically a small amount of labeled data with a large amount of unlabeled data(Xiaojin Zhu, 2008). Furthermore, finding a representative data set is also important for classifiers since the variety of content that can appear in "happy" or "sad" categories is practically unlimited. Research results from psychology, art, musicology, and cinematography may provide some suggestions, but they are far from solving it. In fact, it is already a

considerable challenge in the cognitive domain. From an engineering point of view, increasing the number and types of samples in the database may be feasible.

Physical Space

Selecting sensitive features for different kinds of emotion is a key issue of physical space. The most recent research findings in psychology and cognitive science may be helpful. In addition, new feature selection methods inspired by humans' attention mechanism are also worthy to be expected. Interactive selection may be another approach. Because it is possible to identify human emotion, we may incorporate the human into the sensitive feature selection algorithm. A variety of features and their weights constitute a search space. Users will give the similarity of different media on the psychological or physiological space. By interactive search and optimization, we may obtain the sensitive features and weights.

Introducing new features is also useful here. For music, lyrics, not only melody, are of great importance in evoking emotion. For videos, character dialogue can evoke emotions just through speech. An algorithm that interprets the words and maps the results to a certain emotion is helpful.

Psychological Space

The psychological space may consist of several words or two to three dimensions. Both of them have advantages and disadvantages. For dimension, it is direct and clear, but it is not consistent with people's habits. We tend to use the term "happy movie" rather than "a movie whose valence is 3.0". While for words, there is an ambiguity in terms, and new words cannot be easily added to the existing psychological space. It is, however, consistent with people's habits. A hybrid psychological space with dimension as the lower level and word as the highest level is worthy of study.

Furthermore, relationships between words could be computed. A technique from linguistic analysis may be of use. Kobayashi (2000) built an impression word dictionary including more than 800 adjectives. Concept structure of the dictionary is same as that of WorldNet. Through a semantic network, the dictionary gives not only the relationship of adjectives (synonym, antonym, concepts of high level and low level), but also gives the value of adjectives in the form of fuzzy function.

Physiological Space

Only a few recent studies introduce physiological signals. With the advancement of wearable systems, we may explore as many kinds of physiological signals as possible to help affective multimedia content analysis. In this case, we will also face a feature selection problem that is similar in to that physical space. In addition, the solution may be also similar.

Relationships

Users' emotions are subjective and complex because they are affected not only by the observed media, but also by users' goals and past experiences. They may vary from one individual to another and change over time. So, the mapping between media and users' emotions is highly complex. Although many efforts have been made to accomplish this, it is still in its infancy. Discovering detailed mechanisms of emotion from interdisciplinary study would be helpful, and the introduction of new machine learning methods, such as semi-supervised learning, is another way. Employing information fusion techniques may be also worthy of study, since an observed multimedia consists of many kinds of media. For example, a film includes visuals, motion, speech, background sound, and music. Information fusion techniques and multi-view learning methods may be employed to explore how these media and their combinations induce human emotion.

Individuality has a significant impact on the success of an emotion detection study. Feedback and profiling would be effective for capturing users' preferences. Because users' interests may change over time, interactive, dynamic, and adaptive mechanism are necessary. We may place less weight on the user's older data or redefine the relationships periodically. Alternatively, we may use a dual relationship that classifies instances by first consulting a model trained on recent data, but then delegating classification to a model trained over a longer time period if the recent model is unable to make a prediction with sufficient confidence.

Evaluation

To date, there are no standard database and performance measurements to evaluate the effectiveness of the modeled relationship in affective multimedia analysis. We have discussed the database problem in Section 7.1. For measurements, recognition rate, recall, and precision may be used. But users' emotions that are induced by media are often a complex, rather than pure kind of emotion. The intensity of the emotions should also be considered. Therefore, an empirical evaluation should be used.

In summary, emotion detection from multimedia is still open for discussion. Cooperation among many research fields, such as cognition, psychology, artificial intelligence, signal processing, and wearable computing, will be necessary in the future to realize individual emotion detection.

ACKNOWLEDGMENT

This chapter is supported by National 863 Program (2008AA01Z122), Anhui Provincial Natural Science Foundation (No.070412056) and SRF for ROCS, SEM.

REFERENCES

Alicja Wieczorkowska, P. S., & Zbigniew, W. Ras. (2006). *Multi-Label Classification of Emotions in Music*. Paper presented at the International Conference on Intelligent information Processing and Web Mining, Ustron, Poland.

Arifin, S., & Cheung, P. Y. K. (2007, Sep 17-19). *A novel probabilistic approach to modeling the pleasure-arousal-dominance content of the video based on "Working memory"*. Paper presented at the International Conference on Semantic Computing (ICSC 2007), Irvine, CA.

Bertini, M., Cucchiara, R., Del Bimbo, A., & Prati, A. (2004). *Content-based video adaptation with user's preferences*. Paper presented at the 2004 IEEE International Conference on Multimedia and Expo (ICME), Taipei, Taiwan.

Bianchi-Berthouze, N., & Catarci, T. (2003). K-DIME: An affective image filtering system. *IEEE MultiMedia, 10*(3), 103–106. doi:10.1109/MMUL.2003.1218262

Cabrera, D. (1999). *Psysound: A Computer Program for Psychoacoustical Analysis*. Paper presented at the the Australian Acoustical Society Conference.

Cheng, H.-T., Yang, Y.-H., Lin, Y.-C., Liao, I. B., & Chen, H. H. (2008). *Automatic chord recognition for music classification and retrieval*. Paper presented at the 2008 IEEE International Conference on Multimedia and Expo., Hannover, Germany.

Cho, S., & Lee, J. (2002). A human-oriented image retrieval system using interactive genetic algorithm. *IEEE Transactions on Systems, Man and Cybernetics. Part A, 32*(3), 452–458.

Dan Liu, L. L. Hong-Jiang Zhang. (2003, 27 Oct). *Automatic Mood Detection from Acoustic Music Data*. Paper presented at the International Symposium on Music Information Retrieval, Baltimore, MD, USA.

Dan Yang, W. L. (2004). *Disambiguating Music Emotion Using Software Agents*. Paper presented at the Proc. Int. Conf. Music Information Retrieval(ISMIR), Barcelona, Spain.

Datta, R., Joshi, D., Li, J., & Wang, J. Z. (2006, May). *Studying Aesthetics in Photographic Images Using a Computational Approach*. Paper presented at the European Conference on Computer Vision, Graz, Austria.

Eun-Jong, P., & Joon-Whoan, L. (2008). *Emotion-based image retrieval using multiple-queries and consistency feedback*. Paper presented at the 6th IEEE International Conference on Industrial Informatics, INDIN 2008.

Google. (2009). http://www.google.cn/music/songscreener. Retrieved 10 Oct., 2009

Hajime, H., Takano, A., & Hagiwara, M. (2008, 1-6 June 2008). *Mining KANSEI fuzzy rules from photos on the internet*. Paper presented at the IEEE International Conference on Fuzzy Systems, 2008., Hong Kong, China.

Hanjalic, A. (2001). *Video and image retrieval beyond the cognitive level: The needs and possibilities*. Paper presented at the Storage and Retrieval for Media Databases 2001, San Jose, CA, United states.

Hanjalic, A., & Xu, L. Q. (2005). Affective video content representation and modeling. *IEEE Transactions on Multimedia, 7*(1), 143–154. doi:10.1109/TMM.2004.840618

Hayashi, T., & Hagiwara, M. (1998). Image query by impression words - the IQI system. *IEEE Transactions on Consumer Electronics, 44*(2), 347–352. doi:10.1109/30.681949

He, H., Jin, J., Xiong, Y., Chen, B., Sun, W., & Zhao, L. (2008). *Language feature mining for music emotion classification via supervised learning from lyrics*, Wuhan, China.

Inder, R., Bianchi-Berthouze, N., & Kato, T. (1999). *K-DIME: a software framework for Kansei filtering of internet material.* Paper presented at the IEEE International Conference on Systems, Man and Cybernetics, Tokyo, Jpn.

Jianning, S., & Restrepo, J. (2008). *The harmonics of kansei images.* Paper presented at the 9th International Conference on Computer-Aided Industrial Design and Conceptual Design, 2008., Kunming,China.

Kang, H.-B. (2002). *Analysis of scene context related with emotional events.* Paper presented at the tenth ACM international conference on Multimedia, Juan les Pins, France.

Kang, H.-B. (2003). *Affective Contents Retrieval from Video with Relevance Feedback Digital Libraries: Technology and Management of Indigenous Knowledge for Global Access* (pp. 243–252). Springer Berlin / Heidelberg.

Kim, J., & Andre, E. (2008). Emotion recognition based on physiological changes in music listening. *IEEE Transactions on Pattern Analysis and Machine Intelligence, 30*(12), 2067–2083. doi:10.1109/TPAMI.2008.26

Kim, S.-J., Kim, E. Y., Jeong, K., & Kim, J.-I. (2006, Nov 6-8). *Emotion-based textile indexing using colors, texture and patterns.* Paper presented at the 2nd International Symposium on Visual Computing, Lake Tahoe, NV, United States.

Korhonen, M. D., Clausi, D. A., & Jernigan, M. E. (2006). Modeling emotional content of music using system identification. *IEEE Transactions on Systems, Man, and Cybernetics. Part B, Cybernetics, 36*(3), 588–599. doi:10.1109/TSMCB.2005.862491

Lang, P. J., Bradley, M. M., & Cuthbert, B. N. (2008). International affective picture system (IAPS): Affective ratings of pictures and instruction manual. Technical Report A-8. University of Florida, Gainesville, FL.

Laurier, C., Grivolla, J., & Herrera, P. (2008a). *Multimodal music mood classification using audio and lyrics,* San Diego, CA, United states.

Laurier, C., Grivolla, J., & Herrera, P. (2008b). *Multimodal music mood classification using audio and lyrics.* Paper presented at the International Conference on Machine Learning and Applications, San Diego, CA, United states.

Li, H., Li, J., Song, J., & Chen, J. (2007). *A Fuzzy Mapping from Image Texture to Affective Thesaurus.* Paper presented at the 2007 international conference on Bio-Inspired computational intelligence and applications shanghai,China.

Li, T., & Ogihara, M. (2004). *Content-based music similarity search and emotion detection.* Paper presented at the IEEE Int. Conf. on Acoustics, Speech & Signal Processing, Montreal, Que, Canada.

Liu, C.-C., Yang, Y.-H., Wu, P.-H., & Chen, H. H. (2006). *Detecting and classifying emotion in popular music.* Paper presented at the 7th International Conference on Computer Vision, Pattern Recognition and Image Processing, Taiwan, ROC, Taiwan.

Liu, D., Zhang, N., & Zhu, H. (2003). Form and mood recognition of Johann Strauss's waltz centos. *Chinese Journal of Electronics, 12*(4), 587–593.

Lu, L., Liu, D., & Zhang, H.-J. (2006). Automatic mood detection and tracking of music audio signals. *IEEE Transactions on Audio. Speech and Language Processing, 14*(1), 5–18. doi:10.1109/TSA.2005.860344

Lu, W., & Ni, L. (2005). *Kansei image retrieval based on region of interest.* Paper presented at the SAR and Multispectral Image Processing, Wuhan, China.

Mao, X., Chen, B., & Muta, I. (2003). Affective property of image and fractal dimension. *Chaos, Solitons, and Fractals, 15*(5), 905–910. doi:10.1016/S0960-0779(02)00209-6

MIREX. (2009). Audio Music Mood Classification. from http://www.music-ir.org/mirex/2009/index.php/Audio_Music_Mood_Classification

Moncrieff, S., Dorai, C., & Venkatesh, S. (2001, October 2001.). *Affect Computing in Film through Sound Energy Dynamics.* Paper presented at the the ninth ACM international conference on multimedia, Ottawa, Canada.

Money, A. G., & Agius, H. (2009). Analysing user physiological responses for affective video summarisation. *Display, 30,* 59–70. doi:10.1016/j.displa.2008.12.003

musicovery. (2009). http://musicovery.com/. Retrieved 10 Oct., 2009

Na Yeon, K., Yunhee, S., Youngrae, K., & Eun Yi, K. (2008). *Emotion recognition using color and pattern in textile images.* Paper presented at the 2008 IEEE Conference on Cybernetics and Intelligent Systems, Chengdou,China.

Nack, F., Dorai, C., & Venkatesh, S. (2001). Computational media aesthetics: finding meaning beautiful. *Multimedia, IEEE, 8*(4), 10–12. doi:10.1109/93.959093

Olivier, L., Petri, T., & Tuomas, E. (2009). https://www.jyu.fi/hum/laitokset/musiikki/en/research/coe/materials/mirtoolbox. Retrieved 10 Oct., 2009

Pao, T.-L., Cheng, Y.-M., Yeh, J.-H., Chen, Y.-T., Pai, C.-Y., & Tsai, Y.-W. (2008). *Comparison between weighted D-KNN and other classifiers for music emotion recognition.* Paper presented at the The Third International Conference on Innovative Computing, Information and Control Dalian, Liaoning, China.

Picard, R. W., Vyzas, E., & Healey, J. (2001). Toward Machine Emotional Intelligence: Analysis of Affective Physiological State. *IEEE Transactions on Pattern Analysis and Machine Intelligence, 23*(10), 1175–1191. doi:10.1109/34.954607

Schmidt, S., & Stock, W. G. (2009). Collective indexing of emotions in images. A study in emotional information retrieval. *Journal of the American Society for Information Science and Technology, 60*(5), 863–876. doi:10.1002/asi.21043

Shi, Y.-Y., Zhu, X., Kim, H.-G., & Eom, K.-W. (2006). *A tempo feature via modulation spectrum analysis and its application to music emotion classification,* Toronto, ON, Canada.

Shibata, T., & Kato, T. (1999). *'Kansei' image retrieval system for street landscape-discrimination and graphical parameters based on correlation of two images.* Paper presented at the IEEE International Conference on Systems, Man and Cybernetics, Tokyo, Jpn.

Soleymani, M., Chanel, G., Kierkels, J. J. M., & Pun, T. (2008). *Affective Characterization of Movie Scenes Based on Multimedia Content Analysis and User's Physiological Emotional Responses.* Paper presented at the Tenth IEEE International Symposium on Multimedia, 2008, Berkeley, California, USA.

Soleymani, M., Chanel, G., Kierkels, J. J. M., & Pun, T. (2008). *Affective ranking of movie scenes using physiological signals and content analysis.* Paper presented at the the 2nd ACM workshop on Multimedia semantics, Vancouver, British Columbia, Canada.

Soleymani, M., Davis, J., & Pun, T. (2009). *A collaborative Personalized Affective Video Retrieval System.* Paper presented at the International Conference on Affective Computing and Intelligent interaction.

Soleymani, M., Davis, J., & Pun, T. (2009). *A collaborative Personalized Affective Video Retrieval System.* Paper presented at the International Conference on Affective Computing and Intelligent interaction, Amsterdam, Netherlands.

Sun, K., & Yu, J. (2009). Audience Oriented Personalized Movie Affective Content Representation and Recognition.

Sun, K., & Yu, J. Q. (2007, Sep 12-14). *Video affective content representation and recognition using video affective tree and Hidden Markov Models.* Paper presented at the 2nd International Conference on Affective Computing and Intellegent Interaction, Lisbon, PORTUGAL.

Synak, P., & Wieczorkowska, A. (2005). *Some issues on detecting emotions in music.* Paper presented at the Rough Sets, Fuzzy Sets, Data Mining, and Granular Computing, Regina, Canada.

Tien-Lin Wu, S.-K. J. (2006). *Automatic emotion classification of musical segments.* Paper presented at the 9th International Conference on Music Perception and Cognition Bologna, Italy.

Tobimatsu, S., Zhang, Y. M., Tomoda, Y., Mitsudome, A., & Kato, M. (1999). Chromatic sensitive epilepsy: A variant of photosensitive epilepsy. *Annals of Neurology, 45*(6), 790–793. doi:10.1002/1531-8249(199906)45:6<790::AID-ANA14>3.0.CO;2-7

Toyosawa, S., & Kawai, T. (2009). A video abstraction method based on viewer's heart activity and its evaluations. *Kyokai Joho Imeji Zasshi/Journal of the Institute of Image Information and Television Engineers, 63*(1), 86-94.

Tzanetakis, G. (2009). http://marsyas.sness.net/. Retrieved 10 Oct., 2009

Wagner, J., Kim, J., & Andre, E. (2005). *From physiological signals to emotions: Implementing and comparing selected methods for feature extraction and classification*, Amsterdam, Netherlands.

Wang, C. W., Cheng, W. H., Chen, J. C., Yang, S. S., & Wu, J. L. (2007, Jan 09-12). *Film narrative exploration through the analysis of aesthetic elements.* Paper presented at the 13th International Multimedia Modeling Conference Singapore, SINGAPORE.

Wang, K. C., & Chen, S. M. (2007, Oct 07-10). *Product form design using ANFIS-kansei engineering model.* Paper presented at the IEEE International Conference on Systems, Man and Cybernetics, Montreal, COOK ISLANDS.

Wang, M., Hang, N., & Zhu, H. (2004a). *User-adaptive music emotion recognition.* Paper presented at the International Conference on Signal Processing Proceedings, ICSP, Beijing, China.

Wang, M., Hang, N., & Zhu, H. (2004b). *User-adaptive music emotion recognition*, Beijing, China.

Wang, M., Zhang, N., & Zhu, H. (2006). Emotion recognition of Western tonal music using support vector machine. *Chinese Journal of Electronics, 15*(1), 74–78.

Wang, S. (2002). *Research on Kansei Information Processing and Its Application in Image Retrieval.* Unpublished Doctor dissertation, Universtiy of Science and Technology of China, Hefei, Anhui

Wang, S. F., Chen, E. H., Li, J. L., & Wang, X. F. (2001). Kansei-based image evaluation and retrieval. *Moshi Shibie yu Rengong Zhineng/Pattern Recognition and Artificial Intelligence, 14*(3), 297-297.

Wang, S. F., & Hu, Y. J. (2009). *Emotion valence and arousal recognition on IAPS and IADS.* Paper presented at the Workshop on Specification and Computation of Affect in Collaborative and Social NETworks.

Wang Weining, Y. y. (2005). *Research on Emotion Semantic based image feature extraction, retrieval and classification.* Unpublished doctoral dissertation, South China Universtiy of Technology, Guangzhou.

Watanapa, S. C., Thipakorn, B., & Charoenkitkarn, N. (2008). A sieving ANN for emotion-based movie clip classification. *Ieice Transactions on Information and Systems. E (Norwalk, Conn.), 91D*(5), 1562–1572.

Wei, C.-Y., Dimitrova, N., & Chang, S.-F. (2004). *Color-Mood Analysis of Films Based on Syntactic and Psychological Models.* Paper presented at the IEEE International Conference on Multimedia and Expo.

Wen, W., & Lingyun, X. (2008). *Discriminating mood taxonomy of Chinese traditional music and western classical music with content feature sets.* Paper presented at the 1st International Congress on Image and Signal Processing, Sanya, Hainan, China.

Wieczorkowska, A., & Synak, P. (2006). *Quality assessment of k-NN multi-label classification for music data.* Paper presented at the 16th International Symposium on Methodologies for Intelligent Systems, Bari, Italy.

Wieczorkowska, A., Synak, P., Lewis, R., & Ras, Z. W. (2005). *Extracting emotions from music data.* Paper presented at the 15th International Symposium on Methodologies for Intelligent Systems, Saratoga Springs, NY, United states.

Wieczorkowska, A. A. (2005). *Towards extracting emotions from music.* Paper presented at the Second International Workshop on Intelligent Media Technology for Communicative Intelligence, Warsaw, Poland.

Xu, M., Jin, J. S., Luo, S., & Duan, L. (Eds.). (2008). *Hierarchical movie affective content analysis based on arousal and valence features.* Vancouver, British Columbia, Canada: ACM.

Xu, M. C. L.-T.; Jin, J. (2005). *Affective content analysis in comedy and horror videos by audio emotional event detection.* Paper presented at the IEEE International Conference on Multimedia and Expo, 2005.

Yang, Y.-H., Lin, Y.-C., Su, Y.-F., & Chen, H. H. (2007). *Music emotion classification: A regression approach*, Beijing, China.

Yang, Y.-H., Lin, Y.-C., Su, Y.-F., & Chen, H. H. (2008). A regression approach to music emotion recognition. *IEEE Transactions on Audio. Speech and Language Processing, 16*(2), 448–457. doi:10.1109/TASL.2007.911513

Yang, Y.-H., Liu, C.-C., & Chen, H. H. (2006). *Music emotion classification: a fuzzy approach.* Paper presented at the 14th Annual ACM International Conference on Multimedia, Santa Barbara, CA, United states.

Yanulevskaya, V., van Gemert, J. C., Roth, K., Herbold, A. K., Sebe, N., & Geusebroek, J. M. (2008). *Emotional valence categorization using holistic image features.* Paper presented at the 15th IEEE International Conference on Image Processing, 2008., San Diego, California, U.S.A.

YOO, H.-W. (2006). Visual-Based Emotional Descriptor and Feedback Mechanism for Image Retrieval. *Journal of Information Science and Engineering, 22*(5), 1205–1227.

Yoo, H.-W., & Cho, S.-B. (2007). Video scene retrieval with interactive genetic algorithm. *Multimedia Tools and Applications, 34*(3), 317–336. doi:10.1007/s11042-007-0109-8

Yoshida, K., Kato, T., & Yanaru, T. (1998). *Image retrieval system using impression words.* Paper presented at the IEEE International Conference on Systems, Man, and Cybernetics, 1998, San Diego, California, USA

Zhang, S. L., Huang, Q. M., Tian, Q., Jiang, S. Q., & Gao, W. (2008, Dec 09-13). *Personalized MTV Affective Analysis Using User Profile.* Paper presented at the 9th Pacific Rim Conference on Multimedia, Tainan, TAIWAN.

Zhang, S. L., Tian, Q., Jiang, S. Q., Huang, Q. M., Gao, W., & Ieee. (2008, 26 Aug 2008). *Affective MTV Analysis Based on Arousal and Valence Features.* Paper presented at the IEEE International Conference on Multimedia and Expo (ICME 2008), Hannover, GERMANY.

Zhu, B., Liu, T., & Tang, Y. (2008). *Research on music emotion cognition model based on linguistic value computing*, Chongqing, China.

Zhu, X. (2008). Semi-Supervised Learning Literature Survey. 2010, from http://pages.cs.wisc.edu/~jerryzhu/research/ssl/semireview.html

Zhu, X., Shi, Y.-Y., Kim, H.-G., & Eom, K.-W. (2006). An integrated music recommendation system. *IEEE Transactions on Consumer Electronics*, *52*(3), 917–925. doi:10.1109/TCE.2006.1706489

Chapter 8
Fuzzy Logic for Non–Smooth Dynamical Systems

Kamyar Mehran
Newcastle University, UK

Bashar Zahawi
Newcastle University, UK

Damian Giaouris
Newcastle University, UK

ABSTRACT

Dynamical system theory has proved to be a powerful tool in the analysis and comprehension of a diverse range of problems. Over the past decade, a significant proportion of these systems have been found to contain terms that are non-smooth functions of their arguments. These problems arise in a number of practical systems ranging from electrical circuits to biological systems and even financial markets. It has also been demonstrated that Fuzzy engineering can be effectively employed to identify or even predict an array of uncertainties and chaotic phenomena caused by discontinuities typical of this class of system. This chapter presents a review of the most recent developments concerned with the confluence of these two fields through real-life examples and current advances in research.

1. INTRODUCTION

Bridging the two seemingly unrelated concepts, fuzzy logic and nonlinear piecewise-smooth dynamical systems theory is chiefly motivated by the concept of soft computing (SC), initiated by Lotfi A. Zadeh, the founder of fuzzy set theory. The principal components of SC, as defined in his initiative for soft computing[1], are fuzzy logic (FL), neural network theory (NN) and probabilistic

reasoning (PR), with the latter subsuming parts of belief networks, genetic algorithms, chaos theory and learning theory. SC is essentially distant from traditional, immutable (hard) computing and is much more aligned to the main ideas of Kansei Engineering in that the imprecision, uncertainty and partial truth reflecting the working of the human mind are incorporated into the computing process to form a new paradigm to tackle highly complex, nonlinear systems. The aim of this chapter is to combine FL from general Soft Computing theory and piece-wise smooth dynamical systems from

DOI: 10.4018/978-1-61692-797-4.ch008

the general theory of nonlinear dynamical systems. The main target being to examine their relationship and interaction and to demonstrate that the blending of the two concepts can be effectively used to analyse and control the chaotic and other nonlinear behaviours typical of such systems.

Over the past few decades, there has been a substantial level of interest in fuzzy systems technology and dynamical systems theory shown by almost all hard and soft-science research communities such as theoretical and experimental physicists, applied mathematicians, meteorologists, climatologists, physiologists, psychologists and engineers. More specifically, fuzzy system technology has emerged as an effective methodology to solve many problems ranging from control engineering, robotics, and automation to system identification, medical image/signal processing and Kansei engineering. Meanwhile, dynamical systems theory has proved to be a powerful tool to analyze and understand the behaviour of a diverse range of real life problems. The vast majority of these problems can only be modelled with dynamical systems whose behaviour is characterized by instantaneous changes and discontinuities. These practically ubiquitous dynamical systems are usually referred to as *piece-wise smooth* or *non-smooth* dynamical systems. Examples include mechanical systems with friction, robotic systems, electric and electronic systems employing electronic switching devices, unmanned vehicle systems, biological and biomedical systems, climate modelling and even financial forecasting. The study of these systems is of a great importance, primarily because they have captivating dynamics with significant practical applications and show rich nonlinear phenomena such as *quasi-periodicity* and *chaos*.

Unfortunately, many of the mathematical tools developed for smooth dynamical systems have to-date proven inadequate when dealing with the discontinuities present in non-smooth systems. Furthermore, certain specific approaches are not

well-established and are still in their early stages of development. Not surprisingly, fuzzy system technology, in the context of highly complex nonlinear systems, can be critically intuitive and useful. This belief arises from the fact that fuzzy logic resembles human reasoning in its use of approximate information so it can embody the uncertainty which is the essential part of the mainly event-driven, non-smooth system and its chaotic dynamics. That's why it is possible to believe that FL can lead to a general theory of uncertainty[2].

The chapter does not intend – in fact, is not able – to provide a thorough explanation of the intrinsic relationship between fuzzy logic and dynamical system theory, but attempts to give some heuristic research results and insightful ideas, shedding some light on the subject and attracting more attention to the topic.

The chapter is organised in the following way: it commences with an outline of the fundamental concepts of nonlinear dynamical systems theory, and specifically non-smooth dynamical systems, with examples showing the richness and uniqueness of their nonlinear behaviours. The inherent difficulties in modelling these dynamical systems will be highlighted. This is followed by an examination of how the Takagi-Sugeno fuzzy modelling concept could be extended to overcome these problems. The fuzzy approach is further extended and applied to the stability analysis (in the Lyapunov framework) to predict the onset of structural instability or so-called bifurcations in the evolution of the dynamical system. The chapter ends with an evaluation of the proposed approach in nonlinear system modelling and analysis in general and further discussion about potential forthcoming research.

Although this chapter may raise more questions than it can afford answers, we hope that it nevertheless will open more research avenues and plant the seeds for future developments in this area.

2. BACKGROUNDS

Non-Smooth Dynamical Systems

"Strictly speaking, there is no such thing as a non-smooth dynamical system" says Mario Di Bernardo[3], a leading expert on non-smooth dynamical systems. This might seem somewhat confusing at first, but the statement is true when considering the critical time-scales over which transitions occur between different systems topologies. For instance, in some impacting mechanical systems; the impact takes place over a very short time compared with that of the overall dynamics. Discontinuities or sudden jumps also happen in economic systems such as foreign exchange-rate markets (FOREX) and can lead to full-scale unstable chaotic behaviour, which cannot be understood if we model the dynamics of the market as a smooth system. In truly smooth systems such a scenario normally occurs after a long sequence of bifurcations, such as the Feigenbaum cascade of period-doubling bifurcations.

Another plausible reason for the failure of researchers to appreciate the necessity of establishing appropriate tools and techniques for piece-wise smooth dynamical systems, is that they expostulate many of our assumptions about nonlinear dynamics. Concepts like structural stability, bifurcation and qualitative measures of chaos are either indefinable or need to be redefined to explore the variety of nonlinear phenomena unique to non-smooth systems.

For these particular reasons, we will first outline some elementary but essential concepts of non-smooth dynamical systems and give some case studies and examples arising from different disciplines.

Case Study I: Impact Oscillator

An elastic ball bouncing on a table top is a very simple example of what mechanical engineers call an *impact oscillator*, i.e. a low-degree of

Figure 1. A simple impact oscillator

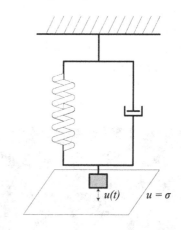

freedom mechanical system with hard constraints that feature impacts (Babitskii, 1978; Feigin). Systems with impacting characteristics are ubiquitous in mechanical systems ranging from gear assemblies and car suspensions to walking robots and many body-particle dynamics (Di Bernardo, Budd, Kowalczyk, & Champneys, 2007). The effect of the impact makes these systems highly nonlinear to the degree that chaotic phenomena turns out to be an inevitable attribute. Figure 1 shows a simple sketch of an impact oscillator. If we think of the motion of a body in one dimension, described by the position $u(t)$ and velocity $v(t)=du/dt$ of its centre of mass, we can visualise this body as a single particle in space. Figure 1 shows that there is a linear spring and dashpot attaching this particle to a datum point in order that its position fulfils the dimensionless differential equation in free motion:

$$\frac{d^2u}{dt^2} + 2\zeta\frac{du}{dt} + u = w(t), \quad if \quad u > \sigma,$$

$$(2.1)$$

where, the mass and stiffness have been scaled to unity, 2ζ denotes the viscous damping coefficient, and $w(t)$ is an applied external force. We assume that motion is free in the region $u > \sigma$, until there is impact with the rigid surface $u = \sigma$ at some time

Figure 2. Oscilloscope trace of the phase portrait of the impact oscillator modelled by an electronic circuit, with the velocity variable v(t) shown vertically and the position variable u(t) horizontally. This experimental result agrees with the solution of (2.1)-(2.3) with σ = 0, r = 0.95, ζ = 0 and ω = 2.76 (M. Oestreich, Hinrichs, & Popp, 1996)

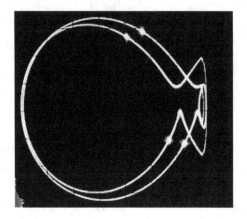

Figure 3. Bifurcation diagram for increasing ω; σ = 0 and r = 0.9 (a) Analytical and (b) experimental results (M Oestreich, Hinrichs, Popp, & Budd, 1997)

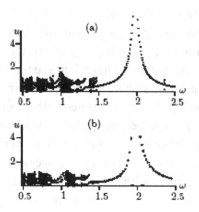

t_0. What actually happens, from the rigorous mathematical point of view, is that $(u(t_0), v(t_0)) := (u_-, v_-)$ is mapped at zero time to (u^+, v^+) via an *impact law*

$$u^+ = u^- \quad and \quad v^+ = -rv^-, \qquad (2.2)$$

where $0 < r < 1$ is Newton's coefficient of restitution. The resulting phenomena in this system can be of course be studied for different types of external forcing function (Bishop, 1994). Here, for the sake of brevity, we focus on a typical sinusoidal forcing function given by:

$$w(t) = \cos(\omega t), \quad with \ period \quad T = \frac{2\pi}{\omega}, \qquad (2.3)$$

The occurrence of impacts introduces *discontinuities* and an ensuing fierce *nonlinearity* into the system; otherwise, the system can be modelled as a smooth system or even a linear system, for

which there are well-established analysis tools. The nonlinearity makes the system acutely sensitive to its initial conditions to the extent that it shows highly irregular chaotic behaviour; not observed in any smooth nonlinear system (Leine & Nijmeijer, 2004). This sensitivity can be easily demonstrated by plotting the solution trajectories of (2.1)-(2.3) in the phase plane *(u,v)*, as shown in Figure 2.

Evidently, the system shows complicated periodic motion intermittent with the chaotic motion at the intervals when we vary, say, the number of impacts per period ω, as a parameter. This can be better seen by the bifurcation diagram of Figure 3, where some measure of the solution state, say oscillator position, is plotted against the parameter ω. As one can notice, there is a striking agreement between the numerically computed bifurcation diagram, resulted from selecting a random set of initial data and solving (2.1)-(2.3) with a numerical software package like Matlab (M. Oestreich, et al., 1996), and the experimental traces resulting from stroboscopic sampling (M Oestreich, et al., 1997).

In a smooth nonlinear system, the characteristic behaviour is for a Fiegenbaum cascade of

Figure 4. Schematic diagram of a DC to DC buck converter

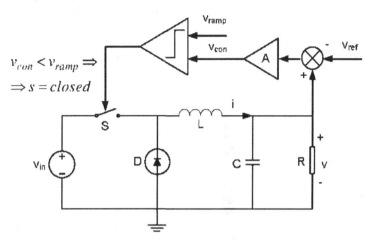

period-doubling bifurcation to $(2^k, 2^k)$ orbits, for $k = 1, 2, ..., \infty$ leading to chaos (Cvitanovic, 1984). This cannot be observed in the impact oscillator, mainly because the resulting orbit of the system loses stability through grazing bifurcations (Di Bernardo, et al., 2007), which can only be observed in non-smooth dynamical systems. That is why in such systems, an unexpectedly different level of complexity is introduced into the *attractors* of the dynamical system or the so-called *ω-limit* sets. In a grazing event, which in a physical sense is the time just before the impact with the rigid surface $u = \sigma$, a periodic attractor can be instantly transformed to a chaotic attractor. Although this chaotic attractor may arise in intervals, it is utterly different in nature from the *period-doubling cascade* associated with the chaotic behaviour of smooth dynamical systems.

Case Study II: Electronic Converters

DC to DC converters have long been regarded as a good example of a nonlinear dynamical system. This might be for the simplicity of its circuit topology but also the variety of observed complex nonlinear phenomena. These circuits are almost omnipresent in our life. The laptop computer and most hand-held devices we use everyday will have one of these circuits to convert DC voltage to another DC voltage in a cheap, energy efficient manner. However, what's really important in our case, is the many possible forms of nonlinear dynamical behaviours the converter can exhibit when operating beyond a set-limit range of their input voltage, output current or other circuit parameters. An ideal representative voltage-mode DC/DC buck converter is shown in Figure 4. What actually makes the converter a non-smooth system, is the toggling between two circuit topologies or, in other words, two sets of differential equations:

$$\frac{di(t)}{dt} = \begin{cases} \dfrac{v_{in} - v(t)}{L}, & S \text{ is blocking} \\[3mm] -\dfrac{v(t)}{L}, & S \text{ is conducting} \end{cases} \quad (2.4)$$

$$\frac{dv(t)}{dt} = \frac{i(t) - \dfrac{v(t)}{R}}{C} \quad (2.5)$$

As apparent from the above equations, the electronic switch S introduces a discontinuity into the right-hand side of (2.4). The system naturally

Figure 5. DC-DC converter bifurcation diagram when the input voltage is varied as a bifurcation parameter. The sudden transition from a periodic to a chaotic attractor, visible as the black band, is quite distinguishable from the ω-limit set of the system

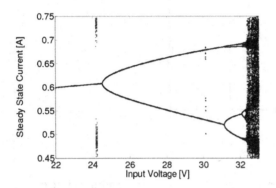

Figure 6. Discontinuity created in the price movement of microprocessors shows that it can be modelled as a non-smooth system

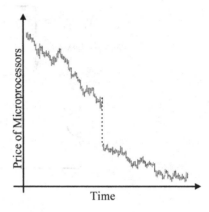

becomes a non-smooth dynamical system, referred to as a Fillipov system. Fillipov-type systems, which get their name from the 18th century Russian mathematician Alexander Fillipov who created the mathematical framework for studying discontinuous systems (Filippov, 1988), are non-smooth systems with a degree of smoothness equal to one (see section 3.1 for a definition).

If, for instance, the input voltage goes beyond the nominal range of the converter, a *Discontinuity-induced bifurcations* (DIB) makes the system lose stability and jump into chaotic behaviour. DIBs are a bifurcation phenomena that occurs only in non-smooth dynamical systems (Di Bernardo, et al., 2007). This is clearly observable in Figure 5, in which a corner-collision bifurcation leads the system to a chaotic attractor sooner than expected in any counterpart smooth system.

Case Study III: Financial Markets

The financial market is in fact one of the most complex nonlinear dynamical system imaginable. Over the years, it's been a long-held assumption that complex phenomena are the outputs of the systems with many degrees of freedom and were analyzed as random process. Simple phenomena were always modelled deterministically. However, as we have learned from the previous case studies, only a few degrees of freedom are necessary to generate complex chaotic motion. One of the most critical points in analyzing and predicting market trends is how to deal with *discontinuities* and their impact.

From the nonlinear dynamical point of view, a discontinuity is an apparent jump caused by a sudden increase in the size of the main attractor (solution space). Any attempt to model such a system using methods derived from smooth function techniques would be doomed to failure. This is as true in economics as it is in electrical and mechanical systems. At the same time, nonlinear mathematics suggests that there are infinitely many possibilities for discontinuities or *non-smoothness,* i.e. many combinations of factors causing jumps. Though many of these jumps can be of small magnitude, they can end up causing a big change in the dynamics of the system. A simple example of this non-smooth behaviour or sudden jump can be seen in the price movement of semiconductor chips (see Figure 6). When a new chip is introduced to the market, the price is relatively high. For the next year or so, the price fluctuates, dropping slowly. However, when the

Figure 7. Attenuating and amplifying of nonlinear factor f in the logistic equation of time series $Z_{(t+1)}$ = f . Z_t , where f itself a variable influenced by bid and ask or f = aX + bY can lead to a DIB and more complex behaviour

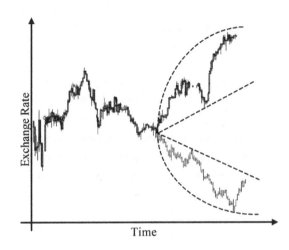

Time

next generation of chip comes out, the price of the old chip would drop sharply before it starts fluctuating again.

This non-smooth behaviour is somehow ever-present in all sorts of markets. One good example is the behaviour of Foreign Exchange Markets or FOREX. This is a currency market where banks and other financial institutions facilitate currency trading, i.e. the buying and selling of foreign currencies. Forex is by far one the most volatile and liquid market in the world, with large numbers of market participations (O'Sullivan & Sheffrin, 2003). One of the evident qualitative factors in this market is *market psychology;* in other words, rumours, trends, envy and greed. There is also a feedback effect in a financial market setting. Markets may have no long-term memory, but individuals who might have burned their fingers or made a fortune form past events have lots of it. If all these factors are considered in a logistic equation, mapping or projecting the time series of the Forex market, the effects of a severe fluctuation (attenuation or amplification) and discontinuity-induced bifurcation (DIB) can be visible.

In October 1992, speculation on the dollar/yen exchange rate attenuated, when the attack on the French Franc verses Deutsche Mark parity took all of the Forex market attention, forcing a *discontinuity* in the parity trend, as it did in the same period with the British Pound and the Italian Lira, devalued by 20 and 30 percent, respectively. A DIBs of the exchange rate price may result, as happened in the early 1980s with the Belgian Franc against other major currencies at the time, which had two values: commercial and financial, both fluctuating with market movements (Figure 7).

Fuzzy Engineering

Informed by the previous case studies, the challenge is how to put known procedures into effect when systems are dynamic and their output presents discontinuities (or non-smoothness) as well as uncertainties[4]. Uncertainties occur when we are not absolutely clear about the information elements at our disposal. The degree of certainty is usually represented by a *quantitative* value. In contrast, most problems encountered in dynamical systems are *qualitative*.

Fuzziness exists when the boundary of information is not clear-cut. Expression such as "more or less", "roughly equal to", "somewhat greater than average" are good examples of this. In some situations, *uncertainty* and *vagueness* may occur simultaneously, and precisely because of this, not every mathematical tool can serve the purpose of tackling piecewise dynamical systems – nor can even the most sophisticated analysis be applied in every situation. For example,

- A polynomial fit that oscillates widely between data points that appear to lie on a *smooth* curve would be a bad choice for *approximating* non-smooth dynamical functions.
- A tool that presupposes crisp (0 and 1 type) data or situations will not answer the chal-

lenges posed by vague conditions involving a significant measure of uncertainty.

The concept of Fuzzy logic, proposed by Zadeh in 1965, is essentially about how to deal with uncertainties. This is made clearer from his recent attempt (Zadeh, 2005) to expand the whole idea to form a generalized theory which can explain and quantify various different forms of uncertainties in existing systems. Uncertainty being the centrepiece of the theory is of prime importance, mainly because it includes both probability and possibility as special constraints.

Fuzzy engineering, in this respect, can really assist in pinpointing these seemingly unpredictable behaviours and identify their overall dynamics. The first stage in this approach is *system identification*. Among the different fuzzy system identification, the Takagi-Sugeno (TS) fuzzy modelling approach (Takagi & Sugeno, 1985) has been more successful in modelling the dynamics of complex nonlinear systems.

Let's understand better the whole modelling procedure of this approach by approximating a simple nonlinear system as an example. Consider the nonlinear system:

$$\begin{cases} \dot{x}_1 = x_2 + 3 \\ \dot{x}_2 = x_1^2 + x_2^2 + 3 + u \end{cases} \tag{2.6}$$

The ultimate goal of modelling the above nonlinear system through the TS fuzzy approach is that the response of the system as a black box with the input u would be the same as the original system. We specify a domain for variables $x_1 \in [0.5, 3.5]$ and $x_2 \in [-1, 4]$ as the area of fuzzy approximation and take advantage of exact linearization as the modelling method (the detailed general procedure of obtaining TS fuzzy model using this method can be found in (Tanaka & Wang, 2001)). The system (2.6) can be equivalently represented as:

$$\dot{x}(t) = \begin{bmatrix} 0 & 1 \\ x_1 & x_2 \end{bmatrix} x(t) + \begin{bmatrix} 3 \\ 3 + u \end{bmatrix}$$

where $x(t) = [x_1(t) \ x_2(t)]^T$. As x_1 and x_2 are nonlinear terms, we choose our fuzzy variables (premise variables) as function of state variables:

$$\begin{cases} z_1 = x_1 \\ z_2 = x_2 \end{cases}$$

The domain of premise variables z_1 and z_2 can be easily obtained from the domain of x_1 and x_2. Therefore, these can be represented by a combination of membership functions:

$$\begin{cases} z_1 = M_1(z_1) \cdot 3.5 + M_2(z_1) \cdot 0.5 \\ z_2 = N_1(z_1) \cdot 4 + N_2(z_1) \cdot (-1) \end{cases},$$

where M_1, M_2, N_1 and N_2 are fuzzy sets, on which the following rules apply

$$\begin{cases} M_1(z_1) + M_2(z_1) = 1 \\ N_1(z_1) + N_2(z_1) = 1 \end{cases},$$

If we name the fuzzy sets respectively as "Positive", "Negative", "Big" and "Small", the rules of the fuzzy system or the so-called model rules can be expressed by a typical fuzzy IF-THEN rule base as:

Model Rule 1:
    IF $z_1(t)$ is "Positive" AND $z_2(t)$ is "Big",
        THEN $\dot{x}(t) = A^1 x(t) + B^1$
Model Rule 2:
    IF $z_1(t)$ is "Positive" AND $z_2(t)$ is "Small",
        THEN $\dot{x}(t) = A^2 x(t) + B^2$
Model Rule 3:
    IF $z_1(t)$ is "Negative" AND $z_2(t)$ is "Big",
        THEN $\dot{x}(t) = A^3 x(t) + B^3$

Model Rule 4:

IF $z_1(t)$ is "Positive" AND $z_2(t)$ is "Small",

THEN $\dot{x}(t) = A^4 x(t) + B^4$,

where the subsystems are determined as:

$$A^1 = \begin{bmatrix} 0 & 1 \\ 3.5 & 4 \end{bmatrix}, A^2 = \begin{bmatrix} 0 & 1 \\ 3.5 & -1 \end{bmatrix},$$

$$A^3 = \begin{bmatrix} 0 & 1 \\ 0.5 & 4 \end{bmatrix}, A^4 = \begin{bmatrix} 0 & 1 \\ 0.5 & -1 \end{bmatrix} \text{ and}$$

$$B^1 = B^2 = B^3 = B^4 = \begin{bmatrix} 3 \\ 3 \end{bmatrix}.$$

The truth value (or activation degree) h^j for the complete rule j is computed using the aggregation operator AND, also called a *t-norm*, often denoted by

$\otimes:[0,1]\times[0,1]\rightarrow[0,1],$

$h^1(z)=M^1(z_1)\otimes N^1(z_2)$

$h^2(z)=M^1(z_1)\otimes N^2(z_2)$

$h^3(z)=M^2(z_1)\otimes N^1(z_2)$

$h^4(z)=M^2(z_1)\otimes N^2(z_2)$

Finally after the defuzzification process, the TS fuzzy model is derived as:

$$\dot{x}(t) = \sum_{j=1}^{4} h^j(z(t))(A^j x(t) + B^j u(t)) \qquad (2.7)$$

The model (2.7) can accurately represents the nonlinear system (2.6) in the region $[0.5, 3.5]'[-1,4]$ in the x_1-x_2 space.

The best choice of the consequent functions (or fuzzy sub-systems) would be the *affine* functions as seen in (2.7); therefore the TS fuzzy model can be generally explained in the form:

$$\dot{x} = \sum_{j=1}^{l} w^j(\theta)(A^j x + B^j u + a^j) = A(\theta)x + B(\theta)u + a(\theta)$$

$$y = \sum_{j=1}^{l} w^j(\theta)(C^j x + c^j) = C(\theta)x + c(\theta),$$

$$(2.8)$$

where $A^j:\mathrm{R}^{n\times n}$, $B^j:\mathrm{R}^{n\times m}$, $a^j\in\mathrm{R}^n$, $C^j:\mathrm{R}^{p\times n}$, $c^j\in\mathrm{R}^p$ and $w^j(\theta)$ is the normalized degree of activation h^j for each model rule j, which we call the weighting functions.

We deliberately said *the best choice* because it has been proven that the affine TS fuzzy system (2.7) can approximate any *smooth* nonlinear function (Tanaka & Wang, 2001). The accuracy of the model will not be affected, whether the TS fuzzy model is obtained from identification of input-output experimental data (Takagi & Sugeno, 1985) or the linearization of the original non-linear function. TS fuzzy identification methods for smooth nonlinear systems are now well-established although there are issues regarding the identification accuracy using input-output data (Tanaka & Wang, 2001).

3. ISSUES AND DIFFICULTIES

Can Current Fuzzy Modelling Approaches Represent a Non-Smooth System?

Sensitive dependence to initial conditions is the signature of nonlinear systems, specially the non-smooth kind. As we saw in section 2.1, a non-smooth system can be much more sensitive to parameter variations; an infinitesimal change in parameter values can change the dynamics of the system from stable period-1 behaviour to a totally unstable chaotic behaviour. In the popular paradigm of chaos theory based on smooth systems, a butterfly flapping its wings in central Asia could start a chain of weather events ending up with a typhoon in a distant place like Florida. Amazingly, if we re-tell the story for a non-smooth nonlinear

Figure 8. Original system (solid) and its Fuzzy approximation (dashed); assuming the existence of fuzzy approximation when losing uniqueness

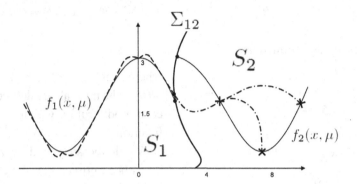

system, a butterfly flapping its wings in central Asia can instantly create a typhoon in Florida! Of course, real dynamical systems around us can be modelled with both smooth and non-smooth functions. However, that modelling of non-smooth systems to single out colourful, complex nonlinear phenomena can be of vital importance.

Despite numerous attempts to model complex nonlinear system using the TS fuzzy approach, there has been no evidence of its universal suitability to the modelling of discontinuous systems. Although it seems, at first, that the system described by (2.8) can approximate any dynamical function, the equation is in fact structurally and mathematically inadequate for the representation or approximation of any discontinuous function. Let's explain this through a simple example:

Consider the approximation of the following non-smooth system by TS fuzzy system (2.8):

$$\dot{x} = \begin{cases} A\sin(x), & S \text{ is ON}, & x \in [-\pi, \pi] \\ A\cos(x), & S \text{ is OFF}, & x \in \left]\pi, 3\pi\right] \end{cases}$$
$$(3.1)$$

When the switch S is ON, the function f behaves as a *sine* function and when S is OFF, the function f behaves as a *cosine* function. We select the off-equilibrium linearization method to obtain our fuzzy model from the original function[5]. The

idea is to carry out a first-order Taylor expansion at different points θ_i and let the rule base describe the validity of the obtained linear model at each point (Tanaka & Wang, 2001). We try to approximate the original system (3.1) over nine (-2.6, -1.57, 0, 1.57, 2.6, 3.63, 4.66, 5.69, 6.72) linearization point which should normally yield enough modelling accuracy. As envisaged in Figure 8, there is no problem approximating the smooth *sine* function when S in ON, but once the switch goes OFF, the problem arises in approximating the rest of the function.

If we consider the system (3.1) as a *non-smooth* flow function $\Phi(x,t)$, it can be specified by finite set of ordinary differential equations (ODEs), $f_1(x,\mu)$ and $f_2(x,\mu)$, and the state space could be partitioned into different regions S_1 and S_2, each partition being associated with a different set of ODEs since the system behaves differently in each region. Therefore, a formal definition of (3.1) could be:

$$\dot{x} = \begin{cases} f_1(x,\mu), & \text{for } x \in S_1, & x \in \Re^n, \mu \in \Re^p \\ f_2(x,\mu), & \text{for } x \in S_2, & x \in \Re^n, \mu \in \Re^p \end{cases}$$

where $\cup_i S_i = D \subset R^n, i=1,2$ and each of S_1 and S_2 has a non-empty interior. The intersection Σ_{12} between the closure of the sets S_1 and S_2, $\Sigma_{12} = \bar{S}_1 \cap \bar{S}_2$, is either an $R^{(n-1)}$ dimensional manifold included in the boundaries ∂S_1 and ∂S_2 (called *discontinuity set* or *switching manifold*) or an empty set. Any non-smooth flow Φ has the *degree of smoothness r*, if the first *(r-1)* derivative of Φ with respect to $x \in X$ exist and are continuous at every point $x \in X$, where X is the state space (Di Bernardo, et al., 2007).

We already know that each vector field f_i is smooth in its region S_1, but the problem arises if we try to define a flow $\Phi(x,t)$ for the behaviour of the system as a whole. To overcome this difficulty, there should be a map to define the *transition* just before the switching manifold to just after the switching manifold, otherwise, the function f or the flow Φ are undefined on the switching manifold Σ_{12} at the switching instant.

In a more rigorous mathematical sense, one of the basic methods to conclude the existence and uniqueness of a differential equation with a vector field satisfying only the *local Lipschitz condition* (Khalil & Grizzle, 1996) is if one has some further knowledge of the behaviour of the system (like if the solution stays in a compact subset[6] of the domain where a local Lipschitz condition is satisfied). Generally, the existence of a unique solution of $\Phi(x,t)$ should be guaranteed only over a small interval, say $[t_0, t_0+T]$ where $T > 0$. We can then expand this interval to $[t_0+T, t_0+2T]$ to guarantee the existence of a unique solution of another part of the $\Phi(x,t)$ until we cover the whole state space. Hence, the fuzzy model (2.8) cannot satisfy the Lipschitz property at the point of discontinuity Σ_{12} (which is an instantaneous interval) where the flow $\Phi(x,t)$ is non-existent for the smooth fuzzy system (2.8). Even if we assume the existence of the fuzzy model approximation of the trajectory of the system (3.1) just after the switching manifold, the flow loses it uniqueness as shown by the two simulated trajectories in Figure 8. This is because a fuzzy model of the form (2.8) is essentially looking for a smooth connection between the linearization points (2.6, 3.63), so it will be confused regardless of how many linearization points we choose for maximum accuracy, whether it continues on the

smooth trajectory as a continuation of the past interval around the linearization point 4.66 or point 5.69 (visible in Figure 8).

Can Current Fuzzy Engineering Tools Tackle the Stability Analysis of Non-Smooth Systems?

Let's transform the nonlinear system (2.6) into a linear system as follows:

$$\begin{cases} \dot{x}_1 = f_1(x) = x_2 + 3 \\ \dot{x}_2 = f_2(x) = x_1 + x_2 + 3 \end{cases} \tag{3.2}$$

This can be described by $\dot{x} = f(x) = Ax + B$ where $A = [0\ 1; 1\ 1]$ and $B = [3\ 3]^T$. The vector $x^0 \in \mathbb{R}^2$ is called an *equilibrium* of the vector field f if $f(x)=0$. The interesting point is that if any trajectory starts from the equilibrium $x^0 = [0\ -3]^T$ of the linear system (3.2), it will stay there forever. However, if a trajectory starts anywhere near x^0, it may completely diverge from or converge to x^0. The primal theorem of stability states that if the eigenvalues of the state matrix A have negative real part, any trajectory starting from any initial condition, will converge to x_0 and the linear system is (globally) exponentially *stable* (Khalil & Grizzle, 1996). Thankfully there is a way to check the stability of a linear system without solving the system.

Revisiting the nonlinear system (2.6)

$$\begin{cases} \dot{x}_1 = f_1(x) = x_2 + 3 \\ \dot{x}_2 = f_2(x) = x_1^2 + x_2^2 + 3 + u \end{cases}$$

The system have multiple equilibrium points $x_1^0 = (-3, -2\sqrt{3})$ and $x_2^0 = (-3, -2\sqrt{3})$. The main difference between a nonlinear system and a linear one is the fact that a nonlinear system may have multiple equilibria and other invariant sets, which may lead to complex dynamics. A smooth (differentiable) dynamical system can have periodic orbits (limit cycles), non-periodic orbits, invariant torus and chaotic attractors (Kuznetsov, 1998). In a way, the easiest way to study stability is to locally linearize the whole system around the equilibrium point or around the orbit in the case of limit cycles (Kuznetsov, 1998). This linearization is achievable through a Taylor series expansion while neglecting higher order terms. The TS fuzzy modelling approach discussed in section 3.1, is one the best ways to achieve accurate linearization around any desirable point. After linearization, it is possible to check the stability of equilibria as linear systems or the stability of limit cycles by calculating the so-called Floquet multipliers (Kuznetsov, 1998) of the system. Floquet multipliers are the eigenvalues of the linearized matrix around the periodic orbit, which ought to have the real part inside the unit circle for the system to be stable.

As previously pointed out in section 2.2, most problems in non-smooth dynamical systems are qualitative. In that respect, the qualitative theory of this kind of nonlinear systems demand different notion of stability, called *structural* stability, a concept tied up with *bifurcation theory*. To better understand these concepts, assume the autonomous nonlinear system:

$$\dot{x} = f(x, \alpha), \qquad x \in \Re^n, \qquad \alpha \in \Re^p$$

where f is smooth. If through a small change in parameter value, for example the input voltage of a dc to dc converter circuit, the invariant set of the system is transformed to another invariant set, a bifurcation occurs and the system is said to have lost its *structural* stability[7].

A new notion of structural stability is demanded in the case of non-smooth dynamical systems. In this, changes to system parameters may cause, for example, a limit cycle of a non-smooth flow to touch the switching manifold Σ_{12} at a grazing point. In this case, the limit cycle (or in general

Figure 9. In the bifurcation scenario above, a new classification of bifurcation, DIB, is visible when the non-smooth flow hits the switching manifold tangentially at the grazing point and its dynamics qualitatively changed (DIB grazing bifurcation (Di Bernardo, et al., 2007))

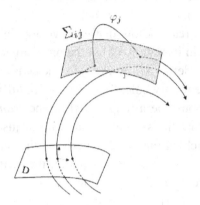

invariant set) qualitatively changes with respect to the switching manifold (Figure 9). It therefore gives birth to a new classification of bifurcation, already mentioned, as a discontinuity-induced bifurcation (DIB) (Di Bernardo, et al., 2007). Interesting verities of DIB exist which cannot be found in smooth dynamical system[8]. Sometimes the DIBs of limit cycles can instantly drive a non-smooth system into chaos.

In the Fuzzy control literature, a dominant tool for stability analysis is the *Lyapunov function* technique (Tanaka & Wang, 2001). For non-smooth systems, proving asymptotic stability (even for a classical notion of stability[9]) can be a very demanding task; so the Lyapunov function technique would be potentially a viable solution. However, it is not clear how existing techniques (which can hardly suffice for the stability analysis of equilibria of a non-smooth system) can tackle structural stability problem?

Basically, the Lyapunov technique is all about finding a *common* Lyapunov function, $V(x)$, which is positive definite and decreasing along the system trajectory in the whole phase space. For a non-smooth system, the function $V(x)$ should be positive definite and decreasing for each of the vector fields defining the system dynamics in each of the phase space regions (Liberzon, 2003). Nevertheless, finding such a Lyapunov function in practice is at best troublesome. Firstly, finding a common Lyapunov function for the whole phase space results in a conservative formulation, this cannot be solved using any analytical or existing numerical method. Secondly, the method is focused on the stability of invariant sets. This second point is of great importance as it stifles the use of Lyapunov theory for proving structural stability. Instead, the dominant stability analysis tool these days is nonlinear discrete modelling, which mainly focuses on examining periodic orbits and their stability by checking the so-called Floquet multipliers of the system (Di Bernardo, et al., 2007; Giaouris, Banerjee, Zahawi, & Pickert, 2008; Leine & Nijmeijer, 2004).

What is the Solution?

One of the main obstacles in studying non-smooth dynamical systems is the lack of rigid procedures for accurate mathematical modelling and numerical simulation. Certainly, wide-spread black-box routines designed to solve smooth dynamical systems cannot be used directly for non-smooth systems since they don't allow for any discontinuous event when the switching manifold Σ_{ij} is crossed. There have been attempts in the past to overcome this problem with two reported methods for numerical simulation of non-smooth system: *event-driven* and *time-stepping* algorithms *(Brogliato, 2000; Brogliato, Ten Dam, Paoli, Genot, & Abadie, 2002)*.

Even though these methods have been applied successfully, depending on the dimension of the specific problem, the modelling and rigorous numerical analysis of non-smooth dynamical systems is still an open research area. Part of the deficiency of the above methods comes from the fact that the modelling, though accurate, ignores

the underlying element of this kind of systems, i.e. uncertainty. On the other hand, current fuzzy modelling approaches (section 2.2) can represents a degree of uncertainty, but they are unable to represent the inherent non-smoothness of the original function. Therefore, if we can find a way to somehow modify the fuzzy model (2.7) to embody the discontinuities, this would be an important advance in the modelling of non-smooth dynamical systems.

Asynchronized discrete event systems are a familiar subject in implementing petri-nets (Cassandras, 1993; Hadjicostis & Verghese, 1999). These systems are usually described by:

$$m^+(t) = \xi(m(t), \sigma(t)),$$

where m is the discrete state variable, σ is the discrete input and ξ is a function describing the change of m. The input σ takes values in a finite set Σ (This Σ should not be mistaken with Σ as discontinuity set or switching manifold), and the elements in Σ are commonly called events. Examples of such events could be "switch S blocking" (case study II) or the "impact with the rigid surface" (case study I). The notation m^+ conveys the next discrete state of m, or in a more accurate sense, $m^+(t) = m(t_{k+1})$ is the successor of $m(t) = m(t_k)$. It is common to drop the time-dependency in m^+ as it's fairly obvious. Now, a non-smooth dynamical system can be obtained if the corresponding TS fuzzy model consists of interacting continuous and discrete event systems. This means that in addition to interpolating between different continuous sub-systems in the TS fuzzy model (2.7), both continuous and discrete states should interpolate with each other. This is possible through synthesizing a new type of fuzzy model of the form:

$$\begin{cases} \dot{x} = \sum_{j=1}^{l_e} w^j(\theta, m)(A^j(m)x + B^j(m)u + a^j(m)) = A(\theta, m)x + B(\theta, m)u + a(\theta, m) \\ m^+ = \xi(x, m) \end{cases}$$

$$(3.3)$$

Figure 10.

$$S_{1,2} = \{x \in \Re^n \mid \xi : m_1 \to m_2\}$$
$$S_{2,1} = \{x \in \Re^n \mid \xi : m_2 \to m_1\}$$

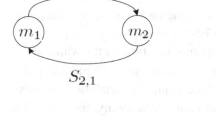

where $x \in R^n$ is the continuous state, $m \in M = \{m_1, ..., m_N\}$ is a discrete state (N possibly infinite), $A^j(m_i) \in R^{n \times n}$, $B^j(m_i) \in R^n$, $a^j(m_i) \in R$, $w^j : R^n \times M \to [0,1]$, $j \in I_{lm}$ are continuous weighting functions satisfying $\sum_{j=1}^{lm} w^j(\theta, m) = 1$ and l_m is the number of fuzzy rules. The state space is the Cartesian product $R^n \times M$. The function $\xi : R^n \times M \to M$ describes the dynamics of the discrete state. The fuzzy model (3.3) basically implies the fuzzy state space F is partitioned to different regions, named $\Omega_q, q \in I_\Delta$, which separated by switching manifold Σ_{ij}. Therefore, each region represents continuous dynamics in the form of set of fuzzy sub-systems

$$\sum_{j \in \{1,2,...\}} w^j(x, m_i)(A^j(m_i)x + B^j(m_i)u),$$
$$i \in I_N = \{1, 2, ..., N\},$$

which we termed *sub-vector field* (K Mehran, D Giaouris, & B Zahawi, 2009) and it is associated with discrete state $m_i \in M$.

For ease of implementation, the switching events can be describe by a number of switch sets $S_{i,k}$, expressed as:

$$S_{i,k} = \{x \in \Re^n \mid m_k = \xi(x, m_i)\}, \quad i \in I_N, k \in I_N,$$
$$(3.4)$$

The switch set (3.4) is actually employed to represents discontinuity sets or switching manifolds Σ_{ij}. Referring to case study II (section 2.1.2.), if we associate the discrete state m_1 with the dynamics in equation (2.4) when switch S is blocking and the discrete state m_2 with the dynam-

ics in equation (2.4) when switch S is conducting, the switch sets explain the system by the state transition diagram[10] in Figure 10.

As we have the fuzzy model structure (3.3) in hand to represent a non-smooth dynamical system, a method can be devised to study the structural stability or even the stability of equilibria of these systems. Fortunately, there is an immense amount of literature on how TS fuzzy systems can be used with Lyapunov techniques to provide an insight into the system. Unfortunately, in the case of non-smooth dynamical systems, the stability analysis would be implausible without having the *right* model. Moreover, the Lyapunov technique itself hasn't showed any promise in tackling structural stability problems. Nevertheless, in the case of non-smooth system, there are ways of formulating the conditions for studying stability and onset of chaos by acquiring the model structure (3.3). First, however, it is necessary to state the basic stability criteria of TS fuzzy systems modelling smooth dynamics by the following theorem:

Theorem 1: The system $\dot{x} = \sum_{j=1}^{l} w^j(\theta) A^j x$ is asymptotically stable if there exists a positive definite and symmetric matrix P such that:

$$(A^j)^T P + PA^j < 0, \quad \forall j = 1, 2, ..., l$$

using the smooth quadratic Lyapunov function $V(x) = x^T P x$, the proof of the theorem fist appeared in (Tanaka & Sugeno, 1992).

As pointed out in section 3.2, the problem of the above formulation (or any other complex formulation) is finding a smooth Lyapunov function over the whole state space. Even for smooth systems, these formulations result in a conservative formulation which in many cases, cannot be numerically solved. After the seminal papers by Paden (Paden & Sastry, 1987; Shevitz & Paden, 1994), it has been shown that the analysis of non-smooth dynamical systems should be based on *discontinuous* or *non-smooth* Lyapunov function. Furthermore, it has been shown, that partitioning the state space into different regions can result in a less conservative (although more complicated) formulation (Johansson, Rantzer, & Arzen, 1999), even in the case of smooth fuzzy systems. Hence, we will base our analysis on *piece-wise* smooth Lyapunov functions, which can be decreasing along the trajectories in *detached* but *flexible* fuzzy state-space regions $\Omega_q, q \in I_\Delta$ (which necessitates that partitioning fulfils $\Omega_1 \cup ... \cup \Omega_\Delta = \Omega$ and $\Omega_q \cap \Omega_r = \varnothing, q \neq r$). This simply means that if the trajectory starts from an initial point in region Ω, $t_k, k=1,2,...$, it can pass through to another region on the condition that $t_k < t_{k+1}$. Not all regions are of the same kind, and there should be a general definition for the regions representing switching manifolds. The existence of this kind of region is of vital importance for the structural stability of non-smooth systems, since it defines the *transition* just before the switching manifold to just after the switching manifold in the fuzzy systems by playing the role of the switching manifold Σ_{ij}. The formal definition is:

$$\Lambda_{qr} = \left\{ x \in \Re^n \middle| \exists t < t_0, \ such\ that\ x(t^-) \in \Omega_q, x(t) \in \Omega_r \right\}$$

where a set of fuzzy continuous states for which the trajectory $x(t)$ with initial condition $(x_0, m_0) \in F_0$ can pass from Ω_q to Ω_r. It is essential for the regions or the sets Ω_q and Ω_r to be next to each other (hence, we call Λ_{qr} a neighbouring region or set). Λ_{qr} can define any hypersurfaces including switching manifolds with the following conditions:

$$\begin{cases} \Sigma_{qr} = 0 \\ \sum_{j \in \{1,2,...\}} w^j(x, m_i)(A^j(m_i)x + B^j(m_i)u) \cdot \nabla\Sigma_{qr} < 0 \end{cases}$$

Since the trajectory should ultimately pass (or in the case of neighbouring regions map) from one region to another, we define another kind of region as:

$$I_\Lambda = \{(q,r) | \Lambda_{qr} \neq \phi\}$$

which is a set of tuples indicating that there is at least one point for which the trajectory passes from Ω_q to Ω_r.

For each fuzzy region, a Lyapunov energy function $V_q : cl \ \Omega_q^x \to R$, $q \in I_\Delta$, (*cl* denotes the closure of a set, which is the smallest closed set containing a set) is assumed to be continuously differentiable on $cl \ \Omega_q^x \to R$, $q \in I_\Delta$. The time derivative of $V_q(x)$ is expressed as:

$$\dot{V}(x) = \sum_{j=1}^{l_m} w^j(\theta, m) \frac{\partial V_q(x)}{\partial t}(A^j(m) + B^j(m)), \qquad (x,m) \in \Omega_q$$

The overall Lyapunov function $V(x)$, composed of local $V_q(x)$, is *discontinuous* at neighbouring regions Λ_{qr} $(q,r) \in I_\Delta$ and with the assumption of $t_k < t_{k+1}$ for every trajectory with an initial point in any region, is *piecewise* with respect to time.

Searching for a Lyapunov function, except in some simple cases, is a very complicated analytical task. The other option is to numerically search for the function, which necessitate formulating the stability conditions as Linear Matrix Inequalities (LMI) which may be solved by interior point methods (Boyd, El Ghaoui, Feron, & Balakrishnan, 1994). Therefore, the first stage here is to define each fuzzy state-space partitions by positive (quadratic) functions. A so-called *S-procedure* technique makes this definition possible by substituting confined conditions with unconfined conditions (Boyd, et al., 1994). To explain the substitution, the procedure is first elaborated in general terms and then applied to the confined conditions of the forthcoming stability theorem (Mehran, et. al., 2009).

$Q_0, ..., Q_s$ being the quadratic function of the variable $x \in R^n$ of the form:

$$Q_k(x) = x^T Z_k x + 2c_k^T x + d_k, \quad k = 0, ..., s, \tag{3.5}$$

where $Z_k = Z_k^T$, we can impose the following condition:

$$Q_0(x) \geq 0 \quad \text{in the region} \quad \{x \in \Re^n \mid Q_k(x) \geq 0, \ k \in I_S\} \tag{3.6}$$

The first two conditions in the stability theorem can be formulated in the form:

$$Q_0(x) \geq 0 \quad \text{in the region} \quad \Omega_q^x, \tag{3.7}$$

where $Q_0(x) \geq 0$ is the corresponding condition in the region. By searching the quadratic functions $Q_0(x) \geq 0$, $k \in I_S$ under the condition $\Omega \in \{x \in \Re^n \mid Q_k(x) \geq 0, \ k \in I_S\}$, it is clear that if condition (3.6) is fulfilled, the condition (3.7) will be automatically fulfilled too. The extreme case would be letting the condition $Q_0(x) \geq 0$ be valid in the entire state space, although this should normally be averted since this conservative formulation may end up not finding a solution for the original condition (3.7). By including Ω in a region specified by the quadratic function, the confined condition (3.6) can be substituted by an unconfined condition through the following Lemma:

Lemma (Boyd, et al., 1994)**:** If there exists $\delta_k \geq 0$, $k \in I_S$, such that

$$\forall x \in \Re^n, \ Q_0(x) \geq \sum_{k=1}^{s} \delta_k Q_k(x)$$

then (3.6) holds. Therefore, by introducing additional variables $\delta_k \geq 0$, $k \in I_S$, the condition (3.7) can be formulated as the following LMI condition:

$$x^T \begin{bmatrix} Z_0 & c_0 \\ c_0^T & d_0 \end{bmatrix} x \geq \sum_{k=1}^{s} \delta_k x^T \begin{bmatrix} Z_0 & c_0 \\ c_0^T & d_0 \end{bmatrix} x \tag{3.8}$$

If the fuzzy region partitions Ω_q, $q \in I_\Delta$ are represented by a single quadratic form, conditions (3.6), (3.7) and the condition of Lemma will be equivalent. We already know that the neighbouring regions are given by the switching manifold. Hence, they can be represented by $Q_k(x) = x^T Z_k x + 2c_k^T x + d_k = 0$, $k \in I_S$, where there is no constrain such as $\delta_k \geq 0$, $k \in I_S$ in Lemma, since Lemma holds regardless of the sign of δ_k[11].

In order to incorporate the candidate Lyapunov functions into an LMI problem, they should be defined as piecewise quadratic with the following structure:

$$(x, m) \in \Omega_q, \ V_q(x) = \pi_q + 2p_q^T x + x^T P_q x$$

where

$$\pi_q \in \Re, \ p_q \in \Re^n, \ P_q = P_q^T \in \Re^n \times \Re^n, \ q \in I_\Delta$$

Therefore the overall *discontinuous* Lyapunov function candidate $V(x)$ is defined as:

$$V(x) = V_q(x) = \begin{bmatrix} x \\ 1 \end{bmatrix}^T \begin{bmatrix} P_q & p_q \\ p_q^T & \pi_q \end{bmatrix} \begin{bmatrix} x \\ 1 \end{bmatrix} = \tilde{x}^T \tilde{P}_q \tilde{x}, \quad (x, m) \in \Omega_q \tag{3.9}$$

Now, by describing $Q_k(x)$ in its matrix form:

$$Q_k(x) = \begin{bmatrix} x \\ 1 \end{bmatrix}^T \begin{bmatrix} Z_k & c_k \\ c_k^T & d_k \end{bmatrix} \begin{bmatrix} x \\ 1 \end{bmatrix} = \tilde{x}^T \tilde{Z}_k \tilde{x}, \quad k = 0, ..., s, \tag{3.10}$$

and by assuming that the fuzzy region partitions Ω_q, $q \in I_\Lambda$ are represented by the LMI form $Q_k^q(x) \geq 0$, $k \in I_{S_q}$, that the neighbouring region Λ_{qr}, $(q,r) \in I_\Lambda$ is represented by the LMI form of $Q_k^{qr}(x) \geq 0$, $k \in I_{S_{qr}}$ and by substituting the conditions given in different fuzzy regions by the LMI condition (3.8), the stability conditions can be formulated as an LMI problem (Mehran, et. al., 2009) as follows:

LMI problem: If there exists $\tilde{P}_q$, $q \in I_\Lambda$, constants $\alpha > 0$, $\mu_k^q \geq 0$, $\nu_k^{qij} \geq 0$, $\eta_k^{qr} \geq 0$ and a solution to min β subject to the following conditions:

1.

$$Q_0(x) \geq \tilde{P}_q - \alpha \tilde{I} + \sum_{k=1}^{s_q} \mu_k^q \begin{bmatrix} Z_k^q & c_k^q \\ (c_k^q)^T & d_k^q \end{bmatrix} \geq 0, \qquad q \in I_\Lambda$$

2.

$$Q_0(x) \geq \beta \tilde{I} + \sum_{k=1}^{s_q} \mu_k^q \begin{bmatrix} Z_k^q & c_k^q \\ (c_k^q)^T & d_k^q \end{bmatrix} - \tilde{P}_q \geq 0, \qquad q \in I_\Lambda$$

3.

$$Q_0(x) \geq -\left((\tilde{A}^j)^T \tilde{P}_q + \tilde{P}_q \tilde{A}^j + \sum_{k=1}^{s_{qij}} \nu_k^{qij} \begin{bmatrix} Z_k^q & c_k^q \\ (c_k^q)^T & d_k^q \end{bmatrix} + \gamma \tilde{I} \right) \geq 0, \qquad (q,i,j) \in I_\Lambda$$

4.

$$Q_0(x) \geq \tilde{P}_q - \tilde{P}_r - \sum_{k=1}^{s_{qr}} \eta_k^{qr} \begin{bmatrix} Z_k^{qr} & c_k^{qr} \\ (c_k^{qr})^T & d_k^{qr} \end{bmatrix} = 0, \qquad (q,r) \in I_\Lambda$$

then, the fixed point is exponentially stable in the sense of Lyapunov[12], where $\tilde{I}$ is the matrix [1 0;0 0].

In the first and second conditions, α and β are constants but originally represent a class K function

$$\alpha(\| x \|), \quad \alpha : \Re^+ \to \Re^+ \text{ and } \beta(\| x \|), \quad \beta : \Re^+ \to \Re^+$$

(the definition of a class K function can be found in (Khalil & Grizzle, 1996)). $\gamma > 0$ is simply a scalar constant. As the forth condition is satisfied on the neighbouring region Λ_{qr} (or the switching manifold) the condition for fuzzy partitions should be given by $Q_k(x) = 0$, $k \in I_S$, where each $Q_k(x)$ has the form (3.6).

The LMI problem can predict the onset of bifurcation or instability leading to chaos for the non-smooth dynamical system represented by the fuzzy model (3.3) through the fixed point of the system's trajectory. The fixed point of the poincaré map is the intersection of the limit cycle with the map. The above stability conditions investigate when the limit cycle loses its stability by checking if the Lyapunov function candidate (3.5) is decreasing along the trajectories in each local fuzzy partition Ω_q, from local partition Ω_q to Ω_k within a fuzzy sub-vector field and most importantly on the neighbouring regions Λ_{qr}, which is the point at which the energy function becomes discontinuous.

To prove the applicability of the theoretical analysis, we applied the TS fuzzy model structure (3.3) and (3.4) to the buck converter (Mehran, Giaouris, & Zahawi, 2008) described in case study II to see if the edge of the bifurcation will be successfully detected by this new method. Figure 11 shows that the bifurcation occurs when the input voltage V_{in} is changed from $24V$ to $25V$. This can also be predicted by the LMI problem showing an infeasible solution when the input voltage is changed to $25V$ but being exponentially stable for $V_{in} \leq 24V$ with the optimal value of $\beta = 2.4962$ (Mehran, et. al., 2008).

4. CONCLUSION AND FUTURE RESEARCH

The proposed TS fuzzy modelling method is able to approximate non-smooth dynamical systems with varying degrees of smoothness. For instance, it is possible to include state jumps in the dynamics of the model (3.3) by another function χ: $D_\chi \to R^n$, where:

$$x^+ = \chi(x, m_i)$$

and the set of states where the state jump takes place for different discrete states can be equivalently explained by the following sets:

Figure 11. The bifurcation diagram of the TS fuzzy model of the converter is well matched with the original bifurcation diagram shown previously. It also shows how the stable limit cycle of the converter loses its stability to a period-doubling bifurcation

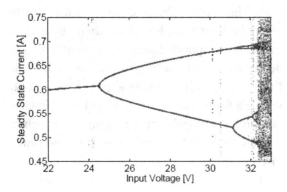

$$J_i = \left\{ \, x \in \Re^n \mid x^+ = \chi(x, m_i) \, \right\}, \qquad i \in I_N$$

Therefore, by letting switch sets $S_{i,j}$ and J_i concur at certain fuzzy continuous states *(x ∈ F)*, a jump can occur at both discrete and continuous states. Moreover, by employing *non-determinism* in discrete event systems and by defining another discrete state, it is possible to represent *sliding mode* behaviour in the model (3.3), which is typical of mechanical relay systems.

One of the difficulties when attempting to simulate a NSDS is that existing *time-stepping* or *event-driven* modelling methods can only be implemented using special purpose software packages. No single software platform is yet available to accurately simulate and study the performance characteristics of these systems. Commercial algorithms have not yet been designed to allow robust numerical computations of all NSDS with different degrees of smoothness; consequently these are computationally expensive options. The proposed fuzzy method may allow the possibility of designing algorithms that do not require special-purpose software platforms. More importantly the new method, although not complicated, is able to approximate the uncertainty inherent in non-smooth systems that tends to be neglected by other available methods for the modelling of discontinuous systems.

Fuzzy engineering has unequivocally shown (at times with other AI-based methods) that it is a powerful tool for system identification. The proposed model structure (3.3) and (3.4) can be especially valuable when obtained from experimental input-output data and in situations when access of the original function is impossible. In this case, the Lyapunov framework proposed for stability analysis is a very useful tool in predicting the onset of dynamic changes (DIBs and chaos) in non-smooth systems. The main reason for this is that the Lyapunov analysis attempts to investigate the stability of the system in an indirect way while other approaches directly target the problem, which in the case of high-order complex non-smooth systems, may result in an incomputable solution.

The last two decades have witnessed considerable efforts in the attempt to control chaotic systems. Chaos control strategies are still difficult to implement and in many cases, still in their theoretical stages. This analysis has shown that a novel TS fuzzy model-based control scheme can be devised, using the LMI formulation, to stabilize the system to its professed period-1 behaviour. One of the design approaches based on the proposed methodology here, is expounded in (Mehran, et. al., 2009).

However, there are some issues that need to be addressed. First, the proposed stability conditions cannot pinpoint the higher period-doubling bifurcation. More sophisticated LMI formulations are needed to specify the kind of instability, which could be an unstable limit cycle, interspersed by some completely chaotic periods. In this respect, the existing interior point methods should be enhanced to better solve those LMI problems.

Second, fuzzy state-space partitioning does not always lead to an actual solution. In some cases, a high number of region partitions, although representing the region more accurately, can end up in formulations which are misleadingly infeasible. Therefore, there is always a delicate balance to strike between high accuracy and complexity. A general guideline for state-space partitioning needs to be developed with some urgency.

Most complex systems in reality, including many Kansei applications where *uncertainty* and *discontinuity* are two essential elements of data gathering and processing, are composed of different nonlinear systems networked together. The behaviour of these systems could be far more complex if they are networks of non-smooth systems. The application of fuzzy engineering in modelling the inner interaction of these complex systems and quantifying their substantial uncertainty is an important subject for future research.

REFERENCES

Babitskii, V. I. (1978). *Theory of Vibroimpact Systems. Approximate methods*. Moscow: Nauka.

Bishop, S. R. (1994). Impact oscillators. *Philosophical Transactions. Physical Sciences and Engineering*, 347–351.

Boyd, S., El Ghaoui, L., Feron, E., & Balakrishnan, V. (1994). *Linear matrix inequalities in system and control theory*. Society for Industrial Mathematics.

Brogliato, B. (2000). Impacts in mechanical systems- Analysis and modeling. *Berlin, Springer-Verlag(Lecture Notes in Physics., 551*. Brogliato, B., Ten Dam, A. A., Paoli, L., Genot, F., & Abadie, M. (2002). Numerical simulation of finite dimensional multibody nonsmooth mechanical systems. *Applied Mechanics Reviews*, *55*, 107. doi:10.1115/1.1454112

Cassandras, C. G. (1993). *Discrete event systems*. New York: Springer.

Cvitanovic, P. (1984). *Universality in chaos*. Bristol: Adam Hilger, Ltd.

Di Bernardo, M., Budd, C. J., Kowalczyk, P., & Champneys, A. R. (2007). *Piecewise-smooth dynamical systems: theory and applications*. New York: Springer.

Feigin, M. I. (1994). *Forced oscillations in systems with discontinuous nonlinearities*. Moscow: Nauka Publication. [in Russian]

Filippov, A. (1988). *Differential equations with discontinuous righthand sides*. Amsterdam: Kluwer Academic Pub.

Giaouris, D., Banerjee, S., Zahawi, B., & Pickert, V. (2008). Stability Analysis of the Continuous-Conduction-Mode Buck Converter Via Filippov's Method. *IEEE Transactions on] Circuits and Systems I: Regular Papers, IEEE Transactions on [Circuits and Systems I. Fundamental Theory and Applications*, *55*(4), 1084–1096. doi:10.1109/TCSI.2008.916443

Hadjicostis, C. N., & Verghese, G. C. (1999). Monitoring discrete event systems using Petri net embeddings. *Lecture Notes in Computer Science*, *1639*, 188–207. doi:10.1007/3-540-48745-X_12

Johansen, T. A., Hunt, K. J., Gawthrop, P. J., & Fritz, H. (1998). Off-equilibrium linearisation and design of gain-scheduled control with application to vehicle speed control. *Control Engineering Practice*, *6*(2), 167–180. doi:10.1016/S0967-0661(98)00015-X

Johansson, M., Rantzer, A., & Arzen, K. E. (1999). Piecewise quadratic stability of fuzzy systems. *IEEE Transactions on Fuzzy Systems*, *7*(6), 713–722. doi:10.1109/91.811241

Khalil, H. K., & Grizzle, J. W. (1996). *Nonlinear systems*. Upper Saddle River, NJ: Prentice Hall.

Kuznetsov, Y. A. (1998). *Elements of applied bifurcation theory*. New York: Springer.

Leine, R. I., & Nijmeijer, H. (2004). *Dynamics and bifurcations of non-smooth mechanical systems.* New York: Springer.

Liberzon, D. (2003). *Switching in systems and control.* New York: Birkhauser.

Mehran, K., Giaouris, D., & Zahawi, B. (2008). Modeling and stability analysis of dc-dc buck converter via takagi-sugeno fuzzy approach. *ISKE 2008, International Conference on Intelligent Systems and Knowledge Engineering, Xiamen, China, (1), 401-406 (selected for publication in the Journal of Donghua University (English version).*

Mehran, K., Giaouris, D., & Zahawi, B. (2009). Stability Analysis and Control of Nonlinear Phenomena in Boost Converter using Model-based Takagi-Sugeno Fuzzy Approach. *Accepted for publication at IEEE Transaction on Circuits and Systems - I: Regular papers.*

O'Sullivan, A., & Sheffrin, S. M. (2003). *Economics: principles in action.* Upper Saddle River, NJ: Prentice Hall.

Oestreich, M., Hinrichs, N., & Popp, K. (1996). Bifurcation and stability analysis for a non-smooth friction oscillator. [Ingenieur Archiv]. *Archive of Applied Mechanics, 66*(5), 301–314. doi:10.1007/BF00795247

Oestreich, M., Hinrichs, N., Popp, K., & Budd, C. (1997). *Analytical and experimental investigation of an impact oscillator.*

Paden, B., & Sastry, S. (1987). A calculus for computing Filippov's differential inclusion with application to the variable structure control of robot manipulators. *IEEE Transactions on Circuits and Systems, 34*(1), 73–82. doi:10.1109/TCS.1987.1086038

Palm, R., Driankov, D., & Hellendoorn, H. (1997). *Model based fuzzy control.* New York: Springer.

Shevitz, D., & Paden, B. (1994). Lyapunov Stability Theory of Nonsmooth Systems. *IEEE Transactions on Automatic Control, 39*(9), 1910–1914. doi:10.1109/9.317122

Takagi, T., & Sugeno, M. (1985). Fuzzy identification of systems and its applications to modeling and control. *IEEE Transactions on Systems, Man, and Cybernetics, 15*(1), 116–132.

Tanaka, K., & Sugeno, M. (1992). Stability analysis and design of fuzzy control systems. *Fuzzy Sets and Systems, 45*(2), 135–156. doi:10.1016/0165-0114(92)90113-I

Tanaka, K., & Wang, H. O. (2001). *Fuzzy control systems design and analysis: a linear matrix inequality approach.* New York: Wiley-Interscience.

Zadeh, L. A. (2005). Toward a generalized theory of uncertainty (GTU)—an outline. *Information Sciences, 172*(1-2), 1–40. doi:10.1016/j.ins.2005.01.017

ENDNOTES

[1] Berkeley Initiative for Soft Computing (BISC) programme: http://www-bisc.cs.berkeley.edu/BISCProgram/default.htm

[2] "Toward a Generalized Theory of Uncertainty (GTU)—An Outline", article by Lotfi A. Zadeh to appear on information sciences, January 20, 2005

[3] Private conversation with author, London June 2009.

[4] Webster's defines uncertainty as the quality or state of being uncertain. An uncertain issue is something not exactly known; not determined, certain, or established; a contingency.

[5] A detail explanation can be found in (Tanaka & Wang, 2001) and good collection of ex-

amples in (Palm, Driankov, & Hellendoorn, 1997) and (Johansen, Hunt, Gawthrop, & Fritz, 1998).

[6] A subset of Euclidean space R^n is called a compact set if it is closed and bounded. For example, in R, the closed unit interval [0, 1] is compact, but the set of Z is not (it is not bounded) and neither is the half-open interval [0, 1) (it is not closed). However, generally, a topological space called compact if each of its open covers has a finite sub-covers. Otherwise it is called non-compact.

[7] Bifurcation theory can be further investigated in (Kuznetsov, 1998).

[8] Bifurcations occurring in smooth systems are termed *smooth bifurcations* because they have nothing to do with switching manifolds.

[9] Stability of equilibria whose eigenvalues are located in the right-half plane.

[10] It is noteworthy that $S_{i,k}$ represents, in general, the set of all values of x that the switching conditions can apply. Therefore, putting them directly on state transition diagram is just for ease of illustration, though, according to formal definition, we should put the switching condition directly on top of each transition arrow.

[11] If in any case, the switching manifold cannot be represented by $Q_k(x)=0$, $k \in I_s$, there is a possibility to represent such manifold by larger switch regions. However, this may end up in a conservative LMI formulation.

[12] The theoretical proof of the theorem can be found in (Mehran, et. al., 2009).

Section 2
Measurement, Analysis, and Representation of Kansei

Chapter 9
An Intimate Relation:
Human Beings with Humanoids

Elisabeth Damour
Act & Be - Creative Management Consultancy, France

ABSTRACT

From the reading of numerous press releases, one may deduce that Japan is a country more and more dedicated to a 'robot world'. Previously, robots were hidden in plants confined within difficult or dangerous tasks: nowadays robots make themselves visible: humanoids and androids offer home services for elderly. Such a situation is questioning the nature of relationships between human beings and humanoids and highlights how we can understand the human's position and identity. In becoming part of a family, we could presume that robots should be considered in the position of a child with his or her parent establishing an amazing couple. We will refer to the works of a renowned psychoanalyst Donald Woods Winnicott to understand the way a child may receive the best conditions to become a mature and independent adult. A child when becoming an adolescent is at risk to show possible antisocial behaviours, as symptoms of delinquency. Human beings would certainly prefer the option of an absolute dependence from their robot-child, keeping it waiting in a sort of perpetual adolescence. In that way, human beings would feel more secure not to be challenged in their unshared human hood. Conversely, humans challenging machines and imagining cyber-bodies are to be found in performances and sports events. Researchers consider that robots would emancipate and create a life of their own. Doing so, they seem to offer new opportunities for developing human creativity, eluding the inexpressible threat: shall humanoids overtake human beings in their capacity to run a creative life?

1. INTRODUCTION

In a country where Sony Aibo robot dogs are treated like family, humanoid and android robots are expected to take place of the workforce and to provide an aging population with a compassionate presence and create one of the greatest new industries of the 21st century. Very soon androids

DOI: 10.4018/978-1-61692-797-4.ch009

will be available in a price range where many people will be able to afford them.

When asked to give a definition of a robot, Katsushi Ikeuchi, a Professor at The University of Tokyo [Ikeuchi, 2008] answers that a robot is an artificial thing with three functions: a function of sensing, one of taking an action and thanks to an artificial intelligence, the capacity of judging and executing by itself. [Ikeuchi, 2008]

A robot with the shape and abilities of a human is an android. An egg shaped lawnmower equipped with eyed- video camera and remote control is a robot but not an android. Anything that can initiate interaction with the outside world like a human being does is a humanoid. For instance, *Asimo* the famous robot, launched by Honda Company in 1996, not only collects information from its environment but also initiates interaction with the outside world: it is an understatement that Asimo is a true humanoid.

For more scientists the goal of an android is to be a domestic servant which is supposed to become as useful as a car. Robots are built mainly to relieve people of dangerous and tiring tasks. It is interesting to notice that robots help human beings enjoy life not only in providing them more time for their leisure but also in providing them with more interesting jobs. It could be foreseen that in the future, any job which is not creative could be performed by a robot. Thus, factory line workers but also dangerous tasks as security guards should be replaced by these new machines. It is worth to mention that robots and androids could be also very efficient machines in spaceships bound for the Moon and further...

Is this trend only restricted to economical stakes dedicated to our wellbeing or is it a main issue for human kind?

2. RELATION & INTIMACY

We can't ignore that the generation of humanoids and androids have a strong humanlike appearance:

this similarity is not resulting from an accident. As Researchers are starting from a human template it is an implicit fact that a robot must resemble a human being.

Robots and humanoids are supposed to interact with people and to be dedicated to live in proximity of the humans. Thus the similarity of appearance with human beings becomes an issue to facilitate interpersonal relationships and is justified by the intimacy with the human models.

The Director of Osaka University Intelligent Robotics Laboratory, Hiroshi Ishiguro [Ishiguro, 2008] wants to investigate human activities from multiple points of view (with cognitive science, behavioural science and neuroscience) and supports this new cross-interdisciplinary framework called android science. He is the creator of *Repliee Q1 the humanoid* which he built by "copying" a real person, Ayako Fuji who is a speaker at NHK TV. Everyone can testify that the result is astonishing: Repliee Q1 is a clone not distinguishable from the person it is supposed to represent. Repliee Q1 is a child of the "Android science." Development of androids occurs to be an important issue.

The resemblance appearance status is not a mere design solution. When the robot android is part of the household and occupies the same space as humans, it is logical that it should resemble the human being not only in function but also in shape.

Katsushi Ikeuchi, Professor at the University of Tokyo ponders upon a robot which could become a true partner of human beings and have a 'normal' dialogue with a human being [Ikeuchi, 2008]. Is this only a fantasy?

In June 2007 a team research has created a robot which was trained physically to show human emotions. *Kansei Robot* through its silicone face frowns or smiles or is scared depending on the selected words it is supposed to react to. Kansei frowns when he hears the word "bomb" smiles at "sushi" and looks afraid and disgusted when someone says "president". 'What we are trying to do here is to create a flow of consciousness in robots so that they can make the relevant facial expressions' said project leader Junichi Takeno, a professor at Meiji University's School of Science and Technology. [Kansei, 2007]

Reportedly, Kansei Robot represents a stake in advanced technology; it is a key to improving communication between humans and robots. Kansei means in Japanese a function of our human brain: special functions as inspiration, creativity, emotion, attachment and curiosity.

All these dimensions are reputed to be exclusively related to human beings. Being creative and having a creative life could be the key role in mankind. Humanlike robots, humanoids, androids and Kansei Robot run the risk of compromising people's comfort zones.

3. BEING IMMORTAL

What people are afraid of? Besides the fact that many people may fear for their jobs when androids appear, what is making them anxious is that androids are the rank result of a remarquable level of intelligence in scientific research.

As the machine shows an ability to solve problems, people are scared to be overtaken by such a *'megamachine'*: a machine which will make a conquest for its needs in a kind of colonisation as defined by the philosopher Günther Anders [Simonelli, 2004]. Androids occur to be very special. They are not a mere machine. We can consider in some cases that androids will be able to repair themselves and to repair other androids - as doctors do with humans. Is this the evidence that androids are not supposed to die: androids will be immortal?

4. A QUESTIONABLE LIKENESS

It is supposed that when a robot's appearance comes to resemble a human's, the degree of intimacy increases. However, a point may be reached at which subtle imperfections create a

sensation of strangeness or uneasiness and then a strong repulsion may appear. This negative emotional reaction is known as the "*uncanny valley*" [Kuniyoshi, 2008] and is part of hypothesis studied by a Japanese researcher in robotics, Masahiro Mori, in the early 70's.

The robot which appears to be humanlike will seem strange to a human being and conduct to a paradox. Being perfectly humanlike or being not is a fundamental paradox in android science.

Conversely, we could encounter a similar *"uncanny valley"* effect when humans want to modify themselves with the aim to improve their abilities beyond what would normally be possible, in an attempt to become 'transhuman'.

5. A CYBER-BODY

In the artistic area, dancing robots are more and more part of choreographic creations. It is the evidence that some persons seem to adapt themselves perfectly well to a virtual world without feeling any reluctance.

The virtual body seems to be echoing to the fantasy of the Golem. The Golem is named from a psalm in the bible and quoted from Jewish Talmudists tradition. Without giving a comprehensive definition of the Golem, the Golem means an unshaped substance to which God gave life.

In our current world the Golem could occurred to be the world of robots and androids. These machines are no more the fruits of the imagination of science fiction authors. In some European cultures, the virtual is equal to escaping from the reality and from the boundaries of the biological organisation. Nevertheless, Japan seems not to be linked to such religious backgrounds: the prerequisites which have facilitate the high inventive level in Japanese research have may be some roots in this cultural gap.

The coming part will focus on the works of a performer Stelios Arcadiou, whose stage name is Stelarc. [Stelarc, 2009]

The Australian born artist has performed in Japan and Europe, especially in dance festivals. Stelarc's work could be considered as being outside the art margins. But it must be also understood as a production from our current years, where the status and position of the body has been modified. In fact, Stelarc may be seen as a 'discoverer' who witnesses his own time. In this perspective, the body seems to loose a sacred position and be driven by off-limit challenges. No doubt that this position sparks off multiple possibilities for any artists eager to question and transform the world and its boundaries.

From the early 70's Stelarc passionately and obsessively pursues the expression of his vision of the body. He explores virtual reality systems and uses Internet in a way which anticipates the future of a body equipped with robotics devices and prosthetics.

Of course his research shows strong fundamental trends: the body is a degenerating body therefore useless in our new worlds and environments [Stelarc, 1999]. To oppose such a pitiful fate Stelarc proposes that the body could be augmented, becoming a host for technology. To provide an example: the inner human body is showing enough room to make it swallow a supervision system. This system allows a medical remote control for permanent check-up of blood, temperature etc.

The consequence of this research is that the body's identity is fading behind the importance of its connectivity and interfacing capacities. Stelarc situates his creations on the transition from psycho-body to cyber system.

Connected to internet, a machine, the Stimbod provides a good example of the way Stelarc eases up an intimate sensation through interface without proximity. The process allows a person to have a sensation of touch through an actuation system by the movement of one another person who is not present.

The Stimbod makes possible the first experimentation of intimacy without proximity and questions the experience of being present.

Instead of seeing the Internet related devices as a means of fulfilling desires of disembodiment, Stelarc sees that it offers powerful individual and collective strategies for projecting body presence and extruding body awareness. For him, the Internet generates new collective physical couplings and a new assessment for subjectivity. One question remains about the capacity of an individual to cope with the experience of absence and of alien action without becoming overcome by metaphysical fears. This is reinforcing the fear to loose individuality and free decision.

When justifying his projects, Stelarc underlines that the current human body becomes inadequate to cope with the future challenges. As humans we experience that the body often malfunctions, that its performances are determined by its age and that it is doomed to a inescapable and early death. It is no longer meaningful to see the body as a site for the psyche. In becoming a mere object, the body is no more an object of desire: if this body has no birth, it has consequently no death. Death would be an evolutionary strategy from the past!

Is Stelarc signing up the end of a traditional philosophy grounded in a limited human physiology? As a result, one can imagine that the reproduction activity of such a cyber-body could be perpetuated by some human-machine interfacing.

It is undeniable that these questions about off-limits options are jeopardizing our Platonic, Cartesian and Freudian models. If referring to these models, we may dare to say that Stelarc's creations might be considered pathological.

Going beyond any limits can't be considered as neutral in the human development steps. This off-boundary behaviour may possibly lead human beings not only to a presumptuous position but further to an illusion upon their omnipotence state.

6. AN OUTMODED BODY

Two years ago, a disabled sprinter from South Africa, asked the Olympic Committee to be allowed to get part of the Olympic Games 2008 as a non disabled athlete. Oscar Pistorius though competing with two legs prosthesis is challenging the best non-disabled sprinters in the world. Pistorius' request has not been accepted, on the plea that the prosthesis turn out to be an advantage.

Pistorius' prosthesis is obviously made from state- of the- art design and material, which is not the case for all disabled persons of course. Nevertheless, prosthesis seems to be no more limited in an amending or substitution position in order to provide disabled persons with a more comfortable daily life. This kind of prosthesis is now playing an active part in the creation of an augmented body.

Oscar Pistorius seems to have fully integrated his body in a fantasized representation of himself as he describes himself as 'the faster 'thing' without legs' in the world. [Pistorius, 2007]

Disabled people can be seen as people with 'less' mobility: definitely we have to consider this point of view as a mere belief to be relinquished to the past. We may figure out that the added body is no more a science-fiction vision! Scientists have informed that in a short while, probably in twenty years ahead, this increasing performances trend will find its conclusion. Athletes will have recourse to the use of prosthesis. We will assist or be part of a change: augmented body will be the standard rule…

What is at stake is to believe the simulacrums provided by the virtual devices to be the truth. How this could be harmful for humanity?

Men have always tried to simulate the reality. We can say that each artistic period has tried to reach a perfect simulacrum of the reality. So that, we can think that the semblance is the real and we are invited to mix the two dimensions. When reality and virtual are tightly mingled, it may happen that people may feel unsteady and confused entering a virtual world not knowing what will happen in the future. Human beings feel afraid that they could lose their identity.

In our current years which are often defined as post-modern, it seems that every limitation must become questionable and especially in the artistic field where artists and performers are overlapping the limits of the human identity almost announcing the death of the body.

When reality and virtual are tightly mingled, it may happen that people may feel unsteady and confused entering a virtual world not knowing what will happen in the future. Human beings feel afraid that they could lose their identity.

7. A SKIN FOR OUR IDENTITY

It is of importance before we could delineate limits applied to human beings, to try to understand what human identity could be. Doing this, we are invited to draw back on a research developped in the mid seventies by a french psychoanalyst.

Didier Anzieu [Anzieu, 1995] considered the skin as the first and natural border where initiates and finishes the personal identity, the 'I'. The membrane which separates our inner space from the outer world is named the *'ego-skin'*. The skin is obviously a barrier, a protective and healthy envelope related to our human capacity to feel real. One can wonder if in showing their tattoos and piercing, young adolescents are seemingly trying to experiment their 'ego-skin' limits.

When performers and artists announce the death of the 'ego-skin' they seem to show the same behaviour as these young adolescents willing to blow out the human body ultimate limit.

Living in the reality is a pre-requisite for acknowledging our limits. The more we are aware of our limited human condition, the more we can develop a potential space for our imagination.

It is part of the human life to accept that limits do exist: obviously they are limiting our capacity in doing what we are abble to imagine. Since the rule of the game is to cross again and again the boundaries, human beings showing a healthy and mature identity do not have to feel jeopardized.

But a question still remains; could all the limits be indefinitely pushed away?

When accepting to live in a human state in a limited skin, individuals won't go through a state of regression, making them go back to what Donald W. Winnicott (1896-1971) called the illusion of an omnipotence state.

8. BECOMING A MATURE HUMAN BEING

In an attempt to describe how humans become human beings, we will restrict here mostly on the human capacity to run a creative life. Previously, we have seen that this condition about creativity seems to be relevant to what is defined as 'life' for robots and androids.

Willingful to go deeper in a comparison between android and human being, we will focus on the works of the British psychoanalyst Donald W. Winnicott who underlined the key role played by what he defined a 'good enough mother' in the child's development. A good development ensures the infant to become capable of mature relations when entering into the social world, the real world.

In the early time of the life's baby the mother adapts herself to his needs and provides him with an optimal environment. By that time infant and mother live in a 'merged couple'. This fusion state has a consequence. The baby considers he is all-powerful and thinks he can create precisely what he desires. All human babies have lived this stage. Living in this *temporary illusion* has an advantage: it prevents the infant from anxiety and is a condition for the baby to feel comfortable. At the same time the baby discover the sense of *subjective omnipotence* [Winnicott, 1964].

This stage of subjective omnipotence doesn't last so long because shortly the mother would begin to recede. Then, the baby will start to realize that the outside world is not always there to fulfil all his desires. When the baby is confronted to an *outside world, to an objective reality,* he experi-

ences for the first time a relationship between the real world and the subjective omnipotence. This relationship is of importance: in it can be found a mature and creative life with a healthy sense of independence, but it has to be underlined that independence will never be reaching to the point of an absolute independence. Obviously, relinquishing the subjective omnipotence is a painful end for magical illusion: fortunately babies have genetically mental mechanism helping them to cope with the insult of the *reality principle*. This step is of crucial importance: because it is the beginning of the feeling of being real. Every human being in his life has lived a first paradox in recognizing and accepting reality.

The little infant has the illusion to create the entire environment with all the objects which are presented to him. Becoming more and more mature the infant becomes confronted to the reality principle and understands that all his desires won't be fulfilled at once anymore.

D. W. Winnicott highlights a fundamental concept: the *reality principle* is the inception of the differentiation principle which *underlines the disparity in years or in gender* ... The reality principle gives the human beings the limits. It is an ultimate principle to prevent the confusion from virtual world and off- limit world. From D. W. Winnicott's perspective, the illusion principle is an important positive aspect of human involvement in the world of experience and in the capacity of running a creative adult life.

9. A SYMBOLIC SPACE

The insult of the reality principle is tolerated and non traumatic only because playing and creating is filling the space between mother and infant. This specific relation about a separation takes place in what Donald Winnicott delineates as a 'potential area'. The potential area is an intermediate area of experiencing, an 'area that is allowed to the infant between primary creativity and objective perception based on reality-testing.' [Winnicott, 1971]

What Winnicott called the *transitional experience* is a transitional zone: it is a middle ground between the *objective reality* that means the real world (the 'not-me') and the *subjective omnipotence* (the 'me'). Only in this zone can be found *creativity* and further the possibility to live a *creative life*.

When the little child is able to cope with the reality principle and start a relationship to external reality - a 'not-me' relation, the infant stands in the threshold of a transition between a state of union with the mother, to the state of relation with her.

In this experience, the pediatrician psychoanalyst underlines the apparition of the 'transitional object' to which every parent remembers of. This object, a teddy bear, a blanket, a bit of cloth, is representing the mother 'when she is absent to feel connected to her.' [Winnicott, 1990]

This object without which the infant could not conceive of going to bed! The transitional object is a fantasy. When a child becomes abble to successfully use symbols, it means that the child has the ability to recognize and accept reality. The use of the first symbolic process when experiencing the detachment and the separation enables the child to stand frustrations and deprivations and to cope with new situations. This process, if planned for androids, would allow them to receive a human breeding! Maybe too human!

In the intimate relationship between human beings and humanoids, we may ponder upon the position of such a robot: being a child or becoming one of a human's transitional objects?

Following this demonstration, which kind of transitional area would be reachable for an android - which kind of transitional object should be convenient to an android when child: a baby android ? This step in the child development is a crucial point for the *concept of being*: it allows the integration of a personal pronoun 'I' that makes possible 'I am', which makes sense of 'I do.' 'This

occurs to be the establishment of an autonomous self at the initial stage.' [Winnicott, 1971]. From Donald W. Winnicott's extensive observation, we may deduce that androids and robots will stay in a dependence state, never to be confronted to an objective reality. Machines are created to be efficient as soon as they are launched in the market. Who will take care of machines and wait for them to grow as babies do.

The concept of potential space has a key role in designing a common place for playing and creating. It is the stage where the child can develop his/her creative self. Playing and creating are natural activities for every individual and are not to be dissociated in 'something that belongs properly to infant experience: the ability to create the world' [Winnicott, 1990] W. Winnicott thought that the experience of creativity was not limited to artistic activity.

D. W. Winnicott was comforted after a conversation with Marion Milner in 1969 [Winnicott, 1971] on the importance of a common interplay in the foundation of our self and personal creative process. *'There is nothing that is outside creativity territory'* [Winnicott, 1990] Thus, it could happen that humanoids lucky enough to be equipped with some consciousness devices should benefit from this possibility.

When giving themselves permissions to create, individuals will directly get in touch with this dedicated area where creating becomes possible as a *symbolic enactment*. When a child is deprived from these positive conditions: 'When the bridge between the subjective and objective is destroyed, or have never been well-formed, the child is unable to operate as a total human being'. [Winnicott, 1971] Deprived from any symbolic mental activity, the child lacks the capacity of escaping from the real by the way of imagination, ideas, language...Such a child and later as an adolescent will only 'enact in the real' with possible delinquent behaviours.

10. FEELING REAL AND BEING ALIVE

According to Winnicott, it is only when playing that an individual is able to be creative and to use his whole personality and discover his self. Donald Winnicott worked on the definition of the 'self' or 'ego' and he makes us discover the differences between false and true self.

The true self is instinctive and occurs to be the true core of the personality, enacting spontaneously, the false self on the opposite reacts to environmental demands. Each person has a polite or socialized self, and also a personal private self that is not available except in intimacy. Most children become able to accept a false self as a sort of 'dishonesty as a price to pay for socialization.' [Winnicott, 1990] Living with a false self leads to the sense of not being alive: In fact, the person has a poor symbolic life. Individuals are in extreme restlessness, inability to concentrate, and a need to react to the demands of the external reality.

What we may observe is that a robot, whatever it is designed for, occurs to stay in an absolute dependence from its creator. This means that robots and humanoids would be cornered in a kind of nursing phase, provided by the facilitating environment of its research team. The team would become the first subrogate mother-figure with which the robot is supposed to relate with. The androids and their teams are representing a sort of a *merged couple*, tight in a dual structure, where any third person as a father-figure would be excluded. Under such a circumstance, no transitional and creative space would create enough permission for the android to become independent and creative.

The further risk is that slightly the creator-conceptor becomes '*all good*' and perfect and not in a *good enough position.*

Due to its peculiar development phases excluding it from playing and creating experience, the android won't have any access to a symbolic mental activity: it is lacking in capacity of escaping from the real. In the 'real space' possible enactments would take place. If we consider the robot as a young man or adolescent, we have to envision which kind of hypothesis could be left.

For instance, if we start from the 'enactment in the real', we may say that environmental conditions could be easily reached for a robot to be on the point of becoming a *time bomb* in delinquency. Should the humanoid behave aggressively and destructively, it will certainly not feel only like truant school-boy: it could become a sort of young asocial delinquent, close to a hooligan figure.

Conversely, if the android would show any behaviour of escaping out of its creators' control, these might, as retaliatory measures cast away their 'creation' like rubbishy goods. It is to consider that robots' users will be very cautious of their androids: these machines are expensive and may be compared to luxury sports cars.

As the cultural life of a delinquent is notoriously thin, all options will be envisioned to avoid such a sad fate. Another option does exist: there is a possibility that the robot develops a devoted and passive behaviour showing tendencies to compliance with a devolving role.

Well briefed and knowing all the ground rules, the android would be able to provide a flawless and up the ante services, that consist in imitating any behaviours and feelings its creators' want it to perform. Subsequently, the robot would be developing what we have identified above as a false self. In that perspective, we may notice that the robot approximates dangerously to human beings.

Is the fate of robots to represent our false self? To an extent they occur to be a sort of coat-rack for our emotional life. Behind a false self the machine gives its allegiance to human kind, but this occurs to be a shift.

That is to say, that a robot has to back up on the span of all human emotions: that means the spectrum from happiness, up to love but also guilt, not to be forgotten aggressive and destructive impulses.

It seems that there is no option left for robots whatever clever they maybe: from delinquent teenagers to coat-rack for mirroring human impulses, they seem to signpost a new territory which could be favourable to a new enslaving civilization.

Representing human false self, would occur a limited and unhappy fate for robots. Though the dependence dimension is envisioned only from the machine point of view, it is interesting to highlight that the absolute dependence could be inverted and become a mutual dependence!

11. NEW ENSLAVING CIVILIZATION

From similar situations in advanced techno-logical devices, we may observe, that 'enslaved machines' become absolutely necessary to there 'masters-users'.

Even though robots creators dictate all the rules, may we be sure that robots users won't be in danger of becoming a mere robots appendage, wavering on the very verge on being managed by their own machine?

Eventually, the position of the robot is similar to a situation where child or adolescent are asked to be prematurely old. Then, adolescents are caught in their own traps and become dictators. *'Immaturity is an essential element of adolescence.'* [Winnicott, 1990]

Once we may assert that the robot is living its robot life in an absolute dependence, to be qualified by immaturity and a sort of perpetual adolescence, following the Winnicott's defini-tion, human beings may feel secure not to be challenged in their unshared human hood. It is an understatement that the enslaving position for robots and androids won't be a convenient place to create intimacy in the parent-child relation: it will create only suffering and envy.

On the opposite point of view this absolute dependence could be a pre-requisite to help us to elude the inexpressible threat: can humanoids emancipate from their creators?

12. CONSCIOUSNESS TO BE SHARED

The task of human beings is to keep exploring uncharted territories and keep ready to cross the threshold of the realms of fancy. *Asimo, Repliee Q1 and Kansei Robot* show the evidences that advanced technological machines will be able to help human hood.

Researchers confess that when they try to de-fine what is humanoid, they feel they are denying some aspects of the human beings! Humanoids, robots and androids can be seen as the result of the evolution of the human hood genius. Robots and humanoids are created by their creators and they are still the expressions of their creators: firstly in their human appearance and secondly they should be similar to human hood in their behaviours.

By now, we are scared by aggressive behav-iours humanoids could adopted for themselves: isn't it interesting that we foreshadow only re-vengeful and aggressive behaviours!

To some extent, our peace of mind would be extremely disturbed listening to the following researchers' visions.

Professor Katsushi Ikeuchi ponders upon creating a consciousness for humanoids. In his vision for the future, Robots would make their own decisions to make themselves to want to get better at things 'making something else happens'. [Ikeuchi, 2008]

The researcher thinks that it is not necessary to implement a model of the will of the human being 'it could be for a robot to have its own will. The desire to make good robots is not the desire to make copies of the human being. I want robots to exist as robots'. [Ikeuchi, 2008]

Professor Katsushi Ikeuchi further confesses that he started wanting to create a robot as a substitute for the human being, which will seem to be equipped with "artificial soul" and "will" [Ikeuchi, 2008].

It is to notice that most of the researchers in robotics testify that humanoids and androids will never be able to overtake human beings!

13. CONCLUSION

From a pragmatic point of view an android is operational when humans are abble to supply it with electricity, its basic need. Why would an android cause harm to someone who is providing it with positive feeding? How would androids try to eliminate humans? Would they kill people one by one? Would it be possible to imagine that when feeling jeopardized by our servant androids we could just unplug them and plug them again when things become better!

In our post-modern and New Age period, adults need to dream and to believe to the magic in the same process than that babies who are marvelled by their power upon the environment. We could be in great danger to feel ourselves over powerful. Thanks to D. W. Winnicott we know the antidote: offering a robot all the good conditions to get access to a symbolic position and be involved in a playing and creating activity, the same way as humans do.

This could be a new kind of training for researchers: becoming subrogates parents to allow humanoids not to be enslaved and providing them all the steps in becoming mature and creative creatures. It seems that androids and humanoids would become benevolent towards humans, grateful and willing to form an alliance toward more peaceful world to the benefit of humanity.

It is unquestionable that researchers in robotics are dedicating themselves for the 21st century in thinking how they should create a rich society. All their contributions are important and need to be supported because they are offering their intelligence to a larger goal which concerns all human hood.

It could be one of our human responsibilities to understand what we want to create. If we want to create a better humanity with compassionate and intimate relations, we need to mobilize any kind of creativity to reach this goal.

Because of our anxiety of being overtaken by the machine, we may forget to find out all the possibilities a robot should display. In some situations, one will find the reversed position of a humanoid parenting a human being and both becoming abble to learn from each other. Therefore, an android like a family pet could allow us to recover a forgotten playful and creative capacity, making our life worth it. From this point of view, humanoids and androids which are supposed to offer services to elderly and disabled people would become a valuable gift to offer for the happiness of the humanity.

REFERENCES

Ikeuchi, K. (2008, September). CREST – *Papers presented at the Symposium 'Can Humanoids Become Human' the Symposium is part of CREST 'Creating 21st Century art from based on digital media –* (Tokyo – University of the Arts - pp. 4-7)

Ishiguro, H. (2008, September*). CREST – Papers presented at the Symposium 'Can Humanoids Become Human' the Symposium is part of CREST 'Creating 21st Century art from based on digital media –* -(Tokyo – University of the Arts - pp. 10-12).

Kansei (2007). *Kansei makes a comeback with reactive facial expressions:.* Wednesday 6 June 2007, 11.00 A.M Reuters Review.

Kuniyoshi, Y. (2008, September). *CREST – Papers presented at the Symposium 'Can Humanoids Become Human' the Symposium is part of CREST 'Creating 21st Century art from based on digital media –* Tokyo – University of the Arts – p. 17

Simonelli, T. (2004). *Günther Anders. The obsolete Man.* Paris: Du Jasmin Ed.

Sterlac, (1999). *Nouvelles de danse - Danse nouvelles et technologies*, 41 p. 80 – 98 Editions Contredanse Bruxelles 1999 n°40-Pistorius, O. (2007) *Blog on Daily motion,* 17 July 2007 Anzieu, D. *The Ego Skin - Dunod.* Paris, 1995, p. 27

Sterlac (2009) *Body mecanics*, p. 37 publication is based on the Sterlac solo exhibition held in the Centre des Arts in Enghien-Les-Bains from 10 April to 28 June 2009.

Winnicott, D. W. (1964). The child, the Family and the Outside world. London: Penguin Books. Reading Massachusetts: Addison-Wesley publishing Co., Inc. p. 128

Winnicott, D. W. (1971). *Playing and Reality.* Tavistock Publication Routledge. (p. 15, p. 148, p.52). [Winnicott, 1990] Winnicott, D. W. (1986) Home is where we start from. First published in the USA by W. W. Norton & Company. Reprinted in Penguin Books. (p. 49, p.40, p.49, p.66, p.160).

Chapter 10
Music and Kansei:
Relations between Modes, Melodic Ranges, Rhythms, and Kansei

Shigekazu Ishihara
Hiroshima International University, Japan

Mitsuo Nagamachi
Hiroshima International University, Japan

Jun Masaki
Nagasaki Prefectural Government, Japan

ABSTRACT

In this chapter, at first the authors review the researches on music in Japan Society of Kansei Engineering. Music related researches are classified into 6 categories; Kansei evaluation methodology, music psychological research, physiological measurement, music theoretical research, Kansei music system and recommendation system. Then, the authors present their approaches for research Kansei on melody and rhythm from the music theoretical aspect. A mode, one of the most elemental structures in music, is a sequence of n musical tones, arranged from the 12 tones, that fall within a one-octave range and are chosen and arranged according to the rules of that mode. In this chapter, the authors analyze, using sound tracks composed automatically by computer software, the relationships between modes and Kansei. "Melodic range" is defined as the high and low extent of the tone movements in a mode. Mode and melodic ranges were the parameters they controlled for evaluation by Kansei. Eighteen sample tracks were automatically composed from combinations of six modes and three ranges. Forty-seven Kansei word pairs were used in the research questionnaire. The results of principal component analysis and an analysis of variance reveal a contrast between tracks with major modes and a larger range and tracks with minor modes and small range. The authors also found that modes and ranges can independently or synergistically affect the Kansei. Based on their results, they have developed a real-time melody recognition program that identifies the mode and its corresponding Kansei from music. The authors also studied rhythm with programmed drum patterns and found that the fluctuation of drum beats relates to the degree of activity, with the interval and complexity of the rhythmic variations relating to the strained to bright axis of a principal components loading map.

DOI: 10.4018/978-1-61692-797-4.ch010

1. INTRODUCTION

Music is one of the most preferred subjects in Kansei engineering research. Numbers of researches had been presented in autumn and spring annual conference of Japanese Kansei Engineering Society (JSKE) and been published in two journals, Journal of Kansei engineering (mainly in Japanese) and Kansei Engineering International (English journal). Kansei related Music researches have different perspectives. We can apply the dichotomous view of fundamental researches and applied approaches.

One aspect of fundamental research is developments of Kansei evaluation methods. Since Kansei engineering is empirical science based on measurement, different Kansei evaluation methods have been developing and been applying.

A most related discipline is music psychology. Music psychology (or under the names of psychology of music, psychomusicology and music perception) researches human responses to the music in empirical and theoretical way (Williams et al., 1981). Not only responses, music generation processes including composition and playing instruments are also becoming attracting researchers (Sloboda (ed.), 1988). Most important reflection to Kansei engineering is researches on music and evoked emotion (i.e, Gabrielsson & Juslin, 2002). Not only cognitive aspects, Psychophysiological aspect are also actively developed in Kansei engineering.

Another related discipline is the music theory. It explains and helps exploration on the structure of music. Music theory has a long tradition at least from 4th century. From Gregorian chants of early medieval age, music was made along with rigorous rules (Stein, 1979).

Applied approaches have two aspects. One aspect is music information processing. Today's developments of computer technology enable high-speed signal processing. Then, music recognition and generation of music those require the large amount of computation become possible.

Another aspect of application is the music recommendation. Recommendation is based on the knowledge of one's preference of tunes. It related to Internet based business and already commercially provided by some companies. It is promising but its methodologies are still developing. Since its beginning, one of the aims of Kansei engineering research is the recommendation system (i.e. Nagamachi et al. 1988), music recommendation is a legitimate subject.

Kansei engineering was pioneered by Nagamachi in early 1970s (i.e. Nagamachi, 1974, 1988, 1995, 2010). Japan society of Kansei engineering was established in October 1998. In Kansei engineering, many researchers have been researched music as one of their research subjects. Methodologies of different disciplines have been utilizing, including psychology, physiology, media art and signal processing engineering

2. REVIEW OF KANSEI ENGINEERING RESEARCHES ON MUSIC

Since the first annual conference of the Japan society of Kansei engineering in autumn of 1999, music related researches are continuously presented and published. We have classified researches into six categories.

The first category is Kansei evaluation methodology. Kansei evaluation is the foundation of an empirical science. Pieces of music are dynamic events in time (Gabrielsson & Juslin, ibid), and unlike other Kansei engineering subjects, music has no visible or tangible shape. Thus, many research methodologies have been actively proposing. Choice of Kansei words for evaluation is crucial, also is for multivariate analysis of evaluation data. Ikeda et al. (2000), Yamawaki & Shiizuka (2007a, 2007b, 2008), Sugihara et al. (2005, 2008) and Okamoto & Kashiwazaki (2005) used statistical multivariate analysis or rough set analysis with a number of Kansei words. Sugihara et al. (2008)

makes a distinction between passive selection (a subject was asked to rate all of Kansei words) and active selection (a subject's spontaneous evaluation words). Kawamura et al. (2003) and Nakai & Mitsuishi (2003) have focused on individual differences. Evaluation on "artificial – natural" (Kawamura et al.) and evaluation of "dark" tunes (Nakai & Mitsuishi) have larger individual differences. Ozawa, Seo & Ise (2007) and Murakami et al. (2007a, 2007b) are analysis of the timbre or frequency spectrum of tunes. Masaki, et al. (2008) investigates road scene and music relations, for proposing of tunes for driving. Yamawaki & Shiizuka (2002, 2005), Kashiwazaki & Okamoto (2007) reported intriguing associations between colors, abstract shapes and tunes.

The second category is music psychological researches. Takahashi et al. (2000) and Kojima et al. (2000) have researched timbre difference and Kansei. Murakami et al. (2008) reported associations between specific Kansei and their dominant frequency zones. Iseki & Ozawa (2005, 2007) investigated the mental set effect on listening. A tune that informed as the computer is playing was poorly evaluated by subjects who have no music playing experience. Experienced subjects have not such mental set. Okamatsu et al. (2007) and Fukumoto (2008) have investigated idiosyncratic relations between Kansei and tempo. Matsuzaki et al. (2005) researched different backing styles. Suk et al. (2007) studied associations between personalities and preferable ring tone melodies. Fujisawa & Saito (2007) found there is no significant relation between music preference and mental tempo, which has been often researched in music psychology. Nagata et al. (2003) tried to use colors as cues to ear training. Ikoma (2007) investigated the difference of absolute pitch recognition while with/without other activities. Aoshima & Toko-sumi (2007) has a unique psychological approach, an analysis of writings of Toru Takemitsu, on his musical pieces.

The third category is the physiological measurement researches. Physiological measurement of Kansei engineering was coined by Prof. Tomoyuki Yoshida, who had been our colleague. He found a significant relationship between subjective comfort and specific statistical distributions of fluctuations ("Yuragi" in Japanese) of alpha wave (8 to 13 Hz), which is measured from the frontal lobe (Fp1, Fp2). Despite of his unforeseen death in 2004, there are many psychophysiological works inspired by Yoshida theory. Higashitani & Yoshida (2004) was almost his last study. They found that combinations of the subject's preferred tunes and not-so-preferred tunes are more comfort than combinations of preferred tunes only. Sixteen classic tunes were used as stimuli. Measurement and analysis were done by Yoshida theory. It can be considered that some kinds of musical diversity will induce comfort.

Murayama et al. (2007, 2009) researched associations of music tempo, heart beat rate and alpha wave fluctuations by Yoshida theory. They reported music tempo close to the heart beat rate induces the fluctuations of the relaxed heartbeat. Slower tempo than the heartbeat induces more relaxed state of alpha wave fluctuation. Fukumoto et al. (2004) gradually slows the tempo of Erik Satie's Gymnopedie No.1, from 66 to 46 bpm by its iterations. They measured synchronization of music tempo and heart beat. During synchronization, $HF / (HF + LF)$ ratio, which shows parasympathetic nerve system activity was increased. HF is the power of high frequency (0.15 to 0.5 Hz). LF is the power of low frequency (0.04 to 0.15 Hz).

Kamei et al. (2006) and Akashi & Uozumi (2008) used NIRS (near-infrared spectroscopy) topography of brain activity. They reported decreased blood flow was induced by music. Yamamoto et al. (2005) and Yoshida et al. (2007) showed the tapping along with/without music. They reported attention and cortical activities with tapping. Shudou (2008) is a biological research using mice and human. After 7 days of listening murmuring of a stream, mouse brain increased serotonin and nor-adrenaline.

The forth category is researches based on music theory. Although music has a long tradition of its theory at least from 4th century (Burns, 1999), there are small number of researches in Kansei engineering, those are directly derived from or analyzed by music theory. Kawase & Tokosumi (2007a, 2007b) analyzed 240 Japanese traditional tunes, and they found local tendency. Analyses of melody transitions were done with an idea of tetrachord, which is proposed by a renowned ethnologist, Fumio Koizumi. Hashida et al. (2005,2007) have investigated individual differences of grouping of melody parts. They found two groups of subjects, a group has weights on accents to the beginning note, and another group has attention to arched change of loudness and tempo. The stimulus they used was Beethoven's piano sonata no.8.

Kansei music system is the fifth category. One of the approaches is mimicking human Kansei. Oonishi et al. (1999), Mieno & Shiizuka (2000), Kobayashi & Haseyama (2007) and Masaki et al. (2007) are attempts to Kansei music recognition system. Kobayashi & Haseyama defined a similarity measure of temporal patterns, and they applied it to find similar tunes. Masaki et al. (2007) is spectrum-based approach for classifying tunes.

Another approach of Kansei music system is assistance of composition. Tokumaru et al. (2004) utilized chaos neural networks. Variations of initial melody were automatically generated. Akabane et al. (2006, 2007) made automatic tuning of synthesizer's sound parameters along with drumming velocity and speed. Hirano & Saito (2008) developed an easy sequencer. Takahashi & Saito (2008) used physical controller for melody improvisation on a collaborative situation. Kanahako et al. (2005) made a system composes a tune from user's color drawings. Tokairin & Shiizuka (2007,2008) made a system consolidate short rock tunes into a complete tune along with Kansei. User chooses preferred Kansei by colors. Moroboshi & Shiizuka (2005a, 2005b) made a composition assistance system of choosing MIDI

loop fragments with KJ method and TRIZ. Fujio & Shiizuka (2005) is semi-automatic tune connecting system for DJ, with beat tracking and time stretching. Ishida et al. (2008, 2009) proposed a system measures walking pitch with an accelerometer, then it recommends a tune that fits the pitch. They used pre-composed 8 beat tunes for the repository. Watanabe & Shiizuka (2004) made a system that shows appropriate dance (choreograph) from the tempo and the key extraction of given tune.

The last category is the music recommendation system. It can be seemed as one of the Kansei music system applications, and is promising in rapidly growing Internet based music industry, like "iTunes Music Store" or "Last.fm". Miura et al. (2000) and Yamashita et al. (2000) made recommendation systems based on Kansei evaluations on various tunes. Another approach is utilizing features of tunes for recommending similar tunes. Yamawaki & Shiizuka (2005) used form, cadence and tempo. Shindo & Shoji (2008) used tags of lyric type, listening situation and tune tempo.

In later part of this chapter, we show out attempts to research music Kansei from the viewpoint of music generation with music theory.

3. KANSEI EVALUATION EXPERIMENT ON MODES AND MELODIC RANGES

Introduction

Many ideas and concepts have been created in the long history of music. Components of musical structure are intervals, mode, rhythm and tempo, melodic properties and timbre (Gabrielsson and Lindström, 2001).

Most of psychological studies on music are based on experimental psychological methods, which focus on empirically noticeable responses and not on differences between controlled variables. Other studies are based on cognitive psychological methods, including the generation of

Table 1. Church modes

		Authentic		Plagal
Minor	I	Dorian	II	Hypodorian
	III	Phrygian	IV	Hypophrygian
Major	V	Lydian	VI	Hypolydian
	VII	Mixolydian	VIII	Hypomixolydian

categories. Burns (ibid.) provides a famous review of experimental and cognitive psychological approaches to studying basic musical structures, including musical modes.

Although music is a great medium for expressing complicated emotion, the relationships between various *Kansei* and musical structure have not been extensively studied. Although several studies have analyzed these associations using psychological rating scales and multivariate analyses, many of studies have using limited and binary judgement tasks (Sloboda, ibid.).

Most of the studies have used existing musical compositions as stimuli. As Gabrielsson and Lindström (ibid.) pointed out, the challenge of using such existing pieces for scientific experiment is that difficult in real pieces to manipulate structural components, such as tempo, rhythm, pitch, melody, and harmony, because they interplay with each other.

Thus, we analyzed the relation between *Kansei* and musical modes and melodic range using musical pieces that were automatically generated by computer program via random numbers.

Background

From the 5th to the 17th centuries A.D., the "mode" was used as an established concept for musical composition. It originated with the theories of Pythagorean scholars in Greece during the 4th century B.C. In the 8th century A.D., with Gregorian chant, the use of modes was firmly established (Burns, ibid.). Gregorian chants were derived from eight different modes using

the names of, but not exactly corresponding to, the ancient Greek modes: Dorian, Hypodorian, Phrygian, Hypophrygian, Lydian, Hypolydian, Mixolydian, and Hypomixolydian (Kennedy and Bourne, 1996). From the 15th century to the 18th century, modes were ordered and they eventually evolved into today's common scales, such as the major scale, the melodic minor scale, and the harmonic minor scale.

By the 18th century, the used of tonic keys was well developed, and mode-based composition was temporarily abandoned. At the end of the 19th century, composers of modern music, such as Debussy, had created several new modes. Some 20th-century contemporary music combines more than two modes. There have been some attempts to re-analyze complicated compositions according to their modal aspects (Martin, 2000). In modern Jazz, mode is the basis of "modal composition and improvisation." In addition, several modes have found in traditional western African music, which suggests that modes are a global musical concept not limited to Western culture (Stevens, 2004, Kolinski, 2009). In today's electronica and ambient music, the mode is often used as a non-chordal (that is, monophonic, unharmonised) compositional concept.

Eight of the church modes are classified in Table 1. The authentic modes were established before the 5th century and the Plagal modes were added at the time of Pope Gregory, during the 5th century (Burns, ibid.). As previously noted, these modes can be roughly classified based on their approximation to major or minor scales. Traditionally, each church mode has its own number.

The Dorian mode is equivalent to the octave of white keys (those used in the C-major scale) on a musical keyboard, but starting on D instead of the standard C; it is denoted Mode I in ecclesiastical music. Although the Dorian mode is similar to a natural minor scale, its sixth note is higher by one-half step. For example, the sixth note on in the Dorian mode is B-natural, compared to B-flat in the D-minor scale. The intervals between notes, by half steps from tonic (the first note of the scale), are 2 1 2 2 2 1 2.

The Hypodorian mode uses the white keys from A and, again using just the white keys, forms a natural minor scale. It represents Mode II in the system of ecclesiastical modes, and is the plagal counterpart of the Dorian mode; its finalis, or the usual final note of a melody in a particular mode, is also D, although its range (ambitus) goes up to A and then down to the lower A. The Hypodorian mode is often referred to as the Aeolian mode in modern music theory. The half-step intervals are 2 1 2 2 1 2 2. The Phrygian mode starts from E on a major scale. Its half-step intervals are 1 2 2 2 1 2 2.

The Lydian mode starts from F and continues through the white keys of the C-major scale. It is similar to a major scale, but the fourth note is raised one-half step from B-flat to B-natural. The half-step intervals are 2 2 2 1 2 2 1.

The Hypolydian starts on C and resembles the major scale, but its finalis is F. The half-step intervals are 2 2 1 2 2 2 1.

The Mixolydian starts from the G of the major scale. It is similar to the major scale, but its seventh note is lowered by one-half step, from F-sharp to F-natural. The half step intervals are 2 2 1 2 2 1 2.

Generated Pieces for Evaluation Samples

In our experiment, we used six different modes, with three melodic ranges within each mode, to generate 18 musical samples.

From the result of exploratory experiment, Hypophrygian and Hypomixolydian are nealy identical to other similar modes and were therefore omitted Kansei evaluation experiment.

Figure 1 shows each mode. Each mode traditionally starts on a different note, and so, for simplicity, we transposed each starting note to G and then G#, as shown.

Figure 2 shows the three different degrees of melodic range of the Lydian mode. The numerals indicate the number of transitions. Frequent transitions are shown by bold arrows. The tones shown in the outer rings are tones one octave higher (in the 5th octave). The left-hand bottom "C" on the larger range represents the C two octaves higher (C_6).

Kansei Evaluation Experiment

As previously mentioned, the experiment used 18 musical samples, generated from six modes and three melodic ranges.

Because it is difficult to manipulate the structural components of real pieces, we used generative music approach. Sample pieces were automatically generated based on random numbers using Koan Pro (SSEYO Inc), within the specified mode. Each sample is 90 s in duration and contains from 60 to 80 notes. Three voices (melodic lines) were used to shape the randomly generated notes into a musical piece. The leading voice, assigned to the "Piccolo timbre" (Standard MIDI #72), randomly moves within a given mode. This modal melody line is transposed to G_4 or $G\#_4$, and starts from G_4 or $G\#_4$.

The first accompanying voice is in the "Pizzicato Strings" timbre (Standard MIDI #45); this follows the leading voice at third degree higher (mediant). The second accompanying voice, which follows the leading voice at third degree lower, is in the "Jazz Guitar" timbre (Standard MIDI #26).

Figure 1. Modes used for the Kansei evaluation. The scales show each original mode, transposed to G, and then to G#)

Kansei Evaluation Experiment and Analysis Results

The 18 samples were evaluated using a five-point Semantic Differential scale questionnaire containing 47 *Kansei* word pairs.

Osgood's original SD scale uses polarized antonyms like "beautiful – ugly" (Osgood, 1957).

In Kansei engineering, we recommend to use the denial word like "beautiful – not beautiful", instead of antonym. In the statistical sense, when measure with "beautiful – ugly" scale, statistical frequency distribution is distorted toward "beautiful" side. Since there is no manufacturer or composer hopes to create "ugly" products or tunes, there are quite few evaluations those rated as "ugly". Then, most

Figure 2. Variations of melodic ranges

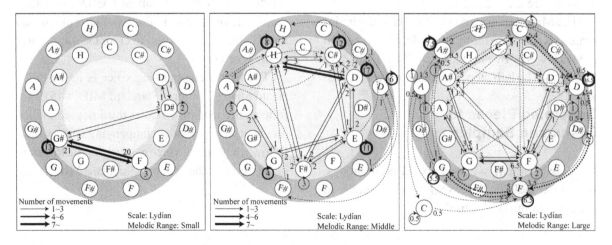

Table 2. Kansei evaluation questionnaire for modes and melodic ranges

bright□□□□□□□□not bright	lively□□□□□□□□not lively
dynamic□□□□□□□□not dynamic	well-organized□□□□□□□□not well-organized
plain□□□□□□□□not plain	innovative□□□□□□□□not innovative
novel□□□□□□□□not novel	refined□□□□□□□□not refined
cheerful□□□□□□□□not cheerful	casual□□□□□□□□not casual
quiet□□□□□□□□not quiet	masculine□□□□□□□□not masculine
serene□□□□□□□□not serene	gorgeous□□□□□□□□not gorgeous
strained□□□□□□□□not strained	polished□□□□□□□□not polished
vivid□□□□□□□□not vivid	adult□□□□□□□□not adult
impressive□□□□□□□□not impressive	individual□□□□□□□□not individual
urban□□□□□□□□not urban	soft□□□□□□□□not soft
up-to-date□□□□□□□□not up-to-date	gloomy□□□□□□□□not gloomy
exotic□□□□□□□□not exotic	simple□□□□□□□□not simple
pleasant□□□□□□□□not pleasant	beautiful□□□□□□□□not beautiful
sunny□□□□□□□□not sunny	expansive□□□□□□□□not expansive
showy□□□□□□□□not showy	translucent□□□□□□□□not translucent
feminine□□□□□□□□not feminine	warm□□□□□□□□not warm
stylish□□□□□□□□not stylish	noisy□□□□□□□□not noisy
easy to listen to□□□□□□□□not easy to listen to	strong□□□□□□□□not strong
clear□□□□□□□□not clear	delicate□□□□□□□□not delicate
relaxed□□□□□□□□not relaxed	keen□□□□□□□□not keen
favourable □□□□□□ □not favourable	clumsy□□□□□□□□not clumsy
natural□□□□□□□□not natural	curative □□□□□□□not curative
amusing□□□□□□□□not amusing	

of evaluation distribution is placed on "beautiful" side and very smaller distribution on "ugly". Such skewed distribution prevents applying of most statistical analysis techniques. In "beautiful – not beautiful", the distribution becomes symmetry and close to the normal (Gaussian) distribution. We have validated various Kansei evaluation data with our modified SD scales. The normality of the multidimensional distributions was shown with various distribution tests (Ishihara, 2010).

We recruited 22 test subjects; 13 were male and 9 were female. At the time of the research, the subjects were around 20 years of age and frequently listened to music. For each subject, all evaluations were done at the same volume using the same audio equipment, and were conducted in the same room. Samples were presented to the subjects in random order. Each subject's evaluation lasted about 30 minute, including a 5-minute break halfway through the session.

Kansei evaluation data was analyzed with Principal Component Analysis. Evaluation value on each Kansei word pair was averaged between subjects. Eigenvalue of the 1st PC (principal component) was 20.50, of the 2nd PC was 12.02 and of the 3rd PC was 0.60. Since a cumulative contribution ratio of the 1st and 2nd PC was 69%, then these two PCs was accounted for further analysis. Figure 3 shows the plot of the same data and results of 2-way analysis of variance. On the

Figure 3. Principal component loadings of Kansei words and the most highly evaluated sample for each word

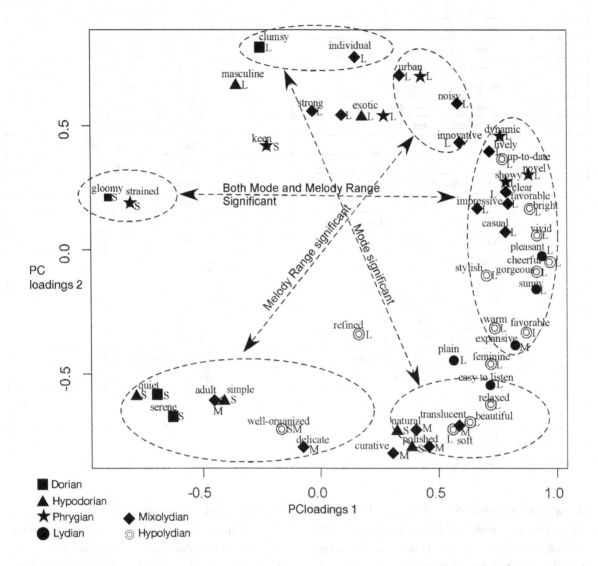

1st PC, positively larger loading Kansei words are *pleasant*, *gorgeous* and *sunny*. Negatively larger loading words on the 1st PC are *gloomy* and *strained*. On the 2nd PC, positively larger loading words are *delicate*, *polished* and *curative*. Negatively larger loading words are *clumsy* and *masculine*.

Two-way ANOVA (analysis of variance) was used to test the effects of modes and melody ranges according to the *Kansei* evaluation. Figure 3 shows the factors having the "main effect", with

the most highly rated music sample shown for each *Kansei* word. The three melody ranges are denoted as L, M, and S. The most significant structures revealed by the ANOVA are:

1. The *kansei* words on the right-hand side of Figure 3 are *dynamic, lively, up-to-date, novel, showy, clear, favourable, impressive, bright, casual, vivid, pleasant, cheerful, stylish, gorgeous, sunny, warm,* and *expansive*. All of the words except *expansive*, match

samples with large melodic ranges. Most of these are in the major modes: Lydian, Hypolydian, and Mixolyidian. The single exception is Phrygian, which corresponds to *dynamic, novel,* and *showy.* The opposite *Kansei* words, on the left side, are *gloomy* and *strained.* The *Kansei* words in this group correspond to a small melodic range and the minor modes of Dorian and Phrygian. Modes and melodic ranges had statistically significant effects on the words in both the right-hand group and in the opposite group.

2. Mode alone (and not the melody range) had a significant effect only on the lower right-hand group and upper central groups of *Kansei* words. The lower right-hand group consists of the *kansei* words *easy to listen* to, *relaxed, beautiful, translucent, soft, natural,* and *polished.* These words correspond to the major modes: Lydian, Mixolydian, and Hypolydian. For the words *natural* and *polished,* Hypodorian produced the same evaluation value as Mixolydian. The top group consists of *clumsy* and *individual,* which were evaluated similarly in the Dorian and Mixolydian modes. These results suggest that major/minor duality can not sufficiently explain the relationship between musical structure and *Kansei.*

3. The words in the upper right-hand, *urban, noisy,* and *innovative,* were related to larger melodic ranges. The lower left-hand group of *quiet, serene, adult, simple, well-organized,* and *delicate,* were related to smaller ranges. Melodic range had a significant effect in these groups, and generated salient opposition between these two groups.

As the above experiment results show, combinations of modes and melodic range have large influences on *Kansei.* However, there are also many *Kansei* affected only by modes or by melodic range. For example, manipulating the melodic range can shift the matching *Kansei* of a piece from *serene* to *urban* without changing the piece's mode. This type of range manipulation within a piece of music is useful for the automatic rearrangement of composed pieces.

A Real-Time Kansei Music Recognition System Based on the Results of the Analysis

Based on our results, we have built a computer system that infers the mode of a musical piece and shows the corresponding *Kansei* word in real-time.

The program was written in Max/MSP 4 (Cycling '74 Inc.), which is an object-oriented graphical programming environment. Our system has three components: 1) audio frequency estimation, 2) notation translation, and 3) search for fulfilling modes.

The audio frequency estimation components translate the audio signal into its frequency. The core of this section is the "Fiddle~" object developed by Puckette & Apel [5], which is a type of likelihood estimation of the musical pitch. The sounds of musical instruments have very rich harmonics, and the different harmonics of the instruments' basic frequencies shape their characteristic timbre. Thus, because of many peaks of frequencies, estimating the basic frequency of the musical instrument is difficult. To do so, the "Fiddle~" object first performs a Fast Fourier Transform (FFT), algorithm and then surveys many candidates for their basic frequency and their various harmonics. The candidate frequency that has largest power and number of harmonics is considered the most plausible basic frequency.

The notation translation routine performs octave normalization. Higher or lower octave notes are normalized by dividing or multiplying them by two or four. In this normalization procedure, the system deals with notes from 110Hz to 1660Hz. The numeric expression of the frequency is then converted into a musical expression such as "G#" and this data packet cascades to the next component.

The search for fulfilling modes component consists of 42 modules of modal note groups (seven pitches of each of six modes), which simultaneously compare the series of notes. The procedure is similar to that of a bingo game. When the seven notes of a module have been fulfilled (matched), the module responds and displays the name of the mode and the corresponding *Kansei*.

Two examples are shown. The first used the tune "Roar to the Sun," by Katsuo Ohno, which is the well-known theme music of a 1970s TV detective drama series. The main melody of the tune was performed on an organ; the system listened and responded with "C-Phrygian" and "F-Hypodorian," and the corresponding *Kansei* words *masculine, exotic, natural, polished, simple, serene, tensioned, keen, urban, dynamic, novel,* and *showy*. Indeed, this tune could be interpreted as being in both modes, and the *Kansei* words generated by the system accurately express the different aspects of a modern detective story. The second example is "Alice Childress" by Ben Folds Five. The system recognizes the music as "H-Lydian" and indicates that it corresponds to *funny, sunny, expansive, plain,* and *easy to listen* to.

From the results mentioned above, the system works very well in mode recognition and in presenting the corresponding *Kansei* (See Figure 4).

4. RHYTHM KANSEI STUDY

Drum Patterns for Evaluation Samples

Rhythm is also a very important musical structure. We have researched rhythm from the viewpoint of statistical fluctuation. In this research, we have used programmed rhythm patterns to study fluctuations in drumming patterns and their relationship with *Kansei*.

Thirty rhythm pattern samples were generated, including samples with 8 beats, 16 beats, and a triplet. The rhythm sound consists of a basic combination of instruments; bass, snare, and hi-hat. Every sample is 2,200 ms in duration and each sample is looped. Each rhythm pattern has 96 steps of resolution. Thus, one step is 2200/96 = 22.9 ms. Samples were made with ReDrum, a software drum machine for the Reason 2.5 virtual studio software (Propellerhead software Inc., Stockholm).

Kansei Evaluation Experiment and Analysis Results

The *Kansei* questionnaire for rhythm contains 28 *Kansei* word pairs on a five-point SD scale. Subjects were asked to fill out the questionnaire during the playback of each sample. The order of presentation of the samples was randomized for each subject. The test subjects were 11 students (10 male and 1 female) who have at least 1 year of experience playing a musical instrument. Audio equipments, loudness, and the listening environment were the same for all subjects.

The resulting *Kansei* structure was studied with principal component analysis. Because the eigenvalues of the principal components abruptly decreased after the third PC, we considered the first and second PCs. The PC loadings map is shown in Figure 5 (left). In the first PC, the words *simple* and *quiet* had the positively largest loading, whereas *noisy, strained, showy, dynamic,* and *innovative* had the largest negative loading. The first PC was labelled the "Activity" axis. In the second PC, the words *gloomy, clumsy* and *strained* showed positively larger loading, whereas *bright, favourable,* and *pleasant* had negatively larger loading. The second PC was labelled the "*strained–bright*" axis.

Figure 5 (right) shows the plot of the PC score of the rhythm samples mapped into the *Kansei* structure. Figure 6 shows the rhythm patterns and distributions of the hi-hat temporal steps. On the first PC of Activity, samples 27 and 6, which correspond to *simple* and *easy-going*, are basic eight-beat patterns, with every drum sound occurring

Figure 4. Real-time Kansei music recognition system

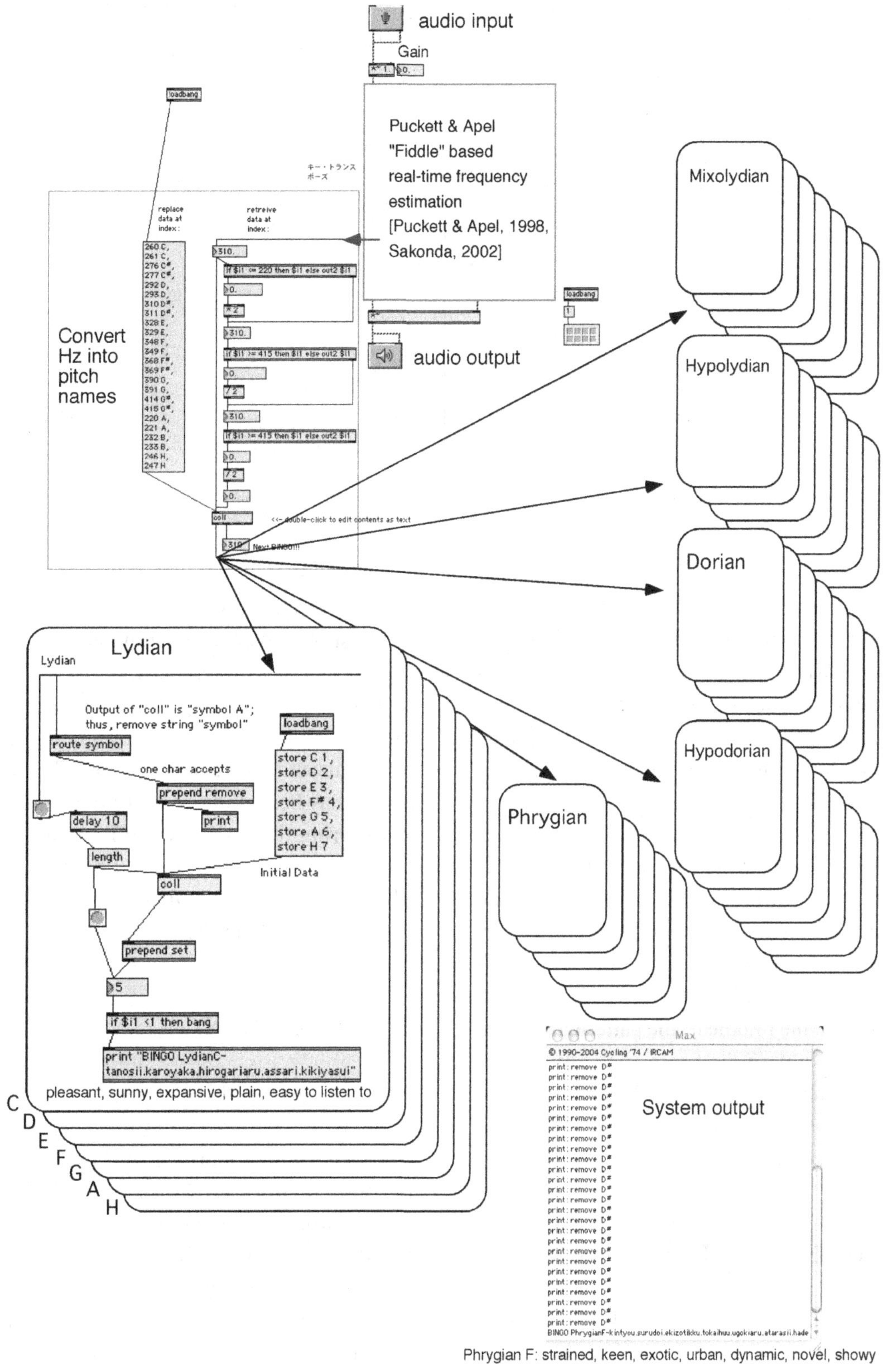

Figure 5. Principal component loadings (left) and scores (right) of rhythm patterns

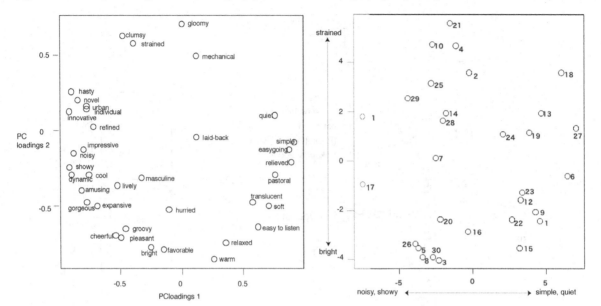

at an equal interval. Samples 11 and 17 have fluctuated intervals in both snare and hi-hat. Histograms of hi-hat interval fluctuation are shown with sample 7, which locates in nearly the center of the map. In the histograms, one unit corresponds to one step in the rhythm programming. A larger fluctuation corresponds to more "Activity."

On the second PC, sample 21, which corresponds to *strained* and *gloomy*, has a less-frequent interval, with a 16-beat hi-hat combined with an equal-interval snare. The bass drum has a four-time beat at equal intervals. Sample 16, which corresponds to *favorable* and *groovy*, has an eight-beat hi-hat. In the middle of the pattern, the snare beats come between the beats of the hi-hat; together, they shape a complex rhythmic pattern. The second PC of *"strained–bright"* relates to interval and complexity.

5. FUTURE RESEARCH DIRECTIONS

Internet-based music services, such as the iTunes Music Store, are now very popular and ubiquitous,

as are proposal-and-suggestion services such as "Last.fm," which recommends music that is matched to user preferences.

However, the sharing of original pieces on such sites as "MySpace" is booming among both professionals and amateur musicians. The next "big thing" may be making or modifying music pieces and sharing them with less effort and less need for technical expertise. *Kansei*-based research is a basic methodology which will open up various opportunities along these lines.

6. CONCLUSION

At the first part of this chapter, we made reviews of the works on music, those were published in conferences and journals of Japan Society of Kansei Engineering. Music related researches are classified into 6 categories; Kansei evaluation methodology, music psychological research, physiological measurement, music theoretical research, Kansei music system and recommendation system. Despite of the diversity of music

Figure 6. Rhythm patterns, fluctuations and interval complexity

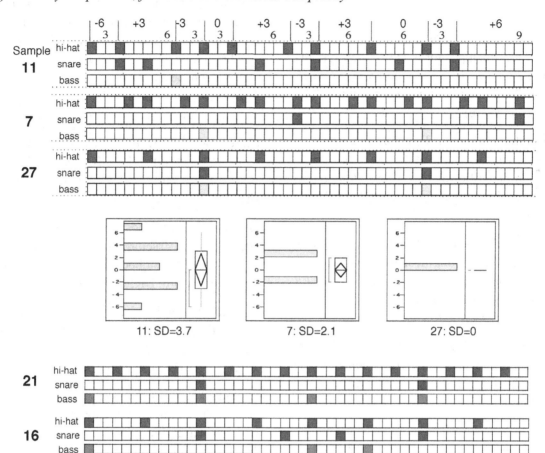

Kansei researches, music structural and theoretical researches are relatively in small numbers.

We have analyzed the relationship of modes and melodic ranges to *Kansei*. For this *Kansei* evaluation, pieces were generated by a computer program. We found that pieces having major modes and larger melodic ranges and pieces those have minor modes and smaller ranges have salient polarized relationships. Although the interaction of modes and melodic ranges has a strong effect, modes and melodic ranges also independently affect other *Kansei*. Using these results, we have developed a real-time *Kansei* music recognition system, which uses sound frequency analysis and mode assessment to produce corresponding *Kansei*.

Mode based approach does not directly deal with hierarchical structure of music. Hierarchical analysis required structured approach, such as Schenkerian analysis (von Cube, 1988, Pankhurst, 2008). It should be incorporated into our further researches.

We also used programmed drum patterns to study rhythm, and found that the fluctuation of beats relates to the degree of activity on the *noisy/ showy* to *simple/quiet* axis, whereas interval and complexity variations are associated with the *strained* to *bright* axis.

Music theory is indispensable for creating music pieces. Exploring various aspects of music theory will make it possible to generate music matching the user's desired *Kansei*.

REFERENCES

Akabane, T., et al. (2006). A proposal for the automatic tone manipulator based on gray systems theory. *Proc. of the 8th annual conf. of JSKE (Japan Society of Kansei Engineering) 2006*, 146. (in Japanese)

Akashi, K., & Uozumi, T. (2008). Evaluation of brain activity by change of the sound source using brain blood flowmeter (NIRS). *Proc. of the 10th annual conf. of JSKE 2008 (CD-ROM)* (in Japanese)

Akibane, T., Yamaguchi, D., & Nagai, M. (2007). Automatic manipulating methods for synthesizer's tone in the development of music. *Proc. of KEER 2007 (International Conference on Kansei Engineering and Emotion Research) (CD-ROM)*

Aoshima, Y., & Tokosumi, A. (2007). Extracting musical concepts from written texts: A case study of Toru Takemitsu. In *Proc. of KEER 2007.* (CD-ROM)

Burns, E. M. (1999). Intervals, scales, and tuning. In Deutsch, D. (Ed.), *The Psychology of Music* (2nd ed.). San Diego, CA: Academic Press. doi:10.1016/B978-012213564-4/50008-1

Fujio, T., & Shiizuka, H. (2005). The automatic DJ mixing system by optimum transformation of MP3 data. [in Japanese]. *Journal of Japan Society of Kansei Engineering, 5*(3), 23–30.

Fujisawa, N., & Saito, M. (2007). Relation of musical impression and mental tempo. In *Proc. of the 9th annual conf. of JSKE 2007* (CD-ROM) (in Japanese)

Fukumoto, M. (2008). Investigation of subjective evaluation for tempo of music. In *Proc. of the 10th annual conf. of JSKE 2008* (CD-ROM) (in Japanese)

Fukumoto, M., Kusunoki, Y., & Nagashima, T. (2004). Synchronization between tempo of music and heartbeat - Detecting synchronization with synchrogram and its influence on relazation effect. [in Japanese]. *Journal of Japan Society of Kansei Engineering, 4*(2), 17–24.

Gabrielsson, A., & Juslin, P. N. (2002). Emotional expression in music. In Davidson, R. J., Scherer, K. R., & Goldsmith, H. H. (Eds.), *Handbook of Affective Sciences*. Oxford, UK: Oxford University Press.

Gabrielsson, A., & Lindström, E. (2001). The influence of musical structure on emotional expression. In Juslin, P. N., & Sloboda, J. A. (Eds.), *Music and Emotion*. Oxford, UK: Oxford University Press.

Hashida, M., Noike, K., Nagata, N., & Katayose, H. (2005). An analysis of musical grouping tencency. In *Proc. of the 1st spring conf. of JSKE 2005, 33-36.* (in Japanese)

Hashida, M., Noike, K., Nagata, N., & Katayose, H. (2007). A study of listening of musical group structure based on performance expression [in Japanese]. *Journal of Japan Society of Kansei Engineering, 7*(2), 327–336.

Higashitani, T., & Yoshida, T. (2004). A prescription of music for healing. In *Proc. of the 6th annual conf. of JSKE 2004, 124.* (in Japanese)

Hirano, M., & Saito, T. (2008). Proposal of phrase production and evaluation support system for music beginner. In *Proc. of the 10th annual conf. of JSKE 2008* (CD-ROM) (in Japanese)

Ikeda, E., et al. (2000). Classification of adjectives expressing sound by Kansei evaluation. In *Proc. of the 2nd annual conf. of JSKE,* (pp.217). (in Japanese)

Ikoma, S. (2007). The relations between absolute-pitch-based recognition for melody and everyday music listening. In *Proc. of the 3rd spring conf. of JSKE 2007,* (P12). (in Japanese)

Iseki, A., & Ozawa, K. (2005). Effect of performer information of music on the Kansei of a listener. In *Proc. of the 7th annual conf. of JSKE 2005*, 189. (in Japanese)

Iseki, A., & Ozawa, K. (2007). Effects of Musical Performer Information on the Kansei of Listeners. In *Proc. of KEER 2007*. (CD-ROM)

Ishida, A., et al. (2008). Development of Music Retrieval System by Analysis of Walking Pattern. In *Proc. of the 10th annual conf. of JSKE 2008* (CD-ROM) (in Japanese)

Ishida, A., Tatsuya, S., Sugihara, R., Omura, T., Ishikawa, T., & Kato, T. (2009). Development of music retrieval system by analysis of walking pattern. [in Japanese]. *Journal of Japan Society of Kansei Engineering*, 8(3), 829–835.

Ishihara, S., & Ishihara, K. (2010). Psychological Methods of Kansei Engineering. In Nagamachi, M. (Ed.), *Kansei / Affective EngineeringBoca*. Raton, FL: CRC press.

Kadotani, A., & Ishihara, S. (2004). Music structures and Kansei – Scales and Kansei. In *Proc. of the 6th annual conf. of JSKE 2004, 191*. (in Japanese)

Kamei, K. (2006). Kansei evaluations of percussion music based on psychological measurements by SD method and physiological measurements by near-infrared spectroscopy (NIRS). [in Japanese]. *Journal of Japan Society of Kansei Engineering*, 6(4), 67–76.

Kanahako, J., et al. (2005). Color based computer aided composition system. In *Proc. of the spring 1st spring conf. of JSKE 2005*, (pp. 81-84). (in Japanese)

Kashiwazaki, N., & Okamoto, K. (2007). Classification of music using Kansei parameter method - Study on Standard parameter values scales for kansei information analyses (1). [in Japanese]. *Journal of Japan Society of Kansei Engineering*, 7(2), 243–249.

Kawamura, T., et al. (2003). A study on individual differences in images roused by music. *Proc. of the 5th annual conf. of JSKE 2003, 208*. (in Japanese)

Kawase, A., & Tokosumi, A. (2007a). A comparative analysis and Regional Classification of Japanese Folk Songs Founded on Pitch Transition Structures. In *Proc. of the 9th annual conf. of JSKE 2007* (CD-ROM) (in Japanese)

Kawase, A., & Tokosumi, A. (2007b). A regional classification of Japanse folk songs. In *Proc. of KEER 2007*. (CD-ROM)

Kennedy, M., & Bourne, J. (1996). *Modes, The Concise Oxford Dictionary of Music*. Oxford, UK: Oxford University Press.

Kobayashi, K., & Haseyama, M. (2007). A Novel Similarity Measurement Using Melody Lines for Music Retrieval. In *Proc. of KEER 2007* (CD-ROM)

Kojima, H., et al. (2000). System of making pleasant sound surroundings based on Kansei. In *Proc. of the 2nd annual conf. of JSKE*, (pp.172). (in Japanese)

Kolinski, M. (2009). Mode. In *Encyclopædia Britannica*. Retrieved July 15, 2009, from Encyclopædia Britannica Online http://www.britannica.com/EBchecked/topic/386980/mode

Martin, H. (2000). Seven steps to heaven: A species approach to twentieth-century analysis and composition. In *Perspective of New Music; 38*(1), 129-168.

Masaki, Y., et al. (2008). An Automatic Music Selection System Considering the Scenery in Car Driving. In *Proc. of the 10th annual conf. of JSKE 2008* (CD-ROM) (in Japanese)

Masaki, Y., Ozawa, K., & Ise, Y. (2007). A consideration on automatic music genre classification using rough sets theory. In *Proc. of the 9th annual conf. of JSKE 2007* (CD-ROM) (in Japanese)

Matsuzaki, Y., et al. (2005). Impressions' variation led by backing-renditions of pop music.In *Proc. of the 1st spring conf. of JSKE 2005,*(pp. 37-40). (in Japanese)

Mieno, Y., & Shiizuka, H. (2000). KANSEI database according to opuses in automatic composition.In *Proc. of the 2nd annual conf. of JSKE,* (pp.65). (in Japanese)

Miura, M., Mitsuishi, T., Sasaki, J., & Funyu, Y. (2000). KANSEI database according to opuses in automatic composition.In *Proc. of the 2nd annual conf. of JSKE,*(pp.66). (in Japanese)

Moroboshi, K., & Shiizuka, H. (2005). Composition support system by TRIZ, In *Proc. of the 7th annual conf. of JSKE 2005*, 191. (in Japanese)

Moroboshi, K., & Shiizuka, H. (2005). Composition support system springing images, In *Proc. of the 1st spring conf. of JSKE 2005,*(p. 41). (in Japanese)

Murakami., et al. (2008). Auditory Feature Parameter Design Based on Frequency Selectivity for Kansei Retrieval of Music. In *Proc. of the 10th annual conf. of JSKE 2008* (CD-ROM) (in Japanese)

Murakami, M., et al. (2007) Auditory features for subjective classification of music.In *Proc. of the 9th annual conf. of JSKE 2007* (CD-ROM) (in Japanese)

Murakami, M., et al. (2007). Study of feature values for subjective classification of music.In *Proc. of KEER 2007.* (CD-ROM)

Murayama, G., Kato, S., Itoh, H., & Kunitachi, T. (2007). Consideration of relationships between pulse and musical tempo, and its effect of relaxation.In *Proc. of the 3rd spring conf. of JSKE 2007,* B31. (in Japanese)

Murayama, G., Kato, S., Itoh, H., & Kunitachi, T. (2009). Analysis of the relationships between pulses and musical tempo, and their effect on relaxation.In*Kansei Engineering International, 8*(1), 91-98.

Nagamachi, M. (1995). An image technology expert system and its application to design consultation. *International Journal of Human-Computer Interaction, 3*(3), 267–279. doi:10.1080/10447319109526012

Nagamachi, M. (1974). A study of emotion-technology [in Japanese]. *The Japanese Journal of Ergonomics, 10*(2), 121–130.

Nagamachi, M. (1988). A study of costume design consultation based on knowledge engineering [in Japanese]. *The Japanese Journal of Ergonomics, 24*(5), 281–289.

Nagamachi, M., & Lokman, A. M. (2010). *Innovations of Kansei engineering*. Boca Raton, Florida: CRC press.

Nagata, N., Waki, S., & Inokuchi, S. (2003). Non-verbal mapping between sound and color- colored hearing possessors as an example.In *Proc. of the 5th annual conf. of JSKE 2003, 207.* (in Japanese)

Nakai, M., & Mitsuishi, M. (2003). Analysis of individual differences in impression evaluations on music phrases by impression words.In *Proc. of the 5th annual conf. of JSKE 2003,* 209. (in Japanese)

Okamatsu, K., Fukumoto, M., & Matsuo, K. (2007). A 'Healing' effect by a tempo of music - Psychological evaluation by a simple sound made from acoustical property of 'healing music'. [in Japanese]. *Journal of Japan Society of Kansei Engineering, 7*(2), 237–242.

Okamoto, K., & Kashiwazaki, N. (2005). Study on factor analysis of Kansei parameters for classification of music genre.In *Proc. of the 7th annual conf. of JSKE 2005*, 190. (in Japanese)

Oonishi, G., Kimura, I., & Yamada, H. (1999). A Kansei model for musical chord progression using recurrent neural networks, Proc. of the 1st annual conf. of JSKE, pp.148. (in Japanese)

Osgood, C. E., Suci, G. J., & Tannenbaum, P. H. (1957). *The Measurement of Meaning*. Urbana, IL: University of Illinois Press.

Ozawa, K., Seo, Y., & Ise, T. (2007). Estimation of the Relative Weights of Timbre Factors for Sound Quality Evaluation, Proc. of KEER 2007. (CD-ROM)

Pankhurst, T. (2008). *SchenkerGUIDE -A Brief Handbook and Website for Schenkerian Analysis*. London: Routledge.

Puckette, M., & Apel, T. (1998). Real-time audio analysis tools for Pd and MSP. *Proceedings of International Computer Music Conference, 1998*, 109–112.

Sakamoto, W., & Ishihara, S. (2005). Kansei on rhythm patterns- statistical analysis of drum sound intervals. *Proc. of the 7th annual conf. of JSKE 2005*, 196. (in Japanese)

Sakonda, N. (2002). Beginning audio programming with Max/MSP – Pitch detection with "fiddle",*Sound & Recording Magazine*, April 2002, 262-263. (in Japanese)

Shindo, K., & Shoji, Y. (2008). A music retrieval system using KANSEI words. *Proc. of the 10th annual conf. of JSKE 2008* (CD-ROM) (in Japanese)

Shudou, F., et al. (2008). Effects of Environmental Auditory Stimulations on Brain Activities in the Humans and the Mice. *Proc. of the 10th annual conf. of JSKE 2008* (CD-ROM) (in Japanese)

Sloboda, J. A. (1988). Preface. In Sloboda, J. A. (Ed.), *Generative processes in music*. Oxford, UK: Oxford University Press.

Stein, L. (1979). *Structure & Style Expanded edition*. Florida: Summy-Birchard Inc.

Stevens, C. (2004). Cross-cultural studies of musical pitch and time. *Acoustical Science and Technology*, 25(6), 433–438. doi:10.1250/ast.25.433

Sugihara, T. (2005). Selecting Kansei words for use in a Kansei-based music retrieval system for young people. [in Japanese]. *Journal of Japan Society of Kansei Engineering*, 5(3), 127–134.

Sugihara, T., Morimoto, K., & Kurokawa, T. (2008). A study of user's strategies with a music information retrieval system with Kansei characteristics: lack attention to the midrange settings. [in Japanese]. *Journal of Japan Society of Kansei Engineering*, 7(4), 665–673.

Suk, H.-J., Kim, B., & Kwon, M.-Y. (2007). The Influence of Ring-Back-Tone (RBT) Music on Evaluation of the Phone-call Receiver's Personality. In *Proc. of KEER 2007*. (CD-ROM)

Takahashi, M., & Saito, T. (2008). Proposal of the musical instrument for cooperative operation. In Proc. *of the 10th annual conf. of JSKE 2008* (CD-ROM) (in Japanese)

Takahashi, T., Matsui, T., & Higashiyama, M. (2000). Tones of Shakuhachi and their wave forms,In *Proc. of the 2nd annual conf. of JSKE*,(pp.81). (in Japanese)

Tokairin, M., & Shiizuka, H. (2007). *Automatic Music Composition System through KANSEI (Sensibility) Adjectives, KEER 2007*. CD-ROM.

Tokairin, M., & Shiizuka, H. (2008). Automatic music composition system through Kansei adjectives. [in Japanese]. *Journal of Japan Society of Kansei Engineering*, 8(1), 119–127.

Tokumaru, M., et al. (2004). Study on music composition system for enjoying music.In *Proc. of the 6th annual conf. of JSKE 2004, 195*. (in Japanese)

von Cube, F.-E. (1988). *The Book of Musical Artwork – An interpretation of the musical theories of Heinrich Schenker*. New York: The Edwin Mellen Press.

Watanabe, C., & Shiizuka, H. (2004). Research of choreograph system by Kansei.In *Proc. of the 6th annual conf. of JSKE 2004, 194.* (in Japanese)

Williams, D. B., Carlsen, J. C., & Dowling, W. J. (1981). Psychomusicology: A position statement. *Psychomusicology, 1*(1), 3–5.

Yamamoto, S., Nakanishi, R., Sagaya, Y., & Takeda, S. (2005). Comparison of EEG alpha-band power variation between beat tracking and listening to music. [in Japanese]. *Journal of Japan Society of Kansei Engineering, 5*(3), 61–70.

Yamashita, Y., Higuchi, Y., & Watanabe, T. (2000). Artists recommend system by taste analysis.In *Proc. of the 2nd annual conf. of JSKE,*(pp.64). (in Japanese)

Yamawaki, K., & Shiizuka, H. (2002). Kansei correspondence between music and color image. In *Proc. of the 4th annual conf. of JSKE, 237.* (in Japanese)

Yamawaki, K., & Shiizuka, H. (2005). Music parameter needed for music recommendation system.In *Proc. of the 1st spring conf. of JSKE 2005,*(pp. 31-32). (in Japanese)

Yamawaki, K., & Shiizuka, H. (2005). Solfege ability and color-heard-sense. [in Japanese]. *Journal of Japan Society of Kansei Engineering, 5*(3), 31–37.

Yamawaki, K., & Shiizuka, H. (2007). Characteristic recognition of the musical piece with correspondence analysis.In *Proc. of the 9th annual conf. of JSKE 2007* (CD-ROM) (in Japanese)

Yamawaki, K., & Shiizuka, H. (2007). Recognition of music characteristic with rough sets. [in Japanese]. *Journal of Japan Society of Kansei Engineering, 7*(2), 283–288.

Yamawaki, K., & Shiizuka, H. (2008). Music recognition system by correspondence analysis. [in Japanese]. *Journal of Japan Society of Kansei Engineering, 7*(4), 659–663.

Yoshida, Tomoyuki. & Iwaki, T. (2000). The study of early emotion processing in the frontal area using a two-dipole source model. *The Japanese Psychological Research, 42*(1), 54–68. doi:10.1111/1468-5884.00131

Yoshida, Tomoyoshi, Nakanishi, S., Yamamoto, S. & Takeda, S. (2007). Measurements of synchronization in musical rhythms and study of effects of rhythms on the EEG. Journal *of Japan Society of Kansei Engineering, 7*(2), 337-344. (in Japanese)

Chapter 11

Analyses of People's Perceptions on Sidewalk Environments Combining Factor Analysis and Rough Sets Approach

Weijie Wang
Southeast University, China

Wei Wang
Southeast University, China

Moon Namgung
Wonkwang University, South Korea

ABSTRACT

This study investigates the relationship between people's perceptions of sidewalk environments and their component elements. Participants are asked to judge the selected twenty sidewalk photographs with the rating scales through a psychological survey. Two perception factors including harmoniousness and openness are specified through semantic differential technique by using factor analysis. In the meantime the physical components of sidewalk environments are surveyed in the field survey. Then the rough sets approach is applied to link people's perception factors and physical components of sidewalk environment. The application of the rough sets approach outputs the most important attributes to people's perceptions, minimal attribute sets without redundancy, and a series of decision rules that represent the relationships between perceptions and physical components of sidewalk environments. The analytical approach helps to better understand people's perceptions to sidewalk environments in a small city and then establish a useful and constructive ground of discussion for walking environment design and management.

DOI: 10.4018/978-1-61692-797-4.ch011

1. INTRODUCTION

Recently, considerable interests in improved *walking environments* have been generated as a result of the desire to encourage no-motorized transportation modes to reduce pollution emissions and to improve public health by increased levels of walking (Evans-Cowley, 2006; Frank and Engelke, 2001; Handy et al., 2002). A large body of research has confirmed that favorable walking environment is a necessary condition for promoting walking and neighborhood interaction (Lindsey and Nguyen, 2004; Clifton et al., 2007; Moudon and Lee, 2003; Williams et al., 2005).

There also have numerous studies on how humans react to walkways or neighborhood environments. However, they suffer from certain limitations. First, most of these studies do not encompass a broad range of *physical components*. For example, Schroeder and Cannon (1987), and Williams (2002) examined the contribution of trees to the visual quality of residential streets. Todorova et al. (2004) explored residents' preferences for the combination of trees and flowers on the street. Nasar and Hong (1999) reported the visual preferences in urban signscapes on the streets. Moreover, these studies usually focus on preference alone, whereas preference constitutes only one response among many psychological mechanisms, ignoring other possible psychological responses of the subject.

Therefore, in this study, we focus on not one single physical component and preference but several physical components or their combinations of sidewalk components and people's perceptions. There can be no doubt that the form of the environment plays an important role in the shaping of people's perceptions. It is on this relation between physical components and perceptions that our interest concerns. Consequently, we try to link people's perceptions and physical components of sidewalk environments and look for the representation of linkages.

However, *human perception* is often subjective and qualitative with uncertainty (Buhyoff and Wellman, 1980; Nassaure, 1980; Shibata and Kato, 1998). Hence, the conventional statistical methods are not suitable due to the unrealistic, rigorous theoretical assumptions, as well as the small number of observations (Baaijens and Nijkamp, 1999; Düntsch and Gediga, 1998). With the development of *artificial intelligence techniques*, Fuzzy set theory, neural network and other methods have been applied widely to deal with vagueness, uncertainty existing in real world (Sriram, 2006). There are some practical applications of these techniques that can be used for references in this study context. Bailey et al. (2001) employed fuzzy set theory to generate a preference knowledge base to investigate and quantify public preference for specific highway design strategies. Ergin et al. (2004) presented a fuzzy logic model to evaluate coastal scenery. Li and Will (2005) proposed a fuzzy logic model to assess the qualitative and subjective views of building scenes. Mougiakakou et al. (2005) applied neural network technology for the classification of landscape images. Naderi and Raman (2005), Raman and Naderi (2006) used decision tree learning to design pedestrian landscapes.

More recently, *rough sets theory,* as one member of artificial intelligence techniques has attracted attention of researchers all over the world and been applied in many different fields (Lin and Crcone, 1997; Pawlak, 1991, 1997; Polkowski et al., 2000; Wu et al., 2004). The rough sets theory uses only internal knowledge and does not rely on prior model assumptions as probabilistic models or fuzzy models do. It has been found that rough sets theory can accept both quantitative and qualitative data, identify important attributes and minimal sets of attributes through elimination of redundancy, and discover hidden facts in data and express them in natural language (Pawlak, 1997; Walczak and Masart, 1999). Due to these advantages, some practical applications of rough sets theory in the study context have been carried out. Hirokane et

Figure 1. Research flow

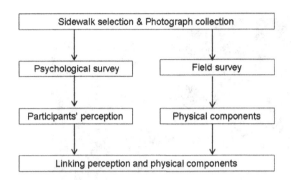

al. (2003) proposed the method of extracting the quantities of characteristics based on the rough sets theory in order to classify bridge images into groups on the basis of similarity. Saito et al. (2005) provided the method of determining the rules of form elements inherent historic buildings by rough sets theory. Wang et al. (2008) developed a rough sets approach to study the relationships between the evaluative image and physical components of sidewalks.

In this study, therefore, rough sets theory becomes our alternative to identify the most important attributes and necessary attribute combinations to people's perceptions, and discover the relationships between people's perceptions and physical components of sidewalk environments. Figure 1 summarizes the research flow of this study. When study objects are selected, we carry out a photograph-questionnaire survey and a field survey to collect subjective and objective data, respectively, and then apply rough sets theory to link these two kinds of data. Useful information may be obtained to better inform our understanding of sidewalk environmental influences on people's perceptions.

2. OBJECTIVES

This study has two objectives as following:

1. To investigate the semantic expressions of sidewalk environment and find the perception factors by factor analysis.
2. To investigate the relationship between participants' perception and component elements of sidewalk environment and find the physical features influencing perceptions by rough sets approach.

3. METHOD AND THE DATA

Sidewalk Photograph Collection

The study area examined in this study locates in Iksan city in the southwest of South Korea, covering approximately $518km^2$ with the population of 310,000. To increase the use of walking mode, the local government has started to improve facilities to be walkable for pedestrians by removing barriers for the handicapped, paving sidewalks colorfully to create good atmosphere. In this study, 20 sidewalks of the city were selected, where the sidewalk improvement project were implemented.

To reduce potential biases from photographic techniques, each scene was photographed in controlled conditions (Hochberg, 1966). The photographs were taken with a 35-mm digital camera using a 50mm lens. Eye-level views, controlled viewing angles and direction of sunlight were adopted. The viewpoints for photographing were located along walkways and central areas.

At each site, three photographs were taken from the perspective of pedestrians. Totally 60 color photographs were taken of various sidewalk environments. Of them, 15 were dropped for problems with focus, distortion, lighting condition or movement, and 20 of the rest were selected as the experimental stimuli, which could most represent typical views of the selected sidewalk environments. The photograph samples are shown in Figure 2.

Figure 2. Photograph samples

The Field Survey

Disaggregating the landscape into component units has been an important method to landscape studies (Ergin et al., 2004; McHarg, 1969; Li and Will, 2005; Raman and Naderi, 2006). In this study, we disaggregated the sidewalk environments into nine parts including sidewalk tree (A), type of surface material (B), surface condition (C), type of land use (D), shrubs (E), signage (F), sidewalk width (G), and percentage of green area (H), percentage of sky area in the photograph (I). A

field reconnaissance of the selected 20 sidewalks was made by trained observers. In addition, green (sky) area in the photographs was measured at the laboratory, and then the ration of green (sky) area in the photograph to the whole photograph area was calculated and recoded. Basing on the field survey data, the nine components of sidewalk environments are categorized three levels (Wang et al., in press). For example, the attribute of sidewalk tree (A) was categorized into one side (A1), both sides (A2) and not applicable (A3). The detailed can be found in table 1.

Table 1. Physical components of sidewalk environment

Attribute	Category
A: Sidewalk tree	A1: one side; A2: both sides; A3: na
B: Type of surface material	B1: asphalt; B2: interlocking block; B3: mixture
C: Surface condition	C1: good; C2: moderate; C3: bad
D: Type of land use	D1: buildings; D2: only vegetation; D3: buildings with vegetation
E: Shrubs	E1: na; E2: yes, tall; E3: yes, short
F: Signage	F1: na; F2: yes, a few; F3: yes, many
G: Sidewalk width	G1: under 2.5m; G2: 2.5m to 3.5m; G3: over 3.5m
H: Percentage of green area	H1: under 20%; H2: 20% to 40%; H3: over 40%
I: Percentage of sky area	I1: under 10%; I2: 10% to 20%; I3: over 20%

na-not applicable.

Semantic Differential Technique and the Psychological Survey

Semantic Differential Technique

Semantic differential technique is the method of measuring the emotional content of a word more objectively, which was developed by psychologist CE Osgood (Osgood et al. 1957; Osgood, 1969) and then was introduced into Kansei Engineering, marketing etc. Typically the adjective pairs with five or seven-point rating scales are used to evaluate the presented objects. For example, a subject might be asked to rate the design of new mobile phone product. An adjective pair such as ugly-beautiful as one of dozen or more pairs, for example, would be presented by the semantic differential scale in the following form:

ugly 1 2 3 4 5 6 7 beautiful

The rating scale ranging from 1 to 7 can represent the subject's opinion or attitude to the design of presented mobile phone. Marking 1 or 7 indicates the subject rate the design to be extremely ugly or beautiful while marking position 4 shows the subject's neutral attitude. This procedure is relatively easily implanted to investigate subjects' attitude, opinion by forcing them to focus on the expected dimensions.

The Psychological Survey

Human being's kansei perceptions can be expressed in attitudes and words. The psychological measurement based on the semantic differential technique is one major approach. The psychological measurement provides a method to measure people's attitude or feelings by evaluating objects with series of adjective emotional words, such as "beautiful - ugly", "expensive - cheap" etc. Through such evaluation, people's feelings can be expressed by emotional dimensions. The method has been applied to environmental psychology area, such as forest scene evaluation (Echelberger, 1979), landscape visual preferences analysis (Kamičaitytė-Virbašienė and Janušaitis, 2004), evaluation of urban street soundscape (Ge and Hokao, 2005), perceptions in housing assessment (Llinares and Page, 2007), tree shape preferences (Müderrisoğlu et al., 2006; Summit and Sommer, 1999), townscape evaluation (Kinoshita et al., 2004), street environment analysis (Shibata and Kato, 1998; Tsumita et al., 2006), virtual landscape evaluation (Lim et al., 2006).

The evaluative scales for semantic differential technique are bipolar adjective pairs like wide-narrow, clean-dirty, which are included in the questionnaire. In order to get a complete selection of adjective words that could measure the different dimensions of people's perceptions on sidewalk environments, we used all available sources about sidewalks, streets and other environments, including manuals, urban design experts' advice, magazines, dictionaries, and especially related research literature (e.g., Shibata and Kato, 1998; Tsumita et al., 2006; Zube et al., 1975). More than 60 words that could describe sidewalk environments were collected. By conducting factor analysis after a pilot study, 14 adjective pairs (See table 2), which showed high loading in the factor and low in other factors, were finally selected and

Table 2. The selected 14 adjective pairs

wide – narrow	tidy - untidy	green – insufficient green	pleasant-unpleasant
bright - dull	soft - hard	light - heavy	natural - man-made
harmonious-discordant	widely spreading - centralizing	beautiful - ugly	varied - monotonous
open - closed	inviting - uninviting		

Figure 3. Scree plot

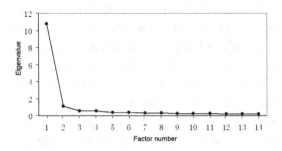

designed by 5-point bipolar semantic differential scales for questionnaire design.

The Summary of the Psychological Survey

The survey was conducted in a seminar room, aided by slide presentation, from August to September, 2005. Each photograph of sidewalks was shown as a slide. To eliminate potential order bias, the photographs were shown in a random order. The survey began with a general introduction, and participants were asked to evaluate the sidewalk environments as pedestrians by rating each adjective pair on a semantic differential scale. In addition, the participants' demographic characteristics and habits as well as the attitude to walking environment were also recorded in the questionnaire form.

Total 105 participants took part in the psychological survey, including 84 university students and 21 residents, of which three surveys were uncompleted, leaving 102(97.1%) valid ones for analysis. Participants' ages varied from 20 to 59 years old, and the average was 25.9 ± 7.4 years old. Of the total participants in the study, 47.1% were male and 52.9% were female. Because most of participants were university students, 80.4% of them were under 30 years old, 16.7% of them were over 30 years old. 80.4% of them lived in the urban community and 19.6% came from the rural. According to the average walking time one day, 55.9% of them spent 60 minutes or over, and

44.1% spent less 60 minutes. 59.8% of them paid much attention to sidewalk environment, 34.3% paid some attention, and 5.9% paid little attention. According to the daily travel modes, walking, bicycling, public transportation and private car were 36.3%, 5.9%, 35.3% and 21.6%, respectively.

4 ANALYSIS AND FINDINGS

Identifying Participants' Perceptions by Factor Analysis

Some variables of theoretical interest cannot be directly observed. These unobserved variables are referred to as either latent variables or factors. Factor analysis is a statistical procedure for uncovering a smaller number of latent variables by studying the covariation among a set of observed variables. This is the fundamental idea underlying the factor analytic model.

Human perception here means people's *emotional responses* to the sidewalk environment, which may be latent in the semantic adjective pairs collected in the psychological survey. This section helps to understand and identify dimensions of participants' perceptions on sidewalk environments, and the identified dimensions of perceptions are regarded as the decision attributes of the rough sets approach.

Determining the Number of Factors

A standard approach to conducting an exploratory factor analysis was followed. Firstly, the scree plot graphed the eigenvalue against the factor number (See Figure 3). From the third factor on, it could be seen that the line is almost flat, meaning the each successive factor is accounting for smaller and smaller amounts of the total variance.

Hence, two meaning factors were identified based on the scree plot. A two-factor solution was supported by the percentage of variance accounted for by each factor. Secondly, the princi-

Table 3. Results of factor analysis

Evaluation item	Perception factors	
	I: Harmoniousness	II: Openness
soft-hard	0.924	
natural-man-made	0.921	
beautiful-ugly	0.912	
harmonious-discordant	0.878	
inviting-uninviting	0.847	
green-insufficient green	0.792	
pleasant-unpleasant	0.726	
diverse-monotonous	0.718	
light-heavy	0.715	
tidy-untidy	0.576	
open-closed		0.951
wide-narrow		0.940
widely spreading-centralizing		0.795
bright-dull		0.531
Eigenvalues	10.757	1.089
% of variance	67.229	6.805
Cumulative %	74.034	

pal component extraction with varimax rotation is conducted and the results are shown in table 3.

Interpreting the Results

It can be seen that in the table, two factors account for 74.034% of the variance among the intercorrelations of the 14 adjective pairs, the first factor, making a large and unique contribution to the variance of the ten item, accounts for 67.229% of the variance, and the second one accounts for an additional 6.805%. The eigenvalues of factors are both over 1.000, which are satisfied with the common requirement.

Table 3 also indicates that the first factor appears to be the pleasingly arranged sidewalk component elements, representing the "Harmoniousness" feature of sidewalk environments and the second factor appears to be the open space of sidewalk environment, representing the "Open-

ness" feature. Thus, the latent perception structure among the 14 adjective pairs is identified.

Constructing Factor Scores for Rough Sets Approach

To perform additional rough sets approach in the following section, the selected twenty sidewalk's factor scores are also calculated (See table 4). The perception factor score for a given factor is a linear combination of all of the fourteen adjective pairs, weighted by the corresponding factor loading. The perception factor score also indicates the degree of participants' perception. We assume that the perception factor score with the value over +0.5 means the positive perception, the one with the value less-0.5 means the negative perception and the one with the value between -0.5 and +0.5 means neutral perception. According to this suggested criteria (HA1 or OP1 = less -0.5, HA2 or OP2 = -0.5 ~ +0.5, HA3 or OP3 = over +0.5), the

Table 4. Scores of extracted perception factors

Photo number	Harmoniousness(HA)	Openness(OP)
01	0.65 (HA3)	0.27 (OP2)
02	-0.94 (HA1)	-0.97 (OP1)
03	-0.10 (HA2)	-0.63 (OP1)
04	-0.67 (HA1)	-0.80 (OP1)
05	0.33 (HA2)	0.76 (OP3)
06	-1.26 (HA1)	-1.18 (OP1)
07	0.43 (HA2)	-0.08 (OP2)
08	0.95 (HA3)	1.19 (OP3)
09	-0.30 (HA2)	-0.60 (OP1)
10	0.54 (HA3)	1.04 (OP3)
11	1.35 (HA3)	0.65 (OP3)
12	-0.46 (HA2)	0.16 (OP2)
13	-0.92 (HA1)	0.26 (OP2)
14	0.80 (HA3)	0.69 (OP3)
15	0.29 (HA2)	0.49 (OP2)
16	-1.24 (HA1)	-1.34 (OP1)
17	0.60 (HA3)	-0.21 (OP2)
18	-1.33 (HA1)	-1.06 (OP1)
19	0.79 (HA3)	0.47 (OP2)
20	0.49 (HA2)	0.90 (OP3)

calculated factor scores that may be used as decision attributes in the following rough sets approach are recoded to 3 levels, which are presented after the original factor score (See table 4).

Linking Perceptions and Physical Components by Rough Sets Approach

This section focuses attention on the physical components of sidewalk environments which relate to people's perceptions. This is a complex process with uncertainty and vagueness. Furthermore, the sidewalk sample of this study is 20, which is rather small, and the collected data is qualitative or categorical information. This means that conventional statistical methods are less appropriate. Rough sets approach may then be very suitable to this study in case of uncertainty, qualitative information and

small sample size (See, for example, Egmond et al., 2003; Medda and Nikjamp, 2003; Water and Scholz, 2007; Wang et al., 2008).

Information System

In any rough sets approach, it is essential to construct an information system with condition and decision attributes. The two decision attributes, identified in the factor analysis, represent people's perceptions with three levels in the psychological survey. The profiles of the 20 sidewalks collected in the field survey are recoded and the nine attributes from A to I become the condition attributes. Thus, two information tables (See Figure 4) are built including the information of physical components of the sidewalks and people's perceptions. They are named "HARMONIOUSNESS" and "OPENNESS" respectively.

Rough Sets Data Explorer (ROSE) system (Predki et al., 1998) is used here for rough sets approach to deal with the two information systems. The software system has an easy user interface and can assess the approximation of decision classes, check dependencies between attributes, identify reduced subsets of attributes and discover hidden facts with induced rules. In this study, we are especially interested in core attributes and induced rules, through which we can identify the most important attributes that are responsible for perception factors and look for relationships between perceptions and physical components of sidewalk environments.

Approximations

There are two measures for the examination of the inexactness of approximate classifications (Pawlak, 1991). The first is the accuracy of classification, which expresses the percentage of possible correct decisions when classifying objects. The accuracy of classification ranges from 0 to 1. If no boundary region exists, it is equal to 1, which means a perfect classification. The other is called

Figure 4. Information table

Information system - "HARMONIOUSNESS"

Photo number	Condition attributes (Physical components of sidewalk)									Decision attribute (Harmoniousness)
	A	B	C	D	E	F	G	H	I	HA
01	A2	B1	C2	D3	E3	F1	G3	H3	I1	HA3
02	A1	B3	C3	D1	E2	F2	G2	H2	I2	HA1
03	A1	B3	C1	D1	E2	F2	G2	H3	I1	HA2
							G1	H2	I1	HA1
18	A3	B2	C3	D1	E1	F2	G1	H1	I2	HA1
19	A2	B3	C2	D2	E3	F1	G2	H3	I2	HA3
20	A2	B3	C2	D2	E3	F1	G2	H3	I2	HA2

Information system - "OPENNESS"

Photo number	Condition attributes (Physical components of sidewalk)									Decision attribute (Openness)
	A	B	C	D	E	F	G	H	I	OP
01	A2	B1	C2	D3	E3	F1	G3	H3	I1	OP2
02	A1	B3	C3	D1	E2	F2	G2	H2	I2	OP1
03	A1	B3	C1	D1	E2	F2	G2	H3	I1	OP1

the quality of approximation, which expresses the percentage of objects correctly classified to classes. The quality of approximation ranges from 0 to 1. The higher the value is, the more correctly the objects are classified.

Approximations of decision classes for two information systems are characterized in table 5. As can be seen, the accuracy and the quality of the rough sets approximations is relatively high both with the values of 0.90, which means that the attributes can provide satisfactory discrimination between the classes.

Reducts and Core Attributes

Some attributes in an information system may be superfluous and dispensable, thus can be eliminated without losing essential classification information. The attributes reduction is the process of removing of superfluous partitions and finding only that part of the really useful knowledge. Intuitively, a reduct of knowledge is its essential part, which suffices to define knowledge, and the elimination of any attribute in it does lead to a less accurate classification. The core is the

Table 5. Accuracy and quality for two information systems

Information system	Class	Number of sidewalks	Lower approximation	Upper approximation	Accuracy	Quality
HARMONIOUSNESS	HA1	6	6	6	1.00	0.90
	HA2	7	6	8	0.75	
	HA3	7	6	8	0.75	
OPENNESS	OP1	7	7	7	1.00	0.90
	OP2	7	6	8	0.75	
	OP3	6	5	7	0.71	

Table 6. Reducts and core attributes for two information systems

Information system	Number of condition attributes	Core attribute	Reduct	Length of reduct
HARMONIOUSNESS	9	D, I	{A, B, D, H, I}	5
			{B, D, E, I}	4
			{A, D, G, I}	4
			{D, E, G, I}	4
OPENNESS	9	I	{A, G, I}	3
			{C, E, G, I}	4
			{A, B, D, E, I}	5
			{A, B, D, H, I}	5
			{B, C, D, E, I}	5

interaction of all reducts and is the set of the most characteristic and important part of knowledge.

In addition, it should be noted that finding a minimal reduct is NP-hard and the reduct of an information system is not unique. There are several methods for obtaining reducts such as exhaustive algorithm and genetic algorithm. The former may calculate all reducts but the operation is time consuming (Rauszer and, Skowron, 1992) while the latter is an approximate and heuristic method (Wroblewski, 1998). The latter method is applied in this study.

The reducts and core attributes for two information systems are calculated next (see table 6). Four and five reducts for HARMONIOUSNESS and OPENNESS are obtained respectively with the length from 3 to 5. It is obvious that the length of reducts is considerably smaller than the total number of condition attributes. From rough sets perspective, the reducts contain only necessary information with fewer attributes. It turns out that there is quite some redundant information in the information systems. We can see that attributes "surface condition (C)" and "signage (F)" never appear in the HARMONIOUSNESS information system and "signage (F)" never appears in the OPENNESS, which indicates that they are redundant. In this study, the reducts, as representative features of sidewalk environments, may be

of particular importance in people's perception process.

Another important question is whether there are condition attributes that are more important than others. From table 6 we can see that "type of land use (D)" and "percentage of sky area (I)" for HARMONIOUSNESS, "percentage of sky area (I)" for OPENNESS are the most pronounced attributes. According to rough sets theory they are the core attributes and the most important factors that are responsible for people's perceptions. In other words, "type of land use (D)" and "percentage of sky area (I)" play the most important role in the shape of harmoniousness perception, while "percentage of sky area (I)" plays the most important role in the shape of openness perception among attributes. We may consider managing the land use and trees to improve people's perceptions.

Induced Rules

In this study, we argue that pedestrians shape their perceptions based on their opinions of how physical features influence the evaluative quality of sidewalk environments. Rough sets approach is able to identify causal linkages between attributes with hidden deterministic rules, which may help to find what features evoke favorable psychological

Table 7. Decision rules for HARMONIOUSNESS

No.	Rules		Strength
	Condition part (If)	Conclusion part (Then)	
1	No shrubs (E1)	Low level of harmoniousness (HA1)	0.83
2	Sidewalk width is 2.5m to 3.5m (G2) & Percentage of sky area is under 10% (I1) or over 20% (I3)	Normal level of harmoniousness (HA2)	0.57
3	Sidewalk tree is both sides (A2) & Type of surface material is mixture (B3) & Type of land use is buildings with vegetation (D3)	Normal level of harmoniousness (HA2)	0.14
4	Type of land use is only vegetation (D2) & Percentage of sky area is under 10% (I1)	Normal level of harmoniousness (HA2)	0.14
5	Sidewalk tree is one side (A1) & Sidewalk width is over 3.5m (G3)	High level of harmoniousness (HA3)	0.43
6	Sidewalk tree is both sides (A2) & Type of surface material is interlocking block (B2) & Percentage of sky area is over 20% (I3)	High level of harmoniousness (HA3)	0.29
7	Sidewalk tree is both sides (A2) & Type of surface material is asphalt (B1) & Percentage of sky area is 10% to 20% (I2)	High level of harmoniousness (HA3)	0.29
8	Type of surface material is asphalt (B1) & Type of land use is buildings with vegetation (D3) & Sidewalk width is over 3.5m (G3)	High level of harmoniousness (HA3)	0.29

responses. We now focus our attention on hidden deterministic rules to identify the causal linkages.

The extended minimal covering method with Laplace measure is adopted and the induced rules for two information systems are presented in table 7 and 8. There are eight rules with relatively high strength for information systems HARMONIOUSNESS and OPENNESS, respectively. The strength of each rule is given in the last column of tables.

The condition part of the rules is comprised of the combination of physical components of sidewalk environment while the conclusion part is comprised of people's perceptions. The rules can express the causal linkages in a relatively straightforward manner. For example, the rule 1 in table 7 can be interpreted as "if there is no shrubs (E1), then the sidewalk is evaluated as low level of harmoniousness (HA1)"; the rule 6 in table 7 can be interpreted as "if sidewalk tree is both sides (A2), type of surface material is interlocking block (B2), and percentage of sky area is over 20% (I3), then the sidewalk is evaluated as high level of harmoniousness (HA3)"; the rule 1

in table 8 can be interpreted as "if sidewalk width is under 2.5m (G1), then the sidewalk is evaluated as low level of openness (OP1) "; the rule 8 in table 8 can be interpreted as "if sidewalk tree is both sides (A2), sidewalk width is over 3.5m (G3), and percentage of sky area is 10% to 20% (I2), then the sidewalk is evaluated as high level of openness (OP3)".

The rules, linking perceptions and physical components of sidewalk environments, can represent feasible cause-effect relationships. We are most interested in the rules for the low and high level of perception. From table 7 and 8, we can see that the rules for the low level of perceptions (HA1 and OP1) are short and simple, which indicates obvious causal linkages, while the rules for the high level of perception (HA3 and OP3) are the combination of two or three condition attributes, and seem to be more complex.

The rules discover the facts and cause-effect relationships hidden in the information systems and express them in the natural language, and can be further analyzed and used to effectively make sidewalk environments more attractive. It should

Table 8. Decision rules for OPENNESS

No	Rules		Strength
	Condition part (If)	Conclusion part (Then)	
1	Sidewalk width is under 2.5m (G1)	Low level of openness (OP1)	0.57
2	Type of surface material is mixture (B3) & Type of land use is buildings (D1)	Low level of openness (OP1)	0.57
3	Sidewalk tree is one side (A1) or not applicable (A3) & Percentage of sky area is over 20% (I3)	Normal level of openness (OP2)	0.43
4	Sidewalk tree is one side (A1) & Surface condition is moderate (C2) & Type of land use is buildings with vegetation (D3)	Normal level of openness (OP2)	0.14
5	Sidewalk tree is both sides (A2) & Percentage of sky area is under 10% (I1)	Normal level of openness (OP2)	0.29
6	Surface condition is good (C1) & Sidewalk width is over 3.5m (G3)	High level of openness (OP3)	0.33
7	Sidewalk width is over 3.5m (G3) & Percentage of green area is 20% to 40% (H2)	High level of openness (OP3)	0.33
8	Sidewalk tree is both sides (A2) & Sidewalk width is over 3.5m (G3) & Percentage of sky area is 10% to 20% (I2)	High level of openness (OP3)	0.33

be mentioned that the rule induction in rough sets approach is deterministic and incorporate a compulsory logic from the given information system. Hence, some of them may be lack of meaningful and theoretical constructs.

5. DISCUSSIONS

Although there are many other factors which may come up during the study, we focus on the physical components of sidewalk environments. The assumption of this study is that the combination of physical components of the sidewalk environments impact on people's perceptions. In this study, the outputs of rough sets approach indicate that attributes "surface condition" and "signage" don't seem to influence participants' perception of harmoniousness while attributes "type of land use" and "percentage of sky area" are very important. At the same time, attribute "signage" seem unimportant to participants' perception of openness while "percentage of sky area" is the most pronounced. Based on that, the collected data is

reorganized with the necessary combinations of attributes, which is called reducts in rough sets theory. Then the decision rules provide the representative features of the sidewalk environments which relate to people's perceptions.

Compared with other studies, the results are not limited to one element such as tree (Wiliams, 2002), signscape (Nasar and Hong, 1999) but a series of physical components of the sidewalk environment. Being similar with the research on representative features of sidewalk (Wang et al., 2008), this study updates the bad and good evaluation to three-level Harmoniousness and Openness perceptions. In one word, this study finds out not only which physical attributes contribute to and which physical attributes don't contribute to designing sidewalk environment relative people's perceptions, but also some hidden relationships between physical components and people's perceptions.

It is necessary to introduce people's perception into the study of walking environment design. The application of rough sets approach proves it is a valuable tool for designers because it can quickly identify features of the physical constructs and output some important information in testing present structure of sidewalk environments, which may help to generate the best design option or make effective decisions. Thus the designers can input necessary design elements to improve user perceptions or increase user satisfaction by utilizing the output information.

6 CONCLUSIONS AND FUTURE DIRECTIONS

This study illustrates the potential usefulness of the rough sets theory as an operational tool for linking participants' perceptions and physical components of sidewalk environments. Understanding people's perceptions of the environment better is necessary through design process. However, conventional statistical methods suffer from limitations of qualitative, categorical information with uncertainty, as well as small sample size. In this context, recent developments in areas outside of the statistical domains may provide new useful solutions forward. Rough sets theory, as nonparametric methods, proves its potential advantages in this study by identifying the most important factors to people's perceptions and discovering the hidden causal relationships between perceptions and physical components of sidewalk environments, which are statistically difficult to judge. Such an analytical activity offers more opportunity to make a better understanding of the relationships between environment and human behavior and to design with evidences from a wide range of field conditions and users' responses. The purpose of this study is to develop new ideas and methods, rather than to prove facts in a final and determinate way. In the future research, the outputs of the rough sets approach can be compared with professional designers' experience, and can also be combined with the simulation tool to realize a more valuable design tool.

REFERENCES

Baaijens, S., & Nijkamp, P. (1999). Time pioneers and travel behaviour: An investigation into the viability of "slow motion". *Growth and Change, 30*(2), 237–263..doi:10.1111/0017-4815.00112

Bailey, K., Brumm, J., & Grossardt, T. (2001). Towards structured public involvement in highway design: A comparative study of visualization methods and preference modeling using CAVE (Casewise Visual Evaluation). *Journal of Geographic Information and Decision Analysis, 5*(1), 1–15.

Buhyoff, G. J., & Wellman, J. D. (1980). The specification of a non-linear psychophysical function for visual landscape dimensions. *Journal of Leisure Research, 12*, 257–272. http://www.cababstractsplus.org/abstracts/Abstract.aspx?AcNo=19811874198.

Clifton, K. J., Smith, A. D. L., & Rodriguez, D. (2007). The development and testing of an audit for the pedestrian environment. *Landscape and Urban Planning, 80*, 95–100..doi:10.1016/j.landurbplan.2006.06.008

Düntsch, I., & Gediga, G. (1998). Uncertainty measures of rough set prediction. *Artificial Intelligence, 106*(1), 109–137..doi:10.1016/S0004-3702(98)00091-5

Echelberger, H. E. (1979). The semantic differential in landscape research. in *Proceedings of Our National Landscape: a Conference on Applied Techniques for Analysis and Management of the Visual Resource*(pp. 524-531). Incline Village.

Egmond, P. V., Nijkamp, P., & Vindigni, G. (2003). A comparative analysis of the performance of urban public transport systems in Europe. *International Social Science Journal, 55*(176), 235–247. doi:. doi:10.1111/j.1468-2451.2003.05502005.x

Ergin, A., Karaesmen, E., Micallef, A., & Williams, A. T. (2004). A new methodology for evaluating coastal scenery: fuzzy logic systems. *Area, 36*(4), 367–386..doi:10.1111/j.0004-0894.2004.00238.x

Evans-Cowley, J. (2006). Sidewalk planning and policies in small cities. *Journal of Urban Planning and Development, 132*(2), 71–75..doi:10.1061/(ASCE)0733-9488(2006)132:2(71)

Frank, L. D., & Engelke, P. O. (2001). The built environment and human activity patterns: Exploring the impacts of urban form on public health. *Journal of Planning Literature, 16*(2), 202–218..doi:10.1177/08854120122093339

Funakoshi, T., & Tsumita, H. (1986). A study of psychological-analysis on street spaces: Study on street spaces (Part I). *Transactions of the Architectural Institute of Japan, 327*, 100-107. http://ci.nii.ac.jp/Detail/detail.do?LOCALID=ART0005211937&lang=en

Ge, J., & Hokao, K. (2005). Applying the methods of image evaluation and spatial analysis to study the sound environment of urban street areas. *Journal of Environmental Psychology, 25*(4), 455–466..doi:10.1016/j.jenvp.2005.10.003

Handy, S. L., Boarnet, M. G., Ewing, R., & Killingworth, R. E. (2002). How the built environment affects physical activity: Views from urban planning. *American Journal of Preventive Medicine, 23*(2), 64–73..doi:10.1016/S0749-3797(02)00475-0

Hirokane, M., Nishimura, F., Morikawa, Y., & Hamaguchi, C. (2003). Rough sets based extraction method of characteristics from bridge images. in *Proceedings of the Seventh International Conference on the Application of Artificial Intelligence to Civil and Structural Engineering*(Paper 68). Scotland: Civil-Comp Press.

Hochberg, J. (1966). Representative sampling and the purposes of research: Pictures of the world and the world of pictures. In Hammond, K. (Ed.), *The Psychology of Egon Brunswik*(pp. 361–381). New York: Holt, Rinehart, and Winston.

Kamičaitytė-Virbašienė, J., & Janušaitis, R. (2004). Some methodical aspects of landscape visual quality preferences analysis. *Environmental Research, Engineering and Management, 3*(29), 51-60. www1.apini.lt/includes/getfile.php?id=201

Kinoshita, Y., Cooper, E. W., Hoshino, Y., & Kamei, K. (2004). A townscape evaluate on system based on kansei and colour harmony models. In *2004 IEEE International Conference on Systems, Man and Cybernetics, 1*, 327-332.

Li, S. P., & Will, B. F. (2005). A fuzzy logic system for visual evaluation. *Environment and Planning. B, Planning & Design, 32*(2), 293–304..doi:10.1068/b31155

Lim, E. M., Honjo, T., & Umeki, K. (2006). The validity of VRML images as a stimulus for landscape assessment. *Landscape and Urban Planning, 77*, 80–93..doi:10.1016/j.landurbplan.2005.01.007

Lin, T. Y., & Crone, N. (1997). *Rough Sets and Data Mining: Analysis for Imprecise Data*. Dordrecht, Boston, London: Kluwer Academic.

Lindsey, G., & Nguyen, D. B. L. (2004). Use of greenway trails in Indiana. *Journal of Urban Planning and Development, 130*(4), 213–217..doi:10.1061/(ASCE)0733-9488(2004)130:4(213)

Llinares, C., & Page, A. (2007). Application of product differential semantics to quantify purchaser perceptions in housing assessment. *Building and Environment, 42*(7), 2488–2497..doi:10.1016/j.buildenv.2006.06.012

McHarg, I. (1969). *Design with Nature*. Garden City, New York: Natural History Press.

Medda, F., & Nijkamp, P. (2003). A combinatorial assessment methodology for complex transport policy analysis. *Integrated Assessment, 4*(3), 214–222..doi:10.1076/iaij.4.3.214.23773

Moudon, A. V., & Lee, C. (2003). Walking and bicycling: An evaluation of environmental audit instruments. *American Journal of Health Promotion, 18*(1), 21–37. http://apt.allenpress.com/perlserv/?request=get-abstract&doi=10.1043%2F0890-1171(2003)018%5B0021%3AWABAEO%5D2.3.CO%3B2.

Mougiakakou, S. G., Tsouchlaraki, A. L., Cassios, C., Nikita, K. S., Matsopoulos, G. K., & Uzunoglu, N. K. (2005). SCAPEVIEWER: preliminary results of a landscape perception classification system based on neural network technology. *Ecological Engineering, 24*(1-2), 5–15..doi:10.1016/j.ecoleng.2004.12.003

Müderrisoğlu, H., Eroğlu, E., Özkan, Ş., & Ak, K. (2006). Visual perception of tree forms. *Building and Environment, 41*(6), 796–806..doi:10.1016/j.buildenv.2005.03.008

Naderi, J. R., & Raman, B. (2005). Capturing impressions of pedestrian landscapes used for healing purposes with decision tree learning. *Landscape and Urban Planning, 73*(2-3), 155–166..doi:10.1016/j.landurbplan.2004.11.012

Nasar, J. L., & Hong, X. (1999). Visual preferences in urban signscapes. *Environment and Behavior, 31*(5), 671–691..doi:10.1177/00139169921972290

Nassauer, J. (1980). A non-linear model of visual quality. *Landscape Research, 5*(3), 29–31. doi:.doi:10.1080/01426398008705956

Nijkamp, P., Rietveld, P., & Spierdijk, L. (2000). A meta-analytic comparison of determinants of public transport use: methodology and application. *Environment and Planning. B, Planning & Design, 27*(6), 893–903..doi:10.1068/b2695

Osgood, C. E. (1969). The nature and measurement of meaning. In Osgood, C. E., & Snider, J. G. (Eds.), *Semantic differential technique: a source book* (pp. 3–41). Chicago: Aldine.

Osgood, C. E., Suci, G. J., & Tannenbaum, P. H. (1957). *The measurement of meaning*. Urbana: The University of Illinois Press.

Pawlak, Z. (1991). *Rough sets: Theoretical Aspects of Reasoning about Data*. Dordrecht, Boston, London: Kluwer Academic.

Pawlak, Z. (1997). Rough set approach to knowledge-based decision support. *European Journal of Operational Research, 99*(1), 48–57..doi:10.1016/S0377-2217(96)00382-7

Polkowski, L., Tsumoto, S., Lin, T.Y. (2000). *Rough Set Methods and Applications: New Developments in Knowledge Discovery in Information Systems*. Heidellberg: Physica-Verlag.

Predki, B., Slowinski, R., Stefanowski, J., Susmaga, R., & Wilk, S. (1998). ROSE-Software implementation of the rough set theory. In Polkowski, L., & Skowron, A. (Eds.), *Rough Sets and current Trends in Computing 1998, LNAI 1424* (pp. 605–608). Heidelberg: Springer Berlin. doi:10.1007/3-540-69115-4_85

Raman, B., & Naderi, J. R. (2006). Computer based pedestrian landscape design using decision tree templates. *Advanced Engineering Informatics, 20*(1), 23–30..doi:10.1016/j.aei.2005.08.002

Rauszer, C., & Skowron, A. (1992). The Discernibility Matrices and Functions in Information. Systems. In Slowinski, R. (Ed.), *Intelligent Decision Support*. Amsterdam: Kluwer Dordrecht.

Saito, A., Munemoto, J., & Matsushita, D. (2005). Study on inference of combination rules of form elements by sensibility evaluation employing rough sets theory - a case of Sanneizaka preservation district for groups of historic buildings. *Journal of Architecture and Planning, 594*, 85–91. http://sciencelinks.jp/j-east/article/200517/000020051705A0688174.php.

Schroeder, H. W., & Cannon, W. N. (1987). Visual quality of residential streets: both street and yard trees make a difference. *Journal of Arboriculture, 13*(10), 236–239. http://joa.isa-arbor.com/request.asp?JournalID=1&ArticleID=2175&Type=2.

Shibata, T., & Kato, T. (1998). Modeling of subjective interpretation for street landscape image. In Neves, J., Santos, M. F., & Machado, J. M. (Eds.), *Progress in Artificial Intelligence, LNCS 1460* (pp. 501–510). Heidelberg: Springer Berlin.

Slowinski, R. (2004).Retrieved from http://www-idss.cs.put.poznan.pl/

Slowinski, R., Greco, S., & Matarazzo, S. (2005). Rough set based decision support. In Burke, E., & Kendall, G. (Eds.), *Search Methodologies: Introductory Tutorials in Optimization and Decision Support Techniques* (pp. 475–527). Boston: Springer-Verlang.

Sriram, R. D. (2006). Artificial intelligence in engineering: Personal reflections. *Advanced Engineering Informatics, 20*(1), 3–5..doi:10.1016/j.aei.2005.12.002

Summit, J., & Sommer, R. (1999). Further studies of preferred tree shapes. *Environment and Behavior, 31*(4), 550–576..doi:10.1177/00139169921972236

Todorova, A., Asakawa, S., & Aikoh, T. (2004). Preferences for and attitudes towards street flowers and trees in Sapporo, Japan. *Landscape and Urban Planning, 69*(4), 403–416..doi:10.1016/j.landurbplan.2003.11.001

Tsumita, H., Sekido, Y., & Hamamoto, S. (2006). A correlation analysis of an atmosphere and indication element of street space by psychological quantity distribution figure: Study of kehai in urban street spaces (Part 2). *Journal of Architecture and Planning, 607*, 41–48. http://ci.nii.ac.jp/naid/110004809771/en.

Walczak, B., & Massart, D. L. (1999). Rough sets theory. *Chemometrics and Intelligent Laboratory Systems, 47*(1), 1–16..doi:10.1016/S0169-7439(98)00200-7

Walter, A. I., & Scholz, R. W. (2007). Critical success conditions of collaborative methods: a comparative evaluation of transport planning projects. *Transportation, 34*(2), 195–212..doi:10.1007/s11116-006-9000-0

Wang, W., Seo, I., Lee, B., & Namgung, M. (2008). Extracting features of sidewalk space using the rough sets approach. *Environment and Planning. B, Planning & Design, 35*(5), 920–934..doi:10.1068/b34045

Williams, J. E., Kirtland, K. A., Cavnar, M. M., Sharpe, P. A., Neet, M. J., & Cook, A. (2005). Development and use of a tool for assessing sidewalk maintenance as an environmental support of physical activity. *Health Promotion Practice, 6*(1), 81–88..doi:10.1177/1524839903260595

Williams, K. (2002). Exploring resident preferences for street trees in Melbourne. *Australia Journal of Arboriculture, 28*(4), 161–169.

Wroblewski, J. Covering with Reducts: A Fast Algorithm for Rule Generation. Proceeding of RSCTC'98 LNAI 1424 Springer Verlag, Berlin, 1998, 402-407.

Wu, C., Yue, Y., Li, M., & Adjei, O. (2004). The rough set theory and applications. *Engineering Computations, 21*(5), 488–511..doi:10.1108/02644400410545092

Zube, E. H., Pitt, D. G., & Anderson, T. W. (1975). Perception and prediction of scenic resource values of the northeast. In E.H. Zube, R.O. Brush, J.G. Fabos (Ed), *Landscape Assessment: Values, Perceptions, and Resources* (pp. 151-167). Stroudsburg: Dowden, Hutchinson & Ross.

Chapter 12
Affective Facial Expressions Using Auto–Associative Neural Network in Kansei Robot "Ifbot"

Masayoshi Kanoh
Chukyo University, Japan

Tsuyoshi Nakamura
Nagoya Institute of Technology, Japan

Shohei Kato
Nagoya Institute of Technology, Japan

Hidenori Itoh
Nagoya Institute of Technology, Japan

ABSTRACT

The authors propose three methods of enabling a Kansei robot, Ifbot, to convey affective expressions using an emotion space composed of an auto-associative neural network. First, the authors attempt to extract the characteristics of Ifbot's facial expressions by mapping them to its emotion space using an auto-associative neural network, and create its emotion regions. They then propose a method for generating affective facial expressions using these emotion regions. The authors also propose an emotion-transition method using a path that minimizes the amount of change in an emotion space. Finally, they propose a method for creating personality using the face.

1. INTRODUCTION

Recently, the robotics research field has been shifting from industrial to domestic applications, and several domestic robots have been developed

DOI: 10.4018/978-1-61692-797-4.ch012

(Murase et al., 2001; Kuroki et al., 2002; Fujita et al., 2000; Kanda et al., 2003). Because these robots are required to work as part of our daily lives, they require interfaces for communicating actively with us. Not only verbal but also non-verbal information is an important part of communication between people. For this reason, communication of mental information, such as emotions and feelings between robots and people has been often studied. For example, Kobayashi et al. (1994) developed an active human interface that allows robots to perceive people's emotions and tell their reactions to people. They also reported a mechanism for controlling the facial expressions of a robot as a way to communicate. Wada et al. (2004) developed a mechanical pet that behaves autonomously, as if it had a mind and emotions, and physically interacts with people. He showed the possibility that this interaction gives people mental effects such as pleasure and calmness. These studies addressed emotions and feelings in communication between people and robots. We aim to develop smooth communication between people and robots by enabling robots to express emotions and feelings.

One useful way to communicate emotions is through facial expressions. In communication between people, an expression of anger threatens the other party, and an expression of happiness extends goodwill. Facial expressions show true emotions. Similarly, in communications between robots and people, if expressions corresponding to the emotions of the robots are generable and the robots can express them, communication becomes smoother.

We developed a Kansei communication robot, Ifbot (BDL, 2009; Kanoh, 2005; Cho, 2009). Ifbot understands speakers' utterances and communicates with people by expressing its emotions. To express its emotions, Ifbot has about 50 expressions and talks while making them. Not only robots but also CGs can communicate with people. However, plasticity, reality, spatiotemporal common feelings etc. help to express sensibility factors because robots are physical entities. Ifbot can make various facial expressions using its complicated mechanisms, so it is especially fit to express sensibility factors. We evaluate the emotional transmission of Ifbot when communicating with people.

Facial robots, which can express their emotions, have been developed such as SAYA (Kobayashi, 1994; Kobayashi & Hara, 1996), Repliee (Mac Dorman & Ishiguro, 2004) and Kismet (Breazeal & Scassellati, 1999). SAYA has human-like skin and creates facial expressions faithfully. Repliee is a common name for two androids, a replica of a five-year-old Japanese girl (Repliee R1) and a woman android (Repliee Q1). Silicon skin covers the entire body of each Repliee, which feels like human skin. SAYA and Repliee are robots that closely resemble humans. On the other hand, Kismet has a simplified face that expresses emotions and interest. Ifbot also has a simplified face. Kismet makes its facial expressions with motors, but Ifbot makes them with motors and LEDs. Motors mounted on eyes, eyelids etc. and colored LEDs create Ifbot's face, which express internal emotions, purposes, and so forth. Using various facial expressions, Ifbot can communicate in an entertaining way. In this chapter, we describe the control of Ifbot's facial expressions using emotion space.

2. IFBOT

Front and side views of Ifbot are shown in Figure 1. Ifbot is 45 cm tall, weighs 9.5 kg, has two arms, and moves on wheels. Ifbot received the 2003 Good Design Award #03A02002 in the product design section and in the amusement products and devices category from the Japan Industrial Design Promotion Organization.

Ifbot's facial expressions are made using ten motors and 101 LEDs, which are diagrammed in Figure 2. The motors move Ifbot's neck, eyes, and eyelids. The neck has two axes (θ_{N1}, θ_{N2}), each eye has two axes (left: $\theta_{E1}^{(L)}$, $\theta_{E2}^{(L)}$; right: $\theta_{E1}^{(R)}$, $\theta_{E2}^{(R)}$), and each eyelid also has two axes (left: $\theta_{L1}^{(L)}$, $\theta_{L2}^{(L)}$; right: $\theta_{L1}^{(R)}$, $\theta_{L2}^{(R)}$). The LEDs are set up for the head (L_H), mouth (L_M), eye color (L_E), cheeks (L_C), and tears (L_T). They emit three colors (orange,

Figure 1. Front and side views of Ifbot

green, and red) in the head, one color (orange) in the mouth, three colors (green, red, and blue) in the eyes, one color (red) in the cheeks, one color (blue) for tears, and one color (orange) in the ears. Using these mechanisms, Ifbot can make various facial expressions.

M is the motor's control parameters, **L** is the LED's control parameters, and Ifbot is controlled using the following facial expression control parameters **s**.

s=(M,L).

3. EMOTION SPACE AND EMOTION REGIONS

Auto-Associative Neural Networks

Multi-layer neural networks can be used for nonlinear dimensionality reductions (Bishop, 1995). We apply a five-layer neural network in the form shown in Figure 3 to extract Ifbot's facial expression characteristics. The network is an auto-associative neural network. The targets used to train the network are simply the input vectors, so the network attempts to map each input onto

Figure 2. Facial expression mechanisms of Ifbot

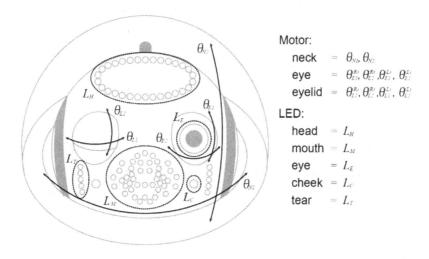

Motor:
  neck $= \theta_{N1}, \theta_{N2}$
  eye $= \theta_{E1}^{R}, \theta_{E2}^{R}, \theta_{E1}^{L}, \theta_{E2}^{L}$
  eyelid $= \theta_{L1}^{R}, \theta_{L2}^{R}, \theta_{L1}^{L}, \theta_{L2}^{L}$

LED:
  head $= L_{H}$
  mouth $= L_{M}$
  eye $= L_{E}$
  cheek $= L_{C}$
  tear $= L_{T}$

Figure 3. Creating emotion space

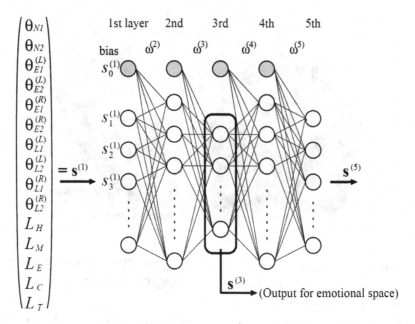

itself. The input information is compressed using a dimensionality reduction process before it is regenerated to recover the original information. In other words, the information is compressed, mixed, and reorganized in the third layer. Similar faces, therefore, are classified as similar values in the third layer when this network is used to extract facial characteristics. Ueki (1994) and Sakaguchi (1997) have focused on this feature and have analyzed and synthesized facial expressions of humans. They used the third layer, which extracts characteristics of facial expressions, as emotion space. We apply this idea in creating Ifbot's emotion space.

We use the following vector to input the network:

$s^{(1)}=(M,L)$,

where **M** and **L** are control parameters of motor and LEDs, respectively. These values are as follows:

$$\mathbf{M} = (\theta_{N1}, \theta_{N2}, \theta_{E1}^{(L)}, \theta_{E2}^{(L)}, \theta_{E1}^{(R)}, \theta_{E2}^{(R)}, \theta_{L1}^{(L)}, \theta_{L2}^{(L)}, \theta_{L1}^{(R)}, \theta_{L2}^{(R)})$$

$$\mathbf{L} = (L_H, L_M, L_E, L_C, L_T)$$

where θ are motor outputs and L are patterns outputted from the LEDs for the head, mouth, eye color, cheeks, and tears.

In the k-th layer, the j-th value $s_j^{(k)}$ of network output is given as:

$$s_j^{(k)} = f(u_j^{(k)}),$$

where $f()$ is a logistic sigmoid activation function, whose outputs lie in the range (0, 1), and each $u_j^{(k)}$ is computed with the following equation:

$$u_j^{(k)} = \sum_i \omega_{ij}^{(k)} s_i^{(k-1)}.$$

Here, $\omega_{ij}^{(k)}$ is a weight, so that each unit computes the weighted sum of its inputs $s_i^{(k-1)}$. Note that we regard the bias parameters as being weights from extra input $u_0^{(k)} = 1$.

The sum-of-squares error E is given as:

Figure 4. Examples of Ifbot's facial sequences

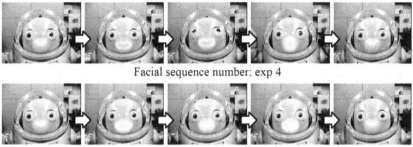

Facial sequence number: exp 4

Facial sequence number: exp 8

$$E = \sum_i \left(s_i^{(1)} - s_i^{(5)} \right)^2.$$

The network can be trained by minimizing error (back propagation):

$$\omega_{ij}^{(k)}(t+1) = \omega_{ij}^{(k)}(t) + \Delta\omega_{ij}^{(k)}(t),$$

where

$$\Delta\omega_{ij}^{(k)}(t) = \varepsilon d_j^{(k)} s_i^{(k-1)} + \eta \Delta\omega_{ij}^{(k)}(t-1) \text{ and}$$

$$d_j^{(k)} = \begin{cases} f'(u_j^{(k)}) \sum_l \omega_{jl}^{(k+1)}(t) d_l^{(k+1)} & (k \neq 5) \\ f'(u_j^{(k)})(s_j^{(1)} - s_j^{(k)}) & (k = 5) \end{cases}.$$

Here $f'()$ is the derivation of $f()$, the term ε is the learning rate, and η is momentum. We used output $\mathbf{s}^{(3)}$ of the network's third layer to map Ifbot's emotion space.

Creating Emotion Space

We first prepared a questionnaire to analyze Ifbot's emotion space, in which we showed 50 respondents 29 of Ifbot's facial sequences[1], and they chose the best emotion corresponding to each sequence. We provided seven options for classifying emotions: six basic emotions (anger, disgust, fear, happiness, sadness, and surprise) (Ekman, 1975) and no classification. Figure 4 shows examples of Ifbot's facial sequences. All facial sequences start with a neutral face, go through expressive faces, and end with the neutral face.

Table 1 lists two facial sequences of each emotion (anger, happiness, sadness, and surprise) that were the most popular in the questionnaire. In the figure, the leftmost column denotes the facial sequence number, and the values in the 2nd to 7th columns indicate support ratings when the sequence denoted in leftmost was shown. Note that disgust and fear did not earn a high support rating in the questionnaire.

We then created an emotion space in Ifbot using the auto-associative neural network described in the previous section. We used the values of 15, 45, 2, 45 and 15 for the number of units in each layer. Note that this type of network extracts characteristics of input data on the third layer, but cannot create meaning on its axes. We, therefore, chose the value of 2 for the number of the third layer's units to visualize and assess the emotion space. We evaluated the emotion space by confirming whether the affective facial sequences listed in Table 1 were classified on it. To train the network, we used the four facial sequences of anger, sadness, happiness and surprise, which earned the best scores in the questionnaire. Control values $\mathbf{s}^{(1)}$ in the sequences are used as inputs and targets of the network.

Figure 5 plots Ifbot's emotion space constructed using the network after the training of the network was completed. The lines in the figure

Table 1. Results of questionnaire (%). This lists that each two- facial sequence of anger, happiness, sadness, and surprise that were the most popular in the questionnaire. Note that disgust and fear did not earn a high support rating in the questionnaire

Facial sequence no.	Recognized emotion (support ratings: %)						
	Anger	Disgust	Fear	Happiness	Sadness	Surprise	No class.
exp 1	78	14	0	0	4	0	4
exp 2	84	4	4	2	0	2	4
exp 3	0	0	0	14	0	66	20
exp 4	0	0	2	22	0	72	4
exp 5	2	6	4	0	86	0	2
exp 6	0	0	8	2	90	0	0
exp 7	0	4	0	84	0	6	6
exp 8	0	0	0	96	0	4	0

are constructed from outputs of the third layer of the network when Ifbot's facial sequences, which earned the best scores, were inputted into the network. You can see that the facial expressions, which best express Ifbot's emotions, are classified in the emotion space.

Emotion Regions

We defined Ifbot's emotion regions based on subjective judgments using a questionnaire with 121 of Ifbot's facial expressions. These facial expressions were extracted according to the following procedure (Gotoh, 2005).

First, we partitioned off the emotion space from 0.0 to 1.0 in units of 0.1 to form a grid and picked out each node. Then, the location of each node was inputted to the third layer of the auto-associative neural network, and facial-expression control parameters were outputted from the fifth layer. We created facial expressions from the facial-expression control parameters. The 20 respondents

Figure 5. Emotion space of Ifbot

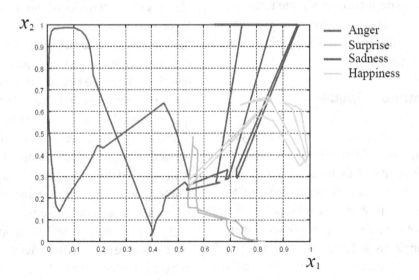

Figure 6. Result of questionnaire

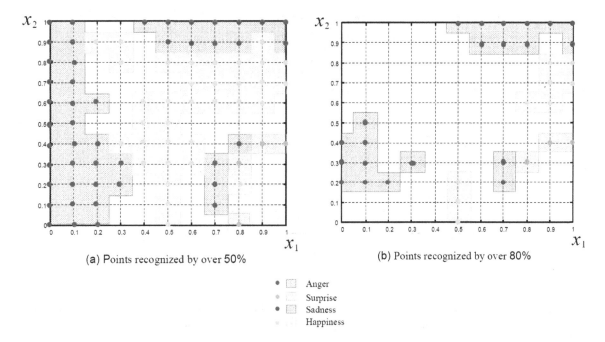

(a) Points recognized by over 50%   (b) Points recognized by over 80%

- Anger
- Surprise
- Sadness
- Happiness

chose the emotion that best corresponded to each expression. We provided seven options for classifying emotions: six basic emotions (Ekman, 1975) and no classification.

The results of the questionnaire are shown in Figure 6. The red points are those perceived as anger, the cyan ones are those perceived as happiness, the blue ones are those perceived as sadness, and the green ones are those perceived as surprise. Figure 6(a) shows points as perceived by over 50% of the respondents, and (b) shows points as perceived by over 80% of the respondents.

In analyzing the results of the questionnaire, we focused on the points that were perceived by 50 to 80% of the respondents and those by over 80% of the respondents. We believe that the same emotion is expressed in a fixed range defined by these points. Therefore, we assumed that the areas defined by the points that were perceived by 50 to 80% of the respondents were regions of weak emotions, and the areas defined by the points that were perceived by over 80% of the respondents were regions of strong emotions. Using these

regions, we defined Ifbot's emotion regions, as shown in Figure 7. In this figure, the dark colors represent regions of strong emotions, and light colors represent regions of weak ones. A model of the emotion regions is shown in Figure 8. Weak happiness is the center of the emotion space, and regions of other emotions surround it. For Ifbot to seem more pleasant, the region of weak happiness is used when Ifbot is neutral. We believe that Ifbot can help people relax by expressing weak happiness when it is neutral. Using these emotion regions, we created facial expressions corresponding to Ifbot's internal emotions.

4. EMOTION EXPRESSIONS

Creating Facial Expressions Using Emotion Regions

Ifbot has many built-in facial expressions for communicating enjoyment. They are used to express its emotions, intentions, and reactions to

Figure 7. Emotion regions based on subjective evaluation

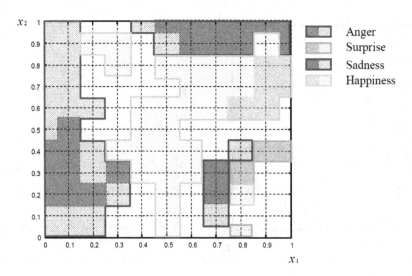

external stimulation. Each of these expressions is a facial sequence that starts with a neutral face, goes through expressive faces, and ends with the neutral face. That is, emotions cannot be expressed continuously, and two facial expressions cannot be smoothly connected. In this section, we use the emotion regions to suitably express emotions.

When Ifbot continuously expresses an emotion, facial expressions with moderate changes are more natural than a fixed one. To express emotions naturally, we developed a method to fluctuate expressions. Ifbot's expression-generation method is outlined in Figure 9. A coordinate point, $P(t)$ = $(x_1(t), x_2(t))^T$, at time t in the emotion space is

Figure 8. Model of emotion regions

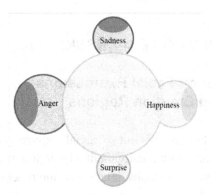

inputted to the third layer of the network, and a facial expression is created. The point is determined using the following procedure.

1. Determining the fluctuation value.

By using the intermittent chaos algorithm (Shinkai & Aizawa, 2006), a fluctuation value, $X_i(t) \in [0,1]$, at time t is given by

$$X_i(t) = \begin{cases} X_i(t-\Delta t) + 2X_i(t-\Delta t)^2 & (0 \le X_i(t-\Delta t) \le 0.5) \\ X_i(t-\Delta t) - 2(1 - X_i(t-\Delta t))^2 & (otherwise) \end{cases},$$

where Δt is a time step. In this section, we consider two fluctuation values, $X_1(t)$ and $X_2(t)$, because we use a two-dimensional emotion space.

2. Determining the direction of point movement.

Using the fluctuation value given in step 1, the direction of movement, $n(t) = (n_1(t), n_2(t))^T$, of a point, $P(t-\Delta t)$, is given by

$$\mathbf{n}(t) = \frac{\mathbf{u}(t)}{|\mathbf{u}(t)|},$$

Figure 9. Outline of facial expression generation method

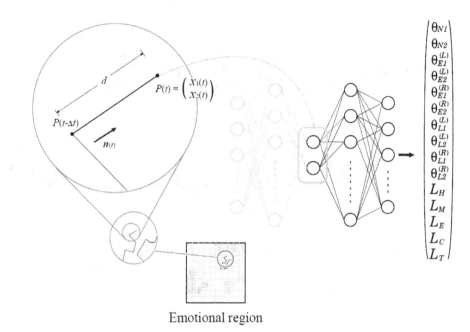

Emotional region

where

$$\mathbf{u}(t) = \begin{pmatrix} X_1(t) - 0.5 \\ X_2(t) - 0.5 \end{pmatrix}.$$

3.   Determining the coordinate point.

The coordinate point, $P(t)$, is determined by moving $P(t-\Delta t)$ in direction $\mathbf{n}(t)$ by a fixed distance, d:

$$P(t) = \begin{pmatrix} x_1(t - \Delta t) + dn_1(t) \\ x_2(t - \Delta t) + dn_2(t) \end{pmatrix}.$$

By repeating the above procedure, Ifbot continuously expresses emotions.

Experiments

When we create facial expressions using emotion regions, we believe we can create more affective faces by using strong emotion regions rather than weak ones. We also believe that impressions of faces change as the time step, Δt, is changed. To test these hypotheses, we conducted two experiments. In Section 4.2.1, we discuss an experiment to verify whether impressions of faces change when we use emotion regions of different strengths (with a fixed time step). Then, in Section 4.2.2, we discuss an experiment to examine how the impressions change when the time step is changed.

Experiment 1

We created eight facial expressions from all the strong and weak regions depicted in Figure 7 and used them to make a questionnaire. Two examples of the expressions used in the questionnaire are shown in Figure 10. Figure 10(a) shows faces created from a strong sad region, and Figure 10(b) shows faces created from a weak sad region. In the questionnaire, we showed eight facial expressions to 20 participants in random order. The participants classified each facial expression into any one of six basic emotions (Ekman, 1975) or no

Figure 10. Facial expressions on questionnaire (sadness)

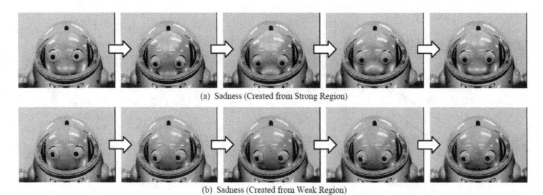

(a) Sadness (Created from Strong Region)

(b) Sadness (Created from Weak Region)

classification. When they chose one of six basic emotions, they were also asked about the strength of the emotion. The strength was rated from 1 to 5 (1, weak; 5, strong). We used Δt=100 (ms) and d = 0.05 for the parameters.

The results of the questionnaires are listed in Table 2. An "S" marks the faces from strong regions, and a "W" marks the faces from weak regions. The scores are listed on the left of each column, and the number of participants who recognized that emotion is listed on the right. If a face has a high score, the emotion it expresses is strong, and if many people recognized the emotion, the expression has a high recognition rate. You can see that the scores of strong regions are higher than those of weak regions. Therefore, we can change the degree of emotion expressed by

changing the strength of the emotion region used. We explain each emotion below.

In faces created from anger regions, both the scores and recognition rates are high, so Ifbot's angry faces were recognized easily. When the face from the weak anger region (Anger (W)) was used, the recognition of disgust increased. This shows that when expressions of anger are decreased, Ifbot's facial expressions tend to be classified as disgust.

The face from the weak happiness region (Happiness (W)) caused many people to think Ifbot felt disgust, and its score was high. Ifbot does not open its eyelids wide in this facial expression. Many participants classified it as disgust because they felt that it lowered its brows.

Table 2. Scores on questionnaire (number of people who recognized each emotion)

	Anger		Happiness		Sadness		Surprise		Disgust		Fear		No class	
Anger (S)	**85**	**(19)**	0		0		0		4	(1)	0			(0)
Anger (W)	**71**	**(16)**	0		0		0		16	(4)	0			(0)
Happiness (S)	0		**53**	**(16)**	7	(3)	0		0		1	(1)		(0)
Happiness (W)	0		**28**	**(10)**	2	(1)	0		20	(7)	2	(1)		(1)
Sadness (S)	0		4	(1)	**69**	**(16)**	0		0		14	(3)		(0)
Sadness (W)	0		3	(1)	**45**	**(16)**	0		4	(1)	6	(2)		(0)
Surprise (S)	1	(1)	4	(2)	0		**28**	**(9)**	3	(1)	1	(1)		(6)
Surprise (W)	0		3	(2)	0		**20**	**(9)**	3	(2)	15	(5)		(2)

No difference was seen between the number of participants who recognized as sadness from the weak sadness region (Sadness (W)) and the strong one (Sadness (S)), but their scores are different. This shows that the face from Sadness (S) expresses sadness more strongly.

Few people recognized surprise, and many of them confused it with other emotions. The scores are different between faces from the strong and weak regions.

Experiment 2

If different impressions of emotions are caused by changing the speed of facial changes, we should be able to change the degree of emotions. We created facial expressions by changing the time step, Δt, in the four emotion regions but using the same lines. The speeds of facial changes are listed in Table 3. In the questionnaire, we showed two facial expressions that changed fast and slow to 15 participants. The participants chose the one that expressed the corresponding emotion more strongly. We told them the emotions that cor-

Table 3. Speed condition

Condition	Δt [ms]	d
Fast	100	0.05
Slow	200	0.05

responded to each facial expression in advance. Four examples of the expressions used in the questionnaire are shown in Figure 11.

The results of the questionnaire are listed in Table 4. The number of people who recognized each emotion when it changed quickly and slowly is given for each facial expression.

For the angry and surprised faces, fast changes were evaluated as expressing the emotion more strongly than slow changes. For happiness, there is no clear difference with Happiness A, but with Happiness B and Happiness C, the faces that changed quickly, were evaluated as expressing the emotion more strongly. For anger, happiness, and surprise, when participants think Ifbot is in a state of high emotion, that is, the speed of ex-

Figure 11. Facial data for questionnaire

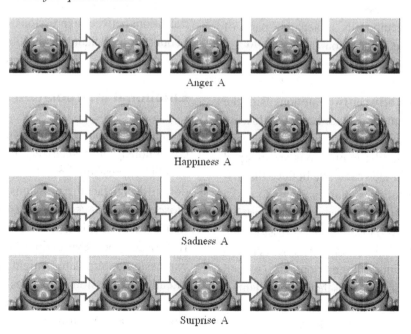

pressions is faster, the strength of the emotion increases.

On the other hand, for sadness, faces that changed slowly were evaluated as expressing the emotion more strongly. When Ifbot expresses sadness, a slow change makes a strong impression.

These results indicate that Ifbot can change the degree of emotions by changing the speed of facial expressions.

5. EMOTION TRANSITION

We did not discuss the transition between expressions of two different emotions in the previous section. In this section, we consider the psychological effects on a person of the change from expression of one emotion to expression of another using the emotion space.

Here, we are going to talk about three methods for the transition between expressions of two different emotions. In the conventional method of changing facial expressions from that conveying one emotion to that conveying another, the robot's motor control values are changed linearly from the start face to the end face (first method). This method may not express natural emotions because it only changes temporally in separate parts of the face, and the impression created between mutually related parts is disregarded. To solve this problem, we suggest a method of changing facial expressions between two emotions using the emotion space. Emotion space has the following features. (1) A facial expression similar to one used as training. (2) Similar expressions are mapped near each other in the space. We believe that using these characteristics enables robots to make facial expressions that do not cause uncomfortable feelings in humans. However, if expressions are generated only by moving in straight lines between two coordinate points in the emotion space (second method), expression changes that disregard intervening emotion space may occur. We especially propose using the route in which the amount of

Table 4. Results of questionnaire in experiment 2

Facial data	Fast condition	Slow condition
Anger A	12	3
Anger B	11	4
Anger C	11	4
Happiness A	8	7
Happiness B	12	3
Happiness C	13	2
Sadness A	4	11
Sadness B	4	11
Sadness C	2	13
Surprise A	11	4
Surprise B	11	4
Surprise C	12	3

change in facial-expression control values in the emotion space is minimized (third method). This route differs from an expression transition executed by linearly changing expression control values and takes into account an emotional change by implication. We believe that this will enable the robot to make facial expressions a person can recognize, which will enhance the sense of compatibility with the robot. We conducted an experiment using the three methods to generate transitions between expressions. The effectiveness of our proposed facial-expression change method is evaluated based on paired comparisons methods.

Emotional Interpolation Method (*EI*)

To enable the robot to change its facial expressions continuously, it is necessary to interpolate two or more expressions smoothly. In general, this is done to design facial expressions and to interpolate those expressions using a linear or nonlinear function. However, this method is time-consuming. If two designed expressions differ greatly, the expression interpolated might differ from the intended expression of the designer. Therefore, our facial-expression change method, *EI*, uses emotion space. We use the following procedure.

First, we input a start face and an end face to the five-layer neural network; we find coordinate points $(x_s, y_s)^T$ and $(x_e, y_e)^T$ in the emotion space from the third layer. Then, we prepare a square with two points that make a diagonal in the emotion space. We divide each side equally in N and the square into a lattice shape (Refer to Figure 12).

The facial expressions outputted from these lattice points are assumed to express emotions. Calculating the amount of change in the facial-expression control parameters from the lattice point (path cost) obtains the path of fewest facial expression changes with the adjacent lattice points. Note that we also use lattice points on opposing corners as adjacent lattice points. The pass search uses dynamic programming.

Pass cost $C(i,j)$ between adjacent lattice points $(x_i, y_i)^T$ and $(x_j, y_j)^T$ is given by

$$C(i, j) = \alpha(\beta \mid \mathbf{M}_i - \mathbf{M}_j \mid + (1 - \beta) \mid \mathbf{L}_i - \mathbf{L}_j \mid),$$

$$\alpha = \begin{cases} \sqrt{2} & (diagonal\ path) \\ 1 & (otherwise) \end{cases},$$

where α is the adjustment constant of the diagonal route, $\mathbf{M}$ is the motor's control parameters, $\mathbf{L}$ is the LED's control parameters, and β is a weighting parameter of the control value of the motors and LEDs. The path search is based on this path cost, and the robot makes the facial expression using the path of lowest cost: $r(k), k=0,\ldots,K$ (K is length of path). That is, coordinate points $(x(t), y(t))^T$ on the emotion space at time t can be given by

$$\begin{pmatrix} x(t) \\ y(t) \end{pmatrix} = \begin{pmatrix} x_{r([Kt/T])} \\ y_{r([Kt/T])} \end{pmatrix},$$

where T is the time that the facial expression changes. The [] function is the floor function as follows:

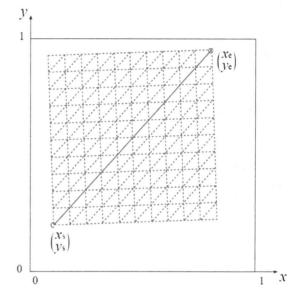

Figure 12. Emotion space search table

$$[x] = \max\{n \in -, n < x\},$$

where $\mathbf{Z}$ is the set of the whole numbers.

Evaluation

To test the effectiveness of our facial expression change method *EI*, we used a paired comparisons method. We now explain the following two other methods for comparing our method. Then, we evaluate the three methods mentioned at the beginning of this section.

Comparative Approach

Linear Interpolation Method (*LI*)

The linear interpolation method (*LI*) interpolates facial expressions by changing the linear control parameter of motors and LEDs. In *LI*, when $\mathbf{s}_s$ is the start facial expression control parameter and $\mathbf{s}_e$ is the end facial expression control parameter, facial expression control parameter $\mathbf{s}(t)$ at time t is given by

$$s(t) = \mathbf{s}_s + \frac{\mathbf{s}_e - \mathbf{s}_s}{T} t,$$

where T is the time that the facial expression changes.

Emotion Space Linear Interpolation Method (*ELI*)

Emotion space linear interpolation method (*ELI*) is a method using coordinate points on a straight line between two points in emotion space. When the coordinate points in emotion space of the start and end faces are (x_s, y_s) and (x_e, y_e), respectively, coordinate points $(x(t), y(t))^T$ in the emotion space at time t are given by

$$\begin{pmatrix} x(t) \\ y(t) \end{pmatrix} = \begin{pmatrix} x_s + \dfrac{x_e - x_s}{T} t \\ y_s + \dfrac{y_e - y_s}{T} t \end{pmatrix}.$$

Expression control parameter $\mathbf{s}(t)$ at time t is generated by the obtained $(x(t), y(t))^T$, and the facial expression is controlled.

Evaluation Experiment

We compared these expression change generating methods *EI*, *LI*, and *ELI*, and we evaluated the effectiveness of using *EI*. Figure 13 shows Ifbot's four emotions: anger, surprise, sadness, and happiness. There are 12 combinations of start and end faces for the four expressions. We generated expression changes using the three methods with each combination. Figures 14 – 16 show examples of facial expressions using each method. We used a questionnaire for the paired comparisons and presented the generated facial expressions to participants. Table 5 lists the content of the questionnaire. Participants compared two presented facial expressions (A and B) and answered whether they were "human-like expres-

Figure 13. Faces used as start and end

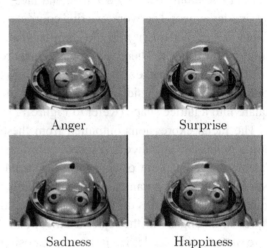

| Anger | Surprise |
| Sadness | Happiness |

sions", "interesting expressions", and "complex emotions". Answers were on a five-point scale from "A, a little A, intermediate, a little B, and B" and were assigned values from -2 to 2 (a five-point scale). If the evaluation of "human-like expression" was high, we took this to mean the robot had changed its expression without causing uncomfortable feelings. If the expression was ranked highly for "interesting expression", we took this to mean the robot could express an entertaining facial expression. Because Ifbot is meant as a domestic partner robot, we hoped that it would score well for this item. If participants ranked "complex emotions" highly, we took it to mean that the robot is expressing different facial expressions with every passing second, though this item is similar to "interesting expression". Even if the expression is uninteresting, a high

Table 5. Questionnaire

Questions	A	A little A	Intermediate	A little B	B
Human-like	2	1	0	-1	-2
Interest-ing	2	1	0	-1	-2
Complex	2	1	0	-1	-2

Figure 14. Facial expressions using LI

Figure 15. Facial expressions using ELI

Figure 16. Facial expressions using **EI**

Figure 17. Human-like. Larger numerical values indicate higher evaluations of Human-like

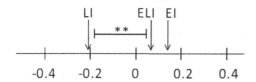

Figure 18. Interesting. Larger numerical values indicate higher evaluations of Interesting

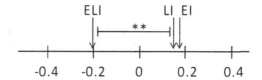

score indicates that the robot has expressed a complex emotion. When an uninteresting and complex expression is expressed, we believe that the entertainment value is low. Therefore, it is inappropriate for Ifbot.

Using the Scheffe's paired comparison, Figures 17, 18 and 19 show the results of "human-like expressions", "interesting expressions", and "complex emotions" respectively. In these figure, larger numerical values indicate higher evaluations. The mark "**" shows when there is a significant difference below significance level 1% in these figures.

First, we explain the results of the comparison of *ELI* and *LI*. Robots using the *ELI* method changed expression in a more human-like way

(p<0.001) than those using *LI*. Also, *ELI* scored low on the interesting (p<0.001) and complicated expression items (p<0.001). To us, Figure 14(c) shows a picture that seems to express a little anger while crying. In the *LI* method, the control information on the emotional expression between each part of the face is not synchronized. Therefore, two mixed emotions or expressions excluding two emotions were often observed. We believe that such expressions influence the scoring of complexity and interest. On the other hand, the *ELI* method generates intermediate expressions between sadness and anger, as shown in Figure 15(b). We believe that, by using emotion space, robots using *ELI* can make human-like expressions. This is born out by the lack of participant

Figure 19. Complex. Larger numerical values indicate higher evaluations of Complex

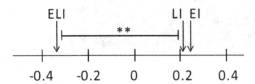

Figure 20. Route example of **EI**

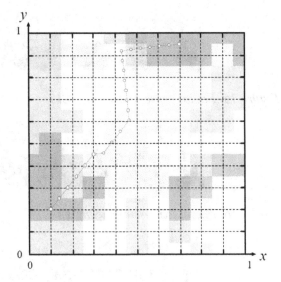

reports of a sense of incompatibility when the robot changed emotions.

Now we turn to the comparison of results for the *EI* and *LI* methods. There is a significant difference in *EI* on human-like expression ($p<0.01$). There is, however, no significant difference between these two methods for the interest and complexity items. For the human-like expression item, *EI* uses the emotion space as well as *ELI*. Therefore, *EI* scored highly because it generates an intermediate (neutral emotion) expression (Refer to Figure 16(c)). The interest and complexity items of *LI* did not decrease more than *ELI*. We explain this as follows.

EI searches for the emotion space and linearly changes the facial expression control parameter as much as possible in the space. The face using *EI* can express the same emotion as the start facial expression longer than with *ELI* because the minimal change of expressions includes successive emotions. Figure 20 shows an example. The panel on the upper-right is a start face (sadness). However, with linear movement using *ELI*, it changes to the emotion regions of happiness soon after the experiment is initiated. In contrast, when *EI* is used, the facial expression of sadness is continuously expressed, as the route in this figure shows. However, a path outside of the emotion regions is often selected, and a facial expression with little relation between the start and end emotions is expressed. It takes less time for a robot using *EI* to make these facial expressions than for one using *ELI* because an emotion is expressed for a long time. We believe that expressing an intermediate facial expression for a short time is an important factor in the evalua-

tion of the interest and complexity items. In this regard, these expressions are based on the teaching data of the auto-associative neural network, and the person might not sense incompatibility from the expression.

Finally we turn to our comparison of results for *EI* and *ELI*. This comparison follows the pattern of the results for *ELI* vs. *LI*, and *EI* vs. *LI*. There is no significant difference between these two methods for the human-like expression item. Robots using *EI* can make expressions that are interesting ($p<0.001$) and complicated ($p<0.001$). Therefore, *EI* (our proposed method) is a method that adds the same degree of human-like facial expression as *ELI* and expresses interest and complexity of *LI*. We believe that *EI* is effective as a facial expression control method of Ifbot because it enables Ifbot to make an entertaining and human-like facial expression.

6. FACIAL EXPRESSIONS OF PERSONALITY

Facial expressions output the following three expressions (Hara & Kobayashi, 2004).

Table 6. Relationship between big five and facial expressions/emotion/decision making

Factors	Facial expressions	Emotion	Decision making
Emotional Stability	Controlled expression	Flat	---
Extraversion	Show emotion	Lots of happiness and surprise	Based on interests in outside
Agreeableness	---	Appropriate response	Aspiring to abnegation and collaboration
Conscientiousness	---	---	Based on ability to concentrate and ambition
Openness	---	---	Based on nous and knowledge

1. His/her personality or character
2. His/her mind and mental (psychological) state.
3. His/her physiological state.

In the above chapters, we described affective facial expressions of Ifbot using the auto-associative neural network. These come under (2) and (3) in the list above. In next stage of robotics, we think that the expressions of information (1) will be important. Personality or character mean particular combination of qualities that makes someone a particular type of person, and they have largely affect communication. In the other words, to build up trustful relations between robots and humans, robots need personality for effective communication is important. In this chapter, we describe how to express the personality of Ifbot using its facial expressions.

Personality by Facial Expressions of Ifbot

Big Five Personality Traits

The "Big five" personality traits are five broad factors or dimensions of personality developed through lexical analysis (Goldberg, 1993; Thurstone, 1934). The five factors are Neuroticism, Extraversion, Agreeableness, Conscientiousness and Openness, and the Neuroticism factor is sometimes referred to as Emotional Stability. We believe that the relationship between the big five personality traits and facial expressions/emotion/decision making, as listed in Table 6. In this research, we assume that the Emotional Stability and Extraversion factors can be expressed by facial expressions. We attempted to express them using Ifbot's face.

Definition of Emotional Stability

When someone is emotionally stable, there are only small emotional ups and downs, and facial expression remains stable. Emotional stability is considered a trend in emotional change, and it does not relate to facial change. However, if someone is afraid or anxious, his/her face expresses emotions such as fright and confusion, that is, these situations make him/her emotionally unstable. Therefore, we define rapidly changing facial expressions as exhibiting low emotional stability.

Expressing Emotional Stability

Emotion space maps similar facial expressions near each other in the space. Using this characteristic, facial expressions related to emotional stability can be created using coordinate points around them obtained using the method proposed in Sections 4 and 5. This is done by drawing circles around a trajectory. Figure 21 shows this creating

Figure 21. Creating method of personality

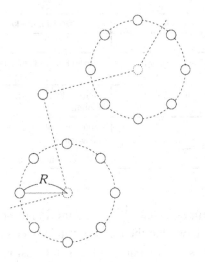

method. The circle-creating parameters are the frequency F of circle occurrence, the number D of facial expressions on the circumference of the circles, and the radius R of the circles. We call these parameters "personality parameters".

Figure 22 (a) shows the trajectory obtained using the method proposed in Sections 4 and 5.

Figure 22 (b) shows the trajectory with personality parameter $F = 2$, $D = 8$, $R = 0.025$.

Subjective Evaluation

We evaluate whether the personality of Ifbot can be changed using personality parameters or not. In this experiment, we created facial expressions adding the personality parameters to facial expressions in Figure 23. We prepared nine patterns in combinations of F, D, R, and time T of face change, and created nine facial changes according to the following procedure.

1. Create angry facial expressions for 1500 ms using the method proposed in Section 4.
2. Create facial changes for T ms using the method proposed in Section 5.
3. Create sad facial expressions for 1500 ms using the method proposed in Section 4.
4. Synthesize trajectories of (1) to (3), and create a facial change by adding personality parameters listed in Table 7.

Figure 22. Trajectory without/with personality parameter in emotion space

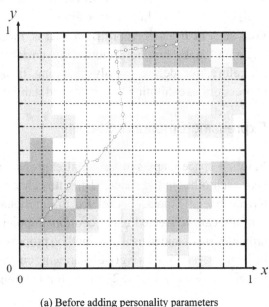

(a) Before adding personality parameters

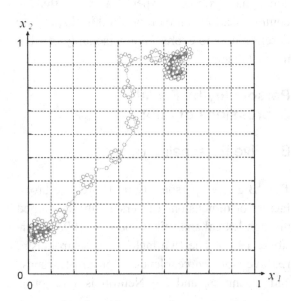

(b) After adding personality parameters

Figure 23. Face change used in questionnaire in Section 6

Table 8 lists the content of the questionnaire. Answers were on a five-point scale. We surveyed 15 people aged 19 to 27.

Figure 24 shows the results of the questionnaire.

First, we focused on the emotional stability score. When personality parameter R increases, the score decreases, except facial change m1. This suggests that personality parameter R decreases emotional stability. The personality parameter was not added to facial change m1, so the m1 looks like the fastest one in all facial changes. We consider that the m1 was evaluated by this fast facial change between two emotions in which emotional stability decreases. This result suggests that if facial change is too fast, facial changes using personality parameter cannot be not properly evaluated.

Next, we investigated extraversion. There is no relation between personality parameter R and extraversion, but the score decreases related to parameter T. We consider that we have the impression of extraversion if facial change is faster. Moreover, the average of score of all facial changes was 0 or more. Participants said that facial changes using anger and sad gives the impression of introversion. We need to investigate facial changes using other emotions for future work.

The human-like expression item was not related to personality parameters. Regarding interesting and mixed scores, if $T = 1500$ and 2000, they increase with parameter R. We assume that entertainment robots should be interesting and have emotional stability. In this experiment, we could not find any parameters that increase emotional stability and interest. Therefore, we have to investigate the parameter satisfying this condition in future work.

Table 7. Personality parameters used in questionnaire

	Personality parameters			
Face number	F	D	R	T [ms]
m1	0	-	-	1000
m2	2	8	0.025	1000
m3	2	8	0.05	1000
m4	0	-	-	1500
m5	2	8	0.025	1500
m6	2	8	0.05	1500
m7	0	-	-	2000
m8	2	8	0.025	2000
m9	2	8	0.05	2000

Table 8. Questionnaire

A	A	A little A	Intermediate	A little B	B	B
Emotional stability	2	1	0	-1	-2	Emotional un-stability
extraversion	2	1	0	-1	-2	Introversion
Human-like	2	1	0	-1	-2	Machine-like
Interesting	2	1	0	-1	-2	Boring
Complex	2	1	0	-1	-2	Simple

Figure 24. Results of questionnaire

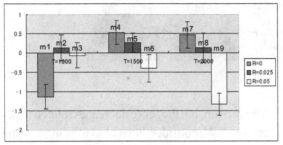

(a) Emotional Stability

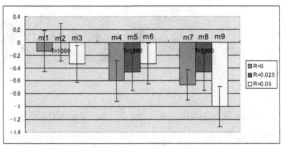

(b) Extraversion

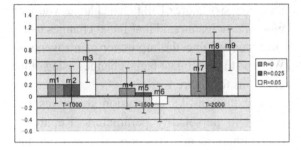

(c) Human-like

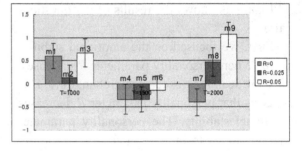

(d) Interesting

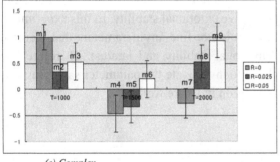

(e) Complex

7. CONCLUSION

In Section 4, we extracted the characteristics of Ifbot's facial expressions by mapping them to its emotion space using an auto-associative neural network. Then, we evaluated the emotion space using people's opinions and created its emotion regions. We developed a method of generating affective facial expressions using these emotion regions. We experimentally showed that people's impressions change depending on the strength of the emotion regions. We also showed that the speed of expression changes change the strength of the

perceived emotion. We created facial expressions corresponding to Ifbot's internal emotions taking the strength of the emotions expressed into account using our method of generating faces from the emotion regions. An emotion continuing for a long time can be expressed, and facial expressions can be changed smoothly as emotions change. Generality is not guaranteed because we evaluated only Ifbot's expressions. However, we hope this research can help the development of emotional expression for future robots.

In Section 5, we proposed a facial-expression method that uses a path that minimizes the amount of change in facial-expression control values in an emotion space. This method is based on an auto-associative neural network. A minimum-change route in the emotion space enables robots to convey human-like expressions because the method differs from expression transitions by linear change in the facial-expression control parameters, and an expression change can be implicitly considered. We experimentally showed that our proposed method has two features, entertainment, which is for linearly changing the expression-control parameter and human, which is linearly moving emotion space.

In Section 6, we proposed a method for expressing personality though the face. The results of experiment suggest that facial changes using personality parameter express emotional stability. We evaluated face changes involving the emotions of anger and sadness. We need to investigate face changes using other emotions. Moreover, we will investigate effects of changing personality parameters F and D and using nonlinearly controlled face changes.

ACKNOWLEDGMENT

Ifbot was produced by an industry-university joint research project of the Business Design Laboratory Co., Ltd., Brother Industries, Ltd., A. G. I. Inc., ROBOS Co., and the Nagoya Institute of Technology. We are grateful for their input. This work was supported in part by Grant-in-Aid for Young Scientists (A) #20680014 of the Ministry of Education, Culture, Sports, Science and Technology.

REFERENCES

BDL. (2009). *Business Design Laboratory*. Retrieved from http://www.business-design.co.jp/en/

Bishop, C. M. (1995). *Neural Networks for Pattern Recognition*. Oxford, UK: Oxford University Press.

Breazeal, C., & Scassellati, B. (1999). A Context-dependent Attention System for a Social Robot. *In Proceedings of the Sixteenth International Joint Conference on Artificial Intelligence*, (pp.1146–1151).

Cho, J. (2009). Bayesian Method for Detecting Emotion from Voice for Kansei Robots. *Kansei Engineering International*, *8*(1), 15–22.

Ekman, P. (1975). *Unmasking the Face*. Upper Saddle River, NJ: Prentice-Hall.

Fujita, M., et al. (2000). *Robot Entertainment, in Robots for Kids: New Technologies for Learning*. In Druin, A. & Hendler, J.(Eds.),(pp.37-70).San Francisco: Morgan Kaufmann Publisher, 37–70.

Goldberg, L. R. (1993). The Structure of Phenotypic Personality Traits. *The American Psychologist*, *48*, 26–34. doi:10.1037/0003-066X.48.1.26

Gotoh, M., et al. (2005). Face Generator for Sensibility Robot based on Emotional Regions. *6th International Symposium on Robotics*, in CD-ROM.

Hara, F. & Kobayashi, H. (2004). *An artificial emotion,,* Kyoritsu suppan. (in Japanese)

Kanda, S. (2003). *Internet-based Robot: Mobile Agent Robot of Next-generation* (MARON-1) [in Japanese]. *Fujitsu*, *54*(4), 285–292.

Kanoh, M. (2005). Emotive Facial Expressions of Sensitivity Communication Robot "Ifbot". *Kansei Engineering International*, *5*(3), 35–42.

Kobayashi, H. (1994). Study on Face Robot for Active Human Interface. [in Japanese]. *Journal of the Robotics Society of Japan*, *12*(1), 155–163.

Kobayashi, H., & Hara, F. (1996). Real Time Dynamic Control of 6 Basic Facial Expressions on Face Robot. [in Japanese]. *Journal of the Robotics Society of Japan*, *14*(5), 677–685.

Kuroki, Y., et al. (2002). A Small Biped Walking Entertainment Robot SDR-4X with a Highly Integrated Motion Control. *The 20ᵗʰ Conf. of Robotics Society of Japan*, (p.1C34). (in Japanese).

Mac Dorman, K. F. & Ishiguro, H.(2004). *The Study of Interaction through the Development of Androids*, IPSJ SIG Technical Report CVIM, 2004 (113), 69-75.

Matsui, Y., et al. (2007). Interaction Effects in Facial Expressions of Emotional Space-using Kansei Robot "Ifbot". *International Conference on Kansei Engineering and Emotion Research 2007*, in CD-ROM.

Murase, Y., et al. (2001). Design of a Compact Humanoid Robot as a Platform. *The 19ᵗʰ Conf. of Robotics Society of Japan*, (pp.789–790). (in Japanese).

Sakaguchi, T. et al.(1997). Construction and Evaluation of 3-D Emotion Space Based on Facial Image Analysis. *IEICE Transactions; J80-A* (8), 1279–1284. (in Japanese).

Shibata, H. (2007). Making Character Using Facial Expressions of Communication Robot. *Forum on Information Technology, 6*, 323–326.

Shinkai, S., & Aizawa, Y. (2006). The Lempel-Ziv Complexity of Non-Stationary Chaos in Infinite Ergodic Cases (Condensed Matter and Statistical Physics). *Progress of Theoretical Physics, 116*(3), 503–515. doi:10.1143/PTP.116.503

Thurstone, L. L. (1934). The vectors of the mind. *Psychological Review, 41*, 1–32. doi:10.1037/h0075959

Ueki, N. et al.(1994). Expression Analysis/Synthesis System Based on Emotional Space Constructed by Multi-Layered Neural Network. *IEICE Transactions; J77-DII* (3), 573–582. (in Japanese).

Wada, K., et al. (2004). *Effects of Three Months Robot Assisted Activity to Depression of Elderly People Who Stay at a Health Service Facility for the Aged*. SICE Annual Conference, 2709-2714.

ENDNOTE

[1]   All of the facial sequences used in this questionnaire are incorporated into the commercial Ifbot. Each sequence is created to project an impression.

Chapter 13
Natural Effect of Spatial and Temporal Color Sequence on Human Color Impression

Naotoshi Sugano
Tamagawa University, Japan

ABSTRACT

The way in which a signal sequence of several colors (temporal information), as well as how a linear, toroidal, or circular sequences of several colors (spatial information) affect human color impression is examined. To investigate spatial or temporal effects of color sequences, a hexagonal projection of an RGB color space is considered. The projected route area indicates the magnitude of naturalness (as in rainbows) of color sequences, with the minimum sequence being similar to the order of rainbow colors. Using the projected route area with route complexity, a simple fuzzy model of human color impression is proposed. Clarifying the relationship between route complexity and the impressions of subjects for a projected route area revealed that the majority (>26%) of subjects of nearly all ages have natural impressions when the minimum route area is large. Thus, this model describes the spatial or temporal nature of natural (or unnatural) multicolored sequences.

1. INTRODUCTION

The degrees of pairs of terms applied to color sequences, such as natural-unnatural, have been investigated previously. Two terms, natural and complex (or unnatural), were described by Ohi & Kawasaki (1996), where after several terms were commonly used to describe the characteristics and associative meanings of colors (Sivik, 1997). In

previous studies by this author, the various effects of temporal color sequences of several colors on human color impression were examined and a hexagonal color model was constructed (Sugano, 2001; Sugano & Matsushita, 2002). To analyze these effects in the current study, human subjects were tested to determine whether a several-color cyclic sequence has a minimum distance in the red, green, blue (RGB) color space."

The various effects of six-colored spatial color sequences on human color impression and

DOI: 10.4018/978-1-61692-797-4.ch013

Figure 1. Relationship between temporal and spatial information

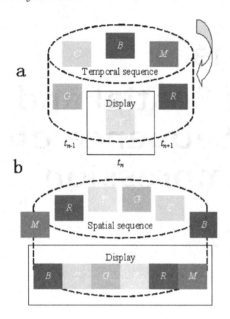

its model (hereafter referred to as the hexagonal color model) have recently been examined using the following four groups of six colors (Sugano et al., 2004; Sugano et al., 2007a):

Type A: six fundamental colors
Type B: five fundamental colors and orange
Type C: six intermediate colors
Type D: six magenta-blue relevant colors

These studies showed that the largest group of subjects (approximately 20%-50%) preferred the minimum sequence when selecting a natural color sequence. However, since only the minimum sequences of the four groups (Type A-D) of six colors were tested (Sugano et al., 2006), a larger projected minimum route area was preferred. That is, the relationship between the route area and the response of subjects was proportional.

More recently, we introduced experiments of human color impression using a tournament-like task (composed of a choice between two alterna-

tives) to compare human color impression and a fuzzy model of human color impression using the projected route area or envelope route with route complexity (Sugano et al., 2009). Since complexity is defined as the ratio of the square of the envelope route distance to the route area, a simple fuzzy model of human color impression is proposed. This model provides spatial (or temporal) color sequences for emotional control, color coordination and similar applications.

2. SPATIAL AND TEMPORAL INFORMATION

Previous studies (Sugano & Nasu, 2000; Sugano, 2001) suggested designs for rows of suitable colors as spatial information and color signal sequences as temporal information for the control of feeling and emotion based on single color effects (Ohmi, 1999). Figures 1(a) and (b) display only one color as temporal information and the simultaneous display of a linear sequence of several colors, respectively, and present these as spatial representations of a several-city Traveling Salesman Problem (TSP) (see Appendix). The letters in Figure 1 denote the following: B; blue, C; cyan, G; green, Y; yellow, R; red, M; magenta, and the time interval is given as $T = t_n - t_{n-1}$.

The system used in this study to represent the three primary colors (red, green, and blue (RGB)) is presented in a cubic color space. As shown in Figure 2, blue, cyan, green, yellow, red, magenta, white, and black are abbreviated as B, C, G, Y, R, M, W, and S, respectively. Several color coordinates—(r_1, g_1, b_1), (r_2, g_2, b_2), ..., (r_n, g_n, b_n)—are selected, where r_n, g_n, and b_n are the red, green, and blue components, respectively, of the nth color. In the cubic color space, RGB values range from 0 to 255, and the minimum distance between coordinates can be computed as shown in Figure 2.

Figure 2. Minimum route projected from six fundamental colors within the RGB color space

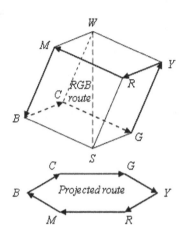

Experimental Design

Four experiments were conducted to test the question, "which sequence is natural?" Figure 3 illustrates the procedures used for the temporal and spatial experiments.

Experiment 1

Trace 1 depicts two routes of one type of temporal sequences (Figure 3 (1)). One route, consisting of seven colors in the right hexagonal diagram, is a projection of a randomly selected sequence in the RGB color space (Figure 2, top). The route shown at left is the minimum route of a projection consisting of several colors (see Sugano (2001), Sugano & Matsushita (2002)).

Experiment 2

Trace 2 depicts four types of spatial sequences (Figure 3 (2)). The Type A route is composed of a projection of six fundamental colors (regular hexagon). Type B is composed of five fundamental colors and orange (irregular hexagon). Type C is composed of six intermediate colors (regular hexagon). Type D is composed of six magenta-blue

relevant colors (irregular hexagon). Only linear sequences (12 routes for A-D types) are used. Figure 4 shows Type A (see Sugano et al. (2007)).

Experiment 3

Trace 3 depicts only the minimum sequences (of 12 routes for A-D types) (Figure 3 (3)). Trace 3 has toroidal, circular and linear sequences where toroidal and circular sequences are the difference between the two. One of 12 routes for each type is used to present toroidal, circular, and linear sequences. The minimum sequences of the four types are compared (see Sugano et al. (2006)).

Experiment 4

Trace 4 shows one type of spatial sequence (Figure 3 (4)). Type A shows one route for the projection of six fundamental colors (regular hexagon), as shown in Figure 4. Toroidal sequences are compared for 12 routes, as shown in Figure 5*b* (see Sugano et al. (2009)).

3. TEMPORAL EXPERIMENTS

Temporal Color Sequences

Experiment 1

The system of the three primary colors (RGB) presented in a cubic color space was used in this study (Sugano, 2001). In this space, seven color coordinates—$(r_1, g_1, b_1), (r_2, g_2, b_2),…, (r_7, g_7, b_7)$—were randomly selected and non-minimum sequences as a seven-color cyclic sequence *(i)* were prepared. The minimum distance of coordinates could be computed using Hopfield networks (three-dimensional (3D) TSP). Minimum sequences having the same colors were prepared as another seven-color cyclic sequence *(ii)*. RGB values ranged from 0 to 255 and the sum of the RGB route distances was 1371.2 and 1164.3 for

Figure 3. Designs of temporal and spatial experiments

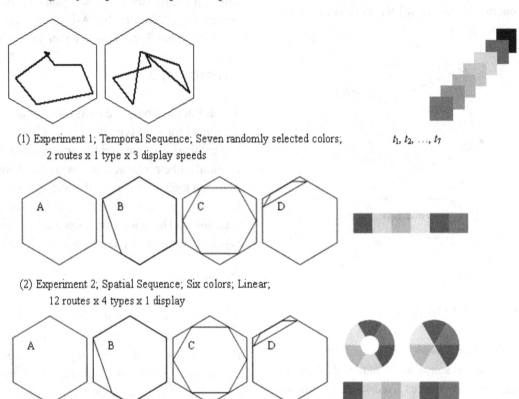

(1) Experiment 1; Temporal Sequence; Seven randomly selected colors;
 2 routes x 1 type x 3 display speeds

$t_1, t_2, ..., t_7$

(2) Experiment 2; Spatial Sequence; Six colors; Linear;
 12 routes x 4 types x 1 display

(3) Experiment 3; Spatial Sequence (*minimum* only); Six colors; Toroidal, Circular, Linear;
 1 route x 4 types x 3 displays

(4) Experiment 4; Spatial Sequence (See Figure 6*b*); Six colors; Toroidal;
 12 routes x 1 type x 1 display

one cycle of the *(i)* non-minimum sequence and *(ii)* minimum sequence, respectively.

The following coordinates describe the randomly selected non-minimum sequence: $(r_1, g_1, b_1) = (117, 76, 209)$, $(r_2, g_2, b_2) = (230, 143, 43)$, $(r_3, g_3, b_3) = (243, 38, 122)$, $(r_4 g_4, b_4) = (181, 202, 235)$, $(r_5, g_5, b_5) = (35, 23, 133)$, $(r_6, g_6, b_6) = (0, 243, 30)$, and $(r_7, g_7, b_7) = (46, 220, 179)$. This is

the computed minimum sequence: $(r_3, g_3, b_3) = (243, 38, 122)$, $(r_2, g_2, b_2) = (230, 143, 43)$, $(r_6, g_6, b_6) = (0, 243, 30)$, $(r_7, g_7, b_7) = (46, 220, 179)$, $(r_4 g_4, b_4) = (181, 202, 235)$, $(r_1, g_1, b_1) = (117, 76, 209)$, and $(r_5, g_5, b_5) = (35, 23, 133)$. The projected coordinates in Trace 1 (Figure 3 (right)) are $(x_1, y_1) = (-29, 92)$, $(x_2, y_2) = (-62, -117)$, $(x_3, y_3) = (-145, -15)$, $(x_4, y_4) = (15, 36)$, $(x_5, y_5) = (-8,$

Figure 4. Twelve typical routes, route areas (dotted areas), and three envelope routes (solid line) projected from six fundamental colors

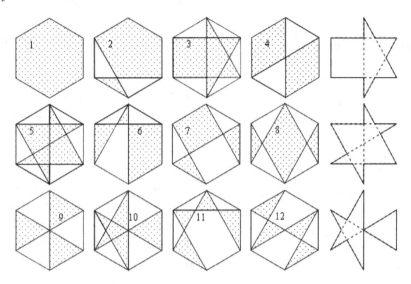

85), $(x_6, y_6) = (172, -75)$, $(x_7, y_7) = (123, 38)$. The origin is the center of the hexagon and (x, y) is the horizontal and vertical coordinate. The display of the sequence is shown in Figure 1a.

Methods

Experiment 1

A total of 73 undergraduate students (70 males and three females) volunteered for the experiments by Sugano & Nasu (2000) and Sugano (2001). The subjects were tested individually, with each seated subject being required to watch a continuous display. The clock intervals for the color signal sequences were 1/3 s, ½ s, and 1 s, or 3, 2, 1 colors/sec (c/s), respectively. One trial (sequence) consisted of the same seven colors displayed in the color coordinates mentioned in the previous section (Temporal Color Sequences Experiment 1) and these seven colors were repeated after approximately 30 s. For example, for a clock interval of 1 s, a seven-color cyclic sequence is $(r_1, g_1, b_1), ..., (r_7, g_7, b_7), (r_1, g_1, b_1), ..., (r_7, g_7, b_7), (r_1, g_1, b_1), ..., (r_7, g_7, b_7), (r_1, g_1, b_1), ..., (r_7, g_7, b_7), (r_1, g_1,$

$b_1), (r_2, g_2, b_2)$. The experiments were performed in an isolated area to direct visual cues ensure subjects' attention was focused on the display.

Experimental Results and Discussion

Experiment 1

Sugano and Matsushita (2001) showed two possible tours of 360 routes in 3D RGB color space. One circuitous route was randomly selected, while the other was selected based on the minimum distance using a Hopfield network (Sugano & Nasu, 2000; Sugano, 2001). The two resulting seven-city TSP tours were thus markedly different, and the complex and the simple routes were visually recognizable (see Figure 2 showing the six-city TSP tour). Then, to determine whether the color impression of these color signal sequences could be expressed using simple adjectives (or adverbs), in the first trials of Experiment 1, 31 subjects reported their impressions freely for the two sequences in which the clock interval of 1 s was used. That is, the subjects were required to

Figure 5. Linear and Toroidal Color Sequences in the Schematic GUI Used in the Questionnaire

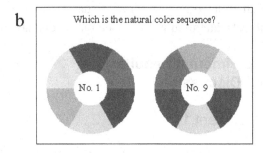

Classification of Human Color Impressions

Simple words describing the impressions expressed by the subjects were classified into Natural, Unnatural, Unknown, and Other impressions. The Natural group included the terms *agreeable, calm, fair, flowing, loose, natural, pleasant, quiet, regularly, relaxed, smooth*, etc., and the Unnatural group included the terms *busy, disagreeable, fidgety, flickeringly, glitter, intense, irregularly, noisy, pit-a-pat, severe, tight, tired, unpleasant*, etc.. The Unknown group included the terms *bad, good, nothing, unknown*, etc., and the Other classification included the terms *dark, deep, fast, light*, etc.

The terms *natural* and *complex* (or *unnatural*), based on the work of Ohi, & Kawasaki (1996), were used in previous studies (Sugano & Nasu, 2000; Sugano, 2001). Subject impressions of the Unknown and Other groups were considered independently of the terms *natural* and *unnatural*, and Other impressions were either color- or speed-related words in this study.

The non-minimum sequences did not evoke natural impressions alone. Unnatural impressions of non-minimum sequences were encountered four times more frequently than the same impressions of the minimum signal sequences. Unknown impressions of non-minimum sequences were more frequent than those of minimum sequences, which were few in number. Other impressions of non-minimum sequences occurred less frequently than those of minimum sequences. The non-minimum sequences only evoked unnatural impressions, while minimum sequences evoked natural impressions implying that the impressions produced by two individual sequences had the opposite effect.

Next, experiments were conducted to examine the references of pairs of terms applied to a color sequence, such as *natural-unnatural*.

The experimental results only showed differences between human color impressions for

select linguistic responses from the list presented in a questionnaire: *agreeable, bad, busy, calm, dark, deep, disagreeable, fair, fast, fidgety, flickeringly, flowing, glitter, good, intense, irregularly, light, loose, natural, noisy, nothing, pit-a-pat, pleasant, quiet, regularly, relaxed, severe, smooth, tight, tired, unknown,* and *unpleasant*. Thus, simple adjectives (or adverbs) were used to convey the impression of the color signal sequences. These impressions were then analyzed to characterize the differences between two sequences.

"natural-unnatural" for the two color signal sequences. The subjects were required to determine whether the natural impression for each color signal sequence was suitable. In the non-minimum sequences, natural impressions were fewer in number than unnatural impressions, except for the 3 c/s display condition. Among the minimum sequences, natural impressions were more frequent than unnatural impressions. Increasing the display frequency appeared to increase the percentage of natural impressions.

How Well Does the Word Natural Suit Color Sequences?

To address this question, the degree of naturalness (or unnaturalness) was defined in the present study. If a subject selected the word *natural*, then the degree of naturalness was positive (+1), whereas if a subject selected the word *unnatural*, then the degree of unnaturalness was negative (−1). The averages were calculated, and the results indicated that the proportion of subjects for which the word *natural* suited each color signal sequence. A positive result denoted the average degree of natural impression, and a negative result denoted the average degree of unnatural impression. The degree of unnaturalness for each non-minimum sequence satisfied the following relation (numbers denote the display conditions in c/s):

Non-minimum (1c/s) > *Non-minimum* (2c/s) > *Non-minimum* (3c/s)

The degree of naturalness for each minimum sequence satisfied the following relation (numbers denote the display conditions in c/s):

Minimum (3c/s) > *Minimum* (2c/s) > *Minimum* (1c/s)

Irrespective of the display condition, human color impression showed a degree of naturalness for minimum sequences and a degree of unnaturalness for non-minimum sequences. In this case, the total degree of the impression (i.e. naturalness or unnaturalness) was 1.02 for the minimum sequences and −0.58 for the non-minimum sequences.

The relationship between the route and distance obtained in the previous experiment was subsequently examined. The 59th route for the non-minimum sequence was randomly ordered and the difference in the distance between the minimum (1st) route (Figure 3, Trace 1 (left)) and the non-minimum (59th) route (Figure 3, Trace 1 (right)) was approximately one-quarter of the difference in the distance between the minimum and the maximum route; the minimum route was approximately 60% of the maximum route (Sugano & Nasu, 2000; Sugano, 2001).

Pairs of Close Components in the Minimum Sequence

The differences between the components of a non-minimum sequence and those of a minimum sequence in the RGB system were then examined, with a particular focus on the number of pairs of close components. The threshold for the closeness of each component was defined as approximately 10% of the maximum value (255), which meant that threshold is therefore 26.0 or less. At the non-minimum distance, only two such pairs existed: ($r_2 = 230$, $r_3 = 243$) and ($g_6 = 243$, $g_7 = 220$). At the minimum distance, seven pairs existed: ($r_3 = 243$, $r_2 = 230$), ($g_6 = 243$, $g_7 = 220$), ($g_7 = 220$, $g_4 = 202$), ($g_5 = 23$, $g_3 = 38$), ($b_2 = 43$, $b_6 = 30$), ($b_4 = 235$, $b_1 = 209$), and ($b_5 = 133$, $b_3 = 122$). In the minimum distance, such a pair did not exist for the 1st and 5th colors. The number of pairs of close components in the minimum sequence was thus clearly more than that in the non-minimum sequence, implying that the number of pairs of close components affected the total distance. Moreover, in the hue, lightness, and saturation (HLS) system, except in the case of the 5th color, all of the hue angles (*h*) were sorted in an order that was similar to that of the rainbow colors which are composed of the following wavelengths: violet (400-430 nm), indigo (440-460 nm), blue (470 nm), green (505 nm), yellow (575 nm), orange (590-620 nm), red (>630 nm), where orange is yellow red, indigo is dull blue, and violet is purple blue (Wooten & Miller, 1997).

Which Route is Most Similar to the Order of Rainbow Colors?

The most similar route was the 3rd route (one route without intersections). The difference between the 1st route minimized and the 3rd route was in the positions of the 1st and the 5th colors. By substituting the 1st color for the 5th color, and vice versa, the order of the seven hues was identical to the order of wavelengths. However, the sum of the distances of routes increased slightly (Sugano, 2001).

4. SPATIAL EXPERIMENTS

Spatial Color Sequences

It is possible to compute the minimum distance of coordinates in the RGB system. Twelve sequences (Figure 4) consisting of the same six fundamental colors (B, C, G, Y, R, and M) were presented in the three spatial experiments shown in Figure 3.

Experiment 2

Four types (Type A: six fundamental colors; Type B: five fundamental colors and orange; Type C: six intermediate colors; Type D: six magenta-blue relevant colors) were prepared as spatial color sequences with minimum distance (Sugano et al., 2004). The minimum cyclic route was B, C, G, Y, R, M, & B again in Type A. For example, the sum of the distances was 2,090 for the non-minimum route (B, C, R, M, G, Y, & B), which is not shown here, and 1,530 for the minimum route (B, C, G,

Y, R, M, & B), shown at the top in Figure 2. The distance of the minimum route was clearly less than that of the non-minimum route (see Appendix Table 1.) The display type of sequences was only linear, as shown in Trace 2 of Figure 3.

Experiment 3

Only the minimum sequence was employed for each type and the subjects compared the sequences. The three sequence display types were toroidal, linear, and circular. As shown in Figure 1b, a linear sequence of six colors was used in Experiment 2. The circular sequences clearly differed from the toroidal sequences with respect to impression, even when the six colors were presented in the same order. The subjects compared four sequences, denoted Types A through D, for the toroidal, linear, and circular display sequence types.

Experiment 4

Only one type (Type A: six fundamental colors) of the previous Experiments 2 and 3 was used and only the toroidal sequence display type was used.

Methods

Experiment 2

In each experiment, either 60 (Types A and B) or 121 (Types C and D) undergraduate students, graduate students, employees, and participants at a university festival volunteered to participate in this study. The subjects were asked to sit in a chair and watch a continuous display showing different sequences of six colors, e.g., $(r_1, g_1, b_1), ..., (r_6, g_6, b_6)$. The experiments were performed in an isolated area to direct visual cues ensure subjects' attention was focused on the display. The following types were used: Type A (six fundamental colors); Type B (five fundamental colors and orange); Type C

Table 1. Summary of characteristics of input sequences and responses

No.	a) Input and output				b) Pre-processed input			
	RGB route distance	Projected route distance	Projected route area	Number of subjects	Route complexity	Envelope route distance	Route area	
							Hexagonal ratio *r*	Area with unit length
1	1530	1247.6	112320	57	13.8	6.00	1	2.60
2	1741	1552.2	87360	19	27.6	7.46	7/9	2.02
3	2139	2064.3	74880	14	32.2	7.46	2/3	1.73
4	1903	1663.6	74880	28	37.0	8.00	2/3	1.73
5	2326	2272.3	62400	10	41.9	7.77	5/9	1.44
6	1928	1760.0	62400	–	49.7	8.46	5/9	1.44
7	1928	1760.0	56160	24	55.1	8.46	1/2	1.30
8	1953	1856.3	62400	–	55.4	8.93	5/9	1.44
9	2090	1871.4	56160	21	62.3	9.00	1/2	1.30
10	2301	2176.0	49920	13	68.7	8.89	4/9	1.15
11	1953	1856.3	37440	10	91.7	8.93	1/3	0.87
12	2115	1968.0	37440	19	102.9	9.46	1/3	0.87

There are no data for the number of subjects for sequences No. 6 or No. 8.

Route area calculated with unit length = hexagonal ratio *r* x regular hexagonal area Δ (=3√3/2).

(six intermediate colors); Type D (six magenta-blue relevant colors).

Subjects selected color sequences that they considered as having a natural impression using a graphical user interface (GUI), as shown in Figure 5*a* (only linear sequences were presented on the GUI). The buttons on the display were pushed in the desired order, as denoted by the numbers. The "@" symbol was used to indicate to subjects, which buttons they pressed. When each button was pushed, the order of each color was stored.

Experiment 3

In the experiments of the present study, 130 subjects volunteered. The subjects compared the four sequence types (A-D) consisting of six colors using a GUI. The projected route areas decreased from Type A to Type D and each subject selected one color sequence (toroidal, circular, and linear) that gave a natural impression.

Experiment 4

In this experiment, 215 subjects were asked to compare two (out of the twelve) typical sequences of six colors each Using the GUI questionnaire (Figure 4 (Type A)). Typical sequences are shown in Figure 5*b*. The subjects were asked to determine which color sequence gave the most natural impression.

Using a tournament-like task consisting of ten (numbered) routes, Sugano et al. (2009) presented subjects with two sequences of six fundamental colors. Two sequences (No. 6 and No. 8) were omitted to reduce the complexity of the task and numbers were randomly selected from ten routes. In nine trials, one suitable color sequence for which the subject reported a natural impression was selected from among the ten sequences.

Sixty routes were reduced to twelve routes, because these routes were based on a regular hexagon with six fundamental colors (see Figure 2 (bottom) and Figure 4, (No. 1)), which meant

Figure 6. Relationship between projected route distance (dotted line), projected route area (solid line), and order of route distance (from the 1st to 60th route). See Sugano et al. (2006)

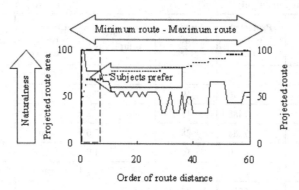

that there were several projected routes with the same shape. In Figure 4, hexagon No. 1 shows the projected minimum cyclic routes (Type A in Figure 3). The ordinate shows the direction from yellow (bottom) to blue (top). The abscissa shows the direction from magenta (left) to cyan (right), or from red (left) to green (right). Thus, projection No. 1 in Figure 4 is turned ninety degrees clockwise to that in Figure 2 (bottom).

Experimental Results and Discussion

This study was/These experiments were conducted to determine whether the color impression for spatial color sequences can be expressed by simple adjectives, such as "natural". One possible tour consisting of 60 routes in the 3D RGB color space was used. Using the questionnaire GUI, the selection of the sequence type (minimum sequence) that gave the subject the most natural impression was investigated.

Experiment 2

Figure 6 shows the relationship between the projected route distance, the projected route area, and the order of the projected route distance in Type A. The majority of subjects reported a "natural"

impression for the minimum sequence, or close to it, which was similar to the order of colors in rainbows. The number of subjects who selected the minimum sequence of each type as a natural color sequence was 21.7% for Type A, 41.7% for Type B, 43.8% for Type C, 49.6% for Type D. Although the route area was considered to indicate the magnitude of naturalness for color sequences in our model, the route area was not proportional to the responses of the subjects. For Type D, subjects with a high-level of human color impression recognized the most confusing task for similar colors.

Experiment 3

Four circuitous routes were selected based solely on minimum distance, and one color sequence – the sequence that conferred a natural impression upon the subject – was selected from the four minimum sequences.

The majority of the subjects (>66%) preferred Type A or Type B minimum sequences. The projected route distances were directly proportional to the projected route areas for the minimum sequence in this case (See Figure 6).

For example, the projected minimum route was formed by *B, C, G, Y, R, M,* & *B* and the projected minimum route area was enclosed by the hexagonal route in Type A (Figure 4). It is clear that the projected route distance and route areas decrease from Type A to Type D.

The relationship between the number of subjects, the projected route distance, and the projected route area were then examined. The number of subjects who responded positively toward the toroidal sequences, linear sequences, and circular sequences followed the same trend as indicated by an exponential approximation. It was clear that the majority of the subjects assigned the impression "natural" to the minimum sequence of a long projected route and a large projected route area. The responses for each type were A: 33.6%, B: 33.1%, C: 23.6%, and D: 9.7%.

In Type A-D, the relationship between the projected minimum route distance and minimum route area was proportional (data not shown), indicating a linear approximation, with characteristics that are dependent on each type.

Model Preparation

In Sugano et al. (2006), two typical projected routes and projected route areas of the human color impression model were investigated using six fundamental colors (using the hexagonal diagram in Figure 4). Each color had maximum saturation, and the projected neighboring colors were widely spread. For example, the non-minimum route (B, C, R, M, G, Y, & B again), shown in Figure 4 (No. 9), included the order of complementary colors. But this was not the result for the maximum route. The minimum route (B, C, G, Y, R, M, & B again) was presented in clockwise direction in the hexagon of Figure 4 (No. 1), where the dotted regions show the projected route areas. If each side of regular hexagon is 1 (unit length), then the ratio of the non-minimum projected route distance to the minimum projected route distance is equal to 1.5, and the ratio of the non-minimum route area to the minimum route area is 0.5 (see Appendix Table 1).

Although the distances were only calculated in the RGB color space, and not in the HLS color space, because hue represents the angle in degrees, the hue, lightness, and saturation of the HLS system are available for the analysis of color sensation. In a previous study (Sugano et al., 2006), hue and saturation, rather than lightness, were found to be important to characterize the difference of routes and almost no difference was observed between the projected routes in the RGB system and those in the HLS system.

Figure 6 shows that the relationship between the order of the projected route distances and route areas decreased and that fluctuations were observed in the six fundamental colors of Type A (Sugano et al., 2004; 2006). Interestingly, these fluctuations increased as the route distance increases.

The simulation for six colors shown in Figure 6 indicated that, as the route distance increases (dotted line), the route area decreases (solid line), and that numerous fluctuations occur. The result for six magenta-blue relevant colors (Type D) was not the same as that obtained for the six fundamental colors (Type A); however, the relationship between the route distances and area showed a similar trend. It was clarified that the characteristics of the color sequences that are considered by subjects was "natural" exist in the dashed rectangle of Figure 6.

This finding implies that the route area indicated the magnitude of naturalness (vertical arrow in Figure 6) for the color sequences in our model. In addition, the route area was found to be roughly proportionally increased to the responses of the subjects (Sugano & Matsushita, 2001a; Sugano & Matsushita, 2001b; Sugano & Matsushita, 2002). The present study clarified that the majority (>66%) of subjects selected the minimum sequence of Type A or Type B (rather than that of Type D), when considering the "naturalness" of a color sequence.

Figure 7. Route complexity (circle) and number of subjects (square) for projected route area in six fundamental color sequences

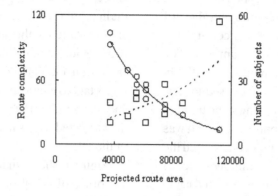

Experiment 4

The purpose of this experiment was to determine whether the subjects, using the GUI shown in Figure 5*b*, selected the minimum route (color sequence) as giving a natural impression.

In addition, the projected route distances and areas are shown in Figure 7. The minimum sequence (Figure 4, No. 1) was preferred by the greatest number of subjects (>26%) (see Appendix Table 1).

Introduction into Complexity

For the projected cross cut routes (broken lines in Figure 4 (right)), in particular, the route distances of sequences No. 3, No. 5, and No. 10, the envelopes were recalculated. If each side of regular hexagon is 1 (unit length), then the envelope route distance and route area (calculated with unit length) were computed. In addition, if the route area of regular hexagon was 100% (unit area) ($\Delta = 3\sqrt{3}/2 = 2.60$), then the route area and the hexagonal ratio were computed. The route area ranged from $\Delta/3$ to Δ (see Appendix).

Next, route complexity c was defined as follows (Minou & Nishida, 1999):

$$c = \frac{d^2}{a} \tag{1}$$

where d is the envelope route distance and a is the route area. For example, for a circle, $c = (2\pi r)^2 / \pi r^2 = 4\pi = 12.6$. For the minimum sequence of six fundamental colors (Figure 4, No. 1), $c = 13.9$ is equal to six intermediate colors (Type C) as reported previously (Sugano et al., 2004; Sugano et al., 2007). Because these color sequences are regular hexagons, the complexity was computed by the envelope and area. Consequently, if the areas were the same, then the order having the lowest complexity was selected as natural.

In Figure 4, the hexagonal diagram corresponds roughly to the hue circle (top view) indicated by both hue and saturation (except for lightness) in the HLS system. For example, the projected minimum route is formed by the order of colors (*B, C, G, Y, R, M,* & *B* again) and the projected minimum route area is the area (dotted region) enclosed by route *B, C, G, Y, R, M,* and *B* in Figure 4 (No. 1).

The projected minimum route could be indicated using a hexagon of route *B, C, G, Y, R, M,* and *B,* as shown at the bottom of Figure 2.

In this experiment, two specific projected routes and projected route areas were considered to construct a human color impression model using six fundamental colors (at the six corners of regular hexagon). Each color had maximum saturation, and the projected neighboring colors were widely spread. As an example, the non-minimum route (*B, C, R, M, G, Y,* & *B* again), No. 9 in Figure 4, has the order of complementary colors. However, this is not so for the maximum route. The minimum route (*B, C, G, Y, R, M,* & *B* again), No. 1 shown in Figure 4, runs in a hexagon in a clockwise direction (Figure 2 bottom). The dotted regions show the projected route areas. If each side of regular hexagon is 1 (unit length), then the ratio of the non-minimum projected route distance to the minimum projected route distance is 9.0/6.0 = 1.5, and the ratio of the non-minimum route area to the minimum route area is 1.3/2.6 = 0.5 (Sugano et al., 2004; Sugano et al., 2007a).

In addition, we also sought to determine whether the color impression for a spatial color sequence can be expressed using the simple adjective "natural". Twelve projections of 60 possible tours in 3D RGB color space are shown in Figure 4. In Figure 4, the order of the projected route areas is from No. 1 (maximum, as "wide") to No. 12 (minimum, as "narrow"). The order of route complexity is from No. 1 (minimum, as "simple") to No. 12 (maximum, as "complex"). The shape of No. 3 is complex, but the route complexity (*c* = 32.2) of No. 3 is lower than that (*c* = 37.0) of No. 4. However, the area of No. 4 is equal to that of No. 3. The envelopes (Figure 4 (right)) were recomputed, excluding the cross cut lines, in three routes (No. 3, No. 5, and No. 10). When the sizes of more than two areas were the same, the route complexities were compared.

The envelopes (Figure 4 (right)) of the No. 3, No. 5, and No. 10 routes in Figure 4 were used to calculate the route complexity. The envelope of the route, especially for the three cross cut routes of No. 3, No. 5, and No. 10, had to be recomputed in this study.

Figure 7 shows the relationship between route complexity and the number of subjects for the projected route areas in six fundamental color sequences. The trends indicate an exponential approximation (dotted curve), while the responses of subjects show a roughly exponential trend (solid curve) to route area in Figure 7. The trend is not a good fit to the dotted curve. In Figure 4, since in No. 5, No. 6, and No. 8, each route area is the same size, 62400 (5Δ/9), No. 6 and No. 8 were omitted from this experiment. The results for six colors indicated that as the route area increased, the route complexity (solid curve with circles) diminished and the number of subjects selecting this route increased (dotted curve with squares). The characteristics of the color sequences for which subjects reported a "natural" color impression were clarified as having a minimum complexity (simple) and maximum route area (wide).

The degree of naturalness β relates to route area *a* for similar hexagons of different size, and the degree of unnaturalness γ relates to route complexity *c* for similar hexagons of different size. These relationships are as follows:

$$\beta \approx \omega_1 a \tag{2}$$

$$\gamma \approx \omega_2 c \tag{3}$$

where ω_1 and ω_2 are unknown constants. Namely, the natural color sequence is evaluated by the projected route area rather than by the route complexity, because the route complexities of the sequences with six colors are exactly the same for different sizes of regular hexagons (similarity).

5. FUZZY MODEL

Figure 8 shows a simple fuzzy model of natural human color impression using the projected route area together with the complexity of six fundamental color sequences (lower trace). Although the medium-sized route area and a medium-sized envelope route distance do not correspond to each

Figure 8. Simple fuzzy model of human color impression (HCI) and determination of naturalness for six fundamental color sequences

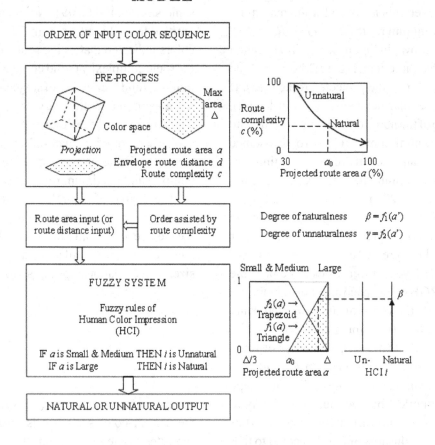

other, the maximum (wide) route area corresponds to the minimum (short) envelope route distance, and the minimum (narrow) route area corresponds to the maximum (long) envelope route distance (see Figure 9 for details).

Although the RGB route distance is the candidate input for a simple fuzzy system, the route complexity (Minou & Nishida, 1999) cannot be computed in 3D. In the pre-process (Figure 8, top trace), by using both the projected envelope route and projected route area, the route complexity can be estimated. However, using route complex-

ity alone is not possible because it is simply a ratio and does not change for different route area sizes (e.g., similarity) in the general model considered herein.

Although the values of route complexity used in the study do not actually exist, those of RGB route distance, projected route distance, envelope route distance, and route area do exist. Therefore, together with route complexity, fuzzy rules of human color impression (HCI) i can be constructed using the projected route area a in Figure 8 (bottom left). These fuzzy rules are as follows:

Figure 9. Relationship between each order of route complexity (twelve levels of twelve routes), RGB route distance (ten levels of twelve routes), envelope route distance (nine levels of twelve routes), and route area (seven levels of twelve routes) of six fundamental color sequences

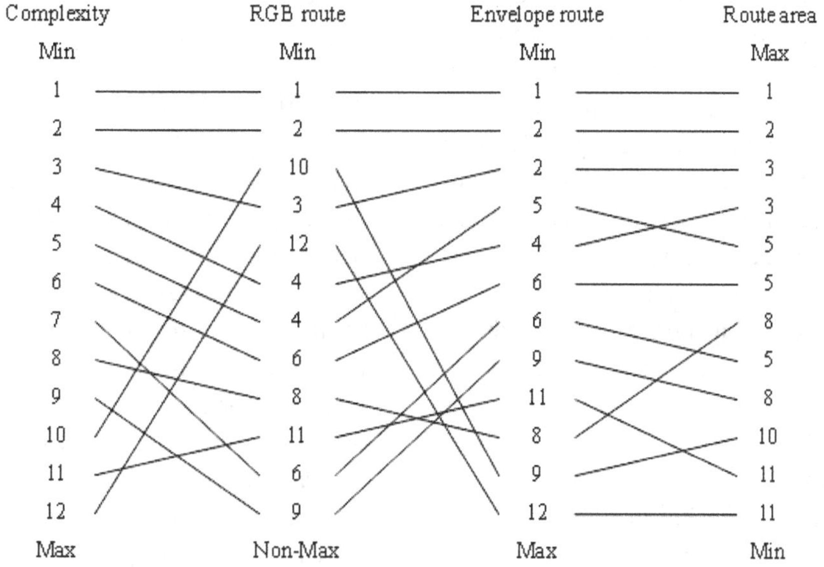

IF a is Small & Medium, THEN i is Unnatural

(4)

IF a is Large, THEN i is Natural (5)

Area a is the input, and HCI i is the output. "Small & Medium" and "Large" are fuzzy values for a, and are expressed by fuzzy sets of a trapezoid and triangle. When an actual input is given, the output is calculated by fuzzy inference. Now, let the input be $a = a'$. From Eq. (2), the triangular membership function f_1 to the route area a' gives the degree of naturalness:

$$\beta = f_1(a')$$

(6)

From Eq. (1) and Eq. (3), trapezoidal membership function f_2 to the route area a' gives the degree of unnaturalness:

$$\gamma = f_2(a')$$

(7)

$$\beta + \gamma = 1$$

(8)

$$f_1(a) = \begin{cases} b(a - a_0), & \Delta \geq a \geq a_0 \\ 0, & a_0 > a > 0 \end{cases}$$

(9)

$$f_2(a) = \begin{cases} -b(a - \Delta), & \Delta \geq a \geq a_0 \\ 1, & a_0 > a > 0 \end{cases}$$

(10)

where the constant $a_0 = 2\Delta/3$ ranges between $\Delta/3$ (minimum area) and Δ (maximum area) and the constant b shows the inclination in Figure 9 (bottom right).

6. DISCUSSION

Figure 9 shows a summary of the relationships presented in this study. The order of route area and envelope distance for six fundamental color sequences are sorted by complexity. A twelve-route complexity is computed, and the RGB route distance is composed of ten levels, where the maximum distance of the RGB route distance is ordered in the fifth trace and does not exist in lower traces. The envelope route distance has nine levels, and the route area has only seven levels, which are the same size in some cases. Excluding the RGB route, the upper traces (1-3), middle and lower traces (3-12) in Figure 9 can be separated. This corresponds to fuzzy sets of "Small & Medium" and "Large" with the membership functions f_1 and f_2 on the route area. Level 3 is a critical situation.

In previous models of six fundamental colors (Sugano et al., 2004; Sugano et al., 2007a), the relationship between the order of RGB route distance and projected route area shows a decreasing trend with fluctuations (Figure 6). These fluctuations become larger with increasing order. That is, the variation of the relationship in Figure 9 causes the fluctuations in Figure 6.

It is thought that route area indicates the magnitude of naturalness (as in a rainbow) for the color sequences in this model, with the minimum sequence being similar to the order of rainbow colors. Conversely, the non-minimum sequence is completely different from the order of rainbow colors.

Although the six colors used in previous studies (Sugano et al., 2004; Sugano et al., 2006; Sugano et al., 2007a) are not distributed as rainbow colors (violet, indigo, blue, green, yellow, orange, and red), and the six-color cyclic sequences are not continuous sequences having gradation, a simple fuzzy model of human color impression using the route area indicated by both hue and saturation is proposed. This model (Sugano & Matsushita, 2001a; Sugano & Matsushita, 2001b; Sugano & Matsushita, 2002) invokes natural impressions when the route area is large and unnatural impressions when the route area is small or medium-sized (Figure 8).

In this study, it is clarified that the majority of subjects choose a large projected route area as the minimum sequence when reporting a "natural" color sequence. When the number of colors is finite, such a simple fuzzy system is useful (Sugano et al., 2007b).

7. CONCLUSION

In the present paper, a simple fuzzy model of human color impression that indicates the degree of perceived naturalness using a projected route area with route complexity is proposed. The simulation results suggest that if the area of the projected route is the maximum, or nearly maximum, the human color impression approaches "natural"; otherwise, the human color impression becomes "unnatural". In addition, route complexity has an inverse relationship to the projected route area.

This model also provides the framework for the design of a row of suitable colors (as spatial information in Figure 1b) for the control of feeling and emotion (for example, in a sign, tiled floor, or garden), as well as a design using a color signal sequence (as temporal information in Figure 1a, for example, in a movie, drama, or play) (Sugano & Nasu, 2000; Sugano, 2001) based on single color effects (Ohmi, 1999).

In future work, new spatial information will be investigated in a block (e.g., a tiled floor) of thirty-six colors composed of linear color sequences in additional experiments.

ACKNOWLEDGMENT

The author would like to thank both present and former members of our laboratory, including M. Matsuura, A. Kojima, Y. Sakai, S. Sato, M. Bando, T. Nasu, Y. Matsushita, S. Nakagawa, Y. Negishi, and T. Ishihara, whose work and ideas have contributed greatly to this project.

REFERENCES

Minou, M., & Nishida, S. (1999). *Information Media Engineering*. Tokyo: Ohmsha. In Japanese

Ohi, Y., & Kawasaki, H. (1996). *Introduction to Color Coordinator, Color*, Japan Color Research Institute (Ed.), Tokyo, Japan Color Enterprise. In Japanese.

Ohmi, G. (1999). *Color Sensation, Data and Test*, Japan Color Research Institute (Ed.), Tokyo, Japan Color Enterprise. In Japanese.

Sivik, L. (1997). Color systems for cognitive research . In Hardin, C. L., & Maffi, L. (Eds.), *Color Categories in Thought and Language* (pp. 163–193). New York: Cambridge University Press. doi:10.1017/CBO9780511519819.008

Sugano, N. (2001). Effect of well-ordered color signal sequence with minimum distance on human color impressions. *Biomedical Soft Computing and Human Sciences*, 7(1), 53–59.

Sugano, N., & Matsushita, Y. (2001a, July). Human color impression model for well-ordered color signal sequence with minimum distance.In *Proc. of Joint 9th International Fuzzy Systems Association World Congress and 20th North American Fuzzy Information Processing Society International Conference, Vancouver* (pp. 2253-2258).

Sugano, N., & Matsushita, Y. (2001b, October). Human color impression model for color signal sequence with minimum distance.In *Proc. of International Symposium: Toward a Development of KANSEI Technology, Muroran* (pp. 157-160).

Sugano, N., & Matsushita, Y. (2002). Effect of color signal sequence with minimum distance on human color impression model. *Biomedical Soft Computing and Human Sciences*, 8(1), 29–35.

Sugano, N., Nakagawa, S., Negishi, Y., & Ishihara, T. (2004, October). Human color impression for color sequence with minimum distance.In *Proc. of IEEE International Conference on Systems, Man and Cybernetics, Hague* (pp. 321-326).

Sugano, N., Nakagawa, S., Negishi, Y., & Ishihara, T. (2007a). Effect of spatial color sequence with minimum distance on human color impression and model behavior.In *Biomedical Soft Computing and Human Sciences, 12* (1), 1-7.

Sugano, N., & Nasu, T. (2000, October). Human color impressions elicited by well-ordered color signal sequences with minimum distance.In *Proc. of 2000 IEEE International Conference on Industrial Electronics, Control and Instrumentation, Nagoya* (pp. 1614-1619).

Sugano, N., Negishi, Y., & Ishihara, T. (2006). Effect of spatial color sequence with minimum distance on human color impression and its model, Proc. of the Institution of Mechanical Engineers, Part I . *Journal of Systems and Control Engineering, 220*(I8), 745–751.

Sugano, N., Negishi, Y., & Ishihara, T. (2007b, September). Effect of route area and route complexity of spatial color sequence on human color impression and simple fuzzy model.In *Proc. of 8th International Symposium on Advanced Intelligent Systems*, Sokcho (pp. 443-448).

Sugano, N., Negishi, Y., & Ishihara, T. (2009). Effect of route complexity of spatial color sequence on human color impression and its fuzzy model . *International Journal of Biomedical Soft Computing and Human Sciences, 14*(1), 131–139.

Wooten, B., & Miller, D. L. (1997). The psychophysics of color . In Hardin, C. L., & Maffi, L. (Eds.), *Color Categories in Thought and Language* (pp. 59–88). New York: Cambridge University Press. doi:10.1017/CBO9780511519819.003

APPENDIX

Traveling Salesman Problems

In an instance of the traveling salesman problem (TSP), we are given a set of cities and a symmetric distance matrix that indicates the cost of direct travel from each city to every other city. The goal is to find the shortest circular tour, visiting each city exactly once, to minimize the total travel cost, which includes the cost of traveling from the last city back to the first city.

In a seven-city problem, for example, 1st-2nd-3rd-4th-5th-6th-7th represents the travel plan that takes the salesman from 1st to 2nd, from 2nd to 3rd... from 6th to 7th, and finally from 7th to 1st again. The cost of this tour is the sum of the distances traversed in each travel segment. The number of possible tours is extremely large ($n!/2n=360$) even for problems containing a small number of cities.

Computation of Route Area

Compute the route area a, as follows:

$$a = \left| \sum_{i=1}^{n} (x_{i+1} - x_{i-1}) y_i \right|$$

where x_i and y_i are color coordinates of an n-color sequence, if $i=n$, $i+1=1$ and if $i=1$, $i-1=n$.

Only three sequences in No. 3, No. 5, and No. 10 of Figure 4 have differences between the route and envelope route projected from the RGB route. We have to consider the intersections of routes in computations of an envelope route area. For example, the envelope route (top right) of No. 3 has 6 colors plus 5 corners as intersections.

Chapter 14
Rural Scenery Narrative and Field Experiences:
From an Aspect of Kansei

Tadashi Hasebe
Tohoku University, Japan

Michiaki Ohmura
Tohoku University, Japan

Hisashi Bannai
Rural Finance Research Institute, Japan

ABSTRACT

Farmers create rural scenery by farming the land. From their memories of the experience of farming the land, they also create their own particular narratives of that rural scenery. Each such narrative differs not only according to the particular environment of each field, but also according to the personal experiences of the farmer. As the narration is repeated, the rural scenery narrative can become the narrative of everyone in the community and this shared narrative can then influence the behavior of all the members in that rural society. The authors call this a 'normative scenery narrative'. This chapters explores how normative scenery narratives differ according to the various experiences of farmers in rural fields and does so by documenting a case study of old Otamachi in Akita Prefecture, Japan.

1. INTRODUCTION

Rural scenery is a byproduct of farmers' efforts to obtain agricultural products through a combination of various types of work and adjustments to changes, both natural and social. Even recent developments of rural scenery are the result of the accumulation of farmers' work experiences as reflected in the physical action of production which has created the rural scenery. Along with the development of the scenery is the development of rural scenery narratives. Apparently no studies, however, have given concern to the relationship between the farmers' field experiences and their rural scenery narratives.

The purpose of this paper is to examine how the scenery narratives of farmers differ according to the farmers' different field experiences as caused by different farmland environments, and then to

DOI: 10.4018/978-1-61692-797-4.ch014

consider how a particular narrative becomes the narrative of everyone in the community as it is repeated many times. In other words, a narrative becomes the norm and influences or controls the behavior of all members of the rural society.

The next section concerns the meaning of 'scenery narrative,' which is perhaps the best translation of the Japanese expression *fukei*. We begin the discussion by adapting Kitarou Nishida's theory of environment for the purpose of explaining a theory of scenery. We then integrate this theory of scenery with Keiichi Noe's narrative theory in order to present the concept of a scenery narrative. Review of research on the narrative approach is also presented. In the subsequent section, we discuss the theoretical relationship between a scenery narrative and previous or current work experiences in the field. Finally, we develop a hypothesis according to the theory of a scenery narrative and test it in a case study.

2. BACKGROUND

Scenery Narrative

This section reviews Hasebe's discussion of scenery narrative (Hasebe, 2005a, 2005b)[1]. We will attempt to explain the creation of scenery from the point of view expressed by Kitaro Nishida (1870-1945, generally considered the most important philosopher of modern Japan); however, in doing so we utilize the logic of Yoshimichi Nakajima whose discussion of the establishment of self is in accordance with the modern European view[2].

Nishida explained that a human as an animate being is not merely created by the environment but is also subjectively a creator of that environment[3]. That is, the environment as the encompassing universe creates a human as an individual by the negation of itself. Reciprocally, a human creates the environment by the negation of himself/herself. This concept of the relationship between the environment and a human derives from Nishida's

concepts of mutual limitation and 'absolute Nothingness'. We apply this framework of mutual control presented by Nishida to the creation of scenery which is part of the environment. We suggest a present scenery world that contains both scenery and society. Similarly, we can suggest an analogous past scenery world. Schematically, a scenery world is a nested structure containing a society, which in turn contains humans. Through that society, humans are in a reciprocal control relationship with a scenery world. In our simplified model, a society is assumed to consist of no less than three persons: the first-person 'I', and two other persons. Philosophically the non-first-person entities are 'the other' and a third party (the other's other). Grammatically, they may be thought of as second and third persons, the addressee and the referred-to object, respectively.

According to Nishida's argument, the human body is an historical body because a human as an individual creates an environment by historical action using his/her body[4]. By extension, a scenery world creates a human and is also created by a human or humans. Because of this reciprocal interaction, a scenery world is also an historical body. According to Yoshimichi Nakajima's discussion on the establishment of self ('I'), self is established by remembering the past and connecting 'I' in the present with 'I' in the past. Nakajima's logic can be applied to help explain the establishment of a scenery world as connecting present and past scenery worlds. We call this an historical scenery world.

We can now introduce the concept of the scenery narrative by applying Keiichi Noe's narrative theory[5]. Noe differentiates a story from a narrative, considering a story to be an objective fact and a narrative to be the discourse that is created through the action of language. By transposing Noe's discussion to an historical scenery world, we can argue that a human creates his narrative on scenery by arranging events in a certain context (See figure 1). The background of this explanation is the theory on remembrance of the past, as

Figure 1. Narrative creation

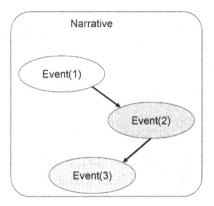

Figure 2. Creation of a scenery narrative

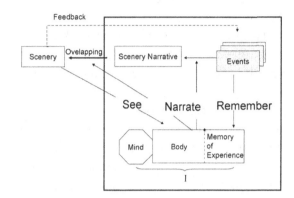

discussed by the contemporary philosopher Shozo Omori (Omori, 1996).

Creation of scenery corresponds to 'active intuition' (*koui-teki chokkan*), which is an important concept from Kitarou Nishida. Nishida established this concept by combining the action of creation with the condition of perception (intuition). Active intuition means integration between body (subject) and scenery (object). Yasuo Yuasa explains that the body has subjectivity to see, and objectivity to be shown (Yuasa, 1991). In the creation of scenery (action), the body as a subject works actively. This effort means the subjectivity of the body. Perceiving scenery (intuition) means interpreting scenery actively, not just passively seeing it.

Each narrative is recreated by new interpretation, because various events occur as a result of interaction between a human and scenery and, possibly, as a result of the body's memories of events (episodic memories). Figure 2 shows the creation of scenery from the viewpoint of 'I' as the individual[6] and how creating a scenery narrative by observing scenery represents the active intuition of Nishida. There are two types of creation: first, creating a scenery narrative by retrieving memories of events in the body, and then overlapping the scenery narrative on a particular scene.

According to Toshio Kuwako's viewpoint from the field of Kansei Philosophy in Kansei Engi-

neering, *Kansei* is "an ability of sympathy between the environmental world and the self body" (Kuwako, 2001, p.32). Because scenery is a part of the environment, a narrative on scenery is an appropriate mode for understanding this ability mentioned by Kuwako[7]. Therefore, it is fundamental to give consideration to this ability of sympathy between the environmental world and the self body when people discuss the problem of maintenance the rural scenery, including agricultural lands.

Scenery Narrative Approach

Recently, the concept of the narrative has been used not only in the fields of literature and philosophy of history, but also in the field of clinical psychology, medicine, nursing, sociology, education and management science[8].

In this chapter, we introduce 'the scenery narrative approach' to interpret the social phenomenon through application of Keiichi Noe's narratology. The scenery narrative is the key concept in our discussion which follows. Noe differentiates a story from a narrative, considering a story to be an objective fact and a narrative to be the discourse that is created through the action of language. According to Noe's discussion, the scenery narrative is created through people's action of using language in relating to the scenery where they live, and in unifying a plurality of events in consideration of a perceived time series order (See figure 1).

There are, however, not so many works in rural landscape research utilizing or incorporating the narrative approach. Lapka and Cudlınová (2003) applied a narrative approach to a management problem in Czech Republic. The method used in their survey involved "intensive interviewing and long-term field-work with families of farmers that provide[d] opportunities to learn about farmers values, attitudes and then to situate their "life-story" within both cultural and social contexts" (Lapka *et al.*, 2003, p.367). Soliva (2007) used the concept of 'ideal type narratives' as a heuristic devise to evaluate changes in land use, landscape and biodiversity in a Swiss mountain area. Four ideal type narratives of change in land use, land-scape and biodiversity, such as a wilderness narrative, a modernization narrative, a subsistence narrative, an endogenous development narrative were made by interaction between interviewees and researchers in the study group of Soliva's and were used for designing questionnaire items.

Hasebe *et al.* (2002) surveyed the attitudes for protecting agricultural farming villages (RFV) in Japan and Korea. In Japan, the attitude for protecting landscape changed, becoming consistent with that for direct payments, which were robust during the time of presenting visual information by photos on nature, usual life, and culture and history. In other words, the consciousness for protecting a specific RFV extends to that of preserving hilly and mountainous village nation-wide. In Korea, the increase of this correlation after giving visual information was very small yet respondents approved a policy of direct payments larger than those in Japan. We think that this difference was caused by the abundance of people having RFV experiences, for many Koreans are more familiar with RFV than Japanese and are prone to evaluate nation-wide RFV in terms of use value in the same way that they evaluate a specific RFV. From the results of this survey, we conceived that people develop different narratives according to

their memories of work experiences that differed because of different environments. We therefore planned a new survey to check whether shared memories or events had an effect on the telling of common narratives. The results of this survey are explained in the forth section.

3. DIFFERENTIATION OF SCENERY NARRATIVES CAUSED BY FIELD EXPERIENCES

We discuss here the relationship between work experiences in a rural field and associated rural scenery narratives.

We begin by assuming the existence of two contrasting districts in a rice-producing area, each exhibiting a different type of paddy field.

1. New reclaimed paddy fields

Wastelands existed because of inadequate water conditions. However, because new water canals were subsequently constructed during a substantial reclamation project, the wastelands could be reclaimed to make paddy fields

2. Old reclaimed paddy fields

Reclamation of paddy fields in earlier times had been possible because of the existence of good water conditions.

Farmers who live in those two different districts were subject to different field experiences. The farmers in the district of the newly reclaimed paddy field had personal and direct experience of the labor needed to reclaim wastelands in order to create paddy fields. Moreover, after reclamation, they had to repair the paddy fields and increase the fertility of the soil in order to cultivate the land successfully. Farmers in the district of the newly reclaimed paddy fields also had to face other difficult challenges. In contrast, the farmers in the district of the old reclaimed paddy fields were able to maintain average production levels through conventional farming. The experiences of these farmers show how different types of work and different accumulations of events contribute to the creation of any particular scenery narrative. Farmers do not simply create rice through agricultural work; in a much more general sense, they also create rural scenery by farming.

Concluding from this discussion, we can propose a sequence of hypotheses which we present now, and in the next section, each followed by explanatory discussion.

A. Scenery narratives are different according to different field experiences.

Farmers tell their narratives according to their field work experiences. Each individual's narrative is necessarily integrated into his or her family's narrative. However, we should also consider change over time and need to focus on the repetition of the scenery narrative and how it evolves, ultimately becoming a part of the family's scenery narrative.

As an example, we present here a hypothetical farmer whose narrative serves as a composite of the fourteen scenery narratives that we collected. We present this narrator as a married man who is a core worker in rice production.

My parents worked hard to reclaim wastelands and make rice paddies. They told of their experiences of reclaiming the land [i.e., their scenery narrative]. They struggled to change the soil, get rid of rocks, and clear the land, and terrace it. During my childhood, I saw this hard work of my parents, and heard them talk of it. I was able to help them sometimes. Now, I am manager of our farm. The agricultural work is not as hard now [i.e. less labor intensive] because of machines, fertilizers, and other chemicals [herbicides and pesticides]. I tell my children and grandchildren about my experiences, and I repeat to them the stories my parents and uncles and aunts told. And

I talk about how agricultural work is changing. I tell the children how things were when I was a child, just as my parents had done, the same with me. I guess everyone does this. It's the history of our family and our village.

A rural scenery narrative is not narrated merely by one person or one family, but also by neighbors. The rural scenery narrative of a group of neighbors was more easily created when there was a mutual aid system (*yui*) for agricultural work because by working together, everyone participated in the creation of the rural scenery, and ultimately contributed to the scenery narrative. Like the scenery narrative of a family, the scenery narrative of a district is repeated and continued over time. Rural residents accept it as the district's history. We can sum up this discussion as follows:

B. A scenery narrative of a family or a district is narrated as mutual language action and becomes the narrative of everyone (=a shared history).

This hypothesis follows from the preceding one and reflects the recognition that farmers work together to produce the conditions that create the rural scenery, and that their narratives of that scenery necessarily share many features.

Having now established both individual and shared narratives, we can look into the effect of such narratives.

4. DIFFERENTIATION OF NORMATIVE SCENERY NARRATIVES CAUSED BY SHARED MEMORIES

In this section we first consider how scenery narratives can affect behavior and then we define those scenery narratives that influence behavior as 'normative scenery narratives.' We establish the validity of their existence as such, by means of presentation of a case study.

Behavior can be Affected by the Acceptance of a Scenery Narrative

As we saw in our composite scenery narrative, a farmer's narrative is made up of his own experiences and the experience of hearing others, especially family members, tell of their experiences. As the farmer incorporates the narratives of family members and neighbors into his own narrative, he and others accept that narrative as historical truth. When a scenery narrative is accepted in that manner, it can affect the views and the decisions of those who accept the narrative as valid. To an extent, therefore, any evolved narrative, which we call here 'a normative scenery narrative,' can potentially control the behavior of those who accept it. The foregoing is a logical outcome of combining hypotheses (A) and (B). As a consequence, we can now create our third hypothesis.

C.   A distinct scenery narrative (=distinct history) is repeated in each family or district where the shared experience of field work is different from that experienced by people of a different family or district, or of a different period of time.

By the act of narrating the same narrative, people acknowledge and accept a shared recognition of reality and experience, and can be logically said to have the same identity[9]. Through repetition of the narration, a scenery narrative therefore can become the norm of everyone who accepts it, and as a norm, it may exert control over their behavior.

From the preceding discussion, we propose our final hypothesis.

D.   The normative scenery narrative of each family, or in each district, differs according to the people's experience of different field work, and this narrative controls the members' behavior.

The validity of this hypothesis will be demonstrated in the discussion of the interview survey presented as follows.

Existence of a Normative Scenery Narrative as Established through a Case Study

We selected old Otamachi in Akita Prefecture (now merged with Daisen City) to analyze hypothesis (D), given above. The construction of the Tazawa-Sosui Canal, begun in the 1930s, allowed wastelands to be converted to paddy fields. Since 1937 about 3500 ha of paddy fields have been reclaimed by this national reclamation project. Those new paddy fields were added to Senboku Plain, and became part of the most productive area in Akita Prefecture. A new reclamation project was begun in 1955, resulting in the establishment of Otamachi. Reclamation works at that time became easier and faster with the usage of heavy, mechanized equipment. New paddy fields were introduced in the eastern part of the town.

After reclamation, however, leakage of water necessitated repair of the paddy fields. Also extensive work was needed to improve the soil because the productivity of the newly reclaimed paddy fields was low. Therefore, labor was intensive in this area and the field work experiences were consequently different for those working in these newly reclaimed district in comparison to those who had worked or were working in the older reclaimed district. This situation is explained in the third section.

To analyze hypothesis (D), we selected nine farmers in the newly reclaimed district, and five farmers in the old reclaimed district.

The main questions in the interviews were:

a.   What physical hardship (specifically related to bodily aches and pains) did you experience when you worked in farming for the first time?

Figure 3. Results of interviews in a newly reclaimed district

No.	Age	Sex	Area	(a) phisical hardship in farming for the first time	(b) the most impressive memory in your agricultural life	(c) the most impressive memory in your agricultural experience in childhood	(d) maintenance and retention of agricultural land
1	71	M	New reclaimed	It was not easy and not hard (refer to the text)	National reclamation was purchased and settled so that I could marry and inherit a house. When I went to work away from home and took charge of the burden of the reclaimed land. These were expected things.	Enjoyment of working with crops.	I must give up agriculture. Most of this village have farms larger than 4 ha. Most villagers don't presume to work under a system of village agriculture. I have only 1.8 ha, and I can not recommend my son be my successor. Rice growing will stop in ten yea
2	72	M	New reclaimed	It was not easy and not hard	The price of the rice rose freely. The achievement of the side business (transport industry) was the best at that time. After that, the price of the rice fell rapidly.	The land that was a wilderness changed into rice fields according to Tazawa-sosui reclamation project.	While I can continue, I want to own it. A son may not necessarily become a successor. I want to leave my agricultural land to a big farmer because I am a small farmer.
3	43	F	New reclaimed	It was hard	Suffering damage from harmful insects and cool summer damage just when agriculture was succeeding, and purchasing a machine to take countermeasures. It was hard.	Enjoying life in the rice field. The mechanization of work in the advanced growing period. The family who used mechanization early was proud. When my parents left agriculture I wanted to carry on.	I will continue working in agriculture, though I won't increase my agricultural land. My forty-year-old son believes that he will inherit my house. My son has been working in the rice field since childhood. A person in the neighborhood is ready to do his
4	66	M	New reclaimed	It was hard	Agricultural mechanization. The progress that one experienced with improvements in farm machinery. Cultivator introduction in 1955 to 1965.	I crouched down in the rice field and weeded. I did rice planting for twelve hours from 6 o'clock in the morning until 6 in the evening. A child worked with Yui to help with manpower.	Possession continues while I can work. I acquired the land when agricultural land was expensive. I don't want to sell it, because I had such difficulty with this land, and because I built it up.
5	54	M	New reclaimed	It was hard	A policy of acreage allotment was started just when I tried to do my best in agriculture. I couldn't expand the area under rice in stony fields, and had difficulty in making a living	Crop work is often supervised by an eldest son working with the youngest child. All crop work was manual. I thought that it was natural that an eldest son succeeded a farmer.	I can't say to my son-in-law (my daughter's husband) that he should live as a peasant. I hope that he will continue to grow rice and manage agricultural land. I may ask a stranger to control the agricultural land. I think that this son's life comes first.

b.   What is the most impressive memory in your agricultural life?

c.   What is the most impressive memory of your childhood experience of agriculture (before the age of fifteen)?

d.   What are your intentions regarding the maintenance and retention of your agricultural land?

In response to question (a), physical hardship, six of the nine farmers interviewed in the newly reclaimed district answered that 'it was hard', and three farmers answered that it was neither easy nor hard, in part because no easy work was commonly available (See Figure 3, Figure 4). To the same question, all five farmers interviewed in the old reclaimed district answered that 'it was hard' (See Figure 5). Although there appears to be a difference, we can conclude that there was no significant difference because the perception of work as "hard" is relative to the individual as well as being a factor of concurrent conditions; moreover, throughout it is apparent that for all workers the work was hard even though those in the newly reclaimed land had benefited from the usage of mechanized equipment from the beginning. Moreover, because question (a) is limited to a particular and limited time, it has a small effect on the creation of a normative scenery narrative.

As for answers to question (b), impressive memories of agriculture life, the nine farmers in the newly reclaimed district listed: 'mechanization', 'acreage allotment', 'increase in rice price' and 'cool summer damage'. The answers of the five farmers in the old reclaimed district were: 'mechanization', 'cooperative labor', 'acreage allotment'. However, as is supported by the responses to question (c), we conclude that there is no significant difference between the two groups (in the different districts) in terms of responses to question (b).

Figure 4. Results of interviews in a newly reclaimed district

No.	Age	Sex	Area	(a) phisical hardship in farming for the first time	(b) the most impressive memory in your agricultural life	(c) the most impressive memory in your agricultural experience in childhood	(d) maintenance and retention of agricultural land
6	41	M	New reclaimed	It was hard.	Not only myself but my parents are doing crop work in the center even now.	Yui (Cooperative work) in the village.	I will continue for the time being. Until a machine breaks, agriculture continues. Though I think about trust. I don't want to stop cultivation, and don't want to sell agricultural land after.
7	43	M	New reclaimed	It was not easy and not hard.	A rise in the price of rice, although harvests decreased markedly because of cool summer damage. The fact that life could be maintained by agricultural mutual aid.	I had no experience of agricultural works because of club activities in a school.	I want to expand the size of the business. There is farm machinery, which would become part of the share of the branch family. I don't want cultivation stopped on the agricultural land that my ancestors cultivated so successfully. I will continue to do crop work while I can.
8	64	F	New reclaimed	It was hard.	When a cultivator was used for the first time. When it was cold, an engine wouldn't start, and there were many stones, and a cultivator couldn't work very well in a rice field. But only one other person used a cultivator, and that was a woman.	I helped with crop work since I was a junior high school student.	I must care for my old mother though I want to continue agriculture by myself. Because my old mother dislikes the nursing and personal care facility, she cannot disagree with me. The son who loses his job and who stays at home fails to gain agricultural experience.
9	61	M	New reclaimed	It was hard.	When reclamation was finished, a policy of acreage allotment soon began. Reclamation work is also a business from the old days.	My impression of crop work isn't especially lasting because it was natural. There was a rest from crop work at least at the time of elementary school.	I have been entrusted with agriculture by the machine use association. The allotted charge of following acreage allotment is expensive, and exceeds farm rent income. The incentive to expand on a reasonable scale is obstructed.

The answers to question (c), childhood memories, for seven farmers in the newly reclaimed district were: 'agricultural labor'. One farmer answered 'no experience of agricultural works because of sports activities in school', and one reported observing the change of the land from wilderness to paddy land, though he did not mention participating in agricultural work. All five farmers in the old reclaimed district answered 'agricultural labor'. Additionally, three of those five farmers stressed 'cooperative labor'. Cooperative labor was important among those engaged in

Figure 5. Results of interviews in an old reclaimed district

No.	Age	Sex	Area	(a) phisical hardship in farming for the first time	(b) the most impressive memory in your agricultural life	(c) the most impressive memory in your agricultural experience in childhood	(d) maintenance and retention of agricultural land
10	59	M	Old reclaimed	It was hard.	Mechanization proceeded and crop work became easy. It felt like doing agriculture by mechanization.	The fact that rice planting was a manual operation.	While I am healthy, I never want to leave it to a stranger. I think this feeling is widespread in all of the villages.
11	66	M	Old reclaimed	It was hard.	Nothing.	Farmers were organized naturally. There was only a cultivator long ago. I wasn't good at agriculture without Yui (Cooperative work).	I don't care even if I have to sell a rice field. The levy money for land improvement is expensive. Growing rice is with a deficit is better than giving up, and only paying levy money. While I am alive, my son doesn't think that agricultural land should be sold.
12	71	M	Old reclaimed	It was hard.	Yui's work of rice planting. The peasant's life leaves a deep impress.	Rice planting and rice reaping took more than twenty days. My waist was painful.	Income and costs discourage rice growing. I don't care even if I sell agricultural land to someone temporarily, although that means consigning to a stranger, after much effort at maintenance. Renouncing cultivation altogether remains a last choice, too.
13	58	M	Old reclaimed	It was hard.	Acreage allotment began the moment I left agricultural high school. I may have given up agriculture if agrotechnology and also farm management had not been learned.	The age of Yui. It was pleasant to listen to a story when older sisters gathered in the rest period.	The future seems totally uncertain. I don't want to damage agricultural land. That is a feeling from childhood. A farmer inside the village is a full time farmer who has a second job. Agriculture should not be done with voluntary labor.
14	57	M		It was hard.	Compost was carried by sled in winter. Snow melted, and compost became a mountain in spring. The original scenery of agriculture is not seen now.	Rice planting. Yui work has a woman at the center. Autumn work was very difficult because of the drying sun.	I will continue the cultivation. But this scale of work is limited under private management. I want to make a corporation, which means producing on a 40 ha scale. I think that those who have a sense of "This is my land" nowadays, will not be able to lower production costs. I think that I should get brid of such a sense, early.

intensive work. In conclusion, 'agricultural labor' was important for all respondents except for one in both districts. It should be mentioned, however, that in terms of agricultural work, the farmers of the newly reclaimed district were more likely to make reference to mechanization, and the farmers of the older reclaimed district were more likely to make reference to cooperative labor (yui), but essentially both groups indicated that the work involved was more than one person alone could handle. For this reason we consider the two groups to be equivalent in this regard.

As stated, there were no significant differences between the farmers in the two districts regarding their answers to questions (a)-(c). However, differences were observed in their answers to question (d), concerning plans for maintenance and retention of their farmland. First we report here the answers of farmers in the newly reclaimed district. Seven farmers answered 'I will continue with agriculture' or 'I don't want to stop farming'. One farmer answered 'I must give up agriculture'. Another one answered, 'I must care for my elderly mother though I want to continue farming by myself'. Apparently most respondents in the newly reclaimed district want to maintain their agricultural land. In contrast, the answers of respondents in the old reclaimed district were different. Two farmers answered 'I will continue farming' and 'while I am healthy, I don't want to leave the land to a stranger'. Two others answered 'I don't care even if I have to sell the rice field' and 'renouncing cultivation altogether remains a last resort'. The fifth one felt that the future was totally uncertain.

The answers to question (d) support hypothesis (D). The scenery narrative depended on the hard field work experiences of reclaiming paddy fields in the newly reclaimed district. Therefore, a normative scenery narrative that includes reclaiming work influences farmers' answers on the maintenance of agricultural land. In contrast, the status of normative scenery narrative in the old reclaimed district is not as apparent. In the newly reclaimed district, the normative narrative of the farmers includes expression of their passionate love for paddy fields connected with the memory of the hard work of reclaiming the land. In contrast, the farmers of the older reclaimed paddy fields do not have such a normative narrative because the memory of hard reclaiming works is absent or less pronounced in their and their parents' generation. Clearly, people in the newly reclaimed district share a common memory of the field experiences of hard reclaiming works. On the other hand, the farmers' negative or passive answers concerning the maintenance of their agricultural land perhaps reflects a lack of a opportunity to share and maintain a normative scenery narrative.

5. CONCLUSION

Farmers narrate their scenery narrative according to their memory of work experience in paddy fields. They narrate a different narrative when their experience changes or is different from that of others. Furthermore, farmers' narratives can become an influential norm after repeated narration, subsequently influencing their own behavior or that of others in their area. Our hypothesis was that there is a shared normative scenery narrative in each family or district where the people share work experiences and that these narratives are distinct from those of people or families in other areas with different work experiences, and that these shared normative scenery narratives influence the members' behavior. Our hypothesis was supported by a case study of rice paddy reclamation in old Otamachi.

Our interview survey was conducted with fourteen farmers, nine from a newly reclaimed paddy-land area and five from older reclaimed paddy lands. Results of the survey reveal that the existence of specific work experiences in agriculture does indeed affect the creation of the farmers' scenery narrative and that their narrative was a narrative shared through acceptance and repetition by others. The results of our interview suggest also that the parent-generation's narrative, which is related to his/her own work experiences, affects the narrative of his/her children. Therefore, co-ownership of the narrative between generations is desirable in order to motivate effective discussions on the maintenance and management of agricultural land.

ACKNOWLEDGMENT

We are grateful to Professor Karen Lupardus of Okinawa International University for her help of revising our early draft.

REFERENCES

Danto, A. C. (1985). *Narration and Knowledge.* New York: Columbia University Press (translated to Japanese by Kawamoto, K. (2000). Tokyo: Kokubunsha).

Hasebe, T. (2005a). Rural Scenery as Norm – Relation to Well-being. *Annual Report of the Tohoku Association of Philosophy*, 21, 45-51 (in Japanese). Hasebe, T. (2005b). Meanings of Narrating a Scenery Narrative. [in Japanese]. *Kansei Philosophy*, 5, 79–94.

Hasebe, T. (2007). Interpretation on Creation of the Street Scenery by Active Intuition. [in Japanese]. *Journal of Rural Economics*, 78(4), 163–173.

Hasebe, T., Kitani, S., & Nomura, N. (2002). Evaluation of Rural Landscape and Consciousness of the Direct Payment for Less Favored Area. [in Japanese]. *Proceedings of Annual Conference of the Agricultural Economics Society of Japan*, 2000, 166–169.

Kakuda, Y. (2001). *A Step for Philosophy of Landscape.* Tokyo: Bunkashobou- Hakubunsha. (in Japanese)

Kashima, T. (2006). *The History as Possibility.* Tokyo: Iwanamishoten. (in Japanese)

Kosaka, K. (2002). *The Thought of Nishida Kitaro.* Tokyo: Koudansha. (in Japanese)

Kuwako, T. (2001). *Philosophy of Kansei.* Tokyo: Nihonhousou-Shuppankyoukai (in Japanese). Lapka, M. & Cudlınová, E. (2003). Landscape Changes and Landscape Scenery: Social Approach. *Ekologia (Bratislava)*, *22*(4), 364–375.

Nakajima, Y. (2002). *The Secret of "I".* Tokyo: Koudansha. (in Japanese)

Nishida, K. (1966). *Collected Works of Kitarou Nishida (Vol. 14).* Tokyo: Iwanamishoten. (in Japanese)

Noe, K. (1996). The Body in History – Philosophy of Nishida and phenomenology . In Ueda, S. (Ed.), *Philosophy of Nishida – Papers of Fifty Years Anniversary after the Death* (pp. 75–100). Tokyo: Iwanamishoten. (in Japanese)

Noe, K. (2005). *Philosophy of Narrative.* Tokyo: Iwanamishoten. (in Japanese)

Noe, N. (1998). Lectures in Seven Days – Narratology of History . In Noe, K. (Ed.), *Iwanami New Lectures on Philosophy 8 History and Theory of Decade End* (pp. 3–76). Tokyo: Iwanamishoten. (in Japanese)

Noguchi, Y. (Ed.). (2009). *A Narrative Approach.* Tokyo: Keisoushobou (in Japanses).

Omori, S. (1996). *Time Does Not Flow.* Tokyo: Seitosha (in Japanese). Yuasa, Y. (1991). *The Body.* Tokyo: Koudansha (in Japanese).

Ricoeur, P. (1990). *Soi-même comme un autre.* Paris: Seuil (translated to Japanese by Kume, H. (1996). Tokyo: Housei U.P.).

Soliva, R. (2007). Landscape stories: Using Ideal Type Narrative as a Heuristic Device in Rural Studies. *Journal of Rural Studies*, 23, 66–74. doi:10.1016/j.jrurstud.2006.04.004

Ueda, S. (Ed.). (2001). *Selected Philosophical Papers of Kitaro Nishida, I, II.* Tokyo: Iwanamishoten. (in Japanese)

ENDNOTES

[1] The best reference on the narrative theory of history is Kashima's *The History as Possibility*, published recently (Kashima, 2006).

[2] The discussion on the establishment of self is based on Nakajima's argument in *The Secret of "I"* (Nakajima, 2002).

[3] We referred to *Selected Philosophical Papers of Kitaro Nishida* edited by Ueda(Ueda ed., 2001) on Kitarou Nishida's theory of environment. We also referred to Kosaka's *The Thought of Kitaro Nishida* (Kosaka, 2002) on the relation between Kitarou Nishida's philosophy and the theory of environment. According to Kakuda, there are no discussions on the theory of scenery in Nishida's works (Kakuda, 2001). Therefore, Hasebe extended Kitarou Nishida's theory of environment to the theory of scenery (Hasebe,

2007) based on Yuasa's *The Body* (Yuasa, 1991).

[4] We referred to "Logic and Life" and "Active Intuition" in *Selected Philosophical Papers of Kitaro Nishida* edited by Ueda (Ueda ed., 2001) and "Historical Body" in Nishida's *Collected Works of Kitarou Nishida*(Nishida, 1966). Keiichi Noe discussed the relationship between Nishida's theory of body and phenomenology (Noe, 1996).

[5] Please refer to Noe's "Lectures in Seven Days" (Noe, 1998) and *Philosophy of Narrative* on his narratology (Noe, 2005). Noe's new book (Noe, 2005) is the enlarged edition, which includes commentaries on main critiques of his theory. Please also refer to Danto's book (Danto, 1985;2000)

[6] Mind and body border each other such that they are inseparable.

[7] Please refer to the Kuwako's book (Kuwako, 2001).

[8] For example, please refer to the book, edited by Noguchi (2009), which includes nine research fields.

[9] Please refer to Ricoeur on the narrative identity (Ricoeur, 1990;1996).

Chapter 15
Psychophysiological Applications in Kansei Design

Pierre Lévy
Eindhoven University of Technology, The Netherlands & Chiba University, Japan

Toshimasa Yamanaka
University of Tsukuba, Japan

Oscar Tomico
Eindhoven University of Technology, The Netherlands

ABSTRACT

In order to describe emerging methods and means for Kansei design, this chapter overviews three approaches involving an intense collaboration between the fields of design and psychophysiology: The use of tools built for psychophysiology and of techniques based on constructivist psychology theory, in order to support designers' inspirational work focusing on human beings' behaviors, experience, and mental constructs; The use of knowledge created by psychophysiological research as an inspirational source of knowledge and as a conveyor of it for all along the design process. This approach takes into account the latest scientific progresses in psychophysiology, and concerns greatly about the scientific nature of the considered knowledge; The use of psychophysiology tools to complete design requirements. Each approach presented here is supported by an applicative example. These interdisciplinary approaches lead towards the structuring of Kansei Design as an application field of Kansei Science.

1. INTRODUCTION

The global aim of Kansei design studies is to bring Kansei related aspects to design methods and means, ultimately targeting the improvement of design outputs. The motivation of such target is to improve the relationship between an individual (the user) and her/his environment (whether it is physical or social one). This can be done by understanding and evaluating better designers and users' Kansei, and by using this knowledge in the design of new products and systems.

To do so, Kansei design studies mainly uses tools and knowledge created by Kansei studies, which gather all the activities aiming together at measuring and evaluating Kansei, and at taking benefit of this to improve the world (through design outputs). Kansei Engineering has been the

DOI: 10.4018/978-1-61692-797-4.ch015

first, and so far the most successful design method created to involve some Kansei considerations in the design process. Yet, other methods have emerged and have considered other approaches than the one of Kansei Engineering. These new approaches we are focusing on in this chapter have brought the particular attention to psychological and psychophysiological tools and techniques in order to deepen the understanding of Kansei impact on users' behavior, focusing on the notions of experience, perception, and mental imagery. Mental imagery is a

quasi-perceptual experience; it resembles perceptual experience, but occurs in the absence of the appropriate external stimuli. It is also generally understood to bear intentionality (i.e., mental images are always images of something or other), and thereby to function as a form of mental representation. (Cornoldi, De Beni, Mammarella, & John, 2008)

Notwithstanding, all these approaches, including obviously Kansei Engineering, share the common aim to increase and to improve Kansei considerations in design.

As measuring other high-functions of the brain, measuring Kansei cannot be acheived directly. What is observed is not Kansei but the causes and the consequences of the Kansei process (Lévy, Nakamori, & Yamanaka, 2008). Therefore, to determine some characteristics of Kansei, researchers often work on correlating different elements "surrounding" Kansei. These can be evaluated by measuring sensory activities, internal factors, psychophysiological and behavioral responses, and finally environmental elements. In the scope of Kansei studies, sensory activities are measured by evaluating the impact of a specific sense stimulus on brain activity. Physiological measures are done by evaluating responses to specific external stimulations.

This chapter proposes a brief overview of emerging methods used in the field of Kansei

design. These methods are all a fruitful output of a collaborative work and exploration between the fields of industrial design and of psychophysiology. By working together, these two fields are aiming at improving knowledge related to both user's and designer's behavior and at producing significant findings for design processes and design output.

After providing an introductive background on Kansei design, this chapter will describe three different approaches involving psychophysiological means in Kansei design processes:

- The use of tools built for psychophysiology and for constructivist psychology in order to support designers' inspiration focusing on human beings' behaviors and mental schemes;
- The use of knowledge created by psychophysiological research as an inspirational source for industrial design, taking into consideration the latest scientific progress in psychophysiology.
- The use of psychophysiology tools to complete design requirements.

These three approaches may not be an exhaustive list of all the design approaches involving psychophysiology (e.g. Schifferstein & Hekkert, 2007). As it will be detailed in the introduction of the next section, other works exist and take a different path than the ones presented here. However, they cover together a significant set of possibilities concerning interdisciplinary collaboration between Kansei design and psychophysiology. Indeed, these three methods points out ways to work with psychophysiological means, methods, and knowledge, in order to contribute to various steps of the design process (ideation, analysis, synthesis, and design requirement achievements).

As a conclusion, a short reflection will be carried out on the specificity of this approach in Kansei design.

2. PSYCHOPHYSIOLOGICAL TOOLS FOR DESIGN INSPIRATION

Description

The use of tools used in psychophysiology and psychology is an emergent activity in Kansei design. The objective in using such tools is to create knowledge related to users' perception, activity and reaction towards products. This knowledge is then used for design recommendations and knowledge applicable for the creation of products more suitable to users and to their own evaluation mental model.

Compared to classic investigations on users' preferences and satisfactions, these approaches focus on the determination of subjective knowledge, which might be output qualitatively or quantitatively. The objectification of investigation results is quite a rare and difficult task (because of the nature of the sampled data), which might not be relevant for the purpose of Kansei design. Mostly, these approaches intend to provide the designer with subjective knowledge that may stimulate her/his inspiration and creativity.

Kansei design investigation may process using two different kinds of tools: psychophysiological and constructivist psychological ones. Their selection for a specific investigation depends on the study objectives, and on the type of knowledge these tools may provide. It is also important to consider these tools not singly but as a set. They provide a set of information which has a global meaning (it tells a certain aspect of the subject's experience), which should not be self contradictory, and which could eventually by self cross-checkable. These two last qualities of the investigation output are crucial to valid the relevancy of the experiment result, and are to be checked.

Psychophysiological means are used to gather real-time information about the subject's experience, at both conscious and unconscious levels. The output is mostly quantitative and is usually very valuable as it may catch unconscious and immedi-

ate user's reactions, which are mostly impossible to point out otherwise. Another characteristic of these means is their great variety, always increasing. Concerning the central nervous responses, brain waves can be measured using (among others) electroencephalograms (EEG) (Maekawa, Nakatsu, Nishina, Fuwamoto, & Ohashi, 1998; Ozaki, 2009) or event-related potential (ERP) (Lévy & Yamanaka, 2009a), and brain cognitive activity using (among others) functional magnetic resonance imagery (fMRI) (Kowatari, et al., 2008) or near-infrared spectroscopy (NIRS) (Kamei, Aoyama, Kinoshita, Cooper, & Hoshino, 2006). Concerning peripheral responses, heartbeats can be measured using electrocardiograms (ECG) (Kohritani, Watada, Hirano, & Yubazaki, 2005), skin conductance using galvanic skin response (GSR) meter (Chung & Min, 2003), and body temperature using infrared thermography (IRT) (Jenkins, Brown, & Rutterford, 2008). Concerning motor responses, eye movements and pupil dilatation can be measured using eye-tracking systems (Kuo, Hsu, & Day), muscle activity using electromyography (EMG) (Maruyama & Nakagawa, 2008), and body movements using 3D-accelerometers and video observation (Kwak & Igarashi, 2008).

Constructivist psychological means intends to understand how human beings create their own construct, i.e. their own mental model to understand and appreciate both their environment and their experience in this environment. Among existing techniques (Sanders, 2001), the repertory grid technique (RGT) holds our attention. Built based on the Kelly's Personal Construct Theory (PCT) (Kelly, 1963), this technique is described as a way for the elicitation of personal constructs. It elicits and gathers information about the user's perception and preference behavior, in her/his own words and descriptive structure, from a subjective experience point of view. Using this technique, the interviewer, who is acting more as a facilitator, can obtain the subject's mental model without

Figure 1. Screenshot of HSK data (translated from Japanese)

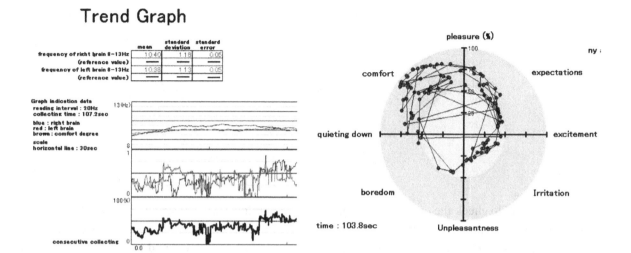

influencing the result significantly (which is the case for most of classic approaches).

Experiment

We propose here to present an experiment that has been using both types of tools described previously. This experiment intends to capture comprehensively a user's behavior and mental model towards the evaluation of pens. The captured information is to be organized to become a usable inspirational material for future pen designs (for details, see (Tomico, et al., 2006)).

Taking place in an environment-controlled laboratory, six pens are successively and randomly presented to the subject. For each pen, the subject is asked successively to observe the pen (no physical contact – 30sec), to manipulate the pen (no writing – 30sec), to write with the pen on a white sheet of paper (60sec), to manipulate again the pen (30sec), and to have a relaxing break for 30sec. While the subject is executing the tasks, brainwaves are recorded thanks to a "HSK centre rhythm monitor device", based on the Yoshida's model (Yoshida, 2002). According to Yoshida comfortableness evaluation model, left frontal

αwave frequency fluctuations express human's valence and the right frontal ones express arousal. The comfort degree is calculated from both left and right frontal αwave frequency fluctuations using the Fast Fourier Transform (FFT) algorithm. When both left and right frontal αwave frequency fluctuations are near the rhythm degree of "1/f fluctuation", it means human is in the state of "calm comfort".

The figure 1 shows a screenshot of the computer screen while using the HSK centre rhythm monitor device. The diagram on the left side shows the evolution of the comfort impression of the subject (with a certain time delay). On the horizontal axis is represented the subject's arousal (from quieting down to excitement) and the vertical axis the subject's valence (from unpleasantness to pleasure). Therefore it is possible to deduce four major zones on the diagram: subject's impression of comfort (pleasure and quiet), of expectations (or positive excitement), of irritation (unpleasant excitement), and of boredom (negative quietness). However, for the experiment and the analysis, only the quantitative data, logged by the software, are taken into considerations. The computer display

Figure 2. HSK Results (averages for each task)

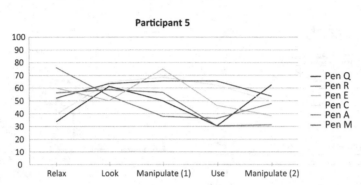

is mainly helpful to check the consistency of the collected data while processing the experiment.

After the experiment, an interview is carried out, using the repertory grid technique (RGT). The pens are presented to the subject in two groups of three:

- As the first step, one group after the other one, the subject is asked to select the preferred pen, which elicit the construct. Then, based on a laddering interview iterative process (Reynolds & Gutman, 2001), the constructs are gathered focusing on the preferred pen and on the least preferred one. To each positive construct (also called positive pole), a negative construct is proposed by the subject, and vice versa. Once the construct elicitation is achieved, an additional and fictitious pen, considered as ideal, is added for the subject to rate each of the seven pens with elicited constructs. Rating is a grade from 1 to 5. The ideal pen is used later to weight each of the constructs. These constructs will provide the designer with guidelines for the structural aspects of the design.

- As the second step, the subject is asked to propose (or to generate) a simple analogy for each of the construct and to justify this analogy. The analogy is another product to which this construct could be also applied

(e.g. to the construct "controllable, easy to work with, use it in multiple ways or clothing" was associated by analogy "a pair of scissors" with the description "direct feedback about what you do with it. Can be used in multiple ways"). These analogies will provide the designer with "experiential material" at the interaction and functional levels of the design.

- Finally, as the third step, the subject is asked to group some of the analogies generated previously and to built a scenario describing an appreciated experience of use of the pen. This scenario will provide the designer with inspirational material for the early creative step of the design process.

The results introduced here have been done with more than thirty subjects, from various nationalities. Yet, for the purpose of the present chapter, and for the ease of its understanding, the result of one subject will be introduced here. The figure 2 shows the main results to be described: the HSK and the RGT ones.

HSK diagram shows the average level of the comfort values for each of the tasks, for each of the pens (each curve). Therefore, it is possible to track the comfortableness changes between each task, for each pen. Different patterns can be then noticed:

- Ascendant patterns can be related to a rising enjoyment during the explorative experience. The user expectations and needs are fulfilled by the different tasks.
- Descendant patterns may express the opposite, in which user's expectations are not met by the product despite the first good impression.
- ∪ patterns with a bottom during the use task may express a nicely designed pen despite the low level of writing qualities.
- ∩ patterns with a peak during the use task may express the writing quality of the pen, but non appreciation of its manipulation by the user.

RGT diagrams show a series of results extracted from the interview:

- The upper illustration is a partial view of the sheet of the subject's constructs. From left to right can be seen the constructs (positive poles, rating of the constructs including the ideal pen, negative poles), the analogies, their explanation, and the scenario. The red lines show global low qualities of current pens (the subject's ratings are globally low for all the pens), which can be seen as great opportunities for design improvements. The blue column is the favored pen by the subjects, also according to the ratings.
- The lower illustration shows a two-dimensional projection of the results, presented to the designer as a mapping of the data. This format is usually more appreciated and more useful for designers. The closer are the constructs or the pens, the more they are considered as similar by the subject. The closer a pen and a construct are, the higher the subject relates to this construct as an evaluation argument for this pen.

Finally, as the last step of the investigation presented in this section, results were presented to four year (senior) students from the Industrial Design Department of Eindhoven University of Technology. During the workshop, the experiment process and the results were explained. Then, they were asked to consider these results for the design of new pens. What has been observed is that students meticulously considered all the data before focusing on a few of them, which they used as a set of important hints from which innovation was both possible and potentially interesting. Moreover, evaluating their work (The output of the workshop consisted in a presentation with the support of drafts, 3-dimensional models, and prototypes), it was pointed out that their design was greatly influenced by the set of important hints, providing a strong case for design innovation. The output was not only satisfying the experiment subjects' constructs, but also original and innovative, for a kind of products for which innovation hardly occurs.

Discussion

The approach introduced in this section shows an interesting way to create knowledge usable by designers as inspirational means. The specificities of this knowledge are its origin and its organization.

First, this knowledge is subjective and cannot be neither objectified nor generalized. What is expressed in this set of subjective knowledge: the actual experience of one individual (the user) at one time, and eventually influenced by the past experiences. Even if this description of the user's experience may not be complete, it is still a direct expression of the user's experience. The experimenter and the designer do not have any (significant) impact on the expression, as the user structured by her/himself the interview, outputting her/his own construct. This points out the originality of both the output from the experiment, and the techniques used to process the experiment.

Figure 3. Cluster structure and mapping of the constructs and samples

negative pole	A	C	E	M	Q	R	Id	positive pole	analogies	description	scenario
too heavy, tends to fall backwards, you have to shift more weight and hold you hand different	4	4	4	3	1	3	5	appropriate weight, nicer to handle, not too heavy in the hand. The balance point is in the front side or the middle of the pen. Airy, it shifts more easily over the paper. Easy and elegant movement	watch	it is not very heavy, you don't feel it when you are wearing it.	In the morning Victor visits this lecture about experience design. During the lecture he wants to make some notes. He takes his pen from his chest pocket and folds the clip as it is integrated in the shaft. This pen is very special to him because it was a present from his past away grandparents. The pen has a simplistic design and on the shaft the sentence "carpe diem" is engraved. The pen is small so it's easy to hide away and has a special prevention for leaking. After making some notes, an idea comes to his mind. He twists his pen switches to pencil and starts to sketch. The organic material of which the pen is made of is high valued and has a neutral light color. The integrated microphone technology makes is possible to make voice recordings if there is no time for writing.
the grip feels cold, doesn't bounce or tends to move when you squeeze it, makes more aware of writting	3	3	3	5	3	2	3	gel grip, makes it nice to handle, the temperature, the texture, feels nicer in my hands. Sticks to the fingers and put a little tension on it. It takes the shape of my fingers. For precise writting	handles of the mountain bike	it forms to your hand while you are cycling. It gives you a strong connection to the diving experience.	
too shiny, too hard reflection, imitation of metal, heavy glossy shine	4	3	2	1	1	1	4	soft shine that emphasizes the line of the pen, like staped from one piece, better finising.	car	emphasizes the way it was modeled, the speed, balance point	
moving clip, too delicate easy to break, not useful. You can't use the clip if you have the pencil.	2	5	4	1	4	4	4	the mecanism, interesting. It does what it has to do. There is a click with an elegant feedback	ipod	the way of interacting, new way. You can hear clicks which seems a mecanical. It is elegant	
Like the mecanism from a kids pen, sliding mechanism. Cheap	2	3	3	1	5	5	4	exclusive, it works turning	mechanical system, door handle	something that you can do wrong but it is straght forward	
you keep it in a pencil box, it will lie arround everywere	3	2	2	1	5	5	4	gives an status. You put in your chest pocket. I will keep it close to me. It is an special gift pen	pocket watch	you got as a present, it creates more value. It is different than a normal watch, the way you use it.	
plastic material, it is easy to throw away, cheap	1	2	2	1	5	5	3	expensive material, al lot of effort put in, metal. You'll try to find refills	ipod	it is minimized, it is technically very high and the measures are really small. The materials are exclusive	
different shapes without a purpose and different colors or materials.	4	5	4	3	3	5	5	simplistic form, stilish, elegant, every line seems to have a purpose, integration of the forms	ipod	straight forward design. It doesn't has lines on it which doesn't have a meaning. No fform lines without a function	
cheap easy to break, delicate, more than one piece. It is bendy	3	4	4	1	5	5	3	robust clip and pen, heavier to move, not easy to break	notebook case	a lot of effort to make it proteck the notebook. Absoves shocks with a rubber pad at the bottom	
imitation, the texture has a silver color and it has a certain grain, not a real	5	4	1	1	2	4	5	emphasize the own properties, it doesn't want to imitate	perspex glasses	perspex is transparant, emphasises the properties of the used material. Doesn't want to imitated.	
clip it doesn't work in the first try	1	5	5	1	5		4	controllable, easy to work with, use it in multiple ways or clothings	a pair of scisors	direct feedback about you do with it. Can be used in multiple ways	
three colored pens with no pencil, provides the same service, no extra value	3	1	1	4	5	5		pen with a pencil, you can sketch with. Work in multiple ways without changing the pen	notebook	multipurpose device provides multiple experiences integrated into one product	
over the top, kich because of the texture, the silver, the shiny plastic, silver dust texture. Imitation of jewery.	4	3	1	2	1	4	5	other materials, like wood ware you can see the texture of it, the grain of it. Natural temperature, you can see the traces of your fingers	tables	often made of wood and you don't want to hide it away and you bring forward the elegance and the beauty of the material it is used.	
something magical, you can't imediately see how it works, it surprised me	5	4	4	4	1	2		simple, i can see the mechanics, give me a clear way about it works. It is not a mistery	interactive installations	i'm wondering how they work, it keeps the mistery, you can't find a solution. Keeps you busy	
heavy color, depressing.	5	1	1	3	1	2	4	it is transparent, light color	lamp shields	with fiber optics, its trnasparent but also creates an interesting conversation with the light from the bulb.	
too round shapes at the edge, the line is not integrated with the shape of the pencil	5	5	5	5	1	5	3	it has a shape of a pencil, there is more speed. The line continues with the tip	car	cars there is a line from the front to the back. Emphasize certain forms in the car, speed, aerodinamics, ··· if you break that like it feels wrong	

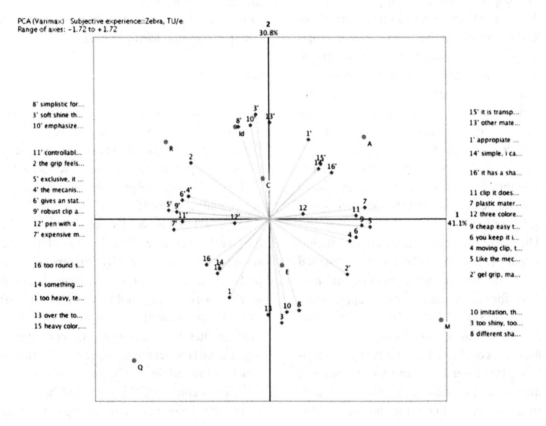

PCA (Varimax)   Subjective experience::Zebra, TU/e
Range of axes: -1.72 to +1.72

Figure 4. Design output (design works made by Annegien Bruins, Joanne Riekhoff, Victor Versteeg, Bart Friederichs, and Bram Steevens – Master students at the Industrial Design department of Eindhoven University of Technology)

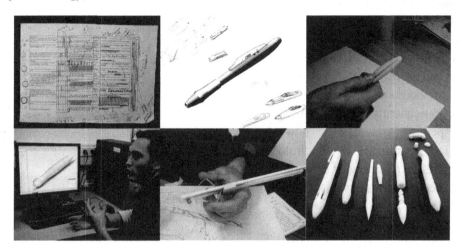

Second, the organization of the output knowledge is well structured for the designer to use efficiently this knowledge. Indeed, it is possible to structure this knowledge into four kinds, depending on which aspect the designer may be informed about the user's experience:

- Time of experience: The HSK centre rhythm monitor device provides information concerning the evolution of the user's comfort in time. Then, it is possible to observe how the user experience the use of the pens, and how her/his appreciation may change depending on the task to perform.
- Concrete level: The interview (exploration tool based on the repertory grid techniques) is situated to a concrete level, in which the subject (or user) refers to physical aspects of the pen.
- Relational level: The analogy generation process, related to a situated level, let the user expressing interaction behavioral aspects of her/his experience and preference.
- Conceptual level: The scenario, situated at a conceptual level, let appear a global

impression of the overall experience and satisfaction at once.

Therefore, based on these two types of evaluation, the designer can gather a great set of knowledge related to the user's experience. Thanks to the content and the way this set in structured, the designer can fully profit from the user experience to get new inspirational matter and to design a new kind of product.

This experiment is an on-going project and had been done with more than 30 subjects, from various nationalities. We expect progressively to determine tendencies towards commonalities depending on each nationality, which could then provide the company with country market characteristics, output directly by their own users.

3. PSYCHOPHYSIOLOGICAL KNOWLEDGE FOR DESIGN INSPIRATION

In this section, we introduce a method using psychophysiological knowledge as an inspiration and investigation means for design. Considering the nature of the source of knowledge involved in this design process, it is suggested that this method may be applied to design projects taking highly into consideration one or more human behavior phenomena, in order to reproduce them artificially or to rely on them for their output (the product) to be relevant and useful.

While the previous section involved psychological tools, consequently requiring the performance of an experiment to create some knowledge, this section focuses directly on psychological knowledge, therefore requiring an exploration in the scientific literature. This design method aims at two objectives:

- Properly integrating the study of psychological knowledge in a design process (target related to the process structure).
- Making sure that both the method and the designer using the method are respecting the scientific quality of the knowledge used as inspirational means (target related to the process content).

Method

The figure 5 shows the main steps of the design method. This method is based on a classic analysis-synthesis cycle process, yet repeated twice with the ideation step as the middle one. The first cycle aims at associating a phenomenon acknowledged by psychophysiology to the design project, in order to emit some design ideas. The second cycle aims at deepening the phenomenon investigation in order to determine elements and mechanisms which could support design decisions.

The design method is processed as follow (cf. Figure 5) (see (Lévy & Yamanaka, 2009b) for details):

- The design project may start from two different start points: from the consideration of a design project or from the consideration of a behavioral phenomenon. In both

Figure 5. The chart flow of the Kansei design method

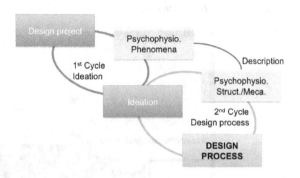

cases, the first investigation is required to acknowledge the actual existence of the phenomenon in the literature and to ensure the consistency and the relevancy of this knowledge for the design project. The higher is the consistency, the lower is the risk of misinterpretation. The higher is the relevancy, the most likely this knowledge will be extensively used in the design process. Yet, this investigation should not be pushed too much, for the designer to keep enough freedom in the mind for the ideation step.

- Based on the acquired knowledge obtained during the previous investigation, the ideation step can be processed. This will help the designer to clarify the opportunities of design supported by the psychophysiological literature.
- Once one or a few ideas are fixed, the designer may investigate more in the literature to validate, to invalidate, or eventually to modify proposed ideas. This step deepens the knowledge related to the phenomenon. At this time, it is very important for the designer to understand properly the mechanism of the phenomenon, the extent of scientific knowledge concerning this phenomenon, the nuances about scientific conclusions (if a fact is proved, is refuted, shows a certain tendency, is believed...),

and the context of the experiment. It is also noted that the designer may choose another model than the "leading" one, as long as the chosen model is both acceptable from a scientific point of view and useful from the design project point of view. This is probably the hardest step for the designer, especially for the one who doesn't have a scientific background. Hence, this step should be considered as crucial, as it is a highly constructive preparation step for the creation of the design solution.

- Based on acquired knowledge extracted from the psychophysiological literature, the designer can process the design project until its conclusion: the design output. The newly acquired knowledge will be helpful to process the design project correctly. Also, the extent of the knowledge will show the time when reasonable speculation and imagination may be required and fully accepted in the design process.

Case Study

The case study introduced here is mostly an explorative project on tangible feedbacks of social virtual network activities: "How can a portable device express the intensity of the virtual network activity surrounding the user in a non-invasive way?" The aim of this project is to inform one about the activity in the virtual world without disturbing one's activity in the tangible world. Therefore the "non-invasiveness" is proposed as a constraint to the design.

As a short reflection on the design problem, it is clear that the target is to tell the user how much her/his virtual life is socially busy, i.e. how much she/he is actively included in a virtual community. Therefore, the user's perception of social inclusion/exclusion is the core of the design project. The literature in psychology describes social exclusion as "a multidimensional process of progressive social rupture, detaching groups and

individuals from social relations and institutions and preventing them from full participation in the normal, normatively prescribed activities of the society in which they live" (Silver, 2007).

A quick investigation in the scientific literature shows that there is a great relation between the perception of social inclusion/exclusion and the feeling of warmness/coldness:

- Two experiments revealed that social exclusion literally feels cold (Zhong & Leonardelli, 2008). The first experiment found that participants who recalled a social exclusion experience gave lower estimates of room temperature than participants who recalled an inclusion experience did. The second experiment found that social exclusion directly induced through an on-line virtual interaction, made "excluded" participants reporting greater desire for warm food and drink than "included" participants did.

- Other researches showed that "warmth" is the most powerful personality trait in social judgment (Williams & Bargh, 2008). Interpersonal warmth refers to a constellation of traits related to perceived peference of the other person's intentions toward us, including friendliness, helpfulness, and trustworthiness. A brief warm or cold physical experience influenced participants' subsequent interpersonal judgments of a target person in the same way that presenting the words "warm" or "cold" was found to affect judgments of the target person in Asch's original study (Asch, 1946). Moreover, participants in this study showed no awareness of the impact of the physical experience on their judgments.

These findings point out a bilateral link between social inclusion and sensation of heat. First, when feeling socially included one feels warmer. Second, the sensation of warmness inclines people to

Figure 6. Effects of the device warming indicator

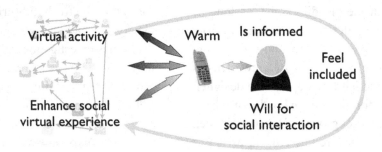

be more perceptive and reactive to the social environment. Therefore, if the portable device from which the user accesses her/his social network may indicate the activity of the social network by a thermal indicator, then the device will not only inform the user in a non-invasive way about the situation of the social network activity, but also motivate her/him towards a prosocial behavior. The indicator has an active effect on the user's behavior towards a positive reaction on the social activity. The thermal indicator is then believed to be a great design idea to solve the design issue.

Investing deeper in the scientific literature, it has been mentioned a possible mental association between physical warmth and psychological warmth (which might be due to frequent early life experiences with the trustworthy caregiver). Indeed, according to Williams et al. (2008), *recent research on the neurobiology of attachment has added further support for the proposed link between tactile temperature sensation and feelings of psychological warmth and trust. This research has revealed that the insular cortex is implicated in processing both the physical and the psychological versions of warmth information. First, the dorsal posterior insula is active during both temperature and touch sensation. For example, activity in the right anterior insular cortex was strongly correlated with normal participants' reported perceptions of the thermal intensity of stimuli, and warm thermal stimulation with a fomentation pack (as compared to neutral thermal*

stimulation) produced an increase in activation of the contralateral insular cortex, among other regions.

The insula is also involved in feelings of trust, empathy, and social emotions of guilt and embarrassment. Indeed, there appears to be specialized neurons for these social functions that have been observed in only two regions of the brain, one of which is the fronto-insular cortex. The insula is more highly activated after social exclusion or rejection than after social inclusion and acceptance, and heightened activity in the anterior insular cortex was associated with the rejection of unfair offers in an economic trust game.

Although a strong neurobiological relation could be built between the perception of warmth and the sensation of social warmth, this investigation did not find out knowledge related to the mechanism performing this connection. This knowledge could have helped to build an original mechanism to associate network activity and physical warmth produced by the device. As this mechanism has not been explained, the design may use any reasonable mechanism, adapted to the task and the technology to be used to make the function possible and consistent for the design.

Discussion

This section has introduced a method aiming at using psychophysiological knowledge as an inspirational and investigation means for design.

Psychophysiological literature contains a great quantity of knowledge describing human behavioral phenomenon and their mechanisms. If considered properly, with respect of its scientific nature, this knowledge can be efficiently used as a means for the design process.

Yet, as this method has been taught to design master students, a great difficulty has been pointed out: the psychophysiological literature is not trivial, and its study can be exhausting. During the class, notable differences of behavior and of results could be observed between students with psychophysiological background (even a light one) and others. The authors believe that the relation between the two fields requires better understanding and more consistent explanation in order to improve this type of interdisciplinary design work.

4. PSYCHOPHYSIOLOGY TO COMPLETE DESIGN REQUIREMENTS

In this last section, we have focused on the use of psychophysiological tools for the completion of design requirements. This approach is fairly close to the one introduced in the first section. However, it differs regarding the design step it is applied to. While the first approach is aiming at providing inspirational means to the early step of the design process, this approach aims at processing design requirements. Therefore, the approach introduced here aims at solving a specific and stated issue in the design requirements.

These characteristics bring the design to adopt objectives and a way of thinking that may be unusual when using psychophysiological tools.

Case Study

MATiK is a computer-mediated communication system (CMC), aiming at improving the quality and the efficiency of information flows in interdisciplinary workgroups. Whereas classic filter systems cut off information flows in order to limit information pollution, the jump analyzer, core function of *MATiK*, creates new information channels for the information to reach all person (in a defined workgroup) likely to be interested by the transferred information. Using the method introduced in the first section (an early version of it), it had been shown that the cocktail party effect, being a psychological phenomenon, was fully relevant to be used as a model for the design and the specification of the jump analyzer.

The cocktail party effect is defined by Barry Arons (1992) as *the ability to focus one's listening attention on a single talker among a cacophony of conversations and background noise*. It is based on three processes performed by the auditory system (Moray, 1959): the stream segregation process, the selective attention process, and the switching process. The stream segregation process separates the incoming auditory signal into individual channels. Cherry (1953) proposed five factors on which the brain process is based to separate the sources: the spatial location of the sources, the visual information (lip-reading, gestures, source displacement, and so on), the differences between voices (pitches, speeds, gender, and so on), the accents, and the transition probabilities (subject matter, voice dynamics, and so on). The selective attention process allows the brain to select a few of the segregated channels, to bring attention to them, and to ignore others. The switching process involves the ability of the brain to switch attention from one channel to another one. This section focuses especially on this switching process, element the cocktail party effect, as it is the one used as a model for the design of the jump analyser.

All messages sent by *MATiK* are filtered by the jump analyzer. Considering not only the content of the message, but various characteristics of the relations between the sender and the potential receivers, the jump analyzer is capable to send messages to people not selected by the sender.

Figure 7. Mechanism of MATiK

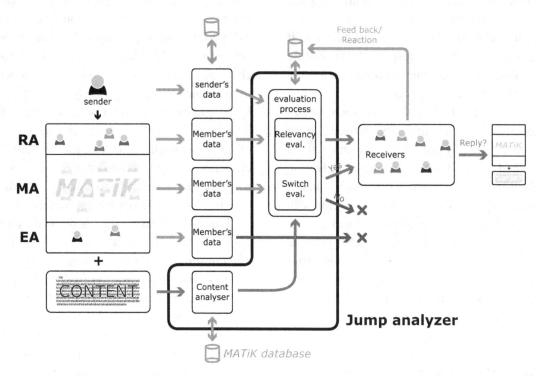

Concerning people selected by the sender as a receiver (RA on Figure 7), the jump analyzer updates its knowledge about the relations between the sender and the receivers. Similar analysis (with different effect) is processed for people rejected as receivers by the sender (i.e. excluded people – EA on Figure 7). Concerning the others (MA on Figure 7), the jump analyzer takes the decision to provide or not the message, or a part of it. In other words, for each of the people in the MA zone, the jump-analyzer as to determine whether a switch should occur or not. During all these processes, the jump-analyzer also updates its understanding of the workgroup flow and members' relationship in order to improve

Therefore, the jump-analyzer has to know permanently the relationship between members of the workgroup, and to evaluate the relevancy of a switch for each message and for each member in the MA. We focus here on the design of the switch.

In order to build the jump analyzer, it is required to determine and weight the criteria to be used to evaluate the relevancy of a switch. For example, an obvious criterion is the 'individual relevancy' of some of the words included in the message: when one hears one's own name, the switch occurs. Which are the criteria? Which one influences more the switch? How can that be quantified (required for the construction of the jump-analyzer)? To answer these questions, following the method introduced here, an experiment based on the measure of cocktail party effect characteristics has been done. The aim is to weight these characteristics by quantification of the reaction of the brain concerning different factors resulting on the switch to unattended channel. The switch reaction in the cocktail party effect is activated based on the following criteria (Cherry, 1953):

Figure 8. Equivalences between criteria of flow jumps in the real world and in MATiK (Lévy, 2006)

Real World		MATiK
Spatial position	⟺	Close activity
Volume	⟺	Message importance
Spoken content	⟺	Written content
Source voice reognition	⟺	History of closeness
Familiar way of speaking	⟺	Discipline level of the content

- The spatial position of the source – This includes not only the interpersonal distance, but also the spatial position of the source (related with the concept of personal space (Hall, 1990; Mehrabian & Ksionzky, 1970)).

- The volume of the message received by the subject – This volume is related with the volume of emission of the source, the importance of the background noises, and the distance between the source and the receiver. The hypothesis is that the louder the stimulus is, the greater the reaction will be.

- The content of the message – This is probably one of the most fundamental criteria launching cocktail party effect. The subject's name or place he/she lives... may be contents being keyword hits for the subject's reaction. The hypothesis is that the greater the 'self-relevance' of the content is, the greater the cognitive reaction is (Gray, Ambady, Lowenthal, & Deldin, 2004).

- Recognizing source voice –This aspect of the stimulus is related with the notion of 'auditory face' (Belin, Fecteau, & Bédard, 2004). Therefore, the hypothesis is that the voice pattern would create a brain reaction, stronger if the voice is already known (i.e. the speaker is known by the subject).

- Familiar way of speaking – This criteria may be wild, but we will limit here to the language pattern (such as the way of speaking, the accent, the intonation...). It is expected that, even if the subject understands a foreign language, a word pronounced in the subject's native language (by a compatriot) would have more impact than the same word pronounced in a foreign language (by a foreigner).

Cherry (1953) proposed some other criteria that are not listed here since they don't correspond with the objective of this study (such as grouping processes, and continuities, visual or timing aspects).

The question this study intends to answer is: Is there any pattern defining the influence of the selected factors structuring the switching ability on the brain reaction? By weighting each of these criteria, we expect to be able to build a structure which contributes to the evaluation of the impact that could have a message for each user of *MATiK*. To be able to answer completely to the question, the equivalences between the cocktail party effect characteristics and the *MATiK*'s ones need to be noticed. These are illustrated by the Figure 8:

The expectation is to find a good correlation between the relative reactions of the subjects on each of these criteria. For the experiment, aiming at measuring the brain reaction to the cocktail party effect events, it had been decided to use event-related potential (ERP) techniques (using 'time-lock' and 'average' methods for calculus). ERP techniques are based on the classical paradigm 'stimulation-response'. The stimulation can be electric or natural (in this chapter, the sound as a natural one) and the response is the brain reaction shown by electrodes. Two types of data can be observed: the latency (in millisecond) and the amplitude (in microvolt) of response. To synchronize the sound player and the ERP measurement system, a trigger system is used. This trigger is activated once, when the sound starts to be played. Then it is possible to know when the sound, controlled by a computer, is played while checking the raw data output from the ERP.

In order to control a maximum of parameters, it was decided that this explorative study will be done in an electro-magnetic isolated laboratory environment. This experiment required the use of a surround technology, supported by a 6.1 channel system. Findings by Kallinen and Ravaja (2007) convinced to prefer the use of headphones to the use of speakers. The fact that the used cordless headphones would not have any impact on the ERP was checked and validated.

A rich literature suggests that two auditory selection processes occur and are elicited by the N100 and the P300 (Hansen & Hillyard, 1983; Hillyard & Picton, 1987; Hink, Fenton, Pfefferbaum, Tinklenberg, & Kopell, 1978; Teder-Salejarvi, Hillyard, Roder, & Neville, 1999). The earlier reflecting an initial selection between channels based on easily discriminatory cues (endogenous criteria). The later indexing a subsequent target selection within each channel following a more elaborated and detailed processing of the relevant stimulus properties (exogenous criteria).

Most of the hypothesis had been already discussed in the literature, besides the volume hypothesis. However, all the hypotheses may be observed, and then validated or undermined, by the ERP analysis. Two great groups of latencies should catch the attention during the analysis: before 100ms for the endogenous-related hypotheses, and around 300ms for the exogenous-related ones. Therefore, the data analysis will be split into two parts according to the two groups of latencies. Also, this literature investigation points out that the amplitude of the ERP peaks are hardly, if ever, communicated or used as quantitative information in ERP analysis. However, a few techniques

were proposed to work on this unused source of information (Carretié, et al., 2004).

The design of the auditory sets (i.e. the auditory content subjects hear) is done by a synopsis precisely defined. This synopsis is used to organize the record of auditory elements, and to organize the auditory sets on the computer. In order to create an environment relevant for the occurrence of the cocktail party effect, an auditory background is made from the mix of conversations. For this purpose, five radio conversation shows had been recorded on the Internet radio, normalized, and included in the audio-editing software. To the mixed conversation were added specific information likely to provoke a cocktail party effect switch based on one of the criteria previously described. As each member switches on different contents (a person may switch on one's name, more hardly on somebody else's name), each auditory set had to be prepared with a prior brief investigation on each subject. For each potential subject, the information was requested in English, in Japanese and in their own native language. Out of thirty persons, four refused to provide information, cancelling their potential participation to the study. According to the requirement of 'known' and 'unknown' speakers, 11 persons read the information previously gathered while being recorded. Then, the recordings were edited and normalized in terms of volume, and the blank parts on the beginning and the end of the sound were trimmed. Finally, the sounds were brought in a surround console (6.1 channels) and spatially placed to create a real-like auditory environment. For each subject, the ten following sequences are created:

- Sequence 1 - The benchmark: This sequence is the benchmark one, with which most of the other sequences are compared ($r=0$ and $\theta=0$).
- Sequence 2 - Front source: This sequence is equivalent to the sequence 1 except that the source location is in front of the subject ($r=1$ and $\theta=0$).

- Sequence 3 - Side source: This sequence is equivalent to the sequence 1 except that the source location is on the left side of the subject (r=1 and θ=π/2). It is used to evaluate the impact of the distance between the source and the listener when the source is on the side. This evaluation is a partial response to the criterion 'the spatial position of the source'.

- Sequence 4 - Back source: This sequence is equivalent to the previous sequence 1 but the source is placed in the back of the subject (r=1 and θ=π).

- Sequence 5 - Loudness: This sequence is equivalent to the sequence 1 except that the source volume is 10dB higher. This evaluation is a response to the criterion 'the volume of the message received by the subject'.

- Sequence 6 - Unknown name: This sequence is equivalent to the sequence 1 except that the content is an unknown name for the listener (the voice is similar). This evaluation is a partial response to the criterion 'the content of the message'.

- Sequence 7 - Own name: This sequence is equivalent to the previous sequence except that the content is the listener's name.

- Sequence 8 - Own country: This sequence is equivalent to the previous sequence except that the content is the listener's own country.

- Sequence 9 - Known voice: This sequence is equivalent to the sequence 1 except that the voice of the speaker is known by the listener (the speaker is still disclosed to the subject). This evaluation is a response to the criterion 'recognizing the voice'.

- Sequence 10 - Native language: This sequence is equivalent to the sequence 8 except that the speaker's native language

Each sequence lasts 200 seconds, with a break of 15 seconds between, and 30 seconds for each of the introduction (fade in) and conclusion (fade out). The auditory set lasts 36:25'.

Three subjects participated to the study (N=3), one female and two males. Each subjects listened to complete auditory set. Relevant raw data were selected, filtered and analyzed to determine relevant peaks, according to the analysis criteria. Few peaks have been found and validated. The lack of relevant data, mainly due to the too few numbers of relevant raw data blocks, prevents to confirm any hypothesis of this study. However, it is possible to show tendencies which goes pro or against the hypothesis. Following the literature, and the actual overview of all the output, the analysis focuses firstly on the 'P300-like peak', noted P300* (positive peak at 300ms, concerning the semantic (exogenous) aspects of the stimulus), and then on the P30* (positive peak at 30ms, concerning physical (endogenous) aspects of the stimulus). Details can be found in (Lévy, 2006).

Concerning the analysis of the P300*, the comparisons 5,6,7,8 are supporting the hypothesis. The first three (subtraction between the sequences 6,7,8, respectively, and 1) point out a tendency that supports the hypothesis related to the self-relevant word (the more the word has a self-relevancy, the more the brain reacts). The comparison 8 (subtraction between the sequences 9 and 1), aiming at determining the impact of the voice (between a known voice and an unknown one), was only measurable for the subject 3, whose reaction supported the hypothesis. The tendency remains weak, because of the lack of support. Nevertheless, the comparison 9 (subtraction between the sequences 10 and 8), which aims at determining the impact of the used language, is in contrast with the hypothesis, as shown by the results found on the subject 1.

Concerning the analysis of the P30*, the comparison 1 (subtraction between the sequences 2 and 1) is contrasting between the subjects 2 and 3. Therefore, no conclusion can be output concerning the impact of the distance between the source and the listener. The comparisons 2 and 3 (subtraction between the sequences 3 and 1, and substraction between the sequences 4 and 1) are supporting the hypothesis since there are both inferior to the comparison 1, and the comparison 3 is also inferior to the comparison 2. This result supports the idea that a frontal position of the source ($\theta=0$) has a greater impact on the brain activity than a lateral position ($\theta=\pi/2$), and even greater on a back position ($\theta=\pi$). The hypothesis of the source position is thus supported by the study analysis. The comparison 4 (subtraction between the sequences 5 and 1) is greatly supported by the results of the subject 3, but slightly contrasting the results of the subjects 1 and 2. Then, no conclusion can be emitted concerning this hypothesis.

Discussion

The study of the P30* supports the hypothesis concerning the lateralization of the source, without supporting (neither invalidating) the effect of the distance. The volume hypothesis is neither validated nor invalidated. As for the P300* analysis, the P30* one cannot bring any proof, but only tendencies. A deeper analysis is required to obtain more relevant results, and to determine quantitative data.

The current state of this explorative study does not provide yet definite results which can be used directly in the design of the jump analyzer. However, from the tendencies described in the analysis, it is possible to validate the relevancy of the criteria used as parameters influencing the switch. Moreover, although this experiment may not bring sufficient and definitive knowledge to build the jump analyzer, it provides a good insight of how psychophysiological tools could be used to fulfill the design requirements.

More work (such as involving more subjects and refining the experiment) is required in order to achieve the objectives of the design project. Involving more subjects is required to improve the relevancy and the stability of the quantified data. Refining the experiment is also required in

order to improve the quality of the output. Refining the experiment may consist into reducing the length of the experiment. A long experiment may eventually makes subjects sleepy (major issue for one of the three subjects), provoking head and eye movements, and therefore noises for the ERP measure. To do so, one subject could be tested only for a part of the sequences, which once again increase the number of required subjects. This suggestion is all the more relevant that the number of occurrences of the stimulus should be increased, to ensure a sufficient number of occurrences usable for the data analysis.

5. CONCLUSION

The overview of these three different approaches emerging in Kansei design shows an interesting insight of the relationship which has risen between design and psychophysiology (which has been associated with constructivist psychology). Although these two fields of research are historically and methodologically very different, they share a common interest in the understanding of the actual human behavior. Both of them wish to understand actual users' (or designers') behavior in real action.

Moreover, tools and methods developed by and for psychophysiology are adapted to design vision, as they capture conscious and unconscious human behavior in a non-invasive way, determining levels of comfort or stress of the subject. The ones of constructivist psychology propose to point out not only what is preferred by the users, but also what is their subjective evaluation model. Therefore, it brings not only a certain evaluation on a design, but also the reason of this evaluation, and some insights regarding possible future behavior. Therefore, all of these tools shape a promising toolbox for Kansei design, interesting in the understanding of human behavior and human Kansei, to design a world in which products, services, and systems make a better link between human Kansei (and perception) and their environment.

This would not be possible with the capability of both domains to interact, to share knowledge and objectives. Forecasting on the future of this collaboration, the authors believe that the interdisciplinary field will progressively lead towards a transdisciplinary domain, becoming a field of application related to Kansei science.

However, for each of the approaches, a common issue seems to appear, related to the relation between the designer and the psychophysiologist. The former intends to remain as concrete as possible, exploring the world and finding new opportunities directly applicable; the later intends to observe the world from a scientific point of view, and to explain behaviors from this point of view. Both have strength; none of them can process a Kansei design project alone. Therefore, the wise behavior is to consider and to achieve design opportunities together. To do so, three requirements have to be followed:

- A clear knowledge and understanding of the problem and the objective of the study for each of the members.
- A permanent and open-minded dialogue between the members concerning the proposition made to progress on the design of the study.
- A systemic reflection on each decision, in order to ensure to reach the best compromise between the involved disciplines without distorting the issue, the method, and the objective of the study.

These three points may seem to be obvious, but one has to have them clearly and permanently in mind to succeed the entire realization of such interdisciplinary and exploratory projects. Therefore, the success of such explorative study cannot be reached only by the strict application of Kansei design methods, but also by acceptance of wise compromises, brought out by human beings.

ACKNOWLEDGMENT

The section entitled "Psychophysiological tools for design inspiration" is part of the "International Program for New Frontiers in Mind and Brain Science", under the "Initiatives for Attractive Education in Graduate Schools", Ministry of Education, Culture, Sports, Science and Technology of Japan. The authors are thankful to Zebra Pen Company for providing a sample of pens from the Japanese market. The section entitled "Psychophysiology to complete design requirements" is a research part of the 21st Century COE program Promotion of Kansei science for Understanding the Mechanism of Mind and Heart, sponsored by the Japanese Ministry of Education, Culture, Sports, Science and Technology. The study protocol was approved by the ethical committee of the University of Tsukuba. The authors are also thankful to Pr. Miyuki Yamamoto and Dr. Yasuyuki Kowatari for their long support to set up the cocktail party effect study and their help to analyze the data.

REFERENCES

Arons, B. (1992). A Review of the Cocktail Party Effect. *Journal of the American Voice I/O Society, 12*, 35 - 50.

Asch, S. E. (1946). Forming impressions of personality. *Journal of Abnormal Psychology, 41*(3), 258–290. doi:10.1037/h0055756

Belin, P., Fecteau, S., & Bédard, C. (2004). Thinking the voice: neural correlates of voice perception. *Trends in Cognitive Sciences, 8*(3), 129–135. doi:10.1016/j.tics.2004.01.008

Carretié, L., Tapia, M., Mercado, F., Albert, J., López-Martín, S., & Serna, J. M. l. (2004). Voltage-Based Versus Factor Score-Based Source Localization Analyses of Electrophysiological Brain Activity: A Comparison. *Brain Topography, 17*(2), 109–115. doi:10.1007/s10548-004-1008-1

Cherry, C. E. (1953). Some Experiments on the Recognition of Speech, with One and with Two Ears. *The Journal of the Acoustical Society of America, 25*(5), 975–979. doi:10.1121/1.1907229

Chung, S.-C., & Min, B.-C. (2003). *Correlation between On-Line Subjective Evaluation and GSR.* Paper presented at the 4th Japan-Korea International Symposium on Kansei Engineering, Tsukuba, Japan.

Cornoldi, C., De Beni, R., Mammarella, I. C., & John, H. B. (2008). Mental Imagery. In Byrne, J. H. (Ed.), *Learning and Memory: A Comprehensive Reference* (pp. 103–123). Oxford, UK: Academic Press. doi:10.1016/B978-012370509-9.00158-3

Gray, H. M., Ambady, N., Lowenthal, W. T., & Deldin, P. (2004). P300 as an index of attention to self-relevant stimuli. *Journal of Experimental Social Psychology, 40*(2), 216–224. doi:10.1016/S0022-1031(03)00092-1

Hall, E. T. (1990). *The Silent Language.* Norwell: Anchor Press.

Hansen, J. C., & Hillyard, S. A. (1983). Selective attention to multidimensional auditory stimuli. *Journal of Experimental Psychology. Human Perception and Performance, 9*(1), 1–19. doi:10.1037/0096-1523.9.1.1

Hillyard, S. A., & Picton, T. W. (1987). Electrophysiology of congnition. In Plum, F. (Ed.), *andbook of Physiology* (*Vol. 5*, pp. 519–584). Bethesda, MD: Wverly Press.

Hink, R. F., Fenton, W. H., Pfefferbaum, A., Tinklenberg, J. R., & Kopell, B. S. (1978). The distribution of attention across auditory input channels: an assessment using the human evoked potential. *Psychophysiology, 15*(5), 466–473. doi:10.1111/j.1469-8986.1978.tb01417.x

Jenkins, S., Brown, R., & Rutterford, N. (2008). *Comparison of thermographic, EEG and subjective measures of affective experience of designed stimuli.* Paper presented at the 6th Conference on Design & Emotion 2008, Hong Kong SAR.

Kallinen, K., & Ravaja, N. (2007). Comparing speakers versus headphones in listening to news from a computer - individual differences and psychophysiological responses. *Computers in Human Behavior, 23*(1), 303–317. doi:10.1016/j.chb.2004.10.014

Kamei, K., Aoyama, M., Kinoshita, Y., Cooper, E. W., & Hoshino, Y. (2006). Kansei Evaluations of Percussion Music Based on Psychological Measurements by SD Method and Physiological Measurements by Near-Infrared Spectroscopy (NIRS). *Journal of Japan Society of Kansei Engineering, 6*(4), 67–75.

Kelly, G. A. (1963). *A Theory of Personality: The Psychology of Personal Constructs.* New-York: W. W. Norton & Co.

Kohritani, M., Watada, J., Hirano, H., & Yubazaki, N. (2005). Kansei Engineering for Comfortable Space Management. In Khosla, R., Howlett, R. J., & Jain, L. C. (Eds.), *Knowledge-Based Intelligent Information and Engineering Systems* (*Vol. 3682*, pp. 1291–1297). Berlin: Springer.

Kowatari, Y., Lee, S. H., Yamamura, H., Nagamori, Y., Lévy, P., & Yamane, S. (2008). Neural Networks Involved in Artistic Creativity. *Human Brain Mapping, 30*(5), 1678–1690. doi:10.1002/hbm.20633

Kuo, F.-Y., Hsu, C.-W., & Day, R.-F. (in press). An exploratory study of cognitive effort involved in decision under framing-an application of the eye-tracking technology. [*Accepted Manuscript.*]. *Decision Support Systems.*

Kwak, Y.-M., & Igarashi, H. (2008, 6-9 October 2008). *Designer's Kansei Feature on Creative Actions by Meta-Cognitive Method.* Paper presented at the 6th Conference on Design & Emotion 2008, Hong Kong SAR.

Lévy, P. (2006). *Interdisciplinary Design for the Cyberspace by an Approach in Kansei Information - Methodology and Workgroup Communication Tool Design.* Tsukuba, Japan: Tsukuba University.

Lévy, P., Nakamori, S., & Yamanaka, T. (2008). *Explaining Kansei Design Studies.* Paper presented at the 6th Conference on Design & Emotion 2008, Hong Kong SAR.

Lévy, P., & Yamanaka, T. (2009a). Design with Event-Related Potentials: a Kansei Information Approach on CMC Design. *International Journal of Product Development, 7*(1/2), 127–148. doi:10.1504/IJPD.2009.022280

Lévy, P., & Yamanaka, T. (2009b). *Prospective Psychophysiological Approach for Kansei Design - Knowledge sharing between psychophysiology and design.* Paper presented at the International Association of Societies of Design Research 2009, Seoul, Korea.

Maekawa, T., Nakatsu, R., Nishina, E., Fuwamoto, Y., & Ohashi, T. (1998). *Alpha-EEG Indicated Kansei Evaluation on Visual Granularity of Still Image.* Paper presented at the Proceedings of the Virtual Reality Society of Japan Annual Conference.

Maruyama, T., & Nakagawa, M. (2008). *Emotion Measurements of Tennis Rackets on the basis of Fractal Analyses of EEG.* Paper presented at the Second International Conference on Kansei Engineering and Affective Systems, Nagaoka, Japan.

Mehrabian, A., & Ksionzky, S. (1970). Models for affiliative and conformity behavior. *Psychological Bulletin, 74*(2), 110–126. doi:10.1037/h0029603

Moray, N. (1959). Attention in dichotic listening: Affective cues and the influence of instructions. *The Quarterly Journal of Experimental Psychology, 11*(1), 56–60. doi:10.1080/17470215908416289

Ozaki, S. (2009). The First Step for Analyzing Kansei by Electrophysiological Technique. *Journal of Japan Society of Kansei Engineering, 8*(3), 432–436.

Reynolds, T. J., & Gutman, J. (2001). Laddering theory, method, analysis, and interpretation. In Reynolds, T. J., & Olson, J. C. (Eds.), *Understanding Consumer Decision Making: The Means-end Approach To Marketing and Advertising Strategy* (pp. 25–62). Mahwah, New Jersey: Lawrence Erlbaum Associates, Inc.

Sanders, E. B.-N. (2001). *A New Design Space.* Paper presented at the ICSID 2001 Seoul: Exploring Emerging Design Paradigm, Seoul, Korea.

Schifferstein, H. N. J., & Hekkert, P. (Eds.). (2007). *Product Experience (Vol. 1).* Amsterdam: Elsevier.

Silver, H. (2007). *Social Exclusion: Comparative Analysis of Europe and Middle East Youth.* Washington, DC: Wolfensohn Center for Development & Dubai School of Government.

Teder-Salejarvi, W. A., Hillyard, S. A., Roder, B., & Neville, H. J. (1999). Spatial attention to central and peripheral auditory stimuli as indexed by event-related potentials. *Brain Research. Cognitive Brain Research, 8*(3), 213–227. doi:10.1016/S0926-6410(99)00023-3

Tomico, O., Mizutani, N., Lévy, P., Takahiro, Y., Cho, Y., & Yamanaka, T. (2006, May 19-22, 2008). *Kansei physiological measurements and contructivist psychological explorations for approaching user subjective experience during and after product usage.* Paper presented at the International Design Conference - Design 2008, Dubrovnik, Croatia.

Williams, L. E., & Bargh, J. A. (2008). Experiencing Physical Warmth Promotes Interpersonal Warmth. *Science, 322*(5901), 606–607. doi:10.1126/science.1162548

Yoshida, T. (2002). An Evaluation-model for 'KAITEKISEI' by Using Frequency-rhythm of Brain Wave. *Japanese Psychological Review, 46*(1), 38–56.

Zhong, C.-B., & Leonardelli, G. J. (2008). Cold and Lonely: Does Social Exclusion Literally Feel Cold? *Psychological Science, 19*(9), 838–842. doi:10.1111/j.1467-9280.2008.02165.x

Chapter 16
Analyzing Coordinate Relations in Handwriting Activity:
Tacit Skill and Individuality

Yusuke Manabe
Chiba Institute of Technology, Japan

Kenji Sugawara
Chiba Institute of Technology, Japan

1. INTRODUCTION

Handwriting activity is one of the intelligent and dexterous movements produced by human. The research on the relation between the movements or character shape in handwriting and writer's personality or individuality has been challenged for a long time. Especially, there is a lot of contribution to person authentication (signature verification) by handwriting features (Nalwa 1997) (Komiya et al. 2001) (Jain et al. 2002) (Li et al. 2006).

Meanwhile the concern with embodied (physical) skill, which is the implicit knowledge the body memorizes, has been growing for the last several years. Such skill is a kind of tacit knowledge, which is presented by Michael Polanyi.

Generally, tacit knowledge is an intelligence that we cannot clearly explain by ourselves in spite of being acquired or learnt. In the light of the concept of tacit skill analysis, conventional studies on handwriting activity and individuality include two problems as follows;

Problem 1: In the conventional studies, handwriting activity is not handled as one of the complicated movements of the whole body. Nicholai A. Bernstein pointed out that human's activity forms a hierarchy and it is based on various coordinations between small activities in various levels. According to Bernstein's hierarchical model, handwriting activity is a kind of *aimed* and *transferring movements*. It leads the pen-tips from somewhere to somewhere on the two dimensional space such as paper. Generally, you may consider that controlling a dominant hand mainly supports handwriting

DOI: 10.4018/978-1-61692-797-4.ch016

activity. However, not only controlling a hand, but also keeping posture is the most fundamental function in handwriting activity. If we do not keep posture, we could not move our hand and lead the pen-tips with sensibility. Therefore, handwriting activity should be analyzed as a movement of the whole body from the multiple view points such as motor skill, how to use the muscle of the neck or the back, how to keep posture as well as pen-tips movement, pen pressure etc..

Problem 2: In the conventional studies, several handwriting features such as character shape, pen pressure, pen-tips coordination, pen azimuth, pen altitude etc., are evaluated independently. Although there is a lot of contribution to use or analyze various features, there are little contribution to analyze the correlations between various features. Recently the coordination between various physical parts or synergy of muscles are treated as important factors in the fields of physical or embodied skill analysis or skill science. Moreover, in Japanese calligraphy "Sho," Syouichirou Otaki pointed out the importance of handwriting activity as the movement of the whole body and coordination of different parts in the physical skill. Therefore, handwriting activity should be analyzed as coordination between various features such as pen-tips movement, pen pressure, pen-incline and motor skill.

These two concepts have brought substantial changes into the idea of human's dexterous activity analysis. It can be possible to find a novel fact or knowledge if the relation between tacit coordination and individuality are revealed in handwriting activity. However, it is difficult to address the handwriting tacit skill because we cannot understand our embedded knowledge by ourselves. Naturally, we cannot express the tacit knowledge as linguistic (symbolic) knowledge.

One of the methods in order to solve the problem is data mining approach. Various human's activities are observed by specific devices and then the observed data should be analyzed. In this approach, tacit knowledge processing is to discover the implicit knowledge from multivariable and nonlinear time series.

Needless to say, soft computing technologies are very suitable tools in finding the knowledge from ambiguous and complex data. Some clustering or self-organizing algorithms can convert nonlinear time series data into symbolic data as well as visualize features. Some learning algorithms or chaotic time series analysis technologies can find causal relation as input-output system. By using soft computing technologies, we can mine and symbolize complex raw signal data as well as we can understand tacit knowledge in activity.

Thus, we propose a framework of tacit skill analysis by soft computing technologies; especially we show the method of handwriting skill analysis. Moreover, a brief experiment of handwriting skill analysis has been done by structural learning of neural network.

2. DEFINITION OF HANDWRITING SKILL AS TACIT KNOWLEDGE

In this section, we discuss about the definition of handwriting skill. First of all, we describe about a concept of "levels of construction of movements" proposed by Bernstein and a concept of tacit knowledge proposed by Polanyi. Based on the relation between tacit knowledge and "levels of construction of movements," we propose that the handwriting skill is a kind of tacit knowledge.

Levels of Construction of Movements and Tacit Knowledge

Dexterous and flexible human's activities are achieved by controlling joints based on muscle coordination. Figure 1 shows the relation between muscles and joint. Most important thing is that the muscle can generate the force not by its stretch but by its contraction, which is represented as outgoing arrows in Figure 1. It needs a couple of flexor and extensor muscle, which is called antagonist

Figure 1. Biceps brachii muscle and triceps brachii muscle

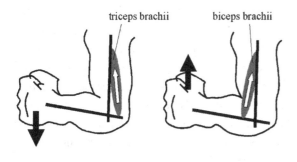

muscle, to control body movements. That's why all of human's activities are controlled by a lot of antagonist muscle.

In case of sophisticated and precise activity such as handwriting, we need to fine-tune our fingers, wrist and elbow. Meanwhile our brain should send signal to those muscles continuously and should process some feedback information from some perceptual organs such as eyes or skin sensibility. As can be seen, human's activity is composed of various muscle coordinations such as controlling some joints.

Nicholai A. Bernstein, who is an outstanding physiologist in Russia (1896-1966), created a new branch of science: physiology of activity. He pointed out that human's activity includes hierarchical feature and it is achieved by coordination of various activity in each level of hierarchy as well as coordination of muscles.

He presented four-level system of movements' construction. Figure 2 shows "levels of construc-

tion of movements" proposed by him. His model consists of level A, B, C and D, which are called level of tonus, level of synergies, level of space and level of actions respectively. The level of tonus is to keep posture by muscular tone. The level of synergies is to coordinate various muscles in order to execute higher levels activities. The level of space is responsible for movements attuned to the environment. The level of action means semantic level, which is the planning, sequencing of goal-directed actions.

This model indicates that performing an action consists of various movements, performing a movement needs various synergies of muscles while keeping posture by muscular tone. That is, higher levels lead lower levels and then lower levels work as background. According to Bernstein, these coordinate relations (coordinate links) are automatically acquired by training, growth and development. Bernstein pointed out that the nature of dexterous human's activity is acquisition of coordinate links between higher level and lower level.

Meanwhile, Michael Polanyi (1891-1976), who is a famous economist and philosopher in Hungary, emphasized the importance of tacit knowledge. What is Tacit Knowledge? He says the following: "We know more than we can tell." This simple and relevant statement is written in his famous book, "Tacit Dimension." He takes face recognition processing as an example to explain function of tacit knowledge in his book. For example, when we meet a person, we can

Figure 2. Bernstein's hierarchical movements model

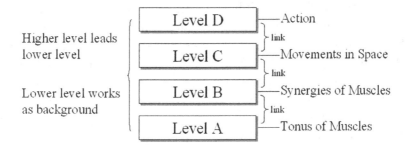

Figure 3. Hierarchical model of handwriting

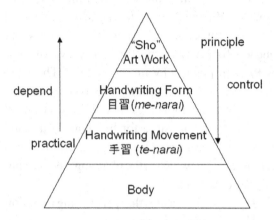

identify whether the person is an acquaintance or not. Nevertheless, we cannot explain the detail of how to recognize one. His statement means that we can acquire various and enormous knowledge by training, growth and development but they are not explicitly expressed by language.

Tacit knowledge is utilized in not only face recognition but also in various skillful activities. We can control our body and perform various actions or movements but we cannot precisely tell how to use our muscles and how to keep posture. Way of using muscles or keeping posture is automatically acquired. This phenomenon is related to the notion previously mentioned. Namely, we can find that tacit knowledge proposed by Polanyi and coordinate relations proposed by Bernstein have same meaning.

Handwriting Skill is Tacit Knowledge

In this subsection, we discuss the handwriting skill. According to the reference (Otaki 1993), Shoichiro Otaki emphasized that handwriting consists of hierarchical activity from the viewpoint of Japanese calligraphy "Sho." Figure 3 shows the hierarchical model of "Sho." The bottom layer denotes body, which is responsible for underpinning of higher level. Second layer denotes handwriting movement, which is training by hand. It is called "te-narai" in Japanese. Third

layer denotes handwriting form, which is training by eye. It is called "me-narai" in Japanese. The top layer denotes art works of "Sho." In this model, the higher layer controls and depends on lower layer. This model resembles Bernstein's model and is true of general handwriting as well as calligraphy. In another reference (Uozumi 2001), Uozumi also says that the mechanism of handwriting is broadly divided into two aspects; memory of characters and its form, memory of technique of handwriting.

From these concepts, we define the handwriting skill as a kind of tacit knowledge. Namely, handwriting skill analysis is finding coordinate relations between various handwriting data corresponding to each hierarchy of handwriting movements.

3. PROCESSING OF HANDWRITING SKILL ANALYSIS

In this section, we describe about a tacit knowledge processing based on levels of construction of movements proposed by Bernstein. Namely, our proposed approach is a kind of data mining approach.

Overview of Processing

Figure 4 shows overview of tacit knowledge processing. Processing is broadly composed of 5 steps; capturing handwriting time series, finding coordinate relations, segmentation and clustering of data, learning coordinate relations between two symbolic time series and extracting linguistic causal rules from trained neural network. In step 1, handwriting trajectory, pen pressure, pen altitude, pen azimuth and so on are measured. It is better to measure two data sets; genuine and forgery data set respectively. In step 2, nonlinear handwriting time series are analyzed based on recurrence quantification analysis (RQA), which is a nonlinear dynamics analysis technique. Moreover,

Figure 4. Overview of handwriting skill analysis

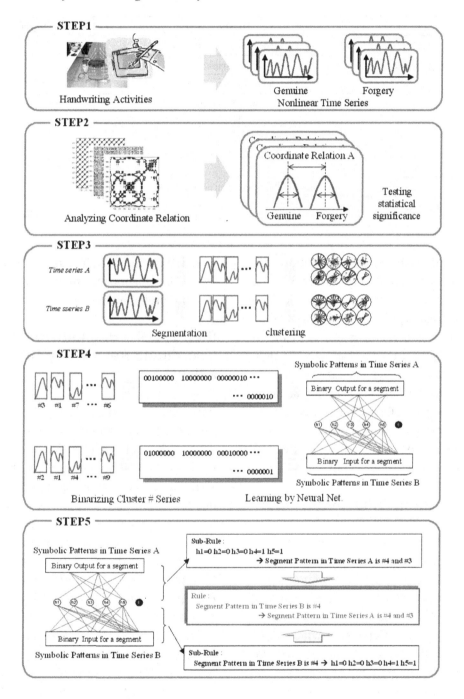

some quantities obtained by RQA for genuine and forgery data set are examined by analysis of variance (ANOVA), which is a statistical hypothesis testing technique. If the objective is to find the better feature for detecting the individuality, it can be fulfilled in 2. However, at this stage the detail relationship between the feature and the notion of individuality is not understood. For extracting the

Table 1. Sensor and data

Sensor Device	Measured Data	Level of Bernstein's Model
Pen Tablet System	pen-tips trajectory (x, y)	C
	pen-pressure	C
	pen-azimuth, pen-altitude	C
Electromyograph	muscle potential of fingers or arm	B
	muscle potential of neck, back or coxa	A
Acceleration sensor	movement of hands, arm or head, swing of body	C
Video camera		
Geomagnetic sensor		

detail of causality in the coordinate relation, step 3, 4 and 5 should be carried out. In step 3, 4 and 5, time series is symbolized by segmentation and clustering, then causal relations between two time series, genuine and forgery data set, are extracted as If-Then rules by structural learning of neural network. In earlier studies, neural network has been recognized as black box learning machine. In last 15 years, a lot of algorithm for extracting knowledge from trained neural network have been proposed and it becomes white box (Tickle *et al.* 1998). Next, we describe the detail for each step.

Step 1: Measuring Time Series Data

In general, handwriting movement can be observed as nonlinear time series data by using observation devices. There are many kinds of time series corresponding to many sensor devices. Then most important thing is to select the device and data from the view point of Bernstein's construction hierarchy. In addition, we should prepare two kinds of data set, which are corresponding to genuine and forgery time series respectively. A data set includes various time series such as pen-tips position (X, Y), pen pressure, EMG data and so on. These time series data should be measured simultaneously. Table 1 shows sensor device and its measured data as well as correspondence to levels of Bernstein's

model. We cannot obtain data for level D because level D is semantic information, which is created and interpreted by human.

Step 2: Detecting Individual Coordinate Relation by CRQA and ANOVA

After capturing handwriting time series, we should analyze captured time series. The analysis method should have the efficiency for analyzing nonlinear time series because the observed time series in general shows complicated behavior due to observation noise and swinging of body based on *Bernstein Problem*, which is called the Degrees-Of-Freedom (DOF) problem. Although DOF is the origin of dexterity in human body movement, it is also the origin of swinging of body movement. This swinging is shown as expansion or contraction of signals for the time axis.

Thus, in this study we utilize recurrence quantification analysis (RQA) for finding coordinate relations. RQA is very useful and powerful tool for nonlinear time series analysis with noise or expansion or contraction. Recently, as analysis tools or programs have been developed (Webber 1996) (Kantz 1999) and published as freeware, it has been widely used. Especially, application to activity data or EMG data analysis has been brought to attention by several contributions in (Riley & Orden 2005) (Shelhamer 2006) (Balasubramaniam *et al.* 2000) and (Shockley *et al.* 2003).

Delay Coordinate Embedding

RQA is based on *delay coordinate embedding*, which is one of the most popular nonlinear time series analysis methods (Abarbanel 1996) (Kantz & Shreiber 2004). In delay coordinate embedding, the relation between a time series and its underlying dynamical system can be expressed by the following equations;

$$u(t+1)=F[u(t)]+\xi(t) \tag{1}$$

$$y(t)=g[u(t)]+\eta(t) \tag{2}$$

where $u(t)$ is the state vector of the dynamical system at time t, the function F represents the state change of dynamical system. $y(t)$ is the observed value at time t while g represents the observation function, $\xi(t)$ and $\eta(t)$ are dynamical noise and observational noise respectively. Then, first of all we should reconstruct the attractor of unknown dynamics in phase space based on embedding theorem. *Embedding theorem*, which is developed by Takens (Takens 1981) and expanded by Sauer *et al.* (Sauer *et al.* 1991), guarantees that we can obtain the following f which has one-to-one correspondence to the original dynamics F from a single observed time series y*(t)*.

$$v(t+1)=f[v(t)] \tag{3}$$

$$v(t)=\{y(t),y(t+\tau),...,y(t+(m-1)\tau)\} \tag{4}$$

where f denotes reconstructed dynamical system, $v(t)$ denotes delay coordinate vector, m is called *embedding dimension* and τ is called *delay time*. In order to reconstruct the attractor correctly, a fine estimation of the parameters (m and τ) is needed. For the estimation of delay time τ, average mutual information (Fraser & Swinney 1986)

at varying sample rates is computed and the first minimum is taken as the appropriate sample rate. The most commonly used techniques to estimate the embedding dimension m are false nearest neighbor (Kennel 1992). There are variety of heuristic techniques for estimating the embedding parameters, m and τ, the details can be found in (Abarbanel 1996) and (Kantz & Shreiber 2004).

Recurrence Quantification Analysis

After reconstructing the attractor from observed time series, next we should examine coordinate relations between two time series by using RQA. RQA method is based on recurrence plot and also called quantification of recurrence plots. Recurrence plot is proposed by Eckmann *et al.* (Eckmann *et al.* 1987), the topological structure of reconstructed attractor is visually characterized on 2-dimensional map. In addition, RQA can analyze for two time series and its analysis is called cross recurrence quantification analysis (CRQA).

A cross recurrence map is drawn by following procedure;

1. Prepare two embedding vectors $v_1(t)$ and $v_2(t)$, which are produced by delay coordinate embedding from observed time series respectively.
2. Number of data of $v_1(t)$ and $v_2(t)$ denotes N_1 and N_2, $N_1 \times N_2$ map is created.
3. Origin is at the bottom left corner of the 2-dimensional map.
4. Recurrence matrix R is created based on the distance between i-th vector and j-th vector defined in the following equation.

$$R(i, j) = \Theta(\varepsilon - \|v_1(i) - v_2(j)\|) \tag{5}$$

where ε denotes threshold and Θ is Heaviside step function as follows;

$$\Theta(x) = \begin{cases} 0 & (x < 0) \\ 1 & (x \geq 0) \end{cases}. \qquad (6)$$

5. According to the above procedure, we can obtain binary matrix $R(i,j)$.
6. Recurrence map is built by painting 2 dimensional pixel map black and white corresponding to $R(i,j)=1$ or 0.

Detecting Individual Coordinate Relation by CRQA and ANOVA

CRQA can quantify determinism or recurrence rate for two time series from pattern map. Recurrence rate is a quantity of proximity between two reconstructed dynamics. If recurrence rate is high, the two dynamics can have similar regularity. Meanwhile determinism is a quantity of obsequiousness between two dynamics and it is responsible to the percentage of similarity of orbital evolution. Recurrence rate %*REC* and determinism %*DET* are respectively calculated as follows;

$$\%REC = \frac{1}{N_1 N_2} \sum_{i=1}^{N_1} \sum_{j=1}^{N_2} R(i, j) \qquad (7)$$

$$\%DET = \frac{L_l}{\sum_{i=1}^{N_1} \sum_{j=1}^{N_2} R(i, j)} \qquad (8)$$

where L_l denotes the number of consecutive diagonal line greater than l, l denotes the number of pixels for minimum length of line (generally $l=2$).

By using these quantities, we can find nonlinear coordinate relation between two time series in the same or another layer level. For example, when two EMG time series, which correspond to muscle of the back and biceps brachii respectively, are collected through a subject performing a specific task such as handwriting, then biceps brachii data is suitable for level B and the back's data is suitable for level A. If determinis m and recurrence rate between these time series are very high, we can find that biceps brachii can be coordinate with the muscle of back for handwriting.

Moreover, in order to detect the individuality in the coordinate relation, recurrence rate %*REC* and determinism %*DET* are calculated from genuine and forgery data set respectively. Here, K denotes number of measured time series in each data set. Then the number of combination of pairs of time series in each data set is ${}_K C_2 = (K \times K - K)/2$ pairs. Recurrence rate and determinism are calculated for the all of combination of a pair of two time series. The calculation for genuine and forgery data set is done separately. In a combination, recurrence rate and determinism in genuine data set are %$REC_g(i)$ and %$DET_g(i)$, where $i=1,2,\ldots,N_g$. In case of forgery data set, recurrence rate and determinism are %$REC_f(j)$ and %$DET_f(j)$, where $j=1,2,\ldots,N_f$. For each %*REC* and %*DET* data set, analysis of variance (ANOVA) of single-factor experiments has been done. ANOVA gives a test of the statistical significant difference of whether the means of two groups, i.e., %$REC_g(i)$ and %$REC_f(j)$ or %$DET_g(i)$ and %$DET_f(j)$, are equal. If the statistical significance is found, one can find individuality in its coordinate relation.

Step 3: Segmenting and Clustering Time Series

In step 3, two time series, one from genuine and one from forgery data set, are picked up and converted into symbolic series by segmentation and clustering.

In segmentation algorithms, reference (Keogh 2003) shows how to approximate a time series with piecewise straight lines. Segmentation algorithms can be grouped into one of the following three categories; sliding windows, top-down and bottom-up. In these algorithms, each segment do not overlap each other and the length of segment is variable because main target of segmentation is to transform time series into a piecewise linear approximation. However, as this study treats with how to convert time series into symbolic series for If-Then rules extraction, it is better that each segment can overlap each other because of high resolution of time series representation. Thus, in this study, time series is converted into segment series by fixed-sliding windows algorithm with overlapping.

After segmentation, segment series are converted into symbolic series by clustering algorithms. There is a lot of clustering algorithm such as k-means, self-organizing map and so on. Before clustering, it may be better to extract feature from each segment by using Fourier Transforms or Wavelets. In many clustering algorithms, clustering result might be different even if number of cluster is same. Thus, the best clustering result is selected based on the following criterion;

$$\frac{The\ Total\ of\ Between-Cluster\ Sum\ of\ Squares}{The\ Total\ of\ Within-Cluster\ Sum\ of\ Squares} \quad (9)$$

By converting non-symbolic signal data into symbolic series data, it is easy to analyze the relations between two time series. The coordinate relations between two cluster number series are trained by neural network in step 4 and they are converted into If-Then rules by using knowledge extraction methods from trained neural network in step 5.

Step 4: Learning Coordinate Relation by Neural Network

The coordinate relations between two cluster number series obtained in step 3 can include nonlinear and complicated coordinate relations. Thus in the step 4, we utilize the strong nonlinear approximation ability of neural network. Neural network and its learning algorithms are powerful and universal nonlinear function approximation tool.

In order to make neural network learn the coordinate relations between two cluster number series, they are converted into binary data pattern. For example, if the number of cluster is C in step 3, a learning data vector is represented as a C bit string such as being shown in Figure 4.

In this study, we want to extract the coordinate relations as If-Then rules in the next step. Thus, we use structural learning algorithm of neural network. Historically, structural learning is characterized as a class of "pruning" (Reed 1993) algorithm. Although pruning algorithms are originally proposed for designing the optimal model for generalization ability, structural learning algorithm can simplify the network topology as well as clarify activation or responsibility of each neuron unit by means of optimizing the number of hidden units and connection weights during learning of the network. This learning algorithm can reveal the internal structure of neural network such as the role of hidden units and extract the If-Then rules from trained neural network. The concept of structural learning is initially proposed by Ishikawa (Ishikawa 1996) (Ishikawa 2000).

In structural learning algorithm, various penalty terms are added in the basic learning criterion such as mean square error. Table 2 shows penalty term variation for eliminating redundant weights and hidden units. w_{ij} denotes connection weight, h_j denotes output of hidden unit, net_j is an interval summation of j-th hidden unit, λ and ξ denote relative weighting for each penalty term. Especially, P_{h3} or P_{h4} are responsible for the clarification of hidden unit activation. These terms modify the outputs of hidden units for become active (1) or inactive (0).

In this study, we utilize multiple criteria with penalty term successively according to (Ishikawa 1996), (Ishikawa 2000), (Kikuchi & Nakanishi 1999) and (Kikuchi & Nakanishi 2003). For example, in Structural Learning with Forgetting (SLF) (Ishikawa 1996), P_{w2} and P_{h3} are applied in order. In addition, in the final phase of learning, criteria with penalty term are selectively applied. For example, P_{w2} is modified as follows;

Table 2. Penalty terms variation

TARGET	PENALTY TERMS	TARGET	PENALTY TERMS
Weights	$P_{w1} = \lambda \cdot \sum_{i,j} w_{ij}^2$ (Chauvin 1989)	Hidden Units	$P_{h2} = \xi \cdot \sum_j \dfrac{h_j^2}{1 + h_j^2}$ (Chauvin 1990)
	$P_{w2} = \lambda \cdot \sum_{i,j} \mid w_{ij} \mid$ (Ishikawa 1996)		$P_{h3} = \xi \cdot \sum_j \min\{h_j, 1 - h_j\}$ (Ishikawa 1996)
	$P_{w3} = \lambda \cdot \sum_{i,j} \dfrac{w_{ij}^2}{1 + w_{ij}^2}$ (Chauvin 1989)		$P_{h4} = \xi \cdot \sum_j \mid h_j - 0.5 \mid$ (Kikuchi 2003)
Hidden Units	$P_{h1} = \xi \cdot \sum_j e(h_j^2)$ (Chauvin 1989)		$P_{h5} = \xi \cdot \sum_j \dfrac{net_j^2}{1 + net_j^2}$ (Manabe 2004)

$$P_{w2}' = \lambda \cdot \sum_{|w_{ij}| < \theta} \mid w_{ij} \mid \qquad (10)$$

where θ is threshold value. This modified criterion contributes to the minimization of training error for fine-tuning because penalty terms prevent the network from training input-output relations. The cost function with penalty terms suppresses emergence of distributed representation of hidden units by introducing a different form of penalty term in the back propagation error function.

Step 5: Rule Extraction from Trained Neural Network

In the step 5, If-Then rules are extracted from the neural network trained in the step 4. Table 3 shows the taxonomy of popular rule extraction methods from trained neural network. In the earlier Andrew *et al.* (Andrew *et al.* 1995) 's contribution, the algorithms of rule extraction from trained neural network are broadly divided into two category; "pedagogical" and "decompositional." The former approach extracts the rules from the global relations between input and output units. On the

Table 3. Taxonomy of rule extraction methods from trained neural network

	Pedagogical	Decompositional
non optimized-structure-based	(Andrews *et al.* 1995), (Craven & Shavlik 1994), (Setiono 2000)	(Garcez et al. 2001), (Fu 1994), (Tsukimoto 2000)
optimized-structure-based		(Setiono *et al.* 1996) (Ishikawa 1996), (Fukumi 1998), (Kikuchi & Nakanishi 1999), (Ishikawa 2000), (Kikuchi & Nakanishi 2003), (Odajima *et al.* 2006), (Wang 2008),

other hand, with the latter approach, the rules are extracted by activations of hidden unit and output unit.

Moreover, decompositional approach is divided into "non-optimized structure" and "optimized structure." Without the optimization method of neural network structure, the extracted rules or extraction algorithm can be complex. For example, IF-THEN rules are successfully extracted from the trained neural network, but knowledge extraction procedures are complicated because of standard back propagation based learning. In case of optimized-structure-based algorithm, by means of simple extraction procedure, IF-THEN rules are extracted from the simple topology of the network.

In this study, we use decompositional and optimized-structure-based approach. Rule extraction procedure is as follows;

1. After learning, all of activation response in input and output units are saved for all of learning data.
2. When an output unit is fired (for example, activation level is greater than 0.9), all of activation of input units is picked up from the data set in procedure 1.
3. The activation pattern of output units is associated with activation pattern of input units.
4. Since activation pattern of output layer and input layer are *winner-take-all* binary pattern, we can build the relations between input cluster vector pattern and output cluster vector pattern easily.
5. Finally, we can obtain If-Then rules from the relations in step 4.

4. EXPERIMENT

Simulation Experiment has been done in order to evaluate our tacit skill analysis framework. This paper shows the analysis result from the view point of 'Problem 2' in Introduction section, that is, analyzing coordinate relations between various handwriting features such as pen-tips movement, pen pressure, pen-incline and so on.

Data Description

Experimental data is a set of handwriting time series, whose kinds are pen-tips position (X, Y), pen-pressure (P), pen-azimuth (Az) and pen-altitude (Al). This data set is obtained by a genuine writer and some forgery writer at least two writers. The number of data set is 40 handwritings: 20 genuine handwritings and 20 forgery handwritings. The data has been pre-processed to scale it from 0.0 to 1.0 because of cross recurrence quantification analysis (CRQA).

Results I (Step 1 and 2)

First, we will provide a comparison of genuine and forgery data set by using CRQA. Since data set includes five kinds of time series, number of combination of a pair of time series is 10 pairs; X-Y, X-P, X-Az, X-Al, Y-P, Y-Az, Y-Al, Az-Al and Al-P. Figure 5 shows average and standard deviation of recurrence rate %*REC* and determinism %*DET* for genuine and forgery data sets when embedding parameters are $m=1$, $\tau=1$. From these graphs, the most obvious results are X-Y relation and Y-P relation. These relations can provide a distinguishable quantity between genuine and forgery by %*DET*. According to ANOVA, %*DET* of genuine and forgery data set indicate statistical significance in both X-Y relation (df = 1/38, F = 48.31, p = 2.869×10^{-8} <.001) and Y-P relation (df = 1/38, F = 37.48, p = 3.871×10^{-7} <.001). We can find that %*DET* of X-Y or Y-P relation can detect the individuality.

Results II (Step 3, 4 and 5)

Next, we analyzed the X-Y relation in detail. Segmentation window length is 20 points and

Figure 5. Coordinate relations for genuine and forgery by RQA

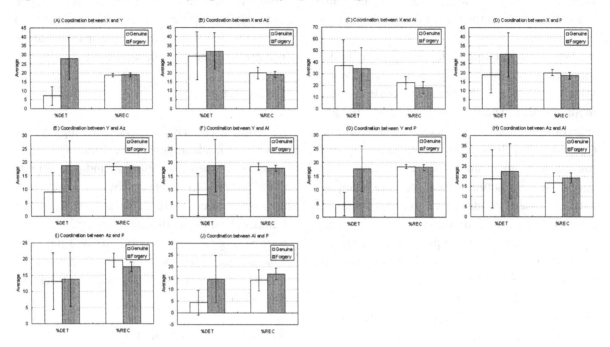

clustering algorithm is k-means method. Number of cluster is 10 and the number of iteration is 5000. The calculation is executed by statistical computing tool R (Crawley 2007). In order to obtain the common cluster vectors for genuine and forgery data set, all of 40 handwritings is used for clustering. Figure 6 shows the obtained cluster vectors for X time series and Y time series respectively. We can find that various time series segments were organized.

After obtaining the result of clustering, X and Y time series are converted into 10 bits binary

Figure 6. Cluster vectors for X time series and Y time series

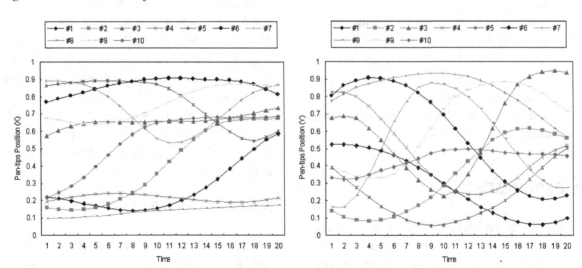

Table 4. # Of output unit (activation level > 0.9)

	Output Unit # (= Cluster # of X)									
	1	2	3	4	5	6	7	8	9	10
# of data pattern	0	113	0	0	99	0	0	0	0	106

pattern series through cluster # series. The two binary pattern series are used as learning data for structural learning of neural network. X binary pattern series are used as teach vectors; Y binary pattern series are used as input vectors. Thus, structure of neural network consists of the number of input units = 10, the number of output units = 10 and the number of hidden units = 20. Learning algorithm is SLF proposed by (Ishikawa 1996). In SLF, three learning criteria are applied in order.

$$J_f = \frac{1}{2} \sum_p (o_p - t_p)^2 + \lambda \cdot \sum_{ij} | w_{ij} | \qquad (11)$$

$$J_h = J_f + \xi \cdot \sum_j \min\{h_j, 1 - h_j\} \qquad (12)$$

$$J_s = \frac{1}{2} \sum_p (o_p - t_p)^2 + \lambda \cdot \sum_{w_{ij} < \theta} | w_{ij} | \qquad (13)$$

In this simulation, parameter settings are as follows; learning rate η=0.1, momentum rate α=0.2, λ=0.0005, ξ=0.05, learning epochs are J_f=2000, J_k=2000, J_s=2000.

Table 4 shows the number of output units when activation level is greater than 0.9 for all of learning data patterns after learning. High activation level indicates that learning of the data patterns have successfully done. We can find that the second, fifth and the tenth output units are aptly associated with input data patterns.

Among 113 learning data patterns, output unit #2 is fired 63.72% (72/113) while input unit #2 is fired and 23.89% (27/113) while input unit #5 is fired. Since input units and output units are correspondent to the cluster # of input vectors and teach vectors, the following two rules are derived;

Rule 1: If input vector is '0100000000' Then output vector is '0100000000'
→ If Y is cluster #2 Then X is cluster #2 (63.72% [72/113])

Rule 2: If input vector is '0000100000' Then output vector is '0100000000'
→ If Y is cluster #5 Then X is cluster #2 (23.89% [27/113])

By the same procedure, the following three rules are derived;

Rule 3: If input vector is '0000100000' Then output vector is '0000100000'
→ If Y is cluster #5 Then X is cluster #5 (84.85% [84/99])

Rule 4: If input vector is '0000000001' Then output vector is '0000000001'
→ If Y is cluster #10 Then X is cluster #10 (49.06% [52/106])

Rule 5: If input vector is '0000000100' Then output vector is '0000000001'
→ If Y is cluster #8 Then X is cluster #10 (37.74% [40/106])

In this simulation, the X-Y relations obtained as rules are plotted in two-dimensional space by using cluster vectors since the selected coordinate relation was X and Y. Figure 7 shows typical stroke trajectories derived by learning result of neural network and cluster vectors. It can be possible to associate these trajectories with individuality through comparing with the result of forgery data analysis.

Figure 7. Typical stroke trajectories generated by cluster vectors

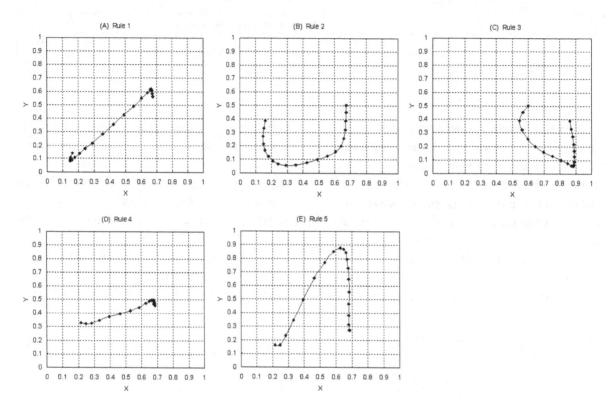

5. CONCLUSION

Tacit skill analysis in handwriting activity is the most interesting and significant processing from the several viewpoints such as handwriting skill understanding, individuality detection and so on. In this chapter, we described a framework of handwriting tacit skill analysis and showed a brief experiment result. First, we pointed out that conventional handwriting analysis includes two problems and we discussed that handwriting activity is a kind of complicated body movements and is composed of coordinate relations based on hierarchy of body movements' construction proposed by Bernstein. Then, we defined the tacit handwriting skill analysis as finding the coordinate relations between various handwriting time series data corresponding with each hierarchy. Moreover, we introduced Recurrence Quantification Analysis (RQA) as a method of analyzing the coordinate relations because observed data of handwriting activity is nonlinear time series. Finally, as rule extraction method to understand the implicit coordination, we introduced structural learning of neural network and its rule extraction approaches. By using structural learning of neural network, we can obtain nonlinear relations between handwriting time series in each level of construction of movements and reveal the relation as If-Then rule form.

In order to evaluate our proposed framework, a brief experiment of skill analysis in handwriting activity has been done. As the result, we found that some relations provide a method to distinguish between genuine handwriting and forgery. In addition, we extracted the detail of coordinate relations as typical stroke trajectories. The extracted stroke patterns can reflect the individuality of a genuine writer.

ACKNOWLEDGMENT

This work was supported by MEXT KAKENHI (21700243).

REFERENCES

Abarbanel, H. D. I. (1996). *Analysis of observed chaotic data.* New York: Springer-Verlag.

Andrews, R., Diederich, J., & Tickle, A. (1995). *A survey and critique of techniques for extracting rules from trained artificial neural networks.* Knowledge-Based Systems.

Balasubramaniam, R., Riley, M. A., & Turvey, M. T. (2000). Specificity of postural sway to the demands of a precision task. *Gait & Posture, 11*(1), 12–24. doi:10.1016/S0966-6362(99)00051-X

Bernstein, N. A. (1996). On Dexterity and Its Development, In Latash, M. L. (Trans.), Latash, M. L. and Turvey, M. T. (Eds.), *Dexterity and Its Development,* (pp.1-244). Mahwah, NJ: Lawrence, Erlbaum.

Chauvin, Y. (1989). A back-propagation algorithm with optimal use of hidden units. In *Advances in neural information processing systems 1* (pp. 519–526). San Francisco: Morgan Kaufmann Publishers Inc.

Craven, M. W., & Shavlik, J. W. (1994). Using Sampling and Queries to Extract Rules from Trained Neural Networks. In *Proceedings of the 11th International Conference on Machine Learning,* (pp. 37-45).

Crawley, M. J. (2007). *The R Book.* England: John Wiley & Sons, Ltd. doi:10.1002/9780470515075

Eckmann, J. P., Kamphorst, S. O., & Ruelle, D. (1987). Recurrence Plots of Dynamical Systems. *Europhysics Letters, 4*(9), 973–977. doi:10.1209/0295-5075/4/9/004

Fraser, A. M., & Swinney, H. L. (1986). Independent coordinates for strange attractors from mutual information. *Physical Review A., 33*, 1134–1140. doi:10.1103/PhysRevA.33.1134

Fu, L. (1994). Rule Generation from Neural Networks. *IEEE Transactions on Systems, Man, and Cybernetics, 24*(8), 1114–1124. doi:10.1109/21.299696

Garcez, A. S. D., Broda, K., & Gabbay, D. M. (2001). Symbolic knowledge extraction from trained neural networks: A sound approach. *Artificial Intelligence, 125*, 155–207. doi:10.1016/S0004-3702(00)00077-1

Ishikawa, M. (1996). Structural Learning with Forgetting. *Neural Networks, 9*(3), 509–521. doi:10.1016/0893-6080(96)83696-3

Jain, A., Griess, F., & Connell, S. (2002). Online Signature Verification. *Pattern Recognition, 35*(12), 2963–2972. doi:10.1016/S0031-3203(01)00240-0

Kantz, H., & Shreiber, T. (2004). *Nonlinear Time series analysis second edition.* UK, Cambridge.

Kennel, M. B. (1992). Determining embedding dimension for phase-space reconstruction using a geometrical construction. *Physical Review A., 45*, 3403–3411. doi:10.1103/PhysRevA.45.3403

Keogh, E., Chu, S., Hart, D., & Pazzani, M. (2003). A Survey and Novel Approach. In *Data mining in time series databases, World Scientific Publishing Company.* Segmenting Time Series.

Kikuchi, S., & Nakanishi, M. (1999). Discovering rules using parallel multi-layer network and modified structural learning with forgetting. *Proc. IASTED Int'l Conf. Artificial Intelligence and Soft Computing,* (pp. 258-262).

Kikuchi, S., & Nakanishi, M. (2003). Recurrent neural network with short-term memory and fast structural learning method. *Systems and Computers in Japan, 34*(6), 69–79. doi:10.1002/scj.1206

Komiya, Y., Ohishi, T., & Matsumoto, T. (2001). A pen input on-line signature verifier integrating position, pressure and indication trajectories. *IEICE Trans. Information and Systems. E (Norwalk, Conn.)*, *84-D*(7), 833–838.

Li, B., Zhanf, D., & Wnag, K. (2006). On-line signature verification based on NCA and PCA. *Pattern Analysis & Applications*, *8*, 345–356. doi:10.1007/s10044-005-0016-4

Nalwa, V. S. (1997). Automatic on-line signature verification. *Proceedings of the IEEE*, *85*(2), 215–239. doi:10.1109/5.554220

Otaki, S. (1993). *"Sho" forumu to shintai –Ryokan, Yaichi, Kazumasa o shudai to shite*. Akita Shoten. in Japanese

Polanyi, M. (1986). *Tacit Dimension*. New York: Smith Peter.

Reed, R. (1991). Pruning Algorithms –A Survey. *IEEE Transactions on Neural Networks*, *4*(5), 740–747. doi:10.1109/72.248452

Riley, M. A., & Orden, G. C. V. (Eds.). (2005). *Tutorials in contemporary nonlinear methods for the behavioral Sciences Web Book*. Retrieved from from http://www.nsf.gov/sbe/bcs/pac/nmbs/nmbs.jsp

Sauer, T., Yorke, J. A., & Casdagli, M. (1991). Embedology. *Journal of Statistical Physics*, *65*(3/4), 579–616. doi:10.1007/BF01053745

Setiono, R. (2000). Extracting M-of-N Rules from Trained Neural Networks. *IEEE Transactions on Neural Networks*, *11*(2), 512–519. doi:10.1109/72.839020

Shelhamer, M. (2006). *Nonlinear Dynamics in Physiology: A State-space Approach*. World Scientific. doi:10.1142/9789812772794

Shockley, K., Santana, M.-V., & Fowler, C. A. (2003). Mutual Interpersonal Postural Constraints Are Involved in Cooperative Conversation. *Journal of Experimental Psychology. Human Perception and Performance*, *29*(2), 326–332. doi:10.1037/0096-1523.29.2.326

Takens, F. (1981). Detecting strange attractors in turbulence. In Rand, D. A., & Young, L. S. (Eds.), *Dynamical Systems and Turbulence, Lecture Notes in Mathematics* (*Vol. 898*, pp. 366–381). New York: Springer-Verlag.

Tickle, A., Andrews, B. R., Golea, M., & Diederich, J. (1998). The truth will come to light: directions and challenges in extracting the knowledge embedded within trained artificial neural networks. *IEEE Transactions on Neural Networks*, *9*(6), 1057–1067. doi:10.1109/72.728352

Webber, C. L. (1996). *RQA Software*, Web site: http://homepages.luc.edu/~cwebber/

Chapter 17
Kansei's Physiological Measurement and its Application (1):
Salivary Biomarkers as a New Metric for Human Mental Stress

Shusaku Nomura
Nagaoka University of Technology, Japan

ABSTRACT

Recent behavioral medicine studies have revealed that various human secretory substances change according to mental states. These substances, the hormones and immune substances show transient increase against mental stress. Therefore it is frequently introduced as an objective index (biomarker) of mental stress. Especially the biomarker which is detectable by human saliva is expected to be a new and practical stress measurement as it can be sampled in less stressful and noninvasive manner unlike blood and urine. In this chapter, the biomarker research, its background, methodology, experiment, and numerical simulation approaches are introduced. Also in the end, it is stated as a possible approach towards a measurement of Kansei.

1. INTRODUCTION

Issues on mental health are an acute and global problem. It is not only a problem for individuals but also a social problem. International Labor Organization (ILO) reported different impacts on the societies, e.g., the social cost of mental health problem in European Union was estimated to be on average 3 to 4% of GNP (Gabriel, 2000). However generally speaking, the mental stress is

quite difficult to be aware of personally. It is hard for anyone to manage mental stress by on his/her own. Therefore it is an urgent task to figure out a "practical" methodology to evaluate, manage and control the mental stresses.

On the other hand, recent developments of the molecular analysis techniques enable scientists to assess tiny amount of substances containing in the human secretory fluids. It has been revealed that some hormones and immune substances secreted within human body change its level in responding to human mental state. For instance, salivary

DOI: 10.4018/978-1-61692-797-4.ch017

Figure 1. Stress reaction pathways

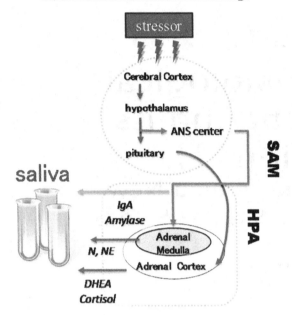

Immunoglobulin-A shows a transient increase against short-term psychological stressors such as mental arithmetic task, stroop task, academic presentation (Valdimarsdottir, 1994). Such a change in the secretion can occur even if a given stressor was relatively mild one by which the heart rate and/or blood pressure could not show any significant change. Thus such a biochemical substance can potentially be a practical biomarker for human mental stress. Currently number of such possible biomarkers have been reported in behavioral medicine and psycho-physiological studies (Izawa, 2004; Wakida, 2004), and it forms a new interdisciplinary research field called psychoneuroendocrinology (PNE) and/or psychoneuroimmunology (PNI) (Ader, 2001) (hereafter, we use the term psychoneuroendocrine-immunology (PNEI) to indicate both PNE and PNI).

PNEI must be a contributory research field which should possibly establish a "practical" criteria for objectively evaluating human mental state, however because PNEI is a new and developing research field basic knowledge on these possible

biomarkers as an objective marker for mental stress have not yet been demonstrated, e.g., the precise stress response of these biomarkers in the time series, the scope of application other than the "acute" stressors, and the relationship with other biological measures for mental stress such as heart rate, blood pressure, and brain waves.

In this chapter, PNEI research, its background, method, experiments, and kinetic model approach are introduced. Also in the end, PNEI is stated as a possible approach towards the measurement of Kansei.

2. BIOMARKERS

HPA and SAM Systems as the Stress Reaction Pathways

An array of secretory substances has already been reported to be changing according to given stressors (Izawa, 2004). Thus, these substances are taken as "biomarkers" for human psycho-physiological state. In the PNEI studies, mainly seven biomarkers falling under the categories of hormones, immune substances, proteins and enzymes; Immunoglobulin A (IgA), cortisol, human Chromogranin A (CgA), alpha-amylase, Dehydroepiandrosterone (DHEA), Dehydroepi-androsterone sulfate (DHEA-S), and testosterone (TE) has been frequently employed (Deguchi, 2006; Bosch, 2002; Michael, 2000; Nakane, 1999; Kirschbaum, 1994).

The reaction mechanism of the substances against the human mental stress is considered in relation with the human physiological stress reaction pathways. The existing two internal stress reaction pathways are namely: (1) hypothalamus-pituitary-adrenal (HPA) and (2) sympatho-adrenal-medullary (SAM) system (Kirschbaum, 1994) as shown in Figure 1. These seven biomarkers are considered to be released into the blood or other secretory fluid and therefore reflecting the activation of either reaction pathways: IgA, CgA, and amylase are considered to reflect SAM activation, and cortisol, DHEA, DHEA-S, and TE are considered to reflect HPA activation.

The purpose of PNEI study is to investigate the activations of these two systems under various stressful situations using secretory hormones and immune substances as a new objective measurement of human mental states. In the following contents, two major biomarkers in the present PNEI study, IgA and cortisol are described with reviewing past PNEI studies.

Salivary Immunoglobulin A (IgA)

Immunoglobulin A (IgA) is one of the most important substances in human immune system (Tsujita, 1999). It is present in almost all human secretory fluids, such as saliva, serum, urine, breast milk et al. IgA works non-specifically and therefore plays a very important role on our health, e.g., preventing bacteria from forming colonies, neutralizing toxins and enzymes produced by bacteria, and inhibiting pathogenic viruses from penetrating into the epithelial cell. This is the reason why IgA, especially the one contained in saliva, called as "the first line of defense" against the influenza or other respiratory tract infection (URTI) illnesses. In fact, clinical studies have suggested the negative correlation between the level of salivary IgA and the incidence of an acute URTI (Jemmott III, 1989). It was also reported the relevance between the level of salivary IgA and caries or periodontitis (Gregory, 1992).

On the other hand, by the 70's behavioral medicine studies, it has been found that salivary IgA changes its level accompanying with various types of psychological factors (Bosh, 2002), such as desirable or undesirable daily events (Stone, 1994), daily hassles (Martin, 1988), negative or positive moods (Martin, 1993), academic stresses such as examination (Jemmott III, 1983) and presentation (Evans, 1994), a short-term stressful cognitive task (Jemmott III, 1989), and relaxation (Green, 1987; Knight, 2001). A review article has

concluded that there are two distinguishable types of stress effects on IgA: 1) increasing IgA secretion immediately after a short-term stress, termed "immediate stress effect", and 2) decreasing IgA secretion several days after or during a long-term stress, termed "delayed stress effect" (Tsujita, 1999). IgA transient secretion by a short-term stress is considered to be regulated by autonomous nervous system (Valdimarsdottir, 1997). Thus it can be taken as a biomarker for SAM system. The change in IgA level during longer period, by contrast, is considered to reflect the change in productivity by long-term stress. Thus it can reflect some sort of longer physiological change derived by long-term stress while it is not necessary to consider reflections on the HPA system.

However, even though the immediate stress effect has been successfully observed by almost all studies targeting on a variety of short-term stressors, the delayed stress effect has not yet been directly observed. A review paper on IgA studies pointed out that studies targeting on a long-term stress had methodological defects such as less control of subjects' physical conditions such as sleep and diet, using inappropriate saliva sampling methods, and introducing non-standardized psychological questionnaires (Bosh, 2002). Moreover, considering the feasibility of which the delayed stress effects might be easily masked by the immediate stress effect, IgA can be a useful stress marker for a short-term stress rather than long-term stress.

There are also studies focusing on the effects of various relaxing factors. Those studies also reported the increase on IgA level is the same as with stress short-term studies. However, because few attempts have been made to investigate the effects of such relaxing factors with/under stressful situation (Valdimarsdottir, 1997), it is not clear whether such an increase on IgA level induced by relaxing factor would be brought from the same physiological mechanism as the immediate stress effect. Some studies investigated on the effect of "psycho-social support", which is an idea encompassed with the quality of life (QOL) regarding with personal relationships in the society, and reported the interventions on IgA secretion against long-term (Jemmott III, 1988) and short-term (Ohira, 2004) stressors.

Salivary Cortisol

Cortisol is the most potent glucocorticoid produced and secreted from adrenal cortex playing a quite important role for maintain our body, e.g., keeping blood glucose level adequately. Cortisol levels can be measured in serum, urine, and saliva. Because cortisol is considered to be released into blood stream via activation of HPA system and a significant positive correlation has been obtained between salivary and blood cortisol, therefore salivary cortisol is assumed as a possible stress biomarker.

In the past cortisol studies, a transient increase of salivary cortisol was observed by short-term stressors, such as mental arithmetic, stroop task, and oral presentation (Dickerson, 2004; Kirschbaum, 1994). It was reported that salivary cortisol also increased daily and/or chronic stressful events, such as job stress (Steptoe, 2000), job loss (Ockenfels, 1995), and divorce (Powell, 2002). Moreover, recently the cortisol released just after awaking is reported to be a suitable measure of chronic stress (Izawa, 2007). Therefore salivary cortisol can be a possible short-term and long-term stress marker.

However as for a stress biomarker, the precise stress responses of salivary cortisol against variety of stressors and its robustness have not yet been fully understood. For an instance, cortisol has been consistently reported to increase against such stressors accompanying with strong tension or threat, whereas it sometimes showed inconsistent result against rather "mild" stressors such as simple arithmetic task or cognitive task (Dickerson, 2004). Some methodological explanations have been made on this discrepancy such as variety of biochemical analysis, saliva collection method,

and subject control. Among that, the variety of the timing of saliva sampling has been frequently indicated, including the past PNEI studies with other biomarkers (Hansen, 2008; Dickerson, 2004; Bosch, 2002; Valdimarsdottir, 1997; Kirschbaum, 1994). Also it should be noted that because the stress reaction of HPA system is truly complicated and potentially mediated by variety of physiological factors, the salivary cortisol cannot be taken as a direct measure of HPA system itself but as rather an "indirect" measure (Hellhammer, 2009).

Other Biomarkers

There are kinds of other substances which are considered to be possible stress/relaxing biomarkers. Dehydroepiandrosterone (DHEA) and Dehydroepiandrosterone sulfate (DHEA-S) is a steroid adrenal cortex hormone like cortisol. Thus it can be a biomarker for HPA system. However, it is considered to function antagonistically with cortisol on the central nervous system and immune system (Wolf, 1999). Few studies have used DHEA to assess the chronic stress; further, depression has been suggested to be associated with low DHEA levels (Izawa, 2008; Michael, 2000).

Chromogranin A (CgA) is known to be released from the adrenal medulla into the blood with catecholamine. Therefore it is considered to be a possible biomarker of SAM system (Winkler, 1992; Nakane, 1999). Its level has been reported to transiently increase in response to short-term stressors such as a calculation test (Nakane, 1999), white noise (Miyakawa, 2006), and a cognitive test (Kanamaru, 2006). On the contrary a recent study showed a transient increase in the CgA level after watching a comic video (Toda, 2007). This study also indicated that the elevation in CgA levels was remarkable in the subjects who experienced lower daily stress.

Alpha-amylase is known to increase along with the activation of sympathetic nervous system mediated via beta-receptor (Stegeren, 2006). Therefore it is also considered to be a possible biomarker of SAM system (Bosch, 2002). Yamaguchi (2004) developed a dry-chemistry devise for quantitative determination of Alpha-amylase. However it is suggested that the activation of parasympathetic nervous system also results in a transient increase of Alpha-amylase (Bosch, 2002).

Free-3-mehoxy-4-hydroxyphenylglycol (free-MHPG) (Buchsbaum, 1981) and testosterone was reported to show transient increase by short-term stressors, while the number of studies targeting on these substances are very small.

Summary of Biomarkers

In the current PNEI studies, it is suggested that the salivary biomarkers can be taken as a possible objective stress measurement. All abovementioned biomarkers show transient increase against short-term stressor by indirectly reflecting human physiological stress reaction pathway, HPA or SAM system. However, because PNEI is relatively a new interdisciplinary study, some basic problems remain unsolved such as sensitivity of these biomarkers against variety of stressful and relaxing factors, precise change of the secretion of biomarkers in the time series, the effects of long-term stress or daily stressful situation which might be reflecting the change in the production speed of these biomarkers rather than a temporal change in the secretion.

3. METHODS OF BIOMARKER STUDIES

Here described are the methods of biomarker studies, its experimental designs, subjects control, preparation of stressors, analysis of biomarkers, etc., which will help students and scientists who are newly entering the field

Saliva Sampling Method

Saliva samples have been collected frequently by "Salivette", which is made of dense plain cotton of a cylindrical shape about 1 cm wide and 3.5 cm long. Salivette is designed for one-time saliva sampling and mostly introduced in diagnosis uses. In other words, it is not suitable for sampling methods of repetitive collection. It has high absorbability and thus deprives far more amount of saliva (around 2 mL per one sampling for 3 minute) for that of necessary to quantitative determination of biomarkers (at most 50 µL of saliva for one biomarker). Excessive saliva collection brings forth the lack of saliva and, as a result, disturbs normal saliva flow. A past study dealing with this problem showed that the repetitive saliva collection in every 5 minutes results in the decrease of saliva volume by sampling time and also the concentration of salivary IgA (Nomura, 2006). Therefore the use of Salivette in case of repetitive sampling is not recommended.

The passive drawing or the use of small cotton is recommended in case of repetitive sampling. The passive drawing is technically ideal method for saliva sampling comparing with the use of cotton, because some substances are known to be absorbed in the cotton. However it requires training session to get used to drawing saliva into small cup or container. Also it might be uncomfortable for some subjects to take saliva in this way. Taking saliva by small cotton is easiest method. Although a certain amount of biomarkers would be absorbed, it might be excluded when one focuses on the relative change in the level of biomarkers. It is important to prepare the same size and volume of cotton in the repetitive sampling, because these would affect the volume of saliva collection. Also the small cotton should be placed under the subjects' tongue so as to collect the fresh saliva.

Experimenter should pay attention in handling the sample saliva to avoid contingent infection of virus or other possible diseases. All experimenters should ware disposable gloves and glasses. The saliva samples should be kept in the freezer below -20 Celsius by the day of the quantitative determination of biomarkers.

Saliva Sampling in the Experimental Design

Because most of biomarkers have diurnal change; the highest level is in the morning and gradually decreases afterwards to the lowest level in the night time, experiments with saliva sampling should be conducted in the afternoon where the secretion of biomarkers are expected to be stable. Postprandial effects on the secretion of biomarkers are considerable. Also pH of saliva could affect the quantitative determination of biomarkers. Therefore subjects are required not to take any food or drink except for water at least an hour prior to the experiment. Hard exercise should be avoided prior to the experiment, because it could also elevate some biomarkers. Moreover it is strongly recommended to take 10 to 30 minutes of an initial rest period before conducting experiment. If subjects were not familiar with or nervous about the experiment, most of biomarkers would be increased by such a negative feeling or strain. Subjects who take any medications, suffer from any disease, are pregnant, or other cases in which physiological states were considered to be unusual should be excluded.

Subjects must be well informed about the objective and method of the experiment. Any experimental design targeting on human mental or physical stress should be approved by a local ethics committee or equivalent organization.

Quantitative Determination of Salivary Biomarkers

The concentrations of salivary biomarkers have frequently been determined by enzyme-linked immunosorbent assay (ELISA). ELISA is nowadays one of major molecular determination techniques.

It is much easier in treatment and cheaper in running cost than other molecular determination techniques, such as the radioimmunoassay (RIA) and the high performance liquid chromatography (HPLC). The treatment of radioactive substance is needed to assess biomarkers by RIA. The cost of determination by HPLC is higher than ELISA for small numbers of samples. Moreover several products which are designed for determination of "salivary" biomarkers, not for blood and/or urine, are provided (e.g., Salivary Secretory IgA Indirect Enzyme Immunoassay Kit, Salimetrics, LLC., USA). By using such a ELISA kit in which all specimens and materials are included, experimenter can easily assay various biomarkers with a minimum knowledge of biochemical analysis.

The principle of ELISA is based on the antigen-antibody reaction which is for capturing a target substance and the enzyme reaction which is for detecting the mass of a target substance via optical density of reaction produced color. The brief description of ELISA (competitive method) is as follows; (1) Thaw saliva samples kept in a biological freezer by moving then into a biological refrigerator (4 Celsius). (2) Centrifuge each saliva samples for 10 minutes at 1500 rpm to precipitate mucins or other solid contents. (3) Add each saliva sample (or known samples for references) into antibody-coated 96-well micro-plate. (4) Add a constant amount of "enzyme conjugate" which is the target biomarker (antigen) combined with horseradish peroxidase (HRP) into the micro-plate and incubate for an hour. In this step, antigen-antibody reaction is occurred competitively between original target in the saliva sample and that in the enzyme conjugate. (5) Wash the micro-plate to flush unbind target. (6) Add TMB (tetramethylbenzidine) solution to induce enzyme reaction with enzyme conjugate which is captured by antigen coated on the bottom of each well of the micro-plate in the step (4). The amount of the bind enzyme conjugate, which is there as a result of competitive reaction process, can be detected as the strength of optimal color

(450nm) cased by enzyme reaction. Therefore this optimal density is inversely proportional to the concentration of target containing in the original saliva sample. (7) Finally, the target concentration in each sample is determined by referencing the optimal density of the reference samples. All analysis procedures take roughly about 3 to 5 hours for one micro-plate. Correct handling of samples and specimens with well calibrated micropipette is critical for all steps.

4. PENI EXPERIMENTAL PROCEDURE AND THE RESPONSE OF BIOMARKERS AGAINST A SHORT-TERM STRESSOR

In this section, the experimental results of our past studies targeting the response of salivary IgA and cortisol against a short-term stressor are reviewed (Nomura, 2006; Nomura 2009). It will provide concrete and practical information on how a biomarker experiment should be designed and conducted and what is expected to be obtained.

Objectives of the Experiment

As described above, in the current PNEI studies variety of salivary substances are considered to be possible biomarkers. However, because PNEI is relatively a new interdisciplinary study, some basic problems remain unsolved. Especially the responses of biomarker (e.g., cortisol) against rather a "mild" stressor have shown inconsistent results in the past studies (Dickerson, 2004). However few studies have ever assessed the precise change of the secretion of biomarkers in the time series. That means if a transient increase of the biomarker derived by a given stressor occur with a certain time delay and saliva samples were collected at inappropriate timing, it would be difficult to obtain a statistically significant difference in a change in biomarkers. Therefore the objective of this experiment is to investigate 1) the precise

stress response of IgA and cortisol in the time series and 2) a congruity of IgA and cortisol as a biomarker for a "mild" mental workload.

Subjects

In our experiment, healthy male university students were frequently recruited. Subjects should follow all the instruction as described above.

A Short-Term Stressful Task

In these experiments, subjects were instructed to perform a simple calculation task as a short-term stressful experience. The calculation task was a simple addition of two double-digit integers, and it was repeatedly presented on a laptop monitor (12.1 inch thin film transistor-liquid crystal display, DELL Inc., USA) every 3.0 seconds with changing the figures. Subjects were instructed to perform this calculation task as correct as possible. Such a simple calculation task is quite similar to so-called Kraepelin psychodiagnostic test, which is frequently introduced for the researches investigating the effects of the mental stress on physiological indices.

Experiments

Two schedule of task/break experimental designs were prepared for this study: 1) in the experiment A, subjects were instructed to perform two sets of 18 minutes of the calculation tasks (T) and 9 minutes of break (B) after that, thus the schedule was as 18(T)-9(B)-18(T)-9(B), and 2) in the experiment B, there were six sets of 6 minutes of the calculation tasks and 3 minutes of break after that, thus the schedule was as 6(T)-3(B)-6(T)-3(B)-6(T)-3(B)-6(T)-3(B)-6(T)-3(B)-6(T)-3(B). Note that the total duration of the calculation and break was 36 and 18 minutes in both experiments. Each subject daily experienced one of these experimental procedures.

Saliva samples were taken by small cotton every three minutes during the calculation tasks and breaks. Saliva was also taken 3, 10 and 20 minutes after the last set of calculation/break. Subjects were instructed to place the cotton under his tongue, not to chew, for three minutes. These cottons were centrifuged at 1500 rpm for 10 minutes to remove mucin, and stored in freezing chamber at –20 Celsius by the day on the quantitative analysis.

Each experiment A and B were conducted in the afternoon for reducing the influence of the diurnal change of biomarkers. The order of these experiments was counterbalanced among the subjects. All the experimental procedures were conducted in a dark and soundproof room one by one.

Physiological and Psychological Measures

Electrocardiogram (ECG) was recorded by a bio-amplifier in 500 Hz (BMS-3201, Nihon-Kohden Co.). By frequency analysis of ECG data, high frequency (0.15-0.40Hz; HF) and low frequency (0.04-0.15Hz; LF) power were found for estimating the autonomous nervous system (ANS) activities. HF and LF/HF rate have frequently been used for the measure of parasympathetic and sympathetic nervous system activity. Salivary cortisol concentration was determined by Enzyme-linked immunosorbent assay (ELISA)

With regard to the psychological test, subjects were required to fill up a "profile of mood state" (POMS) (Japanese version) before the arithmetic task (Yokoyama, 1993). POMS is one of the major questionnaires frequently introduced various psychological studies (McNair, 2003). It consists of 65 items asking about subjects' mood with 5 point scale: not at all, a little, moderately, quite a lot, and extremely. These items are designed to classify into the six identified mood factors: tension-anxiety (T-A), depression-dejection (D), anger-hostility (A-H), fatigue-inertia (F), vigor-activity (V), and confusion-bewilderment (C).

The score of each mood factors is calculated by adding the corresponding items.

Results of the Experiments

POMS and Behavior

Regarding with POMS, only the factor V (vigor-activity) among six mood factors decreased after the arithmetic tasks ($p<.05$, t-test). On the other hand, the task performance, e.g., accuracy and speed of calculation did not show any statistically significant change for six of task period.

Taking these results of POMS and task performance into account, the arithmetic task we introduced for this experiment can work as a "mild" mental workload for participants as we intended.

Profile of IgA

Salivary IgA concentration changes according to the task/break schedule in the experiment A and B, as shown in Figure 2(a) and 2(b). This simple fact demonstrates the congruity of IgA as for a biomarker of a short-term and mild stressor.

In the experiment A, IgA increases immediately after the calculation task and decreases when the task discontinued. In addition, interestingly, the average IgA concentration during the second set of the calculation task in the experiment A was higher than that of the first set ($p<.01$, t-test). That could happen in the case of which the duration of the first break would be not enough to recover for the IgA to the baseline. In experiment B, IgA slightly increases and decreases repeatedly along with the six sets of the task/break. Unlike in the experiment A, the integration of IgA was not observed in the experiment B.

On the other hand, autonomous nervous system (ANS) indices found by ECG signals (HR, HF, and LF/HF) has not showed such an accumulative change in the time series. On the contrary it was changing more like ON/OFF binary response according to task and break periods. Moreover

Figure 2. IgA concentration (a) in the experiment A and (b) experiment B. Error bar indicates standard error. The period indicated as in the gray band represents the calculation task periods

(a)

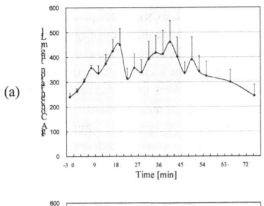

(b)

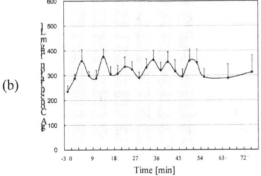

no clear correlation was found among IgA, ANS indices, and saliva flow rate. Therefore the accumulative increase of salivary IgA concentration observed in the experiment A was not merely as a result of the change in saliva flow rate, which is thought to be mediated by the changes in ANS activities, but rather naïve stress response of IgA.

Comparing with the result in experiment A and B, the average baseline of IgA had no significant difference, whereas the average IgA concentration during all through the experiment A was significantly higher than that of the experiment B ($p<.01$, t-test). The differences of the IgA secretion profiles in the experiment A and B are rather intriguing; because the whole task/break periods and its rate (2:1) were the same in both experiments A and B.

It could happen by a nonlinear feature of the IgA secretion depending on the duration of the task. Not only the IgA secretion but also its secretion rate (speed) might increase depending on the duration of the task. That would bring the high IgA concentration in the first set of task period in experiment A. Consequently, it resulted in the accumulative modulation of the IgA because the duration of the intermediate break would not be enough to recover the IgA to the baseline in the experiment A. Therefore, the IgA changing profile in the time series could reflect both the duration and schedule of task/ break.

Seen from another point, it implies that a certain amount of a mild stressor (or that is to say as "mental workload") during a certain period would not necessarily result in the equivalent physiological stress response. In fact, the average IgA during experiment A was significantly higher than that of during B, while the total task/break periods were as the same in both experiments A and B. Therefore, by referring such an accumulative change of IgA in the time series, the physiological effects induced by all different types of long-lasting and intermittent mental workloads can be possibly evaluated. As a whole, our experimental results suggested that the IgA could be a possible stress biomarker upon two aspects: (1) transient short term stress marker and (2) long-lasting or recursive stress marker.

Profile of Cortisol

The accumulative changing profile of salivary biomarker was more remarkable in the profile of cortisol than IgA. The salivary cortisol concentration depicted an accumulative increase all through the task/break schedule even in the experiment B as shown in Figure 3. Moreover it has not recovered to the baseline even by 20 min of the rest period after the task. Autonomous nervous system indices (HR, HF, and LF/HF) and saliva flow rate have no clear correlation with cortisol like as IgA. As abovementioned, there are too physiological stress

Figure 3. Cortisol concentration in the experiment B. Error bar indicates standard error. The period indicated as in the gray band represents the calculation task periods

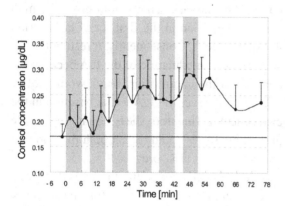

reaction pathways, SAM and HPA, and salivary cortisol is considered to be one of an indirect measure of HPA system activity (Hellhammer, 2009; Dickerson, 2004). Therefore it is natural that cortisol showed such an independent profile from ANS indices.

The accumulative increase of cortisol in our experiment plausibly demonstrates the possible candidacy of cortisol as a biomarker for a "mild" mental workload. In the past cortisol studies, the stress responses of cortisol against rather "mild" stressors, which are as typified by the cognitive tasks without any threat or performance pressure (e.g., passive stroop task and mental arithmetic task), showed inconsistent result, while the stress responses against "acute" stressors such as oral presentation with psychological evaluation (e.g., job interview) showed consistent increase of salivary cortisol (Dickerson, 2004). We by contrast assessed the salivary cortisol every 3 min covering an hour of mental arithmetic task with intermissions and obtained the significant accumulative increase of cortisol concentration. Therefore it is suggested that the scope of application of cortisol as a stress biomarker could be dilatable to even "mild" mental stressors if only salivary

cortisol was assessed by an appropriate timing and duration corresponding to a particular target.

Discussion of the Experiments

The result of the experiments plausibly demonstrates the possible candidacy of IgA and cortisol as a biomarker for a short-term and mild stressful task. Moreover the accumulative changing profiles of these biomarkers are remarkable features in terms of the stress measurement.

In the fields of ergonomics, human interface, or other applied science and engineering, the estimation of mental stress has frequently been assessed by bioelectric indices, such as brain wave (electroencephalogram: EEG), eye movement (electrooculogram: EOG), heart beat (electrocardiogram: ECG), et al. These indices are strongly controlled under the influence of homeostasis. Generally speaking, these bioelectric responses are quite sensitive to the change of psychological state. Nevertheless, in other words, such bioelectrical responses are too fast to evaluate an accumulative affect of long-lasting stressors. For an example, imagine that one faces a stressor in a short period, such bioelectric indices would arise at the moment of the onset of stress and drop back to the base level immediately after the stressor is removed. There would be no accumulative effects even if such a short term stressor was repeated again and again. IgA, cortisol or biomarker, has an edge at this point. Therefore these biomarkers can be taken as a new metric for human mental stress which has different time constant range with conventional bioelectric stress measures.

5. KINETIC MODEL OF BIOMARKERS SECRETION AGAINST A SHORT-TERM STRESSOR

The result of our past study in which the biomarker secretion against a short-term stressor demonstrated an accumulative changing profile led the idea of slow and long-lasting stress response properties of these biomarkers. Subsequently in this section, we propose a mathematical model of such a biomarker response against intermittent type of a short-term stressor.

Basic Assumptions

The mathematical model proposed here consists of following 4 basic assumptions:

1. Biomarkers changes continuously, or gradually, in the time series

Biomarkers are released into a secretion fluid via trans-cytosis. Thus, the amount of biomarkers could change continuously with a certain time delay against stress exposure or removal.

2. Biomarker concentration increases by a stress exposure and decreases to the baseline by its removal.

The result of past PNEI studies have been clearly demonstrated this feature.

3. Biomarkers increase induced by stress exposure is in the nonlinear form regarding the duration of the stressor.

This assumption is led by our past studies. Considering the difference in the accumulative change in profiles between IgA and cortisol as described above, the rate of increase by the duration of the stressor must be different among biomarkers.

4. Biomarker secretion per unit time has lower and upper limits

All living organisms are assumed to possess some sort of self-regulating mechanism as called homeostasis.

Constitution of the Model

As a representation of the most simple and well-consistent with these assumptions, the logistic function is adopted as the basis of this model. The logistic function is a nonlinear ordinary differential equation consisting of the first order of exponential increasing term and the second order of nonlinear decreasing term, as in

$$\frac{dx}{dt} = (a - bx)x$$

where x, t, a, and b are all positive values representing the concentration of biomarker, time, and increasing and decreasing coefficient respectively. The logistic function, or growth curve, has been applied to represent the exponential growth in the number of bacteria, and its decaying caused by environmental deterioration accompanying with an increase of individual density. Moreover, it is the simplest model possessing the homeostatic property.

With regard to the recovering process, a simple exponential decreasing function is introduced, as in

$$\frac{dx}{dt} = -cx$$

where x, t, and c are all positive values representing the concentration of biomarker, integration constant, time, and decreasing coefficient, respectively. The response of biomarker, increase by a short-term stressor and decrease by its removal, was simulated with the same task/break schedule as in the experiment A and B described above.

Result of the Simulation

Figure 4(a) and 4(b) shows the results of the simulation. As we had expected our model, which was designed based on the aforementioned naïve assumptions, successfully illustrated the accumu-

Figure 4. Result of the simulation corresponding to (a) the experiment A and (b) experiment B. Each upper, middle, and lower line is found by the same parameters in (a) and (b), respectively

(a)

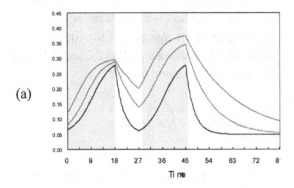

(b)

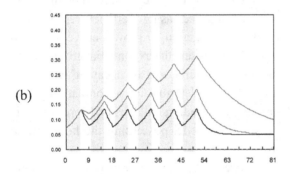

lative changing profile of biomarkers. Moreover by solely changing the increasing and decreasing parameters, *a*, *b*, and c, the degree of such accumulative effects could be changed; actually it was observed in our experiment as the difference in the accumulative changing profile of IgA and cortisol. Therefore the simple nonlinear kinetic model proposed here can be assumed as a basis for the stress induced physiological response in our body. By elaborating this model though a series of experiments targeting on the variety of stressors with different schedule on various biomarkers, the dynamics of human stress reaction pathways, HPA and SAM systems, would be better understood.

On the other hand, such a model can lead to the idea of an estimation of an optimal work/break schedule in the limited time. For instance, when one has to take a long-distance drive and reach at a destination within a limited period of time, one could estimate the optimal timing of the stop for the rest. Also it can be useful for a stress management in the working place, such as VDT workload and monitoring work. The molecular analysis techniques are advancing day by day, real-time monitoring of such a tiny amount of biomarkers might be available in the near future. Remember the difficulty of self-management of the stress and the necessity of introducing objective criteria, as mentioned above. Biomarkers introduced in this manuscript can be a possible solution, even though it remains in the initial step as a research field.

6. LIMITATIONS AND FUTURE WORK

There must be uncountable potential mediators affecting the IgA change, e.g., personality, chronic stress, sex, and age. For an instance, subjects categorized in Type A trait, who are typically represented as short tempered and strong hostile, showed higher baseline of IgA and lower reactivity of IgA against an acute stressor (Ohira, 1999). Moreover, the idea of controllability against an acute stress unconsciously determined the salivary IgA (Ohira, 2001). These studies suggest that the higher cognitive process could mediate the IgA secretion. However, the number of studies targeting these potential mediators remains small, it is necessary to investigate this in future works.

A recent and presently undergoing integrative PNEI research for assessing all different types of biomarkers in blood, such as active natural killer (NK) cell level, varieties of T lymphocyte, dopamine, norepinephrine, and epinephrine, shows a rapid change in the composition of those substances (e.g., Kimura, 2005; Isowa, 2004). It provides quite important information for the better understanding of the human psycho-physiological stress reaction. However such a multi-assessing study is still at its infancy. Far more research needs to be conducted for more discussion.

7. CONCLUSION

In this chapter, we focused on a new biomarker research as a new metric for human mental stress, its background, methods, experiments, and kinetic model approaches were also introduced. Although there are numbers of technical limitation and problems to be solved with regard to the new approach, biomarkers introduced in this manuscript can be a useful and unique measures for human mental states.

Stress estimation by salivary biomarkers has great methodological advantage, because saliva can be collected less-stressfully and in a noninvasive manner unlike blood and urine. Also it is the one and the only secretory fluid that can be collected at anytime and by anyone.

With regard to the *Kansei*, the biomarker research encompasses the idea of *Kansei* measurements. As mentioned above, human secretory biomarkers unconsciously change in responding to one`s psychological state. Moreover they possibly change against not only perceptible psychological states like "stress" but also imperceptible and/ or unverbalized states like "controllability". The Japanese word Kansei is a comprehensive notion encompassing with the idea of emotion, cognition, affection, perception, awareness et al. Biomarkers can reflect all these human psychological and cognitive states. Therefore the biomarker studies will provide an all-new methodology for the researches on Kansei Science and Kansei Engineering.

REFERENCES

Ader, R., Felten, L., & Cohen, N. (Eds.). (2001). *Psychoneruoimmunology* (3rd ed.). Academic Press.

Bosch, J. A., Ring, C., de Geus, E. J., Veerman, E. C., & Amerongen, A. V. (2002). Stress and secretory immunity. *International Review of Neurobiology*, *52*(1), 213–253. doi:10.1016/ S0074-7742(02)52011-0

Buchsbaum, M. S., Muscettola, G., & Goodwin, F. K. (1981). Urinary MHPG, stress response, personality factors and patients with major affective disorders. *Neuropsychology*, *7*, 212–224.

Deguchi, M., Wakasugi, J., Ikegami, T., Nanba, S., & Yamgaguchi, M. (2006). Evaluation of driver stress using motor-vehicle driving simulator. *IEEJ Trans. Sensors and Micromachines*, *126*, 438–444. doi:10.1541/ieejsmas.126.438

Dickerson, S. S., & Kemeny, M. E. (2004). Acute stressors and cortisol responses: A theoretical integration and synthesis of laboratory research. *Psychological Bulletin*, *130*(3), 335–391. doi:10.1037/0033-2909.130.3.355

Evans, P., Bristow, M., Hucklebridge, F., Clow, A., & Pang, F. Y. (1994). Stress, arousal, cortisol and secretory Immunoglobulin A in students undergoing assessment. *The British Journal of Clinical Psychology*, *33*, 575–576.

Gabriel, P., & Liimatainen, M. R. (2000). Mental health in the workplace. *International Labor Organization*. Retrieved August 1, 2009, from http://ilo.org

Green, R. G., & Green, M. L. (1987). Relaxation increases salivary Immunoglobulin A. *Psychological Reports*, *61*, 623–629.

Gregory, R. L., Kim, D. E., Kindle, J. C., Hobbs, L. C., & Lloyd, D. R. (1992). Immunoglobulin-degrading enzymes in localized juvenile periodontitis. *Journal of Periodontal Research*, *27*(3), 176–183. doi:10.1111/j.1600-0765.1992.tb01666.x

Hansen, A. M., Garde, A. H., & Persson, R. (2008). Source of biological and methodological variation in salivary cortisol and their impact on measurement among healthy adults: A review. *Scandinavian Journal of Clinical and Laboratory Investigation*, *68*(6), 448–458. doi:10.1080/00365510701819127

Hellhammer, D. H., Wüst, S., & Kudielka, B. M. (2009). Salivary cortisol as a biomarker in stress research. *Psychoneuroendocrinology*, *34*(2), 163–171. doi:10.1016/j.psyneuen.2008.10.026

Isowa, T., & Ohira, H. &d Murashima, S. (2004). Reactivity of immune, endocrine and cardiovascular parameters to active and passive acute stress. *Biological Psychology*, *65*, 101–120. doi:10.1016/S0301-0511(03)00115-7

Izawa, S., Shirotsuki, K., Sugaya, N., Ogawa, N., Suzuki, K., & Nomura, S. (2004). The application of saliva to an assessment of stress: procedures for collecting and analyzing saliva and characteristics of salivary substances. *Japanese Journal of Complementary and Alternative Medicine.*, *4*(3), 91–101. doi:10.1625/jcam.4.91

Izawa, S., Sugaya, N., Ogawa, N., Nagano, Y., Nakano, M., Nakase, E., et al. (2007). Episodic stress associated with writing a graduation thesis and free cortisol secretion after awakening. *International Journal of Psychophysiology*, *64*, 141-145.

Izawa, S., Sugaya, N., Shirotsuki, K., Yamada, K. C., Ogawa, N., & Ouchi, Y. (2008). Salivary Dehydroepiandrosterone secretion in response to acute psychosocial stress and its correlations with biological and psychological changes. *Biological Psychology*, *79*(3), 294–298. doi:10.1016/j.biopsycho.2008.07.003

Jemmott, J. B. III, Borysenko, J. Z., Borysenko, M., McClelland, D. C., Chapman, R., Meyer, D., & Benson, H. (1983). Academic stress, power motivation, and decrease in secretion rate of salivary secretory Immunoglobulin A. *Lancet*, *1*(8339), 1400–1402. doi:10.1016/S0140-6736(83)92354-1

Jemmott, J. B. III, & Magloire, K. (1988). Academic stress, social support, and secretory Immunoglobulin A. *Journal of Personality and Social Psychology*, *55*(5), 803–810. doi:10.1037/0022-3514.55.5.803

Jemmott, J. B. III, & McClelland, D. C. (1989). Secretory IgA as a measure of resistance to infectious disease: comments on Stone, Cox, Valdimarsdottir, and Neale. *Behavioral Medicine (Washington, D.C.)*, *15*, 63–71.

Kanamaru, Y., Kikukawa, A., & Shimamura, K. (2006). Salivary chromogranin-A as a marker of psychological stress during a cognitive test battery in humans. *Stress (Amsterdam, Netherlands)*, *9*(3), 127–131. doi:10.1080/14769670600909594

Kimura, K. (2005). Isowa, T., Ohira, H., & Murashima, S. (2005). Temporal variation of acute stress responses in sympathetic nervous and immune systesm. *Biological Psychology*, *70*, 131–139. doi:10.1016/j.biopsycho.2004.12.006

Kirschbaum, C., & Hellhammer, D. H. (1994). Salivary cortisol in psychoneuroendocrine research: recent developments and applications. *Psychoneuroendocrinology*, *19*(1), 313–333. doi:10.1016/0306-4530(94)90013-2

Knight, W. E., & Rickard, N. S. (2001). Relaxing music prevents stress-induced increase in subjective anxiety, systolic blood Pressure, and heart rate in healthy males and females. *Journal of Music Therapy*, *38*, 254–272.

Martin, R. A., & Dobbin, J. P. (1988). Sense of humor, hassles, and Immunoglobulin A: evidence for a stress-moderating effect of humor. *International Journal of Psychiatry in Medicine*, *18*, 93–105.

Martin, R. B., Guthrie, C. A., & Pitts, C. G. (1993). Emotional crying, depressed mood, and secretory Immunoglobulin A. *Behavioral Medicine (Washington, D.C.)*, *19*(3), 111–114.

McNair, M., Heuchert, P., & Shilony, E. (2003). *Profile of mood states Bibliography 1964-2002.* Multi-Health-Systems Inc.

Michael, A., Jenaway, A., Paykel, E. S., & Herbert, J. (2000). Altered salivary Dehydroepiandrosterone levels in major depression in adults. *Biological Psychiatry, 48*(10), 989–995. doi:10.1016/S0006-3223(00)00955-0

Miyakawa, M., Matsui, T., Kishikawa, H., Murayama, R., Uchiyama, I., Itoh, T., & Yoshida, T. (2006). Salivary Chromogranin A as a measure of stress response to noise. *Noise & Health, 8*(32), 108–113. doi:10.4103/1463-1741.33951

Nakane, H. (1999). Salivary Chromogranin A as index of psychosomatic stress response. *R&D Review of Toyota CRDL., 34*(3), 17-22.

Nomura, S., Mizuno, T., Nozawa, A., Asano, H., & Ide, H. (2009). Salivary cortisol as a possible physiological biomarker for mild mental workload. *Biofeedback Research., 36*(1), 23–32.

Nomura, S., Tanaka, H., & Moriyama, T. (2006). Pilot Study of SIgA as a Stress Maker with Repetitive Saliva Collection. *Proceedings of the 5th International Conference of the Cognitive Science*, 169-170.

Ockenfels, M. C., Porter, L., Smyth, J., Kirschbaum, C., Hellhammer, D. H., & Stone, A. A. (1995). Effect of chronic stress associated with unemployment on salivary cortisol: overall cortisol levels, diurnal rhythm, and acute stress reactivity. *Psychosomatic Medicine, 57*(5), 460–467.

Ohira, H. (2001). Controllability of aversive stimuli unconsciously determines volume of secretory Immunoglobulin A in saliva. *Japanese Journal of Behavioral Medicine, 6*, 16–28.

Ohira, H. (2004). Social support and salivary secretory Immunoglobulin A response in women to stress of making a public speech. *Perceptual and Motor Skills, 98*, 1241–1250.

Ohira, H., Watanabe, Y., Kobayashi, K., & Kawai, M. (1999). The Type A behavior pattern and immune reactivity to brief stress: change of volume of secretory Immunoglobulin A in saliva. *Perceptual and Motor Skills, 89*, 423–430. doi:10.2466/PMS.89.6.423-430

Powell, L. H., Lovallo, W. R., Matthews, K. A., Meyer, P., Midgley, A. R., & Baum, A. (2002). Physiologic markers of chronic stress in premenopausal, middle-aged women. *Psychosomatic Medicine, 64*(3), 502–509.

Steptoe, A., Cropley, M., Griffith, J., & Kirschbaum, C. (2000). Job strain and anger expression predict early morning elevations in salivary cortisol. *Psychosomatic Medicine, 62*(2), 286–292.

Stone, A. A., Neale, J. M., Cox, D. S., Napoli, A., Valdimarsdottir, H., & Kennedy-Moore, E. (1994). Daily events are associated with a secretory immune response to an oral antigen in men. *Health Psychology, 13*(5), 440–446. doi:10.1037/0278-6133.13.5.440

Toda, M., Kusakabe, S., Nagasawa, S., Kitamura, K., & Morimoto, K. (2007). Effect of laughter on salivary endocrinological stress marker Chromogranin A. *Biomedical Research, 28*(2), 15–18. doi:10.2220/biomedres.28.115

Tsujita, S., & Morimoto, K. (1999). Secretory IgA in saliva can be a useful stress maker. *Environmental Health and Preventive Medicine, 4*, 1–8. doi:10.1007/BF02931243

Valdimarsdottir, H. B., & Stone, A. A. (1997). Psychosocial factors and secretory Immunoglobulin A. *Critical Reviews in Oral Biology and Medicine, 8*(4), 461–474. doi:10.1177/10454411970080040601

van Stegeren, A., Rohleder, N., Everaerd, W., & Wolf, O. T. (2006). Salivary alpha amylase as marker for adrenergic activity during stress: effect of betablockade. *Psychoneuroendocrinology, 31*(1), 137–141. doi:10.1016/j.psyneuen.2005.05.012

Wakida, S., Tanaka, Y., & Nagai, H. (2004). High throughput screening for stress marker. *Bunseki, 2004*, 309–316.

Winkler, H., & Fischer-Colbrie, R. (1992). The chromogranins A and B: the first 25 years and future perspectives. *Neuroscience, 49*(3), 497–528. doi:10.1016/0306-4522(92)90222-N

Wolf, O. T., & Kirschbaum, C. (1999). Actions of Dehydroepiandrosterone and its sulfate in the central nervous system: Effects on cognition and emotion in animals and humans. *Brain Research. Brain Research Reviews, 30*(3), 264–288. doi:10.1016/S0165-0173(99)00021-1

Yamaguchi, M., Kanemori, T., Knemaru, M., Takai, N., Yasufumi, M., & Yoshida, H. (2004). Performance evaluation of salivary amylase activity monitor. *Biosensors & Bioelectronics, 20*, 491–497. doi:10.1016/j.bios.2004.02.012

Yokoyama, K., & Araki, S. (1993). *Nihongo ban POMS tebiki (the guide of profile of mood states Japanese version)* (5th ed.). Tokyo: Kaneko Shobo.

Chapter 18

Kansei's Physiological Measurement and its Application (2):
Estimation of Human States Using PCA and HMM

Santoso Handri
Nagaoka University of Technology, Japan

Shusaku Nomura
Nagaoka University of Technology, Japan

ABSTRACT

Physiological signals or biosignals are electrical, chemical, or mechanical signals that created by biological events such as a beating heart or a contracting muscle producing signals that can be measured and analyzed. These signals are generated from the metabolic activities of human internal organs. Therefore, in certain conditions, physiological signals have different pattern between healthy and unhealthy individuals. Based on this information, generally, physicians take some action and treat their patients. However, utilizing physiological signals is a new approach in Kansei engineering research fields for coping with human sensitivity. This study focuses on the possibility of physiological signal application in Kansei engineering.

1. BACKGROUND

Biosignals are signals that are created by biological events such as a beating heart or a contracting muscle. The electrical, chemical or mechanical activities that occur during these biological events often produce a signal that can be measured and analyzed (Escabi, 2005). Therefore, biosignals

might contain useful information that can be used to understand the relation between biological event and human feeling or perception.

Biosignals can be classified according to various characteristics of those signals; including the waveform shape, statistical structure, and temporal properties. Signals are first detected in a biological medium such as cell or on the skin's surface using a sensor. The sensor converts the

DOI: 10.4018/978-1-61692-797-4.ch018

physical measurand into an electric output and provides an interface between biological systems and electrical recording instruments. The type of biosignal determines what type of sensor will be used. ECGs, for example, are measured with electrodes that have a silver/silver chloride (Ag/AgCl) interface attached to the body that detects the movement of ions. It is very important that the sensor used to detect the biosignal of interest does not adversely affect the properties and characteristics of the signal being measured. After the biosignal has been detected with an appropriate sensor, it is usually amplified and filtered. Operational amplifiers are electronic circuits that are used primarily to increase the amplitude or size of a biosignals. Bioelectric signals, for instance, are often minute and require up to a thousand-fold boosting of their amplitude. An analog filter may then be used to remove noise or to compensate for distortions caused by the sensor. Analog-to-digital (A/D) converters are then used to transform biosignals from continuous analog waveforms to digital sequences. An A/D converter is a computer controller voltmeter, which measures an input analog signal and gives a numeric representation of the signal as its output. The analog waveform, originally detected by the sensor and subsequently amplified and filtered, is a continuous signal. The A/D converters transform the continuous analog signals into discrete digital signals. The discrete signals consist of a sequence of numbers that can easily be stored and processed on a digital computer. A/D conversion is particularly important in that, due to advances in computer technology, the storage and analysis of Biosignals is becoming increasingly computer based.

The operation principles of sensors for measuring signal generated by organs such as heart, brain or muscle are typically based on the potential difference between points (bio-potential), displacement measurement, and temperature difference or chemical substances. Below is description of several types of Biosignals obtained from Escabi, 2005:

Bioelectric Signals

Nerve and muscle cells generate bioelectric signals which result from electrochemical changes within and between cells. If a nerve or muscle cell is stimulated by a stimulus that is strong enough to reach a necessary threshold, the cell will generate an action potential. The action potential, which represents a brief flow of ions across the cell membrane, can be measured with intracellular or extracellular electrodes. Action potentials generated by an excited cell can be transmitted from one cell to adjacent cells via its axon. When many cells become activated, an electric field is generated which propagates through the biological tissue. These changes in extracellular potential can be measured by means of surface electrodes. The electrocardiogram (ECG), electroencephalogram (EEG), and electromyogram (EMG) are all examples of this phenomenon.

Biomagnetic Signals

Different organs, including the heart, brain, and lungs, also generate weak magnetic fields which can be measured with magnetic sensors. Typically, the strength of the magnetic field is much weaker than the corresponding physiological bioelectric signals. Biomagnetism is the measurement of the magnetic signals which are associated with specific physiological activity and are typically linked to an accompanying electric field from a specific tissue or an organ. With the aid of very precise magnetic sensors or SQUID magnetometers it is possible to directly monitor magnetic activity from the brain, peripheral nerves, and the heart.

Biochemical Signals

Biochemical signals contain information about changes in concentration of various chemical agents in the body. The concentration of various ions, such as calcium and potassium, in cells can be measured and recorded. Changes in the partial pressures of oxygen (pO2) and carbon dioxide (pCO2) in the respiratory system or blood are often measured to evaluate normal levels of blood oxygen concentration. All of these constitute biochemical signals. These biochemical signals can be used for a variety of purposes such as determining the level of glucose, lactate, and metabolites and by which providing information about the function of various physiological systems.

Biomechanical Signals

Mechanical functions of biological systems, which include motion, displacement, tension, force pressure, and flow, also produce measurable biosignals. Blood pressure, for example, is a measurement of the force that blood exerts against the wall of blood vessels. Changes in blood pressure can be recorded as a waveform. These upstrokes in the waveform represent the contraction of the ventricles of the heart as blood is ejected from the heart into the body and blood pressure increase to systolic pressure, and the maximum blood pressure.

2. ACQUSITION OF ECG SIGNAL

Biosignals can be acquired in a variety of ways, such as using stethoscope to listen to a patient's heart beat or with technologically advanced biosensors. Data acquisition equipment captures incoming signals and converts them into digital signals that can be processed with a computer. Following the data acquisition, biosignals are analyzed in order to retrieve useful information. Basic methods of signals analysis can be applied to many biosignals. These techniques are generally accomplished with simple electronic circuits or with digital computers. In addition to these common procedures, sophisticated digital processing methods are quite common and can significantly improve the quality of the retrieved data. These include signal averaging, wavelet analysis, and artificial intelligence techniques.

In this study we focus on electrocardiogram (ECG) signal processing. The ECG is an electrical signal generated by the heart's muscular activity. It is usually obtained by using electrodes attached to the skin across different areas of the heart. The placement of the electrodes determines the directional viewpoint of the heart. The standard ECG as recorded by clinicians is the 12-lead ECG, which uses 10 electrodes. A single-lead ECG recorder would typically have three electrodes: the positive electrode, the negative electrode and an indifferent electrode (ground or "right-leg" drive electrode).

Electrodes detect ionic current flow within the body by detecting the potential difference between them as current flows through the resistive tissues. An electrode is labeled as positive when the ECG recording shows a positive signal (upward deflection) corresponding to depolarization propagating towards it. Conversely, if the direction of depolarization is propagating away from it, the result would be a negative signal and will be represented on the ECG as a downward deflection. In nearly all ECG instruments, one electrode is always an indifferent electrode. The indifferent electrode is the "ground" reference of the instrument. While an indifferent electrode could be connected to the instrument ground, most often it would be connected to the output of an amplifier that generates a "right-leg drive" signal. This amplifier inverts and amplifies, generating a "right-leg drive" signal detected at the input electrodes. By feeding back this signal into the body, the common-mode signal at the input is reduced. This connection scheme is commonly referred to as right-leg drive as the electrode is usually attached to the right leg or an electrically equivalent location (Chee and Seow, 2007).

The electrocardiogram (ECG) signal (Figure 1) consists of three basic waves, P, QRS, and T. These waves correspond to the far field induced by specific electrical phenomena on the cardiac surface, namely the atrial depolarization (P wave), the ventricular depolarization (QRS complex), and the ventricular repolarization (T wave). In

Figure 1. Typical ECG signal

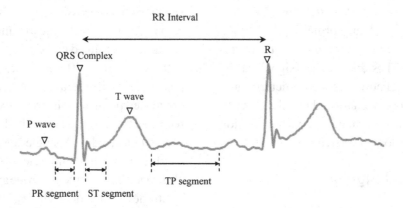

a normal cardiac cycle, the P wave occurs first, followed by the QRS complex and the T wave. The section of the ECG between the waves and complexes are called segments. The ECG is characterized by three segments namely the PR segment, the ST segment and the TP segment. The characteristic time periods in the ECG wave are PR interval, the RT interval and the R-R interval (Kannathal, *et al.*, 2007).

In general terms; the ECG signal is a useful tool for monitoring a patient with conditions of irregular heart rhythms, preventing myocardial infarctions, and diagnosis of ventricular ischemia or hypoxia. As it is well known, the heart rhythm varies according to a person's health, e.g., fatigue, effort, emotion, stress, disease, etc. (S"ornmo and Laguna, 2005).

3. OVERVIEW OF ECG SIGNAL AS FATIGUE INDICATOR

Night shift work has often been associated with increase in the degree and frequency of various psychologic complications. Psychologic disturbances were associated with altered cardiovascular and endocrine responses in healthy nurses after a night time work (Munakata, *et al.*, 2001). Spectral analysis could be a means of demonstrating impairment of autonomic balance of the purpose of detecting a state of fatigue that could result in over-training with a decrease in sympathetic vasomotor and a reduction in diastolic pressure (Portier, *et al.*, 2001). Smoking and overwork such as frequent business trips may amplify the autonomic dysfunction in relation to vital exhaustion (VE) among workers with a pronounced feeling of VE (Watanabe, *et al.*, 2002). It was found that a modulating effect of magnitopuncture on sympathetic and parasympathetic nerve activities in healthy subjects were associated with the acupuncture point. The findings represent physiological evidence that magnitopuncture may reduce mental fatigue in healthy drivers (Li, *et al.*, 2003). The effects of prolonged physical activities on resting heart rate variability (HRV) during a training session attended by cadets of French military academy were studied by Jouanin, *et al.*, 2004. These results suggest that parasympathetic nervous system activity increases with fatigue. It was shown that the modulating effect of acupuncture on heart rate variability not only depends on the points of stimulation such as acupuncture on non-acupuncture points but also on the functional state of the subjects, namely whether the subjects are in a state of fatigue or not (Li, *et al.*, 2006).

This study aims to evaluate mental health problems that are caused by extensive use of personal computer (PC) in various activities. A hike on the level of these activities might cause harmful mental health problems, especially those activities that depend heavily on a visual display terminal (VDT).

4. THE EXPERIMENT PROCEDURE

Subjects

Nine male students between 21 - 23 years olds voluntarily participated in the experiment. Personal data were acquired with a standardized interview before recording physiological information. They did not have any health problem during the experimental period, and that they were not being under any medication. Smoking and hard exercise were also prohibited before the experiment. None of them reported with any cardiovascular disease or neurological disorders in the past. This experiment was conducted in conformity with the Helsinki Declaration. All subjects were well-informed regarding the purpose and the contents of the experiment. The informed consent was obtained before their participation. They were also informed that they had the right to renounce their participation anytime.

Experimental Procedure

Participants were comfortably seated facing an LCD display at about 50 cm distance. A simple calculation task with a laptop computer was taken as a mental workload in this experiment. It is a simple addition of two double-digit integers. These integers were repeatedly presented on the laptop monitor every 3.0 sec with changing figures. The subjects were instructed to input the answer of the addition problem by keyboard as fast and as correct as possible. Such a simple calculation task is quite similar to the so-called *Kraepelin psychodiagnostic* test which has frequently been introduced for

Figure 2. The experiment schedules

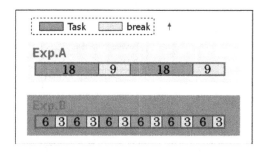

researches investigating physiological responses induced by mental stress. Moreover, the task has typical features of a common mental workload in our daily life such as routine, simple, boring, and unlimited. Thus, the result of the experiment is expected to be a practical model of mental workload in our daily life.

The experiment consisted of two schedules of intermittent calculation tasks: subjects were instructed (1) to conduct two sets of 18 min calculation tasks with 9 min of intermediate breaks (experiment A) and (2) to conduct 6 sets of 6 min tasks with 3 min of breaks between the tasks (experiment B). It should be noted that the total duration of the calculation tasks and breaks was 54 minute in total for each participant doing each experiment as shown in Figure 2. In addition, the subjects were required to fill a profile of mood states (POMS) before and after each experiment. POMS is a measure of six identified mood factors, i.e., tension-anxiety (TA), depression-dejection (D), anger-hostility (A-H), vigor (V), fatigue (F), and confusion (C); it is commonly used for psycho-physiological studies.

Three types of physiological sensors were used during the experiment: electrocardiogram (ECG); electroencephalogram (EEG); and thermograph. The data were recorded using commercial BioPAC MP150 systems for ECG and EEG signal, while the thermograph that uses an infrared camera, monitored the temperature variations on the surface of the subjects' faces.

Figure 3. The conceptual mechanism for understanding human states condition

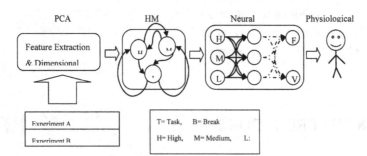

5. PCA AND HMM APPROACH FOR ESTIMATING HUMAN STATES

Reducing the Dimensions of Features Vector Using PCA

PCA is a statistical technique whose purpose is to condensate the information of a large set of correlated variables into a few principal components while not throwing overboard the variability present in the data set (Castells, *et al*, 2007). A recent application of the PCA in ECG signal processing is the robust feature extraction of various waveform properties for the purpose of tracking temporal changes due to myocardial ischemia (Stamkopoulus, *et al*., 1998). Historically, such tracking has been based on local measurements derived from the ST-T segment; however, such measurements are unreliable when the analyzed signal contains considerable amount of noise. With correlation as the fundamental signal processing operation, it has become clear that the use of principal components offer a more robust and global approach to the characterization of the ST-T segment. Signal separation during atrial fibrillation is another recent application of the PCA, the specific challenge being to extract the atrial activity so that the characteristics of this common arrhythmia can be studied without interference from the ventricular activity. Such separation is based on the fact that the two activities originate from different bioelectrical sources; separation may exploit temporal redundancy among suc-

cessive heartbeats as well as spatial redundancy when multilead recordings are analyzed (Laguna, *et al*., 1999, Jager, *et al*., 1992).

The principal components are derived as a linear combination of the variables of the data sets; with weights chosen so that the principal components become mutually uncorrelated. Each component contains new information about the data set, and is ordered so that the first few components account for most of the variability. The objective can be achieved by choosing to analyze only the first few factor principal components. In practice, the choice of the principal components is chosen so that the performance is clinically acceptable and that no vital signal information is lost. In this study, the first 12 principal components are determined by examining the proportion of the total variance over 90% explained by the principal component.

Evaluation Physiological Data Pattern Using Hidden Markov Model (HMM)

The main objective of this section is to develop models and techniques which can be applied in real time to track physiological signals and make inferences about the level of arousal of a particular subject. We envision this study being a useful building block that can be integrated into a computer that uses this information to adapt itself to the needs of the user as shown in Figure 3. This more ambitious idea goes beyond the present scope of this study but is a future research topic in this area.

Human physiology behaves like a complex dynamical system in which several factors, both internal and external, shape the outcome. In approximating such systems, we are interested in modeling its dynamical nature and given that knowledge of all the independent variables that affect the system is limited. We want to approach the problem in a stochastic framework that will help us model the uncertainty and variability that arise over-time. A class of models that has received much attention in the research community over the past years to model complex dynamic phenomena of a stochastic nature is the class of the Hidden Markov Models (HMM). HMMs have been widely used for modeling speech and gesture, and are currently an important block of speech recognition systems. Motivated by their flexibility in modeling a wide class of problem, we decided to study the feasibility of using HMMs to model physiological pattern that are believed to be correlated with different affective states.

A HMM is a stochastic state machine, characterized by the following parameter set:

$$\lambda = (A, B, \pi) \tag{1}$$

where A is the matrix of the state-transition probabilities, B is the observation probability, and π is the initial state probability. The observation of a HMM $0 = (0_1, 0_2, .., 0_T)$ are continuous signal representations, called feature vector, modeled by a Gaussian probability density function of the form:

$$b_j = \frac{1}{\sqrt{2\pi |U_j|}} \exp\left\{ -\frac{1}{2} \left(O_t - \mu_j \right)^T U_j^{-1} \left(O_t - \mu_j \right) \right\} \tag{2}$$

where 0_t is the observation vector at time t, μ_t is the mean vector, and U_j is the covariance matrix at state j. The estimated parameters are obtained by performing the likelihood maximization $P(0|\lambda)$

of the model λ using an iterative procedure such as Baum-Welch method (Rabiner, 1989).

The physiological signal generated by the human body might have strong correlation with the accumulation of the human states. The accumulation of human states may then be seen as one of the HMM problems. Thus, in this study, the HMM network are employed to estimate the accumulation of the human states based on the observed physiological information. The first stage is to build a system adapting the given data by training the HMM network. The purpose of the HMM training is to estimate the model parameters set $\lambda = (A, B, \pi)$ from the observation sequences data O. The HMM parameter estimation is carried out by Baum-Welch method which is similar to the expectation-maximization algorithms. The number of hidden states of the HMM is assumed having three states, i.e., high, medium, and low states. This categorization of hidden states is performed by clustering method, i.e., competitive learning algorithms based on the physiological data representative. This study only considers one Gaussian density function per state. After training, the HMM is then employed to evaluate the probabilities of the human states condition.

Neural Network

Neural Network with a back propagation learning algorithm is well known as a supervised classifier method and suitable for building adaptive pattern recognition system (Duda, Hart, and Stork, 2000). Mapping function of a neuron in a network can be written as

$$y = f_a \left(\sum_i^N w_i x_i + b \right) \tag{3}$$

where y is the output (in this study, the psychological information), f_a is activation function, w_i is weight of input x_i, i.e., output of HMM network, b is a bias term and N is the total number of inputs. In order to determine the mapping function, first,

Figure 4. POMS results of experiment A

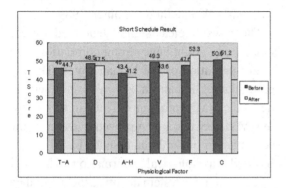

Figure 5. POMS results of experiment B

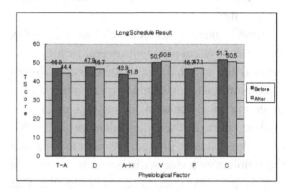

the network needs to be trained by using a sample data. Learning via back-propagation involves the presentation of pairs of input and output vectors. Among several activation functions of Neural Networks, this study uses the sigmoid function as the activation function for the hidden layers. The advantages of the sigmoid functions are that they are easier to train than threshold units, because of better smoothing function in a specific range input-output and they have upper and lower bounds. With the sigmoid function, a small change in the weights will usually produce a change in the outputs, which makes it possible to tell whether that change in the weights is good or not. The selection of an activation function of the output units should suit accordingly with the distribution of the target value. In this study, the identity or linear activation functions are employed.

In this work, Neural Network Toolbox of MATLAB was employed to make use of neural network for pattern recognition. The networks are composed of three layers. The epoch and the learning rate were set to 1000 and 0.01, respectively. The weights were initialized arbitrarily. Further, the network was trained by resilient back-propagation algorithm until the error between the desired and the actual outputs become lower than the threshold value or until the maximum epoch was reached. Once the weights have been determined, the network can be used as a classifier. The network structure was built based on the experiment by

testing several network models and the designed layers were confirmed as the effective network structure for this problem.

6. RESULTS

Subjective Evaluation of Human States

The questionnaire responses are evaluated by POMS method to measure psychological mood index as shown in Figure 4 and Figure 5 for experiment A and B, respectively. The self-report questionnaire reveals the subjects in the session of the pre-experiment and the post-experiment. POMS is a psychological test designed to measure a person's affective states. These include tension-anxiety (T-A), depression (D), anger-hostility (A-H), vigor (V), fatigue (F) and confusion (C). Unlike personality traits, profile mood states are thought to be transitory and specific to a given situation, although moods can also be measured for recent prolonged periods such as the past several months.

As shown in Figure 4 and Figure 5, there are interesting factors, i.e., vigor (V) and fatigue (F) which showed different scoring between experiment A and B. The "vigor" states represent the condition of your enthusiasm at the time of experiment conducted, while "fatigue" is the feeling of extreme tiredness or weakness that can make it difficult to perform an ordinary task. In this study, we are interested in the evaluation of the relationship between psychological mood indices, i.e., vigor and fatigue towards the physiological information.

Performance Evaluation of the Proposed System for Detecting Human States

It is believed that physiological information generated by the human body has strong relations with psychological conditions such as fatigue, vigor and others, which might associate correlation with sensitivity in the Kansei engineering fields. However, monitoring human states at different fractions of time is a difficult task to be performed, even by human. Thus, this study attempts to determine human states based on the psychological and physiological information by employing several information processing techniques.

First, the collected data were subject to analysis using statistical approach. The data were extracted from the segments of the three minute data for all signals. Ten statistical features were calculated for each segment of EEG signal and temperature, i.e., the mean, the standard deviation, the slope mean, the maximum and the minimum. To calculate heart rate variability (HRV) features, the instantaneous heart rate time series derived from ECG was used. The ratio of the low-frequency (LF) band (0.04 – 0.08 Hz) and the high-frequency (HF) band (0.15 – 0.5 Hz) were calculated to produce new data.

The LF/HF is used as an index of sympathetic to parasympathetic balance of heart rate fluctuation. The mean, the standard deviation, the slope mean, the maximum and the minimum of the ratio LF/HF were then used as features. HF is driven by respiration and appears to derive mainly from the parasympathetic nervous systems. The mean, the standard deviation, the slope mean, the maximum and the minimum of HF were used as final features in this experiment. There were 20 features, which

were used to create a single vector representing each of the segments used in the recognition analysis. In total, 324 segments were extracted from experiments A and B, i.e., 216 and 108 from the task and the rest periods respectively. The resulting 324 feature vectors were then analyzed by principal component analysis (PCA).

Second, the obtained feature vectors generated by PCA were reconstructed, so the extracted data belongs to each subject. There were 18 subjects in total. Each feature vector consisted of 12 features and 18 time series data. The extracted data was then set as the training data for HMM network. The parameters of the HMM network were estimated by the given training data.

The output of the HMM, i.e., high, medium, and low states was then used as input training for the neural network. The output of training data consists of psychological mood differences, i.e., vigor and fatigue, between pre-experiment and post-experiment. Then the same input training was employed to evaluate the trained network. The trained network revealed that the correlation coefficient (R) between the output 1 and the target 1 (vigor state) showed moderate result with R_1=0.6257 while the value of the correlation coefficient R_2 (fatigue state) was 0.4480, meaning that there are less variation between the output 2 and the target 2.

The mean absolute error of classification between the target and the output are 13.7% and 21.3% for vigor and fatigue, respectively, as shown in Table 1. Evaluating human states by the proposed method showed that the experiment B has lower psychological states i.e., "vigor" and "fatigue" than those of the experiment A. Demonstrating that the proposed method can distinguish

Table 1. The classification result

	Vigor	Fatigue
Correlation coefficient	0.6257	0.4480
Mean absolute error	13.70%	21.30%

the mental states based on the given task using physiological information, while statistical approach cannot give any differences.

The present study has showed promising results for evaluating human feeling towards the given task using physiological and psychological information, opening possibilities to build systems having the capability to predict human states condition in real time. However, further investigations are necessary to support our claim.

7. CONCLUSION

This study has proposed a method for estimating human states by understanding the physiological and the psychological information using information processing techniques. The results showed that the proposed systems are able to estimate the "Vigor State" in moderate level, and the "Fatigue State" in medium level. These results are promising for understanding the human state conditions more objectively.

However, finding a relationship between the physiological and the psychological information is difficult using the current method. It might be that, firstly, each person has a different capability when handling mental workload. Secondly, the proposed model is not sufficient enough for evaluating human state conditions. Thirdly, the subjective evaluation might not represent the real condition of a person.

This research is still a preliminary study about relations between accumulations of human states and psychological mood indices based on the given task. In the future, the systems which are able to explain relation between the physiological measurements (objective) and the psychological mood indices or human feelings (subjective) should be developed.

This information, in the future, could then be used automatically by the adaptive systems in various ways to help the person better cope with stress, fatigue or even for predicting the occurrence of unwanted events such as heart attack. The example of this might include adaptive systems which are able to analyze the stress level of a person, and give an alert or a suggestion to the person to take a break if required or even sending the critical information to hospital related to the person's condition.

REFERENCES

Castells, F., Laguna, P., Sörnmo, L., Bollmann, A., & Roig, J. M. (2007). Principal Component Analysis in ECG Signal Processing. *EURASIP Journal on Advances in Signal Processing.* 2007(1), 21 pages.

Chee, J., & Seow, S. C. (2007). *The electrocardiogram. U.R. Archarya, J.S. Suri, J.A.E. Spaan, and S.M. Krishnan, Advances in Cardiac Signal Processing.* Berlin: Springer-Verlag.

Duda, R. O., Hart, P. E., & Stork, D. G. (2000). *Pattern Classification (2nd)*. New York: Wiley-Interscience.

Escabi, M. A. (2005). Biosignal Processing. J. Enderle, S. Blanchard, and J. Bronzino, *Introduction to Biomedical Engineering*. Burlinton: Academic Press.

Jager, F. J., Mark, R. G., Moody, G., & Divjak, S. (1992). *Analysis of transient ST segment changes during ambulatory monitoring using the Karhunen-Lo`eve transform: Proceedings of Computers in Cardiology (CIC '92)*, 691–694, Durham, NC, USA.

Jounin, J. C., Dussault, C., Peres, M., Satabin, P., Pierard, C., & Guezennec, C. Y. (2004). Analysis of heart rate variability after a ranger training course. *Military Medicine, 169*(8), 583–587.

Kannathal, N., Rajendra, U., Joseph, P., Min, L. C., & Suri, J. S. (2007). *Analysis of electrocardiograms. U.R. Archarya, J.S. Suri, J.A.E. Spaan, and S.M. Krishnan, Advances in Cardiac Signal Processing*. Berlin: Springer-Verlag.

Laguna, P., Moody, G. B., Garc'ia, J., Goldberger, A. L., & Mark, R. G. (1999). Analysis of the ST-T complex of the electrocardiogram using the Karhunen-Lo`eve transform: adaptive monitoring and alternans detection. *Medical & Biological Engineering & Computing, 37*(2), 175–189. doi:10.1007/BF02513285

Li, Z., Jiao, K., Chen, M., & Wang, C. (2003). Effect of magnitopuncture on sympathetic and parasympathetic nerve activities in healthy driver – assessment by power spectrum analysis of heart rate variability. *European Journal of Applied Physiology, 88*(4-5), 404–410. doi:10.1007/s00421-002-0747-5

Li, Z., Wang, C., Mak, A. F., & Chow, D. H. (2005). Effect of acupuncture on heart rate variability in normal subjects under fatigue and non-fatigue state. *European Journal of Applied Physiology, 94*(5-6), 633–640. doi:10.1007/s00421-005-1362-z

Munakata, M., Ichi, S., Nunokawa, T., Saito, Y., Ito, N., Fukudo, S., & Yoshinaga, K. (2001). Influence of night shift work on psychologic state and cardiovascular and neuroendocrine responses in healthy nurses. *Hypertension Research, 24*(1), 25–31. doi:10.1291/hypres.24.25

Portier, H., Louisy, F., Laude, D., Berthelot, M., & Guezennec, C. Y. (2001). Intense endurance training on heart rate and blood pressure variability in runners. *Medicine and Science in Sports and Exercise, 33*(7), 1120–1125. doi:10.1097/00005768-200107000-00009

Rabiner, L. R. (1989). A Tutorial on Hidden Markov Models and Selected Applications in Speech Recognition. *Proceedings of the IEEE, 77*(2), 257–286. doi:10.1109/5.18626

S"ornmo, L., & Laguna, P. (2005). *Bioelectrical signal processing in cardiac and neurological applications*. New York: Academic Press.

Stamkopoulus, T., Diamantaras, K., Maglaveras, N., & Strintzis, M. (1998). ECG analysis using nonlinear PCA neural network for ischemia detection. *IEEE Transactions on Signal Processing, 46*(11), 3058–3067. doi:10.1109/78.726818

Watanabe, T., Sugiyama, Y., Sumi, Y., Watanabe, M., Takeuchi, K., Kobayashi, F., & Kono, K. (2002). Effects of vital exhaustion on cardiac autonomic nervous functions assessed by heart rate variability at rest in middle-aged male workers. *International Journal of Behavioral Medicine, 9*(1), 68–75. doi:10.1207/S15327558IJBM0901_05

Chapter 19

The China Brain Project:
An Evolutionary Engineering Approach to Building China's First Artificial Brain Consisting of 10,000s of Evolved Neural Net Minsky–Like Agents

Hugo de Garis
Xiamen University, China

Chen Xiaoxi
Xiamen University, China

Ben Goertzel
Novamente LLC, USA & Singularity Institute, USA & Xiamen University, China

ABSTRACT

This chapter describes a 4 year research project (2008-2011) to build China's first artificial brain. It takes an "evolutionary engineering" approach, by evolving 10,000s of neural net modules, (or "agents" in the sense of Minsky's "Society of Mind" [Minsky 1988, 2007]), and connecting them to make artificial brains. These modules are evolved rapidly in seconds on a "Tesla" PC Supercomputer, and connected according to the artificial brain designs of human "BAs" (Brain Architects). The artificial brain will eventually contain thousands of pattern recognizer modules, and hundreds of decision modules that when suitably combined will control the hundreds of behaviors of a walking, talking robot.

1. INTRODUCTION

The Artificial Brain Lab (ABL) (see Figure 1), of the School of Information Science and Technology (SIST) of Xiamen University, Fujian Province, China, has embarked upon an ambitious research project to build China's first artificial brain, over a period of 4 years (2008-2011), with a budget of some 10 million RMB, about 20 people (full and part time), and 250 sq ms of floor space.

The term "artificial brain" is defined here to be a "network of neural networks", where each neural network module (or "agent", to use Minsky's "Society of Mind" terminology [Minsky 1988, 2007]) is evolved in a few seconds in a Tesla PC Supercomputer [NVidia], and then

DOI: 10.4018/978-1-61692-797-4.ch019

Figure 1. Plaque of the Artificial Brain Lab (ABL) at Xiamen University, Xiamen, Fujian Province, China

Figure 2. The French company Aldebaran's 58 cm "NAO" Robot that our 10,000s evolved neural net module artificial brain will control

downloaded into an ordinary PC or supercomputer. This is done 10,000s of times, with each neural net module (or agent) performing some simple task. Human "BAs" ("Brain Architects") then specify the connections between these evolved modules to form networks of networks, or "artificial brains" using special (operating system) software, called IMSI (Inter Module Signaling Interface), which has a double function, firstly to store the humanly (i.e. BA) specified connections between the neural signal outputs and the neural signal inputs of modules, and secondly to perform the neural signaling of the whole brain in real time, defined to be 25 output signals per neuron per second.

The artificial brain is then used to control the 100s of behaviors of a robot (or other appropriate device). These neural net modules can be used to evolve visual (and aural) pattern detectors, e.g. object detectors, face detectors, moving line detectors, color detectors, etc. Thousands of these visual detectors can be placed in an artificial brain consisting of 10,000s of modules.

The artificial brain is used to control the hundreds of behaviors (motions) of a French "NAO" (robo cup standard) robot, shown in Figures 2 and 4. The French company Aldebaran [Aldebaran],

which manufactures this robot also provides motion control software called "Choregraphe", which sends time dependent "angle vectors" to the motors of the robot. These 25 (time dependent) numbers control the angles of the 25 motors of the NAO robot, causing it to move in a desired fashion, e.g. walking straight, turning, etc.

Initially, we thought we would evolve neural net modules to control the robot's motors, but decided against the idea once we saw the results of the Choregraphe software.

Hence, the "China Brain Project" is a hybrid, consisting of a mix of evolved neural net modules, Choregraphe motion control models, and simple conventional code modules (subroutines).

Decision type modules are also evolved, so that an appropriate mapping can be made between stimuli coming from both the external world and the internal world of the robot (e.g. boredom, hunger (i.e. low battery)) and motion generators. With hundreds of motions to choose between, and thousands of pattern detectors and decision modules, we expect that an artificial brain ought to be quite interesting for a human observer to watch.

However, in 2008, before any neural net pattern recognition or decision module could be evolved, we needed to decide initially which neural net evolvable *model* would be used as the basis for all this brain building work. This choice was fundamental to our whole brain building project. Section 2 of this article is devoted to a detailed description of the choice we made (that we called the "Parcone" model, i.e. "Partially Connected Neural Evolutionary" model).

Another important section of this article describes the (operating system) software needed to allow a multi (neural net) module artificial brain to perform its inter module neural net signaling. This software we labeled "IMSI" (Inter Module Signaling Interface). It was written mostly in 2008 as well. In fact, it is fair to say that the first year of this project was devoted primarily to building the "tools" that are now, at the time of writing (Oct 2009) being used to build our first mini brains, as we progress along the path of building ever larger and more capable artificial brains, until we eventually put 10,000s of such modules into our "ABs".

The remaining sections of this article are as follows. Section 2 describes the "Parcone" (evolvable neural net) model, beginning with the motivation for its choice, and followed by a rather detailed description of its structure. Section 3 presents some results of experimental work using the Parcone model. Section 4 is a rather detailed description of the "IMSI" multi Parcone-module operating system software, with its many features. Section 5 describes the hardware "work horse" of our project, namely the NVidia Tesla PC Supercomputer S1070, and its programming language "Cuda". The speed of this remarkably cheap supercomputer allows us to evolve Parcone modules in seconds, thus opening up the exciting possibility of quasi real-time learning. More on this can be found in sections 5 and 10.

Section 6 describes the capabilities of our ABL's NAO robots (shown in Figures 2 and 4). We are very conscious that *"no one will actually see the artificial brain"*. The AB is just a set of neural net weights and connection tables stored in memory, and utterly meaningless to everyone.

The quality of the artificial brain, and the many evolved neural net modules that comprise it, will be judged purely on the basis of the many behaviors of the robot that the artificial brain controls. The robots are the project's "window dressing".

Section 7 describes the interface between the IMSI operating system and Aldebaran's NAO software. For example, the images from the camera eyes of a NAO robot can contain megapixels, too many to be input to the neural net modules, so these images need to be data compressed to thousands of pixels which are then sent to the neural net modules. Behavioral decision signals from the neural net modules then need to be sent back to the NAO robot, that switch on particular behaviors. This section describes how this two way interfacing is performed.

Section 8 deals with NAO's language and cognitive capabilities because the NAO robots are capable not only of walking, but of talking, listening, and understanding as well. The ABL research team consists of several people devoting to the language and cognition aspects of NAO's behaviors (i.e. an American guest professor (Ben Goeretzel) and a PhD student) whose task is to give the robots, i.e. the artificial brain, linguistic and cognitive capabilities, e.g. being able to understand simple instructions (e.g. "Go to the door") and to answer simple questions, e.g. "Who is this?" "It's Tom."

Section 9 is devoted to the presentation and discussion of a series of "Demos" (i.e. demonstrations) that our Artificial Brain Lab (ABL) has committed itself to, aimed at our university's and province's administrations, who are funding us. These "Demos" are progressively ambitious and complex. We plan to show them off at the rate of several per year, for the remaining 3 years of the project. Section 10 is more future oriented. It talks about the main aim and major future challenges of this research project, namely, how to build an artificial brain of 10,000s of Parcone modules, i.e. how to *architect* an artificial brain. Section 11 concludes.

2. THE PARCONE (PARTIALLY CONNECTED NEURAL EVOLVABLE) MODEL

We begin the description of the Parcone model with an explanation as to why we wanted it to be partially connected. In earlier years, the first author evolved fully connected neural net modules [de Garis & Korkin 2002], arguing that they were the "general case". By starting off with every possible connection (i.e. all N^2 of them if there are N neurons in the module) one could let the evolution decide if a particular connection should not exist, by driving down the value of its weighted connection to zero.

This approach was fine, so long as the applications using the fully connected neural net modules did not require too many neurons N. However, in our artificial brain project, we will need the robot to be controlled to have vision, using CCD cameras which output mega-pixels. These images can be preprocessed to condense them to thousands of pixels that can then be input to neural net modules. If the number of pixels falls below the 1000 mark, the quality of the image becomes rather poor and makes recognition between subtly different objects difficult.

Hence we felt that the maximum allowable number of inputs to a neural net module should be in the thousands, and up to ten thousand. If N = 10,000, then in a fully connected neural net, the number of connections would be N^2 = 100,000,000, which is too large. Such a module would take a huge amount of time to evolve and would eat up computer resources (i.e. memory). Hence we decided to modify our old neural net model [de Garis & Korkin 2002] which was fully connected, to make it partially connected.

The moment one makes that decision, one is immediately confronted with the need, for each neuron in the module, to list all the other neurons that that individual neuron connects to. Hence a partially connected neural net model will consist

of a list of lists of inter-neural connections, one list per neuron.

Each neuron in a module is given a unique non negative integer ID, e.g. 18. Since the module is partially connected, the human creator of the module chooses the value of a parameter which specifies the number of inputs and outputs to each neuron in the module (so that every neuron has inputs and outputs, otherwise some would be dysfunctional and would be wasted). For example, imagine this ("maximum connections") parameter = 20, so that each neuron will have 20 other neurons that connect "to" it (called "from" neurons). The integer ID of each of these "from" neurons is stored in the neuron's "connection table", which takes the form of a hash table. If the neuron with ID 161 is a "from" neuron, connecting to the neuron in question (with I.D. 18), then its position in the hash table is found as follows. Choose the largest prime number less than the size of the hash table (which is usually made to be four times the size of the above "maximum connections" parameter (i.e. double the sum of the number of "from" neurons and "to" neurons)). For example, if the parameter value is 20, make the hash table size four times it, say 80, so that the prime would be 79. One then "mods" the "from" neuron ID (i.e. 161) by the prime, to get the position index in the hash table, i.e. 161% 79 = 3.

Actually the hash table position 3 does not contain the ID 161. Instead it contains a pointer to a struct that contains additional information, besides the "from" neuron ID. It contains the bits of the neural weight connecting the "from" neuron (with I.D. 161) to the "to" neuron (with I.D. 18) in question, as well as the weight value. In our Parcone model, these bits are interpreted to be binary fractions, e.g. $0.101_2 = 0.625_{10}$

Figure 3 shows the data structures used in the (C language) coding of the Parcone model. A pointer points to a population of genetic algorithm chromosomes [Goldberg 1989], i.e. pointers to a population of (partially connected) neural network modules. Each pointer in turn points to a further

Figure 3. Data structures for the PARCONE neural net model

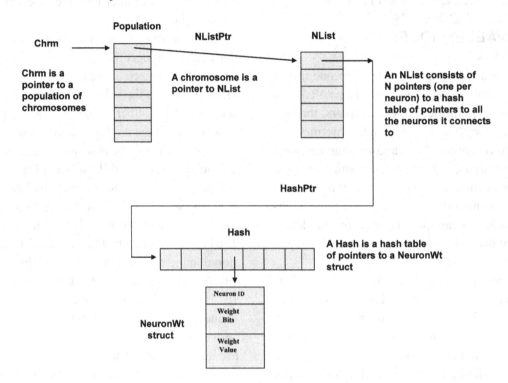

table of pointers, where each pointer points to a hash table for each neuron in the neural net module in question. The hash table contains pointers to structs, each of which contains the integer ID of the "from" neuron that connects to that neuron, the weight bits of the connection, and the weight value. Thus the coding deals with pointers to a nested depth of 4, e.g. datastruct**** Chrom

To calculate the output signal of each neuron (at a given moment, called a "tick", where a "tick" is defined to be the time taken for all neurons in the module (and the artificial brain) to calculate their neural output signals) in the module, its hash table is used. A scan across the length of the hash table is performed. From the previous "tick", a signal table of size N (the number of neurons in the module) is filled with the output signals of all the neurons. Assume the first non NULL pointer in the hash table is found at position (slot) "4". The non zero pointer there is used to find the

"from" neuron ID. Let us say it is 45. The corresponding weight value might be 0.3452

The incoming signal to the neuron at tick "t+1" is found from the 45th slot of the signal table for tick "t". This signal value is multiplied by the connection's weight and the product is added to a running sum of the weighted signals of all the "from" neurons to that neuron. The final sum S is then put through a "squashing" function "f" of the form $f = S/(|S| + c)$, where c is a positive constant, chosen so that in about 95% of cases, the value of "f" lies in the range between +0.8 and -0.8 This value of the output signal of the neuron in question (e.g. with ID 18) is stored in slot 18 of the signal table for tick "t+1". The signal table for tick "t+1" is then used to fill the signal table for tick "t+2", etc. Thus the two signal tables "ping pong" back and forth, each used to fill the other for the following tick.

The user can program the number of input, middle and output neurons contained in the module. For example, if the module is to detect visual patterns, there will need to be several thousand input neurons. Only one output neuron is needed (i.e. with a strong positive valued output signal if the pattern is detected, or a weak (negative valued) one if not), and let us have several hundred middle neurons.

At initialization of the genetic algorithm, random connections between all the input neurons and the middle neurons are made, similarly between the middle neurons and other middle neurons or output neuron(s). Each input neuron is connected to a user specified number of middle neurons. Each output neuron is connected to a user specified number of middle neurons, etc.

Evolution occurs by mutating the weight values, and/or by creating and deleting random connections.

The C code used to implement the above Parcone model was written and debugged in 2008. This code was then given to the supercomputer group in the Artificial Brain Lab (ABL) as well as to the Tesla PC supercomputer group. Both groups have the job to increase the speed of evolution. One of the critical factors in this research project is the speed of evolution.

3. EXPERIMENTAL RESULTS WITH THE PARCONE MODEL

The Parcone model is fairly new at the time of writing, so there has not been a lot of time to truly test its evolvability. The artificial brain project itself is only a bit more than a year old. This section reports on some experimental results using the Parcone model that we have obtained so far.

The first non trivial neural net module we tried to evolve was a pattern recognition module. We created two images of 30*30 (= 900) pixels which were input to 900 input neurons (one pixel per neuron) for a total of 15 ticks each. The two images were black arrows on a white background, one pointing left, the other right. The module was supposed to output as large a positive signal as possible if it was "seeing" a left arrow, and output as large a negative signal if it was "seeing" a right arrow.

This module evolved quickly, giving +ve outputs of about 0.5, and −ve outputs of about -0.5 in about 100 generations, at an evolution rate of about 2 seconds per generation, so only a few minutes were needed.

Our next evolutionary experiment with the Parcone model was to evolve face detectors. We took 5 images of each of two different faces, from 5 different angles, 1) left 40°, 2) left 20°, 3) central, 4) right 20°, 5) right 40°. (See Figure 4). Images 1, 3, and 5 for each person were used for the evolution (the "evolution set"), and images 2 and 4 for testing the evolved result (the "test set"). If a module was to be evolved to give a strong +ve output signal if an image of person "A" was input, and a strong −ve output signal if an image of person "B" was input, then the 3 person A images were called the "positive set", and the images of person B were called the "negative set". For 30 ticks each, the 6 images were input, with a resetting of the internal neural signal values at the tick when the input images were changed.

This face detector module evolved well, so that when the test images were input to see if the evolved face detector module would give the expected output results, i.e. face A test images would give strong +ve output signals, and face B test images would give strong −ve output signals, this is what actually happened. The face detector module "generalized". The 4 test cases were all correct, with output signal values lying in the range of +0.3 to +0.5 for the 2 positive images, and between -0.3 and -0.5 for the 2 negative images. So we felt this initial face detector evolutionary test was a success.

Our next step was to *automate* the evolution of visual pattern detectors. A user could input M +ve images, and N-ve images. The (automated) software, (hardware) then evolved automatically a module that output a strong +ve neural signal

Figure 4. A 60*60 (RGB) pixel image for evolving a face detector module

Evolution Set

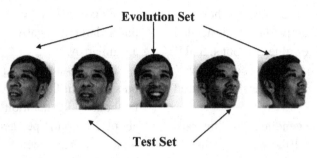

Test Set

for the +ve images, and a strong -ve neural signal for the -ve images. Test images were then used to see how well the evolved pattern detector module was capable of generalizing to unseen test images.

To test this automated version of Parcone, we used a dozen peoples' faces, with an evolution set and a test set with dozens of images in each set. The results on the test sets gave about 80-85% correct. Since we had many faces in the test sets, we placed some of the unsuccessfully detected test set face images into the evolution set and redid the evolution. The success rate on the remaining test set, then climbed into the 90s%. We felt this was also a success, so we then tried something more ambitious, namely facial sex detection, i.e. could an automated Parcone model evolve a male face and female face detector. The result was a bit less successful. Even after using a second pass on the evolution, we only got a correct detection rate with the test set of about 85%. When we looked at the failures, we found they were difficult to classify for humans as well.

We then tried to evolve a color detector. Some undergraduates did a bit of research here and were quite successful. Their positive set was a collection of red images of a variety of different shapes and objects. The negative set was the same but all non red. The correct detection rate of the red and non red test images was very high, around 95%. So we now know we can evolve color detectors. If we can evolve a red detector, presumably we can evolve a blue or purple, or yellow detector etc.

We then tried to evolve a motion detector. This time, the input images were "frozen frames" as on a reel of movie film. Each frame showed an object that was slightly shifted in position relative to the previous frame. We did a "Hubel Wiesel" type experiment. Hubel and Wiesel got a Nobel Prize for discovering "moving line at a given angle" detector cells in the visual cortex of a kitten. So we wanted to see if we could evolve such "HW detectors". Our positive movie was a thick black line moving across a white background at a given speed. Two negative movies were made which were the same arrow moving at two slightly difference angles +/- 20 degrees. This evolved well. When we input test lines at +/- 10 degree differences, we got intermediate output values and negative values for angles greater than 20 degrees. So we feel that we can evolve motion detectors. This will be useful when the time comes to evolve gesture detection modules.

4. IMSI (INTER MODULE SIGNALING INTERFACE) MULTI MODULE OPERATING SYSTEM

The two major software tools constructed in 2008 were Parcone, and IMSI. This section discusses the IMSI (Inter Module Signaling Interface) multi neural net module operating system software.

The primary function of IMSI is to enable multiple evolved neural net modules (up to 10,000s of them) to signal to each other, thus acting as an artificial brain.

From the user's viewpoint, the IMSI software allows him/her to specify the connections between neural net modules, so that an artificial brain can be constructed. A human "BA" (Brain Architect) will have an architecture comprised of interconnected neural net modules that function together (usually) as a component of the overall artificial brain design.

One of the two major functions of IMSI is to prompt the user to specify the connections between modules. Each evolved module is given a unique integer ID, and so is each input and output of that particular module. For example "module 2549: output 1 to module 2837: input 3" means that the neural signal exiting from output number 1 of module number 2549 is connected to input number 3 of module number 2837.

The IMSI software prompts the user to input such connectivity data.Prior to specifying such connectivity, users of IMSI can store the elite chromosome of each evolved neural net module. An example of the data that is stored for each module is shown in the following:-

nbrInNeurons = 2700;
nbrOutNeurons = 1;
nbrInnerNeurons = 600;
nbrInputs = 50;
nbrOutputs = 50;
nbrwtsignbits = 9;
nbrHashTblElmnts= 200;
hashmod = 199;
squashconst = float(1.5);

The artificial neurons in a Parcone module are divided into 3 groups, input neurons, middle neurons and output neurons. In the above example, a 30*30 (RGB) pixel image is input to the module, with one pixel input value per one input neuron, hence 30*30*3 = 2700 (RGB) input neurons are needed. The user has chosen to have 600 middle neurons, and 1 output neuron. The Parcone soft-ware gives each input neuron 50 outputs (i.e. 50 copies); each middle neuron gets 50 input signals, and 50 output signals; each output neuron gets 50 input signals.

nbrwtsignbits = 9;
nbrHashTblElmnts= 200;
hashmod = 199;
squashconst = float(1.5);

The user has chosen to have 8 bits for the fractional weight value and 1 bit for the sign. To calculate the number of hash table elements, (i.e. the number of slots in the hash table), the following rule of thumb is used:- add the number of input signals to a neuron (i.e. nbrInputs = 50;) to the number of output signals from a neuron (i.e. nbrOutputs = 50;), then double this sum, and find the largest prime number less than this sum as the hash table modulus (hashmod = 199;). The last parameter is the squashing function constant (squashconst = float(1.5);) which is used to help generate each neuron's output signal, as explained in section 2 on the Parcone model. These parameters are stored before the weight values in a memory file.

So, in general, a user will evolve a large number of individual neural net modules and save them in memory, being prompted by IMSI to supply a module name, a unique module integer ID, a functional description of the module, etc. The supplied ID is checked to see whether that integer is already used. If not, the elite module is stored.

Once all the modules that a BA needs to make an artificial brain have been stored, then the next step is to specify the connections between the modules. IMSI has functions that prompt the user to input the connections, as exemplified earlier. Note, that an input neuron (in the input group of neurons) will receive only one input signal from another module.

Neural Signaling

Once all the modules have been stored, and all the connections specified, the neural signaling of the whole artificial brain can begin. Actually, that is not quite true. Normally, input from the outside world needs to be data compressed (from digital camera eyes, for example) and fed into the modules. IMSI has routines that allow this too. Instead of connecting an output neuron signal to an input neuron, an external signal is connected.

The IMSI is now ready to "run" the artificial brain, i.e. to calculate the output signal of each neuron in each module for all modules in the brain. IMSI does this by using a table of pointers, where each pointer points to each module. Each module has its own parameters (e.g. how many input neurons, how many middle neurons, etc) which are used in the signal output calculations.

A critical concept here is the notion of a "clock", which is by definition, the time needed for all neurons in the whole brain to calculate their respective neural output signal. The IMSI code contains an outer loop of ticks, so for each tick, the neuron signal for every neural in the brain is calculated. Each module's output neuron(s) is(are) stored in an output table for each tick. The connection tables are then consulted, to find where an output signal at tick t is to be sent to the input table at tick t+1. At the next tick, these input tables are consulted to find the values of signals that are to be input to modules from other modules.

The IMSI multi module operating system has many parts, which a BA can use via a menu driven user interface. The actual details of these menus are as follows. There are two such menus. The first is used to allow the evolution of individual Parcone neural net modules. The second is used to allow Brain Architects (BAs) to connect Parcone modules to build artificial brains.

The first menu is shown in Box 1.

Most of these items are self explanatory. The initialization option creates dynamic data structures for the evolution that is to follow, as well as

Box 1.

```
PARCONE (PARtially COnnected Neural Evolutionary)
Model
                    MENU
  1.  Initialize Population
  2.  Evolve Population
  3.  Store Population
  4.  Load Population
  5.  Test Elite Module
  6.  IMSI (Inter Module Signaling Interface)
  7.  Exit
Choose:
```

random bit strings for the chromosome population that is to be evolved with a genetic algorithm. The second option is to perform the actual evolution of a Parcone module. The whole population of chromosomes can be stored on a hard disk and can be reloaded using the third and fourth options. The fifth option allows a user to input a particular image (e.g. someone's face) and to display the output signals of the elite Parcone module. The sixth option is to open up the second menu, i.e. the IMSI menu.

The second menu is shown in Box 2.

- Option 1 creates dynamic data structures for a modules list, a connections list, etc.
- Option 2 is the same as option 4 of the previous menu, i.e. it loads a whole Parcone module population.
- Option 3 extracts the elite chromosome (Parcone module) from the population loaded by option 2. Only elite modules are used to build an artificial brain.
- Option 4 displays the parameters of a particular module.
- Option 5 creates a new modules list, i.e. an integer ID and module name for each Parcone module to be connected to make an artificial brain.
- Option 6 loads a modules list from the hard disk.
- Option 7 adds a module to the modules list, i.e. the integer ID and name of the module to the list.

Box 2.

```
      INTER MODULE SIGNALING INTERFACE (IMSI)
                        MENU

        1.  INITIALIZE Tables
        2.  Load POPULATION file of chromosomes
        3.  Get/Store ELITE Module's Params & Wts
               from Population
        4.  Show SINGLE Module's Params & Wts
        5.  CREATE New MODULES List
        6.  LOAD MODULES List
        7.  ADD Module to MODULES List
        8.  STORE MODULES List
        9.  CREATE New CONNECTIONS List
        10. LOAD/SHOW CONNECTIONS List
        11. ADD Connection to CONNECTIONS List
        12. Show ONE Module's CONNECTIONS
        13. Show ALL Modules' CONNECTIONS
        14. STORE CONNECTIONS List
        15. CREATE New IMAGE to Modules List
        16. CONNECT an IMAGE to Module
        17. SHOW all IMAGE to Module Connections
        18. STORE IMAGE to Module Connections
        19. LOAD/SHOW All IMAGE to Module
               Connections
        20. Build BRAIN
        21. Run BRAIN
        22. Exit IMSI
      Choose:
```

- Option 8 stores a modules list (prompting the user to give a name to the modules list).

- Option 9 creates a data structure for a new connections list, where a connection is between two neurons, and consists of 4 integers, i.e. the integer ID of the "from" neuron, and the integer ID output number, an integer ID of the "to" neuron, and an integer ID input number.

- Option 10 loads a connections list, and displays all its connections, i.e. the 4 integers of each connection in the list.

- Option 11 adds a connection (i.e. 4 integers) to a connections list.

- Option 12 displays the connections of a particular module in a modules list.

- Option 13 displays all the connections of all the modules in a modules list.

- Option 14 stores a connections list on the hard disk.

- Option 15 creates a new images to modules list, i.e. a list of pairs of integers, where the first integer is an input image number, and the second integer is a module ID.

- Option 16 connects a single input image to a single module, i.e. a pair of integer IDs (one for the image, one for the module).

- Option 17 displays all image to module connections (i.e. all integer pairs of connections between an image and a module).

- Option 18 stores an images to modules connections list onto the hard disk.

- Option 19 loads and displays all image to module connections in a user specified images to modules connections list.

- Option 20 builds an artificial brain, i.e. it uses the above lists to connect the modules of the artificial brain, and created dynamical data structures to store neural signal values etc.

- Option 21 runs the artificial brain, i.e. it calculates the output signal of each artificial neuron and sends the output signals of "from" neurons to the inputs of "to" neurons, etc. The data structures created with option 20 are used to run the artificial brain.

The above options will be added to in time. For example, instead of using evolved neural modules to perform simple decisions, e.g. to decide which of two output signals is stronger. Such decisions ought to be made with simple coding, so some modules are code based rather than neuron based. Further such functionality will be added to the IMSI (multi module operating system) menu.

5. NVIDIA'S TESLA S1070 PC SUPERCOMPUTER

Figure 5 shows the PC Supercomputer that our lab plans to use to evolve neural network modules quickly. This NVidia Tesla PC Supercomputer S1070, has 960 processors, running at 4 Teraflops, and costs only $10,000. It is an amazing machine, delivering supercomputer performance for the price of a high end (single processor) PC. It is not surprising that these machines are selling so well. It is the "workhorse" for our lab. We will use it increasingly in the next few years, as the number of evolved modules inserted into our artificial brains continues to grow. We refer to it simply as the "Tesla". Its programming language is called "Cuda", which is similar to C language, with some additional features allowing it to perform extensive parallel computations. At the time of writing (Oct 2009), we have only recently acquired this machine (and have ordered a second), so we are still learning how to program it. We plan to port the Parcone code to the Tesla, so that ideally, we may be able to speed up the evolution of an individual Parcone neural net module by a factor of about 1000. A PC typically operates at a speed of gigaflops, whereas the Tesla operates at a speed of teraflops, a thousand times faster. If it takes roughly half an hour to evolve a typical Parcone neural net module on a PC, then one thousandth of that time is about 2 seconds, i.e. almost real time. If in the near future, we can evolve Parcone pattern recognition modules in a second or two, this opens up the exciting possibility of performing real time module evolution. For more on this idea, see section 10 on future work and challenges.

The NVidia company will come out late 2009 with a new generation machine to supersede their "Tesla" model, called "Fermi" which will be approximately 4 times faster than the Tesla machine, that our lab currently possesses. We plan to buy a "Fermi", which will make possible the evolution of Parcone neural net modules truly "real time", which in turn opens up exciting possibilities for the years 2010 and 2011. With real time Parcone module evolution it will be possible to have our artificial brain learning in real time, and hence "all the time". This opens up the possibility to create new architectures that are based on a continuous learning of new concepts. This would be like a human baby who is constantly exploring its world, e.g. learning the names of new objects in its environment as supplied by a human teacher. "NAO, this is a key." "NAO, this is a cup."

Figure 6 shows a member of the ABL team next to one of our three NAO robots. As stated in the introduction, no one will see the artificial brain. People will only be able to judge the intelligence and usefulness of the artificial brain by the quality of the behaviors it controls in some visible device, which in our case is a NAO robot. These robots are manufactured by the French company Aldebaran, based in Paris. They are nearly 60 cms

Figure 6. The NAO Robot room with bed, table and chairs

Figure 5. NVidia's PC Supercomputer, Tesla S1070, 960 processors, 4 teraflops, $10,000

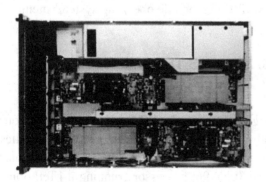

tall, bipedal, two arms, with two fingered hands and opposable thumb. The NAO model robots we bought have two camera eyes, for stereo vision if we choose to pursue that option. The NAOs can speak, listen, walk, turn, etc.

The Aldebaran software used to control the time dependent angles of the 25 motors in each robot is called "Choregraphe". We use this software to generate the motions of the NAO robots. Since this software is commercial and already well developed, we do not describe it here. It is not part of our research to develop this software because it is "off the shelf". Hence the generation of movements of the robot is not a great challenge. The artificial brain is used therefore to decide when to activate a given behavior, based on its current environment and its internal memory.

7. THE INTERFACE BETWEEN THE NAO ROBOT THE IMSI OPERATING SYSTEM

For Demo 1, the two principle software packages (the IMSI operating system code and Aldebaran's control code for the Nao robot) need to interface with each other. The French company Aldebaran which manufactures the Nao robot has software which displays images onto a computer screen that show what the Nao robot's two camera eyes see. These images contain a large number of pixels (actually 160*120 = 19200), which are too many to be input into the Parcone modules of the artificial brain. Hence these visual images need to be data compressed to thousands of pixels, e.g. 53*40 RGB (red green blue) pixels, hence 53*40*3 = 6,360 integers (ranging between 0 and 255 in value) are converted into real numbers by dividing by 255. We took the original 160*120 image, sliced off the last column of pixels, to give a 159*120 pixel image. We then sliced up this image into little squares of 3*3 pixels, and then took the average value of these 9 pixels to create each pixel value of the compressed image. To see

how many 159*120 pixel image frames could be compressed per second we wrote a compression program and tested it. We found experimentally, that the compression rate on an ordinary PC was about 1600 images per second, i.e. effectively real time.

These compressed images are fed (at a rate of one frame per neuron "tick") into an "image buffer" that is an important data structure of the IMSI operating system, that the various visual pattern recognition modules get their input data from to detect their objects. Hence the code that compresses the Nao images is interfaced with the Aldebaran code. The compressed images then interface with the IMSI code. So the 3 codes are integrated.

The artificial brain will eventually output a control signal to the Nao robot telling it to perform some particular action. Hence this control signal from the artificial brain needs to be interfaced with the Nao control code. This is done by inputting the behavior control signals (e.g. the "walk straight" signal, or "turn left" signal, etc) into a piece of conventional software, that calculates the strongest signal input ("winner take all") and then issues the corresponding command to the Nao software to execute the behavior with the strongest neural signal. Note, this interfacing is easily done, since the Nao code, the IMSI code and conventional code are all compiled together into one large program.

8. LANGUAGE & COGNITION

The Nao robot is to be given language and "general intelligence" (i.e. cognitive) capabilities which are implemented in a particular cognitive architecture called "Open Cog". This section describes the contribution to this project of the second author, Ben Goertzel. The Open Cog architecture is not particularly neural net based, instead it uses a mixture of logic and symbolic data structures to enable the Nao robot to listen, understand, and to speak. This is another reason for claiming that the China Brain Project is a hybrid, part neural, part logical/symbolic.

The third author is generally recognized to be the father of "AGI" (Artificial General Intelligence), which attempts to create artificial intelligences that have general problem solving abilities, which absorbs the many specialized branches of "narrow AI".

The Cognition Engine

In [Goertzel, 2006] general intelligence is described as the capability to achieve complex goals in complex environments, using limited computational resources. Using the specific neural net evolution methods described above, one may create a robot able to recognize objects, hear speech, and carry out movements and speech acts. These powerful capabilities are necessary but not sufficient for robotic general intelligence. What is needed is some way to connect the robot's goals with its perceptions and actions: in a word, cognition.

From this perspective, the basic purpose of the Cognition Engine component in the China Brain Project is to, at each time step in the robot's life: Enact a procedure so that, according to its best guess, the probabilistic logical implication *"Context & Procedure ==> Goals"* is true with a high truth value. Here "Context" refers to the current situation as perceived by the robot; and a "Procedure" refers to an "internal program" running within the Cognition Engine, that executes a series of behaviors that the behavior postprocessor knows how to execute. Generally speaking such a procedure will contain an internal control flow involving loops, conditionals, etc. (e.g. "go get the object with ID #764 and bring it to the agent with ID #12"). Such a procedure may be internally represented by a data structure such as a tree or a graph, and may be textualized as a program in a language such as LISP (or, in this project, the LISP-like language Combo), but with special primitives corresponding to the perceptions and behaviors of the robot.

The question then becomes how these probabilistic implications are learned. This of course depends on what Cognition Engine one is using. Here we propose to use OpenCog Prime (OCP), a new system which is a variant of the older Novamente Cognition Engine (NCE) [Goertzel, 2006a]. OCP has two ways of learning implications of the above nature: using an evolutionary learning mechanism (MOSES) that evolves procedures using the truth value of the implication as its fitness function; and a probabilistic logic engine (PLN) that derives the strength of the implication from background knowledge. In the following subsection we describe the NCE approach to cognition in a little more detail (still barely scratching the surface, however.)

Note that multiple representations of truth values are possible; however, one of the distinguishing features of the NCE/OCP approach is the use of multi-component probabilistic truth values such as indefinite probabilities [Goertzel, Ikle' et al, 2008]. The two-component outputs of the neural nets described above are highly appropriate in this context because there exist mathematical formulae for converting them into indefinite probabilities as used in OCP; this would not be the case for neural nets with single-number probability outputs. This is an example of the kind of detail that must be gotten right in order to create a highly effective integrative AI system.

The Novamente Cognition Engine

One way to conceptualize the NCE is to decompose it into five aspects (which of course are not entirely distinct, but still are usefully distinguished):

- *Cognitive architecture* (the overall design of an AGI system: what parts does it have, how do they connect to each other)
- *Knowledge representation* (how does the system internally store declarative, pro-

cedural and episodic knowledge; and how does it create its own representation for knowledge of these sorts in new domains it encounters)

- *Knowledge creation* (how does it learn new knowledge of the types mentioned above; and how does it learn how to learn, and so on)
- *Instructional methodology* (how is it coupled with other systems so as to enable it to gain new knowledge about itself, the world and others)
- *Emergent structures and dynamics* (which arise from the combination of the four previous aspects)

We now briefly review how these four aspects are handled in the NCE. For a more in-depth discussion of the NCE the reader is referred to [Goertzel, 2006] and the OpenCog wiki site (at opencog.org).

The NCE's high-level cognitive architecture is motivated by human cognitive science and is roughly analogous to Stan Franklin's LIDA architecture [Friedlander and Franklin, 2008]. It is divided into a number of interconnected functional units corresponding to different specialized capabilities such as perception, motor control and language, and also an "attentional focus" unit corresponding to intensive integrative processing. A diagrammatic depiction is given in [Goertzel et al, 2004].

Within each functional unit, declarative knowledge representation is enabled via an AtomTable software object that contains nodes and links (collectively called Atoms) of various types representing declarative, procedural and episodic knowledge both symbolically and subsymbolically. Each Atom is labeled with a multicomponent probabilistic truth value object; and also with a multi-component attention value object indicating its short and long term importance.

Procedural knowledge is represented via program trees in a simple LISP-like language

called Combo; and methods exist for translating between Combo and declarative Atoms. Episodic knowledge is represented by the use of Atoms and Combo programs to trigger internal simulations in a UI-free internal virtual world called Third Life, which may be thought of as the system's "mind's eye" running internal (memory-based or hypothetical) movies.

Each unit also contains a collection of MindAgent objects implementing cognitive, perception or action processes that act on this AtomTable, and/or interact with the outside world.

In addition to a number of specialized learning algorithms associated with particular functional units, the NCE is endowed with two powerful learning mechanisms embedded in MindAgents: the MOSES probabilistic-program-evolution module (based on [Looks, 2006], and the Probabilistic Logic Networks module for probabilistic logical inference [Goertzel, Ikle' et al, 2008]. These are used both to learn procedural and declarative knowledge, and to regulate the attention of the MindAgents as they shift from one focus to another, using an economic attention-allocation mechanism [Goertzel, 2006a] that leads to subtle nonlinear dynamics and associated emergent complexity including spontaneous creative emergence of new concepts, plans, procedures, etc.

Regarding teaching methodology, the NCE has been developed in the context of a physically or virtually embodied approach, which integrates linguistic with nonlinguistic instruction, and also autonomous learning via spontaneous exploration of the physical or virtual world. It is the exploration of the world, and the interaction with other (human) minds in the context of the world, that will, we suggest, allow the system's knowledge-based to adapt in such a way as to give rise to the high-level emergent structures characterizing a human-like mind: the phenomenal self [Metzinger, 2004], the illusion of will (Wegner, 2003), the theater of reflective awareness [Baars, 2001].

OpenCog Prime

The NCE is a proprietary software system, but an open-source system has also been created, founded on a number of software objects donated by Novamente LLC and drawn from the NCE codebase. This OSS system is called OpenCog [Hart and Goertzel, 2008], and has two aspects: it is a fairly general framework for the development of AI and AGI systems; and it is also a specific means for the implementation of an AGI design called OpenCog Prime, which is an open-source analogue to the NCE. Our plan in the current architecture is to utilize the OpenCog framework, and in the context of this project to build out key aspects of the OpenCog Prime design.

The RelEx System for Natural Language Comprehension and Generation

OpenCog also contains a significant piece of software, donated by Novamente LLC, which is not strictly a part of the NCE although it interoperates with the NCE: this is the RelEx engine for natural language comprehension and generation. The comprehension aspect of RelEx is more mature and has been briefly described in [Goertzel et al, 2006] in the context of its application to interpreting biomedical research abstracts; the generation aspect is still in prototype phase, but has already been shown to work on simple sentences.

RelEx, in its comprehension aspect, takes English text and maps that text into abstract logical relations, in the Atom format utilized internally by the NCE and OpenCog. Generally speaking it produces multiple interpretations (logical relation sets) for each sentence it processes, and the task of selecting the contextually appropriate interpretation is left to the cognition engine itself. Also, the cognition engine is relied upon to correct errors RelEx may make in areas such as word sense disambiguation and reference resolution. It is anticipated that the sensory data gathered by a robot, regarding the physical and social context of instances of linguistic usages it

produces or hears, may provide data helpful to the cognition engine in executing the linguistic tasks of interpretation-selection, reference resolution and sense disambiguation.

Next, in its generation aspect, RelEx maps logical relation sets (Atom sets) into sets of English sentences. Note that RelEx does not contain any facility for discourse management: this is assumed to be handled within the cognition engine. A design exists for controlling dialogue within OpenCog utilizing a probabilistic implementation of ideas from Rhetorical Structure Theory [Mann and Thompson, 1988], but this still awaits implementation.

RelEx also does not contain any facility for converting speech to text or vice versa. In the proposed integrated architecture for robot control, these conversions will be carried out by existing open-source software and RelEx will be used (together with the Cognition Engine) to select between the multiple outputs of speech-to-text software in an intelligent way.

9. DEMONSTRATIONS ("DEMOS")

An essential feature of this 4 year research project is a series of demonstrations that we refer to colloquially as "Demo 1", "Demo 4" etc. These demonstrations serve to focus the research effort and to assign tasks to the members of the ABL, especially to the PhD students who do most of the real work. Since Xiamen University and Fujian Province have invested a lot of money in this Artificial Brain Lab, they require regular proof that their money is being well spent, so there is a political/economic aspect to these "Demos" as well.

Demo 1: Tools

The first Demo is currently being completed. Its main purpose is to show that the tools, written largely in 2008, are ready and that the real job of designing artificial brains can begin. Demo 1 consists of presenting thick black arrows drawn on white A4 pages to the (two) camera eyes of the NAO robot. If the arrow is pointing towards the left, the robot will turn left. If the arrow points up, the robot will walk straight. If the arrow points right, the robot will turn right. For all this to happen, the following list of tasks had to be completed and tested.

a. The pattern recognition neural net module evolution software (Parcone) had to be programmed and tested. Results of this major component of the whole project were given in section 3.

b. The NAO robot had to be programmed (using Choregraphe software) to walk straight, turn left and turn right. This was not a major challenge, as we used the Choregraphe code supplied by Aldebaran, the French company that manufactured the NAO robot.

c. The megapixel images generated by the two NAO robot cameras were compressed down to tens of thousands of pixels, so that their number could be handled by the Parcone pattern recognition neural net modules. This work was done by a master's student. This image compression was described in section 7 on the NAO-IMSI interface.

d. A Parcone/NAO software interface was written allowing messages to be sent either way between these two sets of software. The NAO software sends image data to be compressed and then input to the Parcone modules. The Parcone modules in the artificial brain instruct the Choregraphe software, which action to perform at a given moment.

e. IMSI (Inter Module Signaling Interface). The IMSI multi-module operating system was described in section 4. It allows many independently evolved neural net modules to signal to each other. The IMSI is effectively the operating system software that allows the artificial brain to function. Along with

the Parcone code, the IMSI code is another of the essential components of the whole artificial brain project.

f. The first (micro) brain architecture. The NAO robot needs to know that when it sees

g. a left pointing arrow that it must activate the "turn left" Choregraphe code to make the robot turn left, etc. This first (micro) brain had only about a dozen Parcone modules, plus a few simple conventional code modules. As the number of modules grows in larger Demos, i.e. larger artificial brains, "administration" type software will need to be written as part of the IMSI operating system that is used to describe each module, e.g. its integer I.D., its name, its function, the functions of its inputs and outputs, its connections to other modules (i.e. their integer IDs), etc. Graphical displays will be needed to show the circuits of which the module is a part. It is anticipated that this "admin" software will become quite elaborate when artificial brains contain thousands of modules.

Demo 2: Language & Cognition

If the key word for Demo 1 was "tools", the key words for Demo 2 will be "language and cognition". Two essential components of the China Brain Project are language and cognition, as described in section 8. Demo 2 will build upon the tools created for Demo 1 by adding language and cognitive capabilities, i.e. speaking, listening, language understanding, and obeying instructions. The details of Demo 2 at the time of writing (Oct 2009) are not yet finalized, but broadly speaking the NAO robot will be asked to follow simple verbal instructions, e.g. "Go to the door", "Point to the window", etc. Demo 2 is effectively an implementation of components of the OpenCog architecture built on top of the tools used in Demo 1.

Demo 3: Hardware Accelerated Parcone Evolution

This demo is to illustrate the acceleration of Parcone neural net module evolution by using the Tesla PC supercomputer. At the time of writing (Oct 2009), we have managed to achieve about a 300 fold speedup (relative to the evolution time on an ordinary PC), using only 1 electronic board of the 4-board computer. We expect to reach at least a 400 fold speed up with 4 boards. When the new "Fermi" model appears early in 2010 (which we will buy), we expect to achieve a 1600 fold speed up. Since typically, it can take an hour to evolve a Parcone neural net, a 1600 fold speed up would mean that that same evolution could be performed in 3600/1600 seconds, i.e. about 2 seconds, which is effectively real time. For the first author, this real time hardware evolution is the achievement of a nearly 2 decade old dream, namely to be able to evolve neural net modules in real time, thus allowing continuous learning of an artificial brain, rather like a human baby, who is learning all the time! We will be able to do the same. As the NAO robot sees something new, for which it has no appropriate detector circuit, then it can learn a new one, and add it to its memory. This prospect is exciting, and will be the main focus of our research work in the year 2010 and 2011.

Demo 4: Real Time Learning

The theme of Demo 4 will be (hopefully) real time Parcone module evolution as executed on the Tesla PC Supercomputer, i.e. to use the results of Demo 3 above. We hope to be able to show off Demo 4 before the end of 2009. If successful, it would be impressive. The Demo itself is as follows. The members of the ABL team stand in a line. All their faces are previously known to "Nao" (the pet name we give to the robot). Nao is asked by one of the members "Who is this? (pointing at some other member). Nao directs its gaze to the person pointed to, recognizes the face and says the name of the person recognized. The second part of the Demo is more ambitious. A stranger to Nao joins the group. Nao is asked by an ABL member (pointing to the stranger), "Who is this?" Nao recognizes that the stranger is not known to it, so replies, "I don't know. What is your name?" The stranger says his/her name and Nao perform two simultaneous functions. One is to evolve in (near) real time, a Parcone module for the stranger's face. This module is stored in the memory of its artificial brain (via the IMSI operating system). The other function is to record and store the name of the stranger. Nao is then asked to name various members of the ABL, by pointing at them. Nao looks at each person pointed to and names them, including the previous stranger!

Demo 5: Gesture Recognition

Demo 5 aims to evolve individual modules that recognize human gestures, e.g. a goodbye wave, a stop sign, and other gestures. Alternatively, one could say that Demo 5 is "movie detection". A movie is just a rapid sequence of stationary images to the human eye. Similarly, one can evolve motion detectors, gesture detectors, by inputting a sequence of stationary images to a Parcone module and evolve it to output a strong signal for a given gesture, and a weak signal for other gestures. The NAO robot will be able to interpret the meaning of these gestures and react appropriately. For example, if given a "come here" gesture, it will approach the person who made the gesture. If given a stop gesture, it will stop moving etc. If given the "Bye now" gesture, it will say "Good bye", etc.

Demo 6: OpenCog and the NAO Robot

Demo 6 is ambitious. It is primarily the work of the second author, and is intended to do with the

NAO robot, what the second author has already done with his virtual dog, i.e. to give cognitive abilities to the NAO robot, so that it can listen and talk intelligently, with inference, learning, etc. Ben Goertzel, the second author, is the father of AGI (Artificial General Intelligence). OpenCog (i.e. a cognitive software system that is open to everyone) is the second author's attempt at creating an AGI. Demo 6 will be effectively Demo 2 + OpenCog.

Demo 7: A 100 Module Artificial Brain: The "BaiNAO" Demo

The "BaiNao" Demo derives it name from the Chinese word for 100, i.e. "bai", and "NAO" is the name of our robot. It also sounds like the English farewell "Bye now". The primary aim of this demo is to create the first fairly substantial artificial brain architecture (with about 100 Parcone modules) that will also test the functionality of the IMSI multi-module operating system software. The IMSI will be used to connect up about 100 previously individually evolved Parcone modules. At the time of writing (Oct 2009) the details of this architecture are yet to be fully formulated, but it will use the fruits of the previous demos, e.g. gesture recognition, etc. This demo will mark the beginning of a long progression of demos that will use a steadily increasing number of Parcone modules, e.g. 200, 500, 1000, 2000, 5000, 10000... One of the basic aims of the whole "China Brain Project" is to build artificial brains with large numbers of evolved neural net modules. Demo 7 is the beginning of this process. We anticipate that each "scaling up" will present its own problems that will have to be overcome. With large numbers of modules, it is obvious that the artificial brain thus constructed, will be capable of ever greater functionality. One of the basic aims of the China Brain Project is to show that building brains using an evolutionary engineering approach is practical.

Demo 8: A 200-500 Module Artificial Brain

Demo 8, which has yet to be formulated in any detail, will probably contain some 200-500 modules. With such a number, and the capability to evolve them very fast using the "Tesla" (and soon, the "Fermi") machine, we can afford to become more ambitious. Our artificial brain architectures can be larger, doing more things. Our brain building team can start looking at the literature to find inspirational ideas to build bigger brains. One obvious source is the work of Minsky [Minsky 1988, 2007] who has not been able to implement his ideas to any real extent, due to the inadequacy of the electronic capacity of machines in the past. However, Moore's Law (that the number of transistors on a chip keeps doubling every 18 months) is now probably in its last decade and the size of the "Moore Doublings" is now gargantuan (with modern chips containing over a billion transistors). Our brain building team feels that the time is now ripe to begin serious attempts at building artificial brains. (In fact the first two authors are currently finishing off the guest editing of a special issue on the topic of "Artificial Brains" for a major journal.)

With 500 modules, the Demo 8 brain could have several hundred pattern recognition modules, and dozens of decision modules. It ought to be able to recognize most of the objects in its special "robot room" that has a table, chairs, bed, etc. (See Figure 6). It may be able to obey instructions such as "NAO, lie on the bed", "Sit down", "Pick up the red ball, put it on the table", etc.

FUTURE CHALLENGES

As stated in the introductory section, and even in the title of this article, the principle aim of the China Brain Project, is to use an *evolutionary engineering* approach to build China's first artificial brain that will contain 10,000s of evolved neural net modules that behave like "Minsky agents" as explained in his "Society of Mind" book [Minsky 1988].

The authors of this article are convinced that modern day electronics allows artificial brains to be built. The most effective and persuasive way to prove to people that this is true, is simply to build one and show what such an artificial brain can do (via a series of demonstrations).

In order to put 10,000s of evolved neural net modules together, in an artificial brain, one will need sophisticated "architectures". One of the major, if not dominant challenges of this research project is "How to architect an artificial brain?" Only a few people have tried to answer this question, e.g. [Minsky, 1988, 2007], [de Garis, 2002]. The approach that we will take we label the "money method", i.e. we will design artificial brains with an increasing number of evolved neural net modules (i.e. Parcone modules). We have begun with about 10 to 20 modules for Demo 1. Demo 2 will probably contain 50 - 100 modules. Demo 3 may contain about 200 modules. One can readily see that the number of modules is increasing roughly in the same size as the denominations of a country's money bills (20, 50, 100, 200, 500, etc).

As each Demo is implemented, we expect that fresh problems, fresh challenges will arise. We expect also to learn from the experiences of these challenges, and benefit from them in planning and implementing the following Demo. We plan by the end of the 4th year to have put 10,000s of modules together, evolving them rapidly on the Tesla, using a small army of master's students.

As the number of modules rises into the thousands, we will be able to tackle far more ambitious Demos, such as creating a "society of mind" a la [Minsky, 1988, 2007]. As the project progresses, more and more emphasis will of necessity be placed on artificial brain architectures. We will be able to structure our artificial brain into functional blocks and sub blocks, etc.

Longer term, we hope that this approach will prove to be inspirational to other research groups so that within 5 to 10 years building artificial brains will be commonplace, occurring in hundreds if not thousands of university computer science departments around the world. Once that happens, the time will be ripe for the creation of national Artificial Brain Administrations (ABAs), similar in structure and scope to America's NASA, i.e. large government run institutions, employing thousands of scientists and engineers to build national artificial brains (ABs). China's could be called "CABA" (i.e. Chinese Artificial Brain Administration).

This project's dean is hoping by the end of this 4 year project, that the ABL will be promoted from a "key province lab" into a "key state (i.e. federal) lab" with much heavier funding. If this were to occur, the following step might be the creation of a CABA. China may become the first country in the world to do such a thing. Considering it is likely by the year 2030, that the home robot industry will be one of the biggest in the world (and that home robots are controlled by artificial brains), promoting the building of artificial brains at federal government level will be of both scientific and economic significance.

CONCLUSION

This article has introduced the "China Brain Project" which aims to build an artificial brain by the end of 2011, which will contain several tens of thousands of evolved neural net modules, in the style of Minsky's "agents" that are interconnected according to the designs of human "BAs" (Brain Architects). These modules are to be evolved rapidly (hopefully in a few seconds each) on a Tesla PC supercomputer that is roughly 1000 times faster than an ordinary PC. If the evolution speed can be made fast enough, real time learning becomes possible, so that for example, pattern recognition modules can be evolved whenever a new pattern appears, and stored in the artificial brain's memory.

The number of evolved neural net modules will grow according to the "money model", i.e. with 20 modules, then 50, 100, 200, 500, 1000, 2000, 5000, 10000, 20000,...

At each stage, the architectural challenge becomes more daunting, i.e. how to design an artificial brain that contains so many modules, that does what? Learning how to design such artificial brains with a large number of evolved neural net modules is the *real* aim of this ambitious project.

In the first year of the project, 2008, the basic tools were constructed, namely the software to evolve the pattern recognition neural net modules (called the "Parcone" (Partially Connected Neural Evolutionary) model). A software operating system (called IMSI (Inter Module Signaling Interface)) was also constructed that allows many evolved neural net modules to be connected and to send neural signals to each other. Once the NAO robots arrived, as well as the Tesla supercomputer, the basic ingredients were in place to begin building the first artificial brains.

Over the course of the next 3 years, a series of "Demos" (technical demonstrations) will be presented, to show off the capabilities of artificial brains with an ever growing number of evolved neural network modules, each with its own little task. As the number of modules in the artificial brain increases, it will become increasingly challenging to architect it. The real aim of this research project is to learn how to architect artificial brains, by actually building a series of them.

If this project is successful, our Artificial Brain Lab (ABL) may be promoted into a federally funded lab ("key state lab") and perhaps after that may serve as a model for a national artificial brain administration "CABA" (Chinese Artificial Brain Administration, comparable in scope with America's NASA), i.e. containing thousands of scientists and engineers to build artificial brains for China's home robot industry and other applications.

REFERENCES

Baars, B. (2001). *In the Theater of Consciousness*. New York: Oxford University Press USA.

de Garis, H., & Korkin, M. (2002). The CAM-Brain Machine (CBM) An FPGA Based Hardware Tool which Evolves a 1000 Neuron Net Circuit Module in Seconds and Updates a 75 Million Neuron Artificial Brain for Real Time Robot Control. *Neurocomputing, 42,* 35–68. doi:10.1016/S0925-2312(01)00593-8

Friedlander, D., & Franklin, S. (2008). LIDA and a Theory of Mind. In Ben Goertzel & Pei Wang (Eds.), *Artificial General Intelligence (AGI-08),* Memphis, TN, USA: IOS Press.

Goertzel, Ben (2006). Patterns, Hypergraphs and General Intelligence. In *Proceedings of International Joint Conference on Neural Networks, (IJCNN 2006),* Vancouver CA

Goertzel, Ben (2006). *The Hidden Pattern*. New York: Brown Walker.

Goertzel, Ben, Matthew Ikle', Izabela Goertzel & Ari Heljakka (2008). *Probabilistic Logic Networks*. New York: Springer Verlag.

Goertzel, Ben, Moshe Looks & Cassio Pennachin (2004). Novamente: An Integrative Architecture for Artificial General Intelligence. In *Proceedings of AAAI Symposium on Achieving Human-Level Intelligence through Integrated Systems and Research,* Washington DC, August 2004

Goldberg, D. (1989). *Genetic Algorithms in Search, Optimization and Machine Learning*. Reading, MA: Addison Wesley.

Hart, D. (2008). *Ben Goertzel*. OpenCog.

Looks, M. (2006). Competent Program Evolution. *PhD thesis, Computer Science Department,* Washington University in St. Louis.

Mann, W., & Thompson, S. (1988). Rhetorical Structure Theory: Toward a Functional Theory of text Organization. *Text*, *8*(3), 243–281. doi:10.1515/text.1.1988.8.3.243

Metzinger, T. (2004). *Being No One*. Cambridge, MA: MIT Press.

Marvin Minsky, *The Society of Mind*, New York: Simon & Schuster.

Marvin Minsky, *The Emotion Machine*. New York: Simon & Schuster.

NVidia Tesla S1070 1U Computing System, Retrieved from http://www.nvidia.com/object/product_tesla_s1070us.ht

Robotics, A Programmable Humanoid Robots, Retrieved from http://www.aldebaran-robotics.com/eng/index.php

APPENDIX

This appendix describes ongoing and future work of the second author, which aims to increase significantly the speed of evolution of Parcone neural net modules. It introduces a modification of the Parcone model, called "CuParcone", which allows high-performance evolution (e.g. 320 (and counting) times faster than on an ordinary PC) of Parcone modules.

Cuparcone: A High Performance Evolvable Neural Network Model

This appendix introduces a partially connected evolutionary neural network model based on a fully optimized CUDA (i.e. the C-like programming language of the NVidia Tesla supercomputer [NVidia]), called the "CuParcone" (i.e. "CUDA based Partially Connected Neural Evolutionary) model. With the innovative use of the powerful parallel computing capability of GPUs (i.e. Graphical Processing Units) CuParcone has achieved a performance increase of about 320 times (in gender recognition of human faces) compared to the comparable Parcone algorithm on a state-of-the-art, commodity single-processor server. The accuracy on this task does not decrease in moving from Parcone to CuParcone, and is comparable to the published results of other algorithms.

Introduction

Evolutionary algorithms have proven to be a powerful tool for learning neural network weights and architectures. One of their drawbacks is generally long computation times; however, compensating for this, they are relatively straightforwardly parallelizable. Here we report on some experiments with a model called "CuParcone", a parallelized version of the Parcone architecture for evolving recurrent neural nets, implemented specially for the CUDA GPU-based parallel architecture. The software we have implemented is quite general in application, and has been created to serve as part of the vision module of humanoid robotic architecture NAO, but for the sake of illustration we focus here on a single, relatively simple application, namely to the problem of gender recognition of human faces.

For the gender recognition task, we found that for 90 positive cases and 90 negative cases of greyscale images of 50×50 (RedGreenBlue) pixels, the training of 40 generations took 33 hours, 48 minutes, and 52 seconds on a PC with Intel Core 2 Duo.On the other hand, using the CUDA (Computing Unified Device Architecture) computing architecture, and using the powerful parallel computing capability of NVidia GPUs, we obtained a performance increase of over 323 times, and with a price far less than that for the traditional CPU MPI cluster. Accuracy in these experiments was comparable to the traditional Parcone model and other image classification algorithms, e.g. for 265 male and 265 female 0°~40° out-of-plane rotated faces randomly selected from the Color FERET database, we obtained an average recognition rate of 90.84%.

Computing Platform

To carry out the work reported here, we built a Tesla high performance computing platform with a Tesla C1060 computing card and a set of graphics workstations, costing about US$7000 and providing a floating point operation throughput of about 250 Gflops, approximately equal to the operational performance of a 200-core CPU computing cluster worth hundreds of thousands of dollars.

Table 1. System architecture

	Host	Device
Hardware configuration	Intel Xeon E3520 8GB (4x2GB) DDR2 RAM 300GB SAS 15K HDD	Tesla C1060
Software	Windows XP sp3 Cudatoolkit 2.2 CudaSDK 2.2 OpenCV 1.0	

Figure 7. System architecture

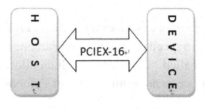

We implemented the CuParcone software using CUDA, an extension to ANSI C that implements several novel features, i.e. threads organized at two levels, shared memory and barrier synchronization. These key features enable CUDA to exploit two levels of parallelism, i.e. thread-level parallelism, that realizes fine grained data parallelism; and task-level parallelism that is more coarse-grained.

More specifically, the CUDA Computing Platform is composed of the host and the device. The host is an ordinary PC workstation. The device can be selected as required. We used a Tesla C1060 computing card. It has a 4G DDR3 onboard video memory, with 240 stream processors in GPU, reaching te computing capacity of CUDA 1.3. The device and host are connected via the PCIE-X16 interface, with the theoretical bandwidth of 4.2G/sec, (See Figure 7).

The Cuparcone Model

The CuParcone partially connected neural evolutionary model is composed of three layers, as shown in Figure 8. They are:

- The input layer that has I neurons. Each neuron can input one pixel of the training or testing image. Each neuron in the input layer can be connected to K neurons of the middle layer.
- The middle layer that has M neurons. Each neuron in the middle layer can be connected to K neurons of the input layer, middle layer and output layer.
- The output layer that has O neurons. Each neuron in the output layer can be connected to K neurons of the middle layer.
- I, M, O and K all can be different in different situations; and N is the total number of neurons in the whole network, N=I+M+O.

In some Parcone experiments, the traditional standardized exponential function was utilized, such as

$$S_i = \left(2.0 \left/ \left(1.0 + e^{-A_i}\right)\right.\right) - 1.0$$

(where Si is the output signal strength of neuron "i", and A is the activation function, i.e. the dot product of the neuron's input signals and their corresponding weights).

However, we found that for applications requiring a large number of neurons, better results were obtained with the following standardized function,

Figure 8. Network structure of the CuParcone model

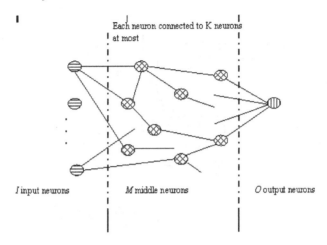

$$S_i = A_i / \left(|A_i| + c \right)$$

The sparse data structure used to implement CuParcone's recurrent neural net is given in Figure 9. Because the neural nets involved are quite sparse, rather than use a full array of connection weights, each neuron is associated with a list of other neurons to which it connects.

Due to the characteristics of the CUDA architecture, when the global memory accesses can be coalesced, the memory bandwidth will reach its maximum, and the costly global memory accesses become the main bottleneck for the performance of the CUDA program. The data structure in Figure 8 was chosen to accommodate this. Each column in CMatrix is a neuron's hash table. And the width of the matrix is $\left\lceil \dfrac{nbrNeurons}{16} \right\rceil \times 16$, which is the minimum multiple of 16 that is not less than the number of neurons, to satisfy the requirements of coalesced access to global memory.

The genetic algorithm used in this application was the same as used in the above Parcone model. In future work we will experiment with more complex GA implementations.

In the data structure of the usual evolvable neural network, in order to change one bit of the weight value during mutation, the connection's weight value is saved as a binary character string. This wastes space, and the floating-point weight value has to be recalculated after each mutation. On the other hand, in our data structure, bit operations were fully utilized, realizing the single bit mutation by directly editing the WeightValue, a strategy which not only saved space, but also increased speed.

Through these innovative data structures, 50% space was saved relative to Parcone, relieving the transmission bottleneck resulting from the slow PCIE bus (with the theoretical value of 4.2G/sec and an actual value usually not exceeding 3G/sec) between the GPU and the CPU.

Design of the Main Algorithms

We now describe the special software design approach that we used to implement the above algorithms in CUDA for use on the NVidia Tesla GPU supercomputer.

Figure 9. Data structures of the CuParcone model

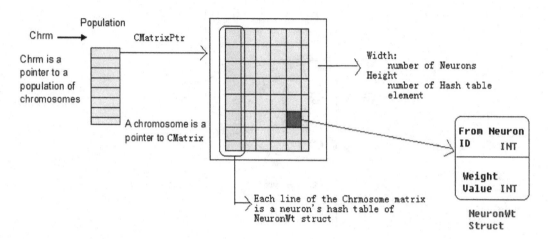

Task Allocation for the GPU and the CPU

Of all components of the CuParcone model, the FITNESS calculation in the genetic algorithm is the most suitable for the SIMD features of the CUDA platform. So we chose to migrate the FITNESS calculation to the DEVICE (TESLA C1060), and leave such operations as mutation and replication on the CPU of the Host.

In more detail our main reasons for this choice were:

a. In the ordinary GA algorithm, FITNESS calculation takes over 75% of the total time, and is the most time-consuming part.

b. In FITNESS calculation, due to the partially connected characteristic of PARCONE, the calculation of the output signals of each neuron in the neural network is essentially a sparse matrix multiplied by a vector. This operation conforms to the Single Instruction Multiple Data (SIMD) feature, and has a good parallel effect.

c. For mutation and replication, the GPU (CUDA) fails to show any advantage over the CPU. Because there are many branch instructions, the computing density is low. And the massive data transmission will influence the speed, for example, if the source gene and the target gene are not in the same card during gene replication, it is required to transmit the source gene back to the host through the PCIE bus first, and then send it to the space where the target gene is located through PCIE bus. As discussed previously, PCIE bus bandwidth is very limited, so this kind of replication is costly.

Design of the DEVICE (CUDA Part)

Algorithm for the Output Signal of the Neuron

In this model, a tick is defined to be the time taken for all neurons in the network to calculate their output signals. In order to calculate the output signal of each neuron in the model at a given moment, we adopted the following approach:

a. If this neuron is an input neuron, initialize its output signal with the input signal at tick=-1. Then the output signal is kept constant. Calculation is not required.
b. If this neuron is not an input neuron, then

Initialize its output signal to be 0 when tick = -1.

For each following tick, scan the connection hash table, and take out the output signal of From Neurons from the current signal table (signow) for each non-null connection. The output signal is multiplied by the corresponding connection's weight, and the product is added to the signal sum (sigsum).

After the end of scanning, the final sigsum is put through a squashing function (Eqn. 2), and the output signal of the current neuron is obtained. This output signal is then stored in the signal table of the next moment (signext)

Under the CUDA architecture, we let a thread correspond to a non-input neuron. Thus, on a single Tesla C1060, calculation of 960 neurons could be performed simultaneously at most.

Memory Access Optimization

To optimize memory access we took the following steps:

a. Based on the design of our data structure, the access to the connection hash table is an aligned access. The access is coalesced into the 128BIT transaction.
b. The texture cache is used to optimize the access to the current signal table.

Usually, the access to the current signal table will be a random access, but due to the characteristics of the hash table, if there is no conflict, the N'th elements in the hash table of different neurons will be the same, exhibiting strong data locality. Texture memory has a 24K cache for every three SMs. If a cache hit occurs, then it is not necessary to obtain data from the global memory. One access to global memory takes 300-400 cycles, whereas only 20-25 cycles are required in the cache, greatly increasing the speed.

Our tests indicated that the performance was improved by 20% after texture optimization compared to without texture optimization.

Selection of Operation Parameters

Threads per block: As shown in Figure 10. the maximum occupancy was achieved for the threads per block of 512, 256 and 128, which are all feasible blocksizes. But the granularity is too coarse for the blocksize of 512, which will influence the degree of parallelism and cause great waste. (An extreme case is when the non-input neuron number is 513, so that there is only one thread in the second block). Our tests indicated that there is no significant difference in the performance between blocksize = 256 and blocksize = 128. According to the recommendation in the NVidia programming guide, 256 was selected as the blocksize.

More Parallelizations

For some input sizes, due to the limit of the network size, the computing power of the GPU cannot be fully utilized. For instance, for a gray-scale image of 50×50 pixels, there are only 768 non-input neurons.

Figure 10. Relationship between the computing throughput and threads per block

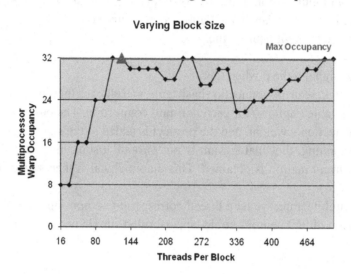

With the blocksize of 256, there are only 3 blocks, and since each card of Tesla has 30 SMs, so at least 30 blocks are required to fill the 30 SMs. According to the NVidia programming guide, the number of blocks should be at least twice the number of SMs. Therefore, we can calculate multiple genes simultaneously on one card. We take $60/\lfloor(nbrNeurons-nbrInNeurons)/256\rfloor$ as the number of genes calculated simultaneously on each card.

Performance Test

We used the task of face-based gender recognition to test the performance of the CuParcone model. First, we randomly selected 530 face images from the Color FERET database (including 265 male faces and 265 female faces). These images include frontal face images as well as side face images between -40° ~ +40°. We randomly selected 90 male images, which were sequentially numbered 1-90, to be positive cases of the training sample set, and randomly selected 90 female images, which were sequentially numbered 1-90, to be negative cases of the training sample set. The other 175 male images and 175 female images constituted the test sample set.

Given a color image, we first cut out the face part from the color image to obtain a second color image, which was then condensed to 50×50 after being sharpened and decolorized to obtain the image used as input to CuParcone.

In our model, the output value (Op) of each neural network is a real number between -1~+1.

When a male test sample is input to the neural network, if the output value of the network Op>0.1, it is considered that the network makes a correct judgment. When -0.1<Op<0.1, it is considered that the network fails to recognize the input sample, and when Op<-0.1, it is considered that the network makes a wrong judgment.

Similarly, when a female test sample is input to the neural network, if the output value of the network Op<-0.1, it is considered that the network makes a correct judgment. When -0.1<Op<0.1, it is considered that the network fails to recognize the input sample, and when Op>-0.1, it is considered that the network makes a wrong judgment.

Table 2. Performance comparison between CuParcone and Parcone

Training generations	Running time	Accuracy rate		Speedup
Parcone	33 hours, 48 minutes, 52 seconds (121732 secs)	Male	77.57%	323.19 times
		Female	88.93%	
CuParcone	6 minutes, 16.65 seconds (376.65 secs)	Male	76.71%	
		Female	89.57%	

We conducted a series of experiments, each involving 50×50 pixel images were taken as the training sample and test sample, prepared as described above.

Our first experiment involved a performance comparison between CuParcone and Parcone. Here there were 60 male images as the positive cases and 60 female images as the negative cases for the training sample, and the test sample included all the 175 male images and 175 female images in the test sample set. After 40 generations of evolution simultaneously in CuParcone and Parcone, the running times and recognition rates for the two models were compared.

The neural network consists of three layers (Figure 2). The neuron number in the input layer I=2500, the neuron number in the middle layer M=767, the neuron number in the output layer O=1, and the number of neurons connected to each neuron K=100. The evolutionary parameter is the population size Popsize=64, and the gene number calculated simultaneously by GPU is 16. The experimental result is shown in Table 2.

In our second experiment, 30 positive cases and 30 negative cases, 60 positive cases and 60 negative cases, and 90 positive cases and 90 negative cases were evolved for 40 generations in CuParcone. The test sample included all the 175 male images and 175 female images in the test sample set. The corresponding running times were recorded. The experimental results are shown in Figure 11.

In our third experiment, there were 90 male images as the positive cases and 90 female images as the negative cases for the training sample, and the test sample included all the 175 male images and 175 female images in the test sample set. After evolution for 20, 40, 60, 80 and 100 generations in CuParcone, the corresponding running times were recorded. The experimental result is shown in Figure 12.

Recognition Results Comparison Based on Feret Database

Our final experiment was oriented toward assessing the accuracy of CuParcone versus other face-based gender recognition methods described in the literature. Again, preprocessed 50×50 pixel images were taken as the training sample and test sample. There were 90 male images as the positive cases and 90 female images as the negative cases for the training sample; and the test sample included all the 175 male images and 175 female images in the test sample set.

After evolution for 700 generations in CuParcone, the accuracy rate was recorded and compared to other famous gender recognition methods.

Further, we note that some of these results from the literature use only straight frontal face images, whereas our training and test sets include side face images between -40°~+40°. We obtained comparable results even under these conditions, which indicates that CuParcone is not only accurate but reasonably robust.

Figure 11. Running time vs. training sample number

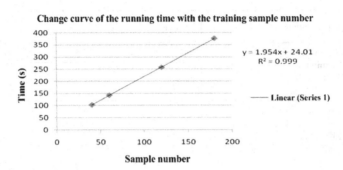

ANALYSIS OF EXPERIMENTAL RESULTS

Analysis of the above experimental results yields the following conclusions:

a.   Although all pixels were taken as the input of CuParcone, CuParcone still could reach stability, and achieve almost the same recognition rate as Parcone. This indicates that CuParcone is a correct implementation of the Parcone algorithm, and can effectively process a large number of input data.

b.   CuParcone shows a great increase in speed compared to Parcone. In experiment 1, the running time was reduced from 33 hours, 48 minutes and 52 seconds to 376.65 seconds, with the performance exceeding 2 orders of magnitude, reaching 323.19 times. An outstanding performance has been obtained with a large number of data. On the face-based gender recognition task, the general running times for CuParcone are at the minute level, a great improvement compared to the original evolution speed that often takes dozens of hours.

c.   When the CuParcone module is used for Gender recognition, the accuracy rate is close to or better than that obtained by standard methods described in the literature.

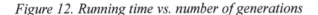

Figure 12. Running time vs. number of generations

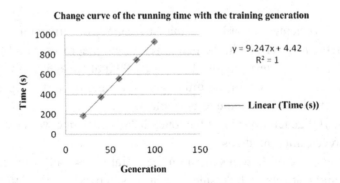

Table 3. Accuracy rate comparison between different methods based on FERET

Method	Accuracy rate
CuParcone with gray images	88.39%
CuParcone with color images	90.75%
PPBTF filtering features	91.75%
Gabor filtering features	85.68%
ICA+COS	85.33%
ICA+LDA	93.33%

CONCLUSION

Our experimental results indicate that the CuParcone model is an efficient partially connected evolutionary neural network model, capable of performing gender recognition without any preliminary phase of feature extraction. Speed-wise, implemented on our Tesla it achieves a performance increase of over 300 times over Parcone while achieving roughly the same accuracy. As the cost of the Tesla is US$7000, roughly 10x the cost of the standard servers normally used to run Parcone, CuParcone vastly increases the amount of processing per dollar achieved.

While the results presented here are restricted to a single task, we are confident that the architecture we have implemented will be more generally applicable. Our intention in implementing CuParcone is to use it for a variety of image and video classification tasks occurring in a humanoid robotics project Nao, and subsequent publications will focus on the accuracy and speedup achievable via CuParcone in this context.

REFERENCES

de Garis, H. (2008). "A "PARtially COnnected Neural Evolutionary" Model Serving as the Basis for Building China's First Artificial Brain", Proceedings of 2008 3rd International Conference on Intelligent System and Knowledge Engineering. China: Xiamen.

Goertzel, Ben & de Garis, Hugo(2008). "XIA-MAN: An Integrative, Extensible Architecture for Intelligent Humanoid Robotics" AAAI Symposium on Biologically-Inspired Cognitive Architectures, Washington DC

Jain, A., Huang, J., & Fang, S. (2005). "Gender Identification Using Frontal Facial Images", 2005 IEEE International Conference on Multimedia and Expo, Amsterdam, Netherlands. Goldberg, David (1989). "Genetic Algorithms in Search, Optimization and Machine Learning" Addison Wesley.

Lu, H., Huang, Y., Chen, Y., & Yang, D. (2008). Automatic gender recognition based on pixel-pattern-based texture feature. *Journal of Real-Time Image Processing*, 3, 109–116. doi:10.1007/s11554-008-0072-2

Compilation of References

A. J. Mansfield &J. L. Wayman (2002), Best Practices in Testing and Reporting Performance of Biometric Devices, Version 2.01. *Centre for Mathematics and Scientific Computing, National Physical Laboratory, Queens Road, Teddington, Middlesex, TW11 OLW*.

A. Martin, G. Doddington, T. Kamm, M. Ordowski, M.Przybocki (1997). The DET curve in Assessment of Detection Task Performance. *Proc. Of Eurospeech '97, 4*, 1895-1898.

A.M. Martinez & R. Benavente (1998). *The AR Face Database*. CVC Technical Report #24.

Abarbanel, H. D. I. (1996). *Analysis of observed chaotic data*. New York: Springer-Verlag.

Abdallah, M. A., Samu, T. I., & Grisson, W. A. (1995). Automatic target identification using neural networks. *SPIE Proceedings on Intelligent Robots and Computer Vision XIV, 2588*, 556–565.

Ackley, D. H., Hinton, G. E., & Sejnowski, T. J. (1985). A learning algorithm for Boltzmann Machines. *Cognitive Science, 9*, 147–169. doi:.doi:10.1207/s15516709cog0901_7

Ader, R., Felten, L., & Cohen, N. (Eds.). (2001). *Psychoneruoimmunology* (3rd ed.). Academic Press.

Adleman, L. (1994). Molecular Computation of Solution to Combinatorial Problems. *Science, 266*(11), 1021–1024. doi:10.1126/science.7973651

Adler, D. W. (2001). DB2 Spatial Extender-Spatial Data with the RDBMS. In *Proceedings International Conference on Very Large Data Bases (VLDB)*, pp. 687-690.

Agrawal, R., & Srikant, R. (1994). Fast Algorithms for Mining Association Rules in Large Databases. *Proceedings of the 20th International Conference on Very Large Data Bases* (pp. 487-499). ACM.

Agrawal, R., Gehrke, J., & Gunopulos, D. (2005). Automatic Subspace Clustering of High Dimensional Data. *Data Mining and Knowledge Discovery, 11*(1), 5–33. doi:10.1007/s10618-005-1396-1

Agrawal, R., Imielinski, T., & Swami, A. (1993). Mining Association Rules between Sets of Items in Large Databases. *Proceedings of the 1993 ACM SIGMOD International Conference on Management of Data* (pp. 207-216). ACM.

Ahonen, H., Heinonen, O., Klemettinen, M., & Verkamo, A. I. (1997). *Applying Data Mining Techniques in Text Analysis* (Technical Report C-1997-23). University of Helsinki.

Aikawa, T., Itoh, T., Takayama, Y., Suzuki, K., & Imamura, M. (2003). A Proposal of a Method of Analysis of Questionnaires Using Text Mining Based on Concept Extraction. *IPSJ SIG Notes*, 2003-FI-70-1, (pp. 1-6). (in Japanese)

Akabane, T., et al. (2006). A proposal for the automatic tone manipulator based on gray systems theory. *Proc. of the 8th annual conf. of JSKE (Japan Society of Kansei Engineering)* 2006, 146. (in Japanese)

Akashi, K., & Uozumi, T. (2008). Evaluation of brain activity by change of the sound source using brain blood flowmeter (NIRS). *Proc. of the 10th annual conf. of JSKE 2008 (CD-ROM)* (in Japanese)

Akibane, T., Yamaguchi, D., & Nagai, M. (2007). Automatic manipulating methods for synthesizer's tone in the development of music. *Proc. of KEER 2007 (International Conference on Kansei Engineering and Emotion Research) (CD-ROM)*

Alicja Wieczorkowska, P. S., & Zbigniew, W. Ras. (2006). *Multi-Label Classification of Emotions in Music.* Paper presented at the International Conference on Intelligent information Processing and Web Mining, Ustron, Poland.

Amari, S. (1988). Mathematical theory of self-organization in neural nets. In Seelen, W. V., Shaw, G., & Leinhos, U. M. (Eds.), *Organization of Neural Networks: Structures and Models*. New York: Academic Press.

Andrews, R., Diederich, J., & Tickle, A. (1995). *A survey and critique of techniques for extracting rules from trained artificial neural networks*. Knowledge-Based Systems.

Antonucci, M., Tirozzi, B., & Yarunin, N. D. (1994). Numerical simulation of neural networks with translation and rotation invariant pattern recognition. *International Journal of Modern Physics B, 8*(11-12), 1529–1541. doi:. doi:10.1142/S0217979294000658

Aoshima, Y., & Tokosumi, A. (2007). Extracting musical concepts from written texts: A case study of Toru Takemitsu. In *Proc. of KEER 2007*. (CD-ROM)

Apolloni, B., Caravalho, C., & De Falco, D. (1989). Quantum stochastic optimization. *Stochastic Processes and their Applications, 33*, 233–244. doi:.doi:10.1016/0304-4149(89)90040-9

Arifin, S., & Cheung, P. Y. K. (2007, Sep 17-19). *A novel probabilistic approach to modeling the pleasure-arousal-dominance content of the video based on "Working memory"*. Paper presented at the International Conference on Semantic Computing (ICSC 2007), Irvine, CA.

Arons, B. (1992). A Review of the Cocktail Party Effect. *Journal of the American Voice I/O Society, 12*, 35 - 50.

Asch, S. E. (1946). Forming impressions of personality. *Journal of Abnormal Psychology, 41*(3), 258–290. doi:10.1037/h0055756

Baaijens, S., & Nijkamp, P. (1999). Time pioneers and travel behaviour: An investigation into the viability of "slow motion". *Growth and Change, 30*(2), 237–263.. doi:10.1111/0017-4815.00112

Baars, B. (2001). *In the Theater of Consciousness*. New York: Oxford University Press USA.

Babitskii, V. I. (1978). *Theory of Vibroimpact Systems. Approximate methods*. Moscow: Nauka.

Bach, E., Condon, A., & Glaser, E. (1998). DNA Models and Algorithms for NP-Complete Problems. *Journal of Computer and System Sciences, 57*(2), 172–186. doi:10.1006/jcss.1998.1586

Baek, S., Cho, M., Hwang, M., & Kim, P. (2006). *Kansei-based Image Retrieval Associated with Color. Lecture Notes in Artificial Intelligence (LNAI) 3849* (pp. 326–333). New York: Springer-Verlag.

Bailey, K., Brumm, J., & Grossardt, T. (2001). Towards structured public involvement in highway design: A comparative study of visualization methods and preference modeling using CAVE (Casewise Visual Evaluation). *Journal of Geographic Information and Decision Analysis, 5*(1), 1–15.

Baker, J. E. (1985). Adaptive selection methods for genetic algorithms In J. J. Grefenstette (Ed.), *Proceedings of 1st International Conference on Genetic Algorithms* (pp. 101-111). Hillsdale, NJ: Lawrence Erlbaum Associates.

Balasubramaniam, R., Riley, M. A., & Turvey, M. T. (2000). Specificity of postural sway to the demands of a precision task. *Gait & Posture, 11*(1), 12–24. doi:10.1016/S0966-6362(99)00051-X

Bandyopadhyay, S., & Maulik, U. (2001). Nonparametric genetic clustering: comparison of validity indices. *IEEE Trans. on Systems, Man, and Cybernetics. Part C: Applications and Reviews, 31*(1), 120–125.

Bandyopadhyay, S., & Pal, S. K. (2007). *Classification and Learning Using Genetic Algorithms: Application in Bioinformatics and Web Intelligence*. Germany: Springer.

Bandyopadhyay, S., Maulik, U., & Wang, J. T. L. (Eds.). (2007). *Analysis of Biological Data: A Soft Computing Approach*. Singapore: World Scientific.

Bandyopadhyay, S., Maulik, U., Holder, L., & Cook, D. (Eds.). (2005). *Advanced Methods for Knowledge Discovery from Complex Data*. London: Springer.

Banerjee, T. P. (2002). An Adapted Lesk Algorithm for Word Sense Disambiguation Using WordNet. *In Proceedings the Third International Conference on Intelligent text Processing and Computational Linguistics*, pp. 136-145.

Baraldi, A., Binaghi, E., Blonda, P., Brivio, P. A., & Rampini, A. (2001). Comparison of the multilayer perceptron with neuro-fuzzy techniques in the estimation of cover class mixture in remotely sensed data. *IEEE Transactions on Geoscience and Remote Sensing*, 39(5), 994–1005. doi:.doi:10.1109/36.921417

BDL. (2009). *Business Design Laboratory*. Retrieved from http://www.business-design.co.jp/en/

Beckmann, N., & Kriegel, H. (1990). The R*-tree: An Efficient and Robust Access Method for Points and Rectangles. In *Proceedings ACM SIGMOD International Conference*, pp. 322-331.

Belin, P., Fecteau, S., & Bédard, C. (2004). Thinking the voice: neural correlates of voice perception. *Trends in Cognitive Sciences*, 8(3), 129–135. doi:10.1016/j.tics.2004.01.008

Benenson, Y., & Gil, B. (2004). An Autonomous Molecular Computer for Logical Control of Gene Expression. *Nature*, 429, 423–429. doi:10.1038/nature02551

Berchtold, S., Keim, D., & Kriegel, H. (1996). The X-tree: An Index Structure for High- dimensional data. In *Proceedings the 22nd International Conference on Very large Data Bases (VLDB)*, pp. 28-39.

Bernstein, N. A. (1996). On Dexterity and Its Development, In Latash, M. L. (Trans.), Latash, M. L. and Turvey, M. T. (Eds.), *Dexterity and Its Development*, (pp.1-244). Mahwah, NJ: Lawrence, Erlbaum.

Bertini, M., Cucchiara, R., Del Bimbo, A., & Prati, A. (2004). *Content-based video adaptation with user's preferences*. Paper presented at the 2004 IEEE International Conference on Multimedia and Expo (ICME), Taipei, Taiwan.

Bezdek, J. C. (1992). On the relationship between neural networks, pattern recognition and intelligence. *International Journal of Approximate Reasoning*, 6, 85–107. doi:10.1016/0888-613X(92)90013-P

Bhattacharyya, S., & Dutta, P. (2006). Designing pruned neighborhood neural networks for object extraction from noisy background. *Journal of Foundations of Computing and Decision Sciences*, 31(2), 105–134.

Bhattacharyya, S., Dutta, P., & Maulik, U. (2008). Self Organizing Neural Network (SONN) based gray scale object extractor with a Multilevel Sigmoidal (MUSIG) activation function. *Journal of Foundations of Computing and Decision Sciences*, 33(2), 131–165.

Bianchi-Berthouze, N., & Catarci, T. (2003). K-DIME: An affective image filtering system. *IEEE MultiMedia*, 10(3), 103–106. doi:10.1109/MMUL.2003.1218262

Bigus, J. P. (1996). *Data Mining With Neural Networks: Solving Business Problems from Application Development to Decision Support*. New York: Mcgraw-Hill.

Bilbro, G. L., White, M., & Synder, W.(n.d.). Image segmentation with neurocomputers. In Eckmiller, R., & Malsburg, C. V. D. (Eds.), *Neural computers*. New York: Springer-Verlag.

Bishop, C. M. (1995). *Neural Networks for Pattern Recognition*. Oxford, UK: Oxford University Press.

Bishop, S. R. (1994). Impact oscillators. *Philosophical Transactions. Physical Sciences and Engineering*, 347–351.

Blackburn, D. M. (2004). *Biometrics 101, version 3.1*. Federal Bureau of Investigation.

Boneh, C. (1996). Breaking DES Using a Molecular Computing. *DNA based. Computer*, 37–66.

Bosch, J. A., Ring, C., de Geus, E. J., Veerman, E. C., & Amerongen, A. V. (2002). Stress and secretory immunity. *International Review of Neurobiology*, *52*(1), 213–253. doi:10.1016/S0074-7742(02)52011-0

Boskovitz, V., & Guterman, H. (2002). An adaptive neuro-fuzzy system for automatic image segmentation and edge detection. *IEEE Transactions on Fuzzy Systems*, *10*(2), 247–262. doi:.doi:10.1109/91.995125

Boyd, S., El Ghaoui, L., Feron, E., & Balakrishnan, V. (1994). *Linear matrix inequalities in system and control theory*. Society for Industrial Mathematics.

Braich, S., Johnson, C., Rothemund, W. K., & Adleman, L. (2001). Solution of a Satisfy Problem on a Gel-based DNA Computer. *The 6th International Workshop on DNA Based Computing, London: Springer-verlag*, 27-42.

Breazeal, C., & Scassellati, B. (1999). A Context-dependent Attention System for a Social Robot. *In Proceedings of the Sixteenth International Joint Conference on Artificial Intelligence*, (pp.1146–1151).

Brogliato, B. (2000). Impacts in mechanical systems-Analysis and modeling. *Berlin, Springer-Verlag(Lecture Notes in Physics., 551*. Brogliato, B., Ten Dam, A. A., Paoli, L., Genot, F., & Abadie, M. (2002). Numerical simulation of finite dimensional multibody nonsmooth mechanical systems. *Applied Mechanics Reviews*, *55*, 107. doi:10.1115/1.1454112

Broomhead, D. S., & Lowe, D. (1988). Multivariate functional interpolation and adaptive networks. *Complex Systems.*, *2*, 321–355.

Buchsbaum, M. S., Muscettola, G., & Goodwin, F. K. (1981). Urinary MHPG, stress response, personality factors and patients with major affective disorders. *Neuropsychology*, *7*, 212–224.

Buhyoff, G. J., & Wellman, J. D. (1980). The specification of a non-linear psychophysical function for visual landscape dimensions. *Journal of Leisure Research*, *12*, 257–272. http://www.cababstractsplus.org/abstracts/Abstract.aspx?AcNo=19811874198.

Burns, E. M. (1999). Intervals, scales, and tuning. In Deutsch, D. (Ed.), *The Psychology of Music* (2nd ed.). San Diego, CA: Academic Press. doi:10.1016/B978-012213564-4/50008-1

Cabrera, D. (1999). *Psysound: A Computer Program for Psychoacoustical Analysis*. Paper presented at the the Australian Acoustical Society Conference.

Carpenter, G. A. (1989). Neural network models for pattern recognition and associative memory. *Neural Networks*, *2*(4), 243–258. doi:.doi:10.1016/0893-6080(89)90035-X

Carpenter, G. A., & Grossberg, S. (1991). *Pattern recognition by self-organizing neural networks*. Cambridge, MA: MIT Press.

Carpenter, G. A., & Ross, W. D. (1995). ART-EMAP: A neural network architecture for object recognition by evidence accumulation. *IEEE Transactions on Neural Networks*, *6*(4), 805–818. doi:.doi:10.1109/72.392245

Carretié, L., Tapia, M., Mercado, F., Albert, J., López-Martín, S., & Serna, J. M. l. (2004). Voltage-Based Versus Factor Score-Based Source Localization Analyses of Electrophysiological Brain Activity: A Comparison. *Brain Topography*, *17*(2), 109–115. doi:10.1007/s10548-004-1008-1

Cassandras, C. G. (1993). *Discrete event systems*. New York: Springer.

Castells, F., Laguna, P., Sörnmo, L., Bollmann, A., & Roig, J. M. (2007). Principal Component Analysis in ECG Signal Processing. *EURASIP Journal on Advances in Signal Processing.* 2007(1), 21 pages.

Cerny, V. (1985). A thermodynamical approach to the traveling salesman problem: an efficient simulation algorithm. *Journal of Optimization Theory and Applications*, *45*, 41–51. doi:.doi:10.1007/BF00940812

Charalampidis, D., Kasparis, T., & Georgiopoulos, M. (2001). Classification of noisy signals using fuzzy ARTMAP neural networks. *IEEE Transactions on Neural Networks*, *12*(5), 1023–1036. doi:.doi:10.1109/72.950132

Chauvin, Y. (1989). A back-propagation algorithm with optimal use of hidden units. In *Advances in neural information processing systems 1* (pp. 519–526). San Francisco: Morgan Kaufmann Publishers Inc.

Chauvin, Y., & Rumelhart, D. E. (1995). *Backpropagation: theory, architectures, and applications*. Hillsdale, NJ: L. Erlbaum Associates Inc.

Chee, J., & Seow, S. C. (2007). *The electrocardiogram. U.R. Archarya, J.S. Suri, J.A.E. Spaan, and S.M. Krishnan, Advances in Cardiac Signal Processing*. Berlin: Springer-Verlag.

Chen, C. T., Chen, K. S., & Lee, J. S. (2003). Fuzzy neural classification of SAR images. *IEEE Transactions on Geoscience and Remote Sensing*, *41*(9), 2089–2100. doi:.doi:10.1109/TGRS.2003.813494

Chen, D., & Bovik, A. C. (1990). Visual Pattern Image Coding. *IEEE Transactions on Communications*, *38*(12), 2137–2146. doi:10.1109/26.64656

Chen, Y., Hwang, H., & Chen, B. (1995). *Color image analysis using fuzzy set theory*. Proceedings of International Conference on Image Processing.(pp. 242-245).

Cheng, H.-T., Yang, Y.-H., Lin, Y.-C., Liao, I. B., & Chen, H. H. (2008). *Automatic chord recognition for music classification and retrieval*. Paper presented at the 2008 IEEE International Conference on Multimedia and Expo., Hannover, Germany.

Cherry, C. E. (1953). Some Experiments on the Recognition of Speech, with One and with Two Ears. *The Journal of the Acoustical Society of America*, *25*(5), 975–979. doi:10.1121/1.1907229

Chiu, W. C., Hines, E. L., Forno, C., Hunt, R., & Oldfield, S. (1990). Artificial neural networks for photogrammetric target processing. *SPIE Proceedings on Close-Range Photogrammetry Meets Machine Vision*, *1395*(2), 794–801.

Cho, J. (2009). Bayesian Method for Detecting Emotion from Voice for Kansei Robots. *Kansei Engineering International*, *8*(1), 15–22.

Cho, S., & Lee, J. (2002). A human-oriented image retrieval system using interactive genetic algorithm. *IEEE Transactions on Systems, Man and Cybernetics. Part A*, *32*(3), 452–458.

Choi, Y., & Krishnapuran, R. (1995). Image enhancement based on fuzzy logic. *Proceedings of International Conference on Image Processing*. (pp. 167-170).

Chua, L. O., & Yang, L. (1988). Cellular network: Applications. *IEEE Transactions on Circuits and Systems*, *35*(10), 1273–1290. doi:.doi:10.1109/31.7601

Chua, L. O., & Yang, L. (1988). Cellular network: Theory. *IEEE Transactions on Circuits and Systems*, *35*(10), 1257–1282. doi:.doi:10.1109/31.7600

Chujo, K., & Utiyama, M. (2006). Selecting level-specific specialized vocabulary using statistical measures. [Elsevier.]. *System*, *34*, 255–269. doi:10.1016/j.system.2005.12.003

Chung, F., & Fung, B. (2003). Fuzzy color quantization and its application to scene change detection. *Proceedings of MIR*, *03*, 157–162.

Chung, S.-C., & Min, B.-C. (2003). *Correlation between On-Line Subjective Evaluation and GSR*. Paper presented at the 4th Japan-Korea International Symposium on Kansei Engineering, Tsukuba, Japan.

Church, K. W., & Hanks, P. (1990). WORD ASSOCIATION NORMS, MUTUAL INFORMATION, AND LEXICOGRAPHY. [Cambridge, MA: MIT Press.]. *Computational Linguistics*, *16*(1), 76–83.

Clifton, K. J., Smith, A. D. L., & Rodriguez, D. (2007). The development and testing of an audit for the pedestrian environment. *Landscape and Urban Planning*, *80*, 95–100..doi:10.1016/j.landurbplan.2006.06.008

Colorni, A., Dorigo, M., & Maniezzo, V. (1991). *Distributed Optimization by Ant Colonies, actes de la première conférence européenne sur la vie artificielle* (pp. 134–142). France: Elsevier Publishing.

Cornoldi, C., De Beni, R., Mammarella, I. C., & John, H. B. (2008). Mental Imagery. In Byrne, J. H. (Ed.), *Learning and Memory: A Comprehensive Reference* (pp. 103–123). Oxford, UK: Academic Press. doi:10.1016/B978-012370509-9.00158-3

Cortes, C., & Vapnik, V. N. (1995). Support vector networks. *Machine Learning, 20*, 273–297. doi:.doi:10.1007/BF00994018

Cox, E. (2005). *Fuzzy Modeling and Genetic Algorithms for Data Mining and Exploration*. San Francisco: Morgan Kaufmann.

Craven, M. W., & Shavlik, J. W. (1994). Using Sampling and Queries to Extract Rules from Trained Neural Networks. In *Proceedings of the 11th International Conference on Machine Learning,* (pp. 37-45).

Crawley, M. J. (2007). *The R Book*. England: John Wiley & Sons, Ltd. doi:10.1002/9780470515075

Cui, G., Li, C., & Zhang, X. (2009). Application of DNA Computing by Self-assembly on 0-1 Knapsack Problem. *Advances in neural networks*, (5583), 684-693.

Cui, G., Niu, Y., Wang, Y., & Pan, L. (2007). A New Approach Based on PSO Algorithm to Find Good Computational Encoding Sequences. *Progress in Natural Science*, (17): 712–716.

Cui, Y. (2003). High-dimensional Indexing. [LNCS]. *Lecture Notes in Computer Science, 2341*.

Cukras, A., Faulhammer, D., & Lipton, R. (1998). Chess Games: A Model for RNA-based Computation. *The 4th International Meeting on DNA based Computer. Baltimore, Penns*, 159-162.

Cvitanovic, P. (1984). *Universality in chaos*. Bristol: Adam Hilger, Ltd.

Dan Liu, L. L. Hong-Jiang Zhang. (2003, 27 Oct). *Automatic Mood Detection from Acoustic Music Data*. Paper presented at the International Symposium on Music Information Retrieval, Baltimore, MD, USA.

Dan Yang, W. L. (2004). *Disambiguating Music Emotion Using Software Agents*. Paper presented at the Proc. Int. Conf. Music Information Retrieval(ISMIR), Barcelona, Spain.

Danto, A. C. (1985). *Narration and Knowledge*. New York: Columbia University Press (translated to Japanese by Kawamoto, K. (2000). Tokyo: Kokubunsha).

Das, A., & Chakrabarti, B. K. (Eds.). (2005). Quantum Annealing and Related Optimization Methods. *Lecture Note in Physics* (*Vol. 679*). Heidelberg: Springer. doi:10.1007/11526216

Datta, R., Joshi, D., Li, J., & Wang, J. Z. (2006, May). *Studying Aesthetics in Photographic Images Using a Computational Approach*. Paper presented at the European Conference on Computer Vision, Graz, Austria.

Davies, D. L., & Bouldin, D. W. (1979). A cluster separation measure. *IEEE Transactions on Pattern Analysis and Machine Intelligence, 1*(4), 224–227. doi:10.1109/TPAMI.1979.4766909

Davis, L. (Ed.). (1991). *Handbook of Genetic Algorithms*. New York: Van Nostrand Reinhold.

de Garis, H., & Korkin, M. (2002). The CAM-Brain Machine (CBM) An FPGA Based Hardware Tool which Evolves a 1000 Neuron Net Circuit Module in Seconds and Updates a 75 Million Neuron Artificial Brain for Real Time Robot Control. *Neurocomputing, 42*, 35–68. doi:10.1016/S0925-2312(01)00593-8

Deguchi, M., Wakasugi, J., Ikegami, T., Nanba, S., & Yamgaguchi, M. (2006). Evaluation of driver stress using motor-vehicle driving simulator. *IEEJ Trans. Sensors and Micromachines, 126*, 438–444. doi:10.1541/ieejsmas.126.438

Deneubourg, J.-L., Aron, S., Goss, S., & Pasteels, J.-M. (1990). The self-organizing exploratory pattern of the Argentine ant. *Journal of Insect Behavior, 3*, 159. doi:.doi:10.1007/BF01417909

Di Bernardo, M., Budd, C. J., Kowalczyk, P., & Champneys, A. R. (2007). *Piecewise-smooth dynamical systems: theory and applications*. New York: Springer.

Dickerson, S. S., & Kemeny, M. E. (2004). Acute stressors and cortisol responses: A theoretical integration and synthesis of laboratory research. *Psychological Bulletin, 130*(3), 335–391. doi:10.1037/0033-2909.130.3.355

Domeniconi, C., & Gunopulos, D. (2007). Locally adaptive metrics for clustering high dimensional data. *Data Mining and Knowledge Discovery Journal, 14*, 63–97. doi:10.1007/s10618-006-0060-8

Dorigo, M. (1992). *Optimization, Learning and Natural Algorithms*. PhD thesis. Politecnico di Milano, Italie.

Dorigo, M., & Gambardella, L. M. (1997). Ant Colony System: A Cooperative Learning Approach to the Traveling Salesman Problem. *IEEE Transactions on Evolutionary Computation, 1*(1), 53–66. doi:.doi:10.1109/4235.585892

Duda, R. O., & Hart, P. E. (1973). *Pattern classification and scene analysis*. New York: Wiley.

Dunning, T. (1993). Accurate Methods for the Statistics of Surprise and Coincidence. [Cambridge, MA: MIT Press.]. *Computational Linguistics, 19*(1), 61–74.

Düntsch, I., & Gediga, G. (1998). Uncertainty measures of rough set prediction. *Artificial Intelligence, 106*(1), 109–137..doi:10.1016/S0004-3702(98)00091-5

Eberhart, R. C., & Kennedy, J. (1995). A new optimizer using particle swarm theory. *Proc. 6th International Symposium on Micromachine and Human Science*, Japan, pp. 39-43.

Echelberger, H. E. (1979). The semantic differential in landscape research. in *Proceedings of Our National Landscape: a Conference on Applied Techniques for Analysis and Management of the Visual Resource*(pp. 524-531). Incline Village.

Eckmann, J. P., Kamphorst, S. O., & Ruelle, D. (1987). Recurrence Plots of Dynamical Systems. *Europhysics Letters, 4*(9), 973–977. doi:10.1209/0295-5075/4/9/004

Edelsbrunner, H., Kirkpatrickand, D. G., & Seidel, R. (1983). On the Shape of a Set of Points in a Plane. *IEEE Transactions on Information Theory, IT-29*, 551–559. doi:10.1109/TIT.1983.1056714

Egmond, P. V., Nijkamp, P., & Vindigni, G. (2003). A comparative analysis of the performance of urban public transport systems in Europe. *International Social Science Journal, 55*(176), 235–247. doi:.doi:10.1111/j.1468-2451.2003.05502005.x

Egmont-Petersen, M., & Arts, T. (1999). Recognition of radiopaque markers in X-ray images using a neural network as nonlinear filter. *Pattern Recognition Letters, 20*(5), 521–533. doi:.doi:10.1016/S0167-8655(99)00024-0

Egmont-Petersen, M., de Ridder, D., & Handels, H. (2002). Image processing using neural networks - a review. *Pattern Recognition, 35*(10), 2279–2301. doi:.doi:10.1016/S0031-3203(01)00178-9

Ekman, P. (1975). *Unmasking the Face*. Upper Saddle River, NJ: Prentice-Hall.

Elke Achtert. & Christian B., et al. (2008). Detection and Visualization of Subspace Cluster Hierarchies. (*LNCS. 4443*, pp. 152-163).

Elsenda, F., Anna, S., & Ramon, E. (2001). Synthesis and Hybridization Properties of DNA and PNA Chimeras Carrying. *Bioorganic & Medicinal Chemistry, 8*, 291–297.

Endou, Y., Ojika, T., Sato, H., & Harada, A. (2001). Construction of Kansei Database with Ise Katagami Lattice and Unit Structure: Extraction and Use of Cognitive Characteristics on Pattern Design. *Bulletin of Japanese Society for Science of Design, 48*(3), 119–124.

Ergin, A., Karaesmen, E., Micallef, A., & Williams, A. T. (2004). A new methodology for evaluating coastal scenery: fuzzy logic systems. *Area, 36*(4), 367–386.. doi:10.1111/j.0004-0894.2004.00238.x

Escabi, M. A. (2005). Biosignal Processing. J. Enderle, S. Blanchard, and J. Bronzino, *Introduction to Biomedical Engineering*. Burlinton: Academic Press.

Eshelman, L. J., & Schaffer, J. D. (1993). Real-coded genetic algorithms and interval schemata. In L. Whitley (Ed.), *Foundations of Genetic Algorithms* (pp 187-202). 2, San Mateo, CA: Morgan Kaufmann.

Eun-Jong, P., & Joon-Whoan, L. (2008). *Emotion-based image retrieval using multiple-queries and consistency feedback.* Paper presented at the 6th IEEE International Conference on Industrial Informatics, INDIN 2008.

Evans, P., Bristow, M., Hucklebridge, F., Clow, A., & Pang, F. Y. (1994). Stress, arousal, cortisol and secretory Immunoglobulin A in students undergoing assessment. *The British Journal of Clinical Psychology, 33,* 575–576.

Evans-Cowley, J. (2006). Sidewalk planning and policies in small cities. *Journal of Urban Planning and Development, 132*(2), 71–75..doi:10.1061/(ASCE)0733-9488(2006)132:2(71)

Feigin, M. I. (1994). *Forced oscillations in systems with discontinuous nonlinearities.* Moscow: Nauka Publication. [in Russian]

Feldman, R., Fresko, M., Kinar, Y., Lindell, Y., Liphstat, O., Rajman, M., et al. (1998). Text Mining at the Term Level. *Proceedings of the Second European Symposium on Principles of Data Mining and Knowledge Discovery* (pp. 65-73). Springer-Verlag.

Feng, Y., & Makinouchi, A. (2006). Dfficient Evaluation of Partially-Dimensional Range Queries Using Adaptive R*-tree. In *Proceedings International Conference on Database and Expert Systems Applications (DEXA),* pp. 687-696.

Filippov, A. (1988). *Differential equations with discontinuous righthand sides.* Amsterdam: Kluwer Academic Pub.

Forrest, B. M. (1988). Neural network models. *Parallel Computing, 8,* 71–83. doi:.doi:10.1016/0167-8191(88)90110-X

Frank, L. D., & Engelke, P. O. (2001). The built environment and human activity patterns: Exploring the impacts of urban form on public health. *Journal of Planning Literature, 16*(2), 202–218..doi:10.1177/08854120122093339

Fraser, A. M., & Swinney, H. L. (1986). Independent coordinates for strange attractors from mutual information. *Physical Review A., 33,* 1134–1140. doi:10.1103/PhysRevA.33.1134

Frege, G. (1893). *Grundlagen der Arithmetik (Vol. 2).* Jena: Verlag von Herman Pohle.

Freud, R., & Păun, G. (1997). Watson-Crick finite Automata. *Proc of the Third Annual DIMACS symp, on DNA Based Computers, Philadephia,* 305-317.

Friedlander, D., & Franklin, S. (2008). LIDA and a Theory of Mind. In Ben Goertzel & Pei Wang (Eds.), *Artificial General Intelligence (AGI-08),* Memphis, TN, USA: IOS Press.

Frutos, A. G. (1997). Demonstration of a Word Design Strategy for DNA Computing on Surface. *Nucleic Acids Research, 25*(23), 4748–4757. doi:10.1093/nar/25.23.4748

Fu, L. (1994). Rule Generation from Neural Networks. *IEEE Transactions on Systems, Man, and Cybernetics, 24*(8), 1114–1124. doi:10.1109/21.299696

Fujio, T., & Shiizuka, H. (2005). The automatic DJ mixing system by optimum transformation of MP3 data. [in Japanese]. *Journal of Japan Society of Kansei Engineering, 5*(3), 23–30.

Fujisawa, N., & Saito, M. (2007). Relation of musical impression and mental tempo. In *Proc. of the 9th annual conf. of JSKE 2007* (CD-ROM) (in Japanese)

Fujita, M., et al. (2000). *Robot Entertainment, in Robots for Kids: New Technologies for Learning.*In Druin, A. & Hendler, J.(Eds.),(pp.37-70).San Francisco: Morgan Kaufmann Publisher, 37–70.

Fukuda, M., & Shibata, Y. (1996). Kansei Retrieval Method Reflecting Shape Pattern of Design Images. *Transactions of Information Processing Society of Japan. DPSWS, 96*(1), 267–274.

Fukuda, M., Katsumoto, A., & Shibata, Y. (1995). Kansei Retrieve Method based on User Model. *Transactions of Information Processing Society of Japan, DPS, 95*(13), 43–48.

Fukumoto, M. (2008). Investigation of subjective evaluation for tempo of music.In *Proc. of the 10th annual conf. of JSKE 2008* (CD-ROM) (in Japanese)

Fukumoto, M., Kusunoki, Y., & Nagashima, T. (2004). Synchronization between tempo of music and heartbeat - Detecting synchronization with synchrogram and its influence on relazation effect. [in Japanese]. *Journal of Japan Society of Kansei Engineering, 4*(2), 17–24.

Fukushima, K. (1980). Neocognitron: A self-organizing multilayer neural network model for a mechanism of pattern recognition unaffected by shift in position. *Biological Cybernetics, 36*, 193–202. doi:.doi:10.1007/BF00344251

Funakoshi, T., & Tsumita, H. (1986). A study of psychological-analysis on street spaces: Study on street spaces (Part I). *Transactions of the Architectural Institute of Japan, 327*, 100-107. http://ci.nii.ac.jp/Detail/detail.do? LOCALID=ART0005211937&lang=en

Gabriel, P., & Liimatainen, M. R. (2000). Mental health in the workplace. *International Labor Organization.* Retrieved August 1, 2009, from http://ilo.org

Gabrielsson, A., & Juslin, P. N. (2002). Emotional expression in music. In Davidson, R. J., Scherer, K. R., & Goldsmith, H. H. (Eds.), *Handbook of Affective Sciences.* Oxford, UK: Oxford University Press.

Gabrielsson, A., & Lindström, E. (2001). The influence of musical structure on emotional expression. In Juslin, P. N., & Sloboda, J. A. (Eds.), *Music and Emotion.* Oxford, UK: Oxford University Press.

Gaede, V., & Gunther, O. (1998). Multidimensional Access Methods. *ACM Computing Surveys, 30*(2), 170–231. doi:10.1145/280277.280279

Garcez, A. S. D., Broda, K., & Gabbay, D. M. (2001). Symbolic knowledge extraction from trained neural networks: A sound approach. *Artificial Intelligence, 125*, 155–207. doi:10.1016/S0004-3702(00)00077-1

Garzon, M., & Neathery, P. (1997). A New Metric for DNA Computing. *Proceedings of the 2nd Annual Genetic Programming Conference GP-97*, 472-487.

Gatterdam, R. (1989). Splicing System and Regularity. *Computer Math, 31*, 63–67.

Ge, J., & Hokao, K. (2005). Applying the methods of image evaluation and spatial analysis to study the sound environment of urban street areas. *Journal of Environmental Psychology, 25*(4), 455–466..doi:10.1016/j.jenvp.2005.10.003

George, A. M. WordNet (1995): a Lexical database for English. *Communications on the ACM.* http://wordnet.cs.princeton.edu/

Giaouris, D., Banerjee, S., Zahawi, B., & Pickert, V. (2008). Stability Analysis of the Continuous-Conduction-Mode Buck Converter Via Filippov's Method. *IEEE Transactions on] Circuits and Systems I: Regular Papers, IEEE Transactions on [Circuits and Systems I. Fundamental Theory and Applications, 55*(4), 1084–1096. doi:10.1109/TCSI.2008.916443

Gillet, A., Macaire, L., Lecocq, C. B., & Postaire, J. G. (2002). Color image segmentation by analysis of 3D histogram with fuzzy morphological filters. *Studies in Fuzziness and Soft Computing, 122*, 153–177.

Glover, F., & Laguna, M. (1997). *Tabu Search.* Norwell, MA: Kluwer.

Goertzel, Ben (2006). Patterns, Hypergraphs and General Intelligence. In *Proceedings of International Joint Conference on Neural Networks, (* IJCNN 2006), Vancouver CA

Goertzel, Ben (2006). *The Hidden Pattern.* New York: Brown Walker.

Goertzel, Ben, Matthew Ikle', Izabela Goertzel & Ari Heljakka (2008). *Probabilistic Logic Networks.* New York: Springer Verlag.

Goertzel, Ben, Moshe Looks & Cassio Pennachin (2004). Novamente: An Integrative Architecture for Artificial General Intelligence. In *Proceedings of AAAI Symposium on Achieving Human-Level Intelligence through Integrated Systems and Research*, Washington DC, August 2004

Goil, S., & Nagesh, H. (1999). *Mafia: Efficient and scalable subspace clustering for very large data sets. Technical Report.* Northwestern University.

Goldberg, D. E. (1989). *Genetic Algorithms: Search, Optimization and Machine Learning.* New York: Addison-Wesley.

Goldberg, L. R. (1993). The Structure of Phenotypic Personality Traits. *The American Psychologist, 48,* 26–34. doi:10.1037/0003-066X.48.1.26

Google. (2009). http://www.google.cn/music/song-screener. Retrieved 10 Oct., 2009

Goss, S., Aron, S., Deneubourg, J.-L., & Pasteels, J.-M. (1989). The self-organized exploratory pattern of the Argentine ant. *Naturwissenschaften, 76,* 579–581. doi:. doi:10.1007/BF00462870

Gotoh, M., et al. (2005). Face Generator for Sensibility Robot based on Emotional Regions. *6th International Symposium on Robotics,* in CD-ROM.

Gray, H. M., Ambady, N., Lowenthal, W. T., & Deldin, P. (2004). P300 as an index of attention to self-relevant stimuli. *Journal of Experimental Social Psychology, 40*(2), 216–224. doi:10.1016/S0022-1031(03)00092-1

Green, R. G., & Green, M. L. (1987). Relaxation increases salivary Immunoglobulin A. *Psychological Reports, 61,* 623–629.

Gregory, R. L., Kim, D. E., Kindle, J. C., Hobbs, L. C., & Lloyd, D. R. (1992). Immunoglobulin-degrading enzymes in localized juvenile periodontitis. *Journal of Periodontal Research, 27*(3), 176–183. doi:10.1111/j.1600-0765.1992. tb01666.x

Grenander, U. (1981). *Abstract Inference.* New York: John Wiley.

Hadjicostis, C. N., & Verghese, G. C. (1999). Monitoring discrete event systems using Petri net embeddings. *Lecture Notes in Computer Science, 1639,* 188–207. doi:10.1007/3-540-48745-X_12

Hajime, H., Takano, A., & Hagiwara, M. (2008, 1-6 June 2008). *Mining KANSEI fuzzy rules from photos on the internet.* Paper presented at the IEEE International Conference on Fuzzy Systems, 2008., Hong Kong, China.

Hall, E. T. (1990). *The Silent Language.* Norwell: Anchor Press.

Handy, S. L., Boarnet, M. G., Ewing, R., & Killingworth, R. E. (2002). How the built environment affects physical activity: Views from urban planning. *American Journal of Preventive Medicine, 23*(2), 64–73..doi:10.1016/S0749-3797(02)00475-0

Hanjalic, A. (2001). *Video and image retrieval beyond the cognitive level: The needs and possibilities.* Paper presented at the Storage and Retrieval for Media Databases 2001, San Jose, CA, United states.

Hanjalic, A., & Xu, L. Q. (2005). Affective video content representation and modeling. *IEEE Transactions on Multimedia, 7*(1), 143–154. doi:10.1109/TMM.2004.840618

Hansen, A. M., Garde, A. H., & Persson, R. (2008). Source of biological and methodological variation in salivary cortisol and their impact on measurement among healthy adults: A review. *Scandinavian Journal of Clinical and Laboratory Investigation, 68*(6), 448–458. doi:10.1080/00365510701819127

Hansen, J. C., & Hillyard, S. A. (1983). Selective attention to multidimensional auditory stimuli. *Journal of Experimental Psychology. Human Perception and Performance, 9*(1), 1–19. doi:10.1037/0096-1523.9.1.1

Hara, F. & Kobayashi, H. (2004). *An artificial emotion,,* Kyoritsu suppan. (in Japanese)

Harada, S., Itoh, Y., & Nakatani, H. (1999). On Constructing Shape Feature Space for Interpreting Subjective Expressions. *Transactions of Information Processing Society of Japan, 40*(5), 2356–2366.

Hart, D. (2008). *Ben Goertzel.* OpenCog.

Hasebe, T. (2005a). Rural Scenery as Norm – Relation to Well-being. *Annual Report of the Tohoku Association of Philosophy, 21,* 45-51 (in Japanese). Hasebe, T. (2005b). Meanings of Narrating a Scenery Narrative. [in Japanese]. *Kansei Philosophy, 5,* 79–94.

Hasebe, T. (2007). Interpretation on Creation of the Street Scenery by Active Intuition. [in Japanese]. *Journal of Rural Economics, 78*(4), 163–173.

Hasebe, T., Kitani, S., & Nomura, N. (2002). Evaluation of Rural Landscape and Consciousness of the Direct Payment for Less Favored Area. [in Japanese]. *Proceedings of Annual Conference of the Agricultural Economics Society of Japan, 2000*, 166–169.

Hashida, M., Noike, K., Nagata, N., & Katayose, H. (2005). An analysis of musical grouping tencency. In *Proc. of the 1st spring conf. of JSKE 2005, 33-36.* (in Japanese)

Hashida, M., Noike, K., Nagata, N., & Katayose, H. (2007). A study of listening of musical group structure based on performance expression [in Japanese]. *Journal of Japan Society of Kansei Engineering, 7*(2), 327–336.

Hayashi, T., & Hagiwara, M. (1998). Image query by impression words - the IQI system. *IEEE Transactions on Consumer Electronics, 44*(2), 347–352. doi:10.1109/30.681949

Hayashida, N., & Takagi, H. (2002). *Acceleration of EC convergence with landscape visualization and human intervention.* doi:10.1016/S1568-4946(01)00023-0.

Haykin, S. (1999). *Neural networks: A comprehensive foundation* (2nd ed.). Upper Saddle River, NJ: Prentice Hall.

He, H., Jin, J., Xiong, Y., Chen, B., Sun, W., & Zhao, L. (2008). *Language feature mining for music emotion classification via supervised learning from lyrics*, Wuhan, China.

Head, T. (1987). Formal Language Theory and DNA: An Analysis of the Generative Capacity of Specific Recombinant Behaviors. *Bulletin of Mathematical Biology, 49*, 737–759.

Head, T., Kaolan, P. D., & Bladergroen, R. (2000). Computing with DNA by Operating on Plasmids [J]. *Bio Systems, 57*, 87–93. doi:10.1016/S0303-2647(00)00091-5

Hellhammer, D. H., Wüst, S., & Kudielka, B. M. (2009). Salivary cortisol as a biomarker in stress research. *Psychoneuroendocrinology, 34*(2), 163–171. doi:10.1016/j.psyneuen.2008.10.026

Hertz, J., Krogh, A., & Palmer, R. G. (1991). *Introduction to the theory of neural computation.* Reading, MA: Addison-Wesley.

Higashitani, T., & Yoshida, T. (2004). A prescription of music for healing. In *Proc. of the 6th annual conf. of JSKE 2004, 124.* (in Japanese)

Hillyard, S. A., & Picton, T. W. (1987). Electrophysiology of congnition. In Plum, F. (Ed.), *andbook of Physiology* (*Vol. 5*, pp. 519–584). Bethesda, MD: Wverly Press.

Hink, R. F., Fenton, W. H., Pfefferbaum, A., Tinklenberg, J. R., & Kopell, B. S. (1978). The distribution of attention across auditory input channels: an assessment using the human evoked potential. *Psychophysiology, 15*(5), 466–473. doi:10.1111/j.1469-8986.1978.tb01417.x

Hirano, M., & Saito, T. (2008). Proposal of phrase production and evaluation support system for music beginner. In *Proc. of the 10th annual conf. of JSKE 2008* (CD-ROM) (in Japanese)

Hirokane, M., Nishimura, F., Morikawa, Y., & Hamaguchi, C. (2003). Rough sets based extraction method of characteristics from bridge images. in *Proceedings of the Seventh International Conference on the Application of Artificial Intelligence to Civil and Structural Engineering* (Paper 68). Scotland: Civil-Comp Press.

Hisamitsu, T., & Niwa, Y. (2001). Topic-Word Selection Based on Combinatorial Probability. *Proceedings of the Sixth Natural Language Processing Pacific Rim Symposium* (pp. 289-296).

Hochberg, J. (1966). Representative sampling and the purposes of research: Pictures of the world and the world of pictures. In Hammond, K. (Ed.), *The Psychology of Egon Brunswik* (pp. 361–381). New York: Holt, Rinehart, and Winston.

Hopfield, J. J. (1984). Neurons with graded response have collective computational properties like those of two state neurons. In *Proceedings of Nat* (pp. 3088–3092). U. S: Acad. Sci.

Huang, J. Z., & Michael, K. (2005). Automated dimension weighting in *k*-means type clustering. *IEEE Transactions on Pattern Analysis and Machine Intelligence, 27*(5), 1–12. doi:10.1109/TPAMI.2005.95

Hui, S., & Zak, S. H. (1992). Dynamical analysis of the Brain-State-in-a-Box (BSB) neural model. *IEEE Transactions on Neural Networks, 3,* 86–94. doi:. doi:10.1109/72.105420

Ikeda, E., et al. (2000). Classification of adjectives expressing sound by Kansei evaluation.In *Proc. of the 2nd annual conf. of JSKE,*(pp.217). (in Japanese)

Ikeuchi, K. (2008, September). CREST – *Papers presented at the Symposium 'Can Humanoids Become Human' the Symposium is part of CREST 'Creating 21st Century art from based on digital media* – (Tokyo – University of the Arts - pp. 4-7)

Ikoma, S. (2007). The relations between absolute-pitch-based recognition for melody and everyday music listening. In *Proc. of the 3rd spring conf. of JSKE 2007,* (P12). (in Japanese)

Inder, R., Bianchi-Berthouze, N., & Kato, T. (1999). *K-DIME: a software framework for Kansei filtering of internet material.* Paper presented at the IEEE International Conference on Systems, Man and Cybernetics, Tokyo, Jpn.

Informix (2004). *Informix Spatial DataBlade Module.* ww306.ibm.com/software/data/ Informix /blades/spatial/ rtree.html).

Iseki, A., & Ozawa, K. (2005). Effect of performer information of music on the Kansei of a listener.In *Proc. of the 7th annual conf. of JSKE 2005,* 189. (in Japanese)

Iseki, A., & Ozawa, K. (2007). Effects of Musical Performer Information on the Kansei of Listeners.In *Proc. of KEER 2007.* (CD-ROM)

Ishida, A., Tatsuya, S., Sugihara, R., Omura, T., Ishikawa, T., & Kato, T. (2009). Development of music retrieval system by analysis of walking pattern. [in Japanese]. *Journal of Japan Society of Kansei Engineering, 8*(3), 829–835.

Ishiguro, H. (2008, September*). CREST – Papers presented at the Symposium 'Can Humanoids Become Human' the Symposium is part of CREST 'Creating 21st Century art from based on digital media* – -(Tokyo – University of the Arts - pp. 10-12).

Ishihara, S., & Ishihara, K. (2010). Psychological Methods of Kansei Engineering. In Nagamachi, M. (Ed.), *Kansei / Affective EngineeringBoca.* Raton, FL: CRC press.

Ishikawa, M. (1996). Structural Learning with Forgetting. *Neural Networks, 9*(3), 509–521. doi:10.1016/0893-6080(96)83696-3

Isowa, T., & Ohira, H. &d Murashima, S. (2004). Reactivity of immune, endocrine and cardiovascular parameters to active and passive acute stress. *Biological Psychology, 65,* 101–120. doi:10.1016/S0301-0511(03)00115-7

Ito, N., Shimazu, Y., Yokoyama, T., & Matsushita, Y. (1995). *Fuzzy logic based non-parametric color image segmentation with optional block processing* (pp. 119–126). ACM.

Izawa, S., Shirotsuki, K., Sugaya, N., Ogawa, N., Suzuki, K., & Nomura, S. (2004). The application of saliva to an assessment of stress: procedures for collecting and analyzing saliva and characteristics of salivary substances. *Japanese Journal of Complementary and Alternative Medicine., 4*(3), 91–101. doi:10.1625/jcam.4.91

Izawa, S., Sugaya, N., Ogawa, N., Nagano, Y., Nakano, M., Nakase, E., et al. (2007). Episodic stress associated with writing a graduation thesis and free cortisol secretion after awakening. *International Journal of Psychophysiology, 64,* 141-145.

Izawa, S., Sugaya, N., Shirotsuki, K., Yamada, K. C., Ogawa, N., & Ouchi, Y. (2008). Salivary Dehydroepiandrosterone secretion in response to acute psychosocial stress and its correlations with biological and psychological changes. *Biological Psychology, 79*(3), 294–298. doi:10.1016/j.biopsycho.2008.07.003

Jager, F. J., Mark, R. G., Moody, G., & Divjak, S. (1992). *Analysis of transient ST segment changes during ambulatory monitoring using the Karhunen-Lo`eve transform: Proceedings of Computers in Cardiology (CIC '92)*, 691–694, Durham, NC, USA.

Jain, A. K., Ross, A., & Prabhakar, S. (2004). An introduction to biometric recognition. *IEEE Transactions on Circuits and Systems for Video Technology, 14*(1). doi:10.1109/TCSVT.2003.818349

Jain, A., Griess, F., & Connell, S. (2002). On-line Signature Verification. *Pattern Recognition, 35*(12), 2963–2972. doi:10.1016/S0031-3203(01)00240-0

Jemmott, J. B. III, & Magloire, K. (1988). Academic stress, social support, and secretory Immunoglobulin A. *Journal of Personality and Social Psychology, 55*(5), 803–810. doi:10.1037/0022-3514.55.5.803

Jemmott, J. B. III, & McClelland, D. C. (1989). Secretory IgA as a measure of resistance to infectious disease: comments on Stone, Cox, Valdimarsdottir, and Neale. *Behavioral Medicine (Washington, D.C.), 15*, 63–71.

Jemmott, J. B. III, Borysenko, J. Z., Borysenko, M., McClelland, D. C., Chapman, R., Meyer, D., & Benson, H. (1983). Academic stress, power motivation, and decrease in secretion rate of salivary secretory Immunoglobulin A. *Lancet, 1*(8339), 1400–1402. doi:10.1016/S0140-6736(83)92354-1

Jenkins, S., Brown, R., & Rutterford, N. (2008). *Comparison of thermographic, EEG and subjective measures of affective experience of designed stimuli.* Paper presented at the 6th Conference on Design & Emotion 2008, Hong Kong SAR.

Jianning, S., & Restrepo, J. (2008). *The harmonics of kansei images.* Paper presented at the 9th International Conference on Computer-Aided Industrial Design and Conceptual Design, 2008., Kunming, China.

Jing, L., Ng, M. K., & Huang, J. Z. (2007). An entropy weighting *k*-means algorithm for subspace clustering of high-dimensional sparse data. *IEEE Transactions on Knowledge and Data Engineering, 19*(8), 1026–1041. doi:10.1109/TKDE.2007.1048

Johansen, T. A., Hunt, K. J., Gawthrop, P. J., & Fritz, H. (1998). Off-equilibrium linearisation and design of gain-scheduled control with application to vehicle speed control. *Control Engineering Practice, 6*(2), 167–180. doi:10.1016/S0967-0661(98)00015-X

Johansson, M., Rantzer, A., & Arzen, K. E. (1999). Piecewise quadratic stability of fuzzy systems. *IEEE Transactions on Fuzzy Systems, 7*(6), 713–722. doi:10.1109/91.811241

Jones, K. S. (1972). A statistical interpretation of term specificity and its application in retrieval. *The Journal of Documentation, 28*(1), 11–21. doi:10.1108/eb026526

Jounin, J. C., Dussault, C., Peres, M., Satabin, P., Pierard, C., & Guezennec, C. Y. (2004). Analysis of heart rate variability after a ranger training course. *Military Medicine, 169*(8), 583–587.

Julia Handl & Joshua D. (2007). An Evolutionary Approach to Multiobjective Clustering. *IEEE Transactions on Evolutionary Computation, 11*(1), 56–76. doi:10.1109/TEVC.2006.877146

Kadotani, A., & Ishihara, S. (2004). Music structures and Kansei – Scales and Kansei. In *Proc. of the 6th annual conf. of JSKE 2004, 191.* (in Japanese)

Kakuda, Y. (2001). *A Step for Philosophy of Landscape.* Tokyo: Bunkashobou- Hakubunsha. (in Japanese)

Kallinen, K., & Ravaja, N. (2007). Comparing speakers versus headphones in listening to news from a computer - individual differences and psychophysiological responses. *Computers in Human Behavior, 23*(1), 303–317. doi:10.1016/j.chb.2004.10.014

Kamei, K., Aoyama, M., Kinoshita, Y., Cooper, E. W., & Hoshino, Y. (2006). Kansei Evaluations of Percussion Music Based on Psychological Measurements by SD Method and Physiological Measurements by Near-Infrared Spectroscopy (NIRS). *Journal of Japan Society of Kansei Engineering, 6*(4), 67–75.

Kamgar-Parsi, B. (1995). *Automatic target extraction in infrared images* (pp. 143–146). NRL Rev.

Kamičaitytė-Virbašienė, J., & Janušaitis, R. (2004). Some methodical aspects of landscape visual quality preferences analysis. *Environmental Research, Engineering and Management, 3*(29), 51-60. www1.apini.lt/includes/getfile.php?id=201

Kanahako, J., et al. (2005). Color based computer aided composition system.In *Proc. of the spring 1st spring conf. of JSKE 2005*,(pp. 81-84). (in Japanese)

Kanamaru, Y., Kikukawa, A., & Shimamura, K. (2006). Salivary chromogranin-A as a marker of psychological stress during a cognitive test battery in humans. *Stress (Amsterdam, Netherlands), 9*(3), 127–131. doi:10.1080/14769670600909594

Kanda, S. (2003). *Internet-based Robot: Mobile Agent Robot of Next-generation* (MARON-1) [in Japanese]. *Fujitsu, 54*(4), 285–292.

Kang, H.-B. (2002). *Analysis of scene context related with emotional events.* Paper presented at the tenth ACM international conference on Multimedia, Juan les Pins, France.

Kang, H.-B. (2003). *Affective Contents Retrieval from Video with Relevance Feedback Digital Libraries: Technology and Management of Indigenous Knowledge for Global Access* (pp. 243–252). Springer Berlin / Heidelberg.

Kannathal, N., Rajendra, U., Joseph, P., Min, L. C., & Suri, J. S. (2007). *Analysis of electrocardiograms. U.R. Archarya, J.S. Suri, J.A.E. Spaan, and S.M. Krishnan, Advances in Cardiac Signal Processing.* Berlin: Springer-Verlag.

Kanoh, M. (2005). Emotive Facial Expressions of Sensitivity Communication Robot "Ifbot". *Kansei Engineering International, 5*(3), 35–42.

Kansei (2007). *Kansei makes a comeback with reactive facial expressions:*. Wednesday 6 June 2007, 11.00 A.M Reuters Review.

Kantz, H., & Shreiber, T. (2004). *Nonlinear Time series analysis second edition.* UK, Cambridge.

Kari, L., & Resenberg. (1998). DNA Computing, Sticker System and Universality. *Acta Informatica, 35*(5), 401–420. doi:10.1007/s002360050125

Karl-Heize, Z. (2002). Efficient DNA Sticker Algorithm for NP Complete Graph Problems. *Computer Physics Communications, 81*, 1–9.

Karypis, G. (2003). *CLUTO: A Clustering Toolkit Release 2.1.1.* (Technical Report: #02-017). University of Minnesota.

Kashima, T. (2006). *The History as Possibility.* Tokyo: Iwanamishoten. (in Japanese)

Kashiwazaki, N., & Okamoto, K. (2007). Classification of music using Kansei parameter method - Study on Standard parameter values scales for kansei information analyses (1). [in Japanese]. *Journal of Japan Society of Kansei Engineering, 7*(2), 243–249.

Katayama, N., & Satoh, S. (1997). The SR-tree: An Index Structure for High-Dimensional Nearest Neighbor Queries. In *Proceedings ACM SIGMOD International Conference*, pp.369-380.

Kawamura, T., et al. (2003). A study on individual differences in images roused by music. *Proc. of the 5th annual conf. of JSKE 2003, 208.* (in Japanese)

Kawase, A., & Tokosumi, A. (2007a). A comparative analysis and Regional Classification of Japanese Folk Songs Founded on Pitch Transition Structures. In *Proc. of the 9th annual conf. of JSKE 2007* (CD-ROM) (in Japanese)

Kawase, A., & Tokosumi, A. (2007b). A regional classification of Japanse folk songs.In *Proc. of KEER 2007.* (CD-ROM)

Kelly, G. A. (1963). *A Theory of Personality: The Psychology of Personal Constructs.* New-York: W. W. Norton & Co.

Kennedy, M., & Bourne, J. (1996). *Modes, The Concise Oxford Dictionary of Music.* Oxford, UK: Oxford University Press.

Kennel, M. B. (1992). Determining embedding dimension for phase-space reconstruction using a geometrical construction. *Physical Review A.*, *45*, 3403–3411. doi:10.1103/PhysRevA.45.3403

Keogh, E., Chu, S., Hart, D., & Pazzani, M. (2003). A Survey and Novel Approach. In *Data mining in time series databases, World Scientific Publishing Company*. Segmenting Time Series.

Khalil, H. K., & Grizzle, J. W. (1996). *Nonlinear systems*. Upper Saddle River, NJ: Prentice Hall.

Kikuchi, S., & Nakanishi, M. (1999). Discovering rules using parallel multi-layer network and modified structural learning with forgetting. *Proc. IASTED Int'l Conf. Artificial Intelligence and Soft Computing*, (pp. 258-262).

Kikuchi, S., & Nakanishi, M. (2003). Recurrent neural network with short-term memory and fast structural learning method. *Systems and Computers in Japan, 34*(6), 69–79. doi:10.1002/scj.1206

Kim, B., Song, J., & Wang, K. (2009). Prostate Cancer Classification Processor Using DNA Computing Technique. *IEICE Elutriations express*, (6), 581-586.

Kim, J., & Andre, E. (2008). Emotion recognition based on physiological changes in music listening. *IEEE Transactions on Pattern Analysis and Machine Intelligence, 30*(12), 2067–2083. doi:10.1109/TPAMI.2008.26

Kim, S.-J., Kim, E. Y., Jeong, K., & Kim, J.-I. (2006, Nov 6-8). *Emotion-based textile indexing using colors, texture and patterns*. Paper presented at the 2nd International Symposium on Visual Computing, Lake Tahoe, NV, United States.

Kimura, K. (2005). Isowa, T., Ohira, H., & Murashima, S. (2005). Temporal variation of acute stress responses in sympathetic nervous and immune systesm. *Biological Psychology, 70*, 131–139. doi:10.1016/j.biopsycho.2004.12.006

Kinoshita, Y., Cooper, E. W., Hoshino, Y., & Kamei, K. (2004). A townscape evaluate on system based on kansei and colour harmony models. In *2004 IEEE International Conference on Systems, Man and Cybernetics, 1*, 327-332.

Kirkpatrick, S., Gelatt, C. D., & Vecchi, M. P. (1983). *Optimization by Simulated Annealing*. Science. *New Series 220.*, *4598*, 671–680.

Kirschbaum, C., & Hellhammer, D. H. (1994). Salivary cortisol in psychoneuroendocrine research: recent developments and applications. *Psychoneuroendocrinology, 19*(1), 313–333. doi:10.1016/0306-4530(94)90013-2

Knight, W. E., & Rickard, N. S. (2001). Relaxing music prevents stress-induced increase in subjective anxiety, systolic blood Pressure, and heart rate in healthy males and females. *Journal of Music Therapy, 38*, 254–272.

Kobayashi, H. (1994). Study on Face Robot for Active Human Interface. [in Japanese]. *Journal of the Robotics Society of Japan, 12*(1), 155–163.

Kobayashi, H., & Hara, F. (1996). Real Time Dynamic Control of 6 Basic Facial Expressions on Face Robot. [in Japanese]. *Journal of the Robotics Society of Japan, 14*(5), 677–685.

Kobayashi, K., & Haseyama, M. (2007). A Novel Similarity Measurement Using Melody Lines for Music Retrieval. In *Proc. of KEER 2007* (CD-ROM)

Kohonen, T. (1995). Self-organizing maps. *Springer Series in Information Sciences, 30*.

Kohritani, M., Watada, J., Hirano, H., & Yubazaki, N. (2005). Kansei Engineering for Comfortable Space Management. In Khosla, R., Howlett, R. J., & Jain, L. C. (Eds.), *Knowledge-Based Intelligent Information and Engineering Systems* (Vol. 3682, pp. 1291–1297). Berlin: Springer.

Kojima, H., et al. (2000). System of making pleasant sound surroundings based on Kansei. In *Proc. of the 2nd annual conf. of JSKE*, (pp.172). (in Japanese)

Kolinski, M. (2009). Mode. In *Encyclopædia Britannica*. Retrieved July 15, 2009, from Encyclopædia Britannica Online http://www.britannica.com/EBchecked/topic/386980/mode

Komiya, Y., Ohishi, T., & Matsumoto, T. (2001). A pen input on-line signature verifier integrating position, pressure and indication trajectories. *IEICE Trans. Information and Systems. E (Norwalk, Conn.), 84-D*(7), 833–838.

Korhonen, M. D., Clausi, D. A., & Jernigan, M. E. (2006). Modeling emotional content of music using system identification. *IEEE Transactions on Systems, Man, and Cybernetics. Part B, Cybernetics*, *36*(3), 588–599. doi:10.1109/TSMCB.2005.862491

Kosaka, K. (2002). *The Thought of Nishida Kitaro*. Tokyo: Koudansha. (in Japanese)

Kosko, B. (1988). Bidirectional associative memories. *IEEE Transactions on Systems, Man, and Cybernetics*, *18*(1), 49–60. doi:.doi:10.1109/21.87054

Kowatari, Y., Lee, S. H., Yamamura, H., Nagamori, Y., Lévy, P., & Yamane, S. (2008). Neural Networks Involved in Artistic Creativity. *Human Brain Mapping*, *30*(5), 1678–1690. doi:10.1002/hbm.20633

Kumar, S. (2004). *Neural networks: A classroom approach*. New Delhi: Tata McGraw-Hill.

Kumsawat, P., & Attakitmongcol, K. (2005). A new approach for optimization in image watermarking by using genetic algorithms. *IEEE Transactions on Signal Processing*, *53*(12), 4707–4719. doi:10.1109/TSP.2005.859323

Kuniyoshi, Y. (2008, September). *CREST – Papers presented at the Symposium 'Can Humanoids Become Human' the Symposium is part of CREST 'Creating 21st Century art from based on digital media* – Tokyo – University of the Arts – p. 17

Kuo, F.-Y., Hsu, C.-W., & Day, R.-F. (in press). An exploratory study of cognitive effort involved in decision under framing-an application of the eye-tracking technology. [*Accepted Manuscript.*]. *Decision Support Systems*.

Kurita, T., Kato, T., Fukuda, I., & Sakakura, A. (1992). Sense Retrieve on an Image Database of Full Color Paintings. *Transactions of Information Processing Society of Japan*, *33*(10), 1373–1383.

Kuroki, Y., et al. (2002). A Small Biped Walking Entertainment Robot SDR-4X with a Highly Integrated Motion Control. *The 20th Conf. of Robotics Society of Japan*, (p.1C34). (in Japanese).

Kuwako, T. (2001). *Philosophy of Kansei*. Tokyo: Nihonhousou-Shuppankyoukai (in Japanese). Lapka, M. & Cudlınová, E. (2003). Landscape Changes and Landscape Scenery: Social Approach. *Ekologia (Bratislava)*, *22*(4), 364–375.

Kuznetsov, Y. A. (1998). *Elements of applied bifurcation theory*. New York: Springer.

Kwak, Y.-M., & Igarashi, H. (2008, 6-9 October 2008). *Designer's Kansei Feature on Creative Actions by Meta-Cognitive Method*. Paper presented at the 6th Conference on Design & Emotion 2008, Hong Kong SAR.

Laguna, P., Moody, G. B., Garc'ıa, J., Goldberger, A. L., & Mark, R. G. (1999). Analysis of the ST-T complex of the electrocardiogram using the Karhunen-Lo`eve transform: adaptive monitoring and alternans detection. *Medical & Biological Engineering & Computing*, *37*(2), 175–189. doi:10.1007/BF02513285

Lai, C. (2005). A novel clustering approach using hierarchical genetic algorithms. *Intelligent Automation and Soft Computing*, *11*(3), 143–153.

Lang, P. J., Bradley, M. M., & Cuthbert, B. N. (2008). International affective picture system (IAPS): Affective ratings of pictures and instruction manual. Technical Report A-8. University of Florida, Gainesville, FL.

Laurier, C., Grivolla, J., & Herrera, P. (2008a). *Multimodal music mood classification using audio and lyrics*, San Diego, CA, United states.

Laurier, C., Grivolla, J., & Herrera, P. (2008b). *Multimodal music mood classification using audio and lyrics*. Paper presented at the International Conference on Machine Learning and Applications, San Diego, CA, United states.

Lee, C.-C., & de Gyvez, J. P. (1996). Color image processing in a cellular neural-network environment. *IEEE Transactions on Neural Networks*, *7*(5), 1086–1098. doi:.doi:10.1109/72.536306

Leine, R. I., & Nijmeijer, H. (2004). *Dynamics and bifurcations of non-smooth mechanical systems*. New York: Springer.

Leondes, C. T. (1998). Neural network techniques and applications. In *Image processing and pattern recognition*. New York: Academic Press.

Lévy, P. (2006). *Interdisciplinary Design for the Cyberspace by an Approach in Kansei Information - Methodology and Workgroup Communication Tool Design*. Tsukuba, Japan: Tsukuba University.

Lévy, P., & Yamanaka, T. (2009a). Design with Event-Related Potentials: a Kansei Information Approach on CMC Design. *International Journal of Product Development*, 7(1/2), 127–148. doi:10.1504/IJPD.2009.022280

Lévy, P., & Yamanaka, T. (2009b). *Prospective Psychophysiological Approach for Kansei Design - Knowledge sharing between psychophysiology and design*. Paper presented at the International Association of Societies of Design Research 2009, Seoul, Korea.

Lévy, P., Nakamori, S., & Yamanaka, T. (2008). *Explaining Kansei Design Studies*. Paper presented at the 6th Conference on Design & Emotion 2008, Hong Kong SAR.

Li, B., Zhanf, D., & Wnag, K. (2006). On-line signature verification based on NCA and PCA. *Pattern Analysis & Applications*, 8, 345–356. doi:10.1007/s10044-005-0016-4

Li, H., Li, J., Song, J., & Chen, J. (2007). *A Fuzzy Mapping from Image Texture to Affective Thesaurus*. Paper presented at the 2007 international conference on Bio-Inspired computational intelligence and applications shanghai,China.

Li, S. P., & Will, B. F. (2005). A fuzzy logic system for visual evaluation. *Environment and Planning. B, Planning & Design*, 32(2), 293–304..doi:10.1068/b31155

Li, T., & Ogihara, M. (2004). *Content-based music similarity search and emotion detection*. Paper presented at the IEEE Int. Conf. on Acoustics, Speech & Signal Processing, Montreal, Que, Canada.

Li, X., Wu, X., Hu, X., Xie, F., & Jiang, Z. (2008). Keyword Extraction Based on Lexical Chains and Word Co-occurrence for Chinese News Web Pages. *Proceedings of the 2008 IEEE International Conference on Data Mining Workshops* (pp. 744-751). IEEE Computer Society.

Li, Z., Jiao, K., Chen, M., & Wang, C. (2003). Effect of magnitopuncture on sympathetic and parasympathetic nerve activities in healthy driver – assessment by power spectrum analysis of heart rate variability. *European Journal of Applied Physiology*, 88(4-5), 404–410. doi:10.1007/s00421-002-0747-5

Li, Z., Wang, C., Mak, A. F., & Chow, D. H. (2005). Effect of acupuncture on heart rate variability in normal subjects under fatigue and non-fatigue state. *European Journal of Applied Physiology*, 94(5-6), 633–640. doi:10.1007/s00421-005-1362-z

Liang, J. J., Qin, A. K., Suganthan, P. N., & Baskar, S. (2006). Comprehensive learning particle swarm optimizer for global optimization of multimodal functions. *IEEE Transactions on Evolutionary Computation*, 10(3), 281–295. doi:10.1109/TEVC.2005.857610

Liberzon, D. (2003). *Switching in systems and control*. New York: Birkhauser.

Lim, E. M., Honjo, T., & Umeki, K. (2006). The validity of VRML images as a stimulus for landscape assessment. *Landscape and Urban Planning*, 77, 80–93..doi:10.1016/j.landurbplan.2005.01.007

Lin, J.-S., Cheng, K.-S., & Mao, C.-W. (1996). A fuzzy Hopfield neural network for medical image segmentation. *IEEE Transactions on Nuclear Science*, 43(4), 2389–2398. doi:.doi:10.1109/23.531787

Lin, T. Y., & Crone, N. (1997). *Rough Sets and Data Mining: Analysis for Imprecise Data*. Dordrecht, Boston, London: Kluwer Academic.

Lindsey, G., & Nguyen, D. B. L. (2004). Use of greenway trails in Indiana. *Journal of Urban Planning and Development*, 130(4), 213–217..doi:10.1061/(ASCE)0733-9488(2004)130:4(213)

Lippmann, R. P. (1987). An introduction to computing with neural nets. *IEEE ASSP Magazine*, 3–22.

Lippmann, R. P. (1989). Pattern classification using neural networks. *IEEE Communications Magazine*, 27, 47–64. doi:.doi:10.1109/35.41401

Lipton, R. (1995). DNA based computers. *Proc of a DIMCS workshop, Princeton.* Kari, L. (1991). On insertion and deletion in formal languages. *University of Turku.*

Lipton. (1996). DNA Solutions of Hard Combinational Problems. *Science, 268,* 542-548.

Liu Yongguo & Y. Mao. P. Jun. (2008). Finding the optimal number of clusters using genetic algorithms. *IEEE Conf. on Cybernetics and Intelligent Systems*(pp.1325-1330).

Liu, C.-C., Yang, Y.-H., Wu, P.-H., & Chen, H. H. (2006). *Detecting and classifying emotion in popular music.* Paper presented at the 7th International Conference on Computer Vision, Pattern Recognition and Image Processing, Taiwan, ROC, Taiwan.

Liu, D., Zhang, N., & Zhu, H. (2003). Form and mood recognition of Johann Strauss's waltz centos. *Chinese Journal of Electronics, 12*(4), 587–593.

Liu, Q., & Frutos, A. G. (2000). DNA Computing on Surface. *Nature, 403,* 175–179. doi:10.1038/35001232

Llinares, C., & Page, A. (2007). Application of product differential semantics to quantify purchaser perceptions in housing assessment. *Building and Environment, 42*(7), 2488–2497..doi:10.1016/j.buildenv.2006.06.012

Looks, M. (2006). Competent Program Evolution. *PhD thesis, Computer Science Department,* Washington University in St. Louis.

Lu, L., Liu, D., & Zhang, H.-J. (2006). Automatic mood detection and tracking of music audio signals. *IEEE Transactions on Audio. Speech and Language Processing, 14*(1), 5–18. doi:10.1109/TSA.2005.860344

Lu, W., & Ni, L. (2005). *Kansei image retrieval based on region of interest.* Paper presented at the SAR and Multispectral Image Processing, Wuhan, China.

Mac Dorman, K. F. & Ishiguro, H.(2004). *The Study of Interaction through the Development of Androids,* IPSJ SIG Technical Report CVIM, 2004 (113), 69-75.

Maekawa, T., Nakatsu, R., Nishina, E., Fuwamoto, Y., & Ohashi, T. (1998). *Alpha-EEG Indicated Kansei Evaluation on Visual Granularity of Still Image.* Paper presented at the Proceedings of the Virtual Reality Society of Japan Annual Conference.

Maio, D., & Maltoni, D. (2005). Real-time face location on gray-scale static images. *Pattern Recognition, 33*(9), 1525–1539. doi:10.1016/S0031-3203(99)00130-2

Mandal, D. P., & Murthy, C. A. (1995). Selection of alpha for alpha-hull and formulation of fuzzy alpha-hull in R^2, *Int. J. of Uncertainty. Fuzziness and Knowledge Based Systems, 3*(4), 401–417. doi:10.1142/S0218488595000207

Mandal, D. P., & Murthy, C. A. (1997). Selection of alpha for alpha-hull in R^2. *Pattern Recognition, 30*(10), 1759–1767. doi:10.1016/S0031-3203(96)00176-8

Mandal, D. P., Murthy, C. A., & Pal, S. K. (1997). Determining the Shape of A Pattern Class From Sampled Points: Extension To R^N. *International Journal of General Systems, 26*(4), 293–320. doi:10.1080/03081079708945187

Mann, W., & Thompson, S. (1988). Rhetorical Structure Theory: Toward a Functional Theory of text Organization. *Text, 8*(3), 243–281. doi:10.1515/text.1.1988.8.3.243

Manning, C. D., & Schütze, H. (1999). *Foundations of Statistical Natural Language Processing.* Cambridge, MA: MIT Press.

Manning, C. D., Raghavan, P., & Schütze, H. (2008). *Introduction to Information Retrieval.* Cambridge, UK: Cambridge University Press.

Mao, X., Chen, B., & Muta, I. (2003). Affective property of image and fractal dimension. *Chaos, Solitons, and Fractals, 15*(5), 905–910. doi:10.1016/S0960-0779(02)00209-6

Martin, C., & Păun, G. (1998). Cooperating Distribute Splicing Systems. *Workshop on molecular computing, Mangalia Romania.*

Martin, H. (2000). Seven steps to heaven: A species approach to twentieth-century analysis and composition. In *Perspective of New Music; 38*(1), 129-168.

Martin, R. A., & Dobbin, J. P. (1988). Sense of humor, hassles, and Immunoglobulin A: evidence for a stress-moderating effect of humor. *International Journal of Psychiatry in Medicine, 18*, 93–105.

Martin, R. B., Guthrie, C. A., & Pitts, C. G. (1993). Emotional crying, depressed mood, and secretory Immunoglobulin A. *Behavioral Medicine (Washington, D.C.), 19*(3), 111–114.

Maruyama, T., & Nakagawa, M. (2008). *Emotion Measurements of Tennis Rackets on the basis of Fractal Analyses of EEG.* Paper presented at the Second International Conference on Kansei Engineering and Affective Systems, Nagaoka, Japan.

Marvin Minsky, *The Society of Mind,* New York: Simon & Schuster.

Marvin Minsky, *The Emotion Machine.* New York: Simon & Schuster.

Masaki, Y., et al. (2008). An Automatic Music Selection System Considering the Scenery in Car Driving. In *Proc. of the 10th annual conf. of JSKE 2008* (CD-ROM) (in Japanese)

Masaki, Y., Ozawa, K., & Ise, Y. (2007). A consideration on automatic music genre classification using rough sets theory. In *Proc. of the 9th annual conf. of JSKE 2007* (CD-ROM) (in Japanese)

Matsui, Y., et al. (2007). Interaction Effects in Facial Expressions of Emotional Space-using Kansei Robot "Ifbot". *International Conference on Kansei Engineering and Emotion Research* 2007, in CD-ROM.

Matsuo, Y., & Ishizuka, M. (2004). Keyword Extraction from a Single Document using Word Co-occurrence Statistical Information. *International Journal of Artificial Intelligence Tools, 13*(1), 157–169. doi:10.1142/S0218213004001466

Matsuzaki, Y., et al. (2005). Impressions' variation led by backing-renditions of pop music. In *Proc. of the 1st spring conf. of JSKE 2005,* (pp. 37-40). (in Japanese)

Maulik, U. (2009). Medical Image Segmentation using Genetic Algorithms. *IEEE Transactions on Information Technology in Biomedicine, 13*, 166–173. doi:. doi:10.1109/TITB.2008.2007301

McHarg, I. (1969). *Design with Nature.* Garden City, New York: Natural History Press.

McNair, M., Heuchert, P., & Shilony, E. (2003). *Profile of mood states Bibliography 1964-2002.* Multi-Health-Systems Inc.

McNicholas, P. D., Murphy, T. B., & O'Regan, M. (2008). Standardising the lift of an association rule. [Elsevier.]. *Computational Statistics & Data Analysis, 52,* 4712–4721. doi:10.1016/j.csda.2008.03.013

McQueen, J. (1967). SOME METHODS FOR CLASSIFICATION AND ANALYSIS OF MULTIVARIATE OBSERVATIONS, *Proceedings of the Fifth Berkeley Symposium on Mathematical Statistics and Probability* (pp.281-297).

Medda, F., & Nijkamp, P. (2003). A combinatorial assessment methodology for complex transport policy analysis. *Integrated Assessment, 4*(3), 214–222..doi:10.1076/iaij.4.3.214.23773

Mehrabian, A., & Ksionzky, S. (1970). Models for affiliative and conformity behavior. *Psychological Bulletin, 74*(2), 110–126. doi:10.1037/h0029603

Mehran, K., Giaouris, D., & Zahawi, B. (2008). Modeling and stability analysis of dc-dc buck converter via takagi-sugeno fuzzy approach. *ISKE 2008, International Conference on Intelligent Systems and Knowledge Engineering, Xiamen, China,* (1), 401-406 *(selected for publication in the Journal of Donghua University (English version).*

Mehran, K., Giaouris, D., & Zahawi, B. (2009). Stability Analysis and Control of Nonlinear Phenomena in Boost Converter using Model-based Takagi-Sugeno Fuzzy Approach. *Accepted for publication at IEEE Transaction on Circuits and Systems - I: Regular papers.*

Melkikh, A. (2008). DNA Computing, Computation Complexity and Problem of Biological Evolution Rate. *Acta Biotheoretica, 56*(4), 285–295. doi:10.1007/s10441-008-9055-8

Metzinger, T. (2004). *Being No One*. Cambridge, MA: MIT Press.

Michael, A., Jenaway, A., Paykel, E. S., & Herbert, J. (2000). Altered salivary Dehydroepiandrosterone levels in major depression in adults. *Biological Psychiatry*, *48*(10), 989–995. doi:10.1016/S0006-3223(00)00955-0

Michalewicz, Z. (1992). *Genetic Algorithms + Data Structures = Evolution Programs*. New York: Springer-Verlag.

Mieno, Y., & Shiizuka, H. (2000). KANSEI database according to opuses in automatic composition.In *Proc. of the 2nd annual conf. of JSKE*, (pp.65). (in Japanese)

Minou, M., & Nishida, S. (1999). *Information Media Engineering*. Tokyo: Ohmsha. In Japanese

MIREX. (2009). Audio Music Mood Classification. from http://www.music-ir.org/mirex/2009/index.php/Audio_Music_Mood_Classification

Miura, M., Mitsuishi, T., Sasaki J., & Funyu, Y. (2002). A Music Retrieval System which Estimates Characteristics of Data based on Users' Sensibility. *Information Processing Society of Japan, SIG Notes*, 2002(3), 129-136.

Miura, M., Mitsuishi, T., Sasaki, J., & Funyu, Y. (2000). KANSEI database according to opuses in automatic composition.In *Proc. of the 2nd annual conf. of JSKE*, (pp.66). (in Japanese)

Miyakawa, M., Matsui, T., Kishikawa, H., Murayama, R., Uchiyama, I., Itoh, T., & Yoshida, T. (2006). Salivary Chromogranin A as a measure of stress response to noise. *Noise & Health*, *8*(32), 108–113. doi:10.4103/1463-1741.33951

Moise, G., & Sander, J. (2008). Robust projected clustering. *Knowledge and Information Systems*, *14*(3), 273–298. doi:10.1007/s10115-007-0090-6

Moncrieff, S., Dorai, C., & Venkatesh, S. (2001, October 2001.). *Affect Computing in Film through Sound Energy Dynamics*. Paper presented at the the ninth ACM international conference on multimedia, Ottawa, Canada.

Money, A. G., & Agius, H. (2009). Analysing user physiological responses for affective video summarisation. *Display*, *30*, 59–70. doi:10.1016/j.displa.2008.12.003

Moray, N. (1959). Attention in dichotic listening: Affective cues and the influence of instructions. *The Quarterly Journal of Experimental Psychology*, *11*(1), 56–60. doi:10.1080/17470215908416289

Moreira, J., & Costa, L. D. F. (1996). *Neural-based color image segmentation and classification using self-organizing maps* (pp. 47–54). Anais do IX SIBGRAPI.

Morita, H., & Nakahara, T. (2005). Data mining from photographs using the KeyGraph and genetic algorithms, *Journal of Economics. Business and Law*, *7*, 73–85.

Moroboshi, K., & Shiizuka, H. (2005). Composition support system by TRIZ, In *Proc. of the 7th annual conf. of JSKE 2005*, 191. (in Japanese)

Moroboshi, K., & Shiizuka, H. (2005). Composition support system springing images, In *Proc. of the 1st spring conf. of JSKE 2005*,(p. 41). (in Japanese)

Motomura, Y., Yoshida, K., & Fujimoto, K. (2000). Generative user models for adaptive Information Retrieval. In *Proceedings IEEE International Conference on System, Man and Cybernetics*, pp. 665-670.

Moudon, A. V., & Lee, C. (2003). Walking and bicycling: An evaluation of environmental audit instruments. *American Journal of Health Promotion*, *18*(1), 21–37. http://apt.allenpress.com/perlserv/?request=get-abstract&doi=10.1043%2F0890-1171(2003)018%5B0021%3AWABAEO%5D2.3.CO%3B2.

Mougiakakou, S. G., Tsouchlaraki, A. L., Cassios, C., Nikita, K. S., Matsopoulos, G. K., & Uzunoglu, N. K. (2005). SCAPEVIEWER: preliminary results of a landscape perception classification system based on neural network technology. *Ecological Engineering*, *24*(1-2), 5–15..doi:10.1016/j.ecoleng.2004.12.003

Müderrisoğlu, H., Eroğlu, E., Özkan, Ş., & Ak, K. (2006). Visual perception of tree forms. *Building and Environment*, *41*(6), 796–806..doi:10.1016/j.buildenv.2005.03.008

Munakata, M., Ichi, S., Nunokawa, T., Saito, Y., Ito, N., Fukudo, S., & Yoshinaga, K. (2001). Influence of night shift work on psychologic state and cardiovascular and neuroendocrine responses in healthy nurses. *Hypertension Research*, *24*(1), 25–31. doi:10.1291/hypres.24.25

Murakami, M., et al. (2007). Study of feature values for subjective classification of music.In *Proc. of KEER 2007*. (CD-ROM)

Murakami., et al. (2008). Auditory Feature Parameter Design Based on Frequency Selectivity for Kansei Retrieval of Music. In *Proc. of the 10th annual conf. of JSKE 2008* (CD-ROM) (in Japanese)

Murase, Y., et al. (2001). Design of a Compact Humanoid Robot as a Platform. *The 19th Conf. of Robotics Society of Japan*, (pp.789–790). (in Japanese).

Murayama, G., Kato, S., Itoh, H., & Kunitachi, T. (2007). Consideration of relationships between pulse and musical tempo, and its effect of relaxation.In *Proc. of the 3rd spring conf. of JSKE 2007,* B31. (in Japanese)

Murayama, G., Kato, S., Itoh, H., & Kunitachi, T. (2009). Analysis of the relationships between pulses and musical tempo, and their effect on relaxation.In*Kansei Engineering International, 8*(1), 91-98.

Murthy, C. A. (1988). *On Consistent Estimation of Classes in R²in The Context of Cluster Analysis*, Ph.D Thesis, Indian Statistical Institute, Calcutta India.

musicovery. (2009). http://musicovery.com/. Retrieved 10 Oct., 2009

Na Yeon, K., Yunhee, S., Youngrae, K., & Eun Yi, K. (2008). *Emotion recognition using color and pattern in textile images.* Paper presented at the 2008 IEEE Conference on Cybernetics and Intelligent Systems, Chengdou,China.

Nack, F., Dorai, C., & Venkatesh, S. (2001). Computational media aesthetics: finding meaning beautiful. *Multimedia, IEEE, 8*(4), 10–12. doi:10.1109/93.959093

Naderi, J. R., & Raman, B. (2005). Capturing impressions of pedestrian landscapes used for healing purposes with decision tree learning. *Landscape and Urban Planning, 73*(2-3), 155–166..doi:10.1016/j.landurbplan.2004.11.012

Nagamachi, M. (1974). A study of emotion-technology [in Japanese]. *The Japanese Journal of Ergonomics, 10*(2), 121–130.

Nagamachi, M. (1988). A study of costume design consultation based on knowledge engineering [in Japanese]. *The Japanese Journal of Ergonomics, 24*(5), 281–289.

Nagamachi, M. (1995). An image technology expert system and its application to design consultation. *International Journal of Human-Computer Interaction, 3*(3), 267–279. doi:10.1080/10447319109526012

Nagamachi, M., & Lokman, A. M. (2010). *Innovations of Kansei engineering.* Boca Raton, Florida: CRC press.

Nagata, N., Waki, S., & Inokuchi, S. (2003). Non-verbal mapping between sound and color- colored hearing possessors as an example.In *Proc. of the 5th annual conf. of JSKE 2003, 207.* (in Japanese)

Nagata, T., Kakihara, K., Ohkawa, T., & Tobita, N. (1994). Concept Space Generation Oriented Design Using Kansei by Individual Subjectivity. *Journal of IEEJ, 116*(4).

Nahm, U. Y., & Mooney, R. J. (2001). Mining Soft-Matching Rules from Textual Data. *Proceedings of the Seventeenth International Joint Conference on Artificial Intelligence* (pp. 979-984).

Nakai, M., & Mitsuishi, M. (2003). Analysis of individual differences in impression evaluations on music phrases by impression words.In *Proc. of the 5th annual conf. of JSKE 2003,* 209. (in Japanese)

Nakajima, Y. (2002). *The Secret of "I".* Tokyo: Koudansha. (in Japanese)

Nakane, H. (1999). Salivary Chromogranin A as index of psychosomatic stress response. *R&D Review of Toyota CRDL., 34*(3), 17-22.

Nalwa, V. S. (1997). Automatic on-line signature verification. *Proceedings of the IEEE*, *85*(2), 215–239. doi:10.1109/5.554220

Nasar, J. L., & Hong, X. (1999). Visual preferences in urban signscapes. *Environment and Behavior*, *31*(5), 671–691..doi:10.1177/00139169921972290

Nassauer, J. (1980). A non-linear model of visual quality. *Landscape Research*, *5*(3), 29–31. doi:. doi:10.1080/01426398008705956

Nene, S. A., Nayar, S. K., & Murase, H. (1996) *Technical Report CUCS-006-96.*

Nijkamp, P., Rietveld, P., & Spierdijk, L. (2000). A meta-analytic comparison of determinants of public transport use: methodology and application. *Environment and Planning. B, Planning & Design*, *27*(6), 893–903.. doi:10.1068/b2695

Nishida, K. (1966). *Collected Works of Kitarou Nishida* (*Vol. 14*). Tokyo: Iwanamishoten. (in Japanese)

Niwa, Y., Nishioka, S., Iwayama, M., Takano, A., & Nitta, Y. (1997). Topic Graph Generation for Query Navigation: Use of Frequency Classes for Topic Extraction. *Proceedings of Natural Language Processing Pacific Rim Symposium*, *97*, 95–100.

Noe, K. (1996). The Body in History – Philosophy of Nishida and phenomenology. In Ueda, S. (Ed.), *Philosophy of Nishida – Papers of Fifty Years Anniversary after the Death* (pp. 75–100). Tokyo: Iwanamishoten. (in Japanese)

Noe, K. (2005). *Philosophy of Narrative*. Tokyo: Iwanamishoten. (in Japanese)

Noe, N. (1998). Lectures in Seven Days – Narratology of History. In Noe, K. (Ed.), *Iwanami New Lectures on Philosophy 8 History and Theory of Decade End* (pp. 3–76). Tokyo: Iwanamishoten. (in Japanese)

Noguchi, Y. (Ed.). (2009). *A Narrative Approach*. Tokyo: Keisoushobou (in Japanses).

Nomura, S., Mizuno, T., Nozawa, A., Asano, H., & Ide, H. (2009). Salivary cortisol as a possible physiological biomarker for mild mental workload. *Biofeedback Research.*, *36*(1), 23–32.

Nomura, S., Tanaka, H., & Moriyama, T. (2006). Pilot Study of SIgA as a Stress Maker with Repetitive Saliva Collection. *Proceedings of the 5th International Conference of the Cognitive Science*, 169-170.

NVidia Tesla S1070 1U Computing System, Retrieved from http://www.nvidia.com/object/product_tesla_s1070us.ht

O'Sullivan, A., & Sheffrin, S. M. (2003). *Economics: principles in action*. Upper Saddle River, NJ: Prentice Hall.

Ockenfels, M. C., Porter, L., Smyth, J., Kirschbaum, C., Hellhammer, D. H., & Stone, A. A. (1995). Effect of chronic stress associated with unemployment on salivary cortisol: overall cortisol levels, diurnal rhythm, and acute stress reactivity. *Psychosomatic Medicine*, *57*(5), 460–467.

Oestreich, M., Hinrichs, N., & Popp, K. (1996). Bifurcation and stability analysis for a non-smooth friction oscillator. [Ingenieur Archiv]. *Archive of Applied Mechanics*, *66*(5), 301–314. doi:10.1007/BF00795247

Oestreich, M., Hinrichs, N., Popp, K., & Budd, C. (1997). *Analytical and experimental investigation of an impact oscillator.*

Ogino, A., & Kato, T. (2006), Kansei System Modeling: Design Method for Kansei Retrieval Systems. *Transactions of Information Processing Society of Japan*, *47.(SIG4) (TOD29)*, pp. 28-39.

Ohi, Y., & Kawasaki, H. (1996). *Introduction to Color Coordinator, Color*, Japan Color Research Institute (Ed.), Tokyo, Japan Color Enterprise. In Japanese.

Ohira, H. (2001). Controllability of aversive stimuli unconsciously determines volume of secretory Immunoglobulin A in saliva. *Japanese Journal of Behavioral Medicine*, *6*, 16–28.

Ohira, H. (2004). Social support and salivary secretory Immunoglobulin A response in women to stress of making a public speech. *Perceptual and Motor Skills*, *98*, 1241–1250.

Ohira, H., Watanabe, Y., Kobayashi, K., & Kawai, M. (1999). The Type A behavior pattern and immune reactivity to brief stress: change of volume of secretory Immunoglobulin A in saliva. *Perceptual and Motor Skills*, *89*, 423–430. doi:10.2466/PMS.89.6.423-430

Ohmi, G. (1999). *Color Sensation, Data and Test*, Japan Color Research Institute (Ed.), Tokyo, Japan Color Enterprise. In Japanese.

Ohsawa, Y., & Nara, Y. (2002). *Modeling the Process of Chance Discovery by Chance Discovery on Double Helix*. AAAI Fall Symposium Technical Report FS-02-01, American Association for Artificial Intelligence, pp.33-40.

Ohsawa, Y., Benson, N. E., & Yachida, M. (1998). Key-Graph: Automatic Indexing by Co-occurrence Graph based on Building Construction Metaphor. *Proceedings of the IEEE International Forum on Research and Technology Advances in Digital Libraries* (pp. 12-18). IEEE Computer Society.

Okamatsu, K., Fukumoto, M., & Matsuo, K. (2007). A 'Healing' effect by a tempo of music - Psychological evaluation by a simple sound made from acoustical property of 'healing music'. [in Japanese]. *Journal of Japan Society of Kansei Engineering, 7*(2), 237–242.

Okamoto, K., & Kashiwazaki, N. (2005). Study on factor analysis of Kansei parameters for classification of music genre. In *Proc. of the 7th annual conf. of JSKE 2005*, 190. (in Japanese)

Olivetti face database, Retrieved from <http://www.cam-orl.co.uk/facedatabase.html>.

Olivier, L., Petri, T., & Tuomas, E. (2009). https://www.jyu.fi/hum/laitokset/musiikki/en/research/coe/materials/mirtoolbox. Retrieved 10 Oct., 2009

Omori, S. (1996). *Time Does Not Flow*. Tokyo: Seitosha (in Japanese). Yuasa, Y. (1991). *The Body*. Tokyo: Koudansha (in Japanese).

Onisawa, T., & Unehara, M. (2005). Application of Interactive Genetic Algorithm toward Human Centered System. *Journal of SICE, 44*(1), 50–57.

Oonishi, G., Kimura, I., & Yamada, H. (1999). A Kansei model for musical chord progression using recurrent neural networks, Proc. of the 1st annual conf. of JSKE, pp.148. (in Japanese)

Osgood, C. E. (1969). The nature and measurement of meaning. In Osgood, C. E., & Snider, J. G. (Eds.), *Semantic differential technique: a source book* (pp. 3–41). Chicago: Aldine.

Osgood, C. E., Suci, G. J., & Tannenbaum, P. H. (1957). *The Measurement of Meaning*. Urbana, IL: University of Illinois Press.

Otaki, S. (1993). *"Sho" forumu to shintai –Ryokan, Yaichi, Kazumasa o shudai to shite*. Akita Shoten. in Japanese

Ouyang, Q., Kaplan, P. D., & Liu, S. (1997). DNA Solution of the Maximal Clique Problem. *Science, 278*, 446–449. doi:10.1126/science.278.5337.446

Ozaki, S. (2009). The First Step for Analyzing Kansei by Electrophysiological Technique. *Journal of Japan Society of Kansei Engineering, 8*(3), 432–436.

Ozawa, K., Seo, Y., & Ise, T. (2007). Estimation of the Relative Weights of Timbre Factors for Sound Quality Evaluation, Proc. of KEER 2007. (CD-ROM)

Paden, B., & Sastry, S. (1987). A calculus for computing Filippov's differential inclusion with application to the variable structure control of robot manipulators. *IEEE Transactions on Circuits and Systems, 34*(1), 73–82. doi:10.1109/TCS.1987.1086038

Paise, C. D. (1990). Another Stemmer. [ACM.]. *ACM SIGIR Forum, 24*(3), 56–61. doi:10.1145/101306.101310

Palm, R., Driankov, D., & Hellendoorn, H. (1997). *Model based fuzzy control*. New York: Springer.

Pankhurst, T. (2008). *SchenkerGUIDE - A Brief Handbook and Website for Schenkerian Analysis*. London: Routledge.

Pao, T.-L., Cheng, Y.-M., Yeh, J.-H., Chen, Y.-T., Pai, C.-Y., & Tsai, Y.-W. (2008). *Comparison between weighted D-KNN and other classifiers for music emotion recognition*. Paper presented at the The Third International Conference on Innovative Computing, Information and Control Dalian, Liaoning, China.

Pao, Y. H. (1989). *Adaptive pattern recognition and neural networks*. New York: Addison-Wesley.

Parsons, L., & Haque, E. (2004). Subspace clustering for high dimensional data: A review. *SIGKDD Explorations Newsletter, 6*, 90–105. doi:10.1145/1007730.1007731

Păun, G. (1996). Regular Extended H systems are Computationally Universal. *Journal of Automata,Languages. Combinatorics, 1*, 27–36.

Păun, G., Rozenberg, & Salomaa, A. (1996). Computing by Splicing. *Theoretical Computer Science, 2*, 332–336.

Pawlak, Z. (1982). Rough sets. *International Journal of Computer and Information Sciences, 11*, 341–356. doi:. doi:10.1007/BF01001956

Pawlak, Z. (1991). *Rough sets: Theoretical Aspects of Reasoning about Data.* Dordrecht, Boston, London: Kluwer Academic.

Pawlak, Z. (1997). Rough set approach to knowledge-based decision support. *European Journal of Operational Research, 99*(1), 48–57..doi:10.1016/S0377-2217(96)00382-7

Pawlak, Z., & Skowron, A. (1994). Rough membership function. In Yeager, R. E., Fedrizzi, M., & Kacprzyk, J. (Eds.), *Advances in the Dempster-Schafer Theory of Evidence* (pp. 251–271). New York: Wiley.

Perlovsky, L. I., Schoendor, W. H., & Burdick, B. J. (1997). Model-based neural network for target detection in SAR images. *IEEE Transactions on Image Processing, 6*(1), 203–216. doi:.doi:10.1109/83.552107

Pham, D. T., & Bayro-Corrochano, E. J. (1998). Neural computing for noise filtering, edge detection and signature extraction. *Journal of Systems Engineering, 2*(2), 666–670.

Phillips, P. J., Grother, P., Micheals, R. J., Blackburn, D. M., Tabassi, E., & Bone, J. M. (2003). *FRVT 2002: Evaluation Report*, from http://www.frvt.org/DLs/FRVT_2002_Evaluation_Report.pdf

Picard, R. W., Vyzas, E., & Healey, J. (2001). Toward Machine Emotional Intelligence: Analysis of Affective Physiological State. *IEEE Transactions on Pattern Analysis and Machine Intelligence, 23*(10), 1175–1191. doi:10.1109/34.954607

Polanyi, M. (1986). *Tacit Dimension.* New York: Smith Peter.

Polkowski, L. (2002). *Rough Sets, Mathematical Foundations.* Advances in Soft Computing, Physica – Verlag, A Springer-Verlag Company.

Polkowski, L., & Skowron, A. (2001). Rough mereological calculi granules: a rough set approach to computation. *International Journal of Computational Intelligence, 17*, 472–479.

Polkowski, L., Tsumoto, S., Lin, T.Y. (2000). *Rough Set Methods and Applications: New Developments in Knowledge Discovery in Information Systems.* Heidellberg: Physica-Verlag.

Porter, M. F. (1980). An algorithm for suffix stripping. *Program, 14*(3), 130–137.

Portier, H., Louisy, F., Laude, D., Berthelot, M., & Guezennec, C. Y. (2001). Intense endurance training on heart rate and blood pressure variability in runners. *Medicine and Science in Sports and Exercise, 33*(7), 1120–1125. doi:10.1097/00005768-200107000-00009

Powell, L. H., Lovallo, W. R., Matthews, K. A., Meyer, P., Midgley, A. R., & Baum, A. (2002). Physiologic markers of chronic stress in premenopausal, middle-aged women. *Psychosomatic Medicine, 64*(3), 502–509.

Predki, B., Slowinski, R., Stefanowski, J., Susmaga, R., & Wilk, S. (1998). ROSE-Software implementation of the rough set theory. In Polkowski, L., & Skowron, A. (Eds.), *Rough Sets and current Trends in Computing 1998, LNAI 1424* (pp. 605–608). Heidelberg: Springer Berlin. doi:10.1007/3-540-69115-4_85

Procopiuc, C. M., & Jones, M. PK. et al. (2002). A Monte Carlo algorithm for fast projective clustering. *Proc. of ACM SIGMOD Int. Conf. on Management of Data.* (pp.418 – 427).

Puckette, M., & Apel, T. (1998). Real-time audio analysis tools for Pd and MSP. *Proceedings of International Computer Music Conference, 1998*, 109–112.

Rabiner, L. R. (1989). A Tutorial on Hidden Markov Models and Selected Applications in Speech Recognition. *Proceedings of the IEEE*, *77*(2), 257–286. doi:10.1109/5.18626

Rajman, M., & Besançon, R. (1998). Text Mining - Knowledge extraction from unstructured textual data. *Proceedings of 6th Conference of International Federation of Classification Societies* (pp. 473-480).

Raman, B., & Naderi, J. R. (2006). Computer based pedestrian landscape design using decision tree templates. *Advanced Engineering Informatics*, *20*(1), 23–30.. doi:10.1016/j.aei.2005.08.002

Rasmussen, E. M. (1992). Clustering Algorithms. In Frakes, W. B., & Baeza-Yates, R. (Eds.), *Information Retrieval: Data Structures & Algorithms* (pp. 419–442). Upper Saddle River, NJ: Prentice-Hall.

Rauszer, C., & Skowron, A. (1992). The Discernibility Matrices and Functions in Information. Systems. In Slowinski, R. (Ed.), *Intelligent Decision Support*. Amsterdam: Kluwer Dordrecht.

Rayner, J. C. W., & Best, D. J. (2001). *A Contingency Table Approach to Nonparametric Testing*. Boca Raton, FL: Chapman & Hall/CRC.

Reed, R. (1991). Pruning Algorithms –A Survey. *IEEE Transactions on Neural Networks*, *4*(5), 740–747. doi:10.1109/72.248452

Reynolds, T. J., & Gutman, J. (2001). Laddering theory, method, analysis, and interpretation. In Reynolds, T. J., & Olson, J. C. (Eds.), *Understanding Consumer Decision Making: The Means-end Approach To Marketing and Advertising Strategy* (pp. 25–62). Mahwah, New Jersey: Lawrence Erlbaum Associates, Inc.

Ricoeur, P. (1990). *Soi-même comme un autre*. Paris: Seuil (translated to Japanese by Kume, H. (1996). Tokyo: Housei U.P.).

Riley, M. A., & Orden, G. C. V. (Eds.). (2005). *Tutorials in contemporary nonlinear methods for the behavioral Sciences Web Book*. Retrieved from from http://www.nsf.gov/sbe/bcs/pac/nmbs/nmbs.jsp

Robotics, A Programmable Humanoid Robots, Retrieved from http://www.aldebaran-robotics.com/eng/index.php

Rosenblatt, F. (1958). The Perceptron: A Probabilistic Model for Information Storage and Organization in the Brain. *Cornell Aeronautical Laboratory. Psychological Review*, *65*(6), 386–408. doi:.doi:10.1037/h0042519

Roska, T., Zarandy, A., & Chua, L. O. (1993). Color image processing using multilayer CNN structure. In Didiev, H. (Ed.), *Circuit theory and design*. New York: Elsevier.

Ross, T. J., & Ross, T. (1995). *Fuzzy logic with engineering applications*. New York: McGraw Hill College Div.

Roth, M. W. (1990). Survey of neural network technology for automatic target recognition. *IEEE Transactions on Neural Networks*, *1*(1), 28–43. doi:.doi:10.1109/72.80203

Roweis, S., Winfree, E., & Burgoyne, R. (1996). A Sticker Based Architecture for DNA Computation. *In Proceeding of Second Annual Meeting on DNA Based Computers, DIMACS: Series in Discrete Mathematics and theoretical Science*, 1123-1126.

Ruiz-del-Solar, J., & Navarrete, P. (2005). Eigenspace-based face recognition: a comparative study of different approaches. *IEEE Transactions on Systems, Man and Cybernetics. Part C*, *35*(3), 315–325.

Rumelhart, D. E., Hinton, G. E., & Williams, R. J. (1986). Learning representations by back-propagating errors. *Nature*, *323*, 533–536. doi:.doi:10.1038/323533a0

S̈ornmo, L., & Laguna, P. (2005). *Bioelectrical signal processing in cardiac and neurological applications*. New York: Academic Press.

Saaid, M., & Ibrahim, Z. (2008). Fuzzy C-Meaus Clustering for DNA Computing Readout Method Implemented on Light Cycler System. *Proceedings of SICE annual conference*, 641-646.

Saito, A., Munemoto, J., & Matsushita, D. (2005). Study on inference of combination rules of form elements by sensibility evaluation employing rough sets theory - a case of Sanneizaka preservation district for groups of historic buildings. *Journal of Architecture and Planning*, *594*, 85–91. http://sciencelinks.jp/j-east/article/200517/000020051705A0688174.php.

Sakaguchi, T. et al.(1997). Construction and Evaluation of 3-D Emotion Space Based on Facial Image Analysis. *IEICE Transactions; J80-A* (8), 1279–1284. (in Japanese).

Sakamoto, W., & Ishihara, S. (2005). Kansei on rhythm patterns- statistical analysis of drum sound intervals. *Proc. of the 7th annual conf. of JSKE 2005*, 196. (in Japanese)

Sakomata, Y., & Kobayashi, S. (2001). Sticker System with Complex Structure. *Soft Computing, 5*, 114–120. doi:10.1007/s005000000074

Sakonda, N. (2002). Beginning audio programming with Max/MSP – Pitch detection with "fiddle",*Sound & Recording Magazine*, April 2002, 262-263. (in Japanese)

Sakurai, Y. (2000), The A-tree: An Index Structure for High-Dimensional Space Using Relative Approximation. In *Proceedings the 26th International Conference on Very Large Data Bases (VLDB)*, pp. 516-526.

Salton, G. (1988). *Automatic Text Processing*. Reading, MA: Addison-Wesley Longman Publishing.

Salton, G., & McGill, J. M. (1983). *Introduction to Modern Information Retrieval*. New York: McGraw Hill New York.

Sanders, E. B.-N. (2001). *A New Design Space*. Paper presented at the ICSID 2001 Seoul: Exploring Emerging Design Paradigm, Seoul, Korea.

Sauer, T., Yorke, J. A., & Casdagli, M. (1991). Embedology. *Journal of Statistical Physics, 65*(3/4), 579–616. doi:10.1007/BF01053745

Sawaki, M., & Hagita, N. (1996). Recognition of Degraded Machine-Printed Characters Using a Complementary Similarity Measure and Error-Correction Learning. *IEICE Transactions on Information and Systems, 79*(5), 491–497.

Schifferstein, H. N. J., & Hekkert, P. (Eds.). (2007). *Product Experience* (*Vol. 1*). Amsterdam: Elsevier.

Schmidt, S., & Stock, W. G. (2009). Collective indexing of emotions in images. A study in emotional information retrieval. *Journal of the American Society for Information Science and Technology, 60*(5), 863–876. doi:10.1002/asi.21043

Schroeder, H. W., & Cannon, W. N. (1987). Visual quality of residential streets: both street and yard trees make a difference. *Journal of Arboriculture, 13*(10), 236–239. http://joa.isa-arbor.com/request.asp?JournalID=1&ArticleID=2175&Type=2.

Schutte, S., Eklund, J., Axelsson, J. R. C., & Nagamachi, M. (2004). Concepts, methods and tools in Kansei Engineering. *Theoretical Issues in Ergonomics Science, 5*(3), 214–232. doi:.doi:10.1080/1463922021000049980

Scott, P. D., Young, S. S., & Nasrabadi, N. M. (1997). Object recognition using multilayer Hopfield neural network. *IEEE Transactions on Image Processing, 6*(3), 357–372. doi:.doi:10.1109/83.557336

Seki, T., Wada, T., Yamada, Y., Ytow, N., & Hirokawa, S. (2007). Multiple Viewed Search Engine for e-Journal - a Case Study on Zoological Science. *Proceedings of the 12th International Conference on Human-Computer Interaction*, Vol. 4553/2007 (pp. 989-998). Springer-Verlag.

Setiono, R. (2000). Extracting M-of-N Rules from Trained Neural Networks. *IEEE Transactions on Neural Networks, 11*(2), 512–519. doi:10.1109/72.839020

Shakhnarovich, G., & Moghaddam, B. (2004). Face Recognition in Subspaces. In Li, S. Z., & Jain, A. K. (Eds.), *Handbook of Face Recognition*. New York: Springer-Verlag.

Shelhamer, M. (2006). *Nonlinear Dynamics in Physiology: A State-space Approach*. World Scientific. doi:10.1142/9789812772794

Shevitz, D., & Paden, B. (1994). Lyapunov Stability Theory of Nonsmooth Systems. *IEEE Transactions on Automatic Control, 39*(9), 1910–1914. doi:10.1109/9.317122

Shi, Y.-Y., Zhu, X., Kim, H.-G., & Eom, K.-W. (2006). *A tempo feature via modulation spectrum analysis and its application to music emotion classification*, Toronto, ON, Canada.

Shibata, H. (2007). Making Character Using Facial Expressions of Communication Robot. *Forum on Information Technology, 6*, 323–326.

Shibata, T., & Kato, T. (1998). Modeling of subjective interpretation for street landscape image. In Neves, J., Santos, M. F., & Machado, J. M. (Eds.), *Progress in Artificial Intelligence, LNCS 1460* (pp. 501–510). Heidelberg: Springer Berlin.

Shibata, T., & Kato, T. (1999). *'Kansei' image retrieval system for street landscape-discrimination and graphical parameters based on correlation of two images.* Paper presented at the IEEE International Conference on Systems, Man and Cybernetics, Tokyo, Jpn.

Shimoji, Y., Wada, T., & Hirokawa, S. (2008). Dynamic Thesaurus Construction from English-Japanese Dictionary. *Proceedings of the 2008 International Conference on Complex, Intelligent and Software Intensive Systems* (pp. 918-923). IEEE Computer Society.

Shindo, K., & Shoji, Y. (2008). A music retrieval system using KANSEI words. *Proc. of the 10th annual conf. of JSKE 2008* (CD-ROM) (in Japanese)

Shinkai, S., & Aizawa, Y. (2006). The Lempel-Ziv Complexity of Non-Stationary Chaos in Infinite Ergodic Cases (Condensed Matter and Statistical Physics). *Progress of Theoretical Physics, 116*(3), 503–515. doi:10.1143/PTP.116.503

Shockley, K., Santana, M.-V., & Fowler, C. A. (2003). Mutual Interpersonal Postural Constraints Are Involved in Cooperative Conversation. *Journal of Experimental Psychology. Human Perception and Performance, 29*(2), 326–332. doi:10.1037/0096-1523.29.2.326

Shudou, F., et al. (2008). Effects of Environmental Auditory Stimulations on Brain Activities in the Humans and the Mice. *Proc. of the 10th annual conf. of JSKE 2008* (CD-ROM) (in Japanese)

Si, J., & Michel, A. N. (1991). *Analysis and synthesis of discrete-time neural networks with multi-level threshold functions.* Proceedings of IEEE International Symposium on Circuits.

Silver, H. (2007). *Social Exclusion: Comparative Analysis of Europe and Middle East Youth.* Washington, DC: Wolfensohn Center for Development & Dubai School of Government.

Simonelli, T. (2004). *Günther Anders. The obsolete Man.* Paris: Du Jasmin Ed.

Sivik, L. (1997). Color systems for cognitive research. In Hardin, C. L., & Maffi, L. (Eds.), *Color Categories in Thought and Language* (pp. 163–193). New York: Cambridge University Press. doi:10.1017/CBO9780511519819.008

Sloboda, J. A. (1988). Preface. In Sloboda, J. A. (Ed.), *Generative processes in music.* Oxford, UK: Oxford University Press.

Slowinski, R. (2004).Retrieved from http://www-idss.cs.put.poznan.pl/

Slowinski, R., Greco, S., & Matarazzo, S. (2005). Rough set based decision support. In Burke, E., & Kendall, G. (Eds.), *Search Methodologies: Introductory Tutorials in Optimization and Decision Support Techniques* (pp. 475–527). Boston: Springer-Verlang.

Sneath, P. H. A. (1957). The Application of Computers to Taxonomy. *Journal of General Microbiology, 17,* 201–226.

Snyman, J. A. (2005). *Practical Mathematical Optimization: An Introduction to Basic Optimization Theory and Classical and New Gradient-Based Algorithms.* New York: Springer Publishing.

Sokal, R. R., & Michener, C. D. (1958). A Statistical Method for Evaluating Systematic Relationships. *University of Kansas Scientific Bulletin, 28,* 1409–1438.

Soleymani, M., Chanel, G., Kierkels, J. J. M., & Pun, T. (2008). *Affective Characterization of Movie Scenes Based on Multimedia Content Analysis and User's Physiological Emotional Responses.* Paper presented at the Tenth IEEE International Symposium on Multimedia, 2008, Berkeley, California, USA.

Soleymani, M., Chanel, G., Kierkels, J. J. M., & Pun, T. (2008). *Affective ranking of movie scenes using physiological signals and content analysis.* Paper presented at the the 2nd ACM workshop on Multimedia semantics, Vancouver, British Columbia, Canada.

Soleymani, M., Davis, J., & Pun, T. (2009). *A collaborative Personalized Affective Video Retrieval System.* Paper presented at the International Conference on Affective Computing and Intelligent interaction, Amsterdam, Netherlands.

Soliva, R. (2007). Landscape stories: Using Ideal Type Narrative as a Heuristic Device in Rural Studies. *Journal of Rural Studies, 23,* 66–74. doi:10.1016/j.jrurstud.2006.04.004

Song, T., Wang, S., & Ma, F. (2008a). *Triple Elements and Adding Elements DNA Encoding Methods.* System Engineering and Electrical Technology. (in Chinese)

Song, T., Wang, S., & Wang, X. (2008b). The Design of Reversible Gate and Reversible Sequential Circuit based on DNA Computing. *Proceedings of 2008 third International Conference on Intelligent System and Knowledge Engineering, IEEE,* 114-118.

Sørensen, T. (1948). A method of establishing groups of equal amplitude in plant sociology based on similarity of species content and its application to analyses of the vegetation on Danish commons. *Biologiske Skrifter, 5,* 1–34.

Srinivas, M., & Patnaik, L. M. (1994). Adaptive probabilities of crossover and mutation in genetic algorithm. *IEEE Transactions on Systems, Man, and Cybernetics, 24,* 656–667. doi:.doi:10.1109/21.286385

Srinivasan, P. (1992). Thesaurus Construction. In Frakes, W. B., & Baeza-Yates, R. (Eds.), *Information Retrieval Data Structures & Algorithms* (pp. 161–218). Upper Saddle River, NJ: Prentice-Hall.

Sriram, R. D. (2006). Artificial intelligence in engineering: Personal reflections. *Advanced Engineering Informatics, 20*(1), 3–5..doi:10.1016/j.aei.2005.12.002

Stamkopoulus, T., Diamantaras, K., Maglaveras, N., & Strintzis, M. (1998). ECG analysis using nonlinear PCA neural network for ischemia detection. *IEEE Transactions on Signal Processing, 46*(11), 3058–3067. doi:10.1109/78.726818

Stein, L. (1979). *Structure & Style Expanded edition.* Florida: Summy-Birchard Inc.

Steptoe, A., Cropley, M., Griffith, J., & Kirschbaum, C. (2000). Job strain and anger expression predict early morning elevations in salivary cortisol. *Psychosomatic Medicine, 62*(2), 286–292.

Sterlac (2009) *Body mecanics*, p. 37 publication is based on the Sterlac solo exhibition held in the Centre des Arts in Enghien-Les-Bains from 10 April to 28 June 2009.

Sterlac, (1999). *Nouvelles de danse - Danse nouvelles et technologies,* 41 p. 80 – 98 Editions Contredanse Bruxelles 1999 n°40-Pistorius, O. (2007) *Blog on Daily motion,* 17 July 2007 Anzieu, D. *The Ego Skin - Dunod.* Paris, 1995, p. 27

Stevens, C. (2004). Cross-cultural studies of musical pitch and time. *Acoustical Science and Technology, 25*(6), 433–438. doi:10.1250/ast.25.433

Stone, A. A., Neale, J. M., Cox, D. S., Napoli, A., Valdimarsdottir, H., & Kennedy-Moore, E. (1994). Daily events are associated with a secretory immune response to an oral antigen in men. *Health Psychology, 13*(5), 440–446. doi:10.1037/0278-6133.13.5.440

Stutzle, T., & Hoos, H. H. (2000). MAX MIN Ant System. *Future Generation Computer Systems, 16,* 889–914. doi:10.1016/S0167-739X(00)00043-1

Sugano, N. (2001). Effect of well-ordered color signal sequence with minimum distance on human color impressions. *Biomedical Soft Computing and Human Sciences, 7*(1), 53–59.

Sugano, N., & Matsushita, Y. (2001a, July). Human color impression model for well-ordered color signal sequence with minimum distance.In *Proc. of Joint 9th International Fuzzy Systems Association World Congress and 20th North American Fuzzy Information Processing Society International Conference, Vancouver* (pp. 2253-2258).

Sugano, N., & Matsushita, Y. (2001b, October). Human color impression model for color signal sequence with minimum distance.In *Proc. of International Symposium: Toward a Development of KANSEI Technology, Muroran* (pp. 157-160).

Sugano, N., & Matsushita, Y. (2002). Effect of color signal sequence with minimum distance on human color impression model. *Biomedical Soft Computing and Human Sciences, 8*(1), 29–35.

Sugano, N., & Nasu, T. (2000, October). Human color impressions elicited by well-ordered color signal sequences with minimum distance.In *Proc. of 2000 IEEE International Conference on Industrial Electronics, Control and Instrumentation,* Nagoya (pp. 1614-1619).

Sugano, N., Nakagawa, S., Negishi, Y., & Ishihara, T. (2004, October). Human color impression for color sequence with minimum distance.In *Proc. of IEEE International Conference on Systems, Man and Cybernetics, Hague* (pp. 321-326).

Sugano, N., Nakagawa, S., Negishi, Y., & Ishihara, T. (2007a). Effect of spatial color sequence with minimum distance on human color impression and model behavior. In *Biomedical Soft Computing and Human Sciences, 12* (1), 1-7.

Sugano, N., Negishi, Y., & Ishihara, T. (2006). Effect of spatial color sequence with minimum distance on human color impression and its model, Proc. of the Institution of Mechanical Engineers, Part I. *Journal of Systems and Control Engineering, 220*(18), 745–751.

Sugano, N., Negishi, Y., & Ishihara, T. (2007b, September). Effect of route area and route complexity of spatial color sequence on human color impression and simple fuzzy model.In *Proc. of 8th International Symposium on Advanced Intelligent Systems,* Sokcho (pp. 443-448).

Sugano, N., Negishi, Y., & Ishihara, T. (2009). Effect of route complexity of spatial color sequence on human color impression and its fuzzy model. *International Journal of Biomedical Soft Computing and Human Sciences, 14*(1), 131–139.

Sugihara, T. (2005). Selecting Kansei words for use in a Kansei-based music retrieval system for young people. [in Japanese]. *Journal of Japan Society of Kansei Engineering, 5*(3), 127–134.

Sugihara, T., Morimoto, K., & Kurokawa, T. (2008). A study of user's strategies with a music information retrieval system with Kansei characteristics: lack attention to the midrange settings. [in Japanese]. *Journal of Japan Society of Kansei Engineering, 7*(4), 665–673.

Suk, H.-J., Kim, B., & Kwon, M.-Y. (2007). The Influence of Ring-Back-Tone (RBT) Music on Evaluation of the Phone-call Receiver's Personality. In *Proc. of KEER 2007.* (CD-ROM)

Summit, J., & Sommer, R. (1999). Further studies of preferred tree shapes. *Environment and Behavior, 31*(4), 550–576..doi:10.1177/00139169921972236

Sun, K., & Yu, J. (2009). Audience Oriented Personalized Movie Affective Content Representation and Recognition.

Sun, K., & Yu, J. Q. (2007, Sep 12-14). *Video affective content representation and recognition using video affective tree and Hidden Markov Models.* Paper presented at the 2nd International Conference on Affective Computing and Intelligent Interaction, Lisbon, PORTUGAL.

Synak, P., & Wieczorkowska, A. (2005). *Some issues on detecting emotions in music.* Paper presented at the Rough Sets, Fuzzy Sets, Data Mining, and Granular Computing, Regina, Canada.

Takagi, T., & Sugeno, M. (1985). Fuzzy identification of systems and its applications to modeling and control. *IEEE Transactions on Systems, Man, and Cybernetics, 15*(1), 116–132.

Takahashi, M., & Saito, T. (2008). Proposal of the musical instrument for cooperative operation.In Proc. *of the 10th annual conf. of JSKE 2008* (CD-ROM) (in Japanese)

Takahashi, T., Matsui, T., & Higashiyama, M. (2000). Tones of Shakuhachi and their wave forms,In *Proc. of the 2nd annual conf. of JSKE,*(pp.81). (in Japanese)

Takens, F. (1981). Detecting strange attractors in turbulence. In Rand, D. A., & Young, L. S. (Eds.), *Dynamical Systems and Turbulence, Lecture Notes in Mathematics* (*Vol. 898,* pp. 366–381). New York: Springer-Verlag.

Tanaka, K., & Sugeno, M. (1992). Stability analysis and design of fuzzy control systems. *Fuzzy Sets and Systems*, *45*(2), 135–156. doi:10.1016/0165-0114(92)90113-I

Tanaka, K., & Wang, H. O. (2001). *Fuzzy control systems design and analysis: a linear matrix inequality approach*. New York: Wiley-Interscience.

Tang, H. W., Srinivasan, V., & Ong, S. H. (1996). Invariant object recognition using a neural template classifier. *Image and Vision Computing*, *14*(7), 473–483. doi:. doi:10.1016/0262-8856(95)01065-3

Tatem, A. J., Lewis, H. G., Atkinson, P. M., & Nixon, M. S. (2001). Super-resolution target identification from remotely sensed images using a Hopfield neural network. *IEEE Transactions on Geoscience and Remote Sensing*, *39*(4), 781–796. doi:.doi:10.1109/36.917895

Teder-Salejarvi, W. A., Hillyard, S. A., Roder, B., & Neville, H. J. (1999). Spatial attention to central and peripheral auditory stimuli as indexed by event-related potentials. *Brain Research. Cognitive Brain Research*, *8*(3), 213–227. doi:10.1016/S0926-6410(99)00023-3

Thurstone, L. L. (1934). The vectors of the mind. *Psychological Review*, *41*, 1–32. doi:10.1037/h0075959

Tickle, A., Andrews, B. R., Golea, M., & Diederich, J. (1998). The truth will come to light: directions and challenges in extracting the knowledge embedded within trained artificial neural networks. *IEEE Transactions on Neural Networks*, *9*(6), 1057–1067. doi:10.1109/72.728352

Tien-Lin Wu, S.-K. J. (2006). *Automatic emotion classification of musical segments*. Paper presented at the 9th International Conference on Music Perception and Cognition Bologna, Italy.

Tobimatsu, S., Zhang, Y. M., Tomoda, Y., Mitsudome, A., & Kato, M. (1999). Chromatic sensitive epilepsy: A variant of photosensitive epilepsy. *Annals of Neurology*, *45*(6), 790–793. doi:10.1002/1531-8249(199906)45:6<790::AID-ANA14>3.0.CO;2-7

Toda, M., Kusakabe, S., Nagasawa, S., Kitamura, K., & Morimoto, K. (2007). Effect of laughter on salivary endocrinological stress marker Chromogranin A. *Biomedical Research*, *28*(2), 15–18. doi:10.2220/biomedres.28.115

Todorova, A., Asakawa, S., & Aikoh, T. (2004). Preferences for and attitudes towards street flowers and trees in Sapporo, Japan. *Landscape and Urban Planning*, *69*(4), 403–416..doi:10.1016/j.landurbplan.2003.11.001

Tokairin, M., & Shiizuka, H. (2007). *Automatic Music Composition System through KANSEI (Sensibility) Adjectives, KEER 2007*. CD-ROM.

Tokairin, M., & Shiizuka, H. (2008). Automatic music composition system through Kansei adjectives. [in Japanese]. *Journal of Japan Society of Kansei Engineering*, *8*(1), 119–127.

Tokumaru, M., et al. (2004). Study on music composition system for enjoying music.In *Proc. of the 6th annual conf. of JSKE 2004, 195*. (in Japanese)

Tomico, O., Mizutani, N., Lévy, P., Takahiro, Y., Cho, Y., & Yamanaka, T. (2006, May 19-22, 2008). *Kansei physiological measurements and contructivist psychological explorations for approaching user subjective experience during and after product usage*. Paper presented at the International Design Conference - Design 2008, Dubrovnik, Croatia.

Toyosawa, S., & Kawai, T. (2009). A video abstraction method based on viewer's heart activity and its evaluations. *Kyokai Joho Imeji Zasshi/Journal of the Institute of Image Information and Television Engineers*, *63*(1), 86-94.

Tsao, E. C. K., Lin, W. C., & Chen, C.-T. (1993). Constraint satisfaction neural networks for image recognition. *Pattern Recognition*, *26*(4), 553–567. doi:.doi:10.1016/0031-3203(93)90110-I

Tsujita, S., & Morimoto, K. (1999). Secretory IgA in saliva can be a useful stress maker. *Environmental Health and Preventive Medicine*, *4*, 1–8. doi:10.1007/BF02931243

Tsumita, H., Sekido, Y., & Hamamoto, S. (2006). A correlation analysis of an atmosphere and indication element of street space by psychological quantity distribution figure: Study of kehai in urban street spaces (Part 2). *Journal of Architecture and Planning, 607*, 41–48. http://ci.nii.ac.jp/naid/110004809771/en.

Tsutsumi, K. (2004). A Development of the Building Kansei Information Retrieval System. In Proceedings *the International Conference on Computing in Civil and Building Engineering, pp.* 174-181.

Tulpan, D., Hoos, H., & Condon, A. (2002). Stochastic Local Search Algorithm for DNA Word Design. *DNA Computing: 8th International Workshop on DNA-Based Computers*, 229—241.

Tzanetakis, G. (2009). http://marsyas.sness.net/. Retrieved 10 Oct., 2009

Tzeng, Y. C., & Chen, K. S. (1998). A fuzzy neural network to SAR image classification. *IEEE Transactions on Geoscience and Remote Sensing, 36*(1), 301–307. doi:. doi:10.1109/36.655339

Ueda, S. (Ed.). (2001). *Selected Philosophical Papers of Kitaro Nishida, I, II*. Tokyo: Iwanamishoten. (in Japanese)

Ueki, N. et al.(1994). Expression Analysis/Synthesis System Based on Emotional Space Constructed by Multi-Layered Neural Network. *IEICE Transactions; J77-DII* (3), 573–582. (in Japanese).

Unehara, M., & Yamada, K. (2008). *Interactive Conceptual Design Support System Using Human Evaluation with Kansei*. Proceesings of 2nd International Conference on Kansei Engineering and Affective Systems, (pp. 175-180).

Valdimarsdottir, H. B., & Stone, A. A. (1997). Psychosocial factors and secretory Immunoglobulin A. *Critical Reviews in Oral Biology and Medicine, 8*(4), 461–474. doi:10.1177/10454411970080040601

van Stegeren, A., Rohleder, N., Everaerd, W., & Wolf, O. T. (2006). Salivary alpha amylase as marker for adrenergic activity during stress: effect of betablockade. *Psychoneuroendocrinology, 31*(1), 137–141. doi:10.1016/j.psyneuen.2005.05.012

von Cube, F.-E. (1988). *The Book of Musical Artwork – An interpretation of the musical theories of Heinrich Schenker*. New York: The Edwin Mellen Press.

Wada, K., et al. (2004). *Effects of Three Months Robot Assisted Activity to Depression of Elderly People Who Stay at a Health Service Facility for the Aged*. SICE Annual Conference, 2709-2714.

Wagner, J., Kim, J., & Andre, E. (2005). *From physiological signals to emotions: Implementing and comparing selected methods for feature extraction and classification*, Amsterdam, Netherlands.

Wakida, S., Tanaka, Y., & Nagai, H. (2004). High throughput screening for stress marker. *Bunseki, 2004*, 309–316.

Walczak, B., & Massart, D. L. (1999). Rough sets theory. *Chemometrics and Intelligent Laboratory Systems, 47*(1), 1–16..doi:10.1016/S0169-7439(98)00200-7

Walter, A. I., & Scholz, R. W. (2007). Critical success conditions of collaborative methods: a comparative evaluation of transport planning projects. *Transportation, 34*(2), 195–212..doi:10.1007/s11116-006-9000-0

Wang Weining, Y. y. (2005). *Research on Emotion Semantic based image feature extraction, retrieval and classification*. Unpublished doctoral dissertation, South China Universtiy of Technology, Guangzhou.

Wang, C. W., Cheng, W. H., Chen, J. C., Yang, S. S., & Wu, J. L. (2007, Jan 09-12). *Film narrative exploration through the analysis of aesthetic elements*. Paper presented at the 13th International Multimedia Modeling Conference Singapore, SINGAPORE.

Wang, K. C., & Chen, S. M. (2007, Oct 07-10). *Product form design using ANFIS-kansei engineering model*. Paper presented at the IEEE International Conference on Systems, Man and Cybernetics, Montreal, COOK ISLANDS.

Wang, M., Hang, N., & Zhu, H. (2004a). *User-adaptive music emotion recognition*. Paper presented at the International Conference on Signal Processing Proceedings, ICSP, Beijing, China.

Wang, M., Hang, N., & Zhu, H. (2004b). *User-adaptive music emotion recognition*, Beijing, China.

Wang, M., Zhang, N., & Zhu, H. (2006). Emotion recognition of Western tonal music using support vector machine. *Chinese Journal of Electronics, 15*(1), 74–78.

Wang, S. (2002). *Research on Kansei Information Processing and Its Application in Image Retrieval.* Unpublished Doctor dissertation, Universtiy of Science and Technology of China, Hefei, Anhui

Wang, S. (2005). Solved Graph Coloring by DNA Sticker Model. *System Engineering and Electrical Technology, 27*(3), 568–573.

Wang, S. F., & Hu, Y. J. (2009). *Emotion valence and arousal recognition on IAPS and IADS.* Paper presented at the Workshop on Specification and Computation of Affect in Collaborative and Social NETworks.

Wang, S. F., Chen, E. H., Li, J. L., & Wang, X. F. (2001). Kansei-based image evaluation and retrieval. *Moshi Shibie yu Rengong Zhineng/Pattern Recognition and Artificial Intelligence, 14*(3), 297-297.

Wang, S., Song, T., & Li, E. (2009). The Design and Analysis of DNA Golay Codes [in Chinese]. *Acta Electronica Sinica, 7*, 1542–1545.

Wang, W., Seo, I., Lee, B., & Namgung, M. (2008). Extracting features of sidewalk space using the rough sets approach. *Environment and Planning. B, Planning & Design, 35*(5), 920–934..doi:10.1068/b34045

Wang, X., Bao, Z.,& Hu, J. (2008). DNA Computing Solves the 3-SAT Problem with a Small Solution Space. *Current nanoscience, 4* (6), 354-360.

Ward, J. H. (1963). Hierarchical Grouping to Optimize an Objective Function. *Journal of the American Statistical Association, 58*(301), 236–244. doi:10.2307/2282967

Watanabe, C., & Shiizuka, H. (2004). Research of choreograph system by Kansei.In *Proc. of the 6th annual conf. of JSKE 2004, 194.* (in Japanese)

Watanabe, T., Sugiyama, Y., Sumi, Y., Watanabe, M., Takeuchi, K., Kobayashi, F., & Kono, K. (2002). Effects of vital exhaustion on cardiac autonomic nervous functions assessed by heart rate variability at rest in middle-aged male workers. *International Journal of Behavioral Medicine, 9*(1), 68–75. doi:10.1207/S15327558IJBM0901_05

Watanapa, S. C., Thipakorn, B., & Charoenkitkarn, N. (2008). A sieving ANN for emotion-based movie clip classification. *Ieice Transactions on Information and Systems. E (Norwalk, Conn.), 91D*(5), 1562–1572.

Webber, C. L. (1996). *RQA Software,* Web site: http://homepages.luc.edu/~cwebber/

Wei, C.-Y., Dimitrova, N., & Chang, S.-F. (2004). *Color-Mood Analysis of Films Based on Syntactic and Psychological Models.* Paper presented at the IEEE International Conference on Multimedia and Expo.

Wen, W., & Lingyun, X. (2008). *Discriminating mood taxonomy of Chinese traditional music and western classical music with content feature sets.* Paper presented at the 1st International Congress on Image and Signal Processing, Sanya, Hainan, China.

Wieczorkowska, A. A. (2005). *Towards extracting emotions from music.* Paper presented at the Second International Workshop on Intelligent Media Technology for Communicative Intelligence, Warsaw, Poland.

Wieczorkowska, A., & Synak, P. (2006). *Quality assessment of k-NN multi-label classification for music data.* Paper presented at the 16th International Symposium on Methodologies for Intelligent Systems, Bari, Italy.

Wieczorkowska, A., Synak, P., Lewis, R., & Ras, Z. W. (2005). *Extracting emotions from music data.* Paper presented at the 15th International Symposium on Methodologies for Intelligent Systems, Saratoga Springs, NY, United states.

Willebrand, M., Andersson, G., Kildal, M., & Ekselius, L. (2002). Exploration of coping patterns in burned adults: cluster analysis of the coping with burns questionnaire (CBQ). [Elsevier.]. *Burns, 28*, 549–554. doi:10.1016/S0305-4179(02)00064-5

Williams, D. B., Carlsen, J. C., & Dowling, W. J. (1981). Psychomusicology: A position statement. *Psychomusicology*, *1*(1), 3–5.

Williams, J. E., Kirtland, K. A., Cavnar, M. M., Sharpe, P. A., Neet, M. J., & Cook, A. (2005). Development and use of a tool for assessing sidewalk maintenance as an environmental support of physical activity. *Health Promotion Practice*, *6*(1), 81–88..doi:10.1177/1524839903260595

Williams, K. (2002). Exploring resident preferences for street trees in Melbourne. *Australia Journal of Arboriculture*, *28*(4), 161–169.

Williams, L. E., & Bargh, J. A. (2008). Experiencing Physical Warmth Promotes Interpersonal Warmth. *Science*, *322*(5901), 606–607. doi:10.1126/science.1162548

Winkler, H., & Fischer-Colbrie, R. (1992). The chromogranins A and B: the first 25 years and future perspectives. *Neuroscience*, *49*(3), 497–528. doi:10.1016/0306-4522(92)90222-N

Winnicott, D. W. (1964). The child, the Family and the Outside world. London: Penguin Books. Reading Massachusetts: Addison-Wesley publishing Co., Inc. p. 128

Winnicott, D. W. (1971). *Playing and Reality.* Tavistock Publication Routledge. (p. 15, p. 148, p.52). [Winnicott, 1990] Winnicott, D. W. (1986) Home is where we start from. First published in the USA by W. W. Norton & Company. Reprinted in Penguin Books. (p. 49, p.40, p.49, p.66, p.160).

Wolf, O. T., & Kirschbaum, C. (1999). Actions of Dehydroepiandrosterone and its sulfate in the central nervous system: Effects on cognition and emotion in animals and humans. *Brain Research. Brain Research Reviews*, *30*(3), 264–288. doi:10.1016/S0165-0173(99)00021-1

Woo, Kyoung-Gu& Lee, Jeong-Hoon et al. (2004). FIN-DIT: A fast and intelligent subspace clustering algorithm using dimension voting. *Information and Software Technology*, *46*(4), 255–271. doi:10.1016/j.infsof.2003.07.003

Wooten, B., & Miller, D. L. (1997). The psychophysics of color. In Hardin, C. L., & Maffi, L. (Eds.), *Color Categories in Thought and Language* (pp. 59–88). New York: Cambridge University Press. doi:10.1017/CBO9780511519819.003

Wroblewski, J. Covering with Reducts: A Fast Algorithm for Rule Generation. Proceeding of RSCTC'98 LNAI 1424 Springer Verlag, Berlin, 1998, 402-407.

Wu, C., Yue, Y., Li, M., & Adjei, O. (2004). The rough set theory and applications. *Engineering Computations*, *21*(5), 488–511..doi:10.1108/02644400410545092

Wu, H. (2001). An Improved Surface-Based Method for DNA Computing. *Bio Systems*, *59*, 1–5. doi:10.1016/S0303-2647(00)00133-7

Wu, Y., Liu, Q., & Huang, T. S. (2000). *An adaptive self-organizing color segmentation algorithm with application to robust real-time human hand localization.* Proceedings of Asian Conference on Computer Vision.

Xu, J. (2004). Stickerter Model(II): Applications. *Chinese Science Bulletin*, *2*, 223–225.

Xu, M. C. L.-T.; Jin, J. (2005). *Affective content analysis in comedy and horror videos by audio emotional event detection.* Paper presented at the IEEE International Conference on Multimedia and Expo, 2005.

Xu, M., Jin, J. S., Luo, S., & Duan, L. (Eds.). (2008). *Hierarchical movie affective content analysis based on arousal and valence features.* Vancouver, British Columbia, Canada: ACM.

*Yale face database,*Retrieved from <http://cvc.yale.edu/projects/yalefaces/yalefaces.html>.

Yamada, Y., Katoh, K., & Hirokawa, S. (2007). Multiple Analysis of Remarks of Elderly and Disabled People by Text Mining. *Proceedings of the International Conference on Kansei Engineering and Emotion Research 2007.*

Yamaguchi, M., Kanemori, T., Knemaru, M., Takai, N., Yasufumi, M., & Yoshida, H. (2004). Performance evaluation of salivary amylase activity monitor. *Biosensors & Bioelectronics*, *20*, 491–497. doi:10.1016/j.bios.2004.02.012

Yamamoto, S., Nakanishi, R., Sagaya, Y., & Takeda, S. (2005). Comparison of EEG alpha-band power variation between beat tracking and listening to music. [in Japanese]. *Journal of Japan Society of Kansei Engineering*, 5(3), 61–70.

Yamashita, Y., Higuchi, Y., & Watanabe, T. (2000). Artists recommend system by taste analysis. In *Proc. of the 2nd annual conf. of JSKE*, (pp.64). (in Japanese)

Yamawaki, K., & Shiizuka, H. (2002). Kansei correspondence between music and color image. In *Proc. of the 4th annual conf. of JSKE, 237*. (in Japanese)

Yamawaki, K., & Shiizuka, H. (2005). Music parameter needed for music recommendation system. In *Proc. of the 1st spring conf. of JSKE 2005*, (pp. 31-32). (in Japanese)

Yamawaki, K., & Shiizuka, H. (2005). Solfege ability and color-heard-sense. [in Japanese]. *Journal of Japan Society of Kansei Engineering*, 5(3), 31–37.

Yamawaki, K., & Shiizuka, H. (2007). Characteristic recognition of the musical piece with correspondence analysis. In *Proc. of the 9th annual conf. of JSKE 2007* (CD-ROM) (in Japanese)

Yamawaki, K., & Shiizuka, H. (2007). Recognition of music characteristic with rough sets. [in Japanese]. *Journal of Japan Society of Kansei Engineering*, 7(2), 283–288.

Yamawaki, K., & Shiizuka, H. (2008). Music recognition system by correspondence analysis. [in Japanese]. *Journal of Japan Society of Kansei Engineering*, 7(4), 659–663.

Yan, H.-B., Huynh, V.-N., Murai, T., & Nakamori, Y. (2008). Kansei evaluation based on prioritized multi-attribute fuzzy target-oriented decision analysis. *International Journal of Information Sciences*, 178(21), 4080–4093.

Yang, Y. X., Wang, A. M., & Ma, J. L. (2009). A DNA Computing Algorithm of Addition Arithmetic. *Proceedings of the first international workshop on education technology and computer science*, 1056-1059.

Yang, Y.-H., Lin, Y.-C., Su, Y.-F., & Chen, H. H. (2007). *Music emotion classification: A regression approach*, Beijing, China.

Yang, Y.-H., Lin, Y.-C., Su, Y.-F., & Chen, H. H. (2008). A regression approach to music emotion recognition. *IEEE Transactions on Audio. Speech and Language Processing*, 16(2), 448–457. doi:10.1109/TASL.2007.911513

Yang, Y.-H., Liu, C.-C., & Chen, H. H. (2006). *Music emotion classification: a fuzzy approach.* Paper presented at the 14th Annual ACM International Conference on Multimedia, Santa Barbara, CA, United states.

Yanulevskaya, V., van Gemert, J. C., Roth, K., Herbold, A. K., Sebe, N., & Geusebroek, J. M. (2008). *Emotional valence categorization using holistic image features.* Paper presented at the 15th IEEE International Conference on Image Processing, 2008., San Diego, California, U.S.A.

Yokomori, T., & Kobayashi, S. (1997). On the Power of Circular System and DNA Computing. *IEEE.* 219-224.

Yokoyama, K., & Araki, S. (1993). *Nihongo ban POMS tebiki (the guide of profile of mood states Japanese version)* (5th ed.). Tokyo: Kaneko Shobo.

YOO, H.-W. (2006). Visual-Based Emotional Descriptor and Feedback Mechanism for Image Retrieval. *Journal of Information Science and Engineering*, 22(5), 1205–1227.

Yoo, H.-W., & Cho, S.-B. (2007). Video scene retrieval with interactive genetic algorithm. *Multimedia Tools and Applications*, 34(3), 317–336. doi:10.1007/s11042-007-0109-8

Yoshida, K., Kato, T., & Yanaru, T. (1998). *Image retrieval system using impression words.* Paper presented at the IEEE International Conference on Systems, Man, and Cybernetics, 1998, San Diego, California, USA

Yoshida, T. (2002). An Evaluation-model for 'KAITEKI-SEI' by Using Frequency-rhythm of Brain Wave. *Japanese Psychological Review*, 46(1), 38–56.

Yoshida, Tomoyoshi, Nakanishi, S., Yamamoto, S. & Takeda, S. (2007). Measurements of synchronization in musical rhythms and study of effects of rhythms on the EEG. Journal *of Japan Society of Kansei Engineering*, 7(2), 337-344. (in Japanese)

Yoshida, Tomoyuki. & Iwaki, T. (2000). The study of early emotion processing in the frontal area using a two-dipole source model. *The Japanese Psychological Research, 42*(1), 54–68. doi:10.1111/1468-5884.00131

Zadeh, L. A. (1965). Fuzzy sets. *Information and Control, 8*, 338–353. doi:.doi:10.1016/S0019-9958(65)90241-X

Zadeh, L. A. (2005). Toward a generalized theory of uncertainty (GTU)—an outline. *Information Sciences, 172*(1-2), 1–40. doi:10.1016/j.ins.2005.01.017

Zhang, C. (2001). On Supporting Containment Queries in Relational Database Management Systems. In *Proceedings ACM SIGMOD International Conference*, pp. 425-436.

Zhang, G. P. (2000). Neural networks for classification: a survey. *IEEE Transactions on Systems, Man and Cybernetics. Part C, Applications and Reviews, 30*(4), 451–462. doi:.doi:10.1109/5326.897072

Zhang, S. L., Huang, Q. M., Tian, Q., Jiang, S. Q., & Gao, W. (2008, Dec 09-13). *Personalized MTV Affective Analysis Using User Profile.* Paper presented at the 9th Pacific Rim Conference on Multimedia, Tainan, TAIWAN.

Zhang, S. L., Tian, Q., Jiang, S. Q., Huang, Q. M., Gao, W., & Ieee. (2008, 26 Aug 2008). *Affective MTV Analysis Based on Arousal and Valence Features.* Paper presented at the IEEE International Conference on Multimedia and Expo (ICME 2008), Hannover, GERMANY.

Zhang, X., Wang, Y., & Cui, G. (2009). Application of a novel IWO to the design of encoding sequences for DNA computing. *Computers & Mathematics with Applications (Oxford, England), 57*(11), 2001–2008. doi:10.1016/j.camwa.2008.10.038

Zhang, Z., Shi, X., & Liu, J. (2008). A Method to Encrypt Information with DNA Computing. *The third international conference on bio-inspired computing: theory and application*, 155-159.

Zhao, W., Chellappa, R., Rosenfeld, A., & Phillips, J. (2003). *Face Recognition: A Literature Survey. Technical Report, CS-TR4167.* Univ. of Maryland.

Zhong, C.-B., & Leonardelli, G. J. (2008). Cold and Lonely: Does Social Exclusion Literally Feel Cold? *Psychological Science, 19*(9), 838–842. doi:10.1111/j.1467-9280.2008.02165.x

Zhu, B., Liu, T., & Tang, Y. (2008). *Research on music emotion cognition model based on linguistic value computing*, Chongqing, China.

Zhu, X. (2008). Semi-Supervised Learning Literature Survey. 2010, from http://pages.cs.wisc.edu/~jerryzhu/research/ssl/semireview.html

Zhu, X., Shi, Y.-Y., Kim, H.-G., & Eom, K.-W. (2006). An integrated music recommendation system. *IEEE Transactions on Consumer Electronics, 52*(3), 917–925. doi:10.1109/TCE.2006.1706489

Zhu, Z. (1994). Color pattern recognition in an image system with chromatic distortion. *Optical Engineering (Redondo Beach, Calif.), 33*(9), 3047–3051. doi:.doi:10.1117/12.177509

Zube, E. H., Pitt, D. G., & Anderson, T. W. (1975). Perception and prediction of scenic resource values of the northeast. In E.H. Zube, R.O. Brush, J.G. Fabos (Ed), *Landscape Assessment: Values, Perceptions, and Resources* (pp. 151-167). Stroudsburg: Dowden, Hutchinson & Ross.

About the Contributors

Ying Dai received her BS and MS degrees from Xian Jiaotong University, China in 1985 and 1988, respectively. After some years working in the same university, she attended Department of Information Engineering, Shinshu University, Japan in 1992. She had a Dr. Eng degree from Shinshu University in 1996. She was granted JSPS Research Fellowships for Young Scientists from 1995 to 1997. She joined the Iwate Pref. University in 1998. She has been an associate professor in the Faculty of Software and Information Science, Iwate Pref. University since 2002. Her main research interests are in the area of Pattern Recognition, Image Understanding, Kansei Information Processing, and Soft Computing Techniques. She is the member of IEEE, IEICE (the Institute of Electronics, Information and Communication Engineers), and JSKE (Japan Society of Kansei Engineering).

Basabi Chakraborty received B.Tech, M.Tech and PhD degrees in RadioPhysics and Electronics from Calcutta University, India. She worked in National Center for Knowledge based Computing Systems and Technology affiliated to Indian Statistical Institute, Calcutta, India until 1990. From 1991 to 1993 she worked as a part time researcher in Advanced Intelligent Communication Systems Laboratory in Sendai, Japan. She received another PhD in Information Science from Tohoku University, Sendai in 1996. From 1996 to 1998, she worked as a post doctoral research fellow in Research Institute of Electrical Communication, Tohoku University, Japan (under Telecommunication Advancement Organization (TAO) fellowship for a period of 10 months). In 1998 she joined as a faculty in Software and Information Science department of Iwate Prefectural University, Iwate, Japan and currently an Associate Professor in the same department. Her main research interests are in the area of Pattern Recognition, Image Processing, Soft Computing Techniques, Biometrics, Trust and Security in Computer Communication Network. She is a senior member of IEEE, member of ACM, Japanese Neural Network Society (JNNS) and Information Processing Society of Japan (IPSJ), executive committee member of IUPRAI (Indian Unit of Pattern Recognition and Artificial Intelligence), IEEE JC WIE (Women In Engineering) and ISAJ (Indian Scientists Association in Japan).

Minghui Shi received his MS degree in 2002 and Dr. degree in 2008 respectively from Jiangnan University and Xiamen University, China. He is currently an assistant professor at Xiamen University. In addition to working as a teacher, he is also a research member of Artificial Intelligence Institute of Xiamen University. His research interests involve Soft Computing Techniques, Machine Learning, Pattern Recognition, Information Processing in TCM (Traditional Chinese Medicine), and Feature Selection.

* * *

Sanghamitra Bandyopadhyay did her B Tech, M Tech and PhD in Computer Science from Calcutta University, IIT Kharagpur and ISI respectively. She is currently an associate professor at the Indian Statistical Institute, Kolkata, India. She has worked at the Los Alamos National Laboratory, Los Alamos, New Mexico, University of New South Wales, Sydney, Australia, University of Texas at Arlington, University of Maryland at Baltimore, Fraunhofer Institute, Germany, Tsinghua University, China, University of Rome, Italy and University of Heidelberg, Germany. She is the first recipient of the Dr. Shanker Dayal Sharma Gold Medal and also the Institute Silver Medal for being adjudged the best all-around postgraduate performer in IIT, Kharagpur, India, in 1994. She has also received the Young Scientist Awards of the Indian National Science Academy (INSA), 2000, the Indian Science Congress Association (ISCA), 2000, the Young Engineer Award of the Indian National Academy of Engineers (INAE), 2002, the Swarnajayanti fellowship from the Department of Science and Technology (DST), 2007, and the prestigious Humboldt Fellowship from Germany, 2009. She has authored/co-authored more than 175 technical articles in international journals, book chapters, and conference/workshop proceedings. She has delivered many invited talks and tutorials around the world, and has been the chair and member of several conference committees. She has published four authored and edited books from publishers like Springer, World Scientific and Wiley. She has also edited journals special issues in the area of soft computing, data mining, and bioinformatics. Her research interests include computational biology and bioinformatics, soft and evolutionary computation, pattern recognition and data mining. She is a senior member of the IEEE.

Hisashi Bannai is a Senior Researcher of Rural Finance Research Institute in Japan. He got MS in the major of Social Economic Thoughts (1981) in Kokugakuin University, and PhD in the major of Resource and Environmental Economics (2004) in Tohoku University. His careers as in rural research field were started as a Senior Researcher of Rural Finance Research Institute collaborating with Prof. Masao Miwa in Graduate School of Economics in Kokugakuin University (1994), doctor course researcher collaborating with Prof. Kazuo Morozumi in Graduate School of Agricultural Economics in Tohoku University (2000). He was awarded the JA Prize (2008) to explore for structural problems of Japanese agricultural cooperatives by Central Union of Agricultural Cooperatives (Zenchu).Now, he dedicates his time to explore a new way of Revival for Japanese rural community applying a revival model based on American rural industry.Japan

Siddhartha Bhattacharyya did his Bachelors in Physics, Bachelors in Optics and Optoelectronics and Masters in Optics and Optoelectronics from University of Calcutta, India in 1995, 1998 and 2000 respectively. He completed PhD in Computer Science and Engineering from Jadavpur University, India in 2008. He is currently a Lecturer in Computer Science and Information Technology of University Institute of Technology, The University of Burdwan, India. He was a Lecturer in Information Technology of Kalyani Government Engineering College, India during 2001-2005. He is a co-author of a book and more than 50 research publications. He was the member of the Young Researchers' Committee of the WSC 2008 Online World Conference on Soft Computing in Industrial Applications. His research interests include soft computing, pattern recognition and quantum computing. Dr. Bhattacharyya is a life member of OSI and ISTE, India. He is a member of IAENG, Hong Kong and IRSS, Poland.

Xiaoxi Chen was born in Xiamen, China, in 1989. He is a sophomore student in the School of Information Science & Technology, Xiamen University. In 2008, he joined the Artificial Brain Lab (ABL)

of Xiamen University, a Fujian Province Key Laboratory, and became the youngest member of ABL. In the lab, he studied with Professor Hugo de GARIS, generally recognized to be the father of the artificial brain. His interests include Artificial Brains, neural networks, GPGPU (General-Purpose computing on Graphics Processing Units) and CUDA parallel computing.

Elisabeth Damour has a Master degree in International Marketing and in Russian Literature: she is a specialist of Chekhov's dramas. She has run an artistic career as a dancer and collaborated with designers in London and in Saõ Paolo. She collaborates as a consultant in Innovation Programs and in the Master Certification in Paris Business Schools. She is a certified Trainer and Coach (member of ICF) in Process Communication, Frederic M. Hudson Institute. As an Expressive Art Therapist and a performer, she runs workshops in Japan and U.K. She is a member of the D. W. Winnicott Association, the Squiggle Foundation in U.K. She is a regular contributor to magazines and a conference speaker in Design International Conferences: in European – Helsinki, Berlin - and Japanese Universities in Sapporo and Osaka.

Madhura Datta is presently a Lecturer in UGC-Academic Staff College of the University of Calcutta. She did her MSc in Computer and Information Science from the University of Calcutta in 2002 and her M.Tech degree in Computer Science and Engineering in 2004 from the same University. She is pursuing her PhD work on face recognition.

Yaokai Feng received his B.E. and M.E. degrees in Computer Science from Tianjin University, China, in 1986 and 1992, respectively. And, he received his PhD degree in Information Science from Kyushu University, Japan, in 2004. From 1986 to 1998, he was with the Department of Computer Engineering and Science, Tianjin University, China, where he was an assistant professor/lecturer and he was studying on fault-tolerant systems and database applications. During his doctoral course in Kyushu University, Japan, he was focusing his attention on the study of database. Now, he is with the Graduate School of Information Science and Electrical Engineering, Kyushu University, Japan, as an assistant professor and faculty of Information Science and Electrical Engineering. Now, his study interests include database (multidimensional indexing and searching, Kansei database, etc.) and pattern recognition (object recognition, localization, etc.).

Hugo de Garis is a Full Professor of Computer Science and Director of the Artificial Brain Lab (ABL) in the Cognitive Science Department of the School of Information Science & Technology (SIST), Xiamen University, Xiamen, Fujian Province. He has a 4 year contract (2008-2011) to build China's first artificial brain, consisting of 1000s of evolved neural net modules to control the behaviors of French NAO robots. He has had two books published, "The Artilect War : Cosmists vs. Terrans: A Bitter Controversy Concerning Whether Humanity Should Build Godlike Massively Intelligent Machines", and "Multis and Monos: What the Multicultured Can Teach the Monocultured: Towards the Creation of a Global State". He is co-guest editor of a special issue of the Neurocomputing journal on the topic of "Artificial Brains", the first of its kind worldwide, and is contracted by World Scientific to write two books on "Artificial Brains" and "Topological Quantum Computing : Making Quantum Computers Robust By Manipulating Quantum Bits in Topological Quantum Fields". Before living in China, he was an Associate Professor of Computer Science at Utah State University, in Utah, USA. He has lived in 7 countries (Australia, England, Holland, Belgium, Japan, America, China).

Damian Giaouris was born in Munich, Germany in 1976. He received the diploma of Automation Engineering from the Automation Department, Technological Educational Institute of Thessaloniki, Greece, in 2000, the MSc degree in Automation and Control from Newcastle University in 2001 and the PhD degree in the area of control and stability of Induction Machine drives in 2004. His research interests involve advanced nonlinear control, estimation, digital signal processing methods applied to electric drives and nonlinear phenomena in power electronic converters. He is currently a lecturer in Control Systems at Newcastle University, England, UK.

Ben Goertzel is CEO and Chief Scientist of AI firm Novamente LLC and bioinformatics firm Biomind LLC, and Director of Research of the nonprofit Singularity Institute for AI. He was a research faculty for 8 years in several universities in the US and Australasia and is the Chair of the Artificial General Intelligence conference series. Dr. Goertzel as authored eight technical monographs in the computing and cognitive sciences, and edited four technical volumes. He has published over 80 research papers in journals, conferences and edited volumes, in disciplines spanning AI, mathematics, computer science, cognitive science, philosophy of mind and bioinformatics; and has developed two AI-based trading systems for hedge funds in Connecticut and San Francisco. AI software created by his teams at Novamente LLC and Biomind LLC has been used in numerous government agencies and corporations.

Santoso Handri is a Post-Doctoral Researcher in the Top Runner Incubation Centre for Academia-Industry Fusion, Nagaoka University of Technology, Nagaoka, Japan. He received the BSc degree in Physics from the University of Indonesia, Depok, Indonesia in 1996. Worked as a Senior Engineer at Yokogawa Indonesia Co. from 1997-2003. He received PhD degree in Information Science and Control Engineering from the Nagaoka University of Technology, Japan in 2008. His research interests include soft-computing approaches to the problems on car detection by in-vehicle camera, human behavior, pedestrian behavior, psychophysiological stress evaluation, epidemic data analysis.

Tadashi Hasebe is a professor of the graduate school of Agricultural Science at Tohoku University, Japan. He received BA, MS and PhD in Agricultural Economics (Agricultural Science), all from Hokkaido University. He was an econometrician of agricultural production and food demand. Recently, major areas of research interests include rural scenery evaluation, sustainability of rural festivals and Kansei philosophy. He teaches Information Economics, Environmental Economics, Landscape Ecology and Ethics of Bio-sphere. He received an award of Tohoku Agricultural Economic Association. He is a member of a board of directors of Japan Association of Human and Environmental Symbiosis.

Sachio Hirokawa is Professor of Research Institute for Information Technology, Kyushu University, Japan. He studied mathematics and computer science at Kyushu University. He was appointed to a research assistant at Shizuoka University in 1979, moved to Kyushu University in 1988 as Associate Professor and Professor in 1996. He received PhD in 1992. He has been involved in research and teaching in the area of mathematical logic and computer science. Since late 90s, his research focuses on search engine and text mining, where frequency analysis and visualization are the key features. He conducted 3 years project on search engine and became founder of start-up company Lafla (http://www.lafla.co.jp) to realize his technologies for commercial services.

Hidenori Itoh completed the doctoral program in electrical and electronic engineering at Nagoya University, Japan, in 1974 and received a D.Eng. degree. From 1974 to 1985, he worked at Nippon Telephone and Telegraph Laboratories, developing systems. From 1985 to 1989, he was with the Institute for New Generation Computer Technology, developing knowledge base systems. He has been a professor at Nagoya Institute of Technology since 1989 and is now affiliated with the Department of Computer Science and Engineering. He has been engaged R&D in the fields of mathematical theory of language, computer network communications, operating systems, knowledge databases, and artificial intelligence. He is a member of the Information Processing Society of Japan, the Institute of Electronics, Information and Communication Engineer, Japanese Society for Artificial Intelligence, the Society for Science on Form, Japan, the Robotics Society of Japan, and Japan Society of Kansei Engineering, and the IEEE computer society.

Shigekazu Ishihara is a professor of Ergonomics and Kansei engineering at the Department of Kansei Design, Hiroshima International University. He obtained PhD from graduate school of engineering, Hiroshima University. His recent research, teaching and consulting activities focus on methodologies and applications of Kansei ergonomics, which is merging Kansei engineering and ergonomics techniques.

Yun Jiang, was born in 1983. Now she is a PhD student in Key Laboratory of Image Processing and Intelligent Control, Department of Control Science and Engineering, Huazhong University of Science and Technology, Wuhan, Hubei, P.R. China. She majors in membrane computing, system biology and parallel and distributed computing, etc. She got her Bachelor's Degree in Huazhong Normal University in Communication Engineering. Till now, she has published several papers and some of them are indexed by EI and SCI.

Masayoshi Kanoh is an assistant professor in the School of Information Science and Technology at Chukyo University, Japan. He received his PhD in Engineering from Nagoya Institute of Technology, Japan, in 2004. His research interests include Kansei robotics, intelligent robotics and human robot interaction.

Kanji Kato is Assistant Director of Communication Design Department, GK Sekkei Incorporated, Japan. He studied design and craft at Okinawa Prefectural University of Arts. He was Associate Professor of User Science Institute, Kyushu University in 2005, moved to GK Sekkei Incorporated as Assistant Director in 2009. Since 2005, his research was the formation of design assessment indicators based on remarks of users. He also focuses on the study of participatory design process at design workshops. He currently designs street furniture, ancillary facilities, and other design components of urban space, for example, the design of city lights, signs, benches, bus stop shelters, and the development of design guideline of townscape.

Shohei Kato received the BS, MS and PhD in Engineering from Nagoya Institute of Technology, Japan, in 1993, 1995 and 1998, respectively. He joined the Department of Electrical and Electronic Engineering at Toyota National College of Technology as a research associate from 1998 to 1999 and as a lecturer from 1999 to 2002. He has been in the Department of Computer Science and Engineering at Nagoya Institute of Technology as an assistant professor from 2002 to 2003 and as an associate professor from 2003 to present. His current research interests include computational intelligence in robotics, artificial life, reasoning under uncertainty, and Kansei engineering. He is a member of the Information Processing Society of Japan, the Institute of Electronics, Information and Communication Engineer, the Japanese Society for Artificial Intelligence, and the Robotics Society of Japan, and Japan Society of Kansei Engineering, and the IEEE.

Pierre Lévy is an assistant professor in the Designing Quality in Interaction Group of the Faculty of Industrial Design of Eindhoven University of Technology. Mechanical engineer from Compiègne University of Technology, he earned his PhD in *Kansei* Science from the Graduate School of Comprehensive Human Sciences of the University of Tsukuba. His current work focuses on sharing, and on its effect on creativity. His research areas of interest include Kansei science, Kansei design, sharing processes, and Occidental/Oriental philosophical differences applied to design.

Shaozi Li is a professor at Xiamen University, China. He is the head of the Department of Cognitive Science, the Deputy Chairman of Fujian Artificial Intelligent Association, the Deputy Director of Fujian Key Lab of the Brain-like Intelligent Systems. His research interests include natural language processing and multimedia information retrieval, moving target detection and recognition, machine learning and computer vision, intelligent Chinese medical information processing. He served as an executive chair in SPCA2006 and a program committee chair in several international conferences, such as ICIS2009, ITME2009, ISKE2008 and ITME2008. He is an associate editor of the International Journal of Computers and Applications. He has lead or participated in multiple National Natural Science Foundation projects, National 863 projects, the Natural Science Foundation projects of Fujian Province, the Science and Technology Key projects of Fujian Province. He has published about 120 academic papers, more than 56 of which collected in SCI/EI Indexes.

Yanping Lu received the BA degree and MA degree in Computer Science from Fuzhou University, China in 2000 and 2005, respectively. She was a PhD candidate in the Department of Computer Science, Xiamen University, China in 2005-09 and a joint PhD candidate in the Department of Computer, University of Sherbrooke, Canada in 2007-09. She obtained one of her two PhD degrees in Artificial Intelligent from Xiamen University and the other one in Computer from the University of Sherbrooke in 2009. Her research interests include evolutionary computation, swarm intelligence, applications of evolutionary computation and particle swarm optimization.

Yusuke Manabe was born in Hokkaido Prefecture, Japan in 1980. He received the Ph.D. degree in software and information science from Iwate Prefectural University, Japan in 2008. Now he is an assistant professor in Faculty of Information and Computer Science, Chiba Institute of Technology, Chiba, Japan. His research interests are in the area of chaotic time series analysis and soft computing, especially artificial neural network.

Jun Masaki obtained PhD from graduate school of engineering, Kyushu University. He has been worked as a researcher of measurements. He has been also involved in Kansei engineering studies. Presently he is working in public works department of Nagasaki Prefectural Government.

Ujjwal Maulik did his BS in Physics and Computer Science in 1986 and 1989 respectively, and MS and Ph.D in Computer Science in 1991 and 1997 respectively. He is currently a Professor in the Department of Computer Science and Technology, Jadavpur University. He has served as the Head of the Computer Science and Technology School of the Government Engineering College in Kalyani, India, during 1996-1999. Dr. Maulik has worked in the Center for Adaptive Systems Application, Los Alamos, New Mexico, USA in 1997, University of New South Wales, Sydney, Australia in 1999, University of Texas at Arlington, USA in 2001, University of Maryland Baltimore County in 2004, Fraunhofer Institute, AiS, Germany in 2005 and Tsinghua University, China in 2007, University of Rome in 2008 and University of Heidelberg, 2009. He received the fellowships from International Center for Pure and Applied Mathematics, CIMPA, France, in 1994, 1996 and 2006, and International Center for Theoretical Physics (ICTP), Italy in 2007. Dr. Maulik is a Fellow of the Institution of Electronics and Telecommunication Engineers (IETE) and Institute of Engineers (IE), India, and a senior member of Institute of Electrical and Electronics Engineers (IEEE), USA. He has edited three books titled "Advanced methods for knowledge discovery from complex data', published by Springer in 2005, "Analysis of biological data: A soft computing approach" published by World Scientific in 2007 and "Computational Intelligence and Pattern Analysis in Biology Informatics", to be published by Wiley Interscience in 2009-2010. He is a co-author of around one hundred seventy technical articles in international journals, book chapters and conference/workshop proceedings. He has served on the program committees of many International Conferences, and has delivered many invited talks and tutorials around the world. He has served as the Program Chair of the Conference on Intelligent Computing and VLSI, 2001 held in Kalyani, India, and Tutorial Co-Chair, World Congress on Lateral Computing, 2004 held in Bangalore, India. His research interests include Soft Computing, Pattern Recognition, Data Mining, Bioinformatics and Parallel and Distributed Systems.

Kamyar Mehran was born in Boston, US, in 1977. He received his BSc degree in Computer Engineering from University of Tehran, Iran, in 1998 and MSc degree in Automation and Control and PhD degree in the area of Artificial Intelligence and Nonlinear Dynamics from Newcastle University, England, in 2004. His professional experience includes 2 years for NIOC as software developer and 3 years for major ICT companies like Sun Microsystems as senior software architect where he focused on Java-based distributed systems. His main research interests involve Artificial Intelligence systems, especially Fuzzy system identification and its application to advanced nonlinear control and nonlinear dynamical system in general. He is currently a researcher at Newcastle University, England, UK.

C. A. Murthy obtained B. Stat (Hons), M. Stat. and PhD degrees from the Indian Statistical Institute (ISI), India. He visited the Michigan State University, East Lansing, USA in 1991-92 for six months, and the Pennsylvania State University, University Park, USA for 18 months in 1996 - 97. He is a Professor in the Machine Intelligence Unit of ISI, Kolkata, India. His research interests include Pattern Recognition, Image Processing, Machine Learning, Soft Computing, Fractals, Wavelets and Data Mining. He has more than 60 papers in international peer reviewed journals, and published more than 150 articles in total. He also has eight US patents. He received the best paper award in 1996 in Computer Science from the Institute of Engineers, India. He received the Vasvik award for Electronic Sciences and Technology for the year 1999. He is a fellow of the National Academy of Engineering, India, and National Academy of Sciences, India.

Mitsuo Nagamachi obtained PhD from Psychology Department, Hiroshima University in 1963 and has been teaching Ergonomics and Management as a professor since then. He was invited by University of Michigan, Transportation Research Institute in 1972 and when returning to Japan he was invited by Japanese Government as a main ergonomist of "Japan Automotive Technology Committee". Since then, he has been consulting Japanese automotive Industries including Toyota, Nissan, Honda, Mitsubishi. His research area has been Manufacturing, TQC, IE, Safety, and Kaizen. He founded "Kansei Engineering" in 1970s, and he endeavored to build Korea Kansei Engineering Society 1n 1997 and Japanese Society of Kansei Engineering in 1998. He has worked for long time to extend Kansei Engineering over the world. He was given "Japanese Government Prize" for his foundation and promotion of Kansei Engineering in 2008. Two books, "Innovation of Kansei Engineering" and "Kansei/Affective Engineering" will be published by CRC Press in 2010.

Tsuyoshi Nakamura received the PhD degree from Nagoya Institute of Technology in 1998, studying computer graphics based on soft computing. He joined Nagoya Institute of Technology as a research associate in 1998. In 2003 and now, he is an associate professor. His research interests include AI, CG, CV, soft computing and emotional information processing.

Moon Namgung is a professor in the Department of Civil and Environmental Engineering since 1992. He received a BS degree in civil engineering from Wonkwang University, Korea in 1984, a M.S. degree in civil engineering from Chonbuk National University, Korea in 1986 and a PhD degree in transportation engineering from Hiroshima University, Japan in 1992. He visited Illinois University at Chicago, USA, Darmstadt University, Germany Hiroshima University, Japan, as an exchanging professor. His research topics focus on travel behavior, traffic safety, ITS, public transportation, Kansei engineering and highway landscape.

Shusaku Nomura is a specially appointed Associate Professor in the "Top Runner Incubation Centre for Academia-Industry Fusion", Nagaoka University of Technology, Nagaoka, Japan. He received the Diploma degree in Physics from Kobe University, Kobe, Japan in 1996, and the PhD degree in computer science from Kobe University Graduate School of Science and Technology, Kobe, Japan, in 2001. He has been engaged in a variety of research topics in biological/medical and ergonomic fields, by theoretical and experimental approaches inclusive of a mathematical model for chemo-taxis of amoeboid organism, data mining analysis for DNA microarray, brain wave studies on the optical illusion, etc. Currently his research interests include measurement of human mental health states by employing physiological biomarkers, which are the hormones and immune substances secreted in human saliva.

Michiaki Omura is an assistant professor of Graduate school of Agriculture, Tohoku University in Japan. He is belonging rural planning laboratory in Innovative Research Center for Agricultural Sciences. His major is environmental impact assessment, such as Life Cycle Assessment. His LCA method was differ from conventional one. In an ordinary way, subject of LCA is a product or a service. But he tried to treat an area by LCA method. Though, he had been actual rural area frequently, and interviewed a lot of rural habitats. That is what he got for interested in consciousness structure of human being. For example, "Why does a farmer insist on his own land? What is that cause?"

Tao Song, was born in 1983. Now is a PhD student in Key Laboratory of Image Processing and Intelligent Control, Department of Control Science and Engineering, Huazhong University of Science and Technology, Wuhan, Hubei, P.R. China. He is Major in DNA computing, Membrane computing,

Bioinformatics, system biology, Gene networks and Metabolic networks etc. He got his Master degree in Shandong University of Science and technology in mathematics and participated in two programs supported by China National Nature funding. Till now, he has published lots of papers and some of them are indexed by EI, SCI and ISTP. He is also a member of Operations Research Society of Hubei and attends some academic conferences. He joins in the reviewing job for the coming book named "Current NanoScience", which will be pressed by Bentham Science Publishers in India.

Naotoshi Sugano was born in Tokyo on December 3, 1951. He received a Doctor of Engineering from Tamagawa University, Tokyo in 1979. He joined Tamagawa University in 1979. From 1981 to 1982, he was a Visiting Fellow at the National Institutes of Health, Maryland. He is currently a Professor at Tamagawa University. His main research interests include color information processing using fuzzy set theory and Kansei information processing for the human interface. Prof. Sugano is a member of the Institute of Electrical and Electronic Engineers, Institute of Electronics, Information and Communication Engineers, Japan Society for Fuzzy Theory and Systems, Japan Society of KANSEI Engineering, Biomedical Fuzzy Systems Association, and Architectural Institute of Japan.

Kenji Sugawara was born in Iwate Prefecture, Japan, in 1950. He received the PhD degree in electrical engineering from Tohoku University, Japan in 1983. He is now a professor in Faculty of Information and Computer Science, Chiba Institute of Technology, Chiba, Japan. His research interests are in the area of knowledge engineering, ubiquitus computing and symbiotic computing. Dr Sugawara is a fellow member of the Institute of Electronics, Informationand Communication Engineer in Japan.

Oscar Tomico is an assistant professor in the Designing Quality in Interaction Group of the Faculty of Industrial Design of Eindhoven University of Technology.). He got his PhD in June 2007 from the Technical University of Catalonia on developing subjective psychological exploration techniques based in the constructivist paradigm for informational and inspirational purposes. His research focuses on exploring relations between physical, social and virtual domains as information interfaces for creating and sharing knowledge. Current projects focus on foreseeing social repercussion of intelligent systems as information platforms (home, shop and library contexts

Weijie Wang is a researcher in School of Transportation, Southeast University, Nanjing, China PR since 2009. He received a B.S. degree in mechanical engineering and marketing from Jingdezhen Ceramic Institute, China PR, in 2002, and a PhD degree in civil and environmental engineering from Wonkwang University, Korea, in 2008. His research topics focus on traffic safety, travel behavior surveying and modeling, human factor, environmental psychology, traffic psychology.

Wei Wang is a professor in School of Transportation, Southeast University, Nanjing, China PR since 1990. He received BS and MS degree in highway engineering in 1982 and 1985, respectively, and a PhD. Degree in traffic engineering from Southeast University in 1989. He has served as Dean of the School of Transportation, Southeast University since 1996. He also serve as Head of Smooth Traffic Project Expert Group, Vice President of China Association of Urban Transportation Planning, Member of the General Assembly and the Scientific Committee of Road Transportation Security Association of China, Member of the China Association for Geographic Information System, Standing Committee Member of China Association of Traffic Engineering, Vice President of Committee of Young Chinese Transportation Professionals in China. His research topics focus on ITS, sustainable transportation system, urban transportation management, traffic flow theory and traffic safety.

Xun Wang was born in 1985. Now is a PHD student in Department of Social Systems and Management in Graduate School Systems and Information Engineering, University of Tsukuba, Tsukuba, Japan. She is Major in combinatorial design, sequence design, DNA sequence design, system biology and Information Science etc. She got her Master degree in GuangXi Normal University in basic mathematics and participated in a program supported by China National Nature funding. Till now, she has published lots of papers and some of them are indexed by EI, SCI and ISTP. Also she attends some academic conferences in recently years.

Shudong Wang graduated from Huazhong University of Science and Technology, and got her Doctor degree in 2004. Her researching interests include Genetic algorithm, the theories and models of DNA computing, system biology and bioinformatics etc. She had published more than 50 papers and a few of them were indexed by SCI and EI. As an author participated in the translating of the book titled "DNA Computing: a new computing paradigm", which is the first book about DNA computing published in China. She has managed two China national natural funding supported programs.

Shangfei Wang received the MS degree in circuits and systems, and the Ph.D. degree in signal and information processing from University of Science and Technology of China, Hefei, China, in 1999 and 2002. From 2004 to 2005, she was a postdoctoral research fellow in Kyushu University, Japan. She is currently an Associate Professor of School of Computer Science and Technology, USTC. Dr. Wang is an IEEE member. Her research interests cover computation intelligence, affective computing, multimedia computing, information retrieval and artificial environment design. She has authored or coauthored over 40 publications.

Xufa Wang received the BS degree in radio electronics from University of Science and Technology of China, Hefei, China, in 1970. He is currently a Professor of School of Computer Science and Technology, USTC, and the Director of the Key Lab of Computing and Communicating Software of Anhui Province. He has published five books and over 100 technical articles in journals and proceedings in the areas of computation intelligence, pattern recognition, signal processing and computer networks. Prof. Wang is the Editorial Board Member of the Chinese *Journal of Electronic, the* Journal of Chinese Computer Systems, and International Journal of Information Acquisition.

Yasuhiro Yamada is an Assistant Professor of Department of Mathematics and Computer Science, Shimane University, Japan. He studied computer science at Kyushu University. He began his career as Technical Staff of Kyushu University in 2006, moved to Shimane University in 2008 as Assistant Professor. He received TELECOM System Technology Award for Student from The Telecommunications Advancement Foundation in 2001. He received PhD in 2008 from Kyushu University. He has been involved in research and teaching in the area of computer science. His research interests are text and Web mining. His research focuses on pattern detection of Web documents and information extraction from the documents based on frequency analysis. His research also focuses on the development of search engines to analyze search results.

Toshimasa Yamanaka is professor of Kansei Information in the Graduate School of Comprehensive Human Sciences and at the Institute of Art and Design of the University of Tsukuba. He teaches undergraduate and graduate courses in Product Design and Kansei Information. He earned his PhD in Kansei Science from the Graduate School of Comprehensive Human Sciences of the University of Tsukuba. His research areas of interest include design process, design analysis, and information design.

Bashar Zahawi received his BSc and PhD degrees in electrical and electronic engineering from Newcastle University, England, in 1983 and 1988, respectively. From 1988 to 1993 he was a design engineer at Cortina Electric Company Ltd, a UK manufacturer of large ac variable speed drives and other power conversion equipment. In 1994, he was appointed as a Lecturer in Electrical Engineering at the University of Manchester, England, and in 2003 he joined the School of Electrical, Electronic and Computer Engineering at Newcastle University, England, where he is currently the Director of Postgraduate Studies. His research interests include power conversion, variable speed drives and the application of nonlinear dynamical methods to transformer and power electronic circuits. Dr. Zahawi is a senior member of the IEEE and a chartered electrical engineer. He is the recipient of the Crompton Premium awarded by the Institution of Electrical Engineers (IEE).

Index